1900 FREDERICK TAYLOR

The "Father of Scientific Management" 

management cooperation, for controllin... methods

1922 MAX WEBER

Defined fully the bureaucratic form of organization

1927 ELTON MAYO

Conducted the famous management study at the Hawthorne Works of the Western Electric Company near Chicago, which examined the relationship between work environment and productivity. These studies were the genesis of the human relations school of management thought

1930 MARY PARKER FOLLET

Developed a management philosophy based on individual motivation and group problem solving— a forerunner of the participatory management idea

1937 LUTHER GULICK
LYNDALL URWICK

Provided the definitive statement of the "principles" approach to management planning, organizing, staffing, directing, coordinating, reporting, and budgeting (in short, POSDCORB)

1938 CHESTER I. BARNARD

Viewed organizations as cooperative systems in which the "functions of the executive" (title of his classic work) were to maintain a balance between the needs of the organization and the needs of the individual and to establish effective communications

1940 ROBERT K. MERTON

Proclaimed that bureaucracy, which Weber (1922) had defined so systematically, had a number of dysfunctions (that is, characteristics that lead to inefficiency)

1943 ABRAHAM H. MASLOW

Developed a theory of human motivation in which men and women move up or down a needs hierarchy as each level is satisfied or threatened

1945 PAUL APPLEBY

Asserted that processes in government organizations are political— at least more than those in business organizations. Philip Selznick, Norton Long, and other writers of the late 1940s were to lend theoretical and empirical support to Appleby's most un-Wilsonian (1887) thesis

1947 HERBERT A. SIMON

In his classic *Administrative Behavior*, Simon, like Merton (1940), attacked the principles approach to management as being often inconsistent and inapplicable. Like Barnard (1938), Simon advocated a systems approach to administration

FOURTH EDITION

Managing the Public Sector

WADSWORTH SERIES IN PUBLIC ADMINISTRATION

The Foundations of Policy Analysis (1983)
Garry D. Brewer and Peter deLeon

Public Administration: An Action Orientation (1991)
Robert B. Denhardt

Public Administration in Action: Readings, Profiles, and Cases (1992)
Robert B. Denhardt and Barry R. Hammond

Theories of Public Organization (1984)
Robert B. Denhardt

The Nonprofit Organization: Essential Readings (1990)
David L. Gies, J. Steven Ott, and Jay M. Shafritz

Organization Theory: A Public Perspective (1987)
Harold F. Gortner, Julianne Mahler, and Jeanne Bell Nicholson

Governmental Accounting and Control (1984)
Leo Herbert, Larry N. Killough, Alan Walter Steiss

Governing Public Organizations (1990)
Karen M. Hult and Charles Walcott

Government Budgeting: Theory, Process, and Politics, Second Edition (1992)
Albert C. Hyde

Democratic Politics and Policy Analysis (1990)
Hank C. Jenkins-Smith

Politics and the Bureaucracy: Policymaking in the Fourth Branch of Government, Third Edition (1992)
Kenneth J. Meier

Applied Statistics for Public Administration, Third Edition (1992)
Kenneth J. Meier and Jeffrey L. Brudney

Fiscal Administration: Analysis and Applications for the Public Sector, Third Edition (1991)
John L. Mikesell

Managing Urban America, Third Edition (1989)
David R. Morgan

Classic Readings in Organizational Behavior (1989)
J. Steven Ott

The Organizational Culture Perspective (1989)
J. Steven Ott

The Job of the Public Manager (1989)
John Rehfuss

Microcomputers and Government Management: Design and Use of Applications (1991)
John F. Sacco and John W. Ostrowski

Classics of Organization Theory, Third Edition (1992)
Jay M. Shafritz and J. Steven Ott

Classics of Public Administration, Third Edition (1992)
Jay M. Shafritz and Albert C. Hyde

Managing the Public Sector, Fourth Edition (1993)
Grover Starling

Strategies for Policy Making (1988)
Grover Starling

Financial Management in Public Organizations (1989)
Alan Walter Steiss

Critical Issues in Public Personnel Policy (1989)
Ronald D. Sylvia

Classics of Public Personnel Policy, Second Edition, Revised and Expanded (1991)
Frank J. Thompson

A Casebook of Public Ethics and Issues (1990)
William M. Timmins

Introduction to Budgeting (1978)
John Wanat

Quantitative Methods for Public Administration, Second Edition (1988)
Susan Welch and John Comer

Managing the Public Sector

FOURTH EDITION

Grover Starling

School of Business
and Public Administration
University of Houston–Clear Lake

Wadsworth Publishing Company
Belmont, California
A Division of Wadsworth, Inc.

© 1993 by Wadsworth, Inc. All rights reserved. No part of this book may be reproduced, stored in a retrieval system, or transcribed, in any form or by any means, without the prior written permission of the publisher, Wadsworth Publishing Company, Belmont, California 94002.

Printed in the United States of America

10 9 8 7 6 5 4 3 2 1—97 96 95 94 93

Library of Congress Cataloging-in-Publication Data

Starling, Grover
Managing the public sector / by Grover Starling. — 4th ed.
p. cm. — (Wadsworth series in public administration)
Includes bibliographical references and index.
ISBN 0-534-19320-X
1. Public administration. I. Title. II. Series.
JF1351.S74 1993
350—dc20 92-5778
CIP

Sponsoring Editor: Cynthia C. Stormer
Editorial Associate: Cathleen S. Collins
Production Coordinator: Fiorella Ljunggren
Production: Greg Hubit Bookworks
Manuscript Editor: Kathleen McCann
Interior Design: John Edeen
Cover Design: Vernon T. Boes
Art and Photo Coordinators: Greg Hubit; Donna Tauscher
Interior Illustration: Susan Rogin
Typesetting: GTS Graphics
Jacket Printing: Phoenix Color Corporation
Printing and Binding: R. R. Donnelley & Sons Company, Crawfordsville

To my wife,
Yolanda Blandón Starling

Preface

My goal for the fourth edition of *Managing the Public Sector* remains the same as that for the first edition—to create a better kind of public administration text. Once again I have tried to make clear the application of management ideas to real problems, to convey to students the intellectual enjoyment of the subject, and to capture some of the excitement, challenge, and adventure of contemporary public administration.

While being faithful to administrative theories and research, I have also identified and discussed emerging trends. For example, few people today would equate government with *quality*, but that could change in the 1990s. Many federal, state, and local officials are embracing the principles of such quality pioneers as W. Edward Deming and Joseph M. Juran. Why quality? Largely because governments are deep in debt and the personal tax rate is at an all-time high. Quality may be one of the best ways to compensate—to deliver better services more cost-effectively.

Two other issues that receive attention throughout the text are *entrepreneurship* and *ethics*. Traditionally, the social sciences have paid little heed to the individual manager as innovator. They have focused on the roles of social movements, interest groups, bureaucratic routines, and institutional processes in effecting change—but seldom on individuals. In fact, some social scientists take a downright pessimistic view on whether leaders in public agencies can make a difference. Unfortunately, this view influences the texts and teaching of public administration and says to society's best potential leaders, "If you are interested in using your talents and energies to accomplish challenging tasks, the public sector is not for you." My own view is much more optimistic. For a model of how government should function, let us look beyond the conventional wisdom to newer works like Doig and Hargrove's *Leaders and Innovation: Entrepreneurs in Government* (1990) and Osborne and Gaebler's *Reinventing Government: How the Entrepreneurial Spirit Is Transforming the Public Sector* (1992).

If academics feel uncomfortable teaching about entrepreneurs in government, they appear only slightly less so when it comes to a subject that is usually the preserve of moral philosophers. Like entrepreneurship, they find ethics a rather messy subject, one with little empirical content. But I think that those who believe ethics to be unteachable are being inconsistent. In no other area of life would they presuppose that one's childhood or high school education provided an adequate resource for coping with situations in adult life. The ethical consequences of administrative action are discussed in every part of this book.

This is the most extensively revised edition of the text yet to appear. The new material covers the following topics:

- The effect of new information technologies (see especially "A Day in the Life of Tomorrow's Public Administrator," which opens Chapter 1, and Chapter 12, "The Information Revolution").
- The growing importance of horizontal coordination, networks, consortia, and privatization rather than vertical command and control (see Chapters 3 and 7).
- The various types of planning with which today's public administrator should be familiar: crisis planning, action planning, growth planning, and so forth (see Chapter 5).
- Communicating in organizations. Given the well-documented fact that communication takes up to 80 percent of a manager's time, I have considerably expanded the discussion of this topic (see Chapter 8).
- The increased importance of teamwork in organizations (see Chapter 8).
- How to design, manage, and evaluate a case-processing system. Public sector organizations devote much time and energy to processing cases: patients in hospitals, welfare clients in human resource departments, labor disputes in labor relations boards, apartment buildings in housing code enforcement offices, grant proposals in foundations, and so on. Yet, the subject receives surprisingly little systematic attention. Chapter 9 will attempt to correct this oversight.
- Increased work-force diversity.

One major goal of this book is to offer better ways of using the textbook medium to convey knowledge about public administration to the reader. To this end, the text offers several innovative features:

- *Photo essays.* A special feature of this book since the first edition has been the use of photographs accompanied by detailed captions that describe the managerial implications of the picture and how they relate to the theme of the chapter. Often pictures can convey a vividness, immediacy, and concreteness not easily achieved by words.
- *"Talking Shop."* These innovative boxed items describe frequently encountered management problems or issues and then provide a no-nonsense discussion of how experts or experienced practitioners would handle them.

These boxes will heighten student interest in public administration and provide a perspective on issues not typically available in textbooks.

- *Working profiles.* Public administration is not just about bureaucratic routines and institutional processes; it is also about the men and women who work in the public sector making things happen (as I suggested earlier). These profiles, which appear at least once in almost every chapter, put students in immediate touch with the real world of public organizations so that they can appreciate the value of the management concepts presented in the chapter.

- *Cases.* Each chapter ends with at least two brief but substantive cases for analysis and discussion. For the most part, they are about real people and real organizations. These cases provide an opportunity for students to apply concepts to real events and to sharpen their diagnostic skills.

Despite these many and substantial changes, the original approach of *Managing the Public Sector* remains the same. The operative word in the title is still *managing.* To many authorities, and surely to most of the American public, the most acute need facing government in the decades ahead will be better management. But "better management" means more than the improvement of basic personnel, budgeting, and administrative practices. It means greater attention to modern analytical, behavioral, and informational techniques that are required to manage any large-scale enterprise successfully.

An introduction to public administration, however, must provide more than an exposure to such business school topics as management by objectives, accrual and cost accounting, microeconomic analysis, decision theory, and job redesign. Otherwise, this book would hardly be necessary—after all, a clutch of business school textbooks are available on all of these topics. No, an introduction to public administration must in at least two ways go beyond an inventory of management techniques. It must, first, place these techniques in the context of the public sector. And by *public sector,* I refer not only to governmental jurisdictions but also to other nonprofit institutions such as hospitals, foundations, and universities.

Second, an introduction must make crystal clear the highly political environment of American public administration. While I am sympathetic to the notion that the environment of private sector management is becoming increasingly similar to that of public sector management, I still see fundamental, and perhaps irreducible, differences. To cite only one: In the private sector, objectives are usually given—they are treated as problems to be solved. In contrast, the public sector's objectives are far less certain, far more debatable. Indeed, the public administrator often participates in the process of determining those objectives. In finding a place for the management expert, we cannot afford to toss out the political scientist.

Besides the strong, though not exclusive, emphasis on management, this book is unusual in avoiding potted summaries of what individual scholars have said. Instead, it provides organizing assumptions, concepts, and definitions that underlie any systematic inquiry and give a field coherence. To provide this coherence, the book builds around three major themes: the sociopolitical environment of public administration (Part I), the management of governmental programs (Part II), and the management of financial, human, and information resources (Part III). This trio forms an integrated whole that attempts to reconcile current thinking on administrative theory.

I should like to conclude on a brief pedagogical note. To ease the reader's journey into what may be entirely unfamiliar terrritory, I have taken several steps. Chapter titles and formats have been carefully drawn to provide a clear and balanced view of the subject. Lists of new terms have been placed at the end of each chapter, and connective summaries appear throughout. I have attempted to make the theoretical parts as clearcut, short, and relevant as possible.

The philosopher and mathematician Alfred North Whitehead (1929:13) once said, "A merely well-informed man is the most useless bore on God's earth." He added, "Above all things we must beware of what I will call 'inert ideas'—that is to say, ideas that are merely received into the mind without being utilized, or tested, or thrown into fresh combinations." To battle the pestilence of inert ideas, I have added to the end of each chapter a set of problems designed not for review but for critical, analytical thinking. These problems are an integral part of the book. They help attain what surely must be our ultimate objective: to improve the quality of thinking about the management of the public sector.

Acknowledgments

For help in preparing this fourth edition, I must express my deepest thanks to Roger Durand, Max Elden, and Kirk Harlow of the University of Houston–Clear Lake and to James I. Scheiner, Secretary of Revenue for Pennsylvania. I also wish to thank Ross A. Webber of the Wharton School, University of Pennsylvania, and Thomas L. Wheeler of the University of South Florida for use of their materials in Chapters 7 and 10. The following reviewers of the manuscript have offered very helpful comments and suggestions, for which I am deeply grateful: Ann Altmeyer of the State University of New York College at Brockport, Mel Arslaner of Drake University, William P. Collins of Samford University, Wilkie A. Denley of South Carolina State University, Betty Hecker of Boise State University, Eugene B. McGregor of Indiana University, Faith Prather of the State University of New York College at Brockport, and James R. Purdy of the University of Central Florida. I also wish to express my appreciation to David N. Ammons of North Texas State University, Rufus Browning of San Francisco State University, Larry Elowitz of Georgia College, and Robert W. Kweit of the University of North Dakota for many valuable suggestions. And I must thank the many instructors and practitioners who took the time to send me useful suggestions based on their experiences with earlier editions of the book. As before, I will greatly appreciate comments from those who use this new book.

All told, I found writing this edition to be a renewed management education for myself. I can only hope that I have made the way a little easier for others.

Grover Starling

Contents

End-of-Chapter Cases

"Talking Shop"

Working Profiles

CHAPTER 1 What Is Public Administration?

Even more important than winning the election is governing the nation. That is the test of a political party—the acid, final test. When the tumult and the shouting die, when the bands are gone and the lights are dimmed, there is the stark reality of responsibility.

Adlai Stevenson, 1952

Introduction

Traditionally, **public administration** is thought of as the accomplishing side of government. It is supposed to comprise all those activities involved in carrying out the policies of elected officials and some activities associated with the development of those policies. Public administration is, as the Stevenson quote suggests, all that comes after the last campaign promise and the election night cheer.

Stevenson's is a fine definition, as far as it goes. But in this book we shall use a broader definition of public administration: *the process by which resources are marshaled and then used to cope with the problems facing a political community.* It is the aim of this introductory chapter to make this definition clear, as well as to show why the traditional one will not do. Perhaps the easiest way to begin is by meeting a couple of public administrators.

Who Public Administrators Are

A Day in the Life of Tomorrow's Public Administrator*

6:10 A.M. It is the year 2010 and another Monday morning has begun for Bill Parma, chief executive for a large, urbanized county. Shutting off his computer alarm, he moves with a quiet economy of effort to his computer terminal to check the weather outlook for Brussels, where he will fly late tonight. He also gives his electronic agent the following tasks:

- Find the date in February that I recorded a phone conversation with Julio.
- Make an appointment for Friday at a tire shop that is on my way home and is open after 6:00 P.M.
- Distribute this draft to the rest of the group, and let me know when they've read it.
- Whenever a paper is published on globalization of municipal finance in the European Community, order a copy for my library.

Meet the public administrator of the future. Our fictitious Bill Parma inhabits a world shaped by high public expectations, public-private and intergovernmental collaboration, technological complexity, and cultural diversity. (For one thing, the public administrator is just as likely to be a woman as a man and—with less than 15 percent of the new entrants to the work force over the next two decades being native white males—will probably manage an older work force made up mostly of women and minorities.)

Parma is comfortable with technology not just because he has been logging onto computers since he was seven years old but also because computers have ceased to be cumbersome machines understood only by a technical elite. They have now evolved into desktop tools that obey the individual. They have thin, flat screens, microphones or styli instead of keyboards, and wireless transmitters rather than cable-bound modems.

An economics honors student with a masters of public administration, the 38-year-old was appointed to his current position by the board of county supervisors after stints with the city government (where he rose to the position of deputy city administrator), a management consulting firm, and the U.S. Navy.

7:20 A.M. Parma and his wife, who heads her own arbitration and mediation firm, put household affairs in order before leaving. They quickly go over the day's schedule for their two children.

* Numerous sources were helpful in the preparation of this hypothetical day. Among the most useful were Cetron and Davies (1991); Garreau (1991); Tesler (1991); Mintzberg (1975); U.S. General Accounting Office (1991); *P.A. Times,* September 1, 1991; *Wall Street Journal,* March 25, 1984, December 7, 1987, and May 2, 1988; *New York Times,* November 28, 1989.

Roaring along a "smart highway," Parma takes only 12 minutes to commute from his home to the "edge city" in which the county's administrative building is located. During the trip he instructs his palmtop computer regarding his priorities for the day and some old acquaintances he wants to call later in the week.

The term *intelligent vehicle and highway systems* (IVHS), or smart highways, refers to a body of technologies that are applied to monitor vehicle transportation and to the transportation system upon which they operate. Through the use of advanced computers, telecommunications, and control technology, the deployment of IVHS early in the 21st century improved communication between drivers and traffic control centers and eventually created an integrated highway transportation system. Although the system was built and operated by the private sector, it was the county government that financed, designed, and coordinated this multibillion-dollar project. Because the system contributed so much to making automobile travel safer, more efficient in time, space, and energy, and more environmentally benign, Parma and his staff are justifiably proud to have played a pivotal role in its development.

Edge cities represent the latest phase of urban America's development. The first phase, contends Joel Garreau, a senior writer for the *Washington Post,* was suburbanization, especially after World War II. Next came the "malling" of America, in the 1960s and 1970s, when marketplaces moved out to where people lived. By 2010, America has moved most of its businesses and jobs to where people already lived and shopped. The edge city that Parma works in has over 5 million square feet of leasable office space, or more than downtown Memphis has today. Welcome to the workplace of the information age.

8:15 A.M. In his high-tech office that doubles as a conference room, Parma merges into his desktop computer the notes he made earlier that morning on his palmtop computer. Then he reviews priorities and schedule for the day with his executive assistant, Randall Brown. Traditional secretaries vanished a decade earlier. Gone too are the "let's do lunch" types who wear red suspenders as accessories to their hand-painted ties (for when they take off their coats "to really get down to business"). The challenges of managing the public sector in the 21st century simply do not allow for excessive office staff.

In their discussion, Parma and Brown touch on a dozen different subjects and issues ranging from air pollution and recycling (since the county has all but run out of landfill space) to stray dogs and local politicians. Just as they begin to discuss the implications of the upcoming mayoral election in the county's largest city, another subordinate, Laura Martin, drops in. She asks a few questions about a personnel problem and then joins the discussion about the election. Parma leaves to get more coffee. Brown and Martin continue their conversation.

8:55 A.M. Parma leaves his office for his first meeting. It is a typical computer-supported meeting. Someone takes notes on the computer as the 30 participants talk. Key points made by the speakers are dutifully typed into the computer (and onto the screen). Everyone at the meeting hears—and sees—the discussion. People watching the flow of comments on the screen begin to say things like, "Hey, this point relates to something that was said earlier," or "Wait a second. Doesn't that contradict what you said ten minutes ago? . . . Let's see." With the tap of a few keys, the screen scrolls back to the desired spot on the list of ideas. Although Parma is the senior official there, he says little, except for the few words needed to keep the discussion on track and to summarize the discussion at the end. After the minutes have been edited on-screen, they are printed. Hard copy is immediately distributed to anybody who needs to know what went on or wants to have a record of the meeting. In other words, the meeting has a product: a document.

Tomorrow's public administrator will be intimately hooked to citizens, elected officials, and outside interest groups and will be knowledgeable about their expectations. Because of individual needs in health care, education, and welfare, the political community will demand customized services and rapid delivery without the red tape. This will force administrators to make swift decisions that now often take months and reams of reports. Instant performance will be expected of them; incompetence will be harder to hide.

Meetings will continue to be the medium with which organizations get people to communicate, coordinate, collaborate, and decide. With computer-supported meetings, words will no longer just float away after the meeting is adjourned, nor will perceptive comments get lost amid the jumble of words spilling over the conference table. By providing an accurate written record of the meeting, computers can help eliminate the "But I thought we had agreed to . . ." problems that occasionally surface weeks or months after the fact.

Participants meeting in this environment will pay more attention to the points displayed on the screen than to the individual making the point. What is on the screen is treated as a creation of the group. One important sociological point: Public administrators will have to be authentic team players in tomorrow's environment. "Me only" administrators all too often cannot lead others effectively or clearly determine their organizations' most important needs. Sooner or later, they run aground.

10:30 A.M. Parma is off to his second meeting. He soon finds himself refereeing for two of his department heads—one Asian, the other European—regarding a proposed project. Parma quickly realizes that this is a cultural, not a strategic or budgetary, clash.

Poor interpersonal skills have always been a major reason for managers' failures, especially in the early and middle stages of their careers. For some, the problem is getting along with subordinates. Managers may not be able to inspire and win the loyalty of subordinates if they are not good listeners, do not give or take criticism well, or view conflict as something bad rather than something inevitable that must be handled.

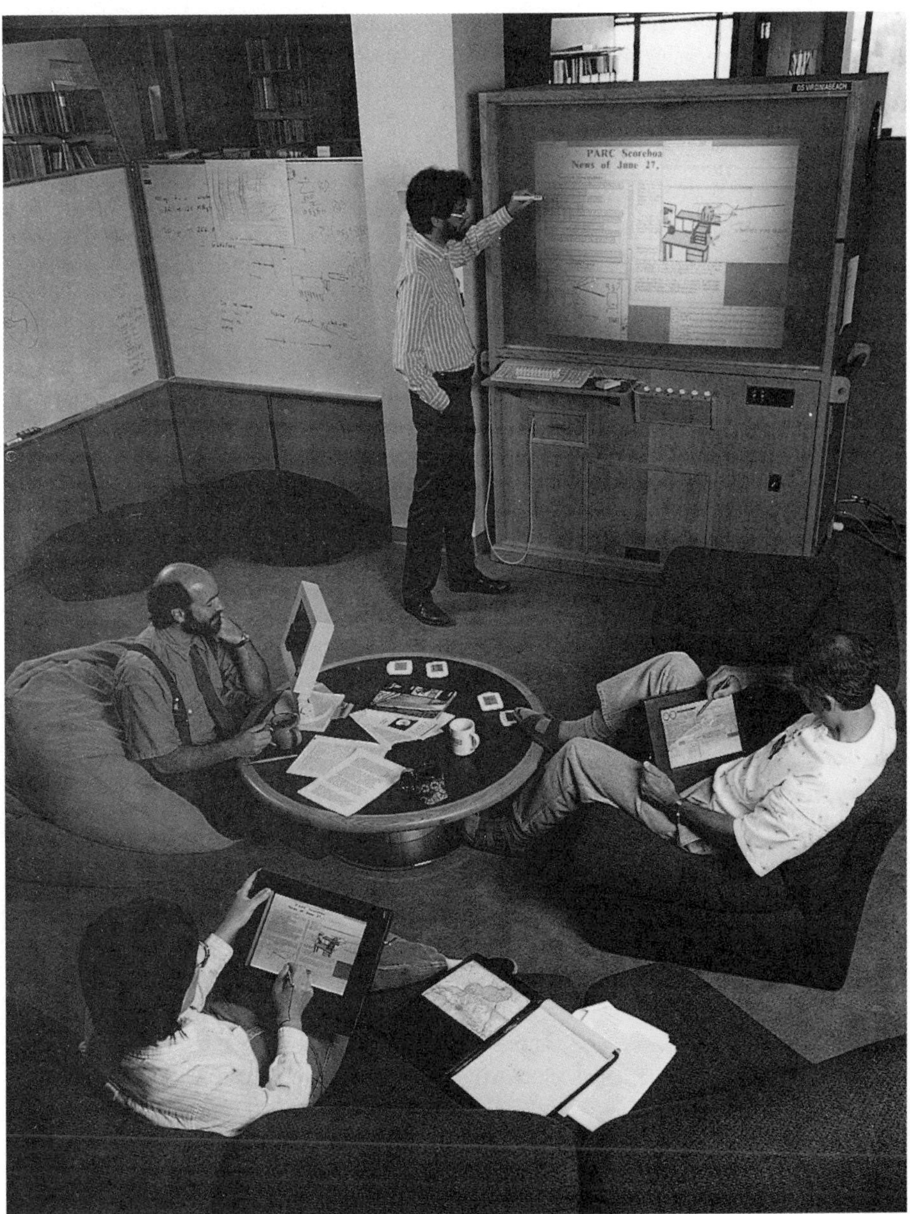

In 2010, computing will be ubiquitous in the workplace. Live boards will replace chalkboards. Live boards can customize the information they display. (Courtesy of Xerox Corporation)

By 2010, managers will have to be especially adept at handling conflict because of the greater cultural diversity. According to Jeffrey Sonnenfeld at Harvard, they will have to understand that employees do not think alike about such basics as "handling confrontation" or "even what it means to do a good day's work." They will also have to find a way to get commitment from employees. In the industrial era, output was the chief objective, and managers sought to motivate employees to higher levels of productivity. In the information age, quality and innovation are the chief objectives, and they require commitment from employees.

12:00 P.M. Parma orders lunch for himself and Brown. Brown comes in and goes over a dozen items. Martin stops by to say that she has already followed up on an earlier conversation. A staff person stops by with some calculations Parma had requested.

12:15 P.M. Lunch arrives. Over lunch, Parma and Brown pursue business and nonbusiness subjects. They laugh at each other's humor. They end the lunch talking about public-private collaboration on an economic development project. After 30 minutes, though, Parma decides to go to his computer to check on the results of the four inquiries he made at home that morning:

- YOU ASKED ME TO FIND OUT WHEN YOU LAST RECORDED A PHONE CONVERSATION WITH JULIO. IT WAS FEBRUARY 27. SHALL I PLAY THE RECORDING?
- YOU SCRIBBLED A NOTE LAST WEEK THAT YOUR TIRES WERE LOW. I CAN GET YOU AN APPOINTMENT ON FRIDAY AT 7:00 P.M.
- LASZLO HAS DISCARDED THE LAST FOUR DRAFTS YOU SENT HIM, WITHOUT READING ANY OF THEM.
- YOU HAVE REQUESTED PAPERS ON GLOBALIZATION OF MUNICIPAL FINANCE IN THE EUROPEAN COMMUNITY. SHALL I ORDER PAPERS ON THE GLOBALIZATION OF PUBLIC FINANCE IN OTHER REGIONS AS WELL?

The computer also reminds Parma that he has a 2:00 P.M. appointment at city hall. "Am I talking?" he asks. The computer assures him that it is only a ceremonial appearance. "Just another pretty face," Parma murmurs to himself.

A key goal for local government will be to establish a positive climate for attracting and keeping local business. Public administrators will continue to improve communications between business and government, respond quickly to the needs and problems of local business, and minimize paperwork and regulatory requirements. If collaborative ventures are to be successful, both sectors will need new skills and new levels of flexibility and adaptability. Local administrators will need to provide the expertise necessary for evaluating potential joint projects and for negotiating contractual arrangements with private sector participants. Business participants will need to develop the necessary skills for negotiating with local governments, recognizing that they cannot dictate the terms of cooperation.

Although technology will provide administrators with easy access to more data than they can possibly use, they will need to develop the ability to synthesize the data in order to make effective decisions. They will also continue to seek "soft" information, especially gossip, hearsay, and speculation. Why? "The reason," Henry Mintzberg (1975:49) of McGill University explains, "is its timeliness; today's gossip may be tomorrow's fact." Consider two of Parma's prime uses for information—to identify problems and opportunities and to build mental models (e.g., how the county's budget process works, how citizens evaluate services, how changes in the state's economy affect his organization). "The evidence suggests that the manager identifies decision situations and builds models not with aggregated abstractions a [computer] provides but with specific tidbits of information" (1975:49). Parma will no doubt use the ceremony today at city hall to gather more tidbits to piece together in his mind.

3:20 P.M. Parma is back from the ceremony at city hall. Two of his subordinates come in to complain that a recent performance bonus payment was not divided equitably. They note rather bluntly that Parma's bonus was more than theirs combined. They even threaten to quit. Parma promises to speak to the board about increasing their bonuses.

The two complaining employees were highly trained professionals and would not be easily replaced. Tomorrow's managers will not only have to share more authority with such people but also have to pay them salaries sometimes in excess of what top management itself makes. Rewarding these people with promotions will not be an attractive option, because the top of the bureaucratic ladder will still be occupied by baby boomers who do not want to retire.

4:00 P.M. The last meeting of the day is a conference via video screen between four members of Parma's staff and a waste-management firm in Toronto. The firm suggests that it can supply a state-of-the-art disposal service for 10 percent less than the county currently pays. The firm tells Parma and his staff how well this service has worked in Monterrey and other towns in Nuevo Leon. Parma and his staff quickly conclude that the deal is not quite good enough for the county to replace the services, which it performs itself, with a private sector contract.

The strength of a market economy is competition for market share. A private company's viability depends on its ability to serve customers with a quality product or service at a fair price. Traditional thinking about local government is that its service-delivery systems are less efficient and responsive and unable to compete with private companies. But many local governments have become lean and mean by 2010. The county that Parma runs has found that competition works. His departments compete head-to-head in a competitive bid process with private companies to deliver county services. And they often win these competitive bids on the basis of service and price.

Local governments are large purchasers of supplies, products, and services. When public administrators understand the workings of the marketplace and the value that their assets bring to this exchange, they can take advantage of the competitive environment to produce better prices and higher returns. Parma's county has committed significant financial and political resources over the last five years to develop computer software for managing municipal finance. Now the county seems poised to export that expertise to France and other countries of the European Economic Community (at this point an even stronger economic power than either the United States or Japan), where the municipal revenue bond market is still not as developed as that in the United States.

6:00 P.M. Parma heads for the airport to catch his Brussels flight to promote his software and perhaps to lure some European businesses into joint and cooperative ventures with the industry in his county. From the airport, he uses a videophone to say good-bye to his children and to talk about the next three day's schedule with his wife. Being reminded that his youngest child has a birthday on Friday, he promises to catch the National Aerospace plane in order to be home on time.

Managing the Olympics

Now let us meet another administrator—Peter Ueberroth, who was president of the nonprofit Los Angeles Olympic Organizing Committee (LAOOC). How he staffed, financed, and managed the 1984 Olympics is a story not without interest to students of public administration.

To protect the taxpayers, the Los Angeles City Council required that LAOOC contract with the city for those municipal services necessary to the games and prohibited the city from spending its general tax dollars on direct Olympic services. Ueberroth's challenge was to open an office for an organization that had no assets and build it into an organization capable of running a two-week sports and cultural event the size of nine Super Bowls. Ueberroth knew that his best chance to get financing was from the television networks. He designed a bold blind-bidding contest that yielded $225 million from ABC. Then he began negotiating contracts with the largest corporations. Colleagues say that his "reverse salesmanship"—earnestly seeming to take the other person's side—was awesome to watch.

As revenue began to increase, building international goodwill became Ueberroth's new priority. In attempting to cultivate the various national ministers of sport, Ueberroth discovered that the political power of athletics and athletic officials around the world was considerable. When foreign officials occasionally asked if he might help change some aspect of U.S. foreign policy, Ueberroth had to explain that sports officials in this country do not have that kind of influence.

His management style throughout was to delegate authority and responsibility. The man who actually ran the games, Harry Usher, says leadership and inspiration, not operations, are Ueberroth's managerial talents. If someone faltered, however, Ueberroth did not hesitate to take charge. To build unity, Ueberroth encouraged staff members to lunch at the cafeteria in the converted hangar that served as the committee's main office. When he saw a staff member not using all of his or her skills, Ueberroth, always the teacher, showed his annoyance; conversely, when someone performed well, he was exhilarated. When the three Olympic villages opened for the athletes two weeks before the games, he seemed to be everywhere at once with an electronic gadget on his hip that delivered printed, urgent messages to him. He particularly sought out the 29 different police forces involved in the games. In working with the police,

*Peter Ueberroth built a travel business from scratch, then sold it to become president of the LAOOC. He set up an administrative structure that was flexible enough to move from planning to operations. He waived his salary for a year as an example to the many volunteers he hoped to recruit; he got more than 50,000 volunteers. What many thought would be a fiasco turned out to be an exciting success. In May 1992, Ueberroth accepted an even bigger challenge when Mayor Tom Bradley appointed him to head the Committee to Rebuild Los Angeles after three days of rioting caused 51 deaths and left over 4000 buildings looted or destroyed. (Heinz Kleutmeier/*Sports Illustrated*)*

Ueberroth's priority was not equipment but attitude: "The law-enforcement people were so upbeat," he explained, "and that affected everyone." (*Time,* January 7, 1985)

The Public Sector in Perspective

Who then, are public administrators? One clear way to answer this question is simply to say that they are people who work at all levels of government. But, as used in this text, the term *public administration* has a more extended meaning—which is one of the reasons why I introduced Peter Ueberroth and the LAOOC into the discussion. Specifically, public administration will refer to running any organization that is not a private, profit-making enterprise. Let's see what kinds of organizations this definition includes.

For starters, it includes numerous quasigovernmental organizations such as the following:

- **Government corporations** (e.g., Pension Fund Guaranty Corporation)
- **Government-sponsored enterprises** (e.g., Corporation for Public Broadcasting)
- **Regulated enterprises** (e.g., private electric utilities)

Whereas a government agency is clearly owned by "the people" and operated with taxpayers' dollars, such is not the case with these three types of organizations. The first is privately funded. The second is publicly funded but privately owned. And the third is neither owned by the public nor funded by it but is regulated by a government-appointed commission—not a privately elected board of directors. (For a further discussion of these distinctions, see Perry & Rainey, 1988.)

Conventional wisdom says that the private sector creates five out of six jobs. While that may have been true in 1929, it is nowhere near the mark today. How can conventional wisdom be so wrong? Part of the problem is that many of the quasi-governmental institutions noted above are classified as private sector enterprises. I would further suggest that categorizing the production of military aircraft by Lockheed and nuclear submarines by General Dynamics as private sector activities obscures the true size of the public sector.

To comprehend the actual dimensions of the **public sector,** one can count the people on the public payroll, as is done in Figure 1-1. But when the wider view is taken and one counts the people who are employed because of government purchases or grants, the public sector accounts for more than a third of the total employment and nearly a third of the gross national product—that is, all the goods and services produced by the American economy in a year (estimated by Ginzberg & Vojta, 1981).

Nor should we overlook in our attempt to define the scope of the public sector the steady growth of what some have called the **third sector,** the thousands of nonprofit but nongovernmental institutions (Drucker, 1989:195–206). These institutions include the majority of U.S. hospitals, schools, colleges, and universities. They also include philanthropic organizations (e.g., American Red Cross), health care groups (e.g., American Heart Association), community service groups (e.g., Salvation Army and Girl Scouts), churches, and cultural enterprises (e.g., symphony orchestras). These institutions are paid mainly by fees and voluntary donations rather than by tax dollars. They are independent and governed by their own volunteer boards. One out of every two adult Americans are estimated to work as volunteers in the third sector, yet few people recognize its importance.

The one thing they have in common—and this factor is surely more significant than being nonprofit or nongovernment—is their purpose, which is *to change people.* Peter Drucker (1989:198–99), a noted management theorist, calls them "human-change institutions": "The product of the hospital is a cured patient. The product of a church is a changed life. The product of the Salvation Army—the one organization that reaches the poorest of the poor regardless of race or religion—is a derelict become a citizen. The product of the Girl Scouts is a mature young woman who has values, skills, and respect for herself."

What Public Administrators Do

However diverse the activities of our two public administrators might seem, research indicates that these activities can be organized into **ten roles** (Mintzberg, 1973; Hales,

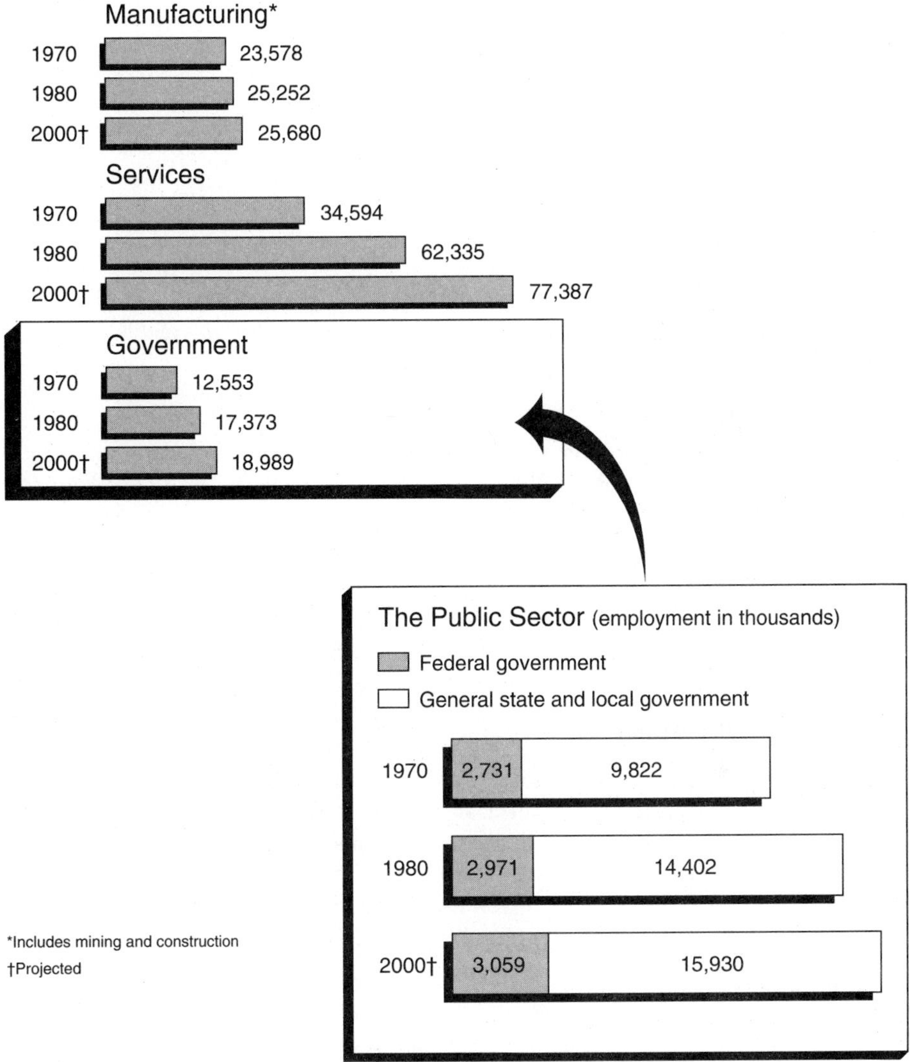

FIGURE 1-1
Putting the Public Sector in Perspective

SOURCE: Data from the U.S. Bureau of Labor Statistics, *Monthly Labor Review,* November 1989.

1986). The ten roles are divided into three categories: interpersonal, informational, and decisional (see Figure 1-2). Although these roles were developed for a "manager," if we keep in mind that a manager is defined as anyone who is in charge of an organization or subunit, then it is obvious that these roles are applicable to public admin-

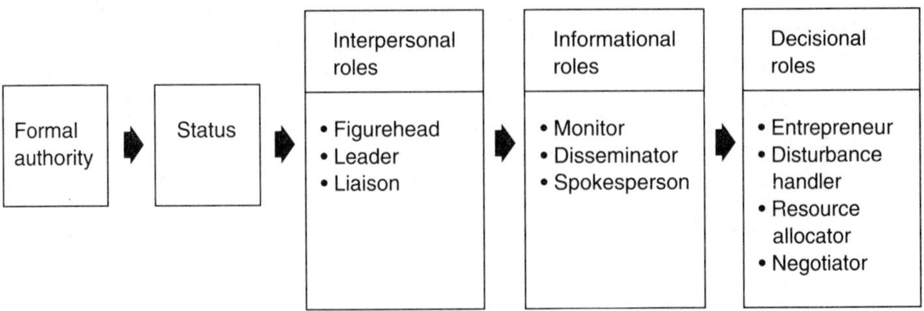

FIGURE 1-2
The Ten Roles of a Manager

SOURCE: Adapted from Henry Mintzberg, "HBR Classic: The Manager's Job," *Harvard Business Review,* March–April 1990, p.168.

istrators.* Indeed, this definition and the concept of roles would apply equally well to conductors, bishops, deans, football coaches, prime ministers, vice presidents for manufacturing, and deputy secretaries of state. All these managers are vested with formal authority over their orchestras, dioceses, schools, teams, governments, divisions, and bureaus. As indicated in Figure 1-2, from formal authority comes status, which leads to certain interpersonal relations. These interpersonal relations, in turn, enable the managers to make decisions and map strategy for their units.

Interpersonal Roles

Interpersonal roles pertain to relationships with others. In an organizational setting, these relations are shaped, in large measure, by the formal authority of the manager. The **figurehead** role involves the handling of ceremonial and symbolic activities for the department or organization. It would be wrong to think that this role is played only by kings, queens, and plenipotentiaries. When managers greet visitors, present awards, or sign documents, they are fulfilling this role. When Bill Parma made his 2:00 P.M.

* Terminological distinctions are important, but a quick trip to the dictionary will do little to untangle the two terms *manager* and *administrator.* The latter does seem to have a more subtle and extended series of meanings than the former. "It is more usually found in the public sector than the private and, in general, carries an implication not of ultimate sovereign control, but of directing and coordinating things on behalf of other people or authorities" (Baker, 1972:12). The term *management,* on the other hand, usually carries a rather different flavor. Drucker (1973) views *management* primarily in terms of a fairly specific set of tasks: to perform the function for the sake of which the institution exists; to make work productive and the worker achieving; to manage the institution's social impacts. But in coordinating complex situations where no criteria really exist, *administration* is probably a more appropriate word. It is also slightly more embracing in that it includes a lot of preparatory and supportive work for higher-level decision making. For our purposes, we will use the terms *public manager* and *public administrator* synonymously.

appearance at city hall, he was fulfilling this role. When Peter Ueberroth wore different uniforms each day during the games—a blue bus driver's suit, a kitchen staffer's whites, a blue and gold usher's suit—he was using symbols to boost morale.

The **leader** role encompasses relationships with subordinates, including motivation, communications, encouragement, and influence. We see this with dramatic clarity in the case of Peter Ueberroth. But recall how Bill Parma was also able to leverage himself and accomplish work through others. "In virtually every contact with the manager," Mintzberg (1973:168) writes, "subordinates seeking leadership clues ask: Does she approve? How would she like the report to turn out? Is she more interested in [performance or costs]?"

The **liaison** role pertains to the development of information sources both inside and outside the organization. In the case of Parma, we saw not only a manager who seemed to make himself readily available to employees but also the way in which modern technology enhances this role by making it easier for managers to extend and maintain a vast network of sources. But technology will never allow managers to ensconce themselves in their offices all day; they will still need to practice what Ueberroth did so well as president of LAOOC: management by walking around (MBWA).

Informational Roles

Given their wide range of personal relations, managers emerge as the nerve center of the organizational unit. Neustadt (1960:153–54) reports that although Franklin Roosevelt may not have known about everything going on in Washington, he likely knew more than any of his subordinates:

> *The essence of Roosevelt's technique for information-gathering was competition. "He would call you in," one of his aides once told me, "and he'd ask you to get the story on some complicated business, and you'd come back after a couple of days of hard labor and present the juicy morsel you'd uncovered under a stone somewhere, and then you'd find out he knew all about it, along with something else you didn't know. Where he got this information from he wouldn't mention, usually, but after he had done this to you once or twice you got damn careful about your information."*

The **monitor** role involves seeking current information from many sources. The **disseminator** role is the opposite: The manager transmits current information to others, both inside and outside the organization, who can use it. The **spokesperson** role pertains to official statements about the agency's programs to people outside the organization. Ueberroth's announcement that ABC had won television rights to the 1984 Olympics is an example of someone acting in the spokesperson role.

Decisional Roles

Information is only a means to an end—namely, decision making. And here again we see managers playing a central role, for only they have the formal authority to commit the organizational unit to a new course of action.

Managers must make choices. Ueberroth (1986:236) puts the idea forcefully: "I learned long ago that if you're going to be in charge, then take charge. Authority is 20 percent given—which was about all the LAOOC board had given me—and 80 percent taken. When you're in charge you assume complete and total authority, and your decisions reduce everything else to mere record keeping and back-up functions."

I am not sure a manager's decision will always "reduce everything else to mere record keeping and back-up functions," but there can be little doubt that a manager's failure to take a decisional role in a timely manner can jeopardize an organization's mission. Consider the case of a personnel manager in a northwestern city who was known to colleagues as the manager who studies everything to death. When asked to recommend a new performance-review system for one department, he immersed himself in studying the current system. By the time he completed his study—more than a year later—the department had a whole new staff and a new boss who already had in place his own performance-review procedures. The personnel manager lost his job over the incident. He had not learned that part of being a manager is taking a leap and bringing things to a head, even when you do not have all the data.

The **entrepreneur** role involves the initiation of change. For example, Parma supervised the implementation of a new roadway system and developed advanced software to handle local government finance.

Unlike their counterparts in business, leaders of American government have not inspired a vast literature about their entrepreneurial achievements. One of the aims of this book is to explore this largely untraveled territory—with real, not hypothetical, examples. In the chapters ahead, you will meet people like Carl Bianchi, under whom the Idaho court system became a national leader in innovation. (Believe me, getting judges and lawyers to innovate is no mean feat.)

The **disturbance handler** role involves resolving conflicts among subordinates or between the manager's department and other departments. While Ueberroth may be smooth, he was severely tested in this role while serving as baseball commissioner from 1987 to 1989. There were frequent clashes with team owners, who felt he wielded too much power, and with the players' union, which complained about his tactics to pressure players into drug testing. (His successor, Bart Giamatti, would also have disturbances to handle, generated not by owners or unions but by a single player: Pete Rose. But that is another story.)

The **resource allocator** role pertains to decisions about how to allocate people, time, equipment, budget, and other resources to attain desired outcomes. For example, recognizing the need for employment programs closely attached to welfare programs, Bill Parma formed an employment bureau coequal in status with the more heavily funded bureaus in his county. For two years, he concentrated department resources on testing and refining a work-force program for food stamp recipients that would become a model for many other jurisdictions in his state.

The **negotiator** role involves formal negotiations and informal bargaining (horse trading) to attain outcomes for the manager's unit of responsibility. Ueberroth's negotiating acumen, tested in one-on-one meetings with television network executives before the Los Angeles Olympics later helped him win a baseball broadcast contract worth more than $1 billion and end strikes by baseball players and umpires.

In sum, the challenges of being a manager in the public sector today are as broad and exciting as contemporary life itself. But the question of what public administrators do raises yet another question: What basic knowledge and skills must they have to fulfill the ten roles outlined above? Mark this question well, for it points squarely in the direction of the subject of this book.

What Public Administrators Need to Know

Each of these ten roles represents activities that managers undertake to ultimately accomplish three functions of public administration: **political management, program management,** and **resources management.** Of course, public administrators really need more than knowledge of these three functions—they also need skills.

Unfortunately, skills cannot be easily learned from a book; they require practice. All is not lost, however. Deep knowledge and objective facts can help practitioners better understand the skills they need, the types of roles they must perform, and the techniques they need to manage public agencies. The fads and trends that will affect the public sector in the decades ahead—whatever they might be—are unlikely to alter in any fundamental way our knowledge of political management, program management, or resources management.

Political Management

The first axiom of administration might be that organizations do not operate in vacuums. Public administrators must have a knowledge of political and legal institutions and processes.

Unfortunately, political knowledge alone is not enough; good administrators must also have political skills—skills to analyze and interpret political, social, and economic trends; skills to evaluate the consequences of administrative actions; and skills to persuade and bargain and thereby further their organization's objective. To put it bluntly: It behooves those people who possess great technical and managerial talent to be skilled politicians. I think society suffers a great loss when outstandingly talented people are so inept in their political skills that they can contribute only a small fraction of their talents. For good reason, Chapter 2 addresses the politics of administration.

An important component of political management is interorganizational relations. This is particularly true in the United States with its federal system of government. As one veteran of public service (Chase, 1984:9–10) has noted:

> *Even after 200 years we will still have not worked out clearly who does what among the three levels of government—federal, state, and local. The result is usually confusion and duplication of effort on overlapping problems. Often the aims of the manager at one level of government must be fulfilled at another*

level. For example, the welfare program, Aid to Families with Dependent Children (AFDC), is regulated and partially funded by the federal government, but it is actually delivered by state governments. Yet, because what one level of government intends is not necessarily what another level wants to do or is capable of doing, the end product is not always what was intended. As the adage goes, "Many a slip occurs between cup and lip."

While pursuing its mission, a government agency must coordinate its effort not only with other levels of government but also with public organizations in its own jurisdiction, private companies with which it has contracts, and various organizations in the third sector. How best to achieve this coordination—which is, essentially, a political question—is the subject of Chapter 3.

Given the public administrator's mandate to manage change in the pursuit of public values, ethical questions lie at the heart of administration. Some examples of those questions are as follows: How do administrators handle conflicts between their personal values and public mandates? When is a public administrator acting responsibly? Irresponsibly? In Chapter 4 we will seek some answers.

Program Management

A **program** is a major organizational endeavor with an objective. In a government agency, programs usually are designed to help fulfill statutory requirements. That is to say, they help to carry out the aims of a **public policy** like the Clean Air Act.

Program management requires a thorough grasp of the five traditional **management functions:** planning, decision making, organizing, leading, and controlling (or, as it is more frequently termed in the public sector, implementation and evaluation). **Planning** defines where the organization wants to be in the future and how it is going to get there. In Chapter 5, we will see how public administrators can define goals for future agency performance and decide on the tasks and the use of resources needed to attain them. We will also see how a lack of planning—or poor planning—can hurt an agency's performance

Closely related to planning is the process of identifying problems and opportunities, generating alternatives, and selecting an alternative. We call this process, which is the subject of Chapter 6, **decision making.** A knack for solving tricky problems is one of the hallmarks of a good administrator. Just consider the problem that Ueberroth faced on the closing day of the Los Angeles Olympics. Closing ceremonies included the award of medals for an equestrian event held miles away that same day. Rather than risk transporting the valuable horses across town, he merely arranged for stand-ins. The doubles, however, were not accustomed to huge crowds and had to be tranquilized. To put it as delicately as I can, while the potent medication calmed the colts in one sense, it excited them in another. Ueberroth's solution: Douse them with a bucket of ice water just before the ceremony (*Wall Street Journal,* 29 March 1989).

Organizing typically follows planning and decision making and, accordingly, will be the subject of Chapter 7. Organization reflects how an agency tries to attain the objectives of its programs; it involves the assignment of tasks ("These are the things we must do") and the grouping of these tasks into various organizational units (e.g., departments, divisions, bureaus, branches, offices, etc.). For example, Bill Parma grouped together a number of existing tasks in his planning department to form a new population division.

The fourth basic management function, described in Chapter 8, is to provide leadership for employees in the organization. **Leading** is the use of influence to motivate civil servants to achieve program objectives. It involves communicating these objectives to employees throughout the agency and developing in them a commitment to perform at a high level.

One of the most exciting things about studying public administration is viewing the way in which the great public executives have performed this function. In the chapters ahead, we will have ample opportunity to do just that. We will see how these men and women made "ungovernable" cities governable once again, made fragile and besieged new agencies viable, revitalized demoralized organization, and created bold new ways of attacking some of society's oldest problems.

Our fifth basic management function is **implementing and evaluating.** Absolutely critical to the success of a program is the monitoring and adjusting of the agency employees' activities to ensure that the program remains on track toward its objectives. Administrators want to know, in particular, two things: program **effectiveness** (the degree to which the program is achieving its objectives) and program **efficiency** (the amount of resources used to obtain a given volume of output). Program implementation and evaluation will be the focus of Chapter 9.

Resources Management

Three kinds of resources are essential to the accomplishment of an agency's mission: people, money, and information. If the agency lacks enough of any one of these three, it will totter like a three-legged stool with a defective leg.

Economists speak of some industries as being capital intensive, meaning that they require heavy investments in plant and equipment. Because public administration is so *people* intensive—about four fifths of a police department budget goes to salaries, for example—superior performance is ultimately based on people in an organization. The right plans, structures, and procedures play an important role, but the capabilities that lead to program success come from people—their skill, discipline, motivation, and intelligence. Leading and developing these people is the heart of successful high-performance administration and the subject of Chapter 10. People make it happen.

An adequate flow of money forms the sinews of public administration. Since few of a government agency's activities are voluntary, little happens unless it is paid for. On a more positive note, the budget can be an effective tool for influencing organizational behavior. In Chapter 11, we will be concerned with how budgets are actually formulated and implemented in government. We will also discuss how public administrators obtain fiscal resources (taxes) from their environment.

The information revolution is sweeping through governments around the world. No public sector organization can escape its effects. Dramatic reductions in the cost of obtaining, processing, and transmitting information are changing the way we manage the public sector. Most practitioners know that the revolution is under way, and few dispute its importance.

As information technology and its effects absorb more and more time and budget, public executives have a growing awareness that technology can no longer be the exclusive territory of the expert. These executives recognize the need to become directly involved in the management of the information now available.

Chapter 12 of this book aims to help public administrators respond to the challenges of the information revolution. For now, however, it is necessary only to understand that information technology is more than computers. It encompasses the information that organizations create and use as well as a wide spectrum of increasingly divergent and linked technologies that process the information. In addition to computers, data-recognition equipment, communications technologies, automation, export systems, and other hardware and software are involved.

In sum, these three functions—political management, program management, and resources management—not only answer the question of what public administrators need to know but also highlight what lies in the chapters ahead (see Figure 1-3).

Essentially, what we will attempt to do in the upcoming chapters is (1) to reconcile the current thinking on administrative theory and then (2) to reconcile that theoretical thinking with the everyday problems of the administrator who stands on the firing line. The operative term is *to reconcile,* and it merits emphasis. To reconcile, as used in item 1 does not mean merely to tie together—in a more or less neat package (usually called a survey)—all the facts, hypotheses, and opinions that happen to be in good currency among the theoreticians of administration. It means instead to inventory systematically the current state of the art; then, to eliminate mercilessly all that is dated, mediocre, irrelevant, or redundant; and last, to present the balance in as clear, concise, and consistent a manner as possible.

How Public and Private Management Differ

By considering who public administrators are, what they do, and what they need to know, we have made considerable progress toward answering the question posed in the chapter title. All that remains is to consider what public administration is not.

At one level of abstraction, we can say that the three core functions just noted are common to both public administration and business administration.* So far so good. But when we begin to consider the relative importance of these functions, sig-

* For those who doubt that business executives must be skilled *political* managers, Copley Place in Boston might provide an illuminating case study. The largest construction project in Boston's history, Copley Place required intense, open consultation by a private developer and the city neighborhoods that his project would affect. The state government insisted that the construction firm "win" its right to a long-term lease by first negotiating an agreement with representations of the affluent Back Bay and the economically, racially diverse South End. The $550 million project represented not only a complex engineering feat but a virtuoso political performance.

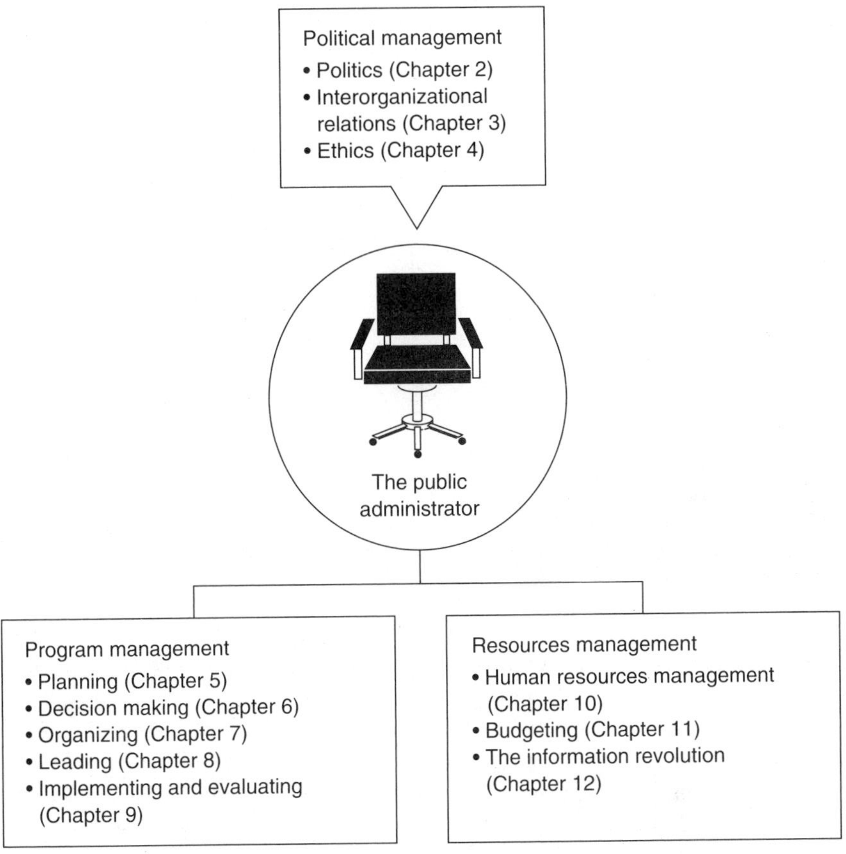

FIGURE 1-3
The Environment and Tasks of the Public Administrator

nificant differences emerge (see Figure 1-4). Moreover, based on the reflections of individuals who have operated in both the public and the private sector, we must conclude that the execution of these three functions is much more difficult in the public sector. Why should this be? Four reasons will be suggested.

Different Structures

One fundamental difference between business administration and public administration is that *responsibility in the latter is blurred.* In other words, government does not give complete authority for government policy to any one individual or institution. Let us hope that the Pod People from the far side of the Great Nebula in Andromeda do not land in Washington, asking to be taken to our leader. It would be embarrassing.

As a consequence of the blurred authority, agency heads, unlike their counterparts in industry, cannot set the level of their agencies' budgets. Rather, budgets must be submitted to department heads, who submit them in turn to the Office of Manage-

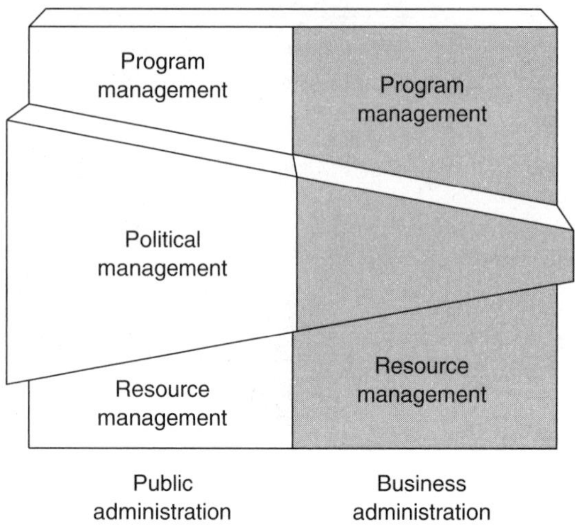

FIGURE 1-4
Relative Time Spent on Three Core Management Elements in Public and Private Sectors

ment and Budget, which submits them in turn to the president, who in turn submits them to Congress. Then things really get complicated.

Needless to say, the time lag in this process makes quick responses to new problems and opportunities—not to mention long-range planning—difficult. Unlike their industrial counterparts, agency heads lack full power to hire and fire. Finally, any planning that public administrations engage in must be shared with legislative bodies, city councils, or governing boards.

Here is how a former president of a life insurance company who became the head of the Small Business Administration explained the difference:

> *At the average company, I would report to only one person—the chairman of the board. Here, in addition to the president, I must report to 535 people. Dealing with Congress takes over 40 percent of my time.*
>
> *In business, I wouldn't have to show up for a week and everything would run smoothly. In government, I can be gone for just a day, and I come back to emergencies. It's difficult to organize well enough to let the ship sail for a few hours alone. (A. Vernon Weaver, quoted in* U.S. News & World Report, *September 25, 1978)*

Different Incentives

The second fundamental difference you may have experienced personally. Because public sector organizations receive a significant amount of financial support from sources other than their clients, *the incentive is to satisfy those who provide resources.* In fact, some agencies even view additional clients not as an opportunity but as an

Talking Shop

What Type of Person Should Become a Public Manager?

Gordon Chase spent over 20 years in government, serving as a member of the White House staff under two presidents, administrator of health services for New York City, and secretary of human services for Massachusetts. He knows well the difficulties and obstacles public administrators had to overcome to get anything done.

Given the differences between the public sector and the private sector, Chase suggests that good public managers should possess all the skills and characteristics of good private managers *plus* these five:

- They need especially good *negotiating skills* and *persuasive abilities* in order to get what they need from others they do not control and who have different agendas and interests.
- They must be able to get and retain *public credibility,* especially through use of the media. Even so, they need a *thick skin* because a certain amount of lumps are inevitable.
- They need to be *quick learners* and *fast movers* because they have little time in office in which to accomplish anything.
- They need good *leadership skills* in order to get high productivity and high-quality work from employees. They have few carrots or sticks.
- Most importantly, they must be *willing to live with uncertainty,* particularly as they rise to the higher levels of the organization.

SOURCE: Based on Gordon Chase, *Bromides for Public Managers,* Case N16-84-586 (Cambridge, Mass.: Kennedy School of Government, 1984).

additional strain on resources. In contrast, the very survival of a business hinges on its ability to get and retain customers. And that is why the attendants at McDonald's are more polite to you than the better-educated, better-paid bureaucrats at the Immigration and Naturalization Service.

Different Settings

Third, public administration could almost be described as business administration in a fishbowl. The press and the public feel that they have a right to know everything that goes on in a public agency, and the Freedom of Information Act makes sure that they can find out if they want to. To quote another businessman-turned-bureaucrat: "My biggest surprise here is how government is ruled by leakage. Employees use the press and Congress to accomplish their goals instead of meeting the issue head-on in an honest fashion. I know that if I make a decision against someone, that person will be on the phone to Congress and the press within an hour." (W. Michael Blumenthal, *Fortune,* January 29, 1979)

In the chapter that follows, you will see the multiple external forces that play on the public administrator. For example, every public administrator is ultimately under some elected official, whose chief concern is likely to center on short-run results rather than on long-run investments. The solar power satellite, which would beam solar energy to earth, may or may not be a good idea. But this much is certain: Few politicians are going to be interested in a multibillion-dollar project that will take 30 years to yield dividends to voters.

In the federal government, a completely new top-management team is possible every four years. Between elections, assistant secretaries average less than two years in the job—not much longer than the time required to find the cafeteria. In contrast, business managers tend to stay with a firm longer and thereby provide continuity. Some authorities argue that one of the strengths of the Japanese management system is that managers tend to stay with a company for a lifetime.

Different Purposes

Both public and private organizations use resources (inputs) to produce goods and services (outputs). In a public sector organization, however, outputs are hard to quantify. The Constitution is just not much help: Congress is to provide "for the common defense and general welfare"; the president is to recommend "such Measures as he shall judge necessary and expedient."

Without a single, broad measure of performance, such as profit, it becomes difficult for governments to delegate important decisions to lower-level managers to the same extent that a business firm can. Moreover, the absence of this measure of performance makes comparison between alternative investments difficult. For example, should the cancer detection program or the school lunch program be funded the extra $10 million? How many main battle tanks equal one guided missile frigate? To save whales should we prohibit Eskimos from slaughtering them, even though their entire culture is built around the whale? If the national speed limit were reduced to 20 miles per hour, the carnage on U.S. highways would be virtually eliminated. Are 30,000 lives worth millions of hours of additional travel time? At this point, the student of public administration is inclined to wonder, "Where is the bottom line around here?" Do not be too discouraged, however. As we shall see in Chapter 9, there *are* performance measures in the public sector—we just have to look a little longer and harder for them.

In sum, business managers look for profitability while public administrators are more concerned with the commonweal, that is, the common or public good. Putting it differently, a private firm is organized for the well-being of its employees and stockholders, while a public agency is supposed to serve the interests of people outside itself. This outside public focus helps to explain why I would categorize the men and women who run an organization like the Ford Foundation as essentially public administrators. Over the years, the foundation has invested heavily in agricultural research overseas and educational reform at home, tried to influence the policies of the United States and other governments, supported scholars, revitalized blighted neighborhoods, and given substantial backing to the civil rights movement.

It also helps to explain why I would categorize Peter Ueberroth's service as president of the LAOOC as public administration; his purpose was not the same as

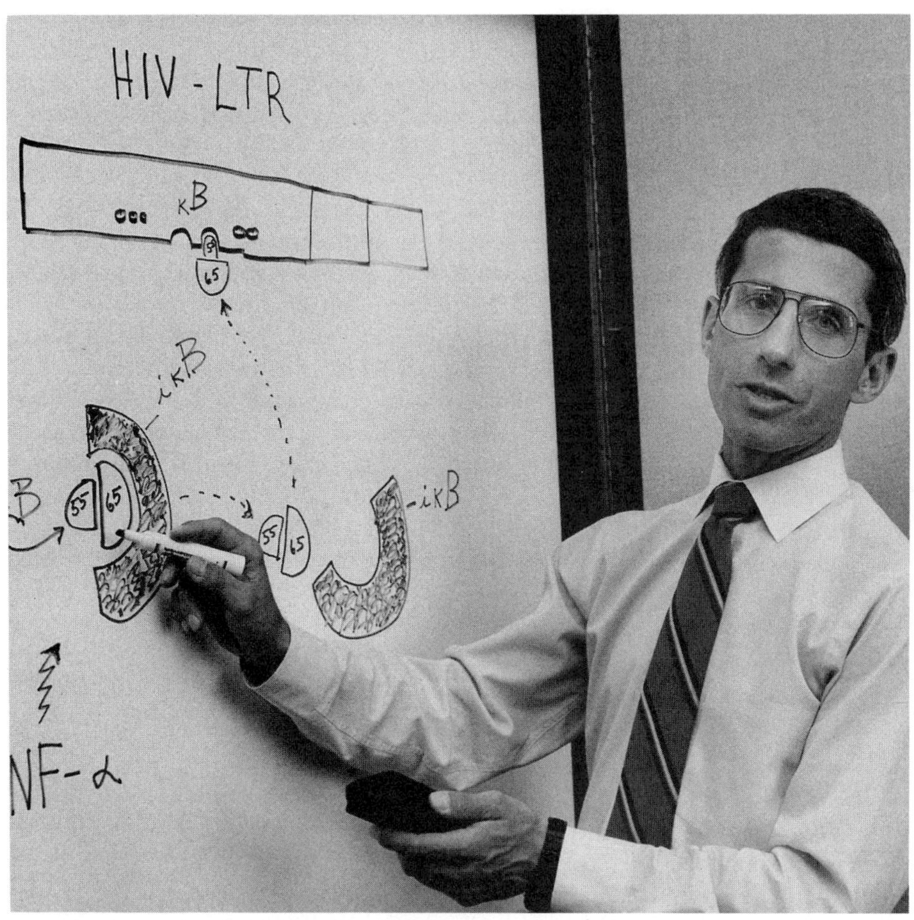

Public administration is grounded in a strong desire to serve the public and solve its problems. A good illustration of this is Dr. Anthony S. Fauci, chief of AIDS work at the National Institutes of Health.

Although government must still ensure that the drinking water is safe, that the homeless have shelter, that social security checks arrive on time, that everyone's civil rights are protected, and that third graders learn to read, many of today's challenges are more complex than those of previous decades. Besides combating the AIDS pandemic, government must also clean up toxic wastes, ensure air safety, deter insider trading, contain terrorism, hold down escalating health care costs, promote competitiveness, and fight drug abuse.

when he ran an airline. Actually, he could be quite imperious with those working for LAOOC whose motivation did not seem appropriate to him. One day in the cafeteria he stopped to talk to some women having lunch. The chat was pleasantly routine until one of the women asked about possible salary increases. Ueberroth, the unsalaried volunteer, turned cold and said angrily: "You shouldn't be working here if you don't understand what we're trying to do." (*Time,* January 7, 1985)

The purpose of the foregoing analysis has been to enumerate four major reasons why public administration tends to be more difficult than business administration. (I freely admit all exceptions to this generalization.) But it would be wrong to say that we are dealing with two separate and distinct categories of management. (Figure 1-4 should have already dispelled that notion.) A more useful way to conclude would be by recognizing that different organizations are managed in different ways. The crucial question then is not whether they are public or private, *but how they are doing.*

Let us also recognize the **interdependence of the two sectors.** While the public sector is dependent on business for resources (especially revenue and the performance of some activities through contracts), the reverse is equally true. Let me be very specific here. California is the richest state in the union—and not merely because of its factories, thriving crops, and private affluence. Little of this would have been possible had it not been for government action. Despite its great natural advantages, California has depended on public investment perhaps more than any other state. If government had not spent billions on irrigation, crops would not have grown. If it had not built up that great intellectual resource, the University of California, agribusiness, Silicon Valley, and other high-tech industries would not have flourished. In short, the public sector performs a large number of functions that are of critical importance to the health of the private sector.

Concepts for Review

- effectiveness
- efficiency
- interdependence of the two sectors
- government corporation, government-sponsored enterprise, and regulated enterprise
- management functions: planning, decision making, organizing, leading, and implementing and evaluating
- political management, program management, and resources management
- program
- public administration
- public policy
- public sector
- ten roles of a manager: figurehead, leader, liaison, monitor, disseminator, spokesperson, entrepreneur, disturbance handler, resource allocator, negotiator
- third sector

Nailing Down the Main Points

1. Traditionally, public administration is thought of as the accomplishing side of government. It comprises all those activities involved in carrying out the policies of elected officials and some activities associated with the development of those policies. This book broadens the definition of public administration: the process by which resources are marshaled and then used to cope with the problems facing a political community. Public administrators are therefore found at all levels of government as well as in a wide variety of nonbusiness institutions.

2. "A Day in the Life of Tomorrow's Public Administrator" introduced a number of important concepts. Managerial activities in the public sector involve variety, fragmentation, and brevity. Public administrators also are expected to perform a great deal of work—often quite complex—at an unrelenting pace. One of the keys to their success will continue to be the ability to deal with a changing work force.

3. Successful public administrators perform well in the ten roles of management: the interpersonal roles of figurehead, leader, and liaison; the informational roles of monitor, disseminator, and spokesperson; and the decisional roles of entrepreneur, disturbance handler, resource allocator, and negotiator.

4. This book builds around three themes: political management (i.e., operating in an environment in which groups have common or overlapping claims concerning the distribution of goods and services), program management, (i.e., formulation and implementation of public policy), and resources management (especially human, fiscal, and information).

5. Public administration differs from business administration in four respects—purpose, structure, incentive, and setting. More specifically, the purpose of public administration is often to produce public goods (things like clean air that can be shared by many members of a political community) rather than private goods (things like skateboards that can be individually owned and enjoyed). At other times, its purpose might be to produce justice; seldom, if ever, will it seek profit.

Problems

1. Donald Trump, the New York real estate executive, was frustrated. After six years of effort and having spent nearly $13 million, the City of New York had still not rebuilt an ice-skating rink. Therefore, Trump offered to take over the rink construction, promising to complete the job in less than six months for $3 million. He would cover cost overruns. He completed the job in less than five months and about $750,000 under budget. What does this story mean? That private enterprise is more efficient than public bureaucracies? Think carefully.

2. Does Bill Parma's day seem chaotic to you? Why or why not?

3. Is business really better run than government? Read one of the following books and report your conclusions.

   Ken Auletta, *The Art of Corporate Success: The Story of Schlumberger* (New York: G.P. Putnam's Sons, 1984.)

   David Halberstam, *The Reckoning* (New York: William Morrow, 1986).

   Lee Iacocca, *Iacocca* (New York: Bantam Books, 1984).

   Tracy Kidder, *The Soul of a New Machine* (Boston: Little, Brown, 1981).

   Michael Moritz, *The Little Kingdom: The Private Story of Apple Computer* (New York: William Morrow, 1984).

John J. Nance, *Splash of Colors: The Self-Destruction of Braniff International* (New York: William Morrow, 1984).

Robert Sobel, *IBM: Colossus in Transition* (New York: Bantam Books, 1983).

J. Patrick Wright, *On a Clear Day You Can See General Motors* (New York: Avon Books, 1979).

Brock Yates, *The Decline and Fall of the American Automobile Industry* (New York: Random House, 1984).

CASE 1.1

Federal Bureau of Investigation

Established in 1908, the Federal Bureau of Investigation (FBI) is the principal investigative arm of the U.S. Department of Justice. The FBI has a special talent for broad, complicated investigations that require a range of resources: accountants to delve into complicated records, technicians to deploy wiretaps and other eavesdropping devises, and surveillance crews that can use such tools as the bureau's 85 airplanes. It has dealt with some of the most important cases of recent years, from congressional corruption to the arrest and conviction in 1992 of John Gotti, the most notorious gangster since Al Capone.

With about 22,400 employees and a budget of $1.4 billion, the FBI is somewhat like a large service company that operates five major "lines of business":

1. *Fighting organized crime.* In the 1960s, the bureau would arrest middle-level gangsters, mainly for gambling, and put them in jail for a few years. Meanwhile, the mob merely replaced them with others. But with the passage of the Racketeer Influenced and Corrupt Organizations Act of 1970, things began to change. By patiently examining the inner machinery of the mob through a network of undercover agents, informants, and wiretaps, the bureau has been able to bring criminal conspiracy charges against nearly 100 Mafia bosses and send them to prison.

2. *Controlling illicit drugs.* For years members of Congress tried to persuade the FBI to take over responsibility for investigating drug trafficking. If the FBI had agreed, it would have meant a big budget increase, but then-director J. Edgar Hoover would not agree. Although the FBI did not enter this field until 1982, today it would command virtually all of the bureau's attention—if managers let it. Leaving most street arrests to local police, the bureau concentrates on major distributors of cocaine and heroin. Agents like narcotics work because good and evil are not blurred as they sometimes can be in white-collar crimes like gambling. Because the drug trade generates so much money, there is a risk that agents might be corrupted. So far that has not happened.

3. *Stopping white-collar crime.* For many years Hoover also resisted enlarging the FBI's activities to include the systematic investigation of organized crime. He justified this with the simple expedient of denying that there was any such thing as organized crime, whether it be called the Mafia, the syndicate, the outfit, or the mob. Today the FBI details 1,600 agents to the pursuit of public officials who take bribes, defense contractors who cheat,

and other swindlers. One recent example of a successful sting operation was an investigation of commodities trading in Chicago. Agents masqueraded as traders at the Board of Trade and the Mercantile Exchange to check out suspicions of widespread cheating. Not only did the bureau have to provide agents with enough cash to make them convincing or affluent traders, but it also had to cover actual trading losses by its agents. Despite this kind of effort, the FBI can stop only a fraction of white-collar crime. It might detect a $300,000 embezzlement in a Memphis bank, but in San Antonio, where agents are overwhelmed with drug traffic, the same felony could go unnoticed.

4. *Countering terrorism.* In the 1970s, terrorism seemed to be on the rise everywhere in the United States, with Puerto Rican nationalists and black militants on the left and the Ku Klux Klan and neo-Nazis on the right. But, in the 1980s, as the FBI became more effective in amassing information on such groups, terrorist bombings and shootings began to subside.

5. *Catching spies.* Even after the collapse of the Soviet Union deterring espionage within the United States remains an important business to the FBI. During World War II, the FBI went to great lengths to defend the United States from encroachment by other agencies. For example, when some officers of the Office of Strategic Services (OSS)—the predecessor of the CIA—were attempting to burglarize a foreign embassy in Washington, Hoover learned of it and sent some FBI agents to prevent it. The OSS head complained to President Roosevelt, but Hoover won. The number of agents assigned to this task is secret, but it could be around 1,800. The biggest success in this business is quietly uncovering a spy and getting him or her to work for the bureau.

The bureau's investigations are conducted through 56 field offices. As in other businesses, the New York City office offers the ambitious agent a particularly good opportunity for advancement. The city is where the work is, and more than 10 percent of the entire force is there. In recent years, the organized-crime field has been the bureau's most glamorous, and the agent who performs well might win a posting as assistant special agent in charge of a small office, a first step on the management ladder.

Perhaps the best job in the FBI is the bureau's version of "district manager": the special agent in charge (SAC) of one of the field offices. Almost all of the SACs come up through the criminal investigations division rather than through counterintelligence. What makes SACs' jobs attractive is considerable prestige in their locale, together with a measure of autonomy from headquarters in Washington. To be sure, headquarters sets priorities, sorting out demands that have accumulated over the years from its "board of directors": the several congressional committees having authority over the FBI and the White House. (We should not, however, overemphasize the influence of the latter; presidents have gone to great lengths to appear to leave the FBI alone ever since the charge was made that Nixon was using the FBI to help cover up the Watergate scandal.) Within this framework, SACs have some freedom to choose which problems to attack in their districts.

During the 1990s, the FBI will undoubtedly face new management challenges. Its overall caseload has risen in the past few years, yet its budget has declined in real dollars. Thus, the FBI's celebrated library of fingerprints is only partly automated and has fallen behind the smaller but more sophisticated operations of states like California and Florida.

Finally, the bureau is about to experience the greatest turnover in personnel in its history. Half of its agents, veterans of

Countering terrorism is only one of the FBI's five major "lines of business." While it may have declined in relative importance in recent years, FBI hostage rescue teams continue to train.

a big expansion in the early 1970s, will retire before the mid-1990s. But this might also be an opportunity to transform a bureau overwhelmingly composed of white men. Today only 9 percent of the agents are women (like the protagonist in the award-winning film *Silence of the Lambs*); only 4 percent, Hispanic; and another 4 percent, black. One suit brought in El Paso by a Hispanic agent, a 26-year veteran of the FBI, charged that his career had been undermined by bigotry at the highest level in the bureau. In a class action, Bernardo (Matt) Perez was joined by fully three quarters of the bureau's Hispanics. The irony is that the FBI should be basking in considerable glory from its success in its five lines of business, but instead its successes have been overshadowed by charges like this one.

Case Questions

1. Discuss the three functions of public administration—political management, program management, and resources management—in the context of the FBI.
2. If you were asked to advise the FBI director on which problems or issues to concentrate, what would you say?
3. How do you measure the bottom line (i.e., performance) in this kind of organization?
4. What do you make of the FBI's reluctance to take responsibility for drug trafficking?

Case References

Gordon Witkin, "The FBI's New Most Wanted List," *U.S. News & World Report,* May 29, 1989; Lee Smith, "The FBI Is a Tough Outfit to Run," *Fortune,* October 9, 1988; James Q. Wilson, *The Investigators* (New York: Basic Books, 1978); Stanford J. Ungar, *FBI* (Boston: Little, Brown, 1975); Peter Maas, "The Struggle Within the FBI," *Parade Magazine,* December 18, 1988.

CASE 1.2

★★★★★★★★★★★★★★★★★★★★★★★★★★★★★★★★★★★

The Transportation Chief

An aide catches New Jersey's transportation commissioner between meetings to say that a reporter has an urgent question for her. Why did she give pay raises to members of her senior staff just before the governor's spending freeze took effect?

She responds without hesitation: "That was in August, right? Well, that's when their annual reviews were due, and I turned them in on time. You just tell that reporter that I take care of my people because they work their asses off."

The answer was pure Hazel Frank Gluck: quick, straightforward, and slightly salty. Gluck has an immediate energetic presence—whether responding to reporters' questions or darting through her suite of offices to chat with staff members. Without exception, they call her Hazel. There is little formality in the Gluck style: She convenes staff meetings with a breezy "Hi guys, what's up?"

Gluck administers the New Jersey Department of Transportation, a relatively small bureaucracy that has jurisdiction over the state's nontoll roads, ferries, bridges, and small airports. But she also chairs the board of New Jersey Transit, the state-run mass transit system. Together these two entities have 16,000 employees and an annual budget of $900 million.

The key to New Jersey's—and Gluck's—success in transportation policy is mobility. If corporations cannot get their employees to work in New Jersey, they will go down the turnpike to Delaware or Pennsylvania, taking thousands of jobs with them. Creating mobility in the nation's most densely populated state, with more cars per mile on its roads than anywhere else in the world, is no easy task.

Gluck was born in Brooklyn, New York, the child of immigrant Jewish parents, and spent the first few years of her life there. She says, "I realized when I got into politics what Brooklyn was all about. It was about street smarts. And it was about understanding certain things that some people never understand unless they have certain experiences in their life." She says that in her current job, working with labor is where her Brooklyn experience really paid off.

Gluck's skills are not the result of formal training. They were acquired in a series of jobs of such short duration that friends teased her about not being able to hold one. Her response is to brag that she has come a long way for a "displaced homemaker." That is because in 1970 she was living in California with her husband, a doctor, and raising their two children; except for selling a little real estate and playing golf, most of her activity was centered on the home.

When the family moved back East, however, Gluck saw a job she really wanted: the first consumer affairs advisor for Ocean County, New Jersey. She got good press coverage for her consumer affairs efforts, and in 1976 was easily elected county commissioner. Three years later, she ran successfully for the New Jersey Assembly, served one two-year term, and then ran against an incumbent state senator. She lost.

So in early 1981, a year after she and her husband were divorced, Helen Gluck found herself "unemployed, at 40-some, with only a degree in speech." Two months later, the new governor asked her to be director of the state lottery. After three years in that position, where she got high marks, the governor appointed her insurance commissioner and then, a scant 14 months later, promoted her to the transportation department.

The agency she inherited is a conglomeration created by the forced marriage of public transit bureaucrats, planners, and old-time highway engineers who believed that a straight line was the shortest distance between two points and built roads that way. Gluck soon revamped the department, breaking up the powerful engineering and operations division and making the policy and planning division the pivotal one in the department.

Next came the problem of ethics. There was, for instance, the questionable use of agency-issued cards—some employees had been using agency-issued credit cards for unauthorized purposes. There were also problems with conflicts of interest—employees going to lunch and dinner with contractors. Although there were policies to cover such matters, there was, in Gluck's words, "so much gray that it allowed them to do a lot of things that you shouldn't do in state government."

She cracked down. A series of retirements and resignations ensued. Morale dropped for a time. But rather than fill vacancies with outsiders, she promoted from within. She articulated positions well and made people feel that what they were doing was important. Morale rose again.

There was still much to do. The four-year transportation trust fund was about to expire and needed renewal—for a longer period of time and with more funding. Knowing it would be hard to convince the state legislature, she started planning her campaign early. Key officials went out to speak to citizens' groups and visit editorial boards. Although Gluck had hoped to raise the gas tax by 5 cents, the governor accepted, in the end, an increase of 4.5 cents.

Whatever Gluck's role in that compromise, most people acknowledged that she had made the best case possible to the governor. Her credibility remained intact.

Gluck needed all her lobbying to push the governor's second major transportation initiative, Transplan. This legislation would allow the state greater authority to limit access to highways and to foster regional planning authorities. The major hurdle to Transplan was the fact that every square mile of New Jersey is incorporated into one of 567 fiercely independent municipalities, each doing its own planning. Persuading these home-rule municipalities to give up some prerogatives would not be easy, but Gluck started to build a consensus with verve. To get the bill passed, she agreed to some compromises but remained adamant on those that "would gut the bill."

Although Hazel Gluck knew very little about transportation when she accepted the job of New Jersey's transportation chief, when she left office she had moved the state a little further away from the near-fatal gridlock that still threatens its future. By the time she left office, she was calling transportation her "passion." She says it was the first job she ever had that did not become boring.

Case Reference

Based on Kathleen Sylvester, "Hazel Frank Gluck: A Transportation Chief Who Can Break Political Gridlock," *Governing,* March 1989.

Case Questions

1. What major public administrator roles are depicted in this case?
2. Why do you think Gluck found her job so satisfying?
3. Compare Gluck's job as transportation chief with her previous jobs. How are they similar? How are they different?

★★★★★★★★★★★★★★★★★★★★★★★★★★★★★★★★★★★

PART I

★ ★

Political Management

CHAPTER 2 The Politics of Administration

Introduction

Today administrators cannot ignore the political environment of their agencies. In the first place, these administrators are involved in both formulation and implementation of public policy. Because policy decisions so profoundly influence who gets what, this involvement in policy inevitably involves them in politics. In the second place, they must deal on a day-to-day basis not only with their immediate supervisors but also with all kinds of external groups and publics. As a result, administrators find themselves in a kind of political force field. Competent administrators do not turn their backs on these matters, however. "The lifeblood of administration is power. Its attainment, maintenance, increase, dissipation, and loss are subjects the practitioners can ill afford to neglect" (Long, 1949:257).

In this chapter, we begin with a couple of examples designed to show how difficult it is for public administrators to ignore the political realm. We then see how the issue of separating politics from administration was debated among the early students of public administration.

That brings us to the heart of the chapter, which can be highlighted with three questions: How is the public administrator involved in the policymaking process? What are the relationships between the administrator and external political forces? And, How can the administrator be more skillful politically?

On the Folly of Separating Politics from Administration

The Case of A. J. Cervantes

In the 1960s, the voters of St. Louis twice elected as mayor a successful insurance executive. His name was A. J. Cervantes, and his message to the voters was plain: "Put government back into the hands of men who know the meaning of the tax dollar, the balanced budget, business methods, and a successful city."

In retrospect, what does Cervantes (1973:19–20) think about this notion—still quite popular—that businesspeople can restore life to American cities? "As one becomes more involved in governing a large city, one learns that in many cases business methods cannot be translated into political reality." To take a word from business, let us consider a couple of his "practical" examples:

- St. Louis has a number of recreation programs operating in school playgrounds and parks. Some programs have many participants, others few. Good management would say to close those programs that have relatively few participants, but this would mean that some neighborhoods would have no programs for those who would use the facilities. Recreation centers must be reasonably close to everyone, so all of them stay open.
- St. Louis needs a new, modern airport suitable for the needs of the 21st century. Federal officials and airlines agree that the best location would be in Illinois, just across the river from St. Louis. Jobs would be created, the area's economy given a boost, and the city's tax base improved. But Missouri interests—union and business—want the contracts and jobs that would flow from the new airport. Even though Missouri does not have a site or funds for the land, they would block the Illinois airport. Would a good manager turn down an investment opportunity because one group of workers or subcontractors received the benefits rather than another? Not one who wanted to survive. Yet political reality forced other government leaders to oppose the Illinois site.

The Case of Jimmy Carter

Before his election in 1976, Jimmy Carter devoted little attention to thinking about major national issues. Until he began his race for the White House, his life had been devoted chiefly to managing a peanut warehouse, serving on community planning boards, and taking care of state business (such as highway construction). Therefore, when he entered the Oval Office, he had to put himself in seclusion and study the issues, from arms control to federal tax systems to U.S. African policy.

This he seemed to enjoy. As Martin Schram wrote: "His was the clockwork presidency. He was chief engineer and operating officer of the United States of America. His role, as he seemed to see it, was to study it all and then engineer the very best program a country could want, send it up to Capitol Hill for enactment, and then wait to sign the measure after congressional enactment" (*Washington Post,* October 27, 1980).

Although this approach has a certain aesthetic appeal, it is no way to run a government. Political realities intrude. Just consider Carter's attempts to reorganize the government. He seemed to ignore the fact that every department and agency was connected to a powerful outside interest. So he proceeded as if he were a student at Harvard Business School facing a Friday deadline on his solution to a management problem. Concentrating on the details, he ignored persuading, cultivating, and even counting key congressional committee leaders. What communication he did have with congressional leadership centered on the economic and managerial advantages of his "solution"—not on why each senator and representative should want to do it for the sake of his or her own career.

Once his plan had taken shape, Carter then turned the awesome responsibility of shepherding it through Congress to an aide. As Schram reports, the aide met alone with Carter on his first visit to the White House but after that consulted with the president mainly by memorandums.

In sharp contrast, Carter's successor, Ronald Reagan, made several dramatic trips to Capitol Hill. Another important contrast was that Reagan knew that priorities had to be set and political strength had to be husbanded for principal goals rather than dissipated on peripheral schemes. Consequently, Reagan focused his persuasive powers on selling his economic policy, whereas Carter dumped a desktop full of major policy proposals on Congress in his first year.

The irony in the Carter record is that a man who had displayed considerable persuasive powers and charm during his 1976 presidential campaign left those vital attributes at the doorstep of the White House. The job of chief executive was a job for an engineer, not a politician. Or so he thought.

Politics and Administration: A Historical Perspective

The point of the preceding examples is obvious. Purely administrative matters can seldom be separated from politics. Yet, interestingly enough, this view could not always be found in the literature of public administration. In fact, for several decades, its antithesis prevailed.

"The field of administration is a field of business," a young academic in the Progressive movement argued in 1887. "It is removed," he continued, "from the hurry and strife of politics." An incredible observation, perhaps; but its author, Woodrow Wilson, did not stand alone. For example, F. Goodnow, often termed the "father of

American administration," and W. F. Willoughby, another early pioneer in the field, also had little trouble dividing government into two functions: political decision and administrative execution. Unlike Wilson and Carter, Goodnow and Willoughby had the good fortune of never having to carry such views into the White House (see Working Profile).

It was not until the end of World War II that these difficulties in politics-administration separation began to be widely recognized. Fritz Morstein–Marx's *The Elements of Public Administration* (1946) pointed out the involvement of administrators in policy formation, in the use of discretionary power, and in the general political process. The following year, Dwight Waldo (1948:121) put the debate into sharp focus: "The disagreement is not generally with politics-administration itself; only with the spirit of rigid separatism. In some measure, this is an advance into realism. In some measure, it flows from a feeling of strength and security, a feeling that the processes and the study of administration have matured, that they no longer need be isolated from the germs of politics. Administration can even think about invading the field of politics, the field of policy determination."

Has the debate ended, as Professor Waldo suggests, by increased realism? The next two sections argue the affirmative. Our approach will be analytic in that we divide the issue into two components. First, we consider the degree to which administration has entered the field of policy determination; second, we consider the degree to which it has entered the field of politics.

Administration in the Field of Policy Determination

We all recall the neat textbook diagrams in Government 101 outlining how a bill becomes a law, that very logical process by which legislative bodies make **policy.** (By *policy,* I mean here simply laws that are, in scope and impact, major attempts to solve problems or to seize opportunities. (Chapter 5 will provide a more rigorous—but not dissimilar—definition of *policy.*) In the process, we were told, the chief executive is the chief legislator, since most major policies—roughly 80 percent over the last two decades—originate with him. Further, we learned that members of Congress submit bills, which must pass through committee, onto the floor and the other chamber, and (prior to a presidential signature) probably to a conference committee. Things were so simple.

The foregoing interpretation of the policymaking process is not so much wrong as it is misleading. In the first place, administrators frequently participate in the process. Chief executives rarely make decisions about issues not presented to them. The issues and solutions, therefore, sometimes bubble up from the echelon of planners just above the career administrators and just below the political appointees of the cabinet and subcabinet.

(text continues on p. 39)

★★★★★★★★★★★★★★★★★★★★★★★★★★★★★★★★★★

WORKING PROFILE

Woodrow Wilson

Woodrow Wilson was that happy exception, a political scientist who had a chance to participate in public affairs at its most elevated level. Let us begin with Wilson the young political scientist.

The Political Scientist

In 1887, Wilson wrote an essay that marks the symbolic beginning of American administration. The essay, which appeared in the *Political Science Quarterly,* was entitled "The Study of Administration." Professor Wilson begins by noting the curious fact that, though the study of politics had begun some 2,200 years ago, it was not until the 19th century that administration ("the most obvious part of government") began to demand attention: "[Administration] is government in action, and one might very naturally expect to find that government in action had arrested the attention and provoked the scrutiny of writers of politics very early in the history of systematic thought." But such was not the case; rather, political writers focused on the constitution of government, the nature of the state, the essence of sovereignty, the monarchy versus democracy, and other lofty, abstract principles.

The question was always: Who shall make the law, and what shall that law be? The other question, how law should be administered with enlightenment, with equity, with speed, and without friction, was put aside as "practical detail" which clerks could arrange after doctors had agreed upon principles.

In Wilson's view, the size and complexity of modern society had grown to a point at which a "science of administration" was essential. The time had come, he argued, to make the execution of government policy more businesslike. "The field of administration is a field of business. It is removed from the hurry and strife of politics." Note how clearly he sees this separation:

Woodrow Wilson as a young lawyer in Atlanta, four years before he wrote his seminal essay on public administration. (Princeton Library)

Public administration is detailed and systematic execution of public law. Every particular application of general law is an act of administration. The assessment and raising of taxes, for instance, the hanging of a criminal, the transportation and delivery of the mail, the equipment and recruiting of the Army, and Navy, et cetera, are all obvious acts of administration, but the general laws which direct these things to be done are as obviously outside of and above administration. The broad plans of government action are not administrative; the detailed execution of such plans are administrative.

Perhaps the most significant issue that Wilson addressed in his 1887 essay concerned the methods by which a science of administration would be developed. He condemned the American tendency to take governing for

(continued)

granted and to overrely on experience and on trial and error. Essentially, he called for Americans to study the administrative methods of the Europeans, which were already highly developed, and to adapt these methods to the American polity.

Although scholars may debate how much direct influence Wilson's essay had on the development of American public administration, few doubt that it foreshadowed the spirit of that development. For the next half century, the emphasis was on finding certain immutable principles of administration and separating administrative questions from political ones. This orthodoxy reached its high noon in 1937 with the publication of Luther H. Gulick and Lyndall Urwick's *Papers on the Science of Administration.* They argued that there are principles that can be arrived at inductively from the study of organizations. Moreover, these principles are universal, applicable to all organizations. Among the more common principles that appeared in the literature of the time were these three:

- Administrative efficiency is increased by *specialization* of the task among the group.
- Administrative efficiency is increased by arranging the members of the group in a determined *hierarchy* of authority or chain of command.
- Administrative efficiency is increased by limiting the *span of control* (i.e., how many people a manager directly supervises) at any point in the hierarchy to a small number (say, three to seven).

As we will see later in the book (Chapter 6), this orthodoxy would be challenged the very next year (in 1938). But now we must consider Wilson the politician.

The University President

One of the shallowest disdains is the sneer against the politician. The invidious implication of the label is, of course, against those who pursue self-interest through political strategies. We forget that few great things are accomplished in public affairs without political calculation. Wilson's life serves as a reminder of this axiom.

Fifteen years after the appearance of his essay, Wilson was chosen president of Princeton University. He immediately began a series of sweeping reforms. First, he endeavored to compel Princeton's relatively affluent and often indolent students to study. Entrance requirements were raised, and those who failed their exams were sent away. (Some undergraduate wiseacre is reported to have said that, if Wilson kept on, he would make Princeton an educational institution.) Next, Wilson introduced an instructional system that brought every student into close relations with a teacher who would introduce the young student to the world of books. In his efforts to raise money for this new and expensive system, Wilson was brought into closer touch with Princeton alumni all over the country, and he became rather well known. Third, he proposed that an elitist club system at Princeton be replaced by dormitories. All students—rich and poor—would live together and have their rooms assigned by lot.

Students, alumni, and some faculty found the pace of these reforms too swift, and they resisted. Apparently, Wilson had forgotten, or chose to ignore, the advice in his own book *The State,* which appeared in 1889. There he advocated a gradualist view of social change: "In politics nothing radically novel may be safely attempted. No result of value can ever be reached except through slow and gradual development, the careful adaptations and nice modifications of growth." It is worth noting that both Harvard and Yale later adopted in essence the plans he proposed for undergraduates.

Although these reforms were popular in educational circles throughout the country, they were halted at Princeton. It was widely rumored that Wilson would resign at commencement in 1910. But Wilson's efforts at Princeton, along with his speeches and articles on political issues of the day, had given him a national reputation. In 1910, he was offered the Democratic nomination for the governorship of New Jersey. He accepted. Politics, he thought, was his real calling. As he had explained to a friend several years earlier:

I do feel a very real regret that I have been shut out from my heart's first—*primary—ambition and purpose, which was to take an active, if possible, a leading part in public life. . . . I have a strong instinct for leadership. . . . I have no patience with the tedious world of what is known as "research." . . . [My] power to write was meant to be a handmaiden to my power to speak and organize action.*

The Politician

As a governor, Wilson was able to provide the necessary leadership for the enactment of a series of bills aimed at election reform, employee compensation, utilities regulation, school reform, and city governance. These successes brought him into the arena of national politics and helped secure for him the Democratic nomination for president in 1912.

His first term as president was as successful as his stint as governor. The first Wilson administration probably produced as much positive legislation as any administration had since Alexander Hamilton who had, as secretary of the treasury under George Washington, presented a far-reaching financial program to the first Congress.

No one, however, has ever explained how Wilson, so deft a politician in 1913, could have made the blunders that he did six years later. In December 1919, Wilson set sail for Europe as head of the U.S. delegation to the Paris Peace Conference. Having supported his war policy of 17 months, Republicans were angry that Wilson did not include any active Republicans or any senator in the delegation. When Wilson returned from Paris with the signed treaty, quarrels over its ratification broke out immediately. Nevertheless, the Senate probably would have ratified the treaty if certain reservations protecting U.S. sovereignty had been added. Wilson refused, however, to compromise even slightly.

If Wilson had been willing to compromise, he could have brought the United States into the League of Nations just as he might have saved his reforms at Princeton. But, when the possibility of rejection by the Senate was presented to him, he snapped: "Anyone who opposes me in that, I'll crush!" As he had written in an article while still a professor: "Tolerance is an admirable intellectual gift; but it is of little worth in politics. Politics is a war of *causes*; a joust of principles. Government is too serious a matter to admit to meaningless courtesies."

Although usually an effective leader, he could, when involved in a great cause, become dogmatic, inflexible, and shortsighted. I suggest, with diffidence, that Wilson did not always fully grasp the relationship between policy and politics.

SOURCES: August Heckscher, *Woodrow Wilson* (New York: Scribners, 1991); and Richard Hofstadter, *The American Political Tradition* (New York: Vintage Books, 1948).

★★★★★★★★★★★★★★★★★★★★★★★★★★★★★★★★★★★

In the second place, administrative decisions may, in effect, produce policy. For example, the choice of new weapon systems, of new state highway routes, of solar energy programs, or of the level of price support for agricultural commodities are all likely to be influenced greatly by administrators. In sum, administrative agencies are influential in both the formulation and the implementation of public policy. This fact is quite important. And at least one political scientist suggested a redefinition of public administration in terms of policymaking: "Public administration is that organized and purposeful interaction of society which, within law, systematically formulates and applies policies of government agencies" (Boyer, 1964). Without necessarily subscribing to this definition, we might at least take a closer look at what the formulation and implementation of policy involves.

Formulation of Policy

Although the main movers and shakers in formulating public policies in the executive branch are the political appointees in departments and bureaus, career civil servants themselves provide a productive source of new ideas. In some instances, an administrative agency may conceive of its function largely as accommodating the needs of some interest group, which is representing its specialized clientele (farmers, truckers, bankers, and so on). Thus, the policy proposal is really designed to further those interests.

Such is not always the case. NASA alone proposed to go to the moon. "Operating pretty much in a political vacuum in terms of policy guidance, and basing their choice on what constituted a rational technical program of manned space flight development, NASA planners chose a lunar-landing objective fully two years before President Kennedy announced his choice of the lunar landing as a national goal." And without the Kennedy decision in 1961, NASA no doubt would have continued pressing for the lunar decision (see Lambright, 1976:195).

Despite the popular perception that civil servants merely execute policies set by their superiors, these officials can at times seize the initiative. Consider these two examples:

- *Presenting the mayor with a fait accompli:* A few years ago, the unit responsible for drug addicts in New York City was the Addiction Services Agency (ASA). Gordon Chase, who was the city's health service administrator, had no direct responsibility for ASA but thought that too little was being done to treat the thousands of addicts on the streets. Lacking formal authority to undertake any new program, Chase nevertheless resolved to establish his own treatment program. His first move was to send the Mayor's Narcotics Control Council a proposal to treat over 15,000 in less than a year. The number was deliberately exaggerated in order to get key officials to think big and create momentum. Then, before he had even heard from the mayor, he began to build a first-rate staff. The head of this new staff immediately began opening treatment programs in existing institutions, pressing to meet deadlines, and overcoming community opposition. In a few months his program had treated 6,000 addicts, and within three years it had risen to over 20,000 (Warwick, 1981).

- *Taking on the legal-judicial establishment:* Carl Bianchi manages the entire Idaho court system for the justices of the Supreme Court. Bianchi thought that court delay, caused by the attitudes of the people involved in the system, was excessive. Therefore he decided to take control of the pace of litigation away from the lawyers and give it to the courts. His first move was to marshal the support of the people he worked for, the Supreme Court justices. Next he went public with the problem, pointing out the number of cases that were over ten years old, telling the media horror stories of how delays had bankrupted farmers and businesses, hammering the message that judges not lawyers should control the pace of the litigation. Then he set time standards for how long a case should take and developed a computer tracking system. Rather quickly, Bianchi disposed of 90 percent of the older cases in the system. Within two years, he reduced by over 47 percent the number of cases that had taken longer than the time standard. The court administrator had changed the legal culture of the state (based on a speech by Bianchi excerpted in Palumbo & Maynard-Moody, 1991).

Agencies also become involved in policy formulation when they recommend to the legislature amendments to existing laws. A large part—perhaps the major portion—of modern legislation is proposed by administrative agencies. This should not be surprising. Agencies are closest to where the action is and therefore are more likely to see imperfection and incompleteness in the laws. Indeed, legislatures *expect* that those who deal continuously with problems will suggest improvements.

In concluding this discussion of the role of the administrator in policy formulation, we ought to note its negative aspect. Bureaucracy *stops* far more policy than it formulates. Is this a bad thing? One close observer of Washington thinks not:

> *As an entity the bureaucracy is no better equipped to manufacture grand designs for government programs than carpenters, electricians, and plumbers are to be architects. But if an architect attempted to build a house, the results might well be disastrous. What the White House identifies as bureaucracy's inherent deficiencies are often its strengths. Effective functioning of the governmental machine requires a high degree of stability, uniformity, and awareness of the impact of new policies, regulations, and procedures on the affected public. (Seidman, 1980:76)*

Implementation of Policy

The formulation of policy ends when the policy becomes law. The annual product of Congress appears in the *Statutes at Large* and the collection of all statutes of the nation still in force appears in the *U.S. Code.*

Now, the implementation begins. In Chapter 9, we shall look at this process from a management perspective, but here our perspective is political. Our aim: to lay bare the ways in which administrative decisions may implement policy. We shall note four: (1) rule making, (2) adjudication, (3) law enforcement, and (4) program operations.

Rule Making. Administrative rule making is the establishment of **prospective rules**; that is, agency statements of general applicability and future effect that concern the rights of private parties. These guidelines have the force and effect of law.

Under the requirements of the **federal Administrative Procedures Act of 1946** (APA), general notice of proposed rule making must be published in the ***Federal Register*** (see Figure 2-1). The *Register,* published five days a week, also contains the latest presidential orders and rules adopted by agencies and a great variety of official notices. Items range from the results of mileage tests on model autos to a notice that the Mississippi conservation director was granted a federal permit to "capture and transport alligators" in that state and move them "to more advantageous locations."

Notices of proposed rules must clearly indicate where the proceedings are to be held, under what legal authority rules are being proposed, and the substance of the proposed rules. After such notice is given, interested parties are to be provided with the opportunity to participate in the rule-making proceedings through the presentation of written data. At the discretion of the agency, oral presentation may be permitted. Unless notice or hearing is required by the statutes governing the agency's operation, notice of rule making can be withheld if the agency considers it to be "impracticable, unnecessary, or contrary to public interest." Although this could potentially exclude many proceedings from public participation, agencies do in practice attempt to conform to the spirit of the APA.

A typical hearing might involve an Environmental Protection Agency (EPA) official discussing proposals to curtail hydrocarbon emission in a city. These might range from controversial (e.g., gasoline rationing and limiting car travel) to mild (e.g., establishing car pools and installing vapor-recovery systems at service stations). In any event, the agency comes up with the final proposals.

Those who wish to change or repeal rules are given the opportunity of petition by the APA, although changes to and repeal of rules on this basis have been extremely rare. Actually, no effective way to compel an agency to alter its policies exists—short of recourse to a superior agency, to the courts, or to the Congress.

In sum, rule making by more than 100 agencies is a continual national activity. Collectively, the volume of rules to a substantial extent is policy. Rule making involves modifying existing policies as well as adopting new ones: The Department of Agriculture describes the labeling requirements for pesticides one day; the Food and Drug Administration (FDA) prescribes safe levels of pesticide residues on plants the next; and an agency in the Interior Department sets a different standard of pesticide toxicity for fish and fowl on another occasion. Moreover, as we shall see in the next chapter, these vertical negotiations with Washington are crisscrossed with horizontal negotiations at the state and local levels.

Adjudication. Another important way in which agencies implement policy is through their adjudicative powers, granted to them by Congress. Adjudication differs from rule making in that it applies only to the specific parties involved in a controversy

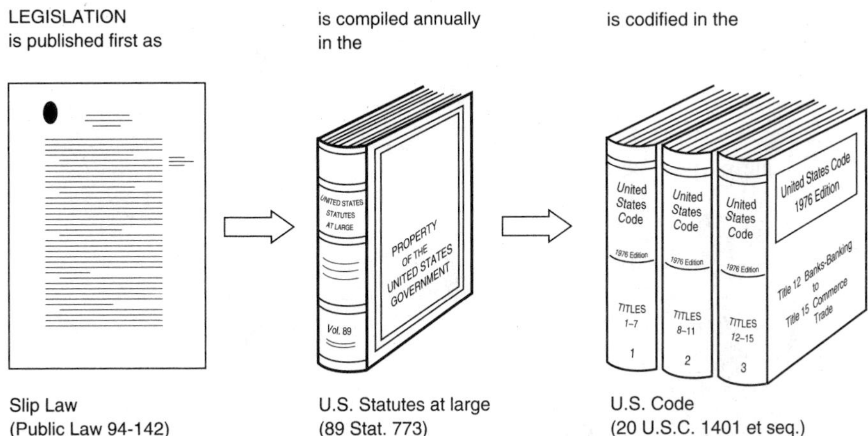

Legislation Is Implemented by Federal Agencies as Rules and Regulations

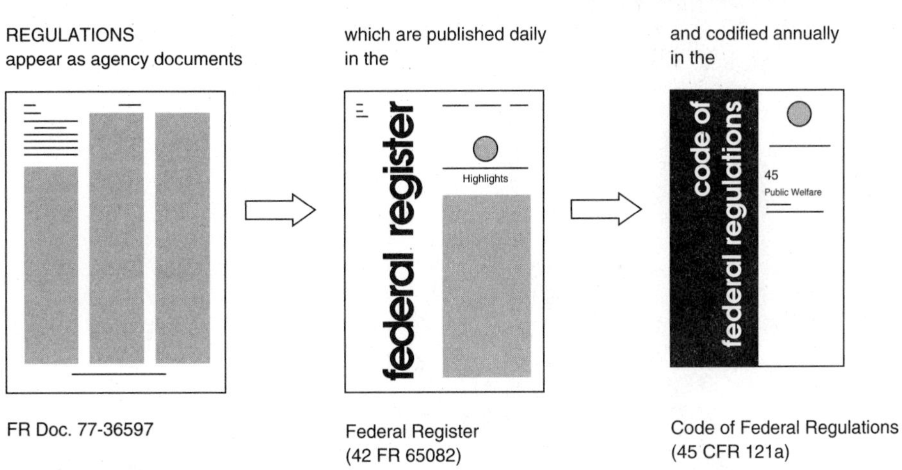

FIGURE 2-1

Parallel Codification of Legislation and Regulation

The Federal Register, *widely considered to be one of Washington's most unreadable publications, has recently been made more readable and useful to ordinary citizens. Its front pages now feature brief highlights of the day's contents. Further, agencies have been required to summarize their rules in language that nonexperts can understand.*

before the agency. Administrative orders have retroactive effect, unlike prospective rule making. In other words, the parties involved do not know how the policy is going to be applied until after the order is issued, giving the agency decision a retroactive effect like a courtroom decision. Deciding policy through adjudication necessarily means that it will be decided on a case-by-case basis. And while the rule of **stare decisis** (i.e., requiring precedent to be followed) does not prevail, over time these cases can mark out public policy and indicate the kinds of practices prohibited.

"So that's where it goes! Well, I'd like to thank you fellows for bringing this to my attention."

Agencies may also influence public policy by the vigor or laxity with which they enforce the law. (Drawing by Stevenson; © 1970 The New Yorker Magazine, Inc.*)*

Essentially, administrative adjudication involves two kinds of cases—accusatory, in which one party is charged with a violation of law, and nonaccusatory, in which a party has applied for permission (say, to offer transportation over a certain route). If the charge in an accusatory case proves true, the agency can impose a fine, revoke a license, or direct the accused to cease and desist.

The APA laid a firm foundation for transforming the agency's hearing officer from a traffic cop into a genuine adjudicator. In 1972, the Civil Service Commission conferred upon these officials the coveted title of administrative law judge (ALJ).

Critics of administrative adjudication argue that the emphasis on trial-type procedures is incompatible with effective rule making. Proceeding case by case can lead to inordinate delay and an incoherent set of policies. Defenders argue that developing coherent policies and standards—not reviewing every decision of an ALJ—is the task of the commission that heads the regulatory agency.

Law Enforcement. Agencies may also implement policy by the vigor or laxity with which they enforce the law. The obvious example is, of course, whether the highway patrol gives you a ticket or a warning.

Less obvious, but more relevant to policymaking than speeding tickets, is the Hepburn Act of 1906. This act authorized the Interstate Commerce Commission (ICC) to regulate rates charged by pipeline companies, but the commission took no action by itself until 1934. In fact, the commission did not complete a pipeline rate proceeding until 1948, and even then no action resulted. Since then, the ICC has continued to do little to carry out this authorization, "essentially substituting a policy of no regulation for the legislatively declared policy of regulation" (Anderson, 1990:194).

Program Operations. Much of an agency's day-to-day operations is not *directly* concerned with rule making, adjudication, or law enforcement. The agency simply administers a program, which means it distributes certain benefits and services, makes loans, provides insurance, constructs dams, and so forth. But the kinds of decisions an agency makes in administering the programs for which it has been given responsibility can, over time, help determine policy. And the more general the language the more this is true. Indeed, some legislative grants of authority to administrators are very broad—for example, the delegation of authority to agencies to make "reasonable" policies for the protection of public health or to eliminate "unfair" trade practices. (What is reasonable? Unfair?) To get a better idea of just how much delegation can be contained in certain legislation, let us consider the Economic Opportunity Act of 1964 for a moment.

Policymakers in the executive branch carefully crafted the bill to grant great discretion to the administrator. The content of the program and the definition of the community were left vague. The new Office of Economic Opportunity would "establish procedures which facilitate effective participation of the states." Formulas for dividing the funds among states and communities were broad. Finally, the act gave the local community the option to designate either a "public or private nonprofit agency" to administer a community action program provided that the program "was developed, conducted, and administered with *maximum feasible participation* of the

"Isn't it about time we issued some new guidelines for something?"

Since it is impossible for legislatures to give specific guidelines to implement public policy, broad grants of authority have been given to agencies. Legislation is implemented by federal agencies as rules and regulations. (Drawing by Alan Dunn; © 1968 The New Yorker Magazine, Inc.*)*

. . . groups served." If there were international contests for ambiguity, the three words that I have italicized would be world-class material. As Harold Seidman (1980:186–87) writes:

> *"Citizen participation" is a very slippery term and means very different things to different people. If participation is measured by the number of people who vote for . . . community action boards, it rests on a very narrow base. Many so-called representatives of the poor were elected by as little as 1 percent of the eligible voters. Citizen participation can be and has been used as a means for transferring power from officials who have at least some political responsibility to the community at large, to self-perpetuating local cliques, or the bureaucracy. It can operate in ways that provide nominal citizen participation but minimal citizen influence and maximum citizen frustration. Fifty-three percent of the funds appropriated for the community action program in 1968 were earmarked for national purposes devised by the Office of Economic Opportunity in Washington, not by the local citizenry.*

Administration in the Force Field of Politics

In the preceding section, we saw how profoundly administrators can influence the formulation and implementation of policy. In this section, we see how public administrators must operate every day in a kind of **political force field.**

Great pictorial convenience results from the use of the field concept. Consider a single, isolated administrator in Figure 2-2. What is the political field surrounding him or her? If arrows are drawn from the administrator through certain individuals and institutions, the resulting porcupine quills provide a two-dimensional picture of the political field. We may attach arrowheads to the radiating lines to indicate the various directions of force being exerted on the administrator.

The lines constructed in this way are called, as in physics, lines of force. They provide a convenient picture of the administrator's political field. Actually, they do even more than this: The thickness and number of the arrows can provide a picture of the strength of a particular field.

To understand the concept of political field is not difficult. The real problem is to understand why this concept is useful. The essential fact to appreciate about a field is that it shatters the older notion of a public administrator sitting at the apex of a **hierarchy.**

The concept of hierarchy is based on the distinction between the roles of superior and subordinate. The former is expected to exercise **authority** over the latter. In other words, the superior has the power to make decisions that will guide the actions of the subordinate. In most organizations, of course, this relationship is carried much further by making one subordinate the superior of another subordinate. The resulting configuration is often shown as a pyramid. The tremendous potential of the pyramidal form for bringing larger numbers of subordinates under central authority should not go unnoticed. Consider a pyramid with only nine levels of administrators and six subordinates for each administrator at the upper eight levels. Under such an arrangement, one executive could exercise formal authority over 2,015,539 people.

In recent years, as observations and insights increased, it became apparent that the single hierarchical picture, especially when applied to public agencies, was inadequate. Why? It is based on the assumption that each subordinate has only one direct supervisor. At the national level, for example, the president is certainly subject to the authority of both the voters and the Congress. In that sense, there is an overhead hierarchy.

This phenomenon of multiple subordination is probably even more widespread at levels below the chief executive offices. Thus, Figure 2-2 shows the administrator not sitting on a pyramid but in a political field. The next several subsections elaborate lines of force at the national level.

Before turning to these linkages, one point regarding Figure 2-2 needs to be made. As drawn, the model refers explicitly to the governmental administrator, but it

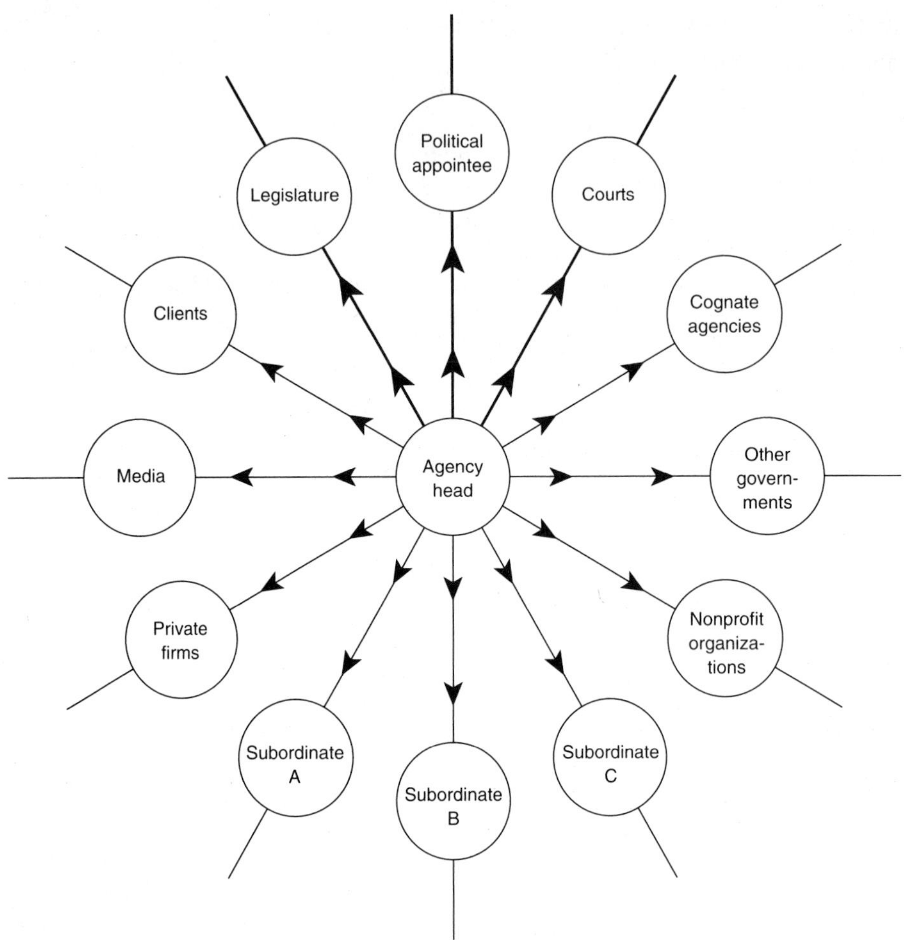

FIGURE 2-2

Pictorial Representation of Political Field Surrounding a Single Public Administrator

The straight lines radiating in all directions from the public administrator indicate the lines of force that constitute his or her daily political environment. While the lines do not quite extend on to infinity, they are likely to extend well beyond any specific individual or constitution appearing in the surrounding circles. For example, beyond the political appointee may be a chief executive or a board of directors; beyond the legislators, the voters; beyond a district court, the Supreme Court; beyond subordinate A, still other subordinates (since everybody within a public agency may feel that he or she has a legitimate piece of the action and must be involved); beyond a client, an interest group or trade association; and so on.

could easily be redrawn for the university president or hospital administrator. Let us consider for a moment the former. When asked to reflect on how their jobs have changed, university presidents invariably reply that they must woo and satisfy new external constituencies. State legislators and federal bureaucracies are becoming increasingly important sources of money for private as well as public institutions. And along with public money comes new requirements, such as federal affirmative action plans (discussed in Chapter 10). The college president's job is probably closer now to that of a big city mayor than a business executive.

The Legislative Connection

One important means by which Congress exercises formal authority over agencies is by setting policy, a process already discussed in this chapter. To the extent that congressional power is fragmented, the programs administered by a federal agency are fragmented. Thus, the chaotic character of social programs can often be traced to congressional sources—specifically, the conflicts between congressional authorization and the appropriations committees, the desire of legislators to author their own pet bills regardless of the narrow structure of the categories found in each, the tendency to legislate redundant programs in order to remain popular with constituents, and the practice of latching onto faddish ideas that seem popular to the public at the expense of more essential programs that are not in vogue. (Richardson, 1973)

Some congressional policies have a pervasive influence on the operations of agencies. The **Freedom of Information Act** (FOIA) of 1966, sunset laws, and sunshine laws are prime examples. The FOIA gave any person the right to request information from agencies and to file action in federal court if the request was denied. With an estimated 6 billion files, the U.S. federal government is the largest single creator and collector of information in the world. This vast storehouse includes well-known files of the FBI and CIA, information on almost every type of product and service the government purchases, safety reports on products it regulates, compliance reports on laws it administered, and written records of official communication and action. The purpose of the 1966 act was, in brief, to give the public the right to know what their government knows (with certain specific exceptions such as national security and law enforcement investigatory records) and to have the data upon which decision making is based. The FOIA requires a reply by agencies to any request within 10 working days and limits duplicating charges to actual costs.

Pioneered by Colorado, **sunset laws** provide that an agency is automatically abolished, or self-destructs, after a period of years (perhaps seven or ten) unless the legislature passes a law extending it. Many states already have such laws, but sunset legislation has been proposed only at the federal level. Another reform, **sunshine laws,** requires that formal business meetings be open to the public. The federal government's Sunshine Act of 1977 requires all independent regulatory commissions to give advance notice of their meetings.

The Sunshine Act was passed to put an end to the infamous smoke-filled room and to give the public "the fullest practicable information regarding the decision-making process of the federal government." Sunlight, as Justice Benjamin Cardozo once said, is the best disinfectant. The act requires 50 or so federal commissions, boards, corporations, and authorities to "conduct their meetings in the open rather than behind closed doors."

On balance, the openness movement has been good, giving us better insight into the rationales behind agency decisions. But the act has also had unintended consequences, especially for collegial decision making. Some agencies have gone to considerable lengths to avoid real debate in these open public meetings. For example, one sees an increasing tendency to arrive at decisions by carefully writing out positions on issues. Commissioners also use their special assistants to relay information, hold closed meetings as trial runs for formal, open meetings, and delegate decision making to staffs (*Wall Street Journal,* September 25, 1986). What one sees less of since the passage of the Sunshine Act is robust discussion and debate. After all, who wants to appear uncertain (by expressing tentative and not fully informed views) or unprincipled (by playing devil's advocate) in a roomful of reporters?

A second means by which Congress exercises control over agencies is the appropriations process. Jamie Whitten, chairman of the House Appropriations Subcommittee on Agriculture, exercises this power shrewdly. His appropriations subcommittee doles out funds for every item in the department's $20 billion budget, and it does not take long for Washington bureaucrats to realize that the chairman's wrath can destroy precious projects and throw hundreds of people out of jobs:

> *The key to this phenomenal power—which goes beyond that of budget control—lies in Whitten's network of informants within the department and his skills in directing their activities and operations. Executive branch officials learn to protect their own jobs, adjusting their loyalties to the legislative branch in a way the Founding Fathers may never have envisioned. (Kotz, 1969)*

A third means by which Congress controls agencies is **oversight.** At its best, oversight involves continuing, systematic congressional checking on the performance of the executive branch—how well government programs are working and how honestly, efficiently, or faithfully the laws are being administered. By and large, though, oversight has been infrequent and slipshod. The reasons are political: There is just more political mileage in running errands for constituents and more satisfaction in passing new laws. Tough oversight, on the other hand, can make enemies among congressional colleagues or powerful interest groups.

Still, some members of Congress practice oversight with a vengeance. Former senator William Proxmire was perhaps the best known watchdog of the bureaucracy. Among his examples of waste have been the supersonic transport plane, federal limousines, and National Science Foundation grants. Each month he gave his own Golden Fleece Award for what he felt was the greatest waste of the taxpayer's money. One award went to the National Institute for Mental Health for funding a study of why bowlers, hockey fans, and pedestrians smile. Another went to the Commerce Department's Economic Development Administration, which had provided Bedford, Indiana, a $200,000 grant to build a limestone model of the Great Pyramid of Egypt. While some of his awards were no doubt deserved, others showed an ignorance of science. Studying the sex habits of the Australian toad might bring congressional guffaws, but medical researchers know that genetic research is no more laughable than birth defects and that the frogs, the research, and the defects are all related.

Legislative oversight is strengthened by the **General Accounting Office** (GAO), an operating staff arm of Congress created in 1921 and originally designed to postaudit government expenditures. Since 1950, the GAO has been moving into what might be called management audits. These audits are policy oriented, seeking to determine what the basis for agency decisions and actions were. (See Chapter 11 for fuller discussion of the GAO.)

As the accompanying box suggests, the multifarious role of Congress in the execution of policy is not without its critics.

The Political Appointee Connection

For a number of reasons, friction tends to exist between the executives appointed by elected officials and the government employees they are supposed to lead. First, agencies form alliances with legislative subcommittees and outside interest groups; this enables, and indeed encourages, them to pursue independent policy courses. We shall discuss these triple alliances later in the chapter. Second, if the president or his appointees can be at cross-purposes with agencies over the *ends* of policy, so too can they be over the *means.* For example, in attempting to attain policy goals, presidents are often driven to economize and to reorganize—two activities that invariably upset some agency interests. Third, agencies have a tendency to become resistant to change due to strong ties to traditional policies and the professional orientation of careerists. Finally, the average tenure of political appointees is only 18 months.

Not surprisingly, presidents wanting to be effective have increasingly circumvented large bureaucracies either by using their own staffs or by setting up new agencies. President John F. Kennedy well understood the difficulty of converting a tradition-ridden bureaucracy into a mechanism for providing information and making decisions. Nevertheless, it was a constant puzzle to him that the State Department remained so formless and impenetrable. He would say, "Damn it, Bundy (one of Kennedy's advisors) and I get more done in one day in the White House than they do in six months in the State Department." Giving the State Department an instruction, he remarked, is like dropping it in the dead-letter box (Schlesinger, 1965:406).

Yet the president and his appointees do not stand helpless. In addition to his formidable command over the public attention and his power to appoint key administrators, the president has the **Office of Management and Budget** (OMB). The largest of the executive office components, the OMB has two main functions. The first is preparation of the budget, a process examined in detail in Chapter 11. The second is **legislative clearance.** Before an agency can submit new legislation to Congress, that legislation must be cleared by the OMB to ensure that it is consistent with the goals and policies of the administration.

The Costs of Micromanagement

The Agriculture Department cannot even study whether potential savings might result from the consolidation of Forest Service regional offices. The secretary of defense cannot even close a small facility in a state where both senators say defense spending should be cut. The Veterans Administration needs congressional approval for any personnel action affecting three or more people. What these three examples illustrate is the increasing tendency for Congress to micromanage administrative agencies.

The cost of micromanagement to the taxpayers may be billions of dollars. For instance, the federal bailout of savings and loan (S & L) institutions is projected to cost more than $400 billion over the 1990s—more than the Vietnam War. Although many individual scandals contributed to this debacle, the central problem might lay with congressional champions of the thrift industry. Key congressional factions entrenched in particular committees and subcommittees were preoccupied with assisting narrowly defined "constituencies" and failed to consider the larger national concerns involved in their intervention in the regulatory process. Whatever disagreements there may be about the proper apportionment of blame, the S & L fiasco illustrates Congress's increased readiness to assert its will in even the smallest details of government programs.

SOURCES: Jeremy Rabkin, "Micromanaging the Administrative Agencies," *Public Interest,* Summer 1990; *Wall Street Journal,* October 18, 1984.

In recent years, the OMB has begun to take on a third function: the coordination and evaluation of executive branch programs. Chapter 9 will be devoted to a few of the management techniques executives at all strata of government have available to gain better control over the bureaucracy.

Problems associated with the bureaucracy should not be overstated. Well-run corporations have long known that challenging, training, and trusting employees is critical to their success. The belief that government employees will not respond to changes in management's policy, though private sector employees will, is simply unfounded. Rather, workers in both sectors tend to behave the way management expects them to behave. For example, former transportation secretary Drew Lewis and General Services Administrator Jerry Carmen were able to get exactly what they expected from their bureaucrats: loyalty and results.

- Lewis had to make large, budget-driven cutbacks in urban mass transit and hazardous materials–transportation safety programs. Instead of prejudging an entrenched bureaucracy's intentions and then proceeding to pick a fight, he relied on career civil servants, who had strong emotional commitments to their programs, to implement the reductions. They were loyal and highly effective in executing their boss's policies.
- Carmen is known for having shaken up the General Services Administration (GSA), but he was effective because of the tough-minded respect he

accorded his bureaucrats. He filled some slots formerly reserved for political appointees with career civil servants. When one high-ranking career employee complained about a GSA program, Carmen let him hold a news conference to vent his views, and then put him in charge of a program to fix it (Christensen, 1984).

The Client Connection

Top administrators are quite sensitive to the dominant interest groups they represent. Nowhere is this more evident than with the federal regulatory agencies. As one Justice Department deputy assistant attorney general put it: In general, there are "incredible love affairs going on between the regulators and the regulated." As a result, critics say, the agencies often condone or even champion monopolistic practices and rubber-stamp higher prices for everything from airline tickets, to natural gas, to telephone calls. Regulators, on the other hand, say that they are not unduly influenced and that they cannot be insulated from the regulated if they do their jobs right.

Every agency, however, has its own constituency that helps it do battle (especially around budget time). The Department of Defense has contractors, the EPA has the Sierra Club, the Foreign Aid Agency has the League of Women Voters, the Labor Department has the unions, the Department of Housing and Urban Development has the National League of Cities, and so on.

To find an explanation for such cozy ties is not hard. As already indicated, agencies need outside support for their programs; thus, a symbiotic relationship emerges. How does it work? Say an agency develops a long-range plan that would, among other things, bring certain benefits to a particular industry. Given this set of circumstances, it would hardly be surprising to find some private industry, say, to sponsor a conference to promote the plan. Another obvious reason for friendly relationships is that some administrators come from the industry they regulate or support.

The Cognate Agency Connection

According to the *Oxford English Dictionary,* the term *cognate* means "kindred, related, connected, having affinity." In considering how government goes about attacking national problems (e.g., decay of city, pollution, regional economic development, and work force development), the expression *cognate agencies* seems a handy way of indicating that seldom will only one agency be involved.

Such a situation breeds not only management problems (e.g., interagency coordination) but also political ones. Agencies compete for specific programs: the Bureau of Reclamation versus the Army Corps of Engineers, the Federal Reserve Board versus the Treasury Department, the air force versus the navy, the Soil Conservation Service versus the Agricultural Extension Service, and so on. In the area of solar energy policy, no less than 15 agencies compete. In the new area of genetic engineering, the National Institutes of Health (NIH), the EPA, the Department of Agriculture, the FDA, and assorted elements of the White House are all jockeying for position.

Is all this jurisdictional and mission overlap, which breeds so much interagency conflict, entirely bad? The problems are clear enough. Agencies become rigid and uncompromising. The results, at best, can be wasted time and money—at worst, policy stalemates in the face of critical problems. Careful. More might be involved here than economy and efficiency. Does not this duplication and overlap provide greater access to and representation of different views and interests? Might not the duplication of mission management and information gathering by cognate agencies provide backups and corrective forces for errors and bad judgments?

Indeed, some would suggest that agencies should have not one but several paths through which policy may be formed and then implemented. Like an electric current in a parallel circuit, formulation and administration of policy in an agency should be able to flow through more than one branch. Thus, the chance for error to be fatal to an agency's policy and administrative responsibilities is lessened. The agency is far less vulnerable to administrative sabotage, while far more capable of policy initiation.

The Media and Other Forces

Suppose one day the president asks his secretary of the treasury to develop a trade policy toward Japan. Almost immediately, scores of people swing into action. The House Ways and Means Committee, the Senate Finance Committee, and virtually every member and staff person on those committees will have an opinion and will seek to exert influence. Also, the Foreign Relations Committee, the oversight committees, and then the interest groups, business, the unions, the State Department, the Commerce Department, the OMB, and the Council of Economic Advisers (and not only the top people, but all their staff) will be mobilized.

Remember, all the president said was "develop a trade policy toward Japan" to his secretary of the treasury. Why is there no limit to the number of people who get in on the act? Why will the secretary of the treasury, who has been assigned lead responsibility, soon find others—who have not been assigned anything—discussing and negotiating Japanese trade policy? Why, in short, are so many so quickly in the loop? To a large extent, the presence of news media explains the phenomenon. All the people mentioned above, you may be sure, are reading *The Washington Post* and *The New York Times.* Much of what they know about new initiatives in trade policy comes from reading the newspapers.

Many would defend the large amount of time and money spent on assembling and disseminating the news on the basis of the public's right to know and as a means by which top administrators can learn about the operations of their programs at the grass roots. Cynics would say the media distort—or, at least, reshape—the process.

The media reshape (perhaps a better word than *distort*) the administrative process in several subtle ways. First, they allow for the disclosure of information—concerning, for example, what the secretary of the treasury is about to recommend on American trade policy toward Japan—through unofficial channels. Of course, not all such disclosures are considered improper by public administrators. For administrators who wish to see something in print but would rather not be on record as formally committed to a particular policy, there is the "authorized leak." In essence a **leak** is a way of testing public opinion.

Reputations in government depend on the press. Glowing press clippings, while one is at the head of an agency, can be a decisive factor in an administrator's promotion to positions of greater responsibility: "A cabinet secretary can become apoplectic when a leading columnist suggests he is losing his clout with the president . . . As long as power depends on the appearance of being listened to by the president, and as long as newspapers are the primary conveyors of that appearance, high officials will always make time for reporters" (Peters, 1980:22).

Finally, what can be said about the remaining components in Figure 2-2? Well, a lot. In fact, we shall devote much of Chapter 3 to the circles labeled "Other Governments" and "Private Firms." Chapter 4 will deal with the circles labeled "Courts" and "Media." And Chapters 7 and 8 will be concerned with relationships with subordinates.

Political Competency

Our discussion has ranged far beyond the pleas of Woodrow Wilson and others for a separation of politics and administration. As we have seen, the administrator is placed squarely in the policymaking process. Further, day-to-day events force administrators to operate in a field crisscrossed by political forces generated by overhead authority (Congress and president), client groups, cognate agencies, other levels of government, and the media. The greater the number of these forces, the more time and energy a public administrator tends to spend on power-oriented behavior.

What follows is neither an essay on realpolitik nor revelations on the political art—the former would be improper, the latter presumptuous. This concluding section only attempts to introduce a few basic political concepts pertinent to good administration. And by good administration, we simply mean administration that can mobilize support for its programs and, in short, get things done. "There is no more forlorn spectacle in the administrative world than an agency and a program possessed of statutory life, armed with executive orders, sustained in the courts, yet stricken with paralysis and deprived of power. An object of contempt to its enemies and of despair to its friends" (Long, 1949:257).

What are these concepts so pertinent to good administration? Recall for a moment the case of A.J. Cervantes, the former mayor of St. Louis, cited at the start of this chapter. If he had decided to attempt to get the airport built in Illinois, then what basic *political* considerations would have been involved? First, he probably would have wanted to assess his strength—or, to put it in the political vernacular, his clout—to see if he should even try. Assuming he did have sufficient political strength, he would then probably have asked himself: Does my objective really merit such an expenditure of political capital?

Let us be clear on the meaning of this second question. If it is financially possible for me to buy a Porsche 928S4, it does not necessarily follow that I should. Where else could I have invested my limited capital? How much would I have left for future contingencies?

We shall assume, however, that Cervantes is in a better position than the author. Therefore, he decides that he has the political capital *and* that the price (in terms of allies lost, favors asked for, and so on) is not too high. Now he must consider the specific strategies and tactics he must use to attain his objective. In sum, the administrator must think through three political questions concerning resources, costs, and strategy. For a less systematic exposition of the subject of power (but I hope equally valuable), see "Talking Shop" on page 58.

Resources

Essentially, the administrator's political resources appear in one of three forms: external support, professionalism, and leadership. The prudent administrator assesses each before attempting any major political act.

External Support. One of the more enduring sources of bureaucratic power is the phenomenon of **subsystem politics,** or **iron triangles.** Agencies ally themselves with congressional committees and interest groups. Examples are legion: agriculture committees, the American Farm Bureau Federation, and agencies within the Department of Agriculture; subcommittees on Indian affairs, the Association on American Indian Affairs, and the Bureau of Indian Affairs; the House Agriculture Committee, the sugar industry, and the Sugar Division of the Department of Agriculture; and so forth. The most immediate consequence of the alliance is that agencies are able to take less seriously supervision by superiors in the executive branch. The two examples below highlight other aspects of the alliance—how it can work and how it can fail to work:

- Both the President's Science Advisory Committee (PSAC) and the air force were unhappy in the early 1960s about the amounts of money NASA was receiving. The basic scientists, who were on PSAC to advise the president, were unhappy because so large a proportion of the nation's scientific talent was being devoted to a spectacular political purpose rather than to basic research. Similarly, the air force (a cognate agency in this case) was unhappy because it would have preferred rocket development to be kept as the means toward air force ends. But, and this is the crucial point, neither the air force nor the basic scientists were able to dent the alliance that NASA had forged with applied scientists and relevant congressional committees.
- The decline of the Interstate Commerce Commission (ICC) can be explained in terms of its alliance with the railroads. More specifically, the commission had tied itself too closely with the railroads. Consequently, nonrailroad interest groups (water, motor, and air carriers) blocked the extension of commission power into their field. The ICC was thus unable to expand its basis of support (Huntington, 1952).

In assessing their own strength, administrators must at the same time assess the strength of their support. But the size alone is not enough; also important are the dispersion and unity of the constituency. For example, the strength of the secretary of interior increased with the establishment of the Bureau of Outdoor Recreation, which broadened the department's base from just the western states to the urban Northeast. For similar reasons, state university systems try to establish satellite campuses in as many state senatorial districts as possible. Regarding the importance of unity, one need only compare the influence of the large, loosely knit consumer movement with the relatively small, tightly knit National Rifle Association.

Professionalism. The second source of agency power is professionalism. In defining a profession, we shall follow Frederick C. Mosher (1968:106): a reasonably clear-cut occupational field that ordinarily requires higher education, at least through the bachelor's level, and offers a lifetime career to its members. As society becomes more specialized and dominated by technological concerns, we can surely expect to see more individuals fitting this description in government agencies. The consequences of this trend are twofold.

Professionals within an organization are obviously in an excellent position to mobilize the support of relevant external professional organizations. Actually, the arrangement is reciprocal, for each profession tends to stake its territory within the appropriate government agency—for example, as does the medical profession within the FDA.

Another consequence of professionalism is that, within the agency, professionals tend to form a kind of elite with substantial control over operations. At least three elements form the base of this power, which can override political control from the top:

Full-time attention to a problem.

Specialization that develops expertise by breaking the function, issue, or problem into subparts.

Monopolization of information.

Leadership. Thus far, we have looked at the political resources of the administrator in terms of interest groups and professional elites. Now we want to consider the political resources that individual administrators themselves can generate.

If leadership is the process by which one person successfully influences another, then power is the means by which he or she does it. Over the years, students of human behavior have identified eight important **bases of individual power:**

1. *Coercive power* derives from a leader's ability to threaten punishment and deliver penalties. Its strength depends on two factors. First is the magnitude of punishment, real or imagined, that the leader controls. Second is the other party's estimate of the probability that the leader will in fact mete out punishment (e.g., undesirable work assignments, reprimands, and dismissal) if necessary.

2. *Connection power* derives from a leader's personal ties with important persons inside or outside an organization. When a junior aide on the president's staff telephones a senior cabinet member and begins by saying "This is the White House calling," he is using connection power. When

(text continues on p. 60)

Talking Shop

Surviving in the Political Force Field

The theme of this chapter has been that there is more to public administration than handling the internal affairs of an agency. Those who might be effective at handling internal operations may become quite uncomfortable when faced with the variety of external factors portrayed in Figure 2-2. Fortunately, there are strategies for coping with some of the most important of these factors.

Managing the Political Boss

More than any other individual, the chief political executive is critical to the success of a public administrator. His or her support will be critical in attaining the agency's goals and missions. Further, nothing else has the effect upon the career advancement of the administrator as does his or her relationship with the boss.

This may sound obvious, but a surprising number of administrators fail at it. For even effective administrators tend to misdefine a "manager" as someone who is responsible for the work of subordinates and thus may ignore their own responsibility for the boss's performance and effectiveness. A better definition of manager would probably be someone who is responsible for the performance of *all* people upon whom his or her performance depends. All these relationships must be consciously managed to obtain the best possible result for the administrator, for the boss, and for the agency. Here then are seven approaches for gaining the chief's backing:

1. Seek information about the boss's goals, problems, and pressures. Be alert for opportunities to question the boss and others around him or her to test your assumptions. Do this continually because priorities and concerns change.
2. Make sure the boss understands what can be expected from you and what you and your people are concentrating on. Recognize how much your boss is dependent on you.
3. Get the boss personally involved in those programs that are near and dear to his or her heart.
4. Adjust your working style in response to the boss's preferred methods for operating. For example, some bosses like to get information in report form so they can read and study it; others work better with information and reports presented in person so they can ask questions.
5. Keep the boss informed. Send regular reports. Let the chief know of potential problems—few like unpleasant surprises.
6. Work to establish a business "friendship" in addition to an effective boss-subordinate relationship. Establish channels of communication other than through work. If the boss likes you, he or she will be more likely to trust you and see you as a member of the team. In any event, never criticize the boss in public. Take the heat and share the credit.
7. Get along with the chief's staff. If they are competent, they can be useful allies. Even if they are not, they control access to the chief and probably have a good sense of his or her views. Pick your fights with them carefully.

Influencing Legislators

Legislatures, cognate agencies, and interest groups also have great influence on an agency's daily operation. Through the budget and oversight process, legislatures have the greatest ability to directly influence agency operations.

Administrators, in turn, have the opportunity to exercise influence over congressional committees, state legislative committees, and city councils. Presenting testimony is one such opportunity. As Thomas P. Lauth reminds us, "If one takes away all the fancy trappings of the hearing room, the committee staff lining the back wall, the klieg lights, the cameras, and the audience, what is left is a group of people sitting at a table and seeking information that will help them perform their jobs and maybe get reelected. If administrators are seen as helpful in those tasks and professional in their approach, the rest should proceed rather well."

Here are some suggestions by Lauth to make one's testimony more effective:

- Prepare as concise a written statement as possible. If it is longer than six pages, prepare a summary.
- Be clear. Use charts, if necessary, but make sure they are not too busy (i.e., contain too much information).
- Master the subject matter as much as time permits.
- Be prepared to respond to any criticisms or recommendations.
- Read the newspaper the day before and the morning of the hearing, for any articles that may come up at the hearing.
- Have a last-minute meeting with staff to go over late-breaking developments.
- Arrive before the hearing starts, and say hello to the committee members and other witnesses.
- Pay special attention to the chairperson's opening statement—it often reflects his or her personal interests.
- Follow the chairperson's instructions on presenting the testimony and offer to summarize the statement before beginning.
- Have as few supporting witnesses at the table as possible.
- Use questions as opportunities to make points.
- Admit mistakes and highlight the corrective actions.

Of course, not all interaction with legislative bodies occurs in such large, formal settings; administrators also influence legislators in one-on-one settings. Assuming the administrator is seeking favorable treatment of a certain program, the thing to understand is what factors will determine a legislator's vote on it.

Political scientists have identified at least four such factors. The first is a legislator's judgments about the merits of the program. The second is the political angle. What will the vote mean in terms of getting reelected? What will it mean in terms of maintaining influence within the legislative body? Will it cause the legislator to lose support on some other program? The third factor is a procedural one. Members do not want to violate the "rules of the game" within their legislative body. Legislators feel, for example, that they should defer, as much as possible, to the recommendations of a committee that has worked intensively to develop those recommendations. Finally, the demands of loyalty and friendship will affect a legislator's vote.

(continued)

In a legislative contest, whoever *defines* the proposal derives powerful advantages both from being able to specify what the proposal will do and from being able to shape what it says to broad publics. For example, in 1991, President Bush was more successful at defining a civil rights bill than the congressional leadership was at defining it an "antidiscrimination" bill.

Dealing with the Media

As Donald Rumsfeld, who served in the Congress and in cabinet offices, explains: "You can communicate with five million people . . . a lot easier through the media than you can through an internal information system. Call a press conference and you can reach almost everybody instantaneously. That tool is not available to business."

Public administrators use the media to highlight important issues and to build and sustain support for them. (A good example of this use appears in the Working Profile of Maxene Johnston in Chapter 5.) Public administrators also rely on the media to educate the public about certain risks like drugs and AIDS. Who has ever experienced a New Year's Eve that was not preceded by an announcement from a police official regarding the expected number of fatalities from drunk driving?

Having to speak through the media, however, has its downside, as Blumenthal discovered: "Not only is what you say used against you—it is also distorted. So what you learn is that you have to build defenses against being misquoted and misunderstood." To avoid media distortion and media wrath, Marvin Linsky offers some basic rules of the game to keep in mind:

- Establish professional working relationships with press members and deal with them as colleagues: "If pol-

John Brademas was swept out of office in 1980, after 22 years in Congress and 4 as House majority whip, he became president of the largest private university in the United States, New York University. Because of his excellent connections, the school thrived. His political connections and his newer contacts—as chairman of the board of directors of the Federal Reserve Bank of New York, a director of the New York Stock Exchange, and chairman of New York Governor Mario Cuomo's Council on Fiscal and Economic Priorities—also played an essential role in the university's fund-raising successes (*Wall Street Journal,* July 15, 1986).

3. *Expert power* derives from a leader's reputation for special knowledge, expertise, or skill in a given area. Lobbyists, who maintain their credibility with members of the legislature, find this kind of power far more effective than the preceding two. One congressman provides us with a good illustration of how David Stockman, who was director of the OMB from 1981 to 1985, used expert power. "Every time a Cabinet secretary comes up here, he brings a battery of assistants and refers everything to them. This guy

icy makers know the conventions of the press, they will be better able to develop their own ways of dealing with journalists so as to maximize their chances of achieving their policy goals."

- Give ample notice when you want the media to cover an event or press conference. Provide them with the information necessary to cover the story, such as press kits. A well-written and carefully constructed press release has a good chance of being quoted verbatim.
- Be honest. Do not think you can fool the media by revealing only part of the story or by distorting the facts. (They usually have more information than you think.)
- Maintain close communication with your agency's press contact people (usually called public information officers). They know the questions the media are likely to ask, the criteria that public service announcements (PSAs) must meet, the deadlines for each station and publication, and so on.

In sum, take an active approach in dealing with the media. As Linsky points out, better media relations will result in better government.

SOURCES: Thomas P. Lauth, "Responding to Public Officials," in James L. Perry, ed., *Handbook of Public Administration* (San Francisco: Jossey-Bass, 1991), pp. 193–207; Steven Cohen, *The Effective Public Manager* (San Francisco: Jossey-Bass, 1988); Philip B. Heymann, *The Politics of Public Administration* (New Haven, Conn.: Yale University Press); John P. Kotter, *Power and Influence* (New York: Free Press, 1985); Charlene Mitchell and Thomas Burdick, *The Right Mores* (New York: Macmillan, 1985); Peter F. Drucker, "How to Manage the Boss," *Wall Street Journal,* August 1, 1986; *Fortune,* September 10, 1979 and January 29, 1979.

[Stockman] comes in all by himself and ticks them off boom, boom. I've never seen anybody who knows the operation like this kid—he's something else, believe me" (*Newsweek,* February 16, 1981).

4. *Dependence power* derives from a people's perception that they are dependent on the leader either for help or for protection. Leaders create dependence through finding and acquiring resources (e.g., authority to make certain decisions, access to important people) that others need for their jobs.

5. *Obligation power* derives from leaders' efforts to do favors for people who they expect will feel an obligation to return those favors and to develop true friendships with those on whom they depend.

6. *Legitimate power* derives from the formal position held by the leader. In recent years, textbooks on the president have tended to emphasize a theory of presidential power based on persuasion. But it could also be argued that ability to persuade affects power at the margins; it does not determine its

use or set its limits. Perhaps the key to understanding presidential power "is to concentrate on the constitutional authority that the president asserts unilaterally through various rules of constitutional construction and interpretation in order to resolve crises or important issues facing the nation" (Pious, 1979: 16). I am inclined to think there is some truth in this. Although persuasion is an important tool, it has limits. To make it work requires time and people who listen; but both are sometimes absent.

The legitimate power of the presidency, if skillfully deployed, its enough to move the nation. George Bush managed to rally a reluctant nation to a successful war in the Persian Gulf not by his powers of persuasion but with four bold, unilateral decisions:

August 7, 1990: Initial American troops deployed.

November 8, 1990: Ground troops doubled.

January 15, 1991: Air war launched.

February 23, 1991: Ground war started.

The remarkable thing about these actions was that each was generally unpopular at the time it was made. Yet, in time, they were seen as correct. His actions, not his words, changed public opinion (*Economist,* March 15, 1991).

7. *Referent power* derives from the identification of others with the leader. This identification can be established if the leader is greatly liked, admired, or respected. "Managers develop power based on others' idealized views of them in a number of ways. They try to look and behave in ways that others respect. They go out of their way to be visible to their employees and to give speeches about their organizational goals, values, and ideas" (Kotter, 1977:131). When Martin Luther King, Jr., gave his famous "I Have a Dream" speech, he was fostering the listener's subconscious identification with his dream.

8. *Reward power* derives from the leader's ability to make followers believe that their compliance will lead to pay, promotion, recognition, or other rewards. Here is a particularly dramatic application of reward power combined with referent power: Early in 1944, General George Patton asked his troops how they would answer when their grandchildren asked them what they did in the war. He then went on to suggest that they could either say they shoveled manure in the states—or say they rode through Europe with Patton's Third Army.

According to John Kotter, managers who successfully exercise power tend to share a number of characteristics. They are sensitive to what others consider legitimate uses of power and the "obligation of power." Consequently, they know when, where, and with whom to use the various types of power. And, they do not rely on any one type of power.

They use all their resources to develop still more power. In effect, they invest in power. For example: "By asking a person to do him two important favors, a manager might be able to finish his construction program one day ahead of schedule. That request may cost him most of the obligation-based power he has over that person, but in return he may significantly increase his perceived expertise as a manager of construction projects in the eyes of everyone in his organization" (Kotter, 1977:136). That is, when the leader has more power, the follower need not have less. Studies by Likert (1961) and Tannenbaum (1968) indicate that in organizations where there is a greater amount of power at all levels, the organization is likely to be more effective and the members more satisfied.

Costs

Virtually every important administrative action has an indirect cost; the economists call such indirect or secondary impacts **externalities,** or spillovers. David Halberstam (1969:302–3), a Pulitzer Prize–winning journalist, provides the following incident from the Kennedy years:

> *In 1962 [Secretary of Defense] McNamara came charging into the White House ready to save millions on the budget by closing certain naval bases. All the statistics were there. Close this base, save this many dollars. Close that one and save that much more. All obsolete. All fat. Each base figured to the fraction of the penny. Kennedy interrupted him and said, "Bob, you're going to close the Brooklyn Navy Yard, with 26,000 people, and they're going to be out of work and go across the street and draw unemployment, and you better figure that into the cost. That's going to cost us something and they're going to be awfully mad at me, and we better figure that in too."*

It was Paul H. Appleby who remarked that the four questions every administrator should always ask before making an important decision are: Who is going to be glad? How glad? Who is going to be mad? And how mad?

Because actions have political costs, administrators can also go into debt. If they use top-level support, it is quite likely that higher officials will later demand bureau backing for other administration programs or demand influence in bureau policy in return. Presidents too sometimes go into the red. As Richard Neustadt (1960:31) suggests, when Truman dismissed General MacArthur he "exhausted his credit"; as a consequence, he was unable to make his case with Congress, court, and public in a steel strike that came the next year.

Strategies

Top administrators have a wide range of strategies available for dealing with the agency's political environment. And all administrators may safely assume that, either voluntarily or otherwise, they will become involved in these strategies. To ignore them, therefore, is to ignore a very big part of day-to-day administration. For purposes of discussion, we shall classify them rather broadly as (1) cooperation, (2) competition, and (3) conflict.

Cooperation. Cooperation is based on the idea that two groups can share compatible goals without one having to completely give in to the other. All parties can be winners, though some more than others. In the language of game theory, a cooperative strategy means the parties are engaged in a **variable-sum game** in which both parties win.

Cooperative strategies come in many varieties. **Persuasion,** for example, is a variety of cooperation, and its essence was stated precisely by Richard Neustadt (1960:46) as follows: To induce someone to believe that what you want of them is what their own appraisal of their own responsibilities requires them to do in their own self-interest. As one aide to President Eisenhower put it: "The people . . . [in Congress] don't do what they might *like* to do, they do what they think they have to do in their own interest as they see it."

Another variety of cooperation is **bargaining;** that is, the negotiation of an agreement for the exchange of goods, services, or other resources. Universities bargain the name of a hall in return for the donor's contribution. The attorney general's antitrust division signs consent decrees with firms that promise not to pursue actions further without first admitting guilt.

To add precision to our analysis, we draw a distinction between two bargaining techniques. **Compromise,** the first, usually results from bargaining over a single, isolated issue when the outcome is one of more or less. Examples would include such matters as busing distances or boundaries; hiring and promotion requirements in government employment; amounts of public housing for ghetto areas; trade-offs between environmental and energy needs; and types of learning programs for the unemployed. Quite clearly, compromise is widely regarded as a positive value in the American political system, but it can lead to ludicrous solutions. In 1961, the director of defense research and engineering had to negotiate between the air force and the navy for the requirements for a fighter to be used by both. The navy argued for a wing span of 56 feet; the air force, 90 feet. Solution? Seventy-three feet, of course.

With the second bargaining technique, **logrolling,** we are concerned with more than one issue. Logrolling, therefore, involves reciprocity of support for different items of interest to each bargainer. For example, a governor's task force on welfare, in return for the support of a powerful advisor to the governor, might be willing to let that advisor's office develop some other plan that would properly belong with the task force. Or when a top administrator from the Department of Labor concedes something to a representative of the U.S. Treasury, he or she can often expect a concession at some later date. Charles Lindblom (1968:96) puts it well: "He has stored up a stock of goodwill on which he can later draw."

In addition to persuasion and bargaining, we might consider the **coalition** as a variety of cooperation. Coalition involves a combination of two or more organizations for a specific purpose. A good example is provided by the Mohole project, which sought to develop new technology that would allow an anchored drilling ship to penetrate the Earth's mantle (see Greenberg 1967:Chapter 9). The original group of sponsoring scientists was concerned with maximizing the scientific returns from the drilling. The contractor understandably sought to confine the project as nearly as possible to a straightforward engineering task. Meanwhile, the President's Office of Science and Technology was concerned with the international and prestige aspects of the success or failure of the project. The National Academy leadership was concerned with preserving the prestige of science, free from controversy. The National Science Foundation sought to sustain the impetus of an important project in earth sciences, but at the same time to support orderly progress in all other fields of science it was sponsoring. Similarly, today we see a coalition of National Aeronautics and Space Association (NASA), air force, and contractors backing the space shuttle program.

What do we know about the art of coalition building? Good administrators have learned that clarity—sometimes but not always—is essential; in other words, if a coalition is to form around a proposal, then that proposal must be as unambiguous as possible. For example, one of the central difficulties of the negative income tax proposal (which would guarantee a minimum income to all Americans), lay in not communicating to the public, to the press, and to Congress exactly how it would work. The NIH provides an example of how such ambiguity might be eliminated. In 1955, the NIH National Microbiological Institute was renamed the National Institute of Allergy and Infectious Diseases. No longer would they be handicapped because "no one died of microbiology" (Seidman, 1980:36).

Coalition builders have also learned the advantage of linking—or repackaging—their agency's proposal with the goals of other agencies and political authorities. Advocates of the nuclear plane in 1953 were successful in linking this proposal in an unmistakable way to a high-priority defense need. Similarly, President Johnson increased the coalition backing the Elementary and Secondary Education Act of 1965 by linking the proposal of federal aid to public schools to his antipoverty program.

Competition. In the last few pages, we have discussed the various forms that a cooperative strategy might take. Now we turn to the second classification of strategy: **competition.** Competition may be defined as a struggle between two or more parties with a third party mediating. Often, in competitive situations, the winnings of one competitor are equaled by the losses of the other. A simple example is when a project is transferred from one agency to another. Game theorists call this kind of competitive situation a **zero-sum game.**

What can an administrator do in a zero-sum situation? Although the alternatives are no doubt many, we shall consider only two examples—seizing the initiative and co-opting the opposition. In the early 1960s, it became apparent to the air force and the navy that the defense secretary was going to choose a single plane, with certain modifications, for both services. The plane would be a modification of either the air force's TFX or the navy's F-4. Under these conditions, the air force immediately and successfully launched a campaign emphasizing the flexibility of *its* plane; at the same time, it glossed over how well the TFX would suit its special needs (Coulam, 1975:1–38).

Administrators sometimes co-opt their adversaries. Philip Selznick (1949) defines **co-optation** as "the process of absorbing new elements into the leadership, as the policy determining structure of an organization, as a means of averting threats to its stability or existence." Co-optation deliberately seeks participation as a means of gaining public agreement to agency programs. In his study of the Tennessee Valley Authority (TVA), Selznick tells how potential opposition from the community and regional groups were brought into the TVA's decision-making process. Awarding lucrative government contracts can provide an enormously flexible way for an agency

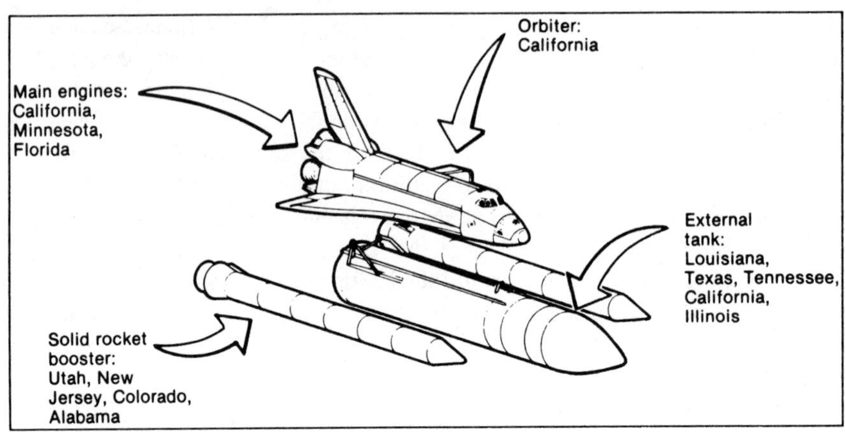

At last! A spacecraft absolutely impervious to attack: It has components manufactured in 300 of the 435 congressional districts. (Only major contractors are shown above.)

to co-opt legislators. (Note the drawing of the space shuttle.) Similarly, certain federal agencies seek to co-opt the scientific community by appointing scientists to advisory boards and giving research grants.

Conflict. Although cooperation and competition are essentially peaceful and governed by formal rules and informal normative constraints, conflict involves situations where actors pursue goals that are fundamentally incompatible. Consider the case of John Kennedy and U.S. Steel. On Tuesday, April 10, 1962, President Kennedy was surprised to note that his appointment calendar included a 5:45 P.M. appointment with Roger Blough, U.S. Steel chairman. The purpose of the Blough visit was to hand the president a press release announcing a $6-a-ton price increase. The president was stunned. He felt his whole fight against inflation was being reduced to tatters. Above all, he felt duped. The man seated on the sofa next to his rocking chair had personally, knowingly, accepted his help in securing from the workers a contract that *would not* lead to an increase in prices. Although being challenged in an area where he had few weapons, the president would not accept this fait accompli without a fight. His main strategy was to divide and conquer; more specifically, he focused his efforts on the Inland Steel Company of Chicago in order to obtain an agreement that they would not follow U.S. Steel's lead. He also followed other courses of action. In brief, he got Senator Kefauver and the Justice Department to begin investigating steel activities, used a press conference to sway public opinion, and made implied threats to cancel certain defense contracts.

Within a period of 72 hours, Blough capitulated before the onslaught. What this event had shown was the ability of the chief executive "to mobilize and concentrate every talent and tool he possessed and could borrow to prevent a serious blow to his program, his prestige, and his office" (Sorensen, 1965:516).

Conflict, of course, occurs at less lofty levels and does not always end in a government victory. Journalist Tom Wolfe (1970:22–23) gives us a vivid picture of how ghetto youth and militants can intimidate the bureaucrats at city hall and in the local Office of Economic Opportunity. Wolfe calls the practice "mau-mauing." One man named Chaser, Wolfe relates, almost gave classes in mau-mauing:

> *Then Chaser would say, "Now when we get there, I want you to come down front and stare at the man and don't say nothing. You just glare. No matter what he says. He'll try to get you to agree with him. He'll say, 'Ain't that right?' and 'You know what I mean?' and he wants you to say yes or nod your head . . . see . . . it's part of his psychological jiveass. But you don't say nothing. You just glare . . . see. . . . Then some of the other brothers will get up on that stage behind him, like there's no more room or like they just gathering around. Then you brothers up there behind him, you start letting him have it. . . . He starts thinking, 'Oh God! Those bad cats are in front of me, they all around me, they behind me. I'm surrounded.' That shakes 'em up.*
>
> *"And then when one of the brothers is up talking, another brother comes up and whispers something in his ear, like this," and Chaser cups his hand around his mouth like he's whispering something. "And the brother stops talking, like he's listening, and the man thinks, 'What's he saying? What kind of unbelievable s—— are they planning now?' The brother, he's not saying anything. He's just moving his lips. It's a tactic . . . you know . . . And at the end I'll slap my hand down on the desk—whop—and everybody gets up, like one man, and walks out of there. And that really shakes 'em up. They see that the people are unified, and disciplined, and mad, and tired of talking and ready for walking, and that shakes 'em up." (Reprinted with the permission of Farrar, Straus & Giroux, Inc., from* Radical Chic & Mau-Mauing the Flak Catchers *by Tom Wolfe. Copyright © 1970 by Tom Wolfe.)*

In conflict situations, the astute administrator needs to keep several things in mind. First is the ever-present danger of **escalation.** This process is characterized by each side in the conflict, repeatedly increasing the intensity of the conflict; if continued with a constant rate of increments, the process is likely to get out of control and end in violence. Suppose that a minor incident occurs in which a black citizen is challenged or wronged by a white police officer and a fracas results. Black witnesses spread the word. As rumors circulate, the hostilities involved become exaggerated. People react angrily and a demonstration takes place, which leads to looting and destruction. The police are ordered to contain what is now a riot; this attempt at control increases the anger of the blacks. Snipers begin to fire at the police and fire fighters. As a result, great resentment spreads, which in turn results in more clandestine attacks, more arson and rioting, and more attacks against the police. The police respond with armored trucks patrolling the streets and more heavy-handed repression. In short, we have a spiral of bloodshed.

Besides attempting to stop the escalation process before it gets out of hand, the administrator should remember in conflict situations to avoid humiliation of the interests that lose out in the policy clash; where an adversary has no honorable path of retreat, conflict can become quite protracted.

Timing and forbearance are also important. In the steel price dispute, Kennedy realized that he had to act swiftly, before a parade of companies, rushing to imitate U.S. Steel's increase, began. But one must also know when to stop pressing the attack—how to avoid overkill. Benjamin Disraeli recognized this factor when he said, "Next to knowing when to seize an advantage, the most important thing in life is to know when to forego an advantage."

Conflict situations, however, do not require backroom politics. They can be managed with forthrightness and even a certain dignity. Indeed, even in the ultimate of conflicts—war—men and women still have this option. The following letter (Churchill, 1959:508) to the Japanese ambassador illustrates my point.

> Sir,
>
> On the evening of December 7th His Majesty's Government in the United Kingdom learned that Japanese forces without previous warning either in the form of a declaration of war or of an ultimatum with a conditional declaration of war had attempted a landing on the coast of Malaya and bombed Singapore and Hong Kong.
>
> In view of these wanton acts of unprovoked aggression committed in flagrant violation of International Law and particularly of Article I of the Third Hague Convention relative to the opening of hostilities, to which both Japan and the United Kingdom are parties, His Majesty's Ambassador at Tokyo has been instructed to inform the Imperial Japanese Government in the name of his Majesty's Government in the United Kingdom that a state of war exists between our two countries.
>
> I have the honour to be, with high consideration,
>
> Sir,
>
> Your obedient servant,
>
> WINSTON S. CHURCHILL

As Churchill (1959:508) noted in his *Memoirs:* "Some people did not like this ceremonial style. But after all when you have to kill a man it costs nothing to be polite."

Concepts for Review

- Administrative Procedures Act
- authority
- bargaining
- bases of individual power

- clients
- coalition
- cognate agencies
- compromise
- cooperation, competition, and conflict
- co-optation
- escalation
- externalities
- *Federal Register*
- Freedom of Information Act
- General Accounting Office
- hierarchy
- leak
- legislative clearance
- logrolling
- Office of Management and Budget (OMB)
- oversight
- persuasion
- policy
- policymaking, policy formulation, and policy implementation
- political force field
- politics administration debate
- professionalism
- prospective rules
- rule making, adjudication, law enforcement, and program operations
- stare decisis
- subsystem politics, or iron triangles
- sunset laws
- sunshine laws
- variable-sum game and zero-sum game

Nailing Down the Main Points

1. Public administrators have learned that to separate administration from politics is impossible; the two are inextricably intertwined. Specifically, today's administrators are intimately involved in policymaking as well as the day-to-day play of politics.

2. The name most commonly associated with the origins of American public administration is that of Woodrow Wilson who, as a young professor at Bryn Mawr, published a precedent-setting and influential article entitled "The Study of Administration." His purpose was the reform of the civil service based on an argument for reform through professional management. Wilson contended that the improvement of the "organization and methods of our government offices" could be achieved through the application of the "science of administration, as it was being invented, developed, and applied by the great corporations and newly created business schools." For Wilson, management was the instrument for reforming the institutions he cared about: "The object of administrative study is to rescue executive methods from the confusion and costliness of empirical experiment and set them upon foundations laid deep in stable principle." Those principles echoed the Progressives' idealistic goals of rationality, science, and individual integrity.

3. Administrators frequently participate in formulation of public policy by making proposals that further their client's interests, originate entirely with the agency, or suggest improvements on existing legislation. Nevertheless, bureaucracy *stops* far more policy proposals than it starts.

4. Implementation of policy begins where formulation ends. Administrative decisions can be crucial in this stage of the policymaking process.

5. Legislative bodies exercise authority over agencies by approving or authorizing the programs that the agencies must administer, by appropriating funds for those programs, and by checking on the agencies' performance (oversight). Thus, the entire policy planning cycle may be thought of as a four-step process:

PROBLEM OR NEED RECOGNITION
↓
POLICY FORMULATION
↓
APPROVAL OR AUTHORIZATION
↓
IMPLEMENTATION

6. Control by the chief executive officer is made difficult by the alliances the agency may form with legislators and clients. Nonetheless, at the national level, the president possesses formidable tools to control agencies: public opinion, appointment power, budget preparation, and legislative clearance. In recent years, presidents have used the OMB for the coordination and evaluation of agency activities. Many governors have adapted this approach.

7. In addition to the varying degrees of control exercised over the agency by legislatures and chief executives, agencies need to consider three other external political bodies: clients, cognate agencies, and the media. Although agencies supposedly regulate these clients, critics charge that, in reality, the relationships become too cozy. Since several agencies can become involved in one policy area, administrators need to consider these cognate agencies when surveying their own political environment. The media also shape the administrative processes in subtle ways.

8. The political resources available to an administrator flow from three chief sources: external support, professionalism, and leadership. In assessing the political consequences of their actions, administrators need to consider, in addition to the resources available, the *political* costs involved.

9. In dealing with the environment, administrators have three broad strategies available: cooperation, competition, and conflict. Although a cooperative strategy might be preferred, administrators should recognize that they can frequently become embroiled in competition or conflict.

Problems

1. An especially important skill in political management is negotiating. According to expert negotiators, some of the following statements are true and some are false. Which do you think are true and which false? Explain.
   a. People are basically the same.
   b. Do not make things personal.
   c. Do your negotiating before a public meeting if possible.
   d. Do not give ultimatums.

e. If you want something, a face-to-face meeting is better than a telephone call.
f. After a meeting, it is better if the other party writes the memo of understanding than if you write it.
g. Do not be afraid to ask the other party for help during a negotiation.

2. Discuss the possibility and implications of citizen participation being overwhelmed during hearings on controversial issues by expert testimony from government and industry representatives. Can you find examples in the local newspapers?

3. Assess the possibility of the adoption in your city of free-fare bus service or some other local issue of your choice. Consider the possibility in terms of (a) possible allies, (b) probable opponents, (c) distribution of resources among the activities, (d) legal constraints, and (e) alternative strategies for achieving it. Begin by completing the following chart:

Actors: list the names of all relevant groups or individuals	(A) Political power: rate each actor on a scale from 1 (weak) to 3 (strong)	(B) Position: rate each actor on a scale from –3 (strongly opposes issue) to +3 (strongly favors issue)	(C) Relative importance: rate each actor on a scale from 1 (low priority) to 3 (high priority)	A X B X C
Total				

4. Look up a major national act in either the *Statutes at Large* or the *Congressional Quarterly Weekly Report,* and then attempt to find applicable executive agency decrees relevant to it in either the *Federal Register* or the *Bureau of National Affairs Reports.* Do you think the law has been perverted to serve the goals of those who enforce it?
5. "The successful executive will readily accede to congressional participation in areas where its committees or members have a proper concern," writes former NASA chief James E. Webb (1969:197–222). Is Mr. Webb naive?
6. Given the prevalence of logrolling, why might an administrator want to keep his or her preferences unclear? What do you think the effect of a ban on logrolling would be?
7. What externalities were involved in the two decisions faced by Mayor Cervantes?
8. Can you see any link between the American party system, which is fairly weak in comparison to that of other Western nations, and the political activism of administrators?
9. "Vote trading and arm twisting are effective when the issue is not that big, when it isn't a glaring national issue. But it doesn't work when you've got the full focus of national attention on it." Do you agree or disagree? Support your answer with recent examples.
10. Redraw Figure 2-2 with a hospital administrator in the center. What do you think the figure would look like with the chief executive of a multinational corporation at its center? The president of Princeton University? Be specific.
11. What kinds of power do even "powerless" people have?
12. Recall situations in which you eagerly or reluctantly did what someone told you to do. What types of power were used in each case? What types of power do you feel most comfortable and/or most awkward exercising?

CASE 2.1

★★★★★★★★★★★★★★★★★★★★★★★★★★★★★★★★★★★

Closing Sydenham Hospital

Unlike other major cities, which have at most 1 municipal hospital, New York City has 17. The smallest of them, Sydenham, was built in the heart of Harlem in 1925. By the 1950s, with modern medicine requiring ever-more space, Sydenham had fallen seriously behind the other city hospitals in providing quality health care. When mayors began to recommend closing it, the Harlem leadership protested vigorously. Sydenham, they argued, was not only a hospital but a cultural landmark.

Nevertheless, in January 1980, the New York Health and Hospitals Corporation (HHC) voted to proceed with the closing of Sydenham. Not surprisingly, the vote caused a furor among black and

Hispanic residents of the area. Fifty percent of New York City Council members urged Mayor Ed Koch to drop all plans to close the hospital. Representative Charles B. Rangel called Koch the most repressive mayor in the city's history and immediately petitioned the Justice Department to block closing, pending investigation by the Office of Civil Rights into charges that the situation would deprive minorities of health care. (Seven months later, the office would conclude that there was no violation of civil rights laws.)

The Politics and Economics of Health Care

Retrenchment has been a common theme in municipal government for nearly a decade, especially in New York City (see Exhibit 1). It was in this context that Mayor Koch decided to close Sydenham. The mayor argued that (1) alternative uses of the hospital were fiscally unsound, (2) federal funds to keep it open would not be sought because the hospital would need $10 million in repairs to bring it into compliance with building codes, and (3) the hospital's patient load could be handled by four other hospitals in the area.

The core economic issue to Koch was empty beds. Sydenham, which had 119 beds, had only 70 or so patients in them because the people of Harlem knew that the care they got at Sydenham was not as good as the care they could get at any of six hospitals between 4 and 12 blocks away. Yet the cost of a bed remained high—$250 to $300 per night—even when it was empty.

Koch's political strategy was simple. According to the experts, two hospitals, Sydenham and Metropolitan, both located in Harlem, met the criteria for closing. So Koch announced that he would close both. Eventually, it became clear to Koch that if both hospitals were closed his administration would lose political support for his other programs. He believed that, by not prematurely indicating a surrender at Metropolitan, he would be in a better position to get federal aid to keep it open. After all, President Carter was running for reelection.

The $42 Million Solution

On March 2, 1980, Mayor Koch and his staff began to put his plan into action. They submitted a $42 million proposal to the U.S. Department of Health, Education and Welfare (HEW)—now the Department of Health and Human Services—calling for federal financing to keep Sydenham and Metropolitan Hospitals open. Under the plan, New York City would have had no financial responsibility to Sydenham after October 1.

On March 29, HEW rejected the proposal, saying that it was too similar to a $30 million rescue of a Brooklyn hospital the previous fall; the department could not justify financing two parallel projects in the same city.

Koch spent the next few weeks urging HEW to save Metropolitan. He warned that unless help came, he would decide the hospital's future on his own. High officials in HEW then began suspecting that Koch preferred to close Metropolitan, thereby saving the hospital's annual $30 million deficit and placing the blame on the department. HEW Secretary Patricia R. Harris found herself spending much of April denying Koch's assertions that she was blocking plans to keep the two hospitals open.

By mid-June an agreement was reached in which the federal government would help fund Metropolitan for at least three years and Sydenham would become, on October 1, a community-operated drug, alcohol, and mental health facility financed by Medicaid funds. At a White House ceremony, Representative Rangel offered Koch stained praise.

Koch Sends in the Police

At about 10:00 P.M. the evening of September 15, Mayor Koch received a call while having dinner in Chinatown. About 60 demonstrators, he was told, had taken

EXHIBIT 1

City of New York Expenditures, Fiscal Years 1975, 1978, 1982
(Dollars in millions)

		Amount	
	1975	*1978*	*1982*
Debt service	$1,896.0	$2,184.0	$1,879.7
Public assistance	1,203.3	1,368.9	1,356.3
Health services	1,007.3	1,052.6	1,271.4
Social services	1,019.6	1,314.6	1,708.5
Housing	169.7	128.5	333.8
Infrastructure projects	893.5	352.7	733.7
Other development programs	3.3	6.8	38.1
Transportation	270.5	374.9	492.0
Education	2,982.2	3,139.6	4,141.4
Criminal justice	1,324.4	1,411.0	1,737.2
General government	1,571.0	1,765.5	2,670.0
Total	$12,340.8	$13,099.1	$16,370.8

SOURCE: Adapted from Annual Reports of the Comptroller of the City of New York as reported in Charles Brecher and Raymond D. Horton, "Expenditures," in Brecher and Horton, eds., *Setting Municipal Priorities, 1984* (New York: New York University Press, 1983), pp. 68–96.

over Sydenham. The media wanted a response.

Koch detailed a response over the phone and the next day held a press conference to tell his side of the story. He said that he would not order the police to forcibly evict the demonstrators, but he refused to accede to their demand that the city negotiate if it wanted to end their occupation. On September 21, some 30 people, including 10 police officers, were injured when demonstrations outside the hospital became violent.

The next day, Koch met with representatives from the Coalition to Save Sydenham. He agreed to postpone the deadline for closing for two weeks to allow more time for the coalition to seek funds to keep Sydenham open as a voluntary general hospital.

Meanwhile, the demonstrators continued their sit-in. Gradually, their numbers thinned to nine. For the next week nothing happened except that the city continuously pulled the plugs on them. First no lights; then no food—except what was supplied by the police; next no telephone; and then no visual contact with the outside. Koch felt that efforts on behalf of the protestors by local politicians during this period were just last-minute posturings. But he wondered: When would it end? As long as the demonstrators were allowed to occupy center stage, the orderly phasing out of Sydenham and the transfer of its employees could not take place.

On Wednesday afternoon, September 24, the Intelligence Division of the New York Police Department advised Mayor Koch that members of the Communist party, white agitators, and others looking for a confrontation might bring guns into the community. Working through Charlie Rangel, Koch let the sit-in demonstrators know that if they would leave, the city would waive criminal and civil sanctions. But they remained adamant.

Koch knew that on Saturday, September 26, there would be a huge demonstration. Therefore, he ordered the police to act; at 2:00 A.M. on the day of the demonstration, the police moved in.

Cops under assault defending Sydenham Hospital from the mob that was bent on forcibly taking it over. (Wide World)

Citicaid

On the afternoon of September 26, Sydenham Hospital, for the first time in nearly 60 years, stood empty. It was ringed with police barriers, and a large contingent of police officers remained on the scene. But the hospital was closed.

Meanwhile, posturing by elected officials continued. For example, Governor Carey, in a surprise move on the day of the huge demonstration, promised to help Harlem community leaders with a plan to convert Sydenham into a private hospital and to help get federal funds to carry out that plan. But the die was cast. Sydenham closed on November 24, and the protracted fight between Koch and community, religious, and political groups had finally come to an end.

All the news, however, was not bad for Harlem that fall. In October, Koch announced that $108 million would be spent over the next five years to provide comprehensive health care in Harlem. The new program, designated Citicaid, would cover indigents who were eligible for Medicaid and 17,000 others who were too poor to afford Blue Cross, did not receive it as an employee benefit, and were not destitute enough to quality for Medicaid. The federal government would pay 50 percent, New York State, 17 percent, and the city, 33 percent. It would be the nation's largest publicly operated health maintenance organization (HMO) in an urban setting.

Case Questions

1. What are Mayor Koch's strengths and weaknesses as a political manager?
2. What was he trying to achieve?
3. What would you have done differently? (Note that the case says nothing about what happened after the police moved in on the morning of September 26.)
4. What is your assessment of what Koch termed "political posturing"?

Case References

Charles Brecher and Raymond D. Horton, *Setting Municipal Priorities, 1982* (New York: Russell Sage Foundation, 1981); Edward I. Koch, *Mayor* (New York: Warner Books, 1984); Karen Gerard, *American Survivors: Cities and Other Scenes* (New York: Harcourt Brace Jovanovich, 1984); *New York Times:* January 22, 1980, February 18, 1980, February 20, 1980, March 1, 1980, March 11, 1980, March 13, 1980, March 30, 1980, April 30, 1980, May 16, 1980, May 30, 1980, June 4, 1980, June 20, 1980, July 13, 1980, September 21, 1980, September 23, 1980, September 24, 1980, September 26, 1980, September 27, 1980, September 28, 1980, October 1, 1980, October 2, 1980, November 21, 1980; *New York Daily News,* September 27, 1980.

CASE 2.2

★ ★

William D. Ruckelshaus and the EPA

"Dead in the Water"

One cannot help seeing the plaque on the wall as you enter the U.S. EPA building in Washington, D.C. On it the agency's mission is inscribed: "To protect the public from environmental hazards." That mission was sidetracked in 1983 when 12 high officials were fired or resigned. A contempt of Congress charge was filed against Anne McGill Burford, the administrator of the EPA, and Rita Lavelle, head of the agency's hazardous-waste cleanup program, was convicted of perjury. As one top administrator observed, the agency was "dead in the water."

Morale was so bad that some loyal, hard-working employees were even ashamed to admit to friends or neighbors that they worked at the agency. Suspicions at EPA headquarters were so intense that a few employees began surreptitiously posting satirical memos attacking their bosses' policies. "There's a bizarre quality to the whole place," a lobbyist for a major chemical company said. "It's turned into a never-never land of rumor, innuendo, and constant bureaucratic upheaval."

Against this backdrop, President Reagan turned to William D. Ruckelshaus, the man who guided the EPA through its first four years (1970–73), to restore the prestige and sense of urgency the agency originally had. Nowhere was the appointment greeted with more enthusiasm than inside the EPA.

Tasks

But Ruckelshaus's job would not be easy. The scientific and regulatory issues that the agency had to handle were more complex in 1983 than they had been in 1973. Furthermore, the Reagan administration had cut the agency's budget by nearly a third and the number of employees had dropped from 14,000 to 11,500.

Ruckelshaus needed to move rapidly to improve the agency's morale and determine its policy direction. Here are the most controversial and pressing issues the new administrator faced:

- Personnel: Ruckelshaus faced a formidable task in filling the vacant slots.
- Legislation: Perhaps the biggest task that faced Ruckelshaus was finding a way to end the two-year-old deadlock on the administration's legislative priorities. The White House had sought but failed to push legislation through Congress to roll back environmental stan-

dards and give states and companies more authority to determine how and when expensive pollution controls would be installed.

■ Enforcement: During 1981, the EPA's enforcement operations were reorganized every few months. The result: Litigation to force companies to clean up pollution virtually came to a halt.

■ International: The EPA was under increasing pressure from the Canadian government and others to crack down on what apparently causes "acid rain" by limiting emissions from power plants and factories, primarily in the Midwest.

■ Regulatory: Ruckelshaus faced a long list of complex, politically explosive decisions that had been put on hold. For example, he had to decide whether to stop millions of dollars in federal aid and impose other sanctions on counties and cities that had not complied with clean-air requirements. He also had to issue rules to protect underground water supplies from toxic chemicals, change some of the air quality standards, and determine whether treated sewage should be dumped into the oceans instead of landfills.

■ Political: Ruckelshaus had to decontaminate the scandal that had toppled his predecessor Anne Burford and stop it from spreading to the White House doors; deal with a hostile Congress that had ordered investigators from six subcommittees to look into the EPA's handling of efforts to clean up the nation's most toxic chemical-waste dumps; mend fences with outraged environmentalists, who accused the Reagan administration of trying to destroy the progress the nation had made in cleaning up its air and water; and come to terms with industry officials, who complained that the agency had lost its efficiency.

Strategy and Tactics

When Ruckelshaus took over as head of the embattled EPA, he followed many of the time-tested rules of thumb that had helped him survive tough periods in the past. Among these "rules," we can note the following:

1. Public officials should think of everything they say or do, even behind closed doors, "as if it were on a billboard." "If you look up and what you see embarrasses you or gives the slightest appearance of impropriety, then don't do it or don't say it."
2. "The best politics is good government: If you start horsing around in areas where the public's health is concerned, you're going to get in trouble."
3. Minimize political miscalculations, assure a sense of calm and serious analysis in the organization, and continue to meet with environmentalists after being confirmed by Congress.
4. When staffing a regulatory agency, "it is probably better if you can find people who are not subject to the charge [of being too close to industry]." If you want people who you can put to work immediately, look to government first, not industry. (This was in sharp contrast to the previous political leadership.)
5. Perceptions are important. Ruckelshaus thought that the Reagan administration had initially misread its mandate from the public on environmental laws. Specifically, it had "confused" the public's wish to improve the *way* the goals of protecting the environment were achieved with a desire to change those goals. This caused the "perception" that the administration was hostile to environmental regulation.
6. Sometimes a "high purpose" of a public executive's office is to "educate" the public. The public cannot be totally protected from environmental hazards—even by statute. Therefore, explain the actual risks of chemicals and other pollutants and the costs of regulating them.
7. Goals in one area of public policy (e.g., protecting health and environment)

must be assessed in the light of other social goals (e.g., more jobs and economic growth).

8. Develop a consistent approach to the management and assessment of risk. His formula was deceptively simple: Obtain the best scientific analysis to determine just how much of a threat to health or environment is posed by some new substance or process.

Managing Internal Components

Ruckelshaus's management style was based on a belief in the quality and dedication of EPA employees. In his opinion, a lot of people within the agency had become discouraged about how environmental laws and rules were working in practice and had ideas about change. But the Reagan administration was suspicious and failed to realize that these bureaucrats had, like the rest of the country, changed their views about regulation.

Accordingly, Ruckelshaus allowed much more participation in decision making. For example:

- One EPA official recalls how the agency decided what to do after traces of the cancer-causing pesticide EDB were discovered in some foods in Florida. "We had to bring extra chairs into [Ruckelshaus's] office in the EDB meetings. It was wall-to-wall people, including all the permanent employees involved—real knockdown, drag-outs."
- Immediately after taking office, Ruckelshaus formed a number of task forces to examine the EPA's policies and options in such areas as ground-water protection, dioxin contamination, and acid rain, as well as the agency's budget and its problems with federal and state programs. All had tight deadlines for reporting back to Ruckelshaus.

Ruckelshaus could be tough when the need arose. For example, when the EPA's top pollution prosecutors gathered in Alexandria, Virginia, in January 1984 for a conference, they got a tongue lashing. After he took over the EPA, Ruckelshaus told agency employees that he expected to find a "bunch of tigers" itching to go aggressively after violators of federal clean air and clean water laws. "But on the basis of what I see here in the past few months, there may be more pussycats in the tank than tigers."

Ruckelshaus knew he would never improve agency morale if he merely sat in Washington mending political fences. Therefore, his first three months as head of the EPA, he visited almost all the agency's regional offices to give staff pep rallies. At every stop, he also made it a point to meet with local environmentalists. This practice is known as "touching all the bases."

Managing External Constituents

To revive a foundering government agency required more than good internal operation. Ruckelshaus had to launch a first-rate public relations offensive. He opened the agency's doors to all—environmentalists, journalists, and industrial executives—to dispel any notion that EPA officials preferred to hear only polluters' pleadings. He even made public his daily appointment book.

Here is how he dealt with other key constituents:

- Congress: To placate congressional critics, Ruckelshaus made frequent trips to Capitol Hill where he personally visited with key legislators. He proposed a budget increase—even when there was a real question about whether the agency could absorb it—partly to appease congressional critics.
- Citizens: In a much publicized action in Tacoma, Washington, Ruckelshaus asked local residents to help the EPA decide on the acceptable level of arsenic emissions from a copper smelter that, if closed down, would have cost the community 575 jobs. He wanted the public to

share with him "the vexing nature of environmental decisions."

■ Industry: Another problem was how to get responsible parties to come up with the money to pay for waste-site cleanups.

To summarize, if Ruckelshaus was the White Knight in 1983, then he was a knight without armor or horse. Surrounding him were many dragons: environmental groups, headline-hunting politicians, scientists, complex technical regulations, the Chemical Manufacturers Association, the American Petroleum Institute, administration budget cutters, waste disposal firms hungry for contracts, sometimes the EPA's own regional offices, the states, and a growing number of disenchanted taxpayers. "It is frustrating," Ruckelshaus said. "There's a lot of history behind these squabbles. It takes time."

Epilogue

In November 1984, the White House announced the resignation of William D. Ruckelshaus. There was almost uniform agreement that he had turned a foundering, dispirited agency into a well-managed organization where a reinvigorated bureaucracy was again confident that its efforts to carry out the environmental laws were supported by the agency's head. EPA employees gave Ruckelshaus an affectionate send-off, with a standing ovation before and after his speech and cheers in between. A hand-lettered sign, hung from the proscenium of the auditorium's stage, said "Thanks Bill!"

Case Questions

1. How did Ruckelshaus's external environment differ from that of a business executive?
2. What do you think might be the basis for the logic behind Ruckelshaus's eight "rules"?
3. When Ruckelshaus was asked to return to the EPA, he was a highly paid business executive. Why do you think he took so large a pay cut?
4. What new political problems does Ruckelshaus allude to in the epilogue? Suggest a strategy for overcoming them.

Case References

"An Old Hand Tries to Clean Up Mess at EPA," *U.S. News & World Report,* April 4, 1983; Andy Pasztor, "In Seeking to Put EPA in Order, Ruckelshaus Is Facing a Tough Job," *Wall Street Journal,* April 29, 1983; Andy Pasztor, "Lots of Controversial Issues Await at EPA as Ruckelshaus Hearings Get Underway," *Wall Street Journal,* May 4, 1983; "Ruckelshaus Vows to End EPA's 'Abuses' of Power," *Wall Street Journal,* May 5, 1983; Andy Pasztor, "Ruckelshaus Seeks Boost in EPA Budget," *Wall Street Journal,* June 15, 1983; Lawrence Mosher, "Ruckelshaus Is Seen as His Own Man in Battle to Renew Clean Air Act," *National Journal,* July 16, 1983; Philip Shabecoff, "Environmental Groups Now Offer Some Praise," *New York Times,* July 19, 1983; Philip Shabecoff, "Ruckelshaus Says Administration Misread Mandate on Environment," *New York Times,* July 27, 1983; "The Environmental Impact of the EPA's New Mr. Fix-It," *Business Week,* August 22, 1983; Alan L. Oten, "Can EPA Be Made Rational?" *Wall Street Journal,* October 19, 1983; "Clearing the Air at EPA," *Time,* December 5, 1983; Andy Pasztor, "Ruckelshaus Criticized by All Sides as Honeymoon at EPA Nears End," *Wall Street Journal,* April 6, 1984; Guy Darst, "Ruckelshaus Gets Praise for Raising Morale at EPA," *Houston Chronicle,* May 20, 1984; Nicholas C. Chriss, "EPA Defining, Assessing Waste Risks," *Houston Chronicle,* May 31, 1984; "Shakeup Sidetracked EPA," *Houston Chronicle,* May 31, 1984; Philip Schabecoff, "Après Ruckelshaus le Deluge?" *New York Times,* December 3, 1984; Philip Shabecoff, "Ruckelshaus Says EPA Is Improved," *New York Times,* December 7, 1984; Michele Perrault, "Ruckelshaus, Thwarted," *New York Times,* December 11, 1984; "Politics of Waste Disposal: Interview with William D. Ruckelshaus," *Governance,* September 1989.

★★

CHAPTER 3 Interorganizational Relations

Introduction

Chapter 2 argued that public administrators find themselves, for better or worse, in a force field of politics. To drive this point home, I presented a simple model of a government agency's universe (Figure 2-2). In that model, the agency is surrounded by legislative bodies, political bosses, courts, cognate agencies, other governments, private firms, nonprofit organizations, the media, subordinates, and, of course, clients. Some of the relationships between the agency and these elements are best characterized as interpersonal; that is, one person dealing with another: the agency head conferring with his or her political boss, trying to persuade a legislator to vote a certain way, giving an interview to a reporter, and so on. But other relations are better characterized as organizational, and it is these relations with which this chapter is briefly concerned.

We begin this chapter by examining the relations between governments: federal to state and local, state to local, state to state, and local to local. The importance of intergovernmental relations to program management cannot be overemphasized. Apart from a few programs, such as the administration of the social security system, the federal government is not a direct provider of domestic public services. Instead, the majority of national domestic programs are implemented through a complex arrangement among federal, state, and local governments. This approach to public service delivery reflects the fact that the United States is a federal system in which responsibilities are both divided and shared among separate levels of government, each possessing a base of legal and fiscal authority.

Furthermore, one government can establish an agreement with another government to provide a particular service for its own citizens. Counties sometimes contract with cities and pay the latter to maintain county roads within city limits. States contract with cities and counties to provide social services to families and individuals. One survey revealed that no less than 62 percent of municipalities in the United States had formal or informal agreements for the provision of services to their citizens by other government units. Figure 3-1, which has been adapted from Figure 2-2, shows this kind of relationship conceptually, with one government (G_2) as the service producer, and another (G_1), as the service arranger who delivers the service to customer (C) (Savas, 1987).

Following our examination of intergovernmental relations, we pause briefly in the second section to consider some of the managerial implications of these relationships.

In the third section, we begin to focus on relationships between the government and the private sector, represented in Figure 3-1 by the circle PF (private firm). We will see that there are at least four types of these relationships: contracting, grant, franchise, and partnership.

In the fourth and final section of the chapter, we look at a concept that really carries us somewhat beyond interorganizational relations: **privatization,** or the move to more market-based arrangements for delivering services. Throughout the chapter emphasis will be placed on the *political* implications of these relationships and how public administrators can best *manage* them.

Intergovernmental Relations (IGR)

Federalism and IGR Compared

Some might say that *IGR* is just another term for **federalism.** But that would not be accurate.

What then is federalism? In its most formal sense, a federal system (such as the United States, Canada, Switzerland, and Germany) stands in contrast to a unitary or centralized system (such as France or Great Britain). A federal system divides power

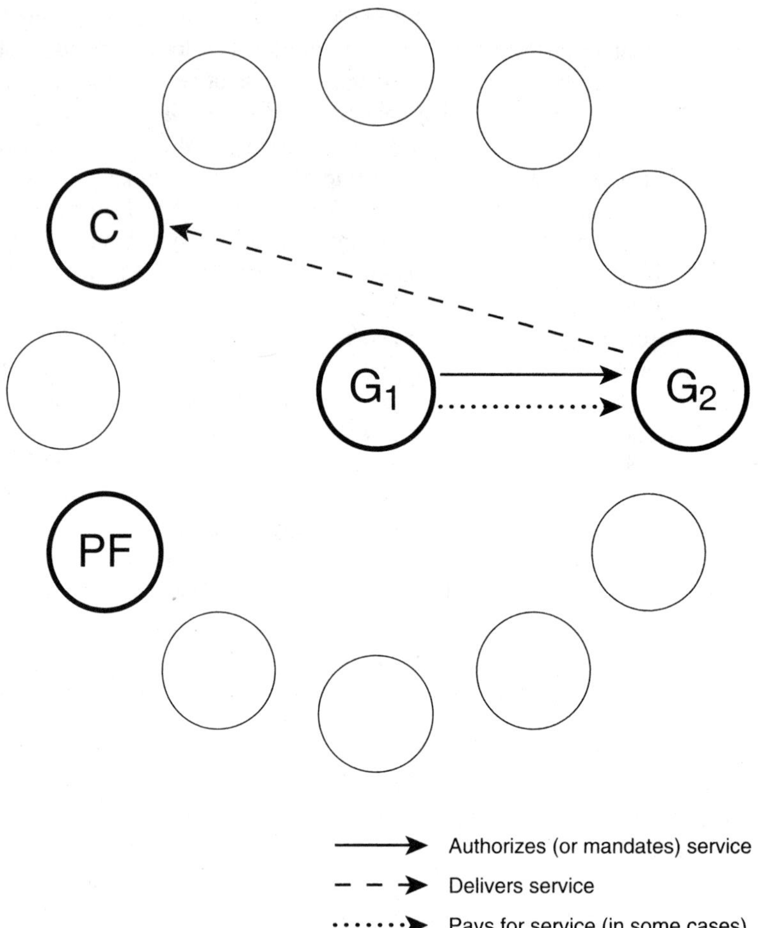

FIGURE 3-1
Intergovernmental Arrangement for Providing Goods and Services

between central government and regional governments (states, provinces, cantons, and lands); each government, central or regional, is legally supreme in its own area of jurisdiction. Thus, in the United States, the federal government controls external affairs, regulates interstate commerce, and establishes rules for immigration and naturalization. But the Constitution reserves certain powers for the states: control of elections, local governments, and public health, safety, and morals. Although some powers are shared between governments—taxing and spending for the general welfare, defining and punishing crimes, and so forth—the traditional, or **"layer cake," model** of federalism assumes that functions appropriate to each level can be defined with reasonable precision and should be kept independent.

Morton Grodzins and Daniel J. Elazar (1966) reject this model of the federal system, preferring a **marble cake model.** According to Grodzins and Elazar, separation of functions is both impractical and undesirable when governments operate in the same area, serve the same clients, and seek comparable goals.

Models should simplify the world, but layer cakes and marble cakes take this simplification a little too far. We need a more accurate picture of how governments operate together in the same program area. That is, what are the *relationships* among administrators in the federal system? We also need to recognize that there are many more governments involved than the concept of federalism implies.

A major deficiency of federalism as a descriptive model is that it tends to recognize mainly national-state and interstate relations but to ignore national-local, state-local, national-state-local, and interlocal relations. In contrast, "IGR includes as proper objects of study all the permutations and combinations of relations among the units of government in the American system" (Wright, 1982).

Local government means much more than the 19,200 cities and the 16,691 townships that can be found in the United States. The populations of the once-powerful cities have spilled over municipal boundaries into the counties. County officials administer a range of federal and state programs, and in many metropolitan areas the county executive spends more money and serves far more people than the mayor of the central city. County officials tend to be more influential with state governments than do their counterparts in the cities. There are some 3,042 counties in the United States. (See "17th Century Countries Struggle with 20th Century Problems" on page 84.)

In addition to cities, townships, and counties are the new special entities that have been created to provide such services as transportation, parks, libraries, hospitals, fire protection, and others that were previously handled by general governments. From 1977 to 1987, the Census Bureau reported, the number of such special purpose districts increased by 2,626—to 29,532. Cities have increasingly set up such districts to serve as separate entities with substantial fiscal independence because they are no longer able to provide these services through general taxes. This has happened even though the authority of the city governments was diminished in the process.

To sum up: While the term *federalism* perhaps helps us distinguish between one general class of government and another class (called unitary), it does not provide the best approach to understanding the kinds of knowledge (useful to administrators) highlighted earlier. For the public administrator at least, the preferable term then is **intergovernmental relations.**

The Evolution of the Intergovernmental System

Talk about the evolution of the intergovernmental system may offend bureaucrats in Washington, a city where a feeling of national dominance and self-importance always seems to be in vogue. It may bore the life out of many journalists, who tend to be preoccupied with what is current rather than long-range historical changes in the relationship among national, state, and local governments and agencies. Nevertheless, the relationship of states to the federal government is the cardinal question of our constitutional system. "It cannot be settled," Woodrow Wilson once wrote, "by the opin-

17th-Century Counties Struggle to Cope with 20th-Century Problems

When NBC's *Today* show decided recently to feature the Miami metropolitan area on a series of broadcasts, its producers were told that by far the most important government in the area was Dade County's, which provides services for close to two million people inside and outside the city, with an annual budget of $1.5 billion. By contrast, the city of Miami encompasses only one-fifth of the county's population and has an annual budget of $253 million. Yet NBC chose to put the mayor of Miami on the air as spokesman for the area. The reason? The producers felt that the county's government, managed by an elected executive with policies set by a board of commissioners, was simply too strange and complicated to explain on television.

"If I could wave a magic wand," says Harvey Ruvin, a Dade commissioner and the immediate past president of the National Association of Counties, "the first thing I would ask for county government would be a change in the nomenclature." County officials, he explains, "are supervisors in California, judges in Texas, jurors in Louisiana, freeholders in New Jersey, county legislators in New York, commissioners in Dade. If I tell somebody from New York I'm a commissioner, they think I'm the dog catcher. No wonder the public and the media focus on governors and mayors."

First formed in colonial America more than 350 years ago to serve rural areas, county government has emerged in the 1980s as the unit of local government under the most stress. It is the unit of government that must deal with many of the most critical social problems, such as health, welfare, and corrections. It must serve urban and suburban areas at the same time that it must tend to rural and agricultural problems.

Yet it is the unit of government most

ion of any one generation, because it is a question of growth, and every new successive stage of our political and economic development gives it a new aspect, makes it a new question." Wilson could not have been more right. As we shall see in this section, IGR have changed greatly since the early 19th century. These changes are closely linked to the overall growth of government in American society. As public administration has come to play a larger and larger role in our lives, the links between the different levels of the federal system have become both tighter and more complex.

The Era of Dual Federalism (1789–1933). The idea that the functions and responsibilities of the federal and state governments are separate and distinct had a long history. For example; in the first half of the nineteenth century, when emerging economic interests sought subsidies or tax breaks, they were likely to go to their state government. But when these interests wanted protection from competition by cheap imports, they had to go to the national government.

Certain political developments reinforced this arrangement, often characterized as **dual federalism.** As the vote was extended to new groups, business elite, who were difficult to change to meet changing needs. For a decade and more, counties have been the fastest-growing general purpose governments in terms of budgets, employees, and constituents. And whether they serve a few hundred people in rural Texas or eight million in Los Angeles County, counties are having a hard time of it.

Counties on the fringe of metropolitan areas, in particular, are being forced to take the lead in dealing with problems of rapid growth, while other counties, chiefly in remote rural areas, must try to reverse chronic economic decline and shrinking tax bases. All share the problem of governing jurisdictions that are superimposed over a vast array of other governments, including municipalities, large or small, and single-purpose districts covering everything from parks to schools.

Not long ago, it was the big cities that were most under stress, weakened by urban riots and reduction of their tax base by movement of the middle class and businesses to the suburbs, and struggling to meet the problems of the growing numbers of poor minorities and elderly left behind.

Now, although many cities remain troubled by drugs, crime and other acute problems, their overall condition has stabilized, aided initially by revenue sharing and other national programs (now shrunken or gone) and more recently by new downtown development.

It is the counties that struggle to cope. Yet most of this growth and turmoil around large cities or decline in the rural areas is obscured from public view by layers of complexity and ambiguity and the diversity of it all.

SOURCE: John Herbers, "17th-Century Counties Struggle to Cope with 20th-Century Problems," *Governing,* May 1989.

interested in a more centralized government, lost influence to farmers and workers, who were less interested in a strong national government.

Roughly speaking, we can say that this era lasted until the New Deal years of the 1930s, despite the fact that cooperation between national and state governments in areas such as railroad construction and banking existed before and during Franklin Roosevelt's administration. But not until the New Deal did the idea really take hold that the national government and the states were complementary parts of a single, governmental mechanism for coping with problems.

The Era of Cooperative Federalism (1933–1960). The Great Depression of the 1930s led to several new and important changes in IGR. The Social Security Act of 1935, for example, included national grants for state and local unemployment and welfare programs; the Housing Act of 1937 was the first instance of national involvement in local public housing. The Tennessee Valley Authority (TVA), created in 1933, was charged with developing the Tennessee River and its tributaries to promote their use for electricity, irrigation, flood control, and navigation (see Working Profile).

During this era of cooperative federalism, IGR became more centralized in Washington, and the role of federal dollars became more important. Without question, the national government had given money to states since its creation; in fact, the first such **grants-in-aid** were used to pay the debts the states had incurred during the American Revolution. In 1802, Congress passed a law providing that revenue from the sale of federal lands be shared with states. Since the early 1800s, however, the tendency has been for the national government to give money for specific purposes. Such **categorical grants**—as they are also called—require that funds be spent for particular programs in particular ways (in other words, "with strings attached").

The Era of "Creative" Federalism (1960–1968). If the great growth in national aid to state and local government began with Franklin Roosevelt's New Deal in 1933, then it is fair to say that the most explosive period of such growth occurred during Lyndon Johnson's Great Society (1963–1968). The number of grant programs grew at an astounding pace—from about 50 in 1961 to some 420 by the time Johnson left office. These programs included legislative landmarks—Medicaid, the Elementary and Secondary Education Act, and the Model Cities program—and smaller initiatives tailored to the interests of narrower constituencies. Federal aid to states and localities in this period almost doubled—from $7.9 billion in fiscal year 1962 to $13.0 billion in fiscal year 1966. Johnson called his program "creative" federalism. Scholars disagree as to the inventive merit, the insight, and the imagination that went into the design of some of these programs, but none dispute Johnson's creation of many new categorical grant programs.

Creative federalism was a turning point in the development of the intergovernmental system for several reasons:

1. The federal government had become a far more significant presence in the daily lives of state and local administrators and in the delivery of government services to citizens, raising practical and philosophical questions. Did the individual programs created in Washington work as intended when implemented in dozens, hundreds, or thousands of state and local sites? What were the limits of purposeful government intervention in the social, economic, and political lives of its citizens? Could sweeping national purposes actually be effectively achieved by planned government activity? Should they be?

2. The intergovernmental system became more difficult to manage. Federal administrators now had to manage a larger number of separate programs, work with many more governmental units, and oversee the expenditure of increasing amounts of money. Moreover, because Congress had prescribed the goals and means of the programs in greater detail, they were more complex than their predecessors' programs (Howitt, 1984).

3. Because governors, mayors, and other state and municipal officials had a growing financial stake in intergovernmental aid, creative federalism developed a strong constituency that was prepared, when necessary, to lobby for the programs. This lobbying activity was carried out either individually or

collectively, through organizations like the National Governors Conference, the Council of State Governments, the U.S. Conference of Mayors, the National League of Cities, the National Association of Counties, the International City Managers Association, and the National Legislative Conference.

4. Categorical grants usually required that the state or local government put up money to match some part of the federal grant. Governors and mayors complained about these categorical grants because their purposes were often so narrow that it was impossible for a state to adapt federal grants to local needs. A mayor seeking federal money to build parks might discover that the city could get money only if it launched an urban renewal program that entailed bulldozing several city blocks.

5. Since grants frequently went directly to the agencies that ran federal programs, governors and mayors found they had less power.

President Nixon, who came into office in 1968, recognized these political realities and created his new policy for IGR accordingly. He would call it the "new federalism."

The Era of New Federalism (1968–1980). To effect the policy of new federalism, Nixon proposed **revenue sharing** in which states and localities would receive funds with virtually no restrictions on how they might be used. He also proposed the consolidation of existing categorical programs into broad-purpose **block grants** in a particular policy area such as education, with relatively few restrictions on their use. The idea of block grants had begun in the mid-1960s, when such a grant was created in the health field.

From 1972 to 1978, categorical grants fell from 90 percent of federal grant money to 73 percent. But President Carter (1977–1981) thought that the no-strings-attached approach led to abuses. By 1981, categorical grants were back to about 80 percent of grant money. In light of what was to come, the Carter administration may be seen as a transition period between an era of expansion and an era of cutback.

Recent Trends

Governors and Local Officials Are Squeezed. The inauguration of President Ronald Reagan in 1981 signaled the arrival at the national level of a chief executive committed to reducing the size and scope of government and creating an intergovernmental system that gave much greater prominence to states and localities. In particular, Reagan wanted to return to a more dual form of federalism by stepping back from the cooperative federalism that had developed over the past 50 years. He also wanted to devolve certain federal responsibilities to the subnational level. Although the president experienced moderate success in these efforts, governors and local officials found that their jobs had become considerably more difficult for two reasons—money and mandates. During the 1980s, there was less of the former and more of the latter.

★★★★★★★★★★★★★★★★★★★★★★★★★★★★★★★★★★★

WORKING PROFILE

David Lilienthal

Early on, David Lilienthal became associated in the public mind with the TVA. More than anyone, he shaped the institution and its relationship with other institutions. While the TVA was created as an autonomous regional public corporation, it had to fight local utilities and national bureaucracies to maintain its autonomy and its beliefs.

That suited Lilienthal fine. He had always fought for his beliefs. As a youth, he played football and boxed. While in college, he used to spar with a professional lightweight—the Tacoma Tiger. He liked debating and verbal sparring in school. He pursued excellence at Harvard Law School and cultivated his professors and other connections, displaying high ideals (Wilsonian liberalism) and extreme vigor. He always tested himself against adversaries and believed that challenge bred creativity. He entered the combative area of labor law and soon achieved wide recognition when he was appointed to the Wisconsin Railroad Commission in 1931.

The act that created the TVA in 1933 left the organizational details and institutional relationships ill-defined. The act included Article 22, a broad grant to develop regional plans. Yet, the new concept of an independent, regional government corporation could take its final form only from experience.

The TVA was run by a three-person board: Lilienthal plus two elder directors, both named Morgan. A. E. Morgan and H. A. Morgan disagreed about the philosophy and goals of the new organization. A. E., who was chairman, believed that the TVA should be more passive and should provide experiments and model plants only. But H. A. believed that, since the TVA could not enforce its plans, it should motivate the region to change by cooperating with local leaders, relying on their "common moorings" in the community. Lilienthal took this idea and developed it into the idea of "grass-roots democracy"—an idea that would come to underlay and direct the entire organization.

A. E. favored cooperation with private power, but H. A. and Lilienthal wanted to fight. Lilienthal had never trusted private utilities and wanted the TVA to have its own distribution systems (a source of political support as well). A. E. was overruled by the

★★★★★★★★★★★★★★★★★★★★★★★★★★★★★★★★★★★

Changing national priorities, tax cuts, and mounting deficits drove federal policymakers to cut funds going to states and localities. In constant 1982 dollars, these funds declined from $109.8 billion in 1978 to $94.7 billion in 1989. But these numbers do not tell the whole story. As Figure 3-2 shows, the composition of funding was also changing.

★★★★★★★★★★★★★★★★★★★★★★★★★★★★★★★★★★★

two-man majority, and his influence began to wane. Eventually, he was dismissed by the president, and Lilienthal became the new chairman.

Lilienthal orchestrated the TVA's rise to dominance in the region. He wrote and lectured throughout the valley. His message was the usefulness of electricity and the promise of the TVA to deliver it cheaply. He molded public opinion for his political battles. He was the itinerant preacher, spreading salvation through electricity and damning the satans of private power and big business.

He was not 'all talk,' however. He offered electricity at one half the rate that the private company charged. He urged the establishment of public cooperatives and municipal cooperations, encouraging them to get Public Works Administration (PWA) funds for their installations. These new entities became the grateful congregants, customers for the cheaper energy. Moreover, Lilienthal supported the creation of an Electric Home and Farm Authority to provide low-interest loans to permit the people to purchase appliances and other electrical equipment cheaply. He also encouraged manufacturers to build cheaper appliances; General Electric was the first to respond to this new market.

Lilienthal first converted the people who in turn won over state and local officials. While he was winning his battles, he was careful to share the glory with President Roosevelt and the New Deal. This political support at the local and federal levels would stand the TVA in good stead when it would have to fight over other issues. For instance, the TVA galvanized local support in 1941 to get the Douglas Dam approved over powerful objections in the Senate. Farmers and other citizens trooped into Washington to lobby for the dam. Similarly, Lilienthal had to call on all his presidential credits in 1939 to fend off the effort by Secretary Harold Ickes to incorporate the TVA into Ickes's Department of the Interior. When David Lilienthal left the TVA in 1946, he could take credit for the successful formation of a new type of organization and for its unique ideology and mission.

In later years, the aura of grass-roots autonomy, which Lilienthal had bequeathed to the TVA, was often used by that organization to protect itself from criticism. In recent times, environmentalists and ratepayers would find the myth to be only partially realized, as ecological concerns grew and utility rates began to rise. Social scientists studying the reality of grass-roots democracy, both under Lilienthal and later, found the rhetoric to be less than real, again because TVA often treated its consumers as captured clients rather than as political constituents.

SOURCES: Erwin C. Hargrove, "David Lilienthal and the Tennessee Valley Authority," in Jameson W. Doig and Erwin C. Hargrove, eds., *Leadership and Innovation: Entrepreneurs in Government,* (Baltimore, Md.: Johns Hopkins University Press, 1990), pp. 25–60; Philip Zelnick, *TVA and the Grass Roots: A Study in the Sociology of Formal Organizations* (Berkeley: University of California Press, 1949); David Lilienthal, *TVA and Democracy on the March* (New York: Harper & Bros., 1944).

★★★★★★★★★★★★★★★★★★★★★★★★★★★★★★★★★★★

Although payments to individuals on welfare, Medicaid, and other programs grew from $35 billion to $50 billion, states had little discretion over how these funds were spent. Block grants, over which they did have discretion within specific functions such as housing and education, were reduced from $50 billion to $25 billion. Revenue sharing, which Nixon had introduced in 1972 as part of his new federalism, had pro-

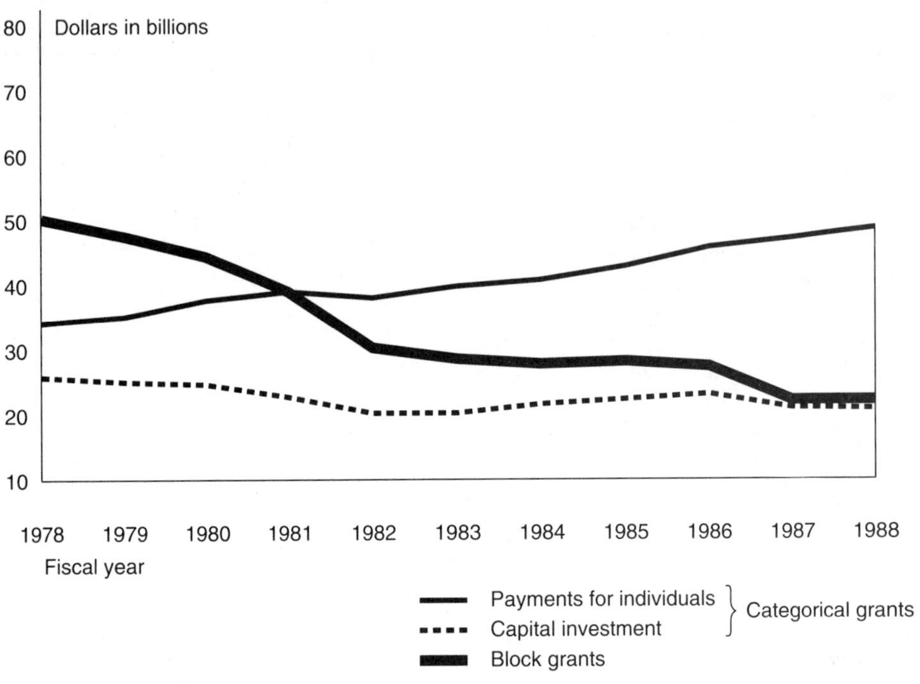

FIGURE 3-2

Changes in the Composition of Federal Aid to States and Localities (1978–1988) (Constant 1982 dollars)

SOURCE: U.S. Office of Management and Budget, *Historical Tables, Budget of the United States Government,* (Fiscal Year 1990) (Washington, D.C.: U.S. Government Printing Office, 1990) p. 240.

vided for the distribution of about $6 billion a year in federal funds with no strings attached but was eliminated for states in 1980 and for local governments in 1986.

The federal role in financing programs and services provided by state and local governments is relatively small when compared with spending for these purposes, which is derived from revenues raised by state and local governments. Yet, federal aid is important because it often signifies strong federal interests (e.g., in health care) or because it is designed to encourage innovation or stimulate spending for particular kinds of services (e.g., in primary and secondary education).

Compounding the money problem was the problem of **mandates.** Although Reagan had pledged to give states and localities more flexibility and authority, that pledge was undercut by an avalanche of mandates imposed in Washington. Indeed, more than a quarter of all statutes in which the federal government preempted state and local laws—setting its own standard and telling the states to enforce them—were enacted in the Reagan years. Most of these requirements dealt with health, safety, and education. Here are a few examples:

- Municipalities were required to monitor pollution from thousands of storm sewers and to test for 77 additional chemicals in municipal water supplies.

Ronald Reagan was committed to reducing the size and scope of the federal government and giving much greater prominence to states. He wanted to step back from the cooperative federalism that had developed over the previous 50 years and return to a more dual form. Governors found that their jobs had become considerably more difficult not only because of the loss of federal money but also because of increased federal mandates.

Nearly half of the $137 billion in federal aid to states and cities consists of direct grants for a variety of purposes, ranging from highways to housing. Through the 1980s the federal role in areas like education and housing—primarily local responsibilities—declined. But grants to individuals (mainly welfare and Medicaid) remained vastly uncontrollable; in 1992 they accounted for 62 percent of federal grants to states and cities. The growth of these programs means that, despite Reagan's cuts, the real value of federal aid to the states was greater in the early 1990s than in the early 1980s. (Cartoon by Bob Englehart, The Hartford Courant*)*

Local governments were also required to control 83 new drinking water contaminants.

- School districts were required to identify asbestos hazards and remove them from local schools.
- States were required to prepare reports on 152 new endangered species.
- States were required to monitor and enforce actions requiring businesses and industries to establish and maintain programs to protect hearing and guard against exposure to certain dangerous chemicals and asbestos.
- States were required to adopt a minimum drinking age of 21 or face a 10 percent reduction in highway aid. (U.S. General Accounting Office, 1990c)

Keep in mind that, although these and many other regulations were being imposed on state and local governments, federal allocations to the state and local governments were falling. It is not hard to see why some governors and mayors complained that they were being squeezed.

States Increase Their Prominence. Over the past decade, states have progressed from a period in which they were sometimes dismissed as mere administrative agents of the federal government to a period in which they are touted as key innovators. They appear today as highly visible leaders in a broad range of policy areas where the federal government was once seen as peerless.

There are a number of reasons for this transformation. First, states improved their capacities by modernizing their institutions and administrations and strengthening their revenue systems. Second, federal budget cuts, tax cuts, and block grants accelerated the rising role of state government in domestic policy in contrast to federal retrenchment. Finally, beginning in 1983, sustained economic growth helped to rebuild state treasuries, providing revenues to fund new initiatives. (See Figure 3.3.)

During the past decade, states broadened their agendas and addressed their social and economic needs in innovative ways. Not all state actions have been uniform. However, many states have been active, and state leadership is now widely recognized and reported. Examples of such leadership include the following, from both traditional and nontraditional state functions:

- *International trade:* State delegations, often headed by governors, now routinely travel to meet with foreign business leaders to secure new markets and solicit investment. Not all such efforts are ad hoc. By one count, 41 states maintained offices in 24 countries worldwide. In fact, by 1989, there were more state offices in Japan (39) than there were in Washington, D.C. (38).
- *The environment:* At least 29 states have implemented their own Superfund programs to clean up toxic-waste sites, and others have created commissions, such as the Chesapeake Bay Commission, to protect and restore the environment.
- *Housing:* States such as Massachusetts have established a trust fund creating a pool of capital for low- and moderate-income housing.
- *Economic development:* Texas has created a department of commerce to encourage and coordinate efforts between public institutions and private institutions with a stake in Texas's economy. To combat urban economic decline, Pennsylvania has created a regional consortium of labor-management committees to improve cooperation, heighten labor's role in industry decision making, and increase productivity. Michigan has created a public venture-capital fund; using 5 percent of the state's public pension funds, this development fund promotes new business and economic enterprises. Arkansas has experimented with a development bank in its efforts to counter rural economic decline. Altogether, 13 states have venture-capital

programs, 30 have established business loan funds, and 31 have created research grant programs to encourage economic development.

- *Growth management:* Florida has enacted legislation aimed at ensuring that adequate infrastructure exists to meet the demands of rapidly growing communities.
- *Health care:* Arizona is experimenting with the use of HMOs, to provide quality health care to the poor under the Medicaid program, while also holding down health care costs.
- *Education:* States across the nation and especially in the South have taken measures to improve their primary and secondary systems. They are raising performance standards; allocating more funds; reducing fiscal disparities; and establishing new modes of delivery, such as expanded parental choice and specialized curricula.

As the federal government became a less dependable source of local government financial assistance, expectations about the role of the states in domestic policy shifted. The fact that states moved to replace some lost federal grant funds to local governments contributed to a widespread sense among observers of the intergovernmental system that states were "on the move."

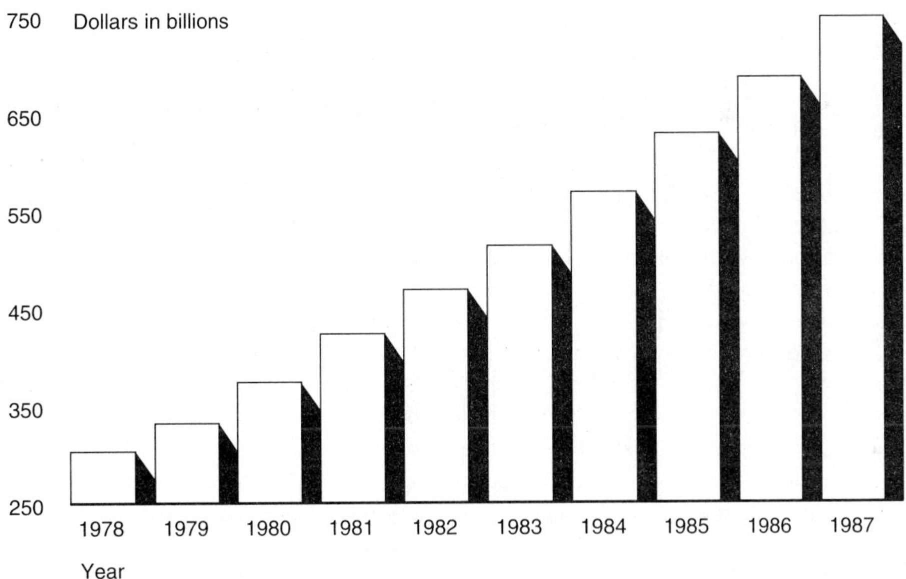

FIGURE 3-3
Growth in State-Local Revenues, Excluding Federal Aid (1978–87)

SOURCE: Advisory Commission on Intergovernmental Relations *Significant Features of Fiscal Federalism,* Vol. 1 (Washington, D.C.: U.S. Government Printing Office, 1989), p. 13.

Cash is not the only connection, however, between states and localities. All units of local government are public corporations created under the authority of state law to provide services that, presumably, could not adequately be provided by the private sector. **Dillon's Rule,** which declares that local jurisdictions are the creatures of the state and may exercise only those powers expressly granted them by the state, has been a guiding doctrine for more than a century. But after creating local units, states tenaciously try to keep them under control.

Although some states have departments to coordinate state and local affairs, administrative relations between the city and the state are generally conducted on a functional basis. Thus, the state department of education supervises the activities of local school districts and the state department of health, the activities of local health departments.

State bureaucracies have several techniques of supervision. First, they can simply require reports from local communities. Reports warn the state agency when trouble spots (e.g., excessive debts) begin to appear. Second, state agencies can, as the federal government does for them, furnish advice and information. Third, with larger budgets and more specialized equipment and personnel, the state can provide technical aid. Finally, if all else fails, the state can use its coercive power. For example, it can grant or withhold permits for certain things (e.g., to dump raw sewage into a stream under prescribed conditions); issue orders (e.g., to prescribe the standards for water supply purification); withhold grants-in-aid; require prior permission from a state agency; and appoint certain local officials or remove them.

Outlook

This section has traced the evolution of the intergovernmental system from the era of dual federalism to its cooperative and creative phases, and it has noted how Richard Nixon coined the slogan "new federalism" and Ronald Reagan rediscovered it ten years later. In his 1991 State of the Union address, George Bush also adopted the devolution of power from Washington as a theme. He proposed to hand $15 billion of programs over to the states in a single, consolidated grant. But the proposal went nowhere in Congress—where members prefer sending money to their districts with strings and bows attached.

When President Bush made his case for the devolution of power to the states, he used the familiar metaphor of "states as laboratories." The idea suggests that the solutions to national problems in health, welfare, crime, and the like can emerge from the experiences of various states. For example, in recent years, states have embraced a rich variety of education reforms: merit pay for teachers, teacher certification through testing, minimum competency standards for high school graduation, and the so-called "no pass, no play" rules for student extracurricular eligibility. In contrast, the federal Elementary and Secondary Education Act and its progeny set up rigid rules, spent billions of dollars on programs to upgrade the education of children with low-income parents, and generally failed in its purpose.

There are other reasons, however, why programs should be forged at the most local level practicable:

Many governors and mayors lamented Ronald Reagan's new federalism. Instead of giving power and flexibility to the states to address their problems, Congress kept giving the states new mandates. "The states are caught in a squeeze," Governor Bill Clinton of Arkansas (left) said. "People who want good things are imposing their priorities on the governors." Robert M. Isaac (right), who was elected president of the U.S. Conference of Mayors in 1991, said, "I don't think there was any New Federalism. I don't think there's been any transfer of power. I think it's gone the other way." Nevertheless, some officials see good in this. The lack of money has forced states and localities to be more innovative and self-reliant in their approaches to governing. (Quotes from New York Times, *May 21, 1990; Clinton photo from Associated Press, Isaac photo from* Colorado Springs Gazette Telegraph)

- Experience shows that state legislative bodies generally are more responsive to constituents than is Congress. State legislatures generally contain fewer members, are more knowledgeable about local conditions, and are less crowded for time than Congress. And malfunctioning state laws that burden all state residents are likely to evoke swift statutory reform. Members of Congress, on the other hand, are frequently ignorant of local conditions or needs because they are preoccupied with major national questions: balanced budget laws, tax reform, defense spending, and so on. In addition, federal statutes that harm only a few states will not usually create the nationwide constituency needed for reform.
- States can tailor policy to their unique circumstances, whereas Congress generally enacts policy nationwide. State policy is thus more likely to satisfy constituent desires. The federal 55-mile-per-hour speed rule is a good example. Although the limit may be desirable in urban states and also may

substantially reduce accidents there, its use makes little sense in rural states such as Idaho or Wyoming.

- Local media are equipped to inform constituents of local political developments, but they ordinarily lack the resources and money to report on the many activities of Congress. Thus, most voters would be more informed about an issue if it was addressed by the state legislature than if the same issue was addressed by Washington (Fein, 1986).

Managerial Implications of IGR

Effective management in an intergovernmental setting requires all skills usually associated with program management—planning (especially anticipating problems), decision making, organizing, implementing, and evaluating. But effective management in this setting also requires political skills such as those discussed in the last chapter. The reason is simple: These relationships are essentially political. Public administrators in these settings must work through organizations that are not necessarily under their direct control; they are in an indirect management situation where authority and responsibility are diffused among many organizations while accountability is relatively concentrated.

These points apply not only to high-profile positions, such as the chairman of the TVA (see Working Profile), but also to lower-level positions with well-defined tasks. Consider, for example, the case of a federal official who is responsible for increasing the fire safety of nursing homes in Massachusetts:

> *A state agency has jurisdiction over the fire inspections he is seeking. To get the inspection carried out, his actions must reach across organizational and jurisdictional lines.*
>
> *The traditional direct management tools and systems are inaccessible to him. He has little or nothing to do with the state agencies; their budget processes; or rewards, punishments, and other aspects of their employees' career paths. In short, if he seeks their "agreement" to carry out these inspections, his ability to manipulate [the consequences of not agreeing] is extremely limited. But the federal official's political and organizational superiors hold him accountable for achieving results. Should there be a disaster in such a federally funded nursing home, he would be held responsible by members of the legislature, the victims, the general public, elements of the media, and, quite conceivably, the courts. (Lax & Sebenius, 1986:315)*

To help administrators who similarly find themselves enmeshed in an intergovernmental setting, a variety of tools have emerged. We begin with the most important of these.

Bargaining

The need to settle differences due to differing interests and perspectives is inherent in IGR. In such situations a first step involves ascertaining the desired results. After a careful attempt to specify the product of the negotiations, a second key step involves specifying the network of linked agreements most likely to yield that product. One should also ask to whose action or inaction is the desired result likely to be vulnerable? Often it is most efficient to begin with the desired result and carefully "map backward" through the necessary chain of actors and events.

Next, one should analyze the bases for potential agreements and decisions. The following procedure evolved from David A. Lax and James K. Sebenius's (1986:314–38) weekly discussions with members of the Negotiations Roundtable, a working seminar of Harvard faculty and graduate students dedicated to learning more about negotiation and its role in management. Their analysis proceeds along the following lines:

1. *Conceive of interests broadly.* People negotiate to further their interests. Although negotiators often focus on the interests of the participants, they conceive of them too narrowly. Negotiators' interests can go beyond the obvious and tangible to include things like self-esteem and saving "face." And since interests are perceived, subjectively what role will information play? The right kind of information can create shared perceptions of the issue and its importance.

2. *Make alternatives to the agreement appear worse than the agreement.* To decide to go along with a proposed measure, a participant in the negotiation must see going along with the agreement as better, from his or her point of view, than not so doing. This focuses central attention on the parties' alternatives to a favorable decision. Managers' lack of measures to affect alternatives to the agreement is perhaps the main difference between traditional management and intergovernmental management. In the latter situation, when A prefers the status quo to Proposal X, then B has only a limited ability to affect A's career prospects, rewards, and punishments.

   Given these realities, B might try to make A's alternative to the proposed action considerably worse through enforcement tools such as fines, adverse publicity, legal sanctions, threats to not renew contracts, funding cutoffs, and the like. Yet bad publicity and a shutdown threat by the federal government against, say, Massachusetts nursing homes that do not meet fire regulations can cause powerful counterresponses. "Those high-handed federal bureaucrats are throwing old people onto the streets," or "Clumsy reliance on real or threatened sanctions can damage one's capacity for cooperative action elsewhere."

   It may be possible to break up sanctions and to threaten milder, more credible measures. For example, a person who has worked for the state may be hired at the federal level to help with state relations, or federal managers may point to an increasingly restive Congress (or some other body) that is likely to take blunt and unwanted action on the problem if a federal-state accord is not reached.

3. *Find alternatives that create values for both sides.* Negotiators of course do not just strive to make alternatives to agreement seem worse than the agreement itself. They also work to make the agreement seem more valuable.

   An obvious first possibility is to appeal to shared goals (e.g., safety of people in nursing homes) or norms and standards that cut across jurisdictional boundaries. Public administrators always have something to trade. For example, officials in Harris County, Texas, agreed to guarantee 100 cell spaces for federal prisoners over a 15-year period. In return, the U.S. Marshal's Service presented the county with a $1 million automated fingerprinting system that state officials had refused to fund. The crucial point is to find an alternative that creates value for both sides.

4. *Change the game.* In IGR-type situations, two types of reconfiguration are common: changing the parties involved in the bargaining or changing the existing organizational structures. The former can occur when federal grant programs build up state capabilities to perform desired functions. Lax and Sebenius (1986:328) explain how the process works:

   As state capacity increases, as a network of beneficiaries of the federal program expands, and as the recipient grows in local political prominence, a subtle but important shift may occur in federal-state bargaining. No longer is it merely the "feds versus the state," but now there is an increasingly powerful ally of the federal agency within the state government. A private sector analogue might be "lending" personnel to another department or unit to ensure a favorable voice in the "other" camp. To be sure, the state entity will have interests other than those of its federal sponsors, but unlike the situation beforehand, an important ally has been created and strengthened with respect to the original federal purposes.

   Administrators may also seek to change the game by changing the existing organizational structure to make it more suitable to IGR tasks. For example, when Caspar Weinberger was secretary of HEW under President Nixon, he tried to push both accountability and authority to the ten regional directors of HEW (see Figure 3-4). The action was never very successful because the regional offices were organized by program. Employees in the regional office had direct links to their counterparts in Washington and thus were able to effectively bypass the regional directors.

   President Carter's secretary of HEW, Joseph Califano, attacked the problem differently, by changing the existing organizational structure:

   Rather than try to devolve authority and accountability to the regions, Califano appointed a Deputy Undersecretary for Intergovernmental Relations in Washington. Officials in the field served as regional "ambassadors" who could go among the various regional programs and convey concerns

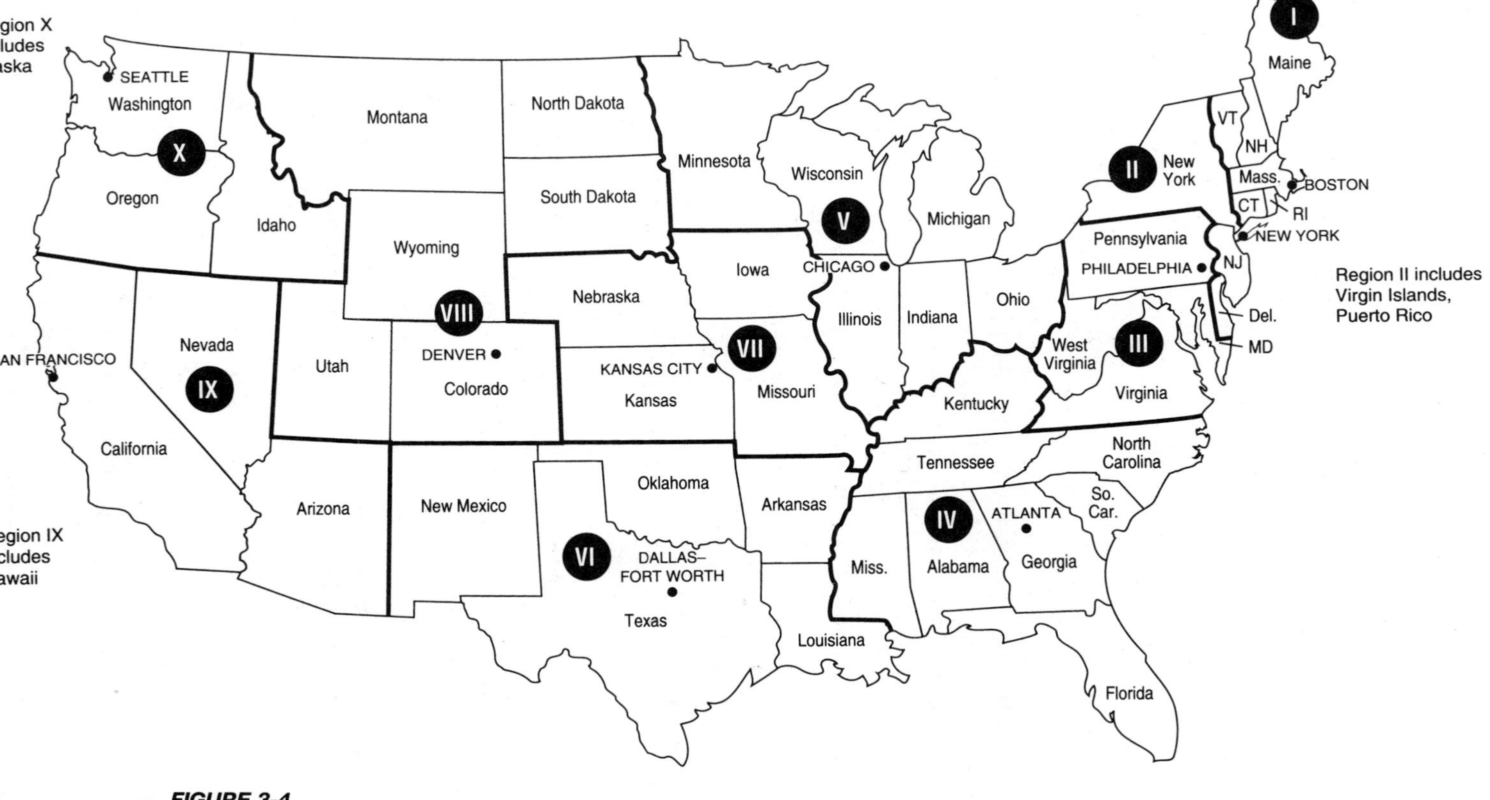

FIGURE 3-4
Map of the United States Showing Federal Administrative Regions

SOURCE: U.S. Bureau of the Census, *Current Population Reports,* Series P-25, No. 533 (Washington, D.C.: Government Printing Office, 1974).

directly to a fairly high level of HEW (the Deputy Undersecretary). At this level, cross trades and program modifications could be made relatively easily. (Lax & Sebenius, 1986:329)

Cooperative Management

The tool of cooperative management involves some form of agreement between jurisdictions. The idea is not new. The Founding Fathers attempted to provide mechanisms to facilitate cooperation between the states. For instance, Article 1, Section 10 of the Constitution permits states to enter into **interstate compacts,** or agreements (with the consent of Congress). The Crime Compact of 1934, which allows parole officers to cooperate across state lines with a minimum of red tape, is now subscribed to by all states. States lacking adequate facilities make compacts with other states to help them with professional education, welfare, tuberculosis, and mental illness.

As state officials have come to realize that problems such as transportation, energy, pollution, water resources, and fishing burst across state boundaries, the number of compacts has risen accordingly. Whereas there were only 24 compacts before the turn of the century, today over 170 are in existence.

One of the most notable and largest interstate agencies established by an interstate compact was the Port of New York Authority. Established in 1921 by New York and New Jersey, the authority constructs and operates bridges, tunnels, terminal facilities, and airports.

Given the interrelationship of society due to modern transportation and communication technology, and given the great number of local governments, it is no surprise to learn that local administrators are meeting with increasing frequency and hammering out cooperative agreements to overcome jurisdictional fragmentation that would otherwise obstruct the delivery of services.

A private organization has few restrictions on the organization of its operations other than the logic of profit or survival.

To see how different things are in the public sector, consider a **standard metropolitan statistical area** (SMSA) is defined as an integrated economic and social unit with a large population nucleus. Generally consisting of a central city with a population of at least 50,000 and the metropolitan area around it, it may include two or more central cities in one area, though it generally does so within one state. In any case, "an integrated economic and social unit" does seem to imply a certain commonality of interest between the central city and the suburbs around it. In short, the SMSA provides a logical basis for administration. In reality, however, the SMSAs are incredibly fragmental. To bring the problem into sharper focus, the Chicago metropolitan area may be taken as an example. As of the early 1970s, it was composed of 6 counties, 114 townships, 250 municipalities, 327 school districts, and 501 special purpose districts. For this metropolitan area, there were 1,198 separate units of government. This represented one local government for every three square miles, or one for every 5,550 inhabitants. Not surprisingly, some of these governments have quite limited functions, such as mosquito abatement or street lighting.

The Houston SMSA might be given as a second example. There, eight government agencies try to enforce protection programs for the environment. The eight agencies are involved only in monitoring, regulating, and carrying out pollution-abatement programs.* But a swarm of additional agencies has an interest and some authority in environmental programs. Among these we might include the U.S. Corps of Engineers, the U.S. Coast Guard, the attorney general's office, the department of health, the Parks and Wildlife Department, the General Land Office, the agricultural departments of the state, various river authorities, the Harris County district attorney and county attorney, and planning agencies such as the Houston Galveston Area Council and the Houston City Planning Division.

Administratively, this overlap and fragmentation is expensive, confusing, and inefficient. But more macabre examples are available—firemen watching houses burn just outside their jurisdiction and police from one town arresting the plainclothes detective of another. We need not go on.

One of the oldest forms of interlocal cooperation to control this confusion is an agreement between two or more adjacent units. One national survey of nearly 6,000 incorporated municipalities revealed that, of 2,248 responding, 61 percent had entered into formal or informal agreements for the provision of services to their citizens by other government units or private firms. As population increases, local government units—especially the smaller ones—will surely tend to turn over the administration of some of their programs (e.g., water supply) to other local units on a contractual basis.

Because politics within most metropolitan areas is not under any kind of central leadership and is, accordingly, carried on by a process of conflict and bargaining, an increasing number of cities and counties are creating **councils of governments** (sometimes known as COGs). These cooperative arrangements facilitate a regional approach to growth, transportation, environment, and other problems that affect a region as a whole.

What happens when cooperative management fails, when the other party will not join into a formal agreement? As discussed in "Talking Shop" on page 102, the enterprising administrator still has options.

Grantsmanship

Although presidents and Congresses have been struggling over the last decade to control the budget deficit, grants are still available for those who know where and how to apply. In fact, J. Robert Dumouchel's *The Government Assistance Almanac 1989–90: The Guide to All Federally Financed and Other Domestic Programs* (Detroit, Mich.: Omnigraphics/Foggy Bottom Publications, 1991) details all 1,117 domestic assistance programs and provides more than 300 pages of information on how to apply.

A distinction should be drawn, however, between formula grants and nonformula discretionary grants. It is the latter that interests the grantsperson. (A formula grant employs a specific decision rule indicating how much money any given jurisdiction

* Houston's eight environmental control agencies are EPA, Texas Water Control Board, Texas Air Control Board, Gulf Coast Waste Disposal Authority, Harris County Pollution Control Department, Air Pollution Division, the Water Pollution Control Division of the City Health Department, and the Waste Water Treatment Division of the City Public Works Department.

Talking Shop

What to Do When the Other Party Says No

When persuasion alone will not get another agency to join into a cooperative agreement, an administrator might try the following:

- *Seize the initiative.* Fill the void that frequently occurs in a joint effort with another organization. The manager who is energetic, skillful, and comfortable with power can assume the lead on a problem. By starting to act, you can make the other agency look bad if it hangs back.
- *Do more than your fair share.* Provide a good example. In a cooperative venture with another agency, you can often get it to move if you go more than halfway yourself. For example, when we were working with the Corrections Department to improve the prison health program, we took on the toughest parts of the problem and attacked them vigorously. This made it difficult for Corrections not to do its share (especially since status meetings were held monthly).
- *Make it easy for them to cooperate.* When you require cooperation from an organization you do not control, bend over backwards to make its work easier. For example, when we were soliciting voluntary hospitals to serve as contracted methadone clinics, we offered to help find space and to train and recruit staff—things not normally done by a contracting agency for a vendor.
- *Expend energy only on those you need.* There are lots of people vying for your time and decisions, many of whom can offer you little in return for your efforts. You should be nice to these people, but do not spend much time with them. Your time is better spent on those with something to offer. Additionally, do not waste your energy trying to gain cooperation from those that "ought" to help but will not, if you can do the job without them.
- *Get people to like you personally.* Remember, most outside groups are not obliged to cooperate with you. The extent to which they do cooperate will depend, at least in part, on whether they like you or not. Be courteous, open, honest, and fair. It is a little more difficult to oppose you or impute bad motives if the outsiders know you as a person. Thus, it is imperative that you get to know these people and meet with them face-to-face, both when you need them and when you do not.

SOURCE: Excerpted with permission from *Bromides for Public Managers,* Kennedy School of Government Case #N16-84-5860. Copyright © 1984 by the President and Fellows of Harvard College.

will receive. For example, money for housing might be distributed to qualified governments based on age and density of residential housing. A nonformula grant, or project grant, makes funds available on a competitive basis.)

The format of a proposal document depends on the requirements of the sponsoring agency to which the grantsperson applies. Most government agencies have application forms with very specific proposal guidelines. Nevertheless, all proposals contain these elements: narrative, evaluation, budget, abstract, and appendixes.

Those skilled in writing proposals carefully follow sponsor guidelines in order not to prejudice sponsor- and address-stated criteria by which the sponsor will judge the proposal. They use clear, precise language aimed at their specific audience. The proposal document should be neat and easy to handle, avoiding fancy covers or too slick an appearance. Finally, the grantsperson has the proposal read by colleagues for both strength of logic and clarity of expression.

Thus, in order to get federal funds for a new library, university presidents must struggle with lengthy applications. For example, Washington might want to know how the proposed project "may affect energy sources by introducing or deleting electromagnetic wave sources which may alter manmade or natural structures or the physiology, behavior patterns, and/or activities of 10 percent of a human, animal, or plant population." The questions go on and on, but you get the idea. (For a detailed discussion of techniques for obtaining grants from government sources, see David G. Bauer, *The "How To" Grants Manual,* [New York: Macmillan, 1984].)

Other Tools

Regulation. Yet another way in which one government can attempt to influence another government is through regulation. Arganoff (1989:136) notes three manifestations of IGR regulation:

1. Regulatory programs that totally or partially preempt state and local actions (e.g., the Occupational Safety and Health Act, the Clean Water Act).
2. Program requirements attached to grants (e.g., the stipulation to provide active treatment for all mentally handicapped persons receiving Medicaid payments).
3. Regulations that make a particular action a condition of receiving federal aid (e.g., highway funds tied to the lowering of the speed limit; grants for urban development tied to environmental-impact reports).

Lobbying. As a result of growth in federal programs, intergovernmental lobbying has increased. The purpose of this lobby is the same as that of any private lobby: to get more money with fewer strings attached and to call for certain policies that accomplish national purposes or redesign existing ones.

The intergovernmental lobby is made up of mayors, governors, superintendents of schools, local police chiefs, and others affected by federal policy or dependent on federal funds. Table 3-1 shows the five largest of these lobbies. Individual states and cities also lobby, and many have opened their own offices in Washington to press for more money for *their* particular jurisdiction.

Program Orchestration. At each level of government, state and local officials must understand and coordinate a wide range of functional programs, vertically structured

(text continues on p. 106)

TABLE 3-1
The Five Largest Lobbies for State and Local Governments

Organization	*Description in Brief*
National League of Cities (NLC) 1301 Pennsylvania Ave., N.W. Washington, D.C. 20004 (202) 626-3000	Formerly the American Municipal Association, founded in 1924 by and for reform-minded state municipal leagues. Membership was opened to individual cities in 1947, and the NLC now has more than eleven hundred direct member cities. All U.S. cities with populations greater than five hundred thousand are NLC direct members, as are 87 percent of all cities with more than a hundred thousand residents. The NLC advocates municipal interests before the Congress, the executive branch, and the federal agencies, and in state capitals across the nation where other matters of importance to cities are decided.  NATIONAL LEAGUE OF CITIES
United States Conference of Mayors (USCM) 1620 I Street, N.W. Washington, D.C. 20006 (202) 293-7330	An organization of city governments founded in 1933. It is a national forum through which this country's larger cities express their concerns and actively work to meet U.S. urban needs. By limiting membership and participation to the 750 cities with over thirty thousand population and by concentrating on questions of federal-city relations, the conference seeks to become a focus for urban political leadership.  UNITED STATES CONFERENCE OF MAYORS

TABLE 3-1
continued

Organization	*Description in Brief*
National Conference of State Legislatures (NCSL) 1050 17th Street Denver, CO 80265 (303) 623-7800	Only nationwide organization representing all state legislators (seventy-six hundred) and their staffs (approximately ten thousand). It seeks to advance the effectiveness, independence, and integrity of the state legislature as an equal coordinate branch of government. It also fosters interstate cooperation and represents states and their legislatures before the Congress and federal agencies. 
National Association of Counties (NACo) 440 1st Street, N.W. Washington, D.C. 20001 (202) 393-6226	The major organization of county government and management officials. Founded in 1935, NACo provides research, reference, and lobbying services for its members. 
National Governors Association (NGA) 444 North Capitol Street Washington, D.C. 20001 (202) 624-5300	Membership organization founded in 1908 that includes governors of the states, commonwealths, and territories. NGA seeks to improve state government through its committees and task forces, provide technical assistance, and faster information sharing among states. NGA endeavors to facilitate intergovernmental relations at the federal-state and state-local levels. 

SOURCE: Descriptions from Jay M. Shafritz, *Dictionary of American Government and Politics* (Chicago: Dorsey Press, 1988).

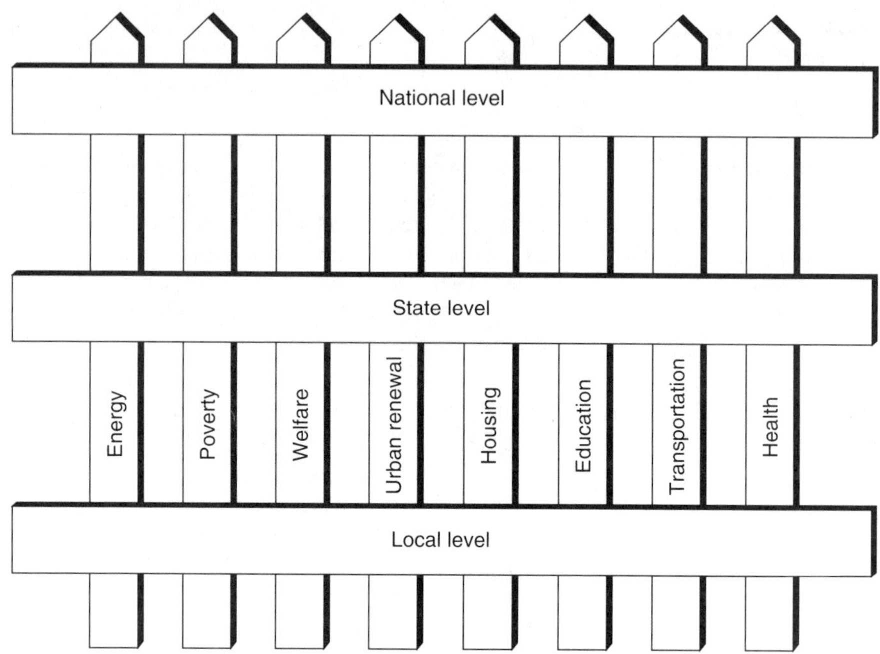

FIGURE 3-5
Picket Fence Federalism
In this model of IGR, specialists at the various levels of government exercise considerable power over intergovernmental programs. Their vertical bureaucracies represent the pickets in the fence. These specialists, however, are likely to be in conflict with the general purpose administrators (governors, city managers, county executives, etc.) who attempt to coordinate the vertical structures, or pickets, to ensure that they work in harmony to meet community needs. These general purpose officials are the crosspieces of the fence.

as shown in Figure 3-5. Just as a conductor must guide performers in tempo and dynamics, so must these officials ensure that the disparate programs work together to meet community needs. For example, a local government might manage multiple state and federal grants and tax incentives to help develop its downtown.

Relations Between Public and Private Organizations

Earlier we examined how government can hire or pay another government to supply a service; we referred to such institutional arrangements as IGR. But government may also establish relations with private firms in order to meet community needs.

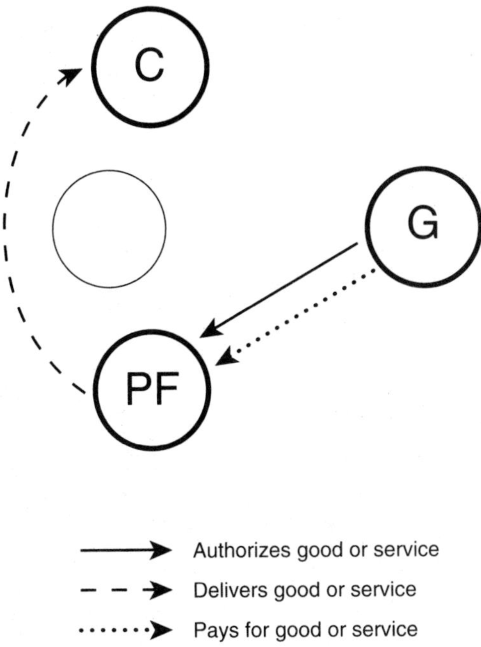

FIGURE 3-6
Contracting Arrangement

This section discusses four such arrangements: contracting, grant, franchise, and partnership.

Contracting

In the contracting arrangement, the private firm is the producer and the government is the arranger that pays the producer and delivers the good or service to the customer (see Figure 3-6).

Many cities are finding that they can increase productivity by hiring profit-making companies to perform such functions as refuse collection, police and fire protection, paramedic services, sewage disposal, accounting, computer operation, and street maintenance (see Figure 3-7). Milwaukee hired a private firm to pick up dead animals; Phoenix replaced the public defender's office with private lawyers; and Scottsdale, Arizona, saves $2 million a year by contracting for fire protection. One third of the refuse in Newark, New Jersey, is privately collected, saving the city $200,000 a year. Dallas closed its municipal late-night gasoline depots; now police cars and some fire vehicles use gas pumps at convenience stores after midnight, saving $200,000 annually. A private firm operates the Orange County, California, computer center at an annual saving of $1.6 million. Butte, Montana, contracted for the private operation of its municipal hospital; annual savings are $600,000. Newton, Massachusetts, saves $500,000 a year through a contract with a firm that supplies the city with paramedical and ambulance service (*New York Times,* March 29, 1984). Although about 99 percent

How Private Company Helps Welfare Clients Find and Keep Jobs

America Works of New York [is] a profit-making company that aspires to be the Federal Express of the welfare system. The efforts of the company and an affiliate in Connecticut over the past few years have helped more than a thousand people to get off welfare and into productive jobs—hardly sufficient to shrink the nation's welfare establishment but successful enough to show that it can be done.

America Works runs an employment service whose clients all come from the welfare rolls. Unlike job-training programs or trade schools that put the unemployed through months of classes and then abandon them during the job search, America Works is a matchmaker. It spends most of its time and resources finding entry-level job openings and candidates to fill them, and then helping monitor and support their clients in the workplace.

Says Lee Bowes, the company's chief operating officer: "We are an old boys' network for very poor people."

A New York state official calls the network's performance remarkable. It is placing more than 300 welfare recipients a year in private-sector jobs that pay an average of $14,000 a year plus benefits. After on-the-job tryouts, some 70 percent of those placed have said goodbye to welfare and become permanent. After one year, 90 percent of them are still working.

"Try before you buy" is a company maxim. Job candidates try working while they are weaned off welfare, a scary prospect for some. Employers, many of whom are initially skeptical of the program, have four months to evaluate candidates on the job without a commitment to hire them permanently. New York State pays America Works $5,000 for each placement, but only after the employee has stayed on the job for seven months. Taxpayers gain because the $5,000 stipend is less than half the $12,000 that the state spends to keep a family of three on welfare for a year.

SOURCE: Based on Ellen Graham, *Wall Street Journal*, May 18, 1990.

of local governments now contract out some functions, full-time city employees still perform over 75 percent of all work.

Contracting by local governments can carry certain risks. In Albany, New York, charges of mismanagement, corruption, and political favoritism in the awarding of contracts resulted in a sharp reduction of that city's use of private contractors. In southern San Francisco, when the city turned over many of its municipal chores to a private firm, residents complained about shoddy work, dozens of city employees were dismissed, staff heads resigned, and morale disintegrated. After nine months, the contract was terminated.

Finally, some charge that initial cost savings can be misleading. Jerry Wurf, past president of the American Federation of State, County, and Municipal Employees, says: "Generally, the savings and improved services turn out to be a very temporary

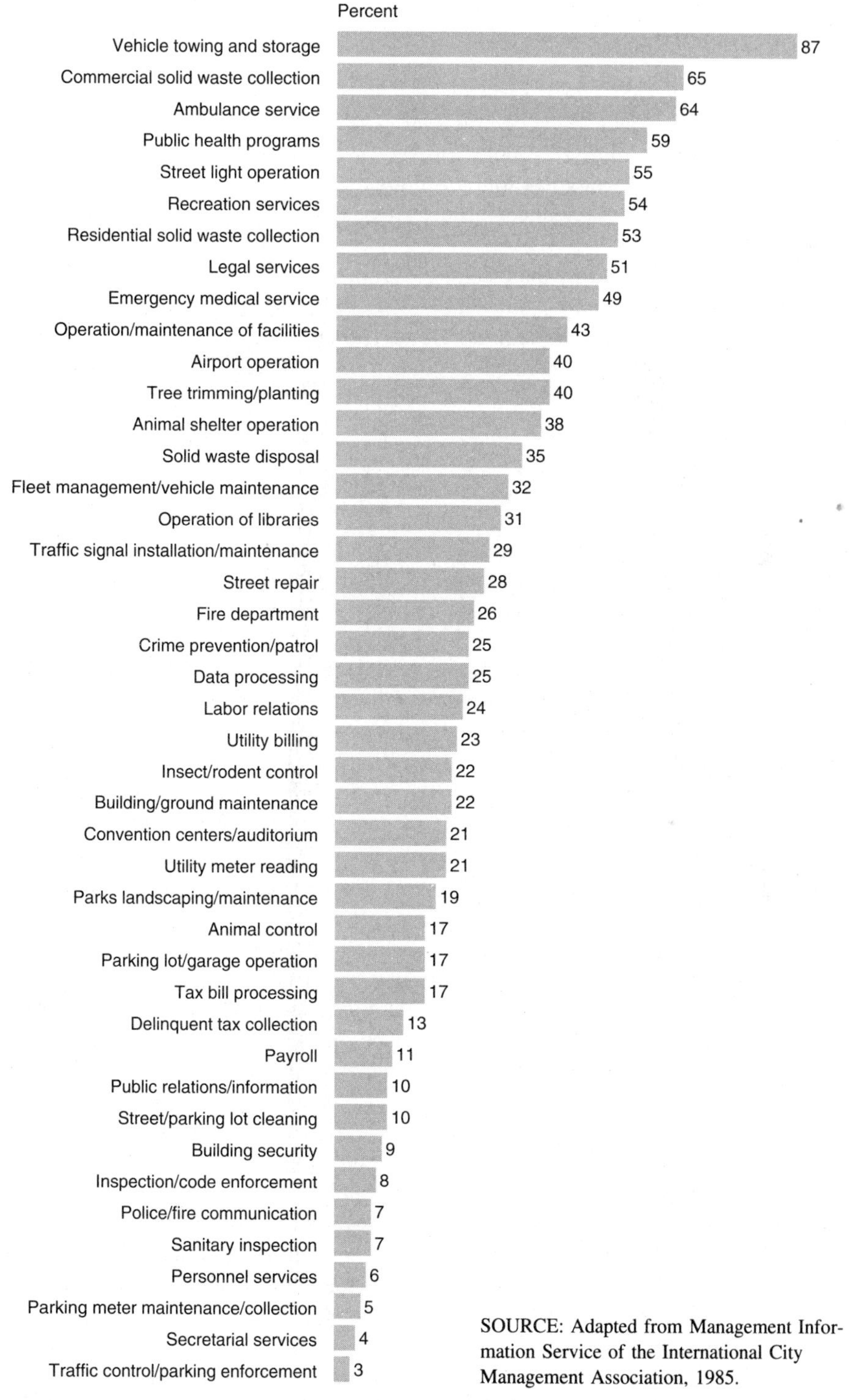

SOURCE: Adapted from Management Information Service of the International City Management Association, 1985.

FIGURE 3-7

Public Services, Private Contracts (Percentage of cities contracting for each service)

situation. . . . The contractor tries to make it look good the first year; then the cost overruns begin to grow and the contracts are renegotiated and somebody's brother-in-law ends up making money" (quoted in *New York Times,* November 23, 1979). By that time, of course, the city has sold its equipment and finds it too costly to get back into business. But union arguments aside, cities appear to be turning increasingly to private contractors.

There is no reason why the federal government cannot realize the sort of savings and benefits that states and localities are enjoying. For instance, by turning over debt collection to private firms, the Farmers Home Administration (FHA) might be able to recoup up to $7.5 billion in delinquent debts for the federal treasury that it has been unable to collect. Or by enlisting private companies for various support services, the Defense Department could pare its massive staff by some 110,000 at savings to the taxpayers of $2 billion. Or by privatizing its power marketing administrations, the Department of Energy could reduce the federal deficit by roughly $1.4 billion in fiscal 1989 and nearly $13 billion over four years.

What are the advantages and disadvantages of contracting? The first advantage is greater efficiency. Certain operations (e.g., trash collection) can be as much as three times more expensive when handled by government rather than private contractor. But this is not always the case.

In Chapter 2, we noted that bureaucracies tend at times to disturb legislative intent. Under the contract system, where performance specification can be written in fairly specific language, such distortion becomes less likely.

A third advantage of contracting is that it may reduce the opportunity for empire building within government. I do not wish to imply, however, that terminating a large-scale project can be done with the stroke of a pen; legislative pressure to keep lucrative projects going can be fierce.

A fourth advantage of contracting is that it would help free public administrators from routine details. As government begins to get out of the "doing," it becomes freer to concentrate its efforts on differentiating public needs from public wants; to sort out who can do what most effectively in society; to consider new approaches to long-standing problems; and to discover and disclose inconsistencies or overlapping among all its interacting parts. In short, government becomes better focused.

But contracting has its disadvantages. Perhaps the most obvious is that too-cozy relationships between business and government contracting personnel might develop. The possible result of such relationships is graft. And some observers, looking further ahead, see totalitarian tendencies resulting. Contracting officers and the contractors could simply begin to bypass both legislative branch and executive branch, enrich themselves, and build a syndicate state, responsive to hardly anyone.

Another fairly obvious disadvantage is that, in certain areas of public policy, contracting seems inappropriate. Should, for example, Westinghouse be responsible for the education of third graders? The implications of a corporation-shaped curriculum for young minds are sobering.

Contracting can also be inappropriate for economic reasons. The managers of one housing project in Brooklyn recently hired four consulting companies to study the idea of using methane from an adjacent sewage plant to heat the apartments. Using a $1.2 million grant from the Department of Energy, the managers were told such a

Talking Shop

Guidelines for Governments Considering Contracting

Over the past decade, contracting out government services grew considerably in popularity. The lessons of that decade provide public administrators with a more sophisticated view of how contracting can be used. For the best chance of success with contracting, these administrators suggest considering at least eight things:

1. Accurately estimate the cost of contracting out a service as compared with performing it in-house. For example, the cost of monitoring a contract is often undervalued because the complications are hard to foresee.
2. Thoroughly analyze the government's own service delivery. Such an analysis might reveal that the high cost is intrinsic to the activity and not simply a matter of who does it.
3. Give the contractor room to innovate. Rather than have interested contractors wade through several volumes of detailed specifications, ask some general questions: Who are you? What do you think ought to be built? What are the financial numbers supporting the project? What do you need from our agency?
4. Allow a government agency to bid as well. This will help ensure that a private firm has competition for a contract.
5. Provide for government employees who could lose their jobs as a result of contracting out. This will help mitigate a major obstacle to contracting: resistance by public employee unions.
6. Look beyond the costs to consider a contractor's experience, performance record, and internal controls. Morton-Thiokol Corporation, designer of the external tank that exploded and destroyed the space shuttle *Challenger,* was a lowest-cost bidder.
7. Follow through. Make sure that the private firm adheres to the contract, properly delivers the service, and handles customer complaints. Ultimately, it is government—not business—that is accountable for the quality and cost of public services, regardless of who delivers them.

SOURCE: Based on Jeffrey L. Katz, "Privatizing Without Tears," *Governing,* June 1991.

system could in fact be built—for as little as $600,000. When the study costs more than the project, we can safely say that the contract for the study was inappropriate.

This leads us to a final disadvantage: How does the government control the quality (as opposed to the cost) of public interest services? Lyle C. Fitch (1974:511) writes: "For goods and services which can be identified, weighed, and measured, or tested as to performance and use, tests concentrate on how well the product meets specifications." But, he continues:

> *Where the product is not easily measurable as to quality* or *quantity, the apparatus of control involves product inspections, investigations of complaints*

(as of faulty service), and monitoring of production processes. Internal controls are subject to various intramural pressures—for example, hostility of administrative agencies toward auditors. External controls are vulnerable to friendly relationships between representatives of contracting agencies and contractors' representatives, political pressure, and outright bribery. In this respect, contracting out has no clear advantages over government in-house account production; in fact, the difficulties of quality control in many cases may be greater with private contractors.

Still, the contract system does not necessarily diminish the government's ability to incorporate political objectives such as small business preference, fair employment practices, labor regulations, and safety standards into their contracts.

Government contracting is an important aspect of public administration that has thus far not been as systematically investigated as other areas. How, for example, do contracting officials balance bureaucratic and elective politics with the frequently repeated goal of acquisition of the best goods and services at the lowest possible price? How should the Defense Department go about improving internal auditing to keep better track of where dollars are spent and to determine the validity of prices charged to the government? (Is it necessary to pay $9,606 for a 12-cent wrench?) What are the trade-offs between letting contractors through **competitive bidding** and letting them on a **sole-source basis**—in which the desired firm is found "uniquely qualified" and all competition is waived? As government contracting continues to be a major instrument for attaining public goals in the 1990s, perhaps these and scores of other critical questions will begin to get the attention they deserve.

Grants

The grant arrangement involves the government subsidizing private firms' production, creating a profit opportunity by lowering their costs of production (see Figure 3-8). Two major examples of grants are wage subsidies to encourage the hiring of disadvantaged workers and capital subsidies to encourage plant locations in economically distressed locations.

A conspicuous example of the latter is enterprise zones. The theory behind them is appealing. By cutting business taxes and regulations in selected areas, government can encourage entrepreneurialism and provide jobs for inner-city residents. The reality is that some 30 states have created between 500 and 700 enterprise zones—with mixed results. The state of Connecticut, for example, claims that it has created or saved 10,000 jobs in enterprise zones; an independent study found that the zones had suffered a loss of 250 jobs. Studies of enterprise zones in Maryland, Illinois, and Louisiana have found little or no effect (Osborne, 1989).

Part of the problem with enterprise zones might be that they offer benefits of relatively little importance to a private firm. Business surveys consistently find that factors such as access to markets, availability of skilled labor, and quality of life carry much greater weight in corporate location decisions than do government-controlled costs or tax incentives. Although states cannot afford unilaterally to abandon their investment incentives for fear of putting themselves at a competitive disadvantage with

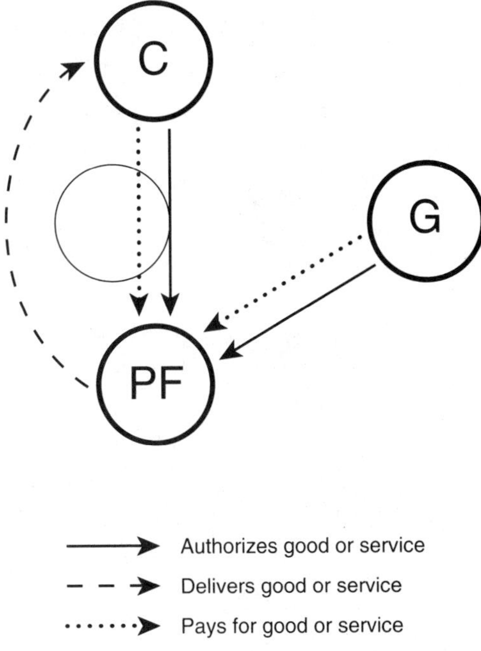

FIGURE 3-8
Grant Arrangement: Government Subsidizes the Producer

their neighbor, they probably should not count on those incentives as a major generator of new investment.

Franchises

In the franchise arrangement, the government assures customers access to a service or product but does not pay the producer for it (see Figure 3-9). Typically, the government designates some private firm as the supplier, usually with some price regulation. Consumers purchase the good or service, usually with some price regulation. For example, the franchise is used for providing toll roads (and automobile service and restaurants along them); common utilities such as electricity, gas, and water; intracity telephone service and cable television; and bus transportation.

These examples are exclusive franchises in the sense that the government does not allow for multiple utilities (each with its own power lines) within its jurisdiction. But nonexclusive or multiple franchises are also awarded, as in the case of taxis and wrecker trucks.

Partnerships

In contrast to contracting, franchise, grant, or other arrangements between the public sector and the private sector, a partnership signifies that both sectors share risks and responsibilities in order to meet critical community needs as defined by the partners.

The desire to replicate California's Silicon Valley, Massachusetts's Route 128, and other high-tech centers has resulted in numerous government policies intended to attract growing industries and nurture new firms. Hundreds, if not thousands, of communities and all 50 states are tying at least part of their economic future to high technology. But grants or subsidies to private firms will not by themselves create such centers. Pools of professional and technical employees and employers, top-rank university research, and sources of seed and venture capital are also critical for high-tech industry. These are not created quickly. (Cartoon reprinted with permission from Minneapolis Star and Tribune.*)*

Shared risk means that both partners could lose resources; it encourages the involvement of both public sector and private sector in ventures that neither could successfully attempt alone. Shared responsibilities include joint decision making by representatives of the different groups that work collaboratively on the project. The partnership (P) arrangement is shown schematically in Figure 3-10.

Today, there is growing interest in public-private collaboration on economic development projects, particularly in larger cities where there are limits to independent initiatives in responding to complex urban economic development programs. The following are examples of collaborative economic partnerships:

- Inner Harbor, a large commercial redevelopment project in Baltimore, includes a world trade center, a new office, new residential units, marina, aquarium, theater, college campus, and parkland, all financed through both private investment and public investment.

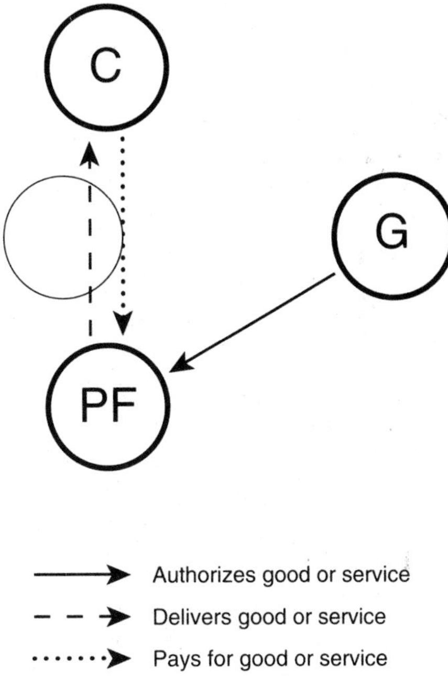

FIGURE 3-9
Exclusive Franchise: Government Authorizes Private Firm to Deliver Service

- Dallas's Reunion Development includes hotel, sports center, terminal building, and recreation area in downtown Dallas. It created over 800 new jobs and was financed through publicly and privately generated funds.
- Wacker Siltronix's silicon-wafer manufacturing plant, when deciding to settle in Portland, Oregon, negotiated an unusual arrangement with the city to hire disadvantaged workers trained under a city-sponsored program.

If collaborative ventures are to be successful, both sectors need new skills and new levels of flexibility and adaptability. Local administrators need to provide the expertise necessary for evaluating potential joint projects and for negotiating contractual arrangements with private sector participants. Business participants must develop the necessary skills for negotiating with local governments, recognizing that they cannot dictate the terms of cooperation.

The private sector can work with local governments to develop the most effective means of providing essential services. Besides contracting with the private sector to reduce costs, communities have the following two additional options for coping with public service problems.

- *Increase revenues.* In addition to raising taxes, businesses can help government develop ways to improve property-tax administration, cut back special

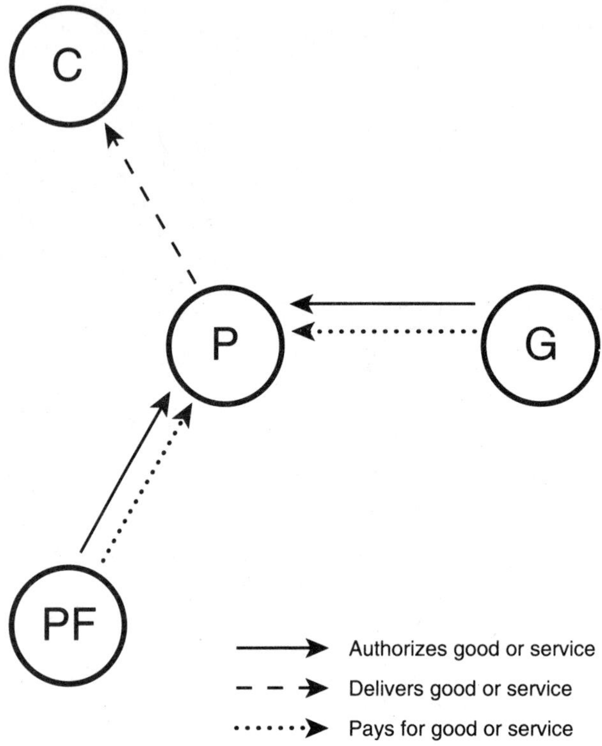

FIGURE 3-10
Partnership Arrangement

tax preferences, broaden the tax base, increase returns on municipal funds, and cooperate to secure funds from state and federal sources.

- *Improve productivity.* Private sector expertise can help raise public sector productivity. Pittsburgh's Committee for Progress in Allegheny County might be cited as a pioneering model for public-private efforts to streamline local government.

Public sector–private sector partnerships at the local level are not a panacea. Thus, the federal government, even in its somewhat reduced capacity, will continue to have an important role in urban development. Furthermore, the federal government will also need to develop its own productive partnership with the private sector.

A case in point is Sematech. In response to losing a significant share of the semiconductor market to Japanese companies in the 1980s, several U.S. semiconductor and computer manufacturers formed Sematech in 1987 to provide the U.S. semiconductor industry with the capability for world manufacturing leadership. Believing that participation in a government-industry consortium furthering semiconductor manufacturing technology was in the nation's economic and security interests, the federal gov-

North Carolina's Research Triangle Park was developed over a period of 25 years. It now has about 50 tenants including (clockwise from top left) International Business Machines Corporation, Becton Dickinson Research Center, MCNC's Center for Microelectronics (Photo by J. Magnum, NSI), *Burroughs Wellcome Co., and Glaxo's Sir Paul Girolami Research Center. In trying to foster economic growth through high technology, states and communities must focus as North Carolina did on what they can control. Although grants or subsidies to private firms cannot create entrepreneurs, public-private partnerships can encourage local entrepreneurs to remain in the area rather than to seek better investment opportunities elsewhere. Partnerships can also bring entrepreneurs together through incubator facilities and integrate universities into civic and economic life. But a partnership must recognize its limited power to speed up the high-tech development process.*

ernment contributed $100 million for Sematech's use in each of the past three fiscal years, matching funds provided by Sematech's 14 member companies.

Beyond Interorganizational Relations: The Concept of Privatization

The word *privatize* did not appear in a dictionary until 1983. Broadly speaking, it symbolizes a new way of thinking about the role of government in addressing a society's needs. E. S. Savas (1987), one of the nation's leading experts on privatization, defines it as the act of reducing the role of government, or increasing the role of the private sector, in an activity or in the ownership of assets.

For a more precise, technical definition of privatization, consider the continuum below:

To privatize means to move leftward from one arrangement to another lower on the continuum.

In this section, we will be discussing the sixth and seventh types of arrangement, voucher and voluntary. What distinguishes this pair from the other types that we have been discussing in this chapter is that they involve little direct relationships between organizations.

Voucher

In the grant system, the government subsidizes the producer and restricts the customer's choice to the subsidized private firm, which provides the medical care, housing, mass transit, or some other good or service. In the voucher system, the government subsidizes customers and permits them to exercise relatively free choice in the marketplace (see Figure 3-11). Rather than subsidize low-cost housing with grants, the government can simply give the customers vouchers to apply toward the rent at a dwelling of their choice. Thus part of the payment comes from government and part from the client.

In 1990, Milwaukee began a voucher system that allowed poor parents to send their children to private schools at public expense. In his budget proposals for 1992, President Bush called for the federal government to help school systems like Milwaukee's. Advocates of the voucher approach to education argue that affluent Americans have always had the opportunity to choose their children's schools—either by sending them to private schools or by moving to neighborhoods with well-regarded

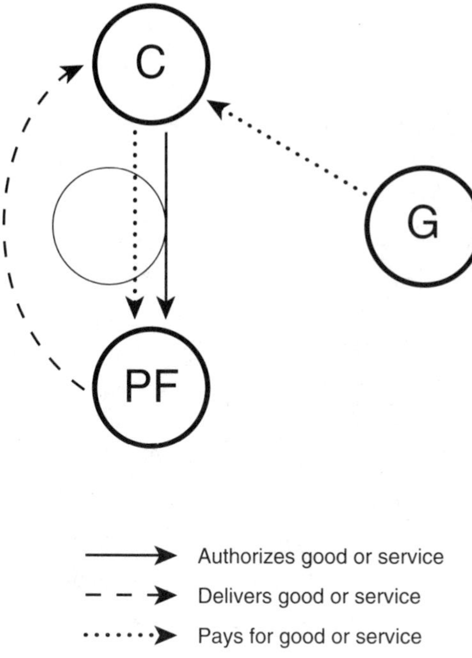

FIGURE 3-11
Voucher Arrangement

systems. Vouchers, they contend, give lower-income families similar options and also improve all schools by forcing them to compete for students with other schools, both public and private.

Voluntary Service

Voluntary associations perform a host of human services that governments are either unwilling or unable to perform. Today a growing number of community groups and block associations work to improve the quality of life in their neighborhoods, plugging gaps in the service of city and county bureaucracy. For example:

- Community leaders in Mountain View, a predominantly low-income neighborhood in Anchorage, Alaska, have organized volunteers to spot and report zoning violations, remove abandoned vehicles and trash piles, and refurbish and maintain neighborhood recreation centers and parks. They were able to obtain free space for a police substation in the neighborhood from a closed branch bank. The Mountain View neighborhood maintains flower beds and parking lots (Fink, 1989).
- The Knox-Gates section of the Northwest Bronx, three large city blocks of five- and six-story apartments, is crowded with working-class families, the

Members of the Morris Avenue Block Association on patrol in the Bronx. (The New York Times/*Keith Meyers*)

poor, and the elderly. The residents are Hispanic, black, Irish, Jewish, Albanian, Korean, and Indian. Threatened by violence and readily available drugs, the Knox-Gates Neighborhood Association has fought to preserve the neighborhood's stability. It tries to prevent deterioration of buildings; it sponsors potluck suppers in the park for a sense of community; it paints garbage cans. The association is also the guiding force behind the new center for the area's children, many of whom are on their own for hours each day (Teltsch, 1989).

- Morris Avenue in the Bronx was the center of an outdoor drug market where customers lined up to make their purchase. Mothers kept young children indoors for fear of violence. Then residents formed the Morris Avenue Block Association and began organizing volunteer patrols to take back their block with the power of the bullhorn. Seven days a week, 25 residents in blue jackets bearing their block association's name take turns walking the street and watching for strangers or suspicious behavior. If they see a drug purchase, they report it on walkie-talkies and call attention to the deal, loudly describing the dealer over a bullhorn. The commotion usually drives off the dealers quickly (Teltsch, 1989).

Voluntary efforts are not limited to trying to lighten the burden of urban problems—drugs, homelessness, dirt, graffiti, unemployment, and loneliness among young and old. Voluntary efforts can and have handled major national undertakings such as the Olympic Games in Los Angeles (Chapter 1).

New Skill Requirements

Because it has changed the character of public administration, privatization has, to a degree, altered the skills that public administrators need. For example, the increasing use of contracting raises the need for well-trained professionals to prepare and monitor contracts. This is a lot harder than it sounds. Problems with private firms occur because of ambiguous, ill-defined, and poorly written contracts that did not include important details and specifications.

A recent report by the National Academy of Public Administration (1989) put the challenge this way:

> *The skills needed by public program managers and their contracting staff today, such as negotiating and using creative incentives to achieve results from parties not under their direct control, are considerably different from, and in some cases contrary to, those formerly deemed crucial by classical public administration theorists. Due to the difficulties involved with inducing private entities to act in a manner consistent with public objectives, current program managers need assistance in adjusting to their new roles as arrangers and administrators instead of doers. Equally important is that future public managers learn different techniques and approaches to accomplish the government's business effectively.*
>
> *Unfortunately, public managers have generally not been receiving such guidance from the academic community. Schools of public administration and policy have generally failed to keep pace with the changes that have altered the role of the program manager. Graduates from these institutions, therefore, do not have a realistic notion of the tasks before them and the mode in which they will operate, nor do they possess the proper knowledge and skills to proceed competently with their work. As Charles Levine wrote recently, "The situation facing federal managers is nearly impossible. . . . They are now operating in uncharted territory with little support from the academic community."*

Concepts for Review

- block grant
- categorical grant
- competitive bidding
- contracting
- cooperative federalism
- council of governments
- creative federalism
- Dillon's Rule

- dual federalism
- federalism
- franchise
- grant
- grants-in-aid
- grantsmanship
- intergovernmental lobby
- intergovernmental relations
- interstate compacts
- layer cake model
- mandates
- marble cake model
- new federalism
- partnership
- picket-fence federalism
- privatization
- revenue sharing
- sole-source basis
- standard metropolitan statistical area
- voluntary association
- voucher

Nailing Down the Main Points

1. *Intergovernmental relations* is a more satisfactory term than federalism to describe the complete governmental structure in the United States. Federalism places too much emphasis on separation of federal, state, and local government and not enough on the intermediate levels of government.

2. The relationship of states to the federal government is the cardinal question of our constitutional system. As Wilson pointed out, every successive stage in the political development of the United States gives IGR a new aspect. The period prior to 1932 may be termed the era of dual federalism. American government had a simple divide: Washington dealt with defense and foreign policy, and the states did everything else, from roads to schools. State spending was twice as big as federal spending. Then Franklin Roosevelt changed the rules. By the 1960s, the federal government was heavily involved in all domestic policies, and its spending had well surpassed that of the states.

3. Partly in reaction to the vast array of categorical grant programs passed under Lyndon Johnson's Great Society, every president since has tried to group programs more rationally—through so-called block grants and other means—and to transfer more operational authority to states and cities. The reasons are clear: Move federal funds closer to the people, cut overhead costs, give states greater spending flexibility, and encourage innovation. President Nixon, who called the idea the new federalism, consolidated related programs in areas like job training and community development. He also initiated general revenue sharing (i.e., money the states could use for any purpose).

4. Former president Ronald Reagan had even more ambitious plans for devolving power, but they were only partially realized. Governors quickly saw that Reagan was, in effect, offering them more control but less money. Congress, meanwhile, was reluctant to let states and cities get credit for spending the money that Congress raises.

5. Like Ronald Reagan, George Bush has also spoken about returning more power to the states but has not really defined the division of labor between the states

and Washington. The critical questions remain. Should Washington pick up a far larger share of the cost of expensive national problems like Medicaid and welfare? Should the states and cities, in exchange, take more responsibility for services better managed locally, like transportation, job training, and education?

6. For the public administrator on the firing line, IGR places a premium on bargaining skills, cooperative management, grantsmanship, lobbying, and program orchestration.

7. While relationships between jurisdictions are important, public administrators must also be concerned with relations with private organizations. Indeed, as the nature of those relations shift from those at the left side of the following continuum to those at the right side, we say that they are being privatized.

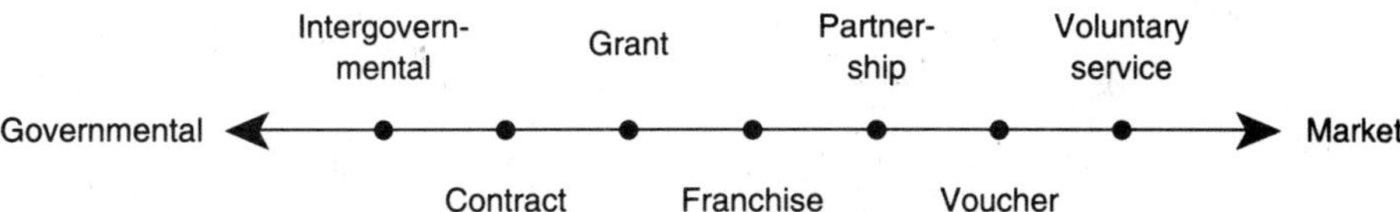

8. Classical public administration assumed that the managers had direct control over operations, but this situation does not pertain under privatization. Perhaps even more than IGR, privatization alters the skills that public managers need.

Problems

1. Alvin Toffler (1980:414) writes:

   A political system must not only be able to make and enforce decisions, it must operate on the right scale, it must be able to integrate disparate policies, it must be able to make decisions at the right speed, and it must both reflect and respond to the diversity of society. If it fails on any of these points it courts disaster. Our problems are no longer a matter of "left-wing" or "right-wing," "strong leadership" or "weak." The decision system itself has become a menace.

   The truly astonishing fact today is that our governments continue to function at all. No corporation president would try to run a large company with a table of organization first sketched by the quill pen of some eighteenth-century ancestor whose sole managerial experience consisted of running a farm. No sane pilot would attempt to fly a supersonic jet with the antique navigation and control instruments available to Blériot or Lindbergh. Yet this is approximately what we are trying to do politically.

   Do you think Toffler overstates the problem? What do you think the optimum size of a city would be? What do you think are the most important factors determining the quality of urban life? (Hint: The Advisory Committee on Intergovernmental Relations suggests four criteria that should provide the basic guidelines in reassigning functions to governmental units: economic efficiency, equality, political accountability, and administrative effectiveness.)

2. Write an essay on whether revenue sharing should be continued.
3. Actually, the areas of federal control are relatively few, compared to those of states and their subdivisions. List those areas in which you think federal policy control is essential. (For example, some would argue that state and local radio stations could not operate effectively unless they were coordinated with commercial stations.)
4. Some of the major social and economic innovations in the United States have begun with small-scale experiments on the state level. Wyoming, for example, permitted women's suffrage 50 years before the 19th Amendment. Can you think of others? What current state experiments might one day be taken up by the federal government?
5. How do you think business executives view centralizing power in Washington rather than decentralizing it via the 50 states?
6. Which government functions should probably never be contracted? Why?

CASE 3.1

★★★★★★★★★★★★★★★★★★★★★★★★★★★★★★★★★★★

Negotiating Nuclear Waste Disposal

How should spent fuel and high-level wastes from commercial nuclear power plants be disposed of? That question, according to one study, has bred more federal-state conflict than any other issue since the battle over desegregation in the South. Another analysis calls the radioactive-waste problem the greatest test of American federalism in this country.

The federal government has accepted responsibility for the long-term management of spent fuel, but potential host states prevented the government from successfully developing disposal sites until Congress passed the Nuclear Waste Policy Act (NWPA) of 1982. The act established immediate development of a permanent disposal of high-level waste in a geological repository (e.g., salt mines) and directed the Department of Energy (DOE) to study the need for engineered temporary storage facilities, termed monitored retrievable storage (MRS), as a fallback position, should the geological repository be delayed.

The act also authorized the DOE to make grants equivalent to the taxes that would be paid on a repository if it was a private facility. Thus, a repository could be a significant revenue source for local governments. Another important feature of the act was that it directed the DOE to "consult and cooperate with" states in which it was considering sites for a facility. This requirement brings states into the siting process at an early stage and provides a legal means to incorporate state and local interests in the decision process. Finally, and most importantly, the act authorized a potential host state to halt development of a site recommended by the president by formally notifying Congress of its disapproval. Congress, however, can override state action by a majority vote in both houses.

Essentially, the NWPA changes the nature of the relationship between local interests and national interests from adjudication (which yields a winner and a loser) to negotiation (which yields all winners); thus, the relationship moves from the courtroom to the bargaining table. The NWPA attempts not to overpower but to accommodate local interests. Besides empowering the DOE to negotiate ("consult and cooperate") with state and local interests and to compensate local interests (through tax equivalency and impact resistance), the NWPA provides for the information requirements of local government through grants for study and monitoring. Paradoxically, granting legal authority to local interests actually weakens local power to obstruct a project, because local opposition is less able to elicit moral outrage by charging that "the feds" are trampling on community interests.

In April 1985, the DOE announced its intention to seek authorization of an MRS facility to receive fuel from reactors in the eastern half of the United States. The new facility would be built either near Hartsville, Tennessee, or at the former Clinch River breeder reactor site within the Oak Ridge city limits. (Oak Ridge has an interesting history. The federal government built the city in the 1940s to house the workers who developed the uranium-235 and plutonium-239 for the atomic bomb. In 1955, the Atomic Energy Commission turned the city over to its residents.)

To study the MRS proposal, the Oak Ridge city council established the Clinch River MRS Task Force. Choosing to ignore the question of whether the facility was needed, the task force focused on the question of how it would affect the local community. The task force concluded that, as proposed, the MRS facility was detrimental to local interests and unacceptable, but the task force also indicated how the DOE might remove these negative effects without significantly changing the facility's physical characteristics. More specifically, the task force wanted *guarantees* of safe operation. It also requested that the facility be taxed as if it were privately owned, that the DOE do business with local private firms, and that it clean up various existing environmental problems. Finally, the task force recommended that the MRS construction be linked to progress with geological disposal; otherwise, the public might think the facility was a substitute for geological disposal.*

Meanwhile, officials in the five counties surrounding the Hartsville site chartered an organization to study the proposal. The Research, Evaluation, Analysis, and Liaison Group (REAL Group) firmly opposed the site. A telephone survey commissioned by the group showed 90 percent of area residents opposed the project.

In Nashville, Tennessee's legislative and executive branches separately stud-

* Concerned that an MRS facility might become a substitute for a permanent repository, the Congress, in the Nuclear Waste Policy Amendments Act of 1987, linked development of an MRS facility to progress in a permanent repository development. For example, the DOE may not build an MRS facility until a license has been issued for construction of the repository. (The amendments also created the independent position of nuclear waste negotiator to work out the terms and conditions under which a state or an Indian tribe would agree to host the repository or an MRS facility.)

ied the proposal. The joint legislative committee was as opposed to the project as was the REAL Group. The governor's cabinet council opposed the project, arguing that it (1) was not needed, (2) would raise electric rates, and (3) might harm tourism and business expansion. Compensation was considered but ruled out. As the governor explained, talk of compensation is inconsistent with opposition.

Case Questions

1. This chapter argued that IGR presents special management problems. What evidence of that did you find in this case?
2. Why do you think that the state and the Hartsville locality ignored the opportunity to seek a mutually acceptable solution?
3. What implications does this case have for other problems involving a facility with negative local costs but widely dispersed benefits?
4. What negotiating strategies would you recommend to the DOE?

Case References

U.S. General Accounting Office, *Nuclear Waste: Operation of Monitored Retrievable Storage Facility* (Washington, D.C.: U.S. General Printing Office, September 1991); Richard C. Kearney and Robert B. Garvey, "American Federalism and the Management of Radioactive Wastes," *Public Administration Review,*, January–February 1982, pp. 12–24; Stephen A. Graham, "The Nuclear Waste Policy Act of 1982: A Case Study in American Federalism," *State Government,* Spring 1984, pp. 7–12; E. Brent Sigmon, "Achieving a Negotiated Compensation Agreement in Nuclear Waste Disposal Siting: The MRS Case," *Journal of Policy Analysis and Management,* 6:2 (1986), pp. 170–79; and Gary L. Downey, "Federalism and Nuclear Waste Disposal: The Struggle Over Shared Decision Making," *Journal of Policy Analysis and Management,* 5:1 (1985), pp. 73–99.

CASE 3.2

★★★★★★★★★★★★★★★★★★★★★★★★★★★★★★★★★★★

The Ben Franklin Partnership

Background: The Pennsylvania Economy

When Richard Thornburgh became governor in 1979, Pennsylvania's unemployment rate was already the ninth highest in the nation. Then the economy fell off a cliff. Between 1979 and 1985, 21.5 percent of all manufacturing jobs in Pennsylvania disappeared. The state's 40 largest corporations were literally cut in half, as their total employment fell from 1.2 million in 1979 to 600,000 in 1986. Unemployment peaked at 14.9 percent. When *Inc.* magazine ranked American cities by their growth in jobs and business start-ups between 1981 and 1985, Pennsylvania had *six* cities in the bottom 20.

The economic crisis created tremendous political pressure on Thornburgh. But the governor wanted nothing to do with expensive subsidies or social welfare programs. Instead, he decided to commission an in-depth study of the state's economy. Called *Choices for Pennsylvanians,* it took almost three years to complete and solicited input from public meetings throughout the state. It then served as the "polar star," in Thornburgh's words, around which all of his efforts revolved.

Forging an Economic Development Program

Among Pennsylvania's greatest strengths, the *Choices* report pointed out, were its universities and its reservoir of technological expertise—its intellectual infrastructure. Pennsylvania graduated more engineers than all but two other states. It had four universities among the nation's top 50 graduate research institutions, with expertise in robotics, computer-assisted design and manufacturing, electronics, computer science, and advanced materials. It ranked fifth among the states on three related measures: the number of scientists and engineers in the state, the number of workers employed in advanced technology industry, and the amount spent on research and development. Yet Pennsylvania had failed to capitalize on these intellectual resources. The kind of interaction between business and academic organizations that had kicked off explosive growth in Massachusetts and the Silicon Valley was absent. Thornburgh and Walt Plosila, a young midwesterner who ran the governor's Office of Policy and Planning, made the creation of that environment their primary goal.

Unlike many state technology programs, which pour money into new buildings and institutes, the Ben Franklin Partnership is essentially a matching grant program. The heart of the program offers "challenge grants" to university-based projects—primarily applied research projects—funded by businesses. . . . The idea is to provide a carrot to get industry and academia interested in working together on research that might result in a marketable (or improved) product or process.

Although the majority of the research projects involve young, entrepreneurial companies, many also fund efforts to help older firms adopt new technologies in order to remain competitive. When the Partnership was created, a debate raged among advocates of industrial policy over the wisdom of targeting sunrise versus sunset industries. Wisely, Plosila and Thornburgh chose to target both. To underscore their commitment, they adopted the term *advanced technology* rather than *high technology.* "What we see in advanced technology is not simply another Silicon Valley," said Thornburgh. "We see new technology clusters emerging; but of equal importance, we see the spinning in of new technology into our traditional industries."

In addition to research, the Partnership also awards challenge grants for education and training programs and for entrepreneurial development activities, again requiring a private-sector match. Examples of the former include programs to help public school teachers achieve computer literacy; a center to train industry personnel in computer-assisted design; and internships in industry for vocational education instructors. Examples of the latter include feasibility studies for small-business incubators; technical assistance for small businesses; and efforts to start "enterprise forums," in which local venture capitalists meet regularly with entrepreneurs who need risk capital.

The program is operated through four Advanced Technology Centers (ATCs), each in a different region of the state. Each center is affiliated with a major university or universities, but every higher education institution in the region is eligible for grants. Each center focuses on two to four technology areas, depending upon the economic strengths of local universities and the region. They include robotics; advanced materials; computer-aided design and computer-aided manufacturing (CAD/CAM); microelectronics; biotechnology; biomedical technologies;

sensor technologies; manufacturing in space; food and plant production and processing; and coal and mineral production and processing. A board made up of regional leaders from academia, business, government, and economic development organizations oversees a staff of 10 to 20 at each center.

Rather than imposing a model on each region, the state allowed each board to craft its own design. Predictably, several of the universities assumed that they could use the money as they would any other research dollars: to finance basic research of interest to their faculty. During the first year, the central Ben Franklin board rejected both Penn State's and the Philadelphia center's proposals and sent them back to the drawing board—whereupon a state legislator from the Penn State area tried to have Plosila fired. To force the centers to focus on projects of value to business, the board decided to make them compete with one another for funding, based on the commercial potential of their projects.

The process works like this. Every spring, each center submits a package of applications for challenge grants. The state board rates each project according to criteria such as potential commercial application; number of jobs created; size of the company (there is a bias toward small firms, on the theory that large corporations do not need as much state help); and quantity and quality of the private-sector match. It also ranks each center according to how well its past projects have done on measures such as job creation, corporate match, and attraction of venture capital. Centers with higher average ratings get more money. They can then divide their allocation up as they wish—providing smaller grants for some projects than originally proposed, for instance, to make the money go further.

In its first four years the Partnership funded close to 1,500 projects, which involved 128 of the state's 135 higher education institutions and 2,500 private firms. With its $77 million in challenge grants, the state claimed to have leveraged $281 million in other investments, the majority of them from private industry.

The Pennsylvania Economic Development Model

The Ben Franklin Partnership is probably the most comprehensive economic development institution in the country. If an entrepreneur needs inexpensive start-up space, Pennsylvania has 30 incubators—more than any other state. If he or she needs technical assistance, each center offers several options. If research is the problem, challenge and seed grants are available, or the local Ben Franklin staff can help the firm apply for a federal grant. If capital is the problem, both seed and traditional venture capital funds are available. If the company needs loans rather than equity, the staff can refer it to local bankers who specialize in its area, or to the right state or regional loan fund. If an older company needs new technology to survive, teams of experts are available to help. "One thing leads to another," says Walt Plosila. "We're trying to build the kind of informal network you see in places like Route 128 and the Silicon Valley."

Equally important, these services are available *locally.* A business person does not have to travel to Harrisburg to deal with any of them. In fact, a business person is hardly aware that he is dealing with a state program. Most of the services—the research, the technical assistance, the analyses of production processes, the venture capital—are *not* provided by state programs. The state simply offers a carrot, a matching grant, to encourage business people to use academic resources, or to create seed funds, or to finance incubators, or to provide technical assistance.

Once those resources are in place, the centers operate sophisticated referral services. The object, as it should be, is to change private-sector behavior in ways that stimulate innovation and productivity.

Case Questions

1. Assess the strengths and weaknesses of this interorganizational approach to economic development.
2. How attractive do you think this approach is politically?
3. Do you think the partnership is aptly named?

Case Reference

Excerpted from David Osborne, *Laboratories of Democracy* (Boston: Harvard Business School, 1990), pp. 45–46, 48–50, and 56–57.

★ ★

CHAPTER 4

Administrative Responsibility and Ethics

Introduction

In Chapter 3, we saw how interorganizational relations complicates even further the already complicated core function of political management. In that chapter, you might recall, our concerns were fairly concrete—block grants, counties, contracts, and so forth. In this chapter, we want to consider several matters more abstract in nature but also affecting political management. One such matter is the value system of the society in which the administrator works.

By values we simply mean things or relationships that people would like to have or to enjoy. Obviously, we cannot—and fortunately we need not—consider the entire complex of values held by American society. We need concern ourselves only with those values that are relevant to administration. What might these be? Most Americans would agree, I think, that government should be responsive, flexible, fair, accountable, honest, and competent. In this chapter, we will use the word *responsibility* as a collective term for values like these, for qualities people would like to see in their government.

Our discussion is in three closely related parts. First, we attempt to clarify how these values relate to public administration and what the ideal of responsibility stands for in the literature of public administration. To speak of an ideal implies an existence not in the actual world but in the mind; it suggests a perfection exceeding what is possible in reality. So it is with the ideal of **administrative responsibility.** It is something to strive toward.

But certain human frailties can make that journey a difficult one. This chapter focuses squarely on three of the most important frailties: greed, or an intense or excessive desire for wealth or possessions; arrogance, or a disposition to claim for oneself more consideration or importance than is warranted or justly due; and cowardice, or lack of courage, especially moral courage.

James Madison and the Founding Fathers understood this problem well. Given human nature, administrative responsibility simply cannot be assumed. Writing in Federalist Paper No. 51, Madison justified the need to protect and foster it:

> *If men were angels, no government would be necessary. If angels were to govern men neither external nor internal controls on government would be necessary. In framing a government which is to be administered by men over men, the greatest difficulty lies in this: you must first enable the government to control the governed; and in the next place to oblige it to control itself. A dependence on the people is, no doubt, the primary control on the government; but experience has taught mankind the necessity of auxiliary precautions.*

Going on the assumption that angels still do not govern, we conclude this chapter by giving some thought to external and internal controls designed to help ensure administrative responsibility. As the chapter title suggests, particular emphasis will be placed on individual ethics. Schematically, the chapter looks something like Figure 4-1.

The Ideal of Administrative Responsibility

While neither exhaustive nor definitive, the following subsections do cover most of the values implied when the term *administrative responsibility* is used.

Responsiveness

The term *responsiveness* refers to the prompt acquiescence by an organization to the popular demands for policy change. Responsiveness can also mean that government does more than merely react to popular demands. In some cases, it can mean that government takes initiatives in the proposal of solutions for problems and even in the definition of problems.

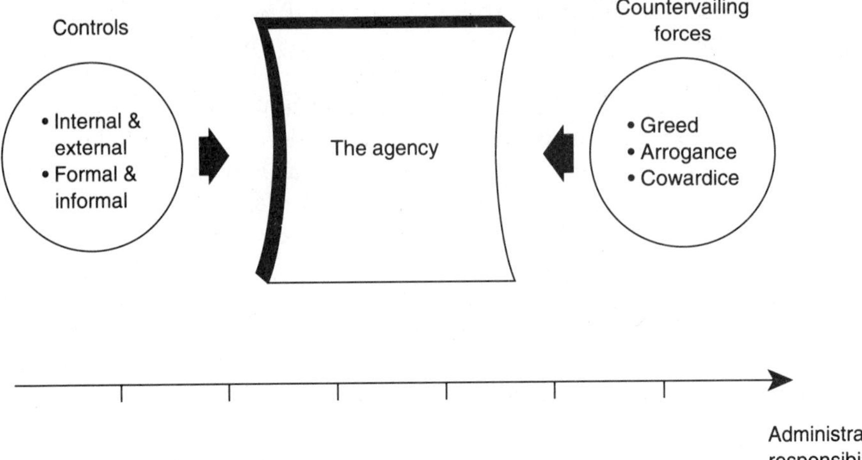

FIGURE 4-1
The Dynamics of Administrative Responsibility: A Chapter Overview

In an effort to determine what people regard as the most significant criticism of the federal bureaucracy, David A. Brown and his students at George Washington University polled 1,470 persons to get their views. The most frequently heard criticism was that bureaucracy is "slow, ponderous; incapable of taking immediate action" (*Public Administration Times,* January 1981).

In fact, organizations might even be classified according to their level of responsiveness to their clients or customers. Philip Kotler and Alan R. Andreason (1991) find four types. First is the unresponsive organization that (1) does nothing to measure the needs, perceptions, preferences, or satisfaction of its constituent publics and (2) even makes it difficult for them to make inquiries, complaints, or suggestions. The prevailing attitude seems to be, "We know what is best." Organizations facing a high and continuous demand for customer needs (such as hospitals) often fall into this category.

Second is the casually responsive organization that *does* show an interest in learning about constituent needs and complaints. Thus, when a college begins to experience a decline in student applications, it begins to listen more to students and to encourage faculty-student committees.

Third is the highly responsive organization that uses systematic information collection procedures (e.g., formal opinion surveys and consumer panels); creates formal systems to facilitate complaints and suggestions (e.g., comment cards); and where called for, takes steps to adjust services and procedures. Large firms such as Sears, Procter & Gamble, General Mills, and General Electric probably have gone the farthest in adopting these characteristics. Sears, for example, uses information from its surveys to chart an attitude index to see if there are *developing* problems requiring attention. Universities, municipalities, and hospitals, however, tend to be rather casual about these matters.

Fourth is the fully responsive organization that overcomes the "us and them" attitude of most organizations by accepting its publics as voting members. Once the principles of a fully responsive organization are fulfilled, then its members will be ready to lend their support and energy. Consider two small examples:

- For years, the Buffalo Philharmonic tried to broaden its audience. It could change its program only so much—after all, Mozart is Mozart. Customers must change *their* attitudes. Research revealed that many consumers thought they might attend a concert if the occasion was not too formal. The orchestra itself was seen as distant, formal, and forbidding. In light of these findings, the Philharmonic began to humanize itself and the concert-going experience. Members began playing shirtsleeve chamber music at local outdoor events and schools. The orchestra itself even performed at halftime at a Buffalo Bills football game. A new conductor, Michael Tilson Thomas, began appearing on local television. Attendance figures soon began to reflect this new customer-centered orientation.
- Also for years, the National Cancer Institute (NCI) tried to communicate the dangers of smoking to a targeted group of smokers. After extensive research, the institute realized that the "product" it was trying to sell (smoking is bad for you) had already been sold. Seven out of eight smokers had tried to quit in the past but had encountered two major barriers to quitting: They did not know of an effective technique; and even if they did, they were reluctant to try because of past failures. Once the NCI understood this consumer perspective, it changed its marketing efforts dramatically. Specifically, efforts were made (1) to develop and get into the field a wide range of quitting techniques and (2) to persuade physicians and health care workers to help smokers cope with their fears of failing. (Kotler and Andreason, 1991:43–44)

Public administrators sincerely interested in the responsiveness of their agencies might find it useful to think of clients as consumers. What this means in practice is that all an agency's efforts should be focused on satisfying consumer needs—instead of producing a good or service and then trying to find a buyer. When an agency tries to find out what the consumer wants and then to produce that good or service consistent with that want, then we say the agency has a marketing (as opposed to a selling) orientation.

Flexibility

In James Jones's novel *From Here to Eternity,* American soldiers are under surprise attack by Japanese planes at Pearl Harbor. The hero, Sergeant Warden, rushes to the arsenal for weapons only to find the door barred by another sergeant loudly proclaiming (over the din of exploding Japanese bombs) that he cannot pass out live ammunition without a written request signed by an officer. But the phenomenon of bureaucratic inflexibility is no fiction. We have all faced—and been frustrated by—instances

(text continues on p. 137)

★★★★★★★★★★★★★★★★★★★★★★★★★★★★★★★★★★★

WORKING PROFILE

William Donald Shaefer

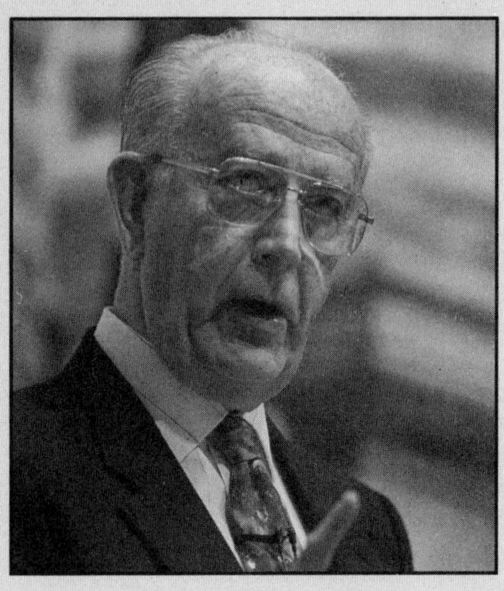

Giving New Meaning to Administrative Responsibility

The mayor of Baltimore is not happy. He holds his big head in his hands and stares into the veneer of the table. Around the table sit members of Don Shaefer's cabinet, fiddling with their legal pads.

He breaks the silence. "I'm not pleased with this. That is *not . . . good . . . enough.*" To help get his message across, he turns to the easel and writes "PEOPLE." For greater emphasis he writes "PEE-PULL" and "WHAT IF YOU LIVE THERE?" He wants the cabinet to empathize with the citizens of Baltimore, whom they govern.

Now the mayor holds up two fingers and pokes them at his eyes. "Do you know what these are? *Do* you? These are *eyes.* I got two and you got two." He grabs a cabinet member and menaces him with fingers in the eyes. So how come my eyes can see and a smart young fella like you can't see a damn thing, huh? How come?"

It is unlikely that Shaefer ever read Aristotle's *Nicomachean Ethics* or Kant's *Foundation of the Metaphysics of Morals,* but some time ago he decided that one of the main shortcomings of public officials was that they just could not see the problems citizens faced. He gave new meaning to the concept of administrative responsibility. Riding around the city on weekends, *he* could see potholes, broken streetlights, caved-in trash cans, dirty parks, housing violations, abandoned cars, crooked traffic signs, dead trees, a missing bus stop, and trash at the curb. "What are they doing with the money?" he would mutter as he got out his pen and his Mayor's Action Memo. The memos would be on the appropriate desks Monday morning.

There are no traces of elitism in Shaefer's city hall. He constantly scolds the bright urban planners and sociologists, who always seem to know what is best for everyone else. A case in point is their careful plans they had made for new suburban-style housing:

"People here want to live in a row house," he told them.

"But, Mayor, there will be grass. Provision is made for a lawn for each, ranging from 26.5 square yards, and for each a tree, with varying placement in . . . "

"I want a row house. I don't want a tree. I don't want a lawn. I live in *Baltimore,* I *like* a row house, I'm gonna *have* my own house. *I am Baltimore, I live in a row house—get it?"*

★★★★★★★★★★★★★★★★★★★★★★★★★★★★★★★★★★★

★★★★★★★★★★★★★★★★★★★★★★★★★★★★★★★★★★★

The Concept of Ownership

Today it is fashionable among students of production and operations management to speak of getting employees to imagine themselves "owning" their program, project, or organizational unit (see, for example, Peters & Austin, 1986:249–95). Fashionable or not, the idea makes eminent good sense—after all, human beings tend to take far better care of things they own than things that they rent, borrow, or have entrusted to them. (Who among us drives a rented car as they would drive their own?)

Don Shaefer is a prime example of how ownership can undergird the principle of accountability. To put it bluntly, Shaefer thinks Baltimore is his. He takes derogatory remarks about the city as personal insults. What other mayor would stop his car to scream at someone who has dropped a paper on the street? That street is Shaefer's street.

A feeling of ownership fosters attention to detail. Take one center-city square. The street actually shines because of his experiment with glasphalt, a pavement made out of bottles from trash. Every corner has a new sidewalk, with curb ramps for the handicapped. Between the curb ramps every block has a couple of orange and white Trashball baskets. (All the litter cans are painted like basketball hoops—"Hook one in," and "Jump one in.") The pedestrian benches are all emblazoned "William Donald Shaefer, Mayor, and the Citizens of Baltimore."

Honest, Competent

In his early years at city hall, Shaefer earned a reputation as an honest, hard-working councilman. As one Baltimore reporter put it, "A dollar wouldn't stick to him if you slapped it on his nose with Super Glue." He often stayed late, working well into the night, conscientiously trying to decide how to vote on upcoming council issues. Sometimes he was outvoted 19 to 1.

Shaefer is credited with transforming Baltimore from the dilapidated, seedy port city known as "Mobtown" or "Survival City" in the early 1970s into a modern tourist center. His most lasting mark on Baltimore was the redevelopment, during his tenure, of a 3.2-acre waterfront site, which became known as Harborplace. The complex includes a network of shops and restaurants developed by urban planner James W. Rouse, adjoining a $21.3 million national aquarium. Shaefer was equally proud of the 2,300 jobs created by Harborplace. When critics maintained that he had established a playground for the affluent, leaving the inner city to rot, he countered by detailing the money that had been invested in neighborhoods and parks and the subsidized housing grants he had won (which amounted to more than for any other city of comparable size).

"Do it Now"

After serving as mayor of Baltimore for 15 years, Shaefer was elected in 1986 as the 58th governor of Maryland by the greatest margin of victory in the state's history, winning 82 percent of the popular vote. His inaugural speech was filled with jokes and homespun wisdom, and in its conclusion he said, "There are certain words I like to use: People . . . Do it now . . . Get it done right the first time."

SOURCES: Richard Ben Cramer, "Can the Best Mayor Win?" *Esquire,* October 1984, pp. 57; Charles Moritz, ed., *Current Biography Yearbook 1988* (New York: H. W. Wilson, pp. 511–14); *Washington Post,* February 7, 1988).

★★★★★★★★★★★★★★★★★★★★★★★★★★★★★★★★★★★

IV. West Central
Third most tolerant (behind New England and Pacific Coast) of different beliefs and lifestyles. Want to increase aid to farmers but not by greater proportions than elsewhere.
III. East Central
Yes, there is a Middle America. In every category of values measured, this region scored at the national average.
I. New England
Unusually tolerant of beliefs and lifestyles different from their own. Freedom of religion important, but relatively few say they are religious. Clear majorities favor almost every type of government assistance for disadvantaged. More pro-business and pro-environment than other Americans.
II. Middle Atlantic
More positive views of government than others, seeing it as an active force for achieving social change. More likely than most to support increased social spending.
V. Southeast
Least tolerant and most conservative in country but, at the same time, view government as a positive force. Religious.
VIII. Pacific (includes Hawaii and Alaska)
Yes, Californians are "laid back." Very tolerant of other lifestyles and not very religious. Want less money spent for military and more for scientific research.
VII. Rocky Mountains
Extremely strong antigovernment attitudes. Support for military programs is higher than other regions.
VI. Southwest
Less tolerant and more religious than elsewhere. Hold a more negative view of government than any other Americans and oppose its use to achieve social change. Most fiscally conservative.
Washington
Oregon
California
Idaho
Nevada
Montana
Wyoming
Utah
Colorado
Arizona
New Mexico
North Dakota
South Dakota
Nebraska
Kansas
Oklahoma
Texas
Minnesota
Iowa
Missouri
Arkansas
Louisiana
Wisconsin
Michigan
Illinois
Indiana
Ohio
Kentucky
Tennessee
Miss.
Alabama
Georgia
Florida
So. Car.
North Carolina
Virginia
West Virginia
Pennsylvania
New York
NJ
Del.
MD
VT
NH
Mass.
CT
RI
Maine

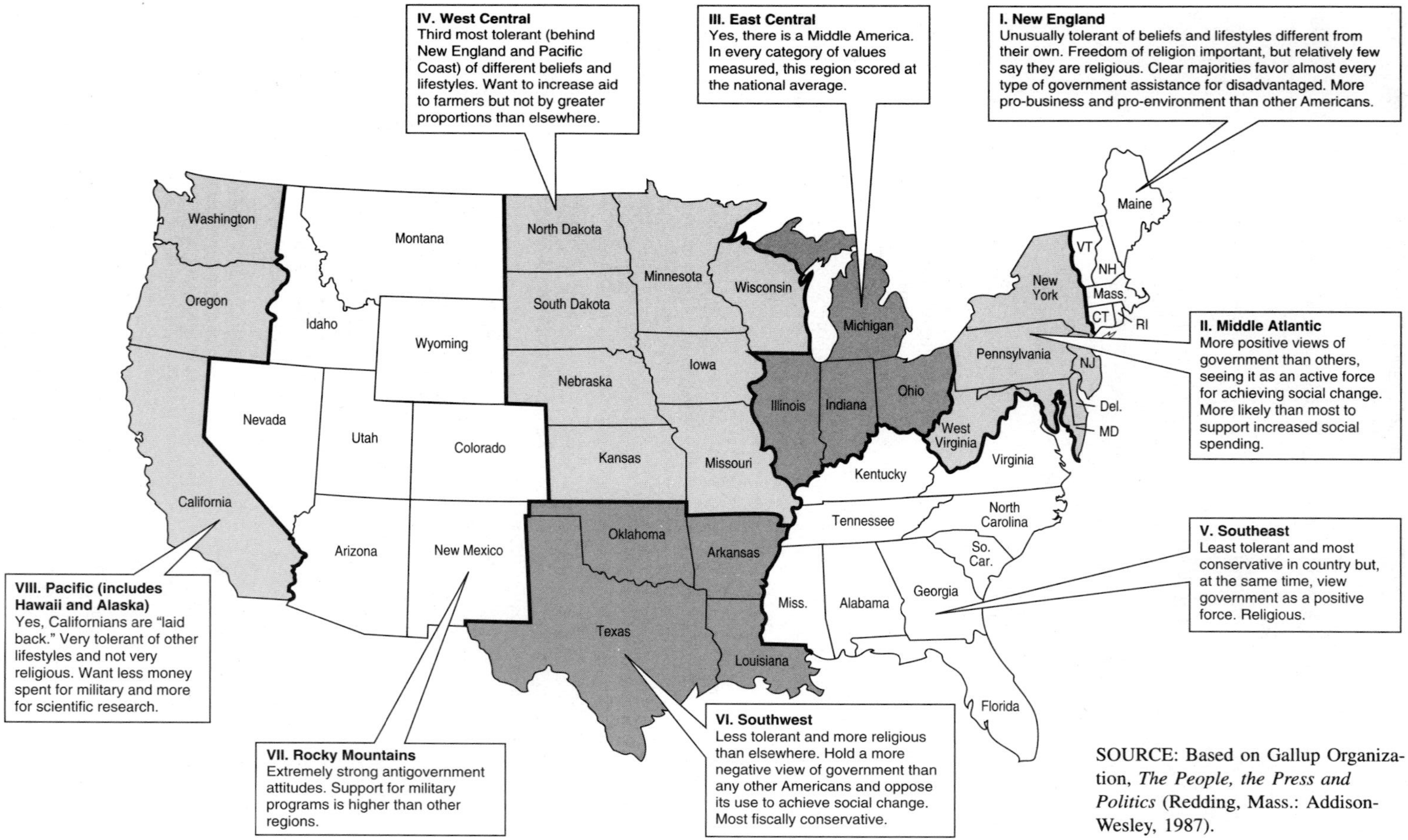

SOURCE: Based on Gallup Organization, *The People, the Press and Politics* (Redding, Mass.: Addison-Wesley, 1987).

FIGURE 4-2 **. . . . .**
American Political and Personal Attitudes

of administrative inflexibility. Buried in almost any daily newspaper can be found an example or two of how some one person was made to suffer while a bureaucrat was making sure all the i's were dotted and all the t's were crossed.

Clearly, in the formulation and implementation of policy, administrators should not ignore individual groups, local concerns, or situational differences relevant to the attainment of policy goals. This imperative applies with particular force in the United States, which has a federal system of government (as discussed in Chapter 3).

To say that the United States is a large and diverse nation surely must be one of the hoariest platitudes around. Yet federal administrators cannot ignore it. When a federal agency suggests legislation, it must be sensitive to the regional biases in Congress. If the legislation passes, the agency then must be sensitive, when it administers the policy, to the different claimants within state boundaries.

A recent survey by the Gallup Organization captures some of this diversity (see Figure 4-2, opposite). It also suggests why uniform economic and social programs stamped out in Washington like so many license plates can sometimes produce gross misallocation of resources.

Flexibility is a value to be sought after at the local levels as well as at the federal and state levels. When Lee Brown was chief of police in Houston, he strongly advocated neighborhood policing but thought that it could work only if the approach was *customized for each neighborhood*: "The overall concept is universal, but the specific tactics to carry it out are not. We analyze the needs of particular neighborhoods and then we create an approach targeted for those needs. We're not doing this as a generic quick fix" (quoted in Persinos, 1989).

But flexibility can be pursued only so far. Treating everyone individually is usually too expensive and impractical for most situations. On the other hand, treating all citizens or clients the same way may achieve economics of scale, but it ignores the diversity of society and probably means that what is offered never meets anyone's needs very well.

Figure 4-3 attempts to illustrate some of the difficulty involved. Figure 4-3A shows a hypothetical market consisting of six persons who share some need in common; no segmentation is required. Figure 4-3B shows the opposite case: Here the orga-

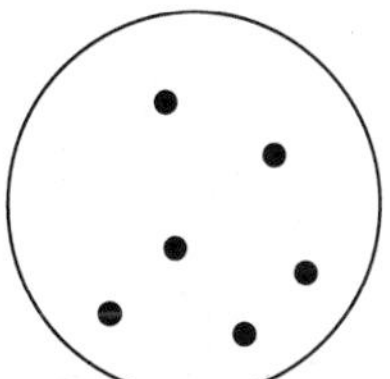

A. No market segmentation

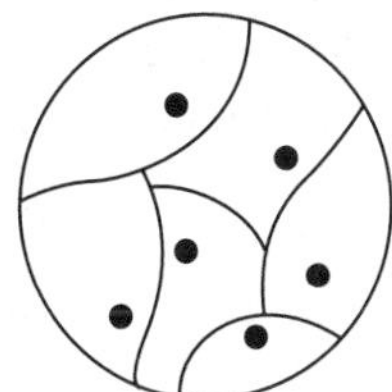

B. Complete market segmentation

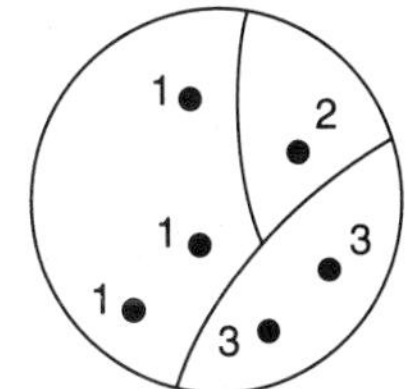

C. Market segmentation by income classes 1, 2, and 3

FIGURE 4-3
Different Approaches to Market Segmentation

SOURCE: Adapted from Philip Kotler, *Marketing for Non-Profit Organizations* (Englewood Cliffs, N.J.: Prentice-Hall, 1975), p. 101.

nization has decided to see each of the six members of this market as being different. But few organizations find it worthwhile to study every individual member and then customize service to each member's need. Instead, organizations generally search for broad groupings that can be approached as segments. The organization can then choose to deal with all these segments or concentrate on one or a few of them. In Figure 4-3C, the organization has taken this approach and used income class as the basis for **market segmentation.** In Chapter 5 we will see how one administrator uses market segmentation with Los Angeles's homeless population.

Of course, many other variables could have been used other than income. The most important fall into three major classes: geographic (by region, county size, climate, and so on), demographic (by age, sex, race, and so on), and psychographic (usage rate, benefits sought, lifestyle, and so on). When governments ignore these kinds of complexities in the formulation and implementation of policy, they tend to fail the standard of flexibility and thereby become a little less responsive.

The concept of client as consumer is potentially a very powerful one in the attainment of responsiveness and flexibility. "Talking Shop" gives you some idea of how a public agency might build on it.

Fairness

To ensure that citizens have a chance to present their cases and be heard fairly, agencies follow the principle of **due process.** To the lawyer, the term *due process* connotes something sufficiently special that cannot be completely encompassed in any other term. The concept of due process is stated for the federal courts in the 5th Amendment and for the state courts in the 14th. It assumes that no citizen should "be deprived of life, liberty, or property without due process of law." In short, it is an assurance that the government will be administered by laws, not by the arbitrary will of people who condemn without a public hearing.

Although the concept of due process originally applied to criminal law, it was later extended to administration. Today, thanks largely to the Administrative Procedures Act of 1946, it serves as a major limitation on administrative discretion. Thus agencies must have jurisdiction over the matters with which they deal; must give fair hearings to all persons affected by their rulings; must give adequate notice of such hearings well in advance of the dates when they are held; and must allow any interested persons to appear. Their officers must be impartial, with no personal interest in the questions upon which they decide. Moreover, their decisions must be based upon substantial evidence. In the orders they issue, specific findings of the law and fact must be set forth. The persons affected by such orders must be permitted counsel and given an opportunity to appeal. This is due process in the *procedural* sense of the term.

The safeguard of law is stressed in both judicial references and literary references. As Justice Louis Brandeis observed over 50 years ago: "Our Government is the potent, the omnipresent teacher. For good or ill, it teaches the whole people by its example. Crime is contagious. If the Government becomes the lawbreaker, it breeds contempt for law, it invites every man to become a law unto himself, it invites anarchy" (cited in U.S. Congress, 1987).

(text continues on p. 142)

Talking Shop ....

Designing a Marketing Mix for a Public Sector Organization

Once a public administrator has identified the market segments, he or she can begin to design a full-fledged marketing program responsive to human needs. It is convenient to refer to the components of such a program in terms of **four *P*s**—produce, price, promotion, and placement. Below we shall discuss a few of the public sector decisions associated with each component.

Product

The crucial point about a consumer's attitude toward any good or service an organization might provide is that it is a mixture of the evaluation of a variety of features. For example, whether a high school student decides to attend a particular college depends on several features: cost, distance from home, number of friends enrolled, and so forth. Of course, the student will weigh (or value) each of these features differently and hold opinions about the probability that the college does in fact offer each of these features. The following formula represents the attitude structure of a citizen toward mass transit:

Overall attitude = (strength of belief that city transit system is *fast*) (importance of speed) + (strength of belief that system is *safe*) (importance of safety) + (strength of belief that system is *clean*) (importance of cleanliness) + . . . + (strength of belief that system is *economical*) (importance of economy).

How can such models help college presidents, directors of city transportation authorities, or hospital administrators (who find that physicians are always recommending somebody else's hospital to their patients)? They tell the administrator what is most affecting consumer's attitudes. The college administrator may be placing too much emphasis on a winning football team when national rankings do not influence applicants—which is what he or she thought.

Public administrators can of course directly measure consumer satisfaction or dissatisfaction. To go solely by level of use, number of clients, or number of public hearings will not do. Instead of writing a better regulation or developing a new service under the assumption that an appreciation of it, or a market for it, will develop later, an agency must consciously try to meet consumer requirements. In this context, public opinion polls and other survey research techniques might help.

Price

What should NASA charge private companies to carry payloads weighing up to 200 pounds and occupying less than 5 cubic feet into orbit aboard the space shuttle? What should a college charge for tuition? A power company, for electricity? A highway commission, for tolls?

Among the pricing strategies a public sector organization might follow are no-fare (e.g., get people to ride buses rather than automobiles), profit maximization (e.g., sell tickets to a charity ball), cost-plus (e.g., open gift shop at museum),

(continued)

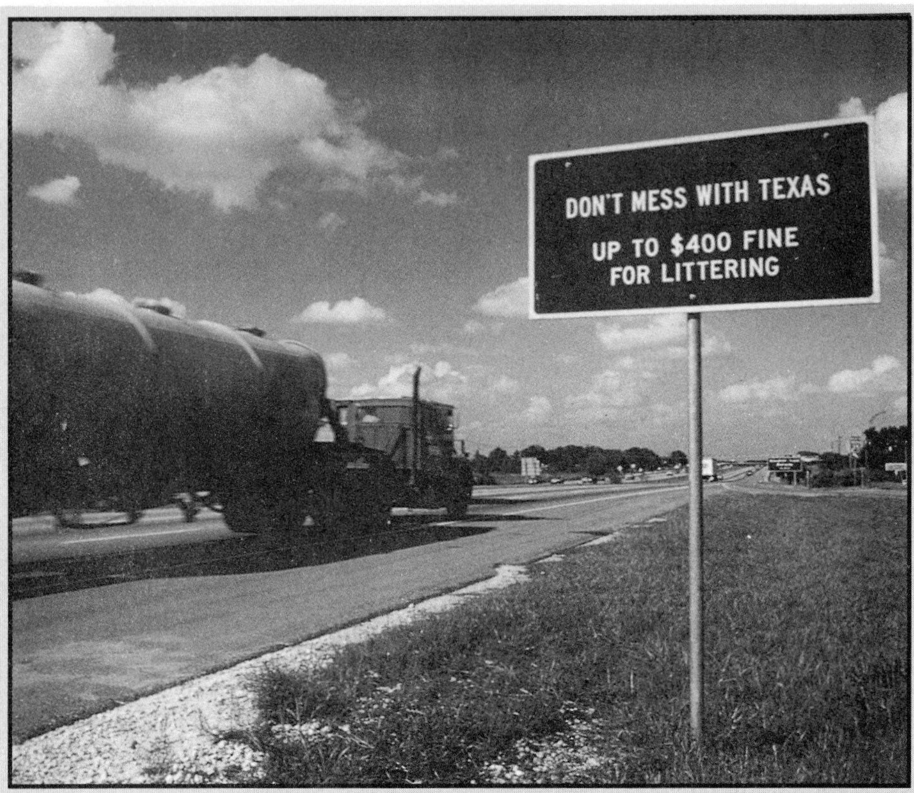

Sign along a road near Midland, Texas, part of campaign to clean up roadside litter. (Texas Department of Transportation)

variable (e.g., charge more for electricity during peak periods), discriminatory (e.g., charge higher tuition to out-of-state students), and cost recovery (e.g., recover a "reasonable" part of a toll road's costs).

Promotion

To promote a service, the agency must communicate with the consumer. As with pricing policies, several strategies are available.

Advertising probably comes first to mind, though its effectiveness is widely overestimated. Nevertheless, the federal government is one of the nation's top 20 advertisers, with outlays rivaling those of such business giants as Coca-Cola and Procter & Gamble. In one year, government advertising costs totaled $200 million.

Market segmentation can help. For example, a small private university in Minnesota might develop three brochures rather than one for prospective students. For inquiries from the West, one brochure might emphasize the winter sports; for inquiries from the East, the teaching excellence; and for inquiries from within Minnesota, the opportunity to go to a national rather than regional university.

In Texas, one year after the Department of Highways and Public Transportation launched its "Don't Mess with Texas" antilitter campaign, litter was down 29 percent on state roads, compared with 10 percent in other states with such programs. The key to Texas's success was research showing that 70 percent of deliberate littering could be attributed to people under 25, most of them male. Therefore the television commercials were aimed directly at the young "Bubbas" in pickup trucks who dispose of burger wrappers and beer bottles the easy way—out the window.

One video had the Fabulous Thunderbirds, a 50s-style rock group from Austin, roaring along in a 1953 convertible singing,

Well you're ridin' down that highway
In your big ol' fancy car.
Got that radio a blastin',
And you're feelin' like a star.
Zoomin' down that Texas highway,
And you've got a heavy load.
Don't you trash that Texas highway.
Don't you throw it in the road.
Don't you mess with Texas.
Don't you mess with Texas.

(continued)

The fourth component in the marketing mix is placement; that is, how the agency plans to make its products or services available and accessible to customers. Avoidable inconveniences should be rooted out. (From The Wall Street Journal, *with permission of Cartoon Features Syndicate.)*

In addition to the Fabulous Thunderbirds, the state has commercials featuring two former Dallas Cowboy football players, Too-Tall Jones and Randy White, picking up trash. Jones steps toward the camera and says, "You see the guy who threw this out the window? . . . You tell him I got a message for him." Mr. White steps forward with a beer can and says, "I got a message for him too." A voice then asks, "What's that?" The player crushes the can with a powerful fist and says threateningly, "Well, I kinda need to see him to deliver it." Too-Tall Jones adds, "Don't mess with Texas."

Besides using television commercials, a public sector organization can communicate with customers directly through personal selling. For example, the administrator of a new hospital might try to visit every physician in the area to explain the hospital's services.

Another promotional technique is in the form of incentives, either in cash or in kind. In the 1960s, the U.S. Soil Conservation Service offered cash payments to farmers to encourage them to adopt conservation practices. In India, the Ministry of Health and Family Planning offered transistor radios to men undergoing sterilization after having two or three children.

Finally, publicity involves stimulating demand for a service or product by planting significant and favorable news about it in the mass media. Because it is not paid for by the sponsor, it has a higher level of credibility than advertising.

Placement

Within cost constraints, a public sector organization should try to make consumer access to the product or service as easy as possible. Hospitals and medical societies can use cable television or prerecorded radio messages to provide useful information to customers. Blood banks can be set up in neighborhood stations to get donations. Subsidized meals can be distributed to disadvantaged and elderly people by having volunteers drive their own cars. Universities can set up ranch campuses, provide courses on commuter trains, or use satellite communication to more remote locations.

The same message appears in Robert Bolt's drama *A Man for All Seasons,* which portrays the martyrdom of Sir Thomas More, Lord Chancellor of England, for refusing to accept Henry VIII's declaration of supremacy over the church. In the following excerpt, Sir Thomas speaks to his son-in-law, William Roper:

Sir Thomas: The law, Roper, the law. I know what's legal not what's right. And I'll stick to what's legal.

Roper: So now you'd give the Devil benefit of law!

Sir Thomas: Yes. What would you do? Cut a great road through the law to get after the Devil?

Roper: I'd cut down every law in England to do that!

Sir Thomas: Oh? And when the last law was down and the Devil turned round on you, where would you hide, Roper, the laws all being flat? (Bolt, 1962:37–38)

Accountability

A good synonym for the term **accountability** is *answerability.* The organization must be answerable to someone or something outside itself. When things go wrong, someone must be held responsible. Unfortunately, a frequently heard charge is that government is faceless and that, consequently, affixing blame is difficult.

Immediately after British troops retook the Falkland Islands from Argentina on June 14, 1982, British Foreign Secretary Lord Carrington resigned his position in Margaret Thatcher's Conservative government. He did so because of the failure of British diplomacy to prevent, and of British intelligence services to anticipate, the Argentine invasion that cost the nation lives, territory, and international embarrassment. Although the recapture of the Falklands proved in time to be a political plus for the Thatcher government (and for British morale), Lord Carrington's action was judged appropriate and was not reversed.

Carrington's action provides an interesting contrast to what happened after the October 23, 1983, bombing of the marine barracks at the Beirut airport in Lebanon. Although the bombing was a severe setback to American interests in the region, no one resigned, no one was disciplined, and no one was fired. President Reagan said no one should have been because "I accepted responsibility." He spoke those words as he flew to Palm Springs for a vacation, which makes one wonder how much he meant them.

Problems of accountability would continue to plague the Reagan Administration. For example, by 1987, it was clear that some of its members—Lt. Col. Oliver North in particular—had secretly sold arms to Iran and had run a clandestine operation to support the rebel forces in Nicaragua. Congressional investigative committees described what they called a "lack of accountability" at the heart of the Iran-contra affair:

> *The confusion, deception and privatization which marked the Iran-contra affair were the inevitable products of an attempt to avoid accountability. Congress, the Cabinet, and the Joint Chiefs of Staff were denied information and excluded from the decision making process. Democratic procedures were disregarded.*
>
> *That is what happened in the Iran-contra affair:*
>
> - *The President's N.S.C. staff carried out a covert action in furtherance of his policy to sustain the contras, but the President said he did not know about it.*
> - *The President's N.S.C. staff secretly diverted millions of dollars in profits from the Iran arms sales to the contras, but the President said he did not know about it and Poindexter claimed he did not tell him.*

Lt. Col. Oliver L. North came to Washington as a major in the Marine Corps to become a junior aide on the staff of the National Security Council (NSC). Eventually, he became the key action officer in a series of covert operations, including the sale of arms to Iran and the diversion of the proceeds to the contras, as the Nicaraguan rebels were called. In testimony before Congress, Colonel North acknowledged that he had lied to members of Congress about the venture. His basic defense before Congress in July 1987 was (1) he was carrying out orders from superiors, and (2) his actions were in the long-term interest of the country. (Photo from The New York Times*)*

- *The Chairman of the Joint Chiefs of Staff was not informed of the Iran arms sales, nor was he ever consulted regarding the impact of such sales on the Iran-Iraq war or on U.S. military readiness.*
- *The Secretary of State was not informed of the millions of dollars in contra contributions solicited by the N.S.C. staff from foreign governments with which the State Department deals each day.*
- *Congress was told almost nothing—and what it was told was false.*

Deniability replaced accountability. Thus, Poindexter justified his decision not to inform the President of the diversion on the ground that he wanted to give the President "deniability." Poindexter said he wanted to shield the President from political embarrassment if the diversion became public (U.S. Congress, 1987).

The utter lack of accountability in dispensing taxpayers' money was well illustrated by Stanford University in the early 1990s. Under criminal penalty, Stanford had certified to the government that its account for expenses on federally funded research projects contained no disallowable charges. But a GAO investigation found that Stanford had charged, on its federal contracts, depreciation expenses on a yacht and silverware, operating expenses for a profit-making shopping center that the university owned, and even $7,000 worth of sheets for the Stanford president's oversized bed. The GAO accused school administrators of blocking access to financial records that could reveal more evidence of overcharges. John D. Dingell, chairman of the House Subcommittee on Oversight and Investigations accused the university administrators of exhibiting a brazen "Catch me if you can" attitude (*Houston Chronicle,* May 9, 1991).

Finally, accountability can refer to the managerial processes of "direction and control." One of the best-known illustrations of control in the federal bureaucracy came from President Franklin D. Roosevelt. Roosevelt reportedly had this exchange with one of his aides (cited in Sherrill, 1974:203):

> *When I woke up this morning, the first thing I saw was a headline in the* New York Times *to the effect that our navy was going to spend $2 billion on a shipbuilding program. Here I am, the commander in chief of the navy having to read about that for the first time in the press. Do you know what I said to that?*
>
> *(Aide): "No, Mr. President."*
>
> *I said: "Jesus Chr-rist!"*

Honesty

When the values of Americans are surveyed, honesty inevitably ranks at the top or quite close to it. Not surprisingly, governments have devoted considerable effort to enforcing honesty—although they have disagreed widely on the means.

Applied to public administration, the principle of honesty has three implications (Warwick, 1981). First is the obligation to avoid lying. The Iran-contra affair again raised the perennial question of whether official lies should be permitted for higher good. When Reagan's national security adviser, John M. Poindexter, was accused by Congress of an "unapologetic embrace of untruth," he replied: "I think the actions I took were in the long-term interest of the country." Even those who might disagree with Poindexter's judgment acknowledge that certain situations warrant deception. But was Poindexter's situation *exceptional enough* to warrant it? Few thought so.

Sissela Bok (1978:12) has put the case against lying succinctly: "Whatever matters to human beings, trust is the atmosphere in which it thrives." In public administration, lying or the suspicion of lying has an added consequence—the proliferation of bureaucracy and regulation. One can safely predict, for example, that the Office of Naval Research will expand its supervision of university contracts in wake of the abuses uncovered at Stanford.

The second implication of honesty is the obligation to be truthful in presenting information to superiors and to the public. Accordingly, it is wrong for an administrator to make exaggerated claims about what a proposed program will do in order to generate enthusiasm for it. But if several agencies are contending for influence on program design, it seems justified for administrators to present just one side of a case. Only through hearing several different perspectives will the public have ample opportunity to sort out the truth.

The third implication of honesty is the obligation to respect the ability of others to gather and present true information relevant to public policy. Honesty would require, in other words, that an administrator does not try to prevent or suppress studies that challenge his or her view.

Competence

Now meet Bob. He is attuned to the ever-changing demands of his agency's clients; he treats clients not as numbers but as individuals; he knows the law and obeys it

(Bob is no Colonel North); he takes full responsibility for all his actions and keeps the agency head fully informed; his reputation for integrity and candor extends well beyond the agency.

But alas, Bob is no paragon of administrative responsibility. His administrative actions are hasty rather than prudent, and they display little concern for consequences. He adheres strictly to an 8-hour, 480-minute day. He never volunteers or demonstrates any initiative. Furthermore, Bob uses his resources poorly—he is always over budget and consistently fails to hit the performance objectives for his administrative unit. His "satisfactory" performance rating satisfies him. He looks forward to retirement.

The public does not want to be served by knaves, nor does it want incompetents. Clearly then, administrative responsibility is a multifaceted concept.

Countervailing Forces

Why is it that the ideal of administrative responsibility described in the previous section seems so hard to realize in practice? For an answer, let us return to James Madison, who is quoted at the beginning of this chapter. Just previous to the marvelous line stating that controls on government would be unnecessary "if men were angels," Madison wrote the following in Federalist Paper No. 10: "Ambition must be made to counteract ambition. . . . It may be a reflection on human nature that such devices should be necessary to control the abuses of government. But what is government itself but the greatest of all reflections on human nature?"

Therefore, the assumption of this section will be explicitly Madisonian: The fundamental deterrents against realizing administrative responsibility are rooted in human nature itself. More specifically, it will be argued that three human weaknesses explain a great deal of administrative action we generally term irresponsible. The first is **greed,** an excessive desire for some benefit or advantage. The second is **arrogance,** a disposition to claim for oneself, often coercively, more consideration or importance than is warranted or justly due. The third is **cowardice,** a lack of courage to face opposition, danger, or hardship. Because cowardice and courage might seem words better suited to battlefields than bureaucracies, we would do well to recall what President John F. Kennedy wrote in his *Profiles in Courage* (1956:3): "For without belittling the courage with which men have died, we should not forget those acts of courage with which men . . . have *lived* . . . . A man does what he must—in spite of personal consequences, in spite of obstacles and dangers and pressures—and that is the basis of all human morality."

Greed

The consequence of greed can be seen on a large scale when one views the scandal at Reagan's Department of Housing and Urban Development (HUD). The cost occurred not just in the estimated direct loss of $6 billion in public money but also in the suffering of millions of people who are poorly housed and in the damage to the reputation of the public service. The process by which the government attempted to pass on a subsidy to poor tenants also provided many opportunities to take slices of that subsidy and make cozy, greedy little deals along the way. The abuses that took place at HUD were surprising in extent though hardly in kind; like other government agencies, HUD has been defrauded before.

Influence peddling and political favoritism, the two main areas of the HUD scandal, are also not uncommon in Washington. An army of lawyers, lobbyists, former members of Congress, and presidential appointees derive handsome incomes from trading on their access to upper levels of the government.

Another Washington phenomenon is the "revolving door" from the government to the private sector. The GAO estimates that about 26 percent of approximately 5,100 former high- and mid-level Defense Department personnel had responsibilities, while they were at the department, for defense contractors for whom they later worked (U.S. General Accounting Office, 1987a). These individuals give the appearance of not having acted in the best interests of the government because they viewed defense contractors as potential employers. A similar problem exists at federal agencies that regulate radio and television stations, banks and savings and loan institutions, trade and tariff levees on imports and exports, oil and gas production, and other lucrative public sector activities.

One need not look long for instances of greed in local government. Entrepreneurs of many kinds want something from the city. Contractors seek business; companies want licenses and privileges; manufacturers need services and not-too-nosy inspectors; and some trades rely on a tolerant police force. Unfortunately, for some of these services, individuals exact a price in the form of bribes or kickbacks.

Of course, George Washington Plunkitt, a ward boss in New York City in the late 1800s, often insisted that *he* had no need for bribes or kickbacks. He favored what he called "honest graft," which he concisely explained as follows: "I might sum up the whole thing by sayin': 'I seen my opportunities and I took 'em.' Suppose it's a new bridge they're going to build. I get tipped off and buy as much property as I can that has to be taken for approaches. I sell at my price later and drop some more money . . . in the bank. It's honest graft, and I'm lookin' for it every day of the year" (Quoted in Steinberg, 1972:6).

(Copyright, 1982, G. B. Trudeau. Reprinted with permission of Universal Press Syndicate. All rights reserved.)

Now fast-forward to 1982. The head of New York City's Parking Violations Bureau (PVB) is having breakfast with a contractor at the Blue Bay Diner in Queens. The PVB, which administers city contracts to firms that collect parking fines, has become by this time the heart of a network of payoffs. Extortion has become the rule. The reluctant executive, between bites of his omelet, tries to beg off from paying bribes by highlighting his company's excellent service record. The PVB official replies, "I'm personally disappointed in you." This is the practiced code of the bagman. (Newfield & Barrett, 1988: 185)

Arrogance

Because noble deeds can flow from base motives and ignoble deeds from lofty ones, a sound intellect will refuse to judge people simply by their outward actions. We must probe the inside and discover what springs set them in motion.

From all indications, what set Poindexter and North in motion during the Iran-contra affair was not greed. What then was it? In 1928 Justice Brandeis got to the heart of the matter when he wrote in *Olmstead*: "The greatest dangers to liberty lurk in insidious encroachment by men of zeal, well-meaning but without understanding."

Government employees, frequently frustrated by the restrictions their agency puts on them, arrogate to themselves the right to expedite what *they* perceive to be of value to the community. The basis of this right might be (1) a zeal for some cause or ideology; (2) a general feeling of superiority; or (3) a purity of intent.

If North and Poindexter provide an example of item 1, we might turn to John Sununu for an example of item 2. During 1991, Sununu, who was President Bush's chief of staff and a former governor of New Hampshire, came under sharp criticism for his use of military jets, government limousines, and corporate aircraft for personal and political trips. Despite the criticism and the distraction it caused the president, Sununu could not bring himself to defuse it by taking a train or riding a bicycle a couple of times. Critics said his egotism and arrogance would not allow it. Susan McLane, a Republican and chairman of the New Hampshire House Ways and Means Committee explains: "It's absolutely typical. Not only does he say 'I know everything' . . . but he goes the next step and says, 'You don't know anything.' Sununu will never apologize because he's never going to think he's wrong. It's an attitude."

For an example of item 3, let us return to the previously mentioned HUD scandal. One agent for HUD funds became known as "Robin HUD" after she told investigators that she had stolen $5.5 million in department money to help the poor (*New York Times,* June 25, 1989). This is a good example of an ignoble deed flowing from a lofty motive.

In the following material I want to focus on three particularly disturbing patterns of behavior that often accompany arrogance: coercion, distortion, and ethnocentrism.

Coercion. Democracy cannot exist without a modicum of consensus. Consequently, the administrative state has what some observers might call an alarming number of programs and techniques for dealing with those who fail to share in the consensus, who dissent from it, and who, in some instances, advocate covertly or overtly its

(Schorr/Kansas City Star)

destruction. Among these sometimes coercive programs and techniques, we might include loyalty oaths, restriction on speech and assembly, lie detector tests, wiretapping, data banks, and behavior modification drugs.

Police agencies, in trying to keep one step ahead of criminals, are sometimes only one step ahead of privacy laws. Across the country, police agencies use invasive high technology to speed the work of catching criminals, tracking stolen goods, and monitoring suspected wrongdoers. For example, in the skies above some cities, unmanned aerial vehicles (UAVs) may look like model airplanes but they are not. Inside them are high-resolution cameras that can make out small objects from hundreds of yards, infrared detectors that can see in the dark, and perhaps even chemical sensors that can pinpoint drugs in an area. Surveillance cameras can now detach pinhead-size lenses operated by remote control. Old-fashioned phone taps have been replaced in some cases by computer technology that can pick out one voice among an entire phone system—and make it impossible for targets to know they are being monitored (*Wall Street Journal,* November 12, 1990).

A milder form of coercion might be called "nannyism." The motive here is not the desire for consensus but the desire to protect—or, more accurately, to overprotect. In this sense, the administrative state becomes a kind of nanny. Frequently cited examples of this phenomenon are the Federal Trade Commission (FTC) and the FDA. A fairly typical criticism of the former, which appeared in *Time,* ran as follows:

> *The commission proposed a truth-in-menu rule that might mean, for example, that no restaurant could offer as Maryland crab any crustacean that had*

crawled into Delaware. The agency intensified a holy war against breakfast cereal companies; it has proposed breaking them up and banning ads for presweetened cereals from Saturday morning's TV cartoon shows. An FTC-proposed rule warned that such ads were enticing children to "surreptitiously" sneak cereals into Mom's shopping cart. Washington wags quipped that the FTC would soon ban peanut butter because it stuck to the roof of the mouth. (Time, *December 3, 1979)*

Meanwhile, the FDA tries to protect consumers by restricting their freedom of choice. Under present law, no new drug or medical device can be made available for sale until it has been officially approved as "safe and effective" by the FDA. Unapproved products like the mechanical heart can be used only in investigational studies when they have been previously cleared by the FDA on application by physicians or their sponsor through a complex approval procedure. Due to lack of FDA approval, numerous cases have been reported in which patients have been unable to obtain investigational drugs, even when suffering from debilitating conditions like arthritis, multiple sclerosis, and cancer.

In theory, the purpose of the FDA regulation is to protect consumers from undue risk. In fact, however, no evidence has ever been produced demonstrating a need for the complex approval procedures. In one study, experts expressed disagreement with FDA decisions in half the approval cases surveyed. The approval system was set up in 1962 after the thalidomide disaster when it was found that more than two million doses of the infamous drug had been distributed to doctors on a promotional basis. Nevertheless, the net toll of thalidomide-caused birth defects in the United States was 10, a tragic cost, but one that was probably far exceeded by the harm resulting from subsequent overregulation (Gieringer, 1985).

Distortion. The management function that assesses public attitudes, identifies the policies of an organization with the public interest, and then executes a program of action to earn public understanding and acceptance is termed **public relations.** Thus, the purposes of an agency's public relations program are to inform and to constructively influence the public. And with both, the risk of distortion needs to be recognized when men and women of zeal take charge.

The importance of keeping the public informed cannot be overemphasized. An informed public is an essential ingredient of democracy. Yet, in practice, some policymakers have found an easy justification for both secrecy and deception. Ordinary citizens, they believe, cannot understand complex decisions like the following:

Do aerosol cans affect the ozone content of the stratosphere?

What should we do about the economy? What is the proper trade-off between deficit reduction and contined growth?

Are we spending too much on AIDS research and not enough on solar energy?

Is our level of defense spending really adequate in comparison with a rapidly changing and inherently unstable Eastern Europe and Russia?

"Fooling some of the people some of the time is good enough for me."

(Drawing by Richter; © 1976 The New Yorker Magazine, Inc.)

The apparent inability of the people to understand these complex problems gives the policymakers—so the argument runs—a kind of "right to deception." Among certain kinds of specialists, even a new ethic has emerged. To wit: Since average citizens cannot possibly know the *whole* truth about specialized subjects, lying to them is permissible—provided there is some good reason. Thus a biomedical researcher might forego getting the informed consent of human subjects on the grounds that those subjects could never be genuinely informed. Similarly, government officials use the same ethic when they decide not to inform citizens of emergency measures or of the risks involved in the transportation of hazardous materials.

As Walter Lippmann noted many years earlier, it is sophistry to think that in a free country certain people have some sort of inalienable or constitutional rights to deceive their fellow humans like this. "There is no more right to deceive than there is a right to swindle, to cheat, or to pick pockets."

The second objective in a public relations program, besides simply providing information, is to influence the public. As we said in Chapter 2, the effective administrators are the ones who can attain their agencies' goals. This task, in turn, frequently *requires* the mobilization of public support. I can cite no better authority on the importance of honest communication than Abraham Lincoln: "In this and like communities public sentiment is everything. With public sentiment nothing can fail; without it nothing can succeed." In a few instances, the agency must actually *persuade* the public to take certain action—for example, participate in immunization programs, use seat belts, and stop smoking.

No official of the federal government has the words *public relations* in his or her title, but the number of government "information specialists" probably runs in the thousands. Critics contend that, in one sense, all of what these information specialists do is propaganda. Nevertheless, reporters need their press releases to keep the public informed:

> *In the typical Washington situation, news is not nosed out by keen reporters and then purveyed to the public. It is manufactured inside the government, by various interested parties for purposes of their own, and then put out to the press in ways and at times that suit the sources. That is how it happens that when the president prepares a message on crime, all the leading columnists suddenly become concerned with crime. That is even how it happens that when the Air Force budget comes up for consideration, some new plane will streak across the continent in record time. (*U.S. News & World Report, *August 27, 1979)*

Public relations operations at the local level, though obviously smaller in scope, are basically no different. Public relations at the local level is not, however, the sole responsibility of community relations officers. The chief administrator certainly has an important role too. "The city manager has an inescapable obligation for public relations, an obligation that is just as compelling as his responsibilities for sound public finance, effective personnel systems, and other areas of management. He must instigate training for employees in all areas of public relations . . . . It is the city manager's job, using all means available, to fashion improvement in the image of the city. He sets the pace for the entire municipality" (Desmond L. Anderson, quoted in Fowles, 1974:282).

Like the chief administrator, the employee in municipal government has a public relations role. Supervisors should make sure that the rank and file are given a preliminary orientation and then kept up to date about the activities of their government. If they do not receive the appropriate information, it is unlikely they will be able to accurately answer questions from the public and thus avoid the negative feelings generated by the dreaded runaround.

Ethnocentrism. We have been discussing some of the disturbing ways in which arrogance—that disposition to claim for oneself more consideration or importance than is warranted or justly due—manifests itself. The first, coercion, involves acts of commission, that is, things an administrator might do to citizens—such as invade their privacy or restrict their freedom of choice. The second, distortion, involves acts of omission, that is, things an administrator might not do for citizens—such as provide truthful, accurate information. In a sense, the third manifestation of arrogance, ethnocentrism, is the most disturbing of all, for it involves simply ignoring the views and aspirations of certain citizens.

Ethnocentrism is the tendency to regard one's own culture (Western, African, Japanese, etc.) as superior and to downgrade other cultures. To survey the contemporary circumstances of minorities and to examine the minority-related programs of the last two decades are objectives beyond the scope of this book. But to briefly consider how the cultures of Mexican-Americans and blacks differ from that of the dom-

Talking Shop

Media Relations

Increasingly, public administrators at all levels are finding it necessary to talk to the media—a task for which they are seldom trained. Moreover, such interviews usually occur after something has gone wrong. Dan Rather (quoted in Dickinson, 1978:159) has given one rule that may be of help: "Stick with one of three responses: (a) I know and I can tell you, (b) I know and I can't tell you, and (c) I don't know." But there are other points worth bearing in mind:

- Use short, concise answers. *Reason:* Much reporting has to be short and snappy. Long, complicated answers can lead to contradictions or revelations you do not wish to make.
- Remain calm and pleasant. *Reason:* Most good journalists are aggressive, but you are not obligated to be.
- Have a prepared statement and adhere to it. *Reason:* Same as the above two.
- Avoid humor. *Reason:* It frequently backfires.

After a two-year study of press officers in government, Stephen Hess (1984) noted three problems. First, even senior press officers are not "in the loop." To the extent that public administrators are heavily dependent on the media—their first and most effective line of communication with the taxpayers—this is somewhat surprising. "To serve effectively as an honest advocate for a political executive and his policies, a press secretary must be in the loop." That means being a part of the inner circle and a party to debates that lead to decisions.

Another problem is that most government public relations programs emphasize information dissemination when they ought to be also providing their chiefs with infiltered information from the field.

A third problem is lack of planning. Managers should set criteria to evaluate the soundness of programs before funding them. Among the standards to be applied to public affairs programs in government are the following: "Does the campaign have clear and meaningful objectives?" "Has the intended audience been precisely targeted?" "What mix of information channels (media, community elements, professional organizations, and so on) are to be utilized?" "Specifically, how is the effectiveness of the campaign to be evaluated—by behavior change, attitude change, dissemination of information?" (U.S. General Accounting Office, 1979).

inant society can be fruitful if it leads to a somewhat better appreciation of the many viewpoints of the various segments of the population in the United States.

Roughly speaking, the worldview of nearly all nonminority Americans can be summarized in terms of the following assumptions: (1) It is natural for individuals to *compete* and to seek to satisfy themselves through *material gain;* (2) it is natural for humans to struggle against and master *nature;* and (3) problems and situations are to be analyzed by means of tangible *evidence* ("hard facts") and the *scientific method.*

In contrast, the worldview of many Mexican-Americans has at least some roots in the Indian worldview that places individualism on a social rather than an economic basis and considers human life inextricably bound up with nature. Mexican-Americans also want to recapture their unique Spanish-Indian heritage and thereby make "la Raza," or "the race," an effective political force. Unlike Mexican-Americans, who tend to envision a multiminority cultural pluralism, blacks emphasize their culture as a prelude to a more far-reaching social change. Blacks are, however, equally sensitive to the necessity of maintaining one's identity.

These different assumptions work to make misunderstandings between people likely and destructive. For example, administrators are apt to take ethnic neighborhoods as slums and classify them for renewal because they do not see the order behind what appears to be disorder:

> *Live, vital, cohesive ethnic communities are destroyed. To make way for a university in Chicago, planners wiped out a Greek and Italian neighborhood, over strong protests. The scars haven't healed yet. It is important to stress that when you scatter such a community, you're doing more than tearing down buildings; you're destroying most of what gives life meaning, particularly for people who are deeply involved with each other. The displaced people grieve for their homes as if they had lost children and parents. (Hall, 1976:97)*

Moreover, most governmental programs designed to aid minorities are based on the dominant worldview. To participate in these programs as a route to progress, minorities must perforce cast aside part of their very identity. Thus they are placed in a dilemma—the implications of which cannot be fully measured by income and employment statistics. Although it is unlikely that public administrators can easily resolve the dilemma, it is inexcusable for them not to recognize it.

Cowardice

As the earlier quote from Kennedy's *Profiles in Courage* suggests, civil action, no less than martial action, requires courage. Courage is more than conquering fear and withholding the legs from flight when an enemy is bearing down on you and the possibility of great pain is imminent. It consists at least as much in steeling the will to do the right thing and in turning the mind relentlessly to seek or face truth. Perhaps nations should also raise monuments to this lonely kind of courage.

The political environment of public administrators puts all sorts of questions to them and tests them in all sorts of ways. Many of these tests they meet by decisions that are relatively easy to make and that can be executed in well-rehearsed ways. But some decisions require steeling of the will as in Martin Luther's dramatic renunciation of papal authority in 1521, when he said, "Here I stand; I can do no other. God help me."

Of course not every administrator handles decisions in this way. His or her calculation might run more along this line: "As long as the behavior of others does not

This building mural in a Hispanic section of Los Angeles symbolizes the importance of localism, the family, and the neighborhood as primary forms of association. (The New York Times/*Michael Tweed)*

affect me directly or attribute blame to my sight of it, I will remain silent. As long as the pain of doing the right thing remains so high, I will remain still. As long as I can plead that I was only following orders, I will comply with a wrongful order." According to the Senate Intelligence Committee report on the Iran-contra scandal, career officials at the CIA knew the proposed deal was wrong yet would not do anything to stop it. Many hundreds of officials in New York City government must have known about the Parking Violations Bureau's network of payoffs, benefited not at all from it, yet refused to speak.

Similar behavior was demonstrated in the Watergate scandal. The White House staff itself planned illegal acts that members *knew* were illegal. Some went along not because of greed or zeal but because of cowardice—they lacked the courage to walk away from the heady power and glory of working directly for the president of the United States and to say, "This is wrong" (see Case 4.2).

To avoid cowardice in decision making, administrators must value certain things as more important than others, so that they are willing to take risks and endure hardships for their sake. This does not mean that administrators can easily ignore the political goals of the party in power and operate the agency as they see fit—that is arrogance. Nor should they leak information to the media at the first hint of transgression.

Rather, they should prudently calculate when the limits of loyalty to a political appointee have been exceeded.

External and Internal Controls

Various measures can and have been taken to counter greed, arrogance, cowardice, and other human frailties that make ensuring administrative responsibility difficult. The table below can help us distinguish and analyze these measures (adapted from Gilbert, 1959):

	Internal	*External*
Formal	Agency head	Legislature Judiciary
Informal	Professional codes Representative bureaucracy Public interest Ethical analysis	Interest group representation Citizen participation The media

This framework divides the measures into four main categories: internal formal, internal informal, external formal, and external informal. The distinction between formal and informal, though not always easy to draw, is roughly this: Informal relationships are those not explicitly provided for in the Constitution. The distinction between internal and external is that between (1) the executive branch of government and the top executives who head it and (2) the rest of society and its political apparatus.

Because we discussed the external formal measures available to Congress (e.g., oversight) and the external informal influence by interest groups and the media, we will need examine here only the remaining seven mechanisms: agency head, judiciary, citizen participation, professional codes, representative bureaucracy, public interest, and ethical analysis.

Agency Head

The personal example of the top administrator in an organization conveys a powerful message to others about what he or she thinks responsible behavior is and is not. Consider the case of the city manager who discovers that an employee on the night shift has programmed the city's computer to cast horoscopes. The horoscopes have become a popular daily practice among employees. The city manager has called the director of finance:

> *Fred, I'm assuming you didn't know this was going on and that it started in your department. Frankly, that's a partial copout for me and not that flattering for you. However, the computer is the city's, paid for by taxpayers, and*

these horoscopes cost time and money. It stops now. Suspend the young man for as long as it takes at his daily rate until he pays back what it cost us for the time it took for the horoscope program. Then, figure out how much it cost the city for each and every one of those horoscopes. Send me a list of every one who got one because I am going to send them a bill. Look, . . . I don't even use the office Xerox for personal stuff—it's not right. (Austern et al., 1978:77)

Here the city manager demonstrates her unequivocal opposition to unethical practices. Using the city's time and equipment to cast horoscopes is wrong. Period. The city manager's follow-up to her employees corrects the problem and reinforces the expected ethical standard.

Now consider the case of President Reagan. Although his personal integrity was seldom questioned, Reagan appeared to do little to foster a high ethical standard in his two administrations. Indeed, much of his time was devoted to defending loyal subordinates such as Michael Deaver who had left the White House staff in 1984 to set up a lucrative lobbying concern. Deaver soon came under criticism for exploiting his public service and personal relationships with Reagan for private gain. President Bush apparently learned some lessons from the Reagan experience. From the start of his administration, Bush stressed that even the *appearance* of wrongdoing would not be tolerated.

In addition to setting the moral climate within his or her organizational unit, the administrator can take a number of concrete steps to ensure proper behavior such as the following:

- Recruiting people whose background has been carefully checked.
- Establishing training programs on proper conduct.
- Reviewing on a regular basis the actions of subordinates.
- Investigating promptly and vigorously allegations of wrongdoing within the organization.

To help in the last-named task, some administrators are able to rely on in-house investigators known as inspectors general (IGs). Congress created an IG corps for the federal government in 1978. Most of the IGs' work involve routine audits of government programs to ferret out billions of dollars worth of waste and abuse. Because the IGs send their findings to Congress, which is often more supportive of them than are the agency heads, IGs have produced some friction within the executive branch.

Judiciary

A Model of the Administrative Process. Many, particularly members of the legal professions, hold that one of the principal arrangements designed to monitor administrative decisions that affect individuals, private organizations, and local communities,

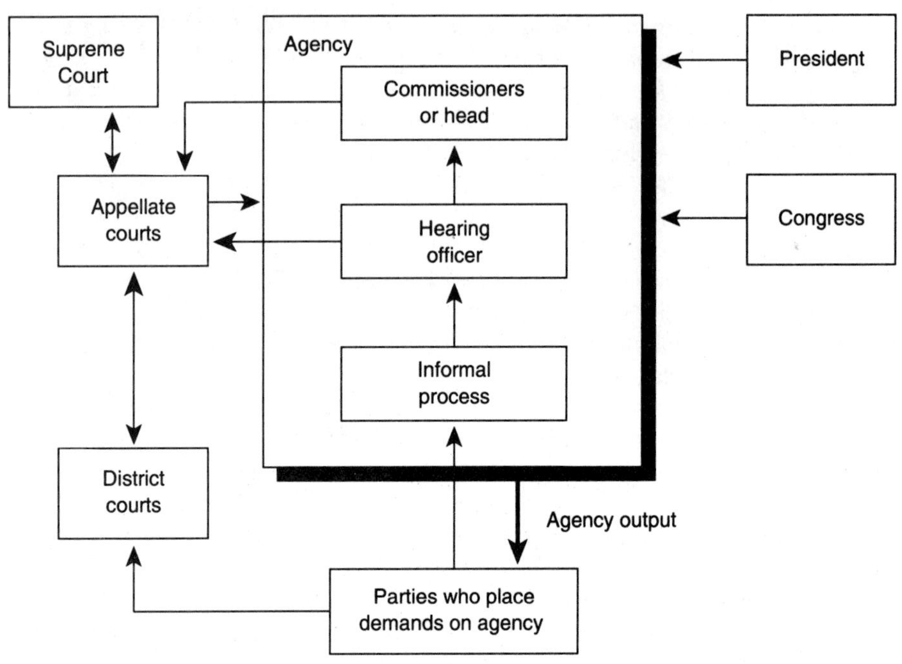

FIGURE 4-4
Judicial Control of a Federal Agency or Commission

is the national court system. After exhausting administrative remedies, individuals in many cases have the opportunity to obtain a judicial review of administrative decisions (see Figure 4-4).

Various parties—Aunt Beth, Engulf & Devour Corporation, and others—make demands on the agency that must first pass through an *informal* screening process. The purpose of this step, which comes before any formal hearing, is to resolve a problem in as economical and flexible a manner as possible. A problem here may involve nothing more than answering a telephone call. ("Where is my social security check?" "What do you mean I underpaid my taxes by $735?") Or it may involve much larger issues. ("May we merge with GM?" "Does our prospectus for a security system look OK?") Even these more complex issues can often be negotiated and resolved congenially.

What triggers *formal* adjudication under the Administrative Procedures Act (APA)? For the formal hearing provisions of the APA to come into play, an agency's authorizing statute must require it. If the statute is vague on this point, the courts will look to the legislative history (i.e., what members of Congress had in mind) and, of course, ensure that constitutional due process governs.

Sometimes the courts favor administrative discretion; other times they favor the benefits of fairness. It all depends.

In cases requiring a more formal process, an administrative law judge generally reviews the evidence and makes preliminary conclusions as to the disposition of the issue. If an appeal is needed, it will usually be an administrative appeal in which the record is examined by other agency officials. Eventually, a final decision is reached. The decision may concern claims and benefits, licenses, rules, rates, routes, or sanctions (for noncompliance). These, in effect, are the output of the administrative agency, and they can have a considerable effect on the involved parties.

Some form of review of agency decisions can be sought in the courts. This review may occur after the administrative procedures have been exhausted. If a case presents important legal questions, there may be appeals leading to the Supreme Court. In Case 4.3 at the end of this chapter, the party circumvented the administrative process by taking his grievance directly to court. The court may set aside any agency action that entailed abuse of discretion, excess of statutory or constitutional authority, improper proceedings, or an action unwarranted by the facts.

Congress appears in the model (Figure 4-4) because that body can define and limit the authority of the agency through law. The president appears because he can issue specific policy directives and executive orders to the agency.

The Importance of Judicial Control. Arguably, the most rapidly expanding control over administration in recent years has been the courts. But it has also been extended to prison administration (e.g., size of cells and number of prisoners per cell), education policy (e.g., routes for buses and content of curriculum), and technical areas like automobile safety standards and resource management. For example, the Supreme Court has ruled that the Federal Communications Commission (FCC) cannot require cable television operators to allow free access to a portion of their broadcast facilities and that the Securities and Exchange Commission (SEC) cannot control private pension plans.

But the court's power is not limited to federal agencies. Sovereign states and independent school districts are also affected. In the state of Alabama, a U.S. district judge, in effect, helped run the state. He supervised the operations of prisons, mental hospitals, highway patrol, and other state institutions. In the Boston school district, another federal judge helped run things. A former superintendent of schools recalls:

> *The scope of the court's intervention . . . was simply staggering and quickly went beyond remedies for specific legal grievances such as classroom segregation. During the first 18 months I was superintendent, the court held 30 hearings, and considered 109 items to assure compliance with more than 200 orders outstanding. Virtually every administrative appointment, and even decisions about curriculum, had to be approved in court-ordered proceedings. The court even held hearings about whether a particular school's auditorium needed roofing. (Wood, 1981)*

What are the limitations to judicial control? The first point to recognize is that responsibility is always after the fact; that is to say, all that courts can do is alleviate or punish wrongs that have already occurred.

A second point about judicial control is that the Supreme Court and its individual members tend to support federal agencies more frequently than they oppose them. In other words, research suggests that the outlook is not altogether promising for individuals who choose to control agency action in court.

Our third point is speculative. The rise of public interest lawyers and a post-Watergate climate of "litigious paranoia" have probably brought the courts into public administration more than at any other time in U.S. history. Harlan Cleveland suggested that the ultimate effect of this phenomenon might be to cause every public agency to write down all its procedures, to put greater power in the hands of lawyers, and to generate in consequence jerky and arthritic administrative procedures.

Fourth, at a time when courts already face huge backlogs of cases, one wonders whether it is even physically possible for them to involve themselves in so many aspects of administration. Of particular concern is judicial decision making in cases involving scientific, technological, and managerial expertise.

Finally, and perhaps most fundamentally, do courts really need to decide whether an agency has "failed to consider all relevant factors" or has "abused its discretion" in writing a regulation on how to label peanut butter? A more useful division of labor might be for the people's representatives to monitor these matters, while courts concentrate on checking on bureaucrats who are accountable in no other way. Assuming agencies are under *political* control, judges can concentrate on their original job of protecting the Bill of Rights. They can let others worry about the hydrogenated vegetable oil in Skippy peanut butter.

Citizen Participation

When William F. Buckley, Jr. wrote that he would rather entrust his governance to the first hundred persons listed in the Cambridge telephone directory than to the faculty of Harvard College, he was simply stating the basic philosophy behind including the citizenry in the public decision-making process. Other observers maintain that citizens, as customers of government, are naturally more responsive to public needs than are government officials. It might even be put forth as a tentative proposition that the poorest moral performances and the least accountability by government are generally associated with conditions in which few citizens have any influence. For these reasons, among others, it is not surprising to see government at all levels trying to facilitate the participation of citizens in the administrative process—sometimes even through the shape of buildings (see boxed insert pp. 162–163).

The most common forms that institutionalized citizen participation assume are the citizen committee as an advisory group, the citizen group as a governing group in a specific policy area, and the idea of neighborhood government, where citizens have direct responsibility in a number of policy areas. Citizens' advisory committees often play important roles in the policymaking process described in Chapter 2.

Advisory groups, as discussed here, refer to the over 1,200 boards, commissions, and committees found within federal executive departments and their regional or district subdivisions and within units of local government. These advisory committees involve more than 20,000 people and cover nearly every imaginable topic—from the President's Council on Energy Research and Development to the Agriculture Department's committee on hog cholera eradication.

Local governments create advisory committees on subjects ranging from community planning and police reform to mass transit and air pollution. Administrators use these bodies to obtain information, advice, and opinions from representatives of affected interests, as this input may aid them in making informed policy decisions.

One shortcoming of citizen participation is that it can take the form of self-serving actions. The objective here is less to advise government than it is to win in the political marketplace. The extension of participatory democracy into the social sphere might even result in antisocial consequences. For example, let us assume

> *that a community exists in which all members freely participate in the decisions that affect their immediate lives. Let us further assume that this community is relatively homogeneous in its ethnic and economic makeup (e.g., a white middle-income community). One of the decisions facing this community is a proposal by the local housing authority to build a low-income housing project in the area. The residents fear the building of this project for two reasons: it would reduce property values, and it might increase crime in the community. After a lengthy and open discussion, the citizens categorically reject the project. Their perceived fears, let us say, are primarily racially motivated, and thus, by direct participatory processes the project is declared politically dead. (Ventriss, 1985:437)*

What other shortcomings to citizen participation might we note? First, it could be argued that some public administrators see the participatory movement as a way to rid themselves of insoluble problems. Given an intractable problem one need only hoist the banner of participatory democracy while transferring responsibility elsewhere. Second, by bringing highly dissatisfied groups into the administrative process, administrators may be able to pacify (or co-opt) them. Third, citizen participation can be used as a vehicle by which a bureaucracy builds a clientele. This technique could be used, for instance, with environmental programs, which have no natural interest group. Enterprising administrators need only form a task force, composed of highly influential citizens, and they would have the nucleus of an effective citizens' lobby for their pet programs.

Professional Codes

This use of professional codes can be traced back at least to the Hippocratic Oath, which has guided the practice of medicine for more than 2,000 years. Next to physicians, lawyers probably have the most stringent set of professional codes to be found. (Interestingly, with few exceptions, the Watergate culprits were lawyers.)

A couple of reasons might be suggested to explain why professional codes have such limited usefulness. To make these concrete, you might want to ask yourself how they might apply to Tables 4-1 and 4-2. First, the scope of activities of an administrator seldom limits itself to one profession; inevitably, questions arise that are outside the code's purview. Similarly, the administrator often finds his or her code in conflict with other loyalties (such as a particular client or geographic region, political leader, social class, or union).

(text continues on p. 164)

How Buildings Encourage Citizen Participation

On October 28, 1943, Prime Minister Winston Churchill, speaking in the Palace of Westminster to urge the reconstruction of the House of Commons exactly as it had been before its destruction in a Luftwaffe air raid, uttered his famous pronouncement about architecture. "We shape our buildings," he said, "and afterwards they shape us." Charles T. Goodsell has examined the implications of that observation for city council chambers in the United States.

Goodsell found that council chambers divide into three district types (as illustrated below):

- *The Traditional (1868–1920).* This room is big, boxy, and ornate. Carved balusters separate its "official" zone from its "public" zone. Every detail, from rostrum height to chair-back height, is calculated to impress upon the visitor the dignity of the proceedings and to create an atmosphere of distant, though legitimate, authority.
- *The Midcentury (1920–1960).* This room is still boxy but less ornate. The utilitarian doors are not great portals, and the ceilings are lower. No longer does the presiding officer sit quite so high. Correspondingly, legislators seated around a concave dais facing the public gain in corporate importance what they lose in individual identity, though the public zone is proportionately larger than in the older, traditional chambers. This is a model of "confronted authority" that parallels the concepts of constitutional government and limited state power.
- *The Contemporary (1960–present).* This room is radically designed: The box has been broken up into asymmetrical sculpted space with curved or angled walls, ceiling, and floors. There is virtually no ornamentation. "Mood cues"—materials, colors, textures—replace direct differentiations of authority and responsibility. The relationship between official and public zones is blurred. The arrangement reflects not only the ethos of participation but also the twin philosophical ideas of political community and direct democracy.

By bringing citizens into the circle of governance itself, the contemporary design projects the citizen participation ideal. Goodsell writes:

According to this idea, citizens do not merely vote or run for office to control their destinies; they become actively and directly involved in the very processes of governance. Citizen participation has its pros and cons, its advocates and detractors. It can be costly in time and money, but under the right conditions, deliberate public involvement can encourage processes of open dialogue and foster a sense of civic responsibility. Citizen participation can also create false expectations and mislead the public on its true role in policy making. The nobility of the concept in terms of fulfilling the potentialities of citizenship can be buried by an empty, hypocritical ritualism that only masks the powerlessness of the ordinary citizen. The Contemporary chamber, then, expresses a noble ideal, but it also offers itself as a setting for the callous corruption of that ideal.

SOURCE: *The Social Meaning of Civic Space: Studying Political Authority through Architecture*, by Charles T. Goodsell, © 1988 by the University Press of Kansas. Reprinted by permission of the publisher.

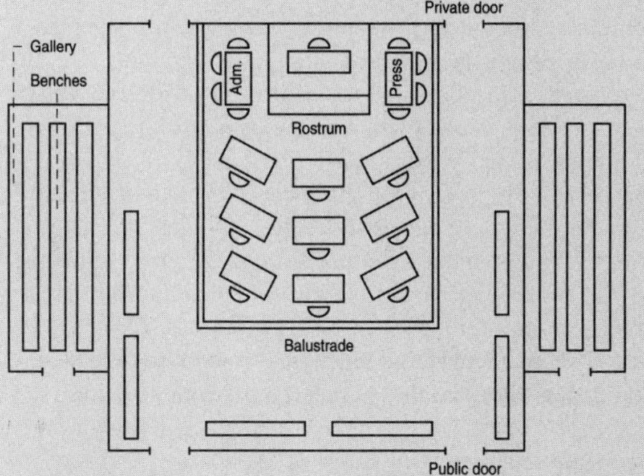

Traditional

Ruling circle of officials confer internally as public observes from afar. Their furniture is much fancier than the public's benches. Clearly, the scene is one of inferiors in the presence of superiors.

Midcentury

Now officials are facing the public rather than having their backs to them. Citizens have individual chairs and their own lecterns. Officials are placed at one end of a longitudinal space; citizens, at the other. This relationship symbolizes the idea that government derives its power from the people and in turn is required to be accountable to them.

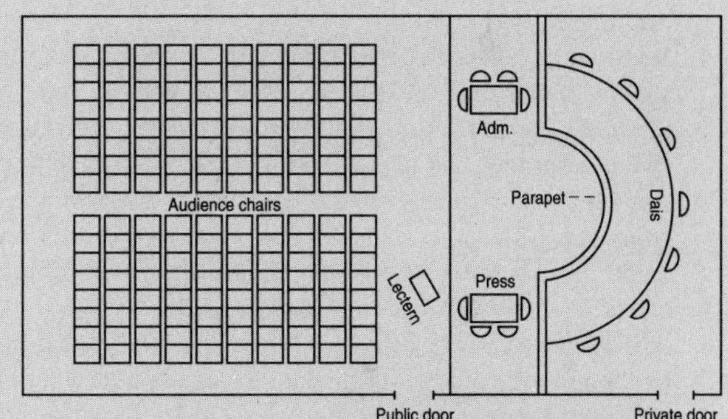

Contemporary

The area reserved for the public has proportionately more seating capacity than ever. Upright barriers that segregate citizens and officials are gone. Seated in an amphitheater, the citizens see themselves as a collective body involved in the process of governance with the officials.

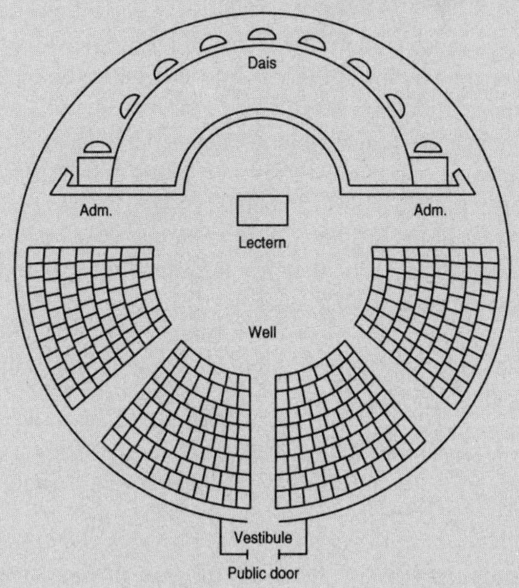

TABLE 4-1

American Society for Public Administration Code of Ethics*

The American Society for Public Administration (ASPA) exists to advance the science, processes, and art of public administration. ASPA encourages professionalism and improved quality of service at all levels of government, education, and the not-for-profit private sectors. ASPA contributes to the analysis, understanding and resolution of public issues by providing programs, services, policy studies, conferences, and publications.

ASPA members share with their neighbors all of the responsibilities and rights of citizenship in a democratic society. However, the mission and goals of ASPA call every member to additional dedication and commitment. Certain principles and moral standards must guide the conduct of ASPA members not merely in preventing wrong, but also in pursuing right through timely and energetic execution of responsibilities.

To this end, we, the members of the Society, recognizing the critical role of conscience in choosing among courses of action and taking into account the moral ambiguities of life, commit ourselves to:

1. Demonstrate the highest standards of personal integrity, truthfulness, honesty, and fortitude in all our public activities in order to inspire public confidence and trust in public institutions.
2. Serve the public with respect, concern, courtesy, and responsiveness, recognizing that service to the public is beyond service to oneself.
3. Strive for personal professional excellence and encourage the professional development of our associates and those seeking to enter the field of public administration.
4. Approach our organization and operational duties with a positive attitude and constructively support open communication, creativity, dedication, and compassion.
5. Serve in such a way that we do not realize undue personal gain from the performance of our official duties.
6. Avoid any interest or activity which is in conflict with the conduct of our official duties.
7. Respect and protect the privileged information to which we have access in the course of official duties.
8. Exercise whatever discretionary authority we have under law to promote the public interest.
9. Accept as a personal duty the responsibility to keep up to date on emerging issues and to administer the public's business with professional competence, fairness, and impartiality, efficiency, and effectiveness.
10. Support, implement, and promote merit employment and programs of affirmative action to assure equal opportunity by our recruitment, selection, and advancement of qualified persons from all elements of society.
11. Eliminate all forms of illegal discrimination, fraud, and mismanagement of public funds, and support colleagues if they are in difficulty because of responsible efforts to correct such discrimination, fraud, mismanagement or abuse.
12. Respect, support, study, and when necessary, work to improve federal and state constitutions, and other laws which define the relationships among public agencies, employees, clients and all citizens.

*Reprinted with permission from *Public Administration Review,* © by the American Society for Public Administration (ASPA), 1120 G Street NW, Suite 700, Washington, DC 20005. All rights reserved.

A second reason for the limitations of professional codes derives from the wording of these guidelines. If too general, they are useless as a guide to action. If specific enough to serve as a guide to action, they might be so numerous, so detailed, as to be unworkable on a day-to-day basis.

TABLE 4-2.
International City/County Management Association (ICMA) Code of Ethics*

The purpose of the International City/County Management Association is to increase the proficiency of city managers, county managers, and other municipal administrators and to strengthen the quality of urban government through professional management. To further these objectives, certain ethical principles shall govern the conduct of every member of the International City Management Associations, who shall:

1. Be dedicated to the concepts of effective and democratic local government by responsible elected officials and believe that professional general management is essential to the achievements of this objective.
2. Affirm the dignity and worth of the services rendered by government and maintain a constructive, creative, and practical attitude toward urban affairs and a deep sense of social responsibility as a trusted public servant.
3. Be dedicated to the highest ideals of honor and integrity in all public and personal relationships in order that the member may merit the respect and confidence of the elected officials, of other officials and employees, and of the public.
4. Recognize that the chief function of local government at all times is to serve the best interests of all the people.
5. Submit policy proposals to elected officials; provide them with the facts and advice on matters of policy as a basis for making decisions and setting community goals, and uphold and implement municipal policies adopted by elected officials.
6. Recognize that elected representatives of the people are entitled to the credit for the establishment of municipal policies; responsibility for public execution rests with the members.
7. Refrain from participation in the election of the members of the employing legislative body, and from all partisan political activities which would impair performance as a professional administrator.
8. Make it a duty continually to improve the member's professional ability and to develop the competence of associates in the use of management techniques.
9. Keep the community informed on municipal affairs; encourage communication between the citizens and all municipal officers; emphasize friendly and courteous service to the public; and seek to improve the quality and image of public service.
10. Resist any encroachment on professional responsibilities, believing the member should be free to carry out official policies without interference, and handle each problem without discrimination on the basis of principle and justice.
11. Handle all matters of personnel on the basis of merit so that fairness and impartiality govern a member's decisions, pertaining to appointments, pay adjustments, promotions, and discipline.
12. Seek no favor; believe that personal aggrandizement or profit served by confidential information or by misuse of public time is dishonest.

*Reprinted with permission of ICMA.

Third, to the extent that many codes posit obedience to authority in one form or another, it could be argued that they are inherently weak, possibly even dangerous. Consider the famous series of experiments on human beings by Stanley Milgram (1974) at Yale University. The participants were led to believe that the purpose of the research project was the "scientific study of memory and learning." By a series of manipulations the participant was chosen to be the "teacher." Next, a fake "learner" was then taken to an adjacent room, strapped into a chair, and manacled with electrodes. Enter a supervisor dressed in a gray technician coat who tells the "teacher" to administer a verbal learning test to the man in the next room. Whenever an incorrect answer is given, the "teacher" is to give the "learner" an electric shock from the "shock generator."

The results of this experiment were surprising and disturbing, for no one refused and walked out of this experiment. In fact, nearly two thirds of the "teachers," who represented a broad cross section of the occupational community, kept pressing away to 450 volts—despite the well-rehearsed shouts and screams of the "learner." The results, obviously, were not what was expected.

Representative Bureaucracy

A representative bureaucracy is, roughly speaking, one that represents its society; that is, the percentage of each minority group in the government approximates the percentage of that group in the entire population. The assumption is, of course, that by hiring more members of some ethnic group the representation of that group's attitudes within the bureaucracy is enhanced.

Does ethnic representation lead to active representation of that group's interest in the bureaucracy? Frank Thompson (1976:576–601), after a rather thorough review of studies on the question, concludes probably not, although the data are quite inclusive.

Consider these findings:

- One study of black and white police in 15 core cities found that the black police viewed ghetto dwellers more positively. They more readily perceived ghetto residents as honest, industrious, respectable, and religious. Other data reveal that black police are more likely to view black citizens as mistreated by the police.
- A study of community development workers in Atlanta revealed that black professionals and paraprofessionals were more likely than white coworkers to perceive their clients as having "positive attitudes." But black welfare workers in 15 cities concluded—to a greater degree than their white colleagues—that black clients did not do enough to improve themselves and that black clients were especially arrogant.
- Similarly, another study of law enforcement personnel in core cities showed that race had little effect on whether police engaged in such potentially controversial practices as searching without a warrant, breaking up loitering groups, and stopping and frisking. Indeed, an analysis of black police in New York City uncovered a "Cossack" disposition. When black police worked with white ones, some of them tended to view black offenders as an embarrassment and treat them harshly. In the words of one black officer, "I have treated many Negroes in a way I wouldn't treat a dog. I am harder on a Negro that commits an infraction than a white person." (Cited in Thompson, 1976:591)

Anthony Downs (1967:233) suggests this explanation for the weak link between ethnic representation and substantive representation: "Officials . . . have no strong incentives to employ representative values in making decisions. The pressure on them to seek representative goals is much weaker than the pressure of their own personal goals or those of their bureaus . . . Neither do officials face reelection, thus having to account for or justify their policies. This lack of any enforcement mechanism further reduces the probability that officials will behave in [a] representative way."

A number of other explanations might be offered: Officials may lack authority to do very much; formal organizational sanction and peer group pressure may reduce gestures of sympathy by public servants from certain ethnic groups (one "gets ahead by going along"); and uncertainty may exist regarding just what the "proper ethnic perspective" is (Thompson, 1976:589–90).

Public Interest

Given the limitations involved in professional codes and representative bureaucracy as internal informal approaches to administrative responsibility, some posit the concept of the public interest as a guide to making administrative decisions. According to this view, the administrator should make decisions based on the best interests of some collective, overarching community or national good rather than on the narrower interest of some small self-serving group.

To discern clearly the public interests is no easy task. Walter Lippmann (1955:42), as lucid a thinker as one is likely to encounter on the subject, could give no better answer than this:

> *There is no point in toying with any notion of an imaginary plebiscite to discern the public interest. We cannot know what we ourselves will be thinking five years hence much less what infants now in the cradle will be thinking when they go into the polling booth. Yet their interests, as we observe them today, are within the public interest. Living adults share, we must believe, the same public interest. For them, however, the public interest is mixed with, and is often at odds with, their private and special interests. Put this way, we can say, I suggest, that the public interest may be presumed to be what men would choose if they saw clearly, thought rationally, acted disinterestedly and benevolently.*

Quite a tall order. But even if the public official could see with this clarity, rationality, and objectivity, would it really be enough? How does one distinguish qualitatively between aggregated private interests (e.g., public opinion polls) and genuine common concerns? How does one distinguish between the various types of public: reasonable and long-range versus passionate and temporary?

During the late 1960s and early 1970s, a number of scholars began advocating a **new public administration.** Although their aims lacked sharp focus, a few tendencies were clear enough. They charged that mainstream public administration in the United States had become too status quo oriented. In particular, the mainstream denied social justice to the disadvantaged members of society. The purpose of public administration should be, therefore, the realization of social equity.

This redefinition of the public interest raises several questions. Why should this particular doctrine (social equity) be adopted over others (e.g., freedom)? The answer seems to derive more from revelation than reason. How does one implement social equity—to what extent should Peter be robbed to pay Paul, and who is Peter and who is Paul? Finally, what are the implications for representative government? Should unelected administrators "correct" the "wrong" decisions of elected officials? By what authority?

The main point about the new public administration is not that it provided a satisfactory definition of public administration but that it caused some rethinking about the nature and scope of the field. Never again would public administration be viewed as purely a matter of efficiency and economy in program execution. Nor would it continue to blithely ignore the needs of clients. Finally, and perhaps most importantly, students of public administration began to talk about ethics.

Ethical Analysis

In examining the Reagan Administration's mismanagement of the Iran-contra affair, the Tower Commission asked, *Quis custodiet ipsos custodes?* or "Who will guard the guardians themselves?" One man who would have thought that question odd was George C. Marshall, Franklin Roosevelt's chief of staff during World War II and Harry Truman's secretary of state. Marshall's approach to public service stressed the duty of those entrusted with official responsibility to maintain *within themselves* appropriate standards of behavior and not to depend on external controls (see Working Profile). Thus, by way of conclusion we focus upon some traditional as well as recent work in the field of ethics. Our immodest goal: to develop a more workable framework of moral choice for the public administrator.

Ethics is the systematic study of values. Before considering the very practical question of why ethical training can help a public administrator, I want to deal briefly with the commonly heard objection that ethics cannot be taught. Most of the resistance to ethics stems from the assumption that no one can say that certain attitudes are really true and others really false. Those who hold this view reject the philosophy and spirit of Plato, Aristotle, Buddha, Christ, Confucius, and Jefferson. They insist that, since there is neither traditional morality nor practical reason to guide us, the right solution to any moral problem "depends on the situation." This insistence is known as situation ethics and was a hallmark of the Nixon White House. John Ehrlichman, who accepted situation ethics when he was President Nixon's domestic policy chief, today rejects it: "The White House should lead in setting standards, morality, and goals. But when you are facing reelection, you look at the polls. When one is not elected, one defers to the guy who is. I never felt I had the right to substitute my judgment for his [Nixon's]" (quoted in *Time,* December 1, 1975).

A more recent practitioner of this moral relativism is the Reverend Jesse Jackson. When Louis Farrakhan publicly threatened the life of a reporter who had disclosed a racial slur Jackson had uttered about New York City's Jewish community, Jackson

(continues on p. 170)

★ ★

WORKING PROFILE

George C. Marshall

When Harvard University awarded Marshall an honorary degree in 1947, the citation read: "To a soldier and statesman whose ability and character brook only one comparison in the history of the nation." It needed no explanation to whom the comparison referred: George Washington.

Our generation has lost touch, to some degree, with the ethical standards that evoked such a unique tribute. Those standards were, for Marshall, very clear: (1) the ability to delegate authority but still accept responsibility, (2) a commitment to democracy, (3) the combination of dignity and humility, and (4) the supremacy of public over personal interest. Here are a few examples of how those standards manifested themselves in concrete action:

- Marshall's management style resembled that of President Reagan's. But there were two critical differences: Marshall made it his business to know the character of those he entrusted with responsibility and, having delegated authority, he backed to the hilt those he had put in charge, even if the outcome was not all he had hoped for. Asked in a 1950 congressional hearing why he had joined in suppressing a report, he replied: "I did not join the suppressing of the report. I personally suppressed it."
- He recognized with great clarity that, given the centrality of the divisions of powers in the Constitution, no important national policy is likely to succeed in the long term—or even to get off the ground at all—without the executive branch's carefully cultivating legislative leaders and attempting to gain their confidence. In this respect, Marshall's character was of extraordinary value. By 1945 his patriotism, integrity, and competence were widely respected on Capitol Hill, where he was recognized as a soldier who neither mixed in politics nor questioned the principle of civilian control over the military.
- Marshall understood well the uses of formality and the dangers of becoming too friendly with those whom he must lead. Yet he inspired great affection among his subordinates. When attending United Nations meetings, he refused to live, as most other diplomats did, at the Waldorf-Astoria. He regularly attended Rotary Club meetings in the small town of Pinehurst, North Carolina, to listen patiently while guest speakers addressed foreign-policy issues.
- When he retired, Marshall rejected opportunities to take well-paid but comfortable and undemanding corporate positions. He repeatedly turned down six- and seven-figure contracts to write his memoirs: He had not, he said, spent a life in public service in order to sell his story.

SOURCE: Forrest C. Pogue, *George C. Marshall: Statesman 1945–1959.* (New York: Viking, 1987).

★ ★

characterized the episode as a "conflict" between "two very able professionals caught in a cycle that could be damaging to their career." Charles Krauthammer (1984) called that characterization "the language of moral equivalence":

> *"Two professionals"—each guy just doing his job—cleverly places the two men on the same moral plane. "Caught"—passive victims, both men done to and not doing—neatly removes any notion of guilt or responsibility. "In a cycle"—no beginning and no end—insinuates an indeterminateness in the relationship between the two men: Someone may have started this, but who can tell and what does it matter?*

Why Study Ethics? There are several practical reasons for studying ethics. First, the study of ethics can help public administrators arrive at decisions more quickly. When confronted with decisions involving conflicting values, the individual who has thought through and clarified his or her own values does not lose time wondering what to do. Such an individual can act more swiftly and assuredly. Consider these two examples:

- Beleaguered by the developing Watergate scandals, President Nixon's counsel, John Dean, produced an "enemies list" and told the Internal Revenue Service (IRS) to harass everyone on it. The IRS asked then Secretary of Treasury Shultz what to do. He remembers the episode well. "I felt," he says, "that this was something we had no business doing. So I just told the IRS, 'Do nothing.' " Soon afterward, an IRS computer kicked out Nixon's tax return for audit. Again, the IRS asked Shultz what to do. "It was an easy question to answer," he recalls. "I said, 'Go audit the president's tax return.' " Nixon was furious (Gwertzman, 1983:15).
- When former Secretary of State Cyrus R. Vance examined President Carter's plan to rescue the 53 hostages in Iran in 1980, he judged the mission profoundly ill-advised. He could have dodged and bluffed his way through questions of whether he supported Carter's move. Or he could have done what he did. Vance said that presidents must have secretaries of state who can support them publicly, and then he resigned, solely over the issue of the mission. Vance did not wait to see how the mission turned out. He saw values in conflict—namely, his ideal of American foreign policy and his loyalty to Carter—and acted swiftly.

A second reason for studying ethics is that it leads to greater consistency in decision making. Administrators who are capable of this are seen by subordinates as fair; they avoid the charge of treating employees unequally.

Third, the study of ethics can reveal the value dimensions of a decision that would otherwise seem value free. For example, consider a fairly straightforward decision involving the U.S. Postal Services' money order operation. The original question is: How could the service make money orders more profitable? But then a different question might be raised: *Should* they be made more profitable, never mind how?

Behind the second question is the recognition that money orders are used primarily by lower-income Americans who do not have checking accounts.

Fourth, the study of ethics can help public administrators make more reflective judgments—ones that can be defended in public. Generally, Americans feel awkward talking about values, as if such talk is something that "real men" do not do. Yet the public and the media continue to clamor for the very qualities that we are reluctant to talk about (honor, enterprise, justice, good faith, mercy, magnanimity, duty, beneficence, and the like). The dangers of flimsy and slipshod arguments arising when we move from ethical principles to their application in the world of administration are plentiful, and we should be aware of them. How then might we be a little more systematic in our ethical analysis?

Some Avenues for Ethical Analysis. The public administrator inevitably faces decisions that have a significant ethical dimension. Sometimes the right course is obvious. Perhaps the cases of Shultz and Vance are examples of such situations. At other times the right course of action is less clear:

- What should an agency do with an employee who thinks that the public interest overrides the interest of the agency and blows the whistle on corrupt, illegal, fraudulent, or harmful activity? In short, how do you handle a **whistle-blower**?
- How far should administrators go in trumpeting the merits of their agencies?
- What do you do if you learn that a 58-year-old employee, who has been a solid performer, lied about his age or education on his resumé?
- Must all decision making be in the open all the time?
- Should Mayor Koch have closed the Sydenham Hospital (Case 2.1)?
- Should President Reagan have fired and refused to rehire the air traffic controllers (Chapter 10)?
- How far may one go in discriminating against whites and males in order to meet affirmative action goals?
- Should regulatory agency employees take jobs with industries they have been regulating?
- What kinds of dress standards (e.g., ties, Mohawks, shorts, and so on) are appropriate—if any?
- Should employees ever be polygraphed? What about employees in the CIA or nursing homes?
- When and how do you fire a marginal employee?
- How does an administrator handle office romances, especially when one or both parties are married to someone else?

In situations like these, administrators need a more or less orderly way of thinking through the ethical implications of a decision—an approach and a language for assessing alternatives from a moral perspective. Although a rigorous review of the many ways philosophers have sought to organize what we are calling ethical analysis is beyond the scope of this book, it is possible to briefly sketch three of the more important views.

One of the most influential ethical views in American society is **contractarianism.** The central idea is that there are certain rights that should not be taken away (e.g., "life, liberty, and the pursuit of happiness") and contractual limitations on what A can do to B. The emphasis here is on the rights of the individual. In an administrative setting, contractarian reasoning manifests itself in concerns about the implications of a decision concerning the rights of an employee and clients and the fair treatment of minorities. One modern, articulate advocate of this view is Robert Nozick (1974:139) who asserts that "The holdings of a person are just if he is entitled to them by the principles of justice in acquisition and transfer."

The second view, **stakeholder analysis,** is based on the early 19th century idea of utilitarianism. Rather than use inalienable rights and contractual limitations to limit the decision maker's power, the standard of value is applied by the principle of utility, which holds that the greatest happiness of the greatest number is the measure of right and wrong. Although this view continues to have influence, it is not always practical. What do we mean by happiness—*anything* that might give an individual pleasure? And how is happiness to be measured in a vast heterogeneous population? The aims of stakeholder analyses are, however, more modest than those of utilitarianism. First, identify all groups that will be appreciably affected by the decision, and then think through how they are affected: adversely or positively—and *how* adversely or positively? At this point, one can begin to make a rough summation of the pluses and the minuses. Only if the pluses outweigh the minuses is the decision right. This approach may seem like common sense masquerading as philosophical insight, but the fact is that decisions *are* commonly made without any attempt to identify *all* potentially affected groups (the obvious ones are easy), or to think through all the implications (again, the obvious ones are easy).

Our third approach to ethical analysis—obligation to rules, principles, or right reason—comes in many versions. But the central idea is not hard to state: In making difficult choices one should adhere to some rule or principle; for example, "Do unto others as you would have them do unto you."

John Rawls provides an interesting application of this approach. Imagine rational, mutually disinterested individuals meeting. But in this hypothetical meeting, rather than make specific decisions, people choose the first principles of a conception of justice. These principles will serve to regulate all subsequent decision making.

But what are these principles they agree to? Rawls maintains they

> *would choose two rather different principles. The first requires equality in the assignment of basic rights and duties, while the second holds that social and economic inequalities . . . are just only if they result in compensating benefits for everyone, and in particular for the least advantaged members of society.*

> *These principles rule out justifying institutions on the ground that the hardships of some are offset by a greater good in the aggregate. It may be expedient but it is not just that some should have less in order that others may prosper. But there is no injustice in the greater benefits earned by a few provided that the situation of persons not so fortunate is thereby improved. (Rawls, 1970:295)*

According to Rawls, these principles are, in essence, a rigorous statement of the traditional Anglo-Saxon concept of fairness. But according to his critics, Rawls's principles are more the application of the handicapper's art to humanity. Compensatory equalization of this sort was the theme of Aristophanes' *Ecclesiazusae,* a play in which the dirty old men of Athens are compensated for their natural handicap by going to the head of the line for access to young women. At the same time, crones have first call on young men—the most cronish first of all.

Another problem with Rawls's theory of justice, at least from the standpoint of the public decision maker, is that it appears somewhat inflexible and, as such, reduces autonomy. "Invocations of justice," Walter Kaufmann writes, "help to blind a moral agent to the full range of his choices. Thus they keep people from realizing the extent of their autonomy." Kaufmann continues: "We can point to examples of love and honesty, courage and humanity. We do not know in the same way what justice is. . . . We cannot point to concrete examples. Solomon's celebrated judgment illustrates his legendary wisdom rather than his justice. What made his judgment so remarkable was that *he managed to get at the facts.*" (Kaufmann, 1973:4; emphasis added)

What Kaufmann seems to be saying here can be illustrated by a recent example. Not long ago, the Wampanoag Indian tribe filed a lawsuit against the town of Mashpee, Massachusetts (example from MacIntyre, 1984:153–54). The tribe members claimed that their tribal lands had been illegally and unconstitutionally appropriated, and they wanted them returned. As the case moved slowly through the court system, property values in Mashpee dropped drastically. In this type of situation, what is just?

Robert Nozick would be of little help since the problem in Mashpee concerns a period of time in which we do not exactly know who had a just title by "acquisition and transfer." Nor would John Rawls help since we do not know which is the least advantaged group in Mashpee. That will depend on the outcome of the case; if the tribe wins, it will be the richest group in town, but for now it is the poorest.

Nonetheless, the tribal claimants have devised a solution that seems to take Kaufmann's approach, namely, all properties of one acre or less on which a dwelling house stands shall be exempted from the suit. Strictly speaking, this solution does not represent the application of a rule; rather, it is the result of rough-and-ready reasoning involving a consideration of all salient facts (e.g., the proportion of the land claimed that comprises such properties and the number of people affected if the size of the property exempted were fixed at one acre rather than more or less).

As Kaufmann sees it, in our time one concept of integrity, which is closely linked with justice, is being replaced by another, which is associated with individual autonomy and honesty. As used here, honesty does not only mean sincerity, credibility, or frankness; rather, it is as justice was to the Greeks, the *sum* of the virtues. Surely, says Kaufmann, that is what we mean when we refer to Abraham Lincoln as "Honest Abe"—not that he could never tell a lie (that was George Washington) but that he was virtuous:

> *High standards of honesty mean that one has a conscience about what one says and what one believes. They mean that one takes some trouble to determine what speaks for and against a view, what the alternatives are, what speaks for and against each, and what alternatives are preferable on these grounds. This is the heart of rationality, the essence of the scientific method, and the meaning of intellectual integrity. (Kaufmann, 1973:178)*

But the newer concept of integrity requires an additional quality: Practice must be integrated with theory. To live in accordance with the new integrity thus requires self-confidence and courage; one must be able to *apply* the canon to the most important questions one faces. Rather than bow to authority, one decides for himself or herself.

Can the New Integrity Work? The question can only be addressed by considering additional cases drawn from the world of administration.

- William T. Coleman, Jr. served as President Gerald Ford's transportation secretary. As his style of decision making began to emerge, it became obvious that Coleman was a man of independence who accepted responsibility. He approached decisions like a judge; that is, he tried to get all the facts and then actually wrote an opinion explaining his decision in an open way. For example, when deciding on a proposed superhighway through the Virginia suburbs, he took the unusual step of personally holding a four-hour public hearing in which both sides gave their arguments. The following year, he faced an even tougher decision: whether the controversial Concorde airplane should be allowed flights into the United States. Taking careful measure of the complex—often conflicting—values of technology, the environment, and world politics, he reached a cautiously balanced decision that established a limited test period for the flights under carefully controlled conditions (Karr, 1975; Lewis, 1975). Typically, the decision was accompanied by a cogently reasoned explanation running 61 pages (*New York Times,* February 17, 1976).
- Harlan Cleveland (1975:214) has had a rich experience as a public executive—foreign aid administrator, magazine publisher, university president, political executive in Washington, and ambassador abroad. First, Cleveland challenges the notion that any one set of principles is going to be much of a guide: "Wise sayings from Mencius and Aristotle, the Bible, and the Founding Fathers, not to mention our own parents, may likewise be useful but hardly controlling: with a little help from a concordance of the Bible or Bartlett's *Familiar Quotations,* it is all too easy to find some pseudoscriptual basis for whatever one really wants to do." Having cleared the brush,

he then gives the key question that he asked himself before getting committed to a line of action. The question is not "Will I be criticized?" (After all, operating in the public sector, the answer to that question is frequently yes.) Rather, it is this: "If this action is held up to public scrutiny, will I still feel that it is what I should have done, and how I should have done it?"

Concept for Review

- accountability
- Administrative Procedures Act
- administrative responsibility
- arrogance
- competence
- contractarianism
- cowardice
- due process
- ethics
- ethnocentrism
- external and internal controls
- flexibility
- four Ps of a marketing program
- greed
- institutionalized citizen participation
- market segmentation
- new integrity
- new public administration
- professional codes
- public interest
- public relations
- representative bureaucracy
- responsiveness
- stakeholder analysis
- whistleblower

Nailing Down the Main Points

1. Given their mandate to change in pursuit of public values, public administrators need to acknowledge personal, organizational, and public values—and how they affect the public service.

2. Administrative responsibility is a collective term that covers those values people generally expect from government. Responsiveness in an organization, one such value, comes in various forms: unresponsive, usually responsive, highly responsive, and fully responsive. (The last type overcomes the "us and them" attitude by accepting its publics as voting members.) Another value associated with responsibility is flexibility, which simply means that administrators do not ignore individual groups, local concerns, or situational differences in formulating and implementing policy. People also expect that government will perform competently, act fairly (i.e., follow due process), remain accountable (not "faceless"), and perhaps above all be honest.

3. Administrative responsibility is, therefore, an ideal—a castle in the sky. Many pitfalls face any public agency trying to attain it. First is the absence within the individual manager of restraint on his or her desire. If the manager is greedy enough, then public objectives will be sacrificed to private goals. Others will be

harmed, and the public trust lost. Another countervailing force is arrogance, the belief that one always knows what is best for everyone else. Arrogance manifests itself in a variety of ways—coercive methods, distorted information, patronizing attitudes, and so forth. Another all-too-human obstacle to administrative responsibility is cowardice, or the lack of courage to do the right thing when one clearly perceives what the right thing is.

4. To help overcome the forces mentioned in the previous point, governments rely on four categories of control: internal formal, internal informal, external formal, and external informal. No writer advocates exclusive reliance upon any one of these four, however.

   Even in combination, measures such as the following have distinct limitations in making the ideal of administrative responsibility a reality: executive, legislative, and judicial control; interest group representation; citizen participation; professional codes; representative bureaucracy; and public interest.

5. Recent work in the field of moral philosophy has, however, sparked renewed interest in moral reasoning. Public administrators can take a number of steps to see and resolve ethical problems. First, by studying ethics, they can learn to think in principled terms and use concepts like justice as fairness, autonomous morality, equity versus efficiency, representativeness versus merit, political responsiveness versus professionalism, and other ethical guidelines suggested in this chapter. These principles are powerful decision criteria that enhance the capacity to discover and communicate ethical alternatives. Studying ethics also allows managers to sort out ethical priorities early, before problems arise. Ethics helps a manager set a good, consistent personal example for employees. This is perhaps the sine qua non for administrative responsibility.

Problems

1. "The decade of the 1980s has seen a dramatic increase in unethical behavior by government employees at all levels. From the inner circle of the White House to local elected and appointed officials, scandal after scandal has been followed by indictments and convictions detailed in banner headlines in newspapers and reported on the evening electronic media. The 1990s will almost certainly witness the unethical fallout of its predecessor decade." Do you think things are as bad as suggested in this quote?

2. Generally, the public accepts the right of business to publicize and advertise, even though the customer pays for it in the long run, but it often regards a similar expenditure of funds for government information as frivolous or a waste of the taxpayer's money. Would you conclude therefore that the public tends to apply a double standard? Why or why not?

3. The aim of the ombudsman, a Swedish idea, is to create a representative or agent of the legislation to protect citizens' rights against bureaucratic abuse.

More precisely, the ombudsman is available to hear complaints of any citizen against erroneous, unfair, or even impolite action by government officials; and then, if necessary, investigate the complaint, publicize any abuse, and recommend corrective action. Research this idea further and then report on whether the United States should have the ombudsman.

4. Toward the end of the 18th century Edmund Burke said: "Constitute government how you please, infinitely the greater part of it must depend upon the exercise of the powers which are left at large to the prudence and uprightness of minister of state." Which ideas expressed in this chapter do you think Burke would be most comfortable with? Least comfortable?

5. Select one of the following works to discuss in class in terms of the ethical or value questions it raises for public administration:
Anouilh, *Antigone.*
Anouilh, *Becket.*
Arden, *Left Handed Liberty.*
Arrighi, *An Ordinary Man.*
Austen, *Mansfield Park.*
Bolt, *A Man for All Seasons.*
Boyer, *Don Juan in Hell.*
Brecht, *Galileo.*
Camus, *Caligula.*
Ibsen, *A Doll's House.*
Ibsen, *Enemy of the People.*
Kippardt, *In the Matter of J. Robert Oppenheimer.*
MacLeish, *J. B.*
Melville, *Billy Budd.*
Shaw, *Mrs. Warren's Profession.*
Stone and Edwards, *1776.*
Vidal, *The Best Man.*
Wolfe, *Bonfire of the Vanities.*

6. "In governing boards (of regents, trustees, or directors), in regulatory commissions, in regular government departments, or in corporate executive suites, there must always be provision for talking out in private the most controversial issues, for compromise and facesaving and graceful backing down. If all boards were required by law to have all their meetings in public, that would just increase the frequency of lunches and dinners among their members, as they negotiate in informal caucus the positions they are going to take in the formal meetings" (Cleveland, 1972:119). Do you agree with this statement? If yes, what are its implications for "sunshine laws" (discussed in Chapter 2)?

7. Should public officials ever lie? (Hint: See Bok, 1978)

8. Suggest a more ethical approach to the treatment of experimental "subjects" than the one you read about on pp. 165–166. Does your university have guidelines for experiments with human subjects?

9. How far should one go in embellishing one's resumé? The governor of a large northeastern state discovered that his newly appointed commissioner of commerce had credentials at variance with the facts. The commissioner, 33 years old, had claimed to have been "a financial adviser to the Vatican" and a "partner" and a "principal" in a New York investment banking concern. Fact: The commissioner had been a low-ranking associate in a London-based investment banking firm that was doing work for the Vatican. Fact: He was not a partner but one of 30 vice presidents. The commissioner told reporters he had attended Oxford University on a scholarship. Fact: Oxford said he was not a scholarship student. The commissioner told reporters that he came from a poor family. Fact: His father was a lawyer who owned a textile mill. Discuss this incident from the governor's standpoint and then from the commissioner's.

10. Explain how you might use ethical analysis to decide the proper action in each of the 12 incidents listed on p. 171.

11. The county official has authorized the purchase of 20 new sedans. State and county practice requires purchase from the lowest bidder. A local dealer will supply the cars for $220,000, while a dealer 30 miles away will do it for $200,000. What should you do? (Based on Steinberg and Austern, 1990:9–10.)

12. What are the major advantages and disadvantages of the two codes of conduct presented in this chapter (pp. 164–165)? Which would you prefer? Why?

13. What do you do when an experienced, valued, and otherwise highly reliable employee confesses that he has been dipping in the till? Although the amounts he "borrowed" from petty cash never exceeded $100, he did write false receipts to cover them until he could make repayment.

CASE 4.1

★★★★★★★★★★★★★★★★★★★★★★★★★★★★★★★★★★★

Doing the Right Thing

One definition of ethics is deciding the right thing to do. What makes this a good definition, besides its brevity, is that the term *deciding* serves to remind us that ethical reasoning is a process, while the verb *do* reminds us that the process should eventually result in some human action.

Perhaps the best place to begin thinking about ethics is with those daily, person-to-person relationships that tie us all together: husband-to-wife, parent-to-child, friend-to-friend.

Derek is a graduating high school senior who has always turned to you for advice. Although he is several years your junior, you have developed a great admiration for this bright young man. Despite the poverty of his family, he has worked hard in school and done quite well.

But today Derek comes to you with anxiety written all over his face. A friend of his, he explains, illegally acquired answers to the college entrance examination, sold them to a few students, and gave him a copy free. Derek used these answers when he took his exam.

Now he is beginning to feel bad. He has once again come to you for advice.

Case Question

Try to imagine this young man sitting across from you. The two of you are alone. As friend and confidant, what do you say to him?

CASE 4.2

★★★★★★★★★★★★★★★★★★★★★★★★★★★★★★★★★★★★

Blind Ambition

Background Note on Watergate

Watergate, the great political scandal of the early 1970s, saw a president manage to avoid impeachment only by resigning from office. The roots of the resignation lay in Richard Nixon's secretive style of governing and in his concern with opposition to the Vietnam War at home. He established his own clandestine group, known as the "plumbers" because they were supposed to stop leaks of government information.

Then, on the evening of June 17, 1971, five men carrying cameras and wiretapping equipment broke into the headquarters of the Democratic National Committee at the Watergate apartment complex in Washington. An alert security guard foiled the break-in, and the men were arrested; two other accomplices, E. Howard Hunt and G. Gordon Liddy, were apprehended soon after. Two of the accused men had worked as security consultants in the White House, a third held a responsible position on the President's reelection committee.

Soon afterward, the cover-up began, with Nixon himself stating "categorically" that "no one in his administration, presently employed, was involved in the bizarre incident." But things began to unravel. Facing conviction and jail, the burglars began to talk. Two reporters from *The Washington Post* kept the story alive. A Senate committee launched an investigation. In May 1973, the committee would hear John Dean, White House counsel, implicate President Nixon in the cover-up. When another aide revealed to the committee that Nixon had a secret taping system, it was no longer simply Dean's word against Nixon's—now it might be possible to find out what actually happened.

At first Nixon stonewalled, refusing to release the tapes in the name of executive privilege and national security. But eventually a lower court forced him to release the tapes. They were heavily edited and contained a suspicious 18-minute gap during which Nixon had met with his top two aides, Haldeman and Ehrlichman, three days after the break-in. On August 5, 1973, the Supreme Court ruled unanimously that Nixon must release the unexpurgated tapes, which contained shocking evidence that he had ordered the cover-up. It became apparent that he had lied to the American people. Four days later Nixon became the first American president to resign from office.

But this case is about neither Nixon nor Constitutional crises. It is about a young man, John Dean, and what might be termed a "power fix." The case begins on a warm afternoon in May 1970, when Dean, who had a relaxed and enjoyable job at the Justice Department, was asked if he would be interested in working at the White House.

Reaching for the Top

Not long after he indicated his interest in the position, Dean found himself on his way to the President's home in San Clemente, California, to meet with Haldeman. As Dean drove his Porsche to the airport, he fantasized how he might beat a speeding ticket simply by saying he was on his way to the Western White House.

When Dean finally arrived at his destination, he was pleasantly embarrassed when an officious airline executive whisked him off the plane ahead of the other passengers and handed his suitcase to a young marine lieutenant who took him to a waiting helicopter. Controlling his excitement, Dean thought that, if nothing else came of the trip, at least he could call the stewardess for a date. She must have been wondering who he was. Dean was wondering too.

Later that day, Dean met for the first time Bob Haldeman, Nixon's chief of staff, who described the job of president's counsel. It would not involve program or policy development but rather keeping the White House informed about domestic disorders and antiwar demonstrations, investigating possible conflicts of interest among staff, and generally assisting staff with legal problems. Or, as Haldeman said with a smirk, "doing whatever you goddamn lawyers do for those who need you."

The next day Dean was ushered in to meet the president for the first time. Nixon asked Dean if he was interested in the job. With a tremble in his voice, Dean replied that it would be an honor.

The Greasy Pole

Dean quickly adapted to the White House routine and formulated a plan of advancement. As he saw it, he and his small staff would have to build a practice just like any other law firm. To convince his principal client, the president, that his law office was the "best in town," he would have to convince the people surrounding the president first.

The plan worked and Dean was soon enjoying many coveted White House status symbols (e.g., a daily copy of the president's news summary and an Army Signal Corps telephone in his home). His small law firm grew.

By the beginning of 1971, Dean was scouting for more important cases, even though the members of his staff were hopelessly overworked. He realized that his office could perform intelligence work for the White House—after all, he was already doing investigative work in conjunction with his conflict-of-interest duties. It should be relatively easy to search the military records of some antiwar Vietnam veterans, to answer questions about directors of films that satirized Nixon, to find out what reporters really knew about other politicians, and so forth. He advertised his office as the place where questions would be answered. Dean figured that intelligence would be more valuable to policy makers than dry legal advice. Dean was quickly finding out what interested his bosses.

By April 1971, it became apparent to Dean that the president's reelection was the highest priority in the White House. Accordingly, Dean began to expand the role of the counsel's office to all intelligence that would be of interest to the president in his campaign. This required that he work closely with the Committee to Reelect the President (CREEP), which had its own intelligence operation headed by G. Gordon Liddy.

Damage Control

At 2:00 A.M. on Saturday, June 17, 1972, Liddy's team was caught and arrested in the Watergate office of the Democratic National Committee. Their mission had been to replace an electronic eavesdropping device in the telephone of the committee chairman.

A few days later Dean met with Haldeman and Ehrlichman to discuss whether Dean's old boss, Attorney General John

Mr. and Mrs. Nixon in the Oval Office as some family business is conducted. White House Counsel John Dean (right) looks on. (Official White House photo)

Mitchell, should be removed as head of the reelection committee. Dean felt a surge of importance at the thought of sitting in judgment of a man of such consequence. Be that as it may, a few days later Mitchell was gone. Dean was becoming possessed of the "toughness" he imagined generals displaying in combat when sacrificing lives for the overall objective.

Haldeman's staff was now allowing Dean access to the executive mess. Others on the White House staff began to sense Dean's new importance. His travel requests were no longer questioned; he was above bureaucratic hassles. Dean even broke off relations with his fiancée, reasoning that his prospects as a bachelor were now looking too good.

As the cover-up progressed through July and August, Dean was amazed at how successful it was. At the end of August, the president, whose popularity remained quite high, held a news conference. Dean turned on his television set, listening with one ear as he continued to work. The conference dragged on until suddenly something caught Dean's attention.

In response to a reporter's question, Nixon was explaining that a special prosecutor was unnecessary because no fewer than five investigations were already under way, all of which, he said, had received "at my direction" the "total cooperation" of the White House. Dean was stunned because these five investigations were precisely the ones that he had been trying to delay, deflect, and contain. What Nixon said next was even more shocking: "In addition to that within our own staff, under my direction, the counsel to the President, Mr. Dean, had conducted a complete investigation of all leads which might involve any present members of the White House staff or anybody in the government. I can say categorically that his investigation indicates that no one in the White House staff, no one in this Administration, presently employed, was involved in this very bizarre incident."

Even though it was a brazen lie, Dean was ecstatic to be so recognized by the president on national television. Obviously, Nixon knew how hard Dean had been working to keep the Watergate mess from spilling over everyone. The fact that Dean had never heard of a "Dean investigation," much less conducted one, did not seem important to him. He was basking in the glory of being publicly perceived as the man the president turned to with a difficult problem like Watergate. Later, upon sober reflection, Dean began to wonder if he was being set up. Could he become the fall guy?

In any event, the Dean-engineered cover-up continued. Each day brought new threats, new dramas, and more legal strategies. There were clandestine conversations about hush money, attaché cases filled with FBI reports, fights to stall discovery proceedings in civil suits, crisis calls, coaching sessions for witnesses being interviewed by the FBI, reports on the criminal case involving the burglars, payment of money to defendants, and shredding of documents.

Riding high from the cover-up success, Dean was not bashful in expanding even more the power and perquisites of his office. He redecorated his office for the sake of redecorating. The president was now taking Dean into his confidence more and more. Near the president and his aides, Dean felt tough and hopeful, but away from them he had doubts about the ultimate success of the cover-up.

Closing In

By December, Haldeman and Ehrlichman were increasing pressure on Dean to transform his mystical "investigation" into a historical reality. They told him it would "clear the decks" for the president's second term. The Dean Report would put Watergate behind them. Dean did not like the idea, since a public report with his name on it would associate him even more with Watergate. Yet his ambition kept him from flatly saying no. Haldeman and Ehrlichman continued to maneuver Dean into preparing the report. Dean spent most of his evenings at home, escaping with liquor the events of the days.

On February 7, 1973, the Senate established a select committee to investigate the Watergate break-in and related 1972 campaign improprieties. Ehrlichman and Haldeman redoubled their efforts to get Dean to prepare the Dean Report. They put it bluntly: It would give the President a public alibi if the cover-up were to collapse.

Breaking Point

Dean spent a few days in March at Camp David, ostensibly to write the long-awaited Dean Report. He was accompanied by his new wife, Maureen. She wanted to talk about what was in his head:

"You didn't have anything to do with that stupid break-in, I hope."

"Not directly. That's not my problem. It's what happened after those guys got arrested."

"Is the President in trouble? I thought you were going to warn him."

"I did, but I was like Caspar Milquetoast going in to the boss for a raise. I went in there Wednesday and tried to paint a picture of what the problems were. I tried to be as dramatic as I could. He listened, but by the end of our meeting he had turned me around again. Out I went, almost thanking him for not listening to me. Just call me Mr. Milquetoast, dear."

"Are you afraid of the President?"

I paused to think about the question. "Yeah, kinda. I'm not really afraid of the man who is President of the United States anymore. He's really no different than any-

John W. Dean III. (A photo taken in March 1973, when the Watergate cover-up was first unraveling.) (Official White House photo)

body else. That was something that I had to realize slowly. But I'm afraid of who he really is and the power he commands as he sits in the Oval Office. If this cover-up goes on, he's going to be in really serious trouble, and I can't believe he doesn't recognize that. He knows he's got a problem, and he knows there is no easy answer, because I'm not the only one working for him who's got a serious problem."

"You mean Haldeman is involved, too?" she asked.

"Yep, and Ehrlichman and Mitchell and others."

"That's awful, John. What are you all going to do?"

"Let's talk about it after I sort it all out. I'm thinking of getting myself a lawyer, some guy who really knows the criminal law, and having him tell me how serious my problem is."

As we came out of the woods near the helicopter pad, Mo asked, "That report you're writing—is this what it's all about?"

"Not exactly. In fact, not at all. It's an idea of Ehrlichman's to protect the President by giving him a report that says everything is okay and no one in the White House has any problems. It says everything is just hunky-dory."

"That's not true, though, is it?"

"No, it's not."

"Then, John, you shouldn't write that report. That's not very smart."

She was right, but her innocence annoyed me. She seemed so far removed from all the shadings of lies that make up political life. How could she possibly understand the pressure to just do something when the President wants it, regardless of whether you think it's dumb or wrong? Or that my doing such things had enabled her to enjoy Camp David and countless other White House privileges? Still, even though she knew nothing of the details of Watergate, or the rationale behind the report, or all that had gone on before, she had hit the mark intuitively.

Case Questions

1. What are the issues raised in this case? What is the most striking aspect of this portrait to you?
2. How would you characterize John Dean? What motivated him?
3. What might Dean have done that he did not do?
4. After studying Dean's crimes, one young attorney said, "There but for fortune go I." Do you agree or disagree?

Case Reference

John Dean III, *Blind Ambition* (New York: Simon & Schuster, 1976). Copyright © 1976 by John W. Dean. Reprinted by permission of Simon & Schuster.

CASE 4.3

★★★

Eldridge's Complaint

The Letter

The warm May sun shined friendly on Norton, Virginia, a small coal-mining town in the southwestern corner of the state. George Eldridge noticed a kindly western wind beginning to blow down from the mountains as he journeyed out to his mailbox. Even with his arthritis and diabetes, he felt pretty good—at least until he saw the legal-sized envelope with the Social Security Administration (SSA) logo. His name had been typed—this was no form letter announcing something innocuous like a ZIP code change. He immediately ripped it open and began to read, all the way to the last line: "unless additional evidence is submitted which shows that you are still unable to work because of your impairment."

Eldridge had had problems with the SSA before. Five years earlier, in 1967, when he first applied for complete disability benefits, his application was rejected. He requested a hearing before a hearing examiner and received a favorable ruling.

All went well for a couple of years, then, after reviewing his case but without seeing him or performing any medical tests, the state agency administering the disability program for SSA decided to terminate Eldridge's benefits.

Eldridge again requested that the agency reconsider his case. Feeling that the SSA decision-making process had been unfair and arbitrary, he also decided to challenge SSA on constitutional grounds. Specifically, Eldridge's attorney would argue that it was a violation of due process of law (protected by the Fifth Amendment) for Secretary David Mathews, who was responsible for SSA, to terminate a disability recipient's benefits without first affording that person an oral hearing. In other words, administrators should not be able to make decisions that will severely jeopardize a citizen's liberty or property without holding a hearing.

It was not until March 1971 that Eldridge got his hearing. The administrative law judge ordered payments resumed; accordingly, the district court declared the constitutional case moot. Eldridge remembered these past battles all too well. Now, it looked as though he and his attorney would have to fight them again.

The Road to the Supreme Court

Eldridge could have chosen again to battle his way through reconsideration, hearing, and SSA Appeals Council (a process known as "exhaustion of administrative remedies") to get to the district court. There, a judge would have reviewed the record to see if there was substantial evidence to support SSA's decision (a process known as the "substantial evidence rule"). But Eldridge and his attorney, Donald Earls, were willing to concede that the agency had abided by all statutes and regulations. The crux of their argument was to be that those regulations were unconstitutional. Therefore, they took the issue directly to court.

On April 9, 1973, a federal district judge held that the government must provide a predetermination hearing for those receiving disability benefits under Title II of the Social Security Act, just as the Supreme Court had required a hearing for those receiving benefits under Title IV, Aid to Families with Dependent Children (*Goldberg v. Kelly*). The government had argued that a decision in favor of Eldridge would result in an intolerable financial and administrative burden, but the judge concluded that procedural due process does not exist to minimize costs and maximize efficiency.

The government promptly appealed this decision to the U.S. Circuit Court of Appeals and lost. The government then appealed to the Supreme Court.

The Arguments

On October 6, 1975, the Supreme Court heard oral arguments from Eldridge's attorney and Solicitor General Robert H. Bork. The fact that the solicitor general himself would make the argument was an indication of how important the case was to the government.

Essentially, there were three parts to Bork's argument:

- Existing procedures are fair; Eldridge just lacked the patience to use the available alternatives.
- Because the statute does not require proof of indigence, disability recipients are not as needy as welfare recipients.
- The interests of the government in avoiding excessive administrative costs outweigh Eldridge's interest in continued receipt of benefits. Moreover, a pretermination hearing requirement would pose costs that the government cannot at this time afford.

Bork elaborated on the last point as follows:

We are, in effect, dealing with a cost benefit judgment; and so viewed the question becomes really how many? The decision of this case will have a heavy impact upon the decision of how many decisional processes of government must be conformed to a judicial model rather than to an administrative model. I think that is important and clearly there has to be a stopping point somewhere to the imposition of judicial models upon governmental decision making because it is very expensive; and in some circumstances, which I would contend this is one, adds little or nothing to the alternative procedures provided. . . .

It would be nice to say, I suppose, that the system must be perfect. Nobody must ever be terminated, no matter how temporarily, but indeed I don't think any legal process, any chemical process, or any industrial process ever can afford to remove the last bit of impurities in that process. It gets extraordinarily expensive. Indeed, it begins to defeat the ends of the process. I can put an approximate dollar value on both sides of this due process equation. [The total figure he calculated for increased costs to government was $25 million per year.]

As Bork returned to his seat, Eldridge's attorney, Donald Earls, rose to make his argument:

- Eldridge had already been completely through the administrative process twice. Both times he had lost on the paper review but prevailed in the hearing. In one case, 18 months had elapsed between the termination decision and the hearing.
- Welfare was not a viable option to support him while he exhausted his

administrative remedies, since welfare benefits (1) may require more stringent standards than qualification for disability and (2) begin only after a lengthy investigation.

■ Eldridge had as much entitlement to an opportunity for an evidentiary hearing concerning his termination of disability benefits as a welfare recipient concerning his or her welfare check. In each of the following instances, case law mandates a prior hearing: a wage earner concerning his or her paycheck, a parolee concerning his or her freedom, a prison inmate concerning his or her good-time credits, a consumer concerning his or her old stove, an uninsured motorist concerning his or her license, an elderly person concerning his or her Medicare benefits, a student concerning his or her suspension from school.

Earls attacked Bork's contention that a claimant would not suffer because of lost benefits: "I feel in the George Eldridge case, where Mr. Eldridge was required to sleep in one bed with five children, lost his home that he had worked all his life for [first] as a laborer on the railroad and then as a soda distributor, driving a truck and carrying cases of soda: there certainly he lost everything which could not be recouped . . . . This is what happened in the George Eldridge case, and this is what happens in many of the cases."

Case Questions

1. If you were on the Supreme Court, how would you decide? Support your decision.
2. What is the public interest in this case?

Case References

Matthews v. Eldridge, 424 U.S. 319 (1976); Philip J. Cooper, "*Matthews v. Eldridge:* The Anatomy of an Administrative Law Case," *Public Law and Public Administration,* (Palo Alto, Calif.: Mayfield, 1983), pp. 355–401.

CASE 4.4

★★★★★★★★★★★★★★★★★★★★★★★★★★★★★★★★★★★

Relocating a State School

The division of corrections in a midwestern state has decided that the state boys' school is grossly inadequate and is a dangerous firetrap. After some struggle, the state legislature has appropriated $6 million for a new reformatory.

The division wishes to build the reformatory in a state forest. Such a location would provide attractive surroundings, isolation from cities, and constructive work for the boys.

Unfortunately, conservation groups issue vehement protests and threaten court action to block the move. They also start a public campaign to force the governor and the state corrections board to reverse the decision. Meanwhile, the community in which the present reformatory is located organizes a committee to keep it there. The new reformatory appears to be in deep trouble.

Case Question

As a public relations director for the welfare department, what are your recommendations?

Case Reference

Based on Scott M. Cutlip and Allen H. Center, *Effective Public Relations* (Englewood Cliffs, N.J.: Princeton-Hall, 1982), p. 521.

★★★★★★★★★★★★★★★★★★★★★★★★★★★★★★★★★★★

PART II

★ ★ ★ ★ ★ ★ ★ ★ ★ ★ ★ ★ ★ ★ ★ ★ ★ ★ ★ ★

Program Management

CHAPTER 5 Planning

Introduction

Planning is the keystone of the arch of program management, and government success is often synonymous with planning success. Quite properly, then, Part II of this book on managing the public sector begins with planning.

As will be explained shortly, planning covers a far wider spectrum of meanings than can be encompassed in this chapter. Indeed, many of the things said in Chapter 2 about policymaking apply to planning, which we interpret in this chapter quite broadly: reasoning about how an organization will get where it wants to go.

The essence of planning is to see opportunities and threats in the future and to exploit or combat them by deci sions taken in the present. It is therefore hardly an overstatement to say that planning, as defined here, shapes the whole field of public administration. It determines the limits of government responsibility, the allocation of resources and distribution of costs, the division of labor, and the extent of public controls. Nor is it an overstatement to say that the magnitude of current problems—such as pollution of air and water, exploitation of natural resources, and decline in the quality of urban life—are related to our inability to plan effectively.

If planning is an important area of public administration, it is also a relatively neglected one. Recent attempts to remedy this neglect of planning in the literature of public administration have yielded almost as much confusion as progress. For this reason, we begin our discussion by attempting to clarify what we mean, and what we do not mean, by planning. Then, we examine the rational model of the planning process. The importance of this model should be underscored: It sets a framework for organizing our thinking about the planning process and foreshadows the chapters that follow.

But this formal, rational model must be reconciled with the messy political realities we discussed in Part I. The third section therefore presents another view of planning—logical incrementalism—that builds on the first model yet takes into account the realities of planning in a world of politics.

By the end of the third section, the main goals of this chapter will essentially have been achieved. Nevertheless, two more sections follow. The fourth section discusses forecasting techniques. If, as we said, the essence of planning is to see opportunities and threats in the future, then the link between planning and this section should be fairly obvious. The fifth and final section reviews the different ways in which the term *planning* is used in public administration. Although I am convinced that the model of the planning process presented in the earlier sections has the widest application, students of public administration should still be conversant with more specialized types of planning.

Toward a Definition of Planning

Since the thrust of this book is toward the integration—not the fragmentation—of thought, planning will be treated as a general process, recognizable in a great number of human situations. The definition of planning that opened this chapter reflects this more general approach. Planning is reasoning about how an organization will get where it wants to go. Its essence is to see opportunities and threats in the future and to exploit or combat them by decisions taken in the present.

To really grasp the dynamics of this process, it is of course necessary to understand its components. What, for example, is a plan? How does a plan differ from a policy? From a program? For our purposes, a **policy** is a statement of goals and of the relative importance attached to each goal. It is translated into a **plan** by specifying the objectives to be attained. A proposed set of specific actions intended to implement a plan is called a **program.**

A simple example will perhaps clarify these terse terminological stipulations. Assume that the mayor of a city has among his or her goals an increase in the physical safety of the city's inhabitants and an improvement in housing conditions. The mayor might then announce a policy that these goals, in the order stated, are to have priority over all other goals. A plan to implement this policy might specify the objectives of (1) reducing the rate of crimes of violence in the city and the death rate from traffic accidents by 25 percent and (2) providing an additional 10,000 housing units. A program would spell out in detail the action to be taken to achieve these objectives; for example, increasing the police force by 1,000 and providing city-backed, long-term loans to construction firms (Helmer, 1968:14–16).

The crucial difference among the terms *policy, plan,* and *program* is level of generality. More specifically, an increasing number of writers suggest that the term *policy* should be reserved for statements of intention and direction of a relatively high order. Harold Lasswell (1951:5–8) put it succinctly: "The word *policy* is commonly used to designate the *most* important choices made either in organized or in private life." The emphasis, then, is not upon the topical issues of the moment but upon the fundamental problems of society.

As we shall see below, these terminological stipulations are more than mere academic hairsplitting; they help to make better policy. Possibly, Confucius had something like this in mind when he said that because actions follow words, he would, if ruler of the world, fix the meaning of words.

The Rational Planning Model

To provide a meaningful and systematic framework for understanding the planning process, the now familiar and well-established model of the rational planning process is presented. According to this model, a planner is acting rationally if he or she undertakes the following five interrelated steps:

1. Identify the problem or problems to be solved and the opportunities to be seized upon.
2. Design alternative solutions or courses of action (i.e., policies, plans, and programs) to solve the problems, or seize upon the opportunities and forecast the consequences and effectiveness of each alternative.
3. Compare and evaluate the alternatives with each other and with the forecasted consequences of unplanned development, and choose the alternative whose probable consequences would be preferable.
4. Develop a plan of action for implementing the alternative selected, including budgets, project schedules, regulatory measures, and the like.
5. Maintain the plan on a current basis through feedback and review of information.

Although these steps are treated separately and in linear sequence, in actual practice, they represent a cyclic process. Evaluation procedures, for example, enter into the

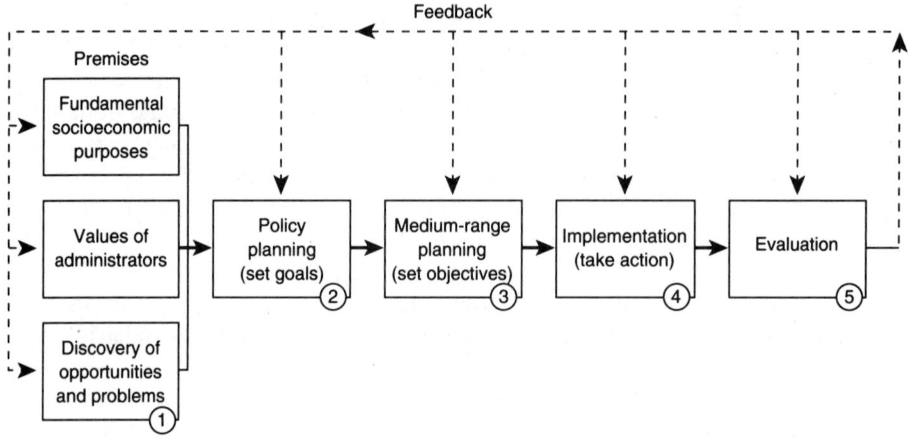

FIGURE 5-1
Basic Rational Planning Model

process at the outset in the identification of problems and opportunities; they also influence the design of alternative solutions. Likewise, the problems of implementation enter into the design stages as constraints that must be taken into account. For this reason, it is probably preferable to present the model not as a list of steps but as a dynamic and iterative process. In this model, shown in Figure 5-1, the five steps have been rearranged in the form of a dynamic model and are indicated by the circled numbers.

Premises

At the left of the model are three underlying foundations of any government planning effort. The first, fundamental organizational socioeconomic purposes, refers to those underlying ends that society expects of its governmental institutions. Basically, this means that society demands that governments utilize the resources at their disposal to satisfy the wants of society. It is important for administrators to keep in mind this underlying reason for the existence of government. It explains why, as governments become larger and society becomes more complex, the things society wants from government become more numerous and sometimes contradictory.

The second fundamental set of foundations for planning are the values the top administrators hold—for example: conservation of resources, efficiency, beauty, equity, pluralism, individuality, and participation. Included here too would be the values of the elected officials, both executive (e.g., president, governor, and mayor) and legislative (e.g., Congress, legislature, and council). In fact, in the earlier stages of the planning process, where policy decisions are made, the influence of this group—especially through legislation—is usually decisive. Needless to say, their values do not always coincide with those of the administrator.

We now come to the final foundation of any government planning effort. A cardinal purpose of planning is to discover future opportunities and make plans to exploit them. Likewise, basic to planning is the detection of obstructions or problems that must be removed from the road ahead. The most effective plans are those that exploit opportunities and remove obstacles on the basis of an objective and systematic survey of the future. There is, in short, an enormous payoff to the skilled probing of the future and to relating the results of that probing to an unbiased study of an agency's strengths, weaknesses, and purpose. For example, if a city is planning for orderly community development, the regular forecasting of change is vital. What should such a forecast include? At least such factors as number of people, number of school children, number and types of new residential and other buildings, and number and location of automobiles. Whenever possible, the forecast should include changes in the characteristics of the population, of land use, of the economic conditions, and of transportation patterns.

Our third premise of planning implies, however, more than good forecasts. The effective planner must also be able to discern clearly and accurately what the problem is. As the French novelist Georges Bernanas once wrote, the worst, the most corrupting, of lies are problems poorly stated. How one defines a problem is of crucial importance. In the 1960s, Washington planners defined the war in Vietnam as a "classic revolutionary war." Accordingly, President Kennedy reacted to that definition with the doctrine of counterinsurgency. But with hindsight it is clear that this approach was wrong. The guerrillas in South Vietnam did *not* achieve decisive results on their own; there was no popular uprising. They merely served to harass and distract both the United States and South Vietnam so that North Vietnam regular forces could win in conventional battles (Summers, 1982).

Today politicians and social scientists continue to struggle to understand the problem of poverty in America's inner cities. If one defines poverty in terms of a lack of certain necessities (dental care, food, education, etc.), then the solution will be a variety of government programs designed to provide each of those necessities (as did President Johnson's Great Society). If, however, one defines poverty as simply a lack of money—and social science as well as common sense suggest that well-being rises with income—then the solution will be something like a guaranteed income (as was proposed by President Nixon). If one defines poverty in terms of a lack of jobs, then the solution will be enterprise zones to encourage businesses to expand in inner cities or a job corps in which government provides a job to every able-bodied citizen. Finally, if one defines poverty in terms of a breakdown of family values and the attendant growth in unwed teenage mothers, then the strategy will be more or less hands-off, since governments are not particularly good at changing values. Clearly, how one defines a problem makes a big difference.

Attention to the definition of problems, however, must not replace attention to the discovery of opportunities. Actually, by consistently directing performance toward opportunity rather than toward problems, the administrator will tend to foster high morale. In contrast, the problem-focused organization is an organization on the defensive; it feels that it has performed well if things do not get worse. In short, administrators who want to create and maintain the spirit of achievement in their agencies stress opportunity.

Policy Planning

The next major structural element in Figure 5-1 is policy planning. Policy planning is the process of determining goals and their priorities. It is at this point in the planning process that the influence of political leadership is especially important.

According to journalist David Halberstam (1969:370–71), during the Vietnam War the highest level of American policymakers refused to accept the necessity for making decisions at this level. They tried to delay such decisions and thus buy a little more time. These policymakers "were above all functional, operational, *tactical* men, not really intellectuals, and tactical men think in terms of options, while intellectuals less so; intellectuals might think in terms of the sweep of history and might believe that 12 months would make little difference in Vietnam."

Daniel P. Moynihan, who served in the executive branch under three presidents before entering the Senate, argues that one of the more important things about the structure of American government is that too much public policy is defined in terms of *program* rather than true *policy.* The problem with the program approach is that it deals only with a part of the system; policy, on the other hand, seeks to respond to the system in its entirety:

> *The idea of policy is not new. We have for long been accustomed to the idea of foreign policy, including defense policy. Since 1946 Congress has mandated an employment and income policy more or less explicitly based on a "general theory" of the endlessly intricate interconnections of such matters. Yet our ways of behavior resist this: only great crises, great dangers, seem to evoke the effort. Or have seemed able to do so in the past. I believe, however, that a learning process of sorts has been going on. Increasingly the idea of system-wide policies commends itself to persons of responsibility in public affairs as an approach both desirable and necessary. (Moynihan, 1973:273)*

Apparently, President Carter was unable to act on this principle. He came to the presidency with no agenda. He did not see the presidency as a chance to put any program into effect but rather as a job to be performed skillfully. Rather than *tell* his energy secretary, in broad outline, what energy policy he wanted developed, he *asked* the secretary for a policy.

Carter's economic policy pleased neither conservatives nor liberals. Consider these zigzags: During his campaign, Carter endorsed standby wage and price control authority; between election and inauguration, he became an opponent. A week after inauguration, he declared the economy stagnant and proposed a package of stimulative spending increases and tax cuts; less than three months later, he abandoned the cornerstones of the package and, citing inflation as the principal economic menace, proposed the first of four anti-inflation programs. A year later, he again asked for a major tax cut, only to have to again delay it and scale it back in response to inflationary pressures. In 1978, he offered his second and third anti-inflation programs. But after a week of adverse reaction, the administration turned to the Federal Reserve for a sharp increase in interest rates as a rescue. In 1979, Carter began the decontrol of crude oil prices, having failed two years earlier to win approval of a tax that would have continued those price controls.

"Each time a policy was developed, the policy was too weak for the problems that appeared," Barry P. Bosworth, Carter's director of the Council on Wage and Price Stability and now a Brookings Institution economist said. "We had no overall framework of what are the things we stand for and what are our priorities" (*New York Times,* March 23, 1980).

By way of contrast, let us consider the clear goals of the Apollo mission. Write Sayles and Chandler (1971:21):

> *While both purposes and plans need to have a great deal of flexibility to allow for changes in sentiment, new information, and unforeseen problems and opportunities, objectives need to be relatively fixed and highly specific. They become the emotional symbols, the universally visible target that attracts and holds political support. They can also become the catalyst that mobilizes resources and encourages whole new technologies by capturing the imagination, the commitment, and the dedication of both those who will support the program and those who will actually do the work.*

Medium-Range Planning

The best policy is only a policy—that is, good intentions—unless it is transformed into action. Medium-range planning is an important step in that direction. At this stage in the planning process, detailed, coordinated, and comprehensive plans are made for an agency to deploy the resources necessary to attain the goals laid down in the policy-planning stage. We are concerned, in particular, with two aspects of this stage: (1) the design of alternatives and (2) the analysis of each alternative in terms of its consequences.

Design of Alternatives. Let us return for a moment to the issue of poverty. It can be said that in the last three years of the Johnson administration there was fairly wide agreement that the existing welfare system constituted a major problem. Further, there was even considerable consensus on the goals of the welfare problem: to raise incomes of the poor; to narrow disparities among states in benefit levels; to reduce inequities in treatment of different kinds of poor people; to increase incentives to work; to remove incentives to break up families. But on the question of how to achieve these goals—that is, what the objectives should be—polarization was the rule.

According to Alice M. Rivlin (1971:19–21), who served as assistant secretary for planning and evaluation during the Johnson administration, at least three alternative strategies on how to attain these goals were available and each had its spokespeople both within and outside the administration. One of these approaches was to improve the existing welfare system by a series of amendments to make it more uniform and more nearly adequate. Another was put forth by the advocates of a negative income tax. And the third was family or children allowance.

It would be a serious mistake to jump to the easy conclusion that the existence of such widely divergent alternatives is a bad thing. Consider the 1964 planning group headed by William Bundy. This group also presented President Johnson with a set of three alternatives—but these concerned the Vietnam War. The first alternative was light bombing with more reprisals and more use of covert operations. The second was very heavy massive bombing, including the Phuc Yen airfield at Hanoi and the rail links with China. And the third was a moderate solution—a slow squeeze, which allowed the United States to put increasing pressure on Hanoi while "keeping the hostage alive" but still permitting it to pull back if it wished. What was significant about these proposals of course was that all three included bombing; there was, in other words, really no political option at all.

What lesson is to be derived from these two cases? Simply this: Effective planning calls for a multiplicity of inputs. To achieve this multiplicity, the planner must studiously avoid becoming the captive of any one group of advisors or experts. To emphasize this point, we might cite one more example—this time from the Kennedy administration.

Shortly after the Bay of Pigs disaster, a number of members of the Kennedy circle became increasingly uneasy with the decision-making processes of the administration. Arthur Goldberg, the new secretary of labor, finally asked the president why he had not consulted more widely, why he had taken such a narrow spectrum of advice, much of it so predictable. Kennedy said that he meant no offense, that even though Goldberg was a good man, he *was* in labor, not in foreign policy.

"You're wrong," Goldberg replied, "you're making the mistake of compartmentalizing your cabinet." The secretary then went on to point out—much to the president's surprise—that the two men in the cabinet who should have been consulted were Orville Freeman, the secretary of agriculture, and himself. Freeman had been a marine, made amphibious landings, and knew how tough such landings can be; and Goldberg had been in the Office of Strategic Services (the forerunner of the CIA) during World War II and had run guerilla operations (Halberstam, 1969:90).

Analysis of Consequences. After an adequate list of alternatives is developed, the next step is to consider their consequences. In this respect, the case of the Family Assistance Plan (FAP) is again instructive. In the first place, thanks to the development in early 1969 of a simulation model (discussed in the next chapter), it was possible to actually test and cost out the various versions of FAP. The use of this technique, probably without precedence in the development of major social legislation in the opinion of Moynihan, did much to discipline and inform debate.

In the second place, the case of FAP is instructive because it involved the use of experimentation. Hence, those wanting to know the consequences of the various versions of FAP merely had to examine the preliminary results from carefully designed negative income tax experiments in New Jersey, Iowa, and North Carolina.

The case of FAP involved the use of yet a third procedure to scrutinize the consequences of the alternatives: congressional hearings. While not as modern as computer simulation and social experimentation, it is, all in all, just as effective. In fact, it was this process more than the other two that proved most effective in exposing the undesirable consequences of FAP.

In 1979, a series of case studies by the Advisory Commission on Intergovernmental Relations (ACIR) revealed that much of the growth of the federal government in recent years had been accidental. Simply put, many of the larger and more controversial federal programs were adopted *without much consideration of their long-range significance.* For this reason, the ACIR concluded, "the construction of the contemporary leviathan state must be judged in part to be simply a mistake." Consider this pair of examples:

- In 1977, an apparently minor amendment was voted by Congress into the Small Business Administration's Disaster Loan Program, making farmers as well as businesspeople eligible for benefits. The program was budgeted at $20 million, but within several months applications from farmers came to $1.4 billion.
- When Congress enacted disability insurance in 1956, sponsors estimated that costs by 1980 would be $860 million for one million workers. But the costs surpassed that figure in the 1960s. From 1970 to 1978, costs quadrupled to about $13 billion and for 1980 there were 5.4 million beneficiaries on the rolls, more than five times the original estimate.

Not surprisingly, techniques to scrutinize consequences were certainly atrophied if not totally absent, in planning the war in Vietnam:

> *In early March 1965, a pessimistic Emmitt John Hughes, a former White House aide under Eisenhower, went to see McGeorge Bundy. What, Hughes asked, if the North Vietnamese retaliate by matching the American air escalation with their own ground escalation. Hughes would long remember the answer and the cool smile. "Just suppose it happens," Hughes persisted. Bundy answered, "We can't assume what we don't believe." (Halberstam, 1969:640)*

These three anecdotes bring to mind an aphorism by the German philosopher Nietzsche: "A very popular error: having the courage of one's convictions; rather it is a matter of having the courage for an *attack* on one's convictions!!!" Good philosophy, good administration.

Implementation

The planning process began, it will be recalled, on a lofty plane, where goals are set and policy established. That stage then merged into a consideration of alternatives and their consequences. Now we arrive at the point where these alternatives must be divided into specific targets that need to be met and actions that need to be taken in order that the objectives are attained. At this point in the process, money must be set aside or budgeted for these programs and actions.

A program is thus a governmental action initiated in order to secure objectives whose attainment is by no means certain without human effort. The degree to which the predicted consequences take place we call successful implementation. To put it inelegantly, implementation is the nuts and bolts of the planning process. (Programming or implementation is similar to what private sector managers call control.)

Consider policies with the objective of improving environmental quality. A variety of specific actions are available to give effect to environmental policies. These approaches to policy objectives fall into four general sets (Caldwell, 1972). In brief:

1. Self-executory: for example, the pricing of pollution and other forms of environmental degradation through taxes, licenses, and rebates.
2. Self-helping: for example, establishment of environmental rights that may be enforced through judicial action.
3. Technological: for instance, specifications regarding applications of technology; assistance for development of ameliorating technological innovations.
4. Administrative: for instance, air and water quality standards; controls over emissions, land use, water disposal, and other environment-affecting behaviors.

What, then, should those at the top do? Perhaps the most important rule to follow is: Do not divorce programming or implementation from policy. Later we shall see that this rule is more than a homily. Chapter 9, which is concerned largely with implementation, focuses on a number of specific steps that the planner can take to tie policy and implementation together. Among such steps, we shall consider the role of incentives, penalties, and rewards; the reduction of the length and unpredictability of necessary decision sequences; and the creation of an effective communication system.

Evaluation

The last stage in our rational planning model is evaluation. It is axiomatic that effective planning requires periodic review to ensure not only that the plans are carried out in the prescribed manner but also that they are achieving the expected results—an axiom of administration not always honored.

This task, in turn, requires that the output of public services be measured. A relatively new and important area of social research, evaluation techniques, is discussed in Chapter 9 along with implementation.

The feedback loop, or information loop, plays a decisive part in the operation of the rational planning model. Feedback allows the policymaker to make adjustments in the policy according to how well or poorly it has been working and according to changes in the environment. The 1972 National Water Pollution Abatement Program provides a good illustration of feedback. The original goal called for universally clean water by 1985. By 1979, with $28 billion in federal money committed, it was rather apparent that the program needed technical, financial, and administrative adjustments. The federal government estimated that to make all the country's waterways "fishable and swimable" by 1985 would require at least $106 billion more. Communities, which had supported the goal of clean water, were aghast when their sewer rates tripled and they learned they faced further hikes. Once they realized how onerous the obligations were, they began asking elected officials to set more realistic goals and to look at the cost-effectiveness (Chapter 6) of current expenditures.

There are two kinds of feedback loops. Positive feedback loops contain the dynamics for change in a system (growth, for example). Negative feedback loops represent control and stability, the reestablishment of equilibriums.

What happens when planning takes place without feedback? For one thing, organizations continue to perform outdated tasks. A notable example is the Rural Electrification Administration (REA), begun in 1935 to provide electricity to rural America. Today, 99 percent of rural homes have electricity, but the REA is still around and is getting bigger. A less well-known example that illustrates the positive results of paying attention to feedback can be found among certain religious organizations. The success of the evangelical churches (relative to mainline churches) may well be based less on their conservatism than on their willingness to face up to the fact that in today's over-institutionalized society the first job of the minister is no longer to run a social agency—the job that made the American Protestant church so effective in the early years of the century. Today the priority may be to "minister" to the spiritual needs of the individual.

By and large, however, few public sector organizations attempt to think through the changed circumstances in which they operate. Most believe that all that is required is to run harder (in the same direction) and to spend more money on the same program.

In the Working Profile of Maxene Johnston, I hope to make our conceptual model even more concrete. Note how such concepts as planning premises, policy planning, medium-range planning, implementation, and evaluation help us organize and make sense of the multifarious activities at her Weingart Center.

Reconciling the Rational Model with Political Realities

The rational planning model (Figure 5-1) deemphasizes the role of politics, human behavior, and other qualitative and subjective factors in policy planning. This section will try to present a more accurate model of how planning unfolds in the real world of public administration. This model, which we shall call **logical incrementalism,** preserves the strengths and purges the weaknesses of the rational model. In this sense, it is more a refinement of than an alternative to the rational model. That being the case,

(text continues on p. 205)

★★★★★★★★★★★★★★★★★★★★★★★★★★★★★★★★★★★
WORKING PROFILE

Maxene Johnston

While working as program manager for medical services of the Los Angeles Olympic Organizing Committee (see Chapter 1), Maxene Johnston got a call from an executive search firm. The firm was seeking a highly experienced executive for a "once in a lifetime" opportunity to turn around an exciting new center in Los Angeles and make it viable. She was intrigued. Then she was told it was in skid row.

Johnston is proud to point out that 6 out of 10 of the people who receive meals, counseling and other services at Weingart Center don't go back to the streets. (Eric Sanders/ Gamma Liaison)

Background

Business and community leaders created the Weingart Center as a response to the *Sundance* decision of 1978. In that decision, the Los Angeles Superior Court ruled that public inebriates should not be thrown into jail—the criminal justice system was too costly and inappropriate for dealing with their problems. The decision mandated referral to civilian diversion agencies for rehabilitation, but there were not enough facilities to deal with the growing number of alcoholics on the streets.

A blue-ribbon panel of leaders was formed to develop solutions. The Weingart Foundation, a major Los Angeles philanthropy, donated an old downtown hotel to be converted into a rehabilitation facility. After a $2.2 million renovation, the Weingart Center was born.

The public-private partnership, however, soon ran into serious financial difficulties. The Weingart Center Association, a group of local business leaders, recognized the need to improve the center's management and to better address the area's growing homeless problem. So they turned to Johnston. Her job was to turn the center around and make it financially sound.

The Problem

The problem of the homeless has probably received as much media attention as any domestic social issue. Yet do we really understand the problem? Johnston thinks not:

Until now our difficulty has been compounded by the very term "homeless." If we define the problem as a lack of homes, then on its face the solution appears to be the construction of more affordable living units. This misdirects the search for answers while grossly understating the real needs of the urban poor. Among their growing ranks are 4 million unemployed, underemployed, sick

★★★★★★★★★★★★★★★★★★★★★★★★★★★★★★★★★★★

and mentally ill American citizens. The fact that they are without adequate housing, important as that is, is just one piece in the homeless puzzle; it is impossible to think that we could create, overnight, all the affordable housing that ostensibly would put roofs over their heads.

Johnston sees the problem quite differently than did the architects of the Great Society of the 1960s (discussed in Chapter 3). Band-Aid solutions, handout programs, and overnight shelters are common from coast to coast, but they tend to offer too-little-too-late remedies for the growing problem. Conditions have changed: The kinds and numbers of jobs available yesterday are scarce today, delivery of welfare services is highly fragmented, and of course drug addiction is much more critical. "It's too late to do away with the homeless problem," Johnston argues. "The issue is how to manage it."

As she sees it, the heart of the problem is that welfare services and agencies are "fragmented, scattered, poorly integrated—all working alone to do their best with no system helping them work more effectively, let alone synergistically." Once she concluded that the system was not user-friendly, she asked herself: "Where was the quality, value, and convenience in circumstances where homeless persons would spend an entire day being sent from one office to another gathering pieces of a puzzle that would, most likely, fall apart by nightfall?"

Johnston's Values

Suffice it to say Johnston's values are not quite the same as those of typical welfare or missionary workers. Prior to directing medical services for the Olympics, she held high-ranking positions at several Los Angeles hospitals. This business background shapes the way she views and speaks about the homeless. To her they are unused human capital rather than souls in search of salvation.

She has little patience for status quo social programs. In her opinion, the area of human services is one of the most lethargic sectors of society:

By and large, most agencies and institutions providing human services are over-managed and under-led. I think in the past these organizations have suffered from unfocused leadership and a lack of efficiency.
It wasn't long ago that people considered business and health care as compatible as oil and water. But we can't afford to think that way anymore. To exist in today's world, where we all are competing for the same dollar, you have to be efficient and be able to produce. . . . You don't have to go broke solving social problems, even though the economic realities and competition faced by service agencies will require new skills and strategies to survive.

Also shaping her worldview is her training in cognitive and behavioral science. Over ten years ago, after reading Margaret Mead's autobiography, *Blackberry Winter,* Johnston followed in Mead's steps by enrolling in graduate school in anthropology. From Mead's teachings, she learned that understanding the cultural beliefs and context in which problems occur could help her in looking at problems in society.

"We've Got to Make This a More *Planned* Community"

Based on the center's mandate and Johnston's own problem analysis and value system, a new strategy eventually began to emerge. In a recent speech, she explained how:

(continued)

While there was much about our "business" we did not know at the outset, there were some things we did know. We knew, for example, that perceptions matter. People do see pieces of reality. Perceptions of our problems and the events around them influence the way we all deal with reality.

We also knew that, while many questions needed answers, the overarching question we faced was: What industry are we in and how does it work? Obviously this is the quintessential marketing question.

To respond, we had to look at all critical components. We needed to know about the investors, brokers, companies and customers—just like any other enterprise.

First, we needed to know who—in general—were the investors (the underwriters and funders). Who were they in particular and what did they want as a return on investment in our territory?

Second, we needed to know who were the brokers in this field. Who in particular were they and which specific brokers could provide resources to our venture?

Third, we needed to know who were the companies (colleagues and "competitors" in the emerging "homeless" industry). What types of organizations were in this field already? And, specifically, what did they do?

Finally, and most importantly, we needed to know who our customers were. We needed demographic information about our customers, people who were poor and homeless. We needed to know more about the size of this marketplace and its needs related to Weingart Center products and services.

After gathering this information, we began to focus on identifying a specific business niche for the Center. We studied other well-managed service companies to gain perspective. For example, the Rolex company is not in the business of selling expensive watches; they are in the business of selling luxury and status. Federal Express is not just in the business of delivering overnight mail; they sell peace of mind. And Scandinavian Airlines does not just fly airplanes; they focus their business on moving people and provide them the on-time service they want.

In short, we found that each of these successful ventures had one thing in common. They often appear to be in one type of business but, in actuality, occupy a rather different market niche. If I may use a capitalistic concept for a humanistic effort, we subsequently concluded that the Weingart Center should be in the "opportunity business," not in the food and shelter business. We defined a service niche and geared our product and service lines to selling government the opportunity to get its many "goods" and services to the marketplace, i.e., our customers, in a more cost-efficient and effective way. We also provided a new opportunity to the marketplace itself to more easily access and use available government benefits.

She then developed four objectives for reaching this goal:

1. *Identify the major segments in the marketplace.* Such a differentiation would enable the center to better match supply and demand and identify customer service requirements.

   One segment consisted of the "have-nots": working Americans temporarily derailed by economic downturn or family crisis. They need relatively little support to provide for themselves and their families. Johnston's strategy for this group was to "give them an immediate remedy to keep them from becoming so emotionally or economically disabled that they fall into the 'can-not's' category."

   The "can-nots" consisted of those disabled by mental illness, drug or alcohol addiction, poor health, or inadequate education. Johnston's short-term strategy for this group was to link them to existing benefits and programs so that they can lead relatively self-sufficient lives with minimal supervision. The aim is to prevent them from becoming completely dysfunctional.

Last are the highly visible "will-nots." Distraught and incapacitated from years of mental illness and living on the streets, they are amenable to only limited assistance. "While we should not turn our backs on this group, our time and resources should first be invested in services for the two segments of the homeless population that still have the ability and desire to help themselves."

2. *Maintain a strict orientation to customer-driven services.* Although Weingart Center customers are poor and often homeless as well, almost all of them need the same service qualities sought by the general public. They value convenience, accessibility, consistency, affordability, and rapid response. Unfortunately, they generally face a large service system so complex that, with the case management orientation of various professionals rather limited, customer service is often not "user-friendly." Organizations in this system often arrange their services to meet internal institutional agendas rather than the needs of customers.

   From this observation emerged the concept of service brokers. The aim is to get the best the marketplace has to offer the customer by brokering the system on his or her behalf. Anyone serving the customer in this framework has the responsibility to ensure customer satisfaction.

3. *Build a multiservice organization.* Johnston did not want the center to be in the welfare business. ("Everyone is in the welfare business.") Rather the center would find the best in the system, then screen, refer, and broker. The center would become, in short, a clearinghouse, a "one-stop-shopping center" for the poor.

4. *Change expectations.* What people see is what they expect. Johnston knew that she had to change expectations if the center was to improve services and satisfy the desire for exits out of the cycle shared by both customers and investors. So she set out to repeat the course of many successful service companies by setting new expectations—and delivering still more.

5. *Satisfy investor orientations.* In an era of pervasive, instantaneous communications, it was clear to Johnston that the media could be a major tool for getting the center's message out and generating support. "Too often," she says, "people operate under the assumption that good work will generate good press."

Implementation

Once Johnston had thought through her objectives, she immediately set to work attaining them.

Services at the center are organized in two clusters: housing services and transition services. The first includes 600-bed, short-term housing and full-service cafe; subsidized cafeteria adjacent to the hotel; and staff that is professionally trained in hotel and food management. The second cluster includes screening and referral service (the heart of the center's operation); alcoholism detoxification and recovery program; mental health clinic; primary health care clinic; adult literacy program; employment referral and preparation program; veterans' services; and even cultural enrichment program. Nine agencies serve the homeless through the center:

- Alcoholics Anonymous
- American Red Cross
- Community Redevelopment Agency, City of Los Angeles
- Department of Corrections, State of California
- Department of Health Services, County of Los Angeles

(continued)

- Department of Mental Health, County of Los Angeles
- Department of Public School Services, County of Los Angeles
- Department of Veterans Affairs
- Volunteers of America, Alcoholism Services Division

Making the center effective not only meant arranging for services but also changing people's perceptions. One of Johnston's first actions was to paint the former El Rey Hotel.

The Former El Rey Hotel

Street people remembered the former El Rey Hotel, where the center has now located, as the "Death-a-day El Rey" because of the violence and drug and alcohol deaths that occurred there; some said that police would not even go beyond its second floor. Therefore, one of Johnston's first actions was to paint it white, with smart blue trim. Atop the 12-story Weingart Center roof, she placed a big flag—in aqua, no less—with a big *W* on it, the center's logo. "Eighty percent of communications is nonverbal," she explains, "so I felt that Weingart Center's renovation had to be complete. When people looked at it, they had to know something different was going on inside."

She made sure that all the fixtures worked, decorated hallways with fresh flowers and artwork, and made sure the huge hotel was clean. In a clean environment, she said, she can help people in need get their lives back on track. She believes community and human redevelopment must go hand in hand. "As I started to repair the center," she says, "I felt it was symbolic of people walking in, hopefully, to repair their lives. Not only did we need to rebuild pride and self-respect back into the community, through our efforts, but people coming through the doors of the center had to rebuild pride in themselves."

Johnston also helped restore the pride of her staff (many of whom came out of the poor and homeless population, got volunteer jobs at the center, then were hired in paid positions). She gave the staff aqua paper aprons to distinguish them from the residents. "We have our Weingart patrol in yellow jackets," says Johnston, "and they are our 'bumble bees,' buzzing around, making sure the center is safe." These security guards—called "ambassadors"—constantly circle the center to make sure that people who need service get in, and that those who abuse the streets stay away.

From the outset, Johnston also made it a point to get to know key television and radio station general managers, programming directors, publishers, and editorial boards. She quickly learned which reporters covered which issues in order to alert them to developments breaking on a topic. "As demand for services from the nonprofit sector soars while funding remains static or shrinks, the media is the message. Nothing can help persuade large numbers of potential volunteers or contributors—including key corporate, foundation and governmental decisionmakers—that yours is an eminently worthy cause like good media coverage."

Equally impressive as her handling of media relations is her ability to combine hard-nosed business planning with inventive financing. For example, in 1989, the center introduced a $2.50 meal coupon that individuals, companies, and organizations can buy to distribute directly or indirectly to homeless men and women. Each coupon can be exchanged for a hot, nutritious breakfast, lunch, or dinner at the Weingart Center's bright and spacious cafeteria.

The coupons, packaged in books of ten, are distributed in a variety of ways. Organizations can buy books and donate them to skid row service agencies, which then can give the coupons to needy clients. Companies, too, can buy and give the coupons to employees, who, in turn, can hand them out to homeless people they meet on the street. And individuals buy them for one-on-one distribution. The people who hand the coupons to the homeless have said they feel better offering the coupon rather than cash, knowing that their money will be spent on food, not drink or drugs.

Evaluation

Johnston rattles off facts and figures with a speed that leaves some listeners three steps behind her. (One reporter characterized her as a cross between Mother Theresa and Joan Rivers.) In any event, she is aware that running a nonprofit organization does not excuse a manager from measuring its performance.

The center serves more than 2,000 people a day and she says that 63 percent of the people in its program within a few months find employment and other professional help and move off the street. She estimates that the center saves up to $3 million a year in city and county jail and hospital services. But no evaluation of such an organization can or should be restricted to purely quantitative data. Consider this comment by a 41-year-old unemployed carpenter: "You get to sleep at night knowing you'll wake up the next morning and that you'll have the chance to fix yourself up to look for a job. I'm very thankful for this place." Surely that is worth something.

SOURCES: Maxene Johnston, "Non-Traditional Tools Get Results with Traditional Problems," adaptation of remarks at the Foundation for American Communication Symposium, Scottsdale, Arizona, January 24, 1990; Marsha Vande Berg, "Success on Skid Row," *Golden State Report* iv, October 1988; Kathleen MacKay, "Tackling Social Ills with Business Skills," Southwest Airlines *Spirit* Magazine, September 1987; Weingart Center Association "Backgrounder," March 1990; Maxene Johnston, "Homeless Are More Than Homeless," *Los Angeles Times,* June 29, 1988.

★★★★★★★★★★★★★★★★★★★★★★★★★★★★★★★★★★★★★

let us begin by summarizing the strengths and weaknesses of the rational model before we try to define logical incrementalism.

Strengths and Weaknesses of the Rational Planning Model

If not followed too rigorously, the rational model can help public administrators avoid several serious mistakes.

The first thing the rational model alerts the administrators to is the need to translate lofty goals into concrete actions. To speak always of goals is to ensure that nothing will be accomplished.

The second thing the rational model helps guarantee is that priorities will be set and adhered to. Without concentration on priorities, efforts will be diluted over several objectives and squandered in areas where the payoff is low. Congressional investigations, for example, made it clear that outside critics were right when they complained that J. Edgar Hoover, former FBI director, had squandered bureau resources on penny-ante cases involving stolen cars and bank robberies. These made for impressive charts at budget hearings but had little real impact on crime. A GAO study that was commissioned by an oversight committee headed by Representative Don Edwards, Democrat of California who is a former FBI agent, showed that much of the bureau's domestic surveillance had been of questionable value.

The third thing the rational model can do is remind the administrator that structure follows strategy, that is, designing an effective organization should occur *after* goals have been set. Not all organizational structures are equally well suited to accomplishing a particular goal.

Fourth and equally important, the rational model alerts the administrator to the ever-present need to analyze, experiment, or evaluate to see what works before launching a program on a grand scale.

Fifth, the rational model highlights the vital and continuing role of feedback in the planning process. Only if the organization continues to learn through feedback can its performance improve and can it know when to abandon programs and activities that are no longer producing results.

Sixth, the rational model reminds administrators that they must periodically scan their environments for new threats and opportunities. Which is to say, rational model planning systems force operating administrators to extend their time horizons and see their work in a larger, dynamic framework. Henry Kissinger (1979) explains why such a forcing mechanism might be necessary: "The analysis of where one is overwhelms the consideration of where one should be going. Serving the machine becomes a more absorbing occupation than defining the purpose."

Seventh, to the extent that they require rigorous communications about goals, alternatives, and resource allocations, rational models help create a network of information that probably would not have otherwise been present in the agency.

Against these strengths, however, we must weigh several weaknesses. For example, the rational model suggests that executives should announce explicit goals. Yet research suggests that effective executives often proceed quite differently. Why? Quinn (1980:65–96) suggests the following reasons:

- Goal announcements centralize and freeze the organization by telling subordinates that certain issues and alternatives are closed.
- Explicitly stated goals provide focal points against which an otherwise fragmented *opposition* can organize. This is what often happens when a town reveals its land use plan. It also explains why presidents keep their specific budget cuts as fuzzy as possible for as long as possible.
- Once top administrators announce their goals, those goals are difficult to change; the administrators' egos and those of the people in supporting programs become identified with them. To change the goal is to admit to error. Thus, government plunges ahead with obsolete military, energy, and social programs.

As Figure 5-2 suggests, a few goals at least should be specific, though they should be generated with care. Why so much care? "Effective strategic goals do more than provide a basis for direction setting and maintaining freedom, morale, and timely problem sensing in an enterprise. The benefits of effective goal setting are greatest when people throughout the organization genuinely internalize goals and make them their own." (Quinn, 1980:81)

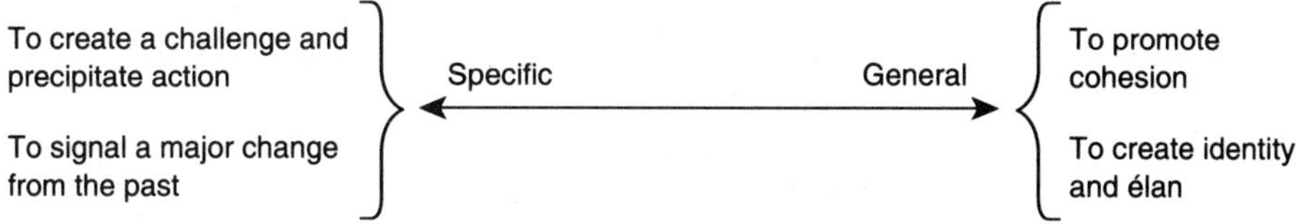

FIGURE 5-2
How Specific Should Goals Be?
SOURCE: J. B. Quinn, *Strategies for Change: Logical Incrementalism* (Homewood, Ill.: Richard D. Irwin, 1980), pp. 72–81.

A second weakness of the rational model is that it is based on a most dubious assumption—namely, that the planner can peer clearly and deeply into the future. In reality, a host of unforeseen problems and events can sweep down upon the set of new directions an agency might develop. Although many frustrated Americans might wish for a more specific, cohesive energy policy, logic dictates that massive resource commitments be made as late as possible consistent with the information available. To begin "to go solar" today means that the United States must begin to build a solar industry at least on the scale of the automobile industry. But there are so many social, political, economic, and technological unknowns hiding between here and the year 2010 that logic dictates a more incremental, step-by-step approach.*

A third shortcoming of our rational model is that it fails to account for the politics within and outside the organization. In fact, one could argue that some planning decisions are the result of various bargaining games among the political leadership. Although this was not quite the thesis of Chapter 2, it was suggested there that politics and administration cannot be easily separated. It could be also argued that some planning decisions are more the result of regular patterns of behavior than of any rational analysis. Faced with a problem, the administrator simply adapts certain standard operating procedures and the fixed routines, or "drills," of the agency to formulate a strategy (Allison, 1971).

The fourth and final weakness in the rational model is not easily defined. Crudely put, the rational model discounts the role of subjective and qualitative factors in the policy-planning process. Its step-by-step view of the planning process is hard to reconcile with the experienced observations of flesh and blood administrators. Perhaps the following two quotes by practicing managers come closer to capturing the realities of planning than the five-step model outlined on page 192:

- I start conversations with a number of knowledgeable people . . . . I collect articles and talk to people about how things get done in Washington in this

* For example, people might begin to seriously practice conservation, which would make massive solar investment less necessary. Or they might decide that acres and acres of solar collectors are an eyesore, which would make tomorrow's solar industry as besieged as today's nuclear industry. Political upheavals overseas might cut off the U.S. supply of raw materials needed to make photovoltaic cells. Even more likely are technological breakthroughs like fusion energy and hydrogen fuel (from water) that could make solar energy economically less attractive.

particular field. I collect data from any reasonable source. I begin wide-ranging discussions with people inside and outside the corporation. From these a pattern eventually emerges. It's like fitting together a jigsaw puzzle. At first the vague outline of an approach appears like the sail of a ship in a puzzle. Then suddenly the rest of the puzzle becomes quite clear. You wonder why you didn't see it all along. And once it's crystallized, it's not difficult to explain to others. (Quoted in Quinn, 1980:35)

- Typically you start with general concerns, vaguely felt. Next you roll an issue around in your mind till you think you have a conclusion that makes sense for the company. You then go out and sort of post the idea without being too wedded to its details. You then start hearing the arguments pro and con, and some very good refinements of the idea usually emerge. Then you pull the idea in and put some resources together to study it so it can be put forward as more of a formal presentation. You wait for "stimuli occurrences" or "crises," and launch pieces of the idea to help in these situations. But they lead toward your ultimate aim. You know where you want to get. You'd like to get there in six months. But it may take three years, or you may not get there. And when you do get there, you don't know whether it was originally your own idea—or somebody else had reached the same conclusion before you and just got you on board for it. You never know. The president would follow the same basic process, but he could drive it much faster than an executive lower in the organization. (Quoted in Quinn, 1980:102)

A New Synthesis: Logical Incrementalism

The challenge to students of public administration is, therefore, easy enough to state: How can you build on the strengths of the rational model without including its weaknesses? James Brian Quinn, a professor of management at Dartmouth College, has suggested a possible solution. It is a synthesis of various behavioral, power-dynamic, and formal analytical approaches that more closely approximates the policy-planning process in major organizations (see Figure 5-3). Because the process does not result solely from power-political interplays, it is not what Charles E. Lindblom (1959, 1963) and others have called "muddling through" or "disjointed incrementalism." Because it does not explore all alternatives and factors, nor try to treat them quantitatively, it is not the rational model. Quinn (1980:58) explains:

The most effective strategies of major enterprises tend to emerge step by step from an iterative process in which the organization probes the future, experiments, and learns from a series of partial (incremental) commitments rather than through global formulations of total strategies. Good managers are aware of this process, and they consciously intervene in it. They use it to improve the information available for decisions and to build the psychological identification essential to successful strategies. The process is both local and

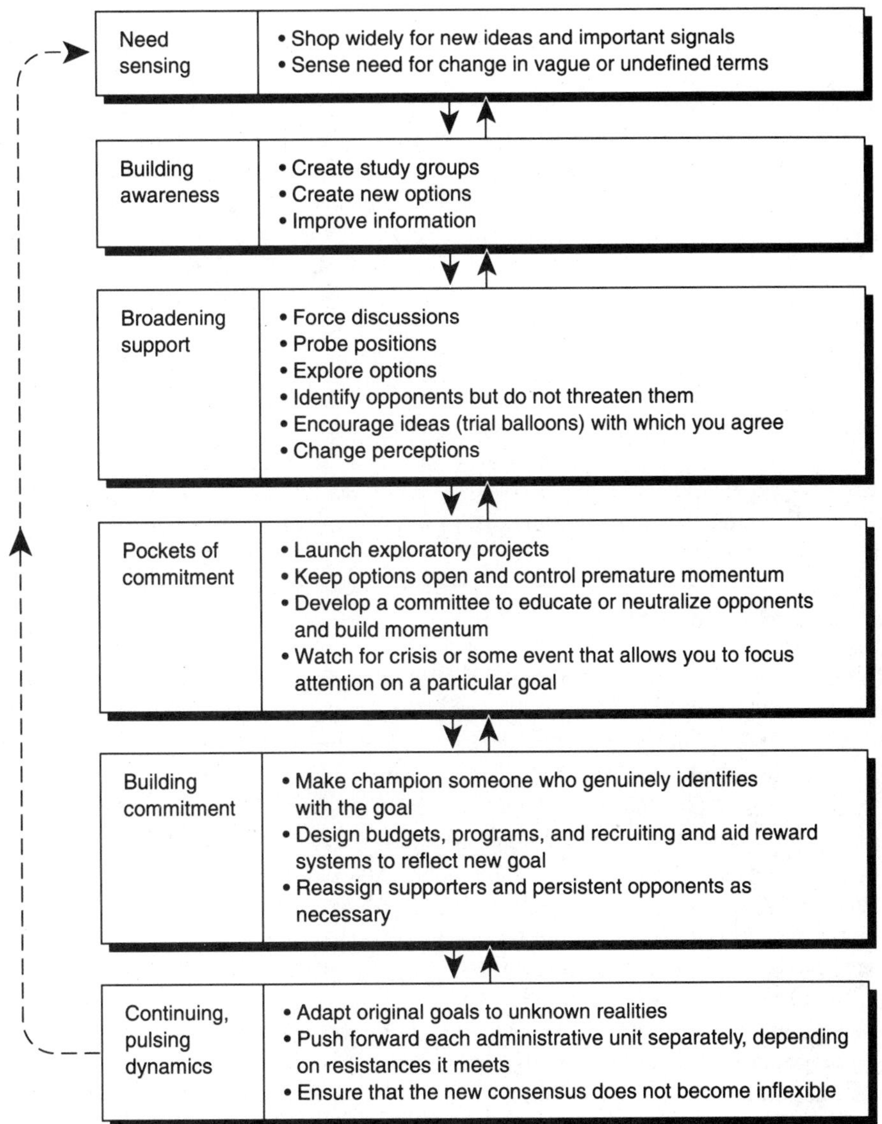

FIGURE 5-3
The Logical Incremental Planning Model

incremental. Such logical incrementalism is not muddling, *as most people understand that word. Properly managed, it is a conscious, purposeful, proactive, executive practice. Logical incrementalism honors and utilizes the global analyses inherent in formal strategy formulation models. It also embraces the central tenets of the political or power-behavioral approaches to such deci-*

(text continues on p. 212)

Talking Shop

Eight Mistakes in Planning

1. Trying to Do Too Much

It is easy to be impressed by the scope of a problem and to want to solve it all at once. Yet an incremental approach, though not as aesthetically pleasing as a comprehensive approach, may be more realistic to implement. You can build a comprehensive system as you go. For example, if you cannot solve all the problems of child health in a large city, then perhaps you can make progress with a series of categorical programs (lead-poisoning screening, rat control, immunization, sickle-cell testing).

2. Expecting Continuance of the Status Quo

Too many managers only spend time coping with the problems they see now, but situations change and a manager should be just as prepared to cope with different circumstances. Ask yourself, If I had to bet my right arm, what would I think is likely to happen? Administrators must constantly think aloud about their programs, try to foresee problems before they arrive, and instill this same attitude in their subordinates. Frequently ask yourself, Is there anything else we should be doing that we are not now doing? But administrators must also recognize that they cannot anticipate everything—some things are bound to go wrong.

3. Trying the Impossible

Public administrators should develop the skill of discerning what is possible and what is impossible, because many of the problems in the public sector are totally intractable. They should not waste valuable time and resources trying to do the impossible. This does not mean they should not tackle tough problems, but rather that they should define *realistic* goals.

It is especially important when taking over an organization—whatever its size—to pick a problem that is important and quickly solvable. Then launch a program to fix it. This quick success helps establish credibility.

4. Getting Emotionally Involved

When managers get emotionally involved in their plans, they resist changes in it. No plan is inviolate, nor did one, in and of itself, ever make anyone healthy. Planners should see their work as a living thing that can and should be improved upon even after implementation has begun.

5. Overplanning

Managers should not be too concerned with details. Sometimes it is better to forsake the next increment of effort required to get it perfect, because the payoff is not worth it. Be flexible in your plan—change it as you go. Very little is irreversible. Likewise, the implementation plan should be simple and realistic.

6. Focusing on Trivia

Planners have a tendency to want a lot of extras that would be nice if they happened but that are not crucial to achieving the objectives of the program. Therefore they should identify the factors in a program that, if absent, will cause a program to fail. For example, in setting up a large lead-poisoning screening program, a good reporting system, in order to increase the productivity of testing personnel, would be a sine qua non. It would have been *nice* to have Red Cross mobile vans help in the program, but they would not be critical to getting the program off the ground.

7. Understanding the Importance of Organizational Structure

Some new, large programs fail because no organization is built to support it and to allow for managerial control. This happens to numerous low-income housing programs where money is distributed to various community groups and contractors before adequate accounting and auditing systems are established. Questions to ask are, How will the program play with the informal organization? Can a coalition be formed within the organization to champion this program? How decentralized (or centralized) should control be? Chapter 7 will suggest a number of other pertinent questions that should be addressed during the planning process.

8. Understanding the Importance of Leadership

In Chapter 3, we saw the critical role that David Lilienthal played in making the TVA's rural electrification program a success. But a manager's entrepreneurial spirit can also cause programs to happen that others have never thought of or have thought impossible. There are plenty of vacuums in government, and some managers move with alacrity to fill them. When they propose a new program, everyone will force them to justify why. That is a legitimate question, but it is also legitimate to ask, Why not? In Chapter 8, we will see how one entrepreneurial-minded manager changed the entire court system in Idaho.

Public agencies and nonprofit organizations are relatively limited in their planning by highly contained mission definitions; still, a number of possibilities exist for expanding their domain without reducing the commitment to the core mission. One such strategy is piggybacking. For example, the Boston Symphony Orchestra (BSO) established the Boston Pops. The Pops uses the same concert hall and concessions as the BSO while providing an extra source of income for its parent organization.

SOURCES: Based on Bozeman and Straussman (1990), and Chase (1984).

sion making. But it does not become subservient to any one model. Instead each approach becomes simply a component in a logical process that improves the quality of available information, establishes critical elements of political power and credibility, creates needed participation and psychological commitment, and thus enhances both the quality of strategic decisions and the likelihood of their successful implementation.

In sum, a kind of logical incrementalism usually dominates policy planning in the real world of public administration. The process is, according to Quinn, "purposeful, politically astute, and effective." Like the rational model it begins with needs that may only be vaguely sensed at first. But the managers who follow the logical incremental model usually do not jump next to an articulation of specific goals; rather, they will steadily build within the organization support for and eventually commitment to new goals. Some common steps in this process and relevant management techniques are set forth in Figure 5-3. "Talking Shop" (pp. 210–211) highlights several common mistakes that effective planners try to avoid.

Forecasting—A Critical Planning Ingredient

To plan is to make assumptions about the future. Unfortunately, the assumptions are usually made semiconsciously, but if articulated, they would sound something like this: "Tomorrow will be like today, only more so."

The error of this mindset can be seen clearly in the planning of Miami's Metrorail. Six months after the first 11 miles of elevated track were opened, average daily ridership was a paltry 9,500—about 10 percent of what had been expected. Why was the patronage estimate so far off the mark? The main reason is that the planners assumed that the costs of operating an automobile—gasoline, oil, parking fees, and maintenance—would increase severalfold between 1975 and 1985. As car costs rose, the planners believed, more people would switch to public transportation. When this forecast was made, tensions were high between the United States and the Middle East, and the United States was experiencing gas shortages and sharp price increases. Tomorrow, transit planners assumed, would bring more of the same. But tomorrow was different, and by 1985 the public transit system's deficits had risen significantly.

What was the bottom line in this story? Miami's elevated rapid transit system cost the federal government over $700 million but attracted only 10 percent as many riders as projected. It would have been cheaper to give each new rider $100,000!

What Is a Forecast?

Erich Jantsch (1967:15) provides us with this definition of a forecast: a probabilistic statement, on a relatively high confidence level, about the future. A prediction, in contrast, is a nonprobabilistic statement (*X will* occur). Jantsch also distinguishes between two types of forecasts. **Exploratory forecast** starts from today's knowledge and attempts to say what is likely to occur in the future. **Normative forecast,** however, starts in the future, assessing goals, needs, desires, and so forth. It then works backward to the present, attempting to spell out what should be done to attain, at some time in the future, the desired goal.

So much for definitions. How does this relate to the task of the administrator? In brief, forecasting provides a means of discovering and articulating the more important opportunities and problems in the future. Further, it provides a systematic method for estimating the trajectory likely to be produced by contemplated or existing governmental programs.

The number of forecasting methods available is vast. Below we discuss only four of the more basic methods: expert forecasting, trend extrapolation, leading indicators, and impact assessment.

Expert Forecasting

The expert forecast is the oldest and the most intuitive of the methods. Here, if one wants to know what is likely or unlikely to happen, one simply goes to the expert. The science fiction writer Arthur C. Clarke documents the limitations to this approach by citing numerous failures by experts.

Lord Rutherford, for example, was certainly an expert on the atom—more than any other scientist he helped to lay bare its internal structure. But, as Clarke (1963:14) notes:

> *Rutherford frequently made fun of those sensation mongers who predicted that we would one day be able to harness the energy locked up in matter. Yet, only five years after his death in 1937, the first chain reaction was started in Chicago. What Rutherford, for all his wonderful insight, had failed to take into account was that a nuclear reaction might be discovered that would release more energy than that required to start it.*
>
> *. . . The example of Lord Rutherford demonstrates that it is not the man who knows most about a subject, and is the acknowledged master of his field, who can give the most reliable pointers to its future. Too great a burden of knowledge can clog the wheels of imagination; I have tried to embody this fact of observation in* Clarke's law, *which may be formulated as follows: When a distinguished but elderly scientist states that something is possible, he is almost certainly right. When he states that something is impossible, he is very probably wrong.*

To help overcome such limitations in forecasting by individual experts, consensus methods were developed. By far, the best known of these is the **Delphi technique.** Generally, a Delphi exercise asks a group of experts on a certain subject—economics, medicine, automation, population, education, and so forth—to state *anonymously* when a future event might occur. Their answers, with their reasons, are summarized and fed back to the entire group for a second round. This process may be repeated several times with the hope that eventually there will be a narrowing of the initial spread of opinions.

Trend Extrapolation

If one buys the assumption that trends established in recent history will continue, then trend extrapolation might be used. A parameter—for example, U.S. population, maximum aircraft speed, or even the world record in the 1500-meter run (see Figure 5-4)—is plotted on a graph against time. The analyst then extends the curve either by an "eyeball" extension or by a quantitative curve-fitting method.

As I see it, the biggest limitation to this method is the assumption that past trends hold, that we *know* what the curve is. Say that an analyst has the plot of historical data shown in Figure 5-5. How does this person know whether A or B is the proper extension? The first curve, represented by A, shows an exponential increase with no flattening in the time range considered. For our purposes, we may think of an exponential growth curve as one that shows a constant *rate* of change; that is, the increase in December was greater than that in November which, in turn, was greater than the increase in October, and so on. This characteristic is exhibited by a number of parameters (e.g., maximum transport aircraft speed and energy conversion efficiency in illumination technology) at least until certain limits are hit (e.g., Concorde and the gallium arsenide diode).

Not all trends, however, are exponential. And when one ignores the possibility of an S-shaped curve, such as that represented by B, ludicrous forecasts can sometimes result.

For example, the growth in the number of scientists between 1850 and 1950 was very steep and probably followed roughly the path of the solid line in Figure 5-5. Someone who ignored the possibility of saturation might be led to the mind-boggling conclusion that, by the end of the century, all the Earth's inhabitants over the age of six would be holding doctorates in science. One also should be open to the possibility of certain external events or breakthroughs. In London in the latter part of the 19th century, with the horse as the principal means of rapid intracity transportation, the accumulation of manure in the streets was cause for no little concern. Naive extrapolation, ignoring the possibility of the technological breakthrough such as the automobile, would have forecasted a city buried in 30 years.

Leading Indicators

One of the more fascinating methods is Graham T. T. Molitor's (1975:204–10) schema of forecasting public policy change through leading indicators. Basically, Molitor suggests that by monitoring events, intellectual elites, literature, organizations, and political jurisdictions, the policy analyst can develop a better idea of what to expect in the future. The premise upon which this method builds goes something like this. Issues of public policy are almost always the result of unusual events that give rise to abuse or excess so extreme that public action eventually is required. Between the occurrence of the first isolated event and the creation of public policy, Molitor thinks a fairly consistent pattern of behavior unfolds. The analyst's job, then, is one of monitoring

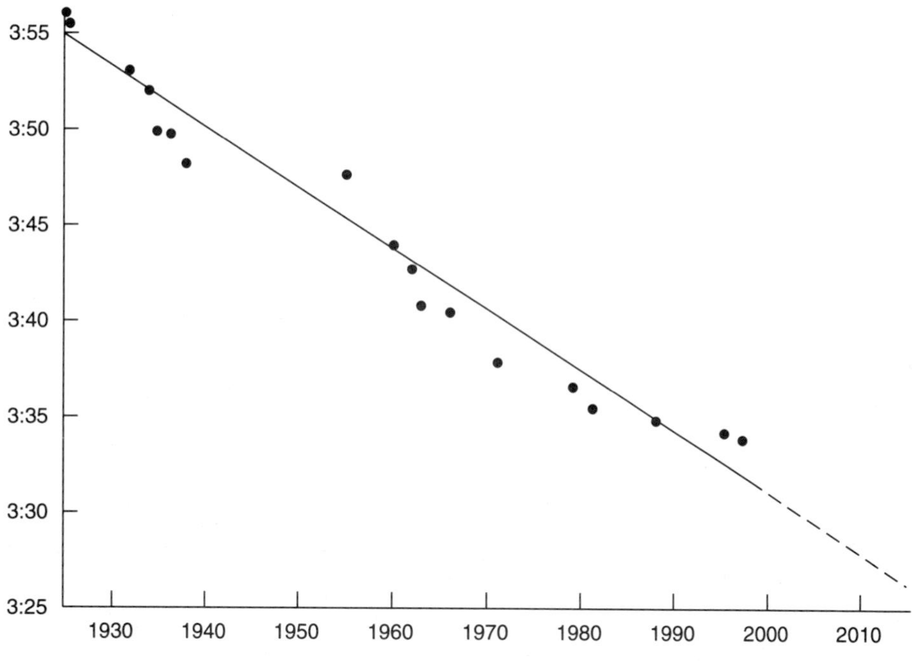

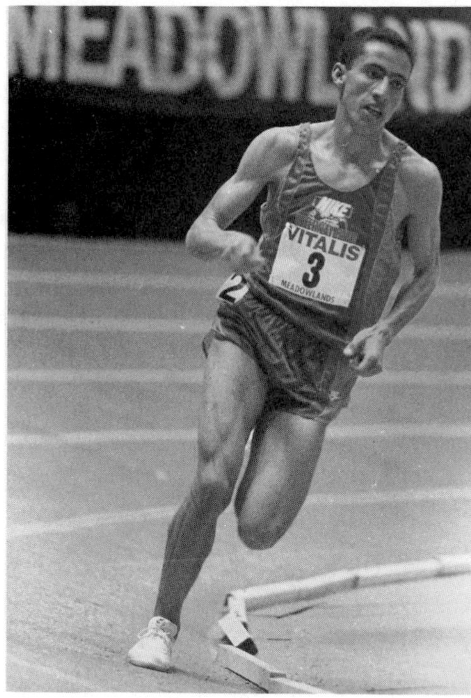

3:56.2	Paavo Nurmi (Fin)	1/6/25
3:55.8	Lloyd Hahn (US)	2/21/25
3:53.4	Gene Venzke (US)	2/27/32
3:52.2	Glenn Cunningham (US)	2/24/34
	Bill Bonthron (US)	2/24/34
3:50.5	Cunningham	2/23/35
3:49.9	Venzke	2/22/36
3:48.4	Cunningham	2/26/38
3:48.3	Wes Santee (US)	2/5/55
3:44.6	Siegfried Hermann (EG)	2/28/60
3:43.2	Jim Beatty (US)	2/10/62
3:41.6	Tom O'Hara (US)	3/6/64
3:40.7	Michel Jazy (Fra)	2/27/66
3:37.8	Harald Norpoth (WG)	2/13/71
3:37.4	John Walker (NZ)	1/6/79
3:35.6	Eamonn Coghlan (Ire)	2/20/81
3:35.4	Marcus O'Sullivan (Ire)	2/13/88
3:34.20	Peter Elliott (GB)	2/27/90
3:34.16	Noureddine Morceli (Alg)	2/28/91

FIGURE 5-4

Progress in the 1500-Meter Run

SOURCE: Data from *Track & Field News,* April 1991, p. 37; photo by AP/Wide World.

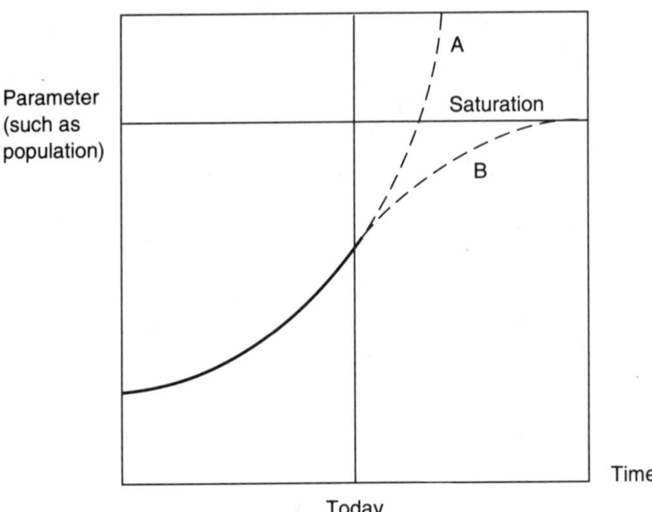

FIGURE 5-5
Trend Extrapolation Dilemmas

this pattern as it unfolds. For example, we know that intellectual elites, who analyze and articulate social problems, tend to emerge around issues. Similarly, the victimized express their feelings and thus become powerful symbols for change. "By monitoring these . . . vanguards, whose ideas ultimately are diffused widely, early indications of change can be forecasted" (Molitor, 1975:206).

Meanwhile, the sequence by which different types of literature build up and provide a permanent written analysis and wider publicity of the new ideas and concepts follows a rough pattern. The sequence, which might cover over 100 years, could go like this. At first, the early warnings about emerging problems appear in the more visionary classes of literature. (For example, it would appear that the poet Blake was one of the first to recognize the arrival of the Industrial Revolution and its social implications.) Then, the idea is rendered into specifics in monographs and speeches in specialized journals. Next, these phases occur: corroboration of details; institutional responses through journals for the cause; consideration in the mass media; and politicization of the issue in government reports and a diffusion of the idea among opinion leaders.

Translating a cause into public policy, however, requires more than advocates and articles—it requires organizational support: "Growth of institutional backing for a cause—whether measured by number of organizations, persons involved, or resources committed—follows exponential increases which tend to force serious consideration of the issue by public policymakers" (Molitor, 1975:209).

Ultimately, political officials become involved. Certain leading political jurisdictions invariably are among the first to implement new policy solutions. These early innovators and experimenters show the way to others; then, after the idea is proven, other jurisdictions emulate.

Generally speaking, there are 5 states where most social invention occurs. The other 45 states usually follow. California is the key indicator state with Florida a close second. The other three trendsetting states are Washington, Colorado, and Connecticut (Naisbitt, 1980).

Impact Assessment

Inherent in all planning is the problem of unexpected consequences. The more profound and longer-term the program, the greater the possibility of horrendous side effects, yet people tend to ignore the potential dangers from the secondary effects of benevolent enterprises and good intentions. Can our late 20th-century public administrators overcome such a tendency? I think that a method is already in place that can help them look ahead more realistically. The general name for this method is impact assessment, though it takes a variety of forms.

The first of these is the **environmental impact statement** (EIS). An EIS is a document prepared either by a governmental agency or private concern that outlines how a proposed action (e.g., construction of a new dam or highway) might affect the quality of the human environment. The requirement for EISs began with the passage of the National Environmental Policy Act (NEPA) of 1969. Section 102(2)(c) of the act sets forth the EIS requirement. The significance of this requirement was not initially apparent to most government agencies or to private industry. Today, the number and variety of EISs required at all levels of government are enormous.

A basic framework for an EIS might be something like the following: (1) describe present conditions; (2) describe proposed action (e.g., new highway or housing project); (3) describe probable impacts of each alternative to soil conditions, wildlife, climate, existing pollution, transportation congestion, aesthetics, and so forth; (4) identify the alternative chosen; (5) describe probable impacts of proposed action in detail; and (6) describe techniques to be used to minimize harm.

Similar to the writing of an EIS is **technology assessment.** Joseph F. Coates (1971:225) defines technology assessment as "the systematic study of the effects on society that may occur when a technology is introduced, extended, or modified, with a special emphasis on the impacts that are unintended, indirect, and delayed." Technology assessment became firmly established as a decision-making tool in 1972 when Congress created the Office of Technology Assessment. Figure 5-6 shows the seven major steps in technology assessment.

Either directly or indirectly, technological advance brings certain risks. One need look no further than the headlines of the press for evidence. Surely government has some responsibility to look for the side effects of new technology.

Let me give just one example. By 1980, evidence had begun to pile up that conserving energy can damage your health. More exactly, energy-efficient buildings can be dangerous because they not only prevent warmed (or cooled) air from escaping but also prevent pollutants from escaping. According to one World Health Organization expert, indoor pollution is already doing more damage to human health than the outdoor pollution that regulatory authorities are fighting against throughout the industrialized world (*New Scientist,* May 4, 1980).

Step 1	DEFINE THE ASSESSMENT TASK Discuss relevant issues and any major problems. Establish scope (breadth and depth) of inquiry. Develop project ground rules.
Step 2	DESCRIBE RELEVANT TECHNOLOGIES Describe major technology being assessed. Describe other technologies supporting the major technology. Describe technologies competitive with the major and supporting technologies.
Step 3	DEVELOP STATE-OF-SOCIETY ASSUMPTIONS Identify and describe major nontechnological factors influencing the application of the relevant technologies.
Step 4	IDENTIFY IMPACT AREAS Ascertain those societal characteristics that will be most influenced by the application of the assessed technology.
Step 5	MAKE PRELIMINARY IMPACT ANALYSIS Trace and integrate the process by which the assessed technology makes its societal influence felt.
Step 6	IDENTIFY POSSIBLE ACTION OPTIONS Develop and analyze various programs for obtaining maximum public advantage from the assessed technologies.
Step 7	COMPLETE IMPACT ANALYSIS Analyze the degree to which each action option would alter the specific societal impacts of the assessed technology discussed in Step 5.

FIGURE 5-6

Seven Major Steps in Making a Technology Assessment

SOURCE: Mitre Corporation, A Technology Assessment Methodology (Washington, D.C.: Office of Science and Technology, 1971).

Consider the case of builders who install double insulation, triple-glazed windows, polyurethane caulking, and other advanced conservation measures to produce a house that uses only one third to one half as much energy as a conventional one. To their horror, they discover they have also produced one dangerous to inhabit—with very high levels of humidity, odors, pollutants, and even an accumulation of radioactive radon gas. The effect of swapping ventilation for energy conservation is a buildup in the house of pollutants from furniture polish, deodorants, hair sprays, and carpet adhesives. In less than an hour, a gas stove in the kitchen can produce levels of carbon monoxide that exceed standards for the outside. High humidity makes matters worse. In areas where sulphur emissions from coal combustion are high, the result can be indoor "acid rain" as the sulphur combines with oxygen to form sulphate. The sulphate then deposits to eat away at furniture—and lung tissue.

Safety equipment and emission-control technology on the automobile can even kill you. Lester B. Lave, a senior fellow at the Brookings Institution, estimates that reducing the size of automobiles increases fatalities by 1,400 a year and significantly increases serious injuries (*Science,* May 22, 1981).

What can public administrators do about risks? They must begin by recognizing that to head off undesirable side effects, a good tactic is prudence. Instead of proceeding full speed with any new technology, they can wait a bit, mull over any distant warnings, and approach risk in an incremental, experimental, trial-and-error way, and thus improve, reinvent, or redesign processes and devices. To succeed at risk management, the government bureaucracy will need unbiased feedback that is direct, immediate, and continuing on both the effects of new technology and the effects of government action. Finally, it needs to use technology assessment more extensively to attempt to see in advance the unintended, unexpected consequences of current action. Otherwise, the bureaucracy will find itself experiencing even more technological blunders such as toxic seepage from chemical dumps.

Variations on a Theme: The Many Types of Planning

To better appreciate the wide variety of meanings that managers have affixed to the single word *planning,* think back to your kindergarten career. Remember alphabet-based word games that taught you how to read? A is for apple, B is for bird, and so on. The same approach can help decipher the word *planning.* To be sure, the following review of planning meanings is somewhat simplistic, so consider it nothing more than a "short course" in what you can expect when you hear the word *planning* bandied about in the workplace.

Action Planning. In the early 1990s, Gwendolyn S. King faced a mess at the Social Security Administration. The agency, which she now headed, had been battered throughout the previous decade by staff reductions and general management chaos. Many in Washington were speaking of "a system on the verge of collapse."

Like Gwendolyn King, public administrators are continually faced with the need to tackle many difficult tasks in a finite amount of time. Some of these must be completed immediately and have important near-term implications. Some do not seem as difficult (e.g., congratulating an employee, moving offices to new buildings, etc.); but the administrator's action must nevertheless be thought through. Still other tasks encompass longer time frames. In each of these three cases, public administrators need to help them accomplish these tasks. We call this planned sequence of actions an action plan because it spells out the specific behavioral steps that the administrator intends to carry out. It may exist only in the administrator's mind or it may be written down, as was King's: (1) Send four strike teams to the agency's ten regions to investigate problems; (2) lift the hiring freeze in field offices with the most pressing staff shortages; (3) abolish rigid numerical performance goals; (4) appoint persons to take confidential complaints from employees; and (5) encourage beneficiaries to call the agency's toll-free line during off-peak hours.

This ability to think through and act out a coherent sequence of behaviors will determine as much as anything an administrator's effectiveness. Why? Because action planning helps the administrator to go beyond understanding and analyzing the issue and take action that effectively addresses the issue at hand.

Business Planning. Cal Worthington has cars, and he wants to sell them—lots of them. To accomplish this, he develops a plan. A business plan is a written document that specifies what is to be done ("We will increase last year's sales by 12 percent"), who will do the work, and when the work will be completed. Although each business plan is tailored to the company, most contain elements like the following: potential market, store locations, negotiations with vendors, inventory control systems, pricing, and advertising.

Crisis Planning. Early one afternoon in late October, about a dozen city and industry officials gathered for a casual discussion on the "what ifs" of coping with disaster in their area. In less than five hours, that abstract discussion in Texas City turned terribly real as the same officials scrambled to cope with 53,000 pounds of hydrofluoric acid, escaping from a Marathon Petroleum Company tank in a deadly cloud that stretched at least 2 miles northeast. The planners suddenly found themselves reacting.

Without prior planning, things no doubt would have been much worse. Emergency management coordinations between city and company did go fairly well. Still, the plan had its gaps. For example, it failed to address the issue of how the public would be educated as to what the sirens meant and what citizens should do when they heard them.

Crises such as the Challenger space shuttle explosion, the Exxon *Valdez* oil spill, earthquakes in California and Mexico, terrorism, or the AIDS epidemic appear so random that public administrators find themselves at a loss to take preventive action. Although a few administrators might actually believe their own organization to be somehow immune, most would probably hope that there might be a rational way to select which potential crises an organization should prepare for and which can be safely ignored.

Ian I. Mitoff (1988) has developed two portfolios that can give organizations a way to think about crisis planning. First, crises can be grouped according to their underlying structural similarity into five families: (1) mega damage (e.g., poor security, employee errors, and computer breakdowns; (2) breaks (e.g., poor security, employee errors, and computer breakdowns); (3) external information attacks (e.g., rumors); (4) psycho damage (e.g., terrorism and boycotts); and (5) external economic attacks (e.g., bribery). Administrators should pick at least one crisis from each of the families and then plan for that crisis. Why?

> *Since the other members of the family are related to one another, preparing for one crisis in each family provides some preparation for each of the others.*

> *This point becomes more clear when we note that the purpose of crisis planning is* not *the preparation of a thick set of plans that sits on a shelf. Rather, crisis planning is a process of continually asking "what if" a set of crises hits us simultaneously. What are we prepared to do? Are we trained both intellectually and emotionally to handle a major crisis? In other words, the purpose of crisis management is to teach an organization to confront, in advance, the stress that will arise when a crisis happens. Crisis planning teaches an organization to roll with the punches. (Mitoff, 1988: 15–20)*

Mitoff also recommends a crises-prevention portfolio. There are four families of preventive actions that organizations can take to blunt crises: (1) audits; (2) external information/communications (e.g., Texas City took this action with industry but not with the public); (3) internal repair design (e.g., improved safety); and (4) internal emotional preparation (e.g., whistleblowers). Thus an organization would have two portfolios. The first one would prepare for the worst possible crisis out of each family group and the second one would consider the best preventive action for blunting crisis potential.

Developmental Planning. The desire to improve material well-being—dry houses, dry feet, sewers, hot water, baths, electricity, automobiles, good roads, vacations away from the village, varied diets, theatres, orchestras, bands—spurs an interest in developmental planning in the poorer countries of Asia, Africa, and Latin America. Can a relatively poor country plan the way it uses its resources—human, natural, financial, and technological—to maximize economic growth? Economists and political scientists have intensely debated this question since the end of World War II.

An important issue facing the governments of most less-developed countries is the extent to which they want to promote a balance between the agricultural and industrial sectors of the economy. Another very important issue for some is overpopulation; as total output has increased, these gains have been offset by population increases.

Economic Planning. Since the presidency of Franklin Roosevelt, there have been periodic demands to impose upon the American economy a system of planning, meaning comprehensive and detailed control or selective influence by government over investment, production, pricing, wage-setting and other decisions in the private economy. Obviously this goes well beyond the government's conduct of its taxing and spending functions and control of the money supply (see "Keynesian Economic Planning"). The current version of this demand is the call for "industrial policy." The cornerstone of most industrial policies is a strategic consensus among government, industry, and labor as to the basic direction in which the economy ought to move. Most industrial policies have three operating arms: a government agency to partially finance civilian cooperative research (see discussion of DARPA—a specialized unit within the R&D side of the Defense Department—in Chapter 7), efforts by government to reduce cost and increase availability of capital to business, and some systematic procedure for dealing with ailing industries.

The American people have shown little interest in proposals for economic planning in peacetime, except for Roosevelt's National Recovery Administration and Nixon's wage and price controls. Simply put, they think it would interfere with a market system that has worked reasonably well. Who is correct? Advocates of industrial policy would look under "Japanese Planning" to support their position. Opponents would look no further than the next entry.

Five-Year Plan. The Soviet Union used a central plan to control the production and distribution of most goods and services from the time of Lenin until the fall of Gorbachev. A central plan calls for the establishment of plans outlining production goals for a five-year period and detailing how they are to be met. The concept is riddled with problems.

First, production goals are extremely ambitious and hence seldom met. Second, almost all rewards to managers are based on fulfillment of the production target. If we assume that the target for a bolt factory is so many kilograms of bolts, then a manager's incentive is to make huge bolts; but if the target becomes a certain number of bolts, the manager's incentive might be to make tiny ones. Whether the manager's shenanigans meet customer needs is, to the manager at least, beside the point. Third, because the incentive system's aim is to fulfill the target, managers are not concerned with quality, research and development, or maintenance.

Growth Planning. Back in the United States of America, Florida is falling away, piece by piece, mile by mile. With nearly 12 million residents and more newcomers pouring in at the rate of 1,000 a day, the state's beauty is eroding as fast as the fragile beaches. State planners say that each new migrant to Florida eventually requires $10,000 worth of public services. With 7,000 new arrivals a week, projections call for the statewide costs of services to nearly double by the year 2000. Few can agree on how to slow down this influx.

Across the continent, voters in San Francisco know how to deal with this problem. Proposition M, which they passed in 1986, set the limits to office expansion through 1998. The city's downtown plan had already imposed strict architectural requirements for the size, height, and shape of each building. Developers are required to provide a certain amount of open space, to create plazas, and to put up pieces of art. Taken together, these requirements add an extra $15 per square foot to the cost of development—life as usual in the City on the Bay.

Even more conservative Los Angeles has joined the no-growth movement. It halved the maximum permissible density on 85 per cent of commercial and industrial land. One reason for this change, after years of real estate boom, is that millions of jobs are now being created at the outskirts of our metropolitan areas, and politically active suburbanites do not want office buildings and industrial parks rising near their neighborhoods and attracting traffic to their own quiet streets.

The crux of the problem for growth planners, then, is this: how to devise a way that a town can grow fast but with class and can add new industries and residences—without quick, cheap, land-gorging, environmentally insensitive strip development. Consider a university town on the Front Range of the Rockies. Since World War II, its population has grown from 12,000 to 85,000—an even faster rate than Florida's. Yet Boulder has a vibrant downtown, minimal unemployment, beautiful views of the mountains unmarred by billboards, and plenty of open lands. The reason is that Boulder has followed intelligent growth-planning principles.

For example, in 1959, when it appeared that a big convention-hotel center would be built between the city and its mountains, citizens raised the money to buy and protect the property as open space. Twelve years later, the city devised a comprehensive plan specifically indicating which land can be built on and which cannot. The city also got the county government to let it control all its surrounding territory. It limits its annual growth to 2 percent and gives preference to multifamily housing when issuing building permits. All Boulder housing projects must set aside 15 percent for moderate- and low-income families. Recently, when U.S. West, the big telephone company, wanted to build a research center near an open space of land, the city guided the company to an acceptable location and, unlike other towns, offered no tax write-offs or free land (Pierce, 1989). Boulder has controlled its own destiny.

Housing Planning. See "Transportation Planning." The two go together.

Indicative Planning. France has developed a method of economic planning called indicative planning, a name meant to suggest planning by voluntary compliance and agreement rather than by government coercion. Under this system, representatives of government, industry, and labor, along with technical experts, hammer out and agree to a national economic plan. The aim is to achieve some coordination of economic activity simply by passing both information and ideas back and forth among all the parties.

It sounds good, but the bottom line is that the economic performance of France never really matched that of Germany (to which it is always comparing itself). Although it would be wrong to say that France has abandoned indicative planning, its government has in recent years been less obtrusive in the economy.

Japanese Planning. Japan, like France, has a long history of economic planning by government. In particular, the Ministry of International Trade and Industry (MITI) has been singled out as an important element in this system. MITI can designate special regions as industrial parks, target certain industries for growth, plan research efforts by firms in the targeted industry, and impose trade barriers to protect those firms from foreign competition.

Keynesian Economic Planning. The British economist John Maynard Keynes (1883–1946) has had a profound influence on every American president since Herbert Hoover, with the possible exception of Ronald Reagan. Essentially, Keynes argued that, since the private economy may not reach full employment on its own, government should plan to spur it along. When political officials advocate priming the pump—by establishing or escalating government programs to get the country moving again or by slashing taxes to boost consumption—they are following Keynesian economics.

Long-Range Planning. Unlike action planning (described above), long-range planning means dealing with future implications of present decisions on setting goals. It looks five or more years ahead.

Military Planning. One of the oldest forms of planning is found in the military. When things have gone well on the battlefield, it means that the plan and its execution were good and that there was minimal enemy interference with the operation. This, of course, was the case in 1991 with Operation Desert Storm, one of the most stunning and one-sided victories in history.

The U.S. Armed Forces operates with a system adapted from the General Staff system introduced in Prussia in 1809. In such a system, determining whether good performance in planning and execution is due to the staff system and the quality of its people or to the genius of the commander is not always easy. In any event, when planning the battle, General Schwarzkopf and his staff applied a doctrine that is both old and new: the AirLand Battle Doctrine. It is new to the extent that it tries to take maximum advantage of the most modern developments in technology. It is old because it emphasizes the application of the new technologies in accordance with the classic **principles of war.** The principles are worth repeating here because of their obvious applicability to effective planning in civil affairs:

1. *Objective.* Every operation must be directed toward a decisive, obtainable objective.
2. *Offensive.* Only offensive action achieves decisive results.
3. *Simplicity.* Too many things can go wrong when plans are complicated. This rule is also known as the "KISS principle" (Keep It Simple, Stupid).
4. *Unity of command.* Every person is held accountable to only one supervisor.
5. *Mass.* Maximum available resources must be applied at the point of decision.
6. *Economy of forces.* Minimum essential means must be employed at points other than that of decision.
7. *Maneuver.* Maneuver must be used to alter the relative combat power of opposition.
8. *Surprise.* Surprise may decisively shift the balance of combat power in favor of whoever achieves it.
9. *Security.* Security is essential to the application of the other principles.

National Planning. See "Economic Planning."

Operational Planning. Sometimes it is useful to distinguish planning efforts in terms of their scope. Planning of the broadest scope, setting general goals, is called strategic. When the Allies decided to defeat Germany before Japan or to land at Normandy rather than southern France, they were engaged in strategic planning. When a company commander orders the first platoon to swing in a large arc to the right and attack the enemies' left flank, that commander is engaged in tactical planning. In scope and detail, operational planning falls somewhere between these two.

Planning-Programming-Budgeting System (PPBS). This budget system attempts to interrelate and coordinate the three management processes constituting its title. Planning is related to programs that are keyed to budgeting. To further emphasize the planning aspect, the system requires that agencies push their time horizons out five years, making five-year forecasts for program plans and cost estimates (see also Chapter 11).

Quality Planning. Quality planning has become about as fashionable in the 1990s as PPBS was in the 1960s. Planning should be a key part of quality control. Everything that happens in a quality system must be a result, not a reaction. More specifically, quality planning involves the following tasks: (1) Providing a basic plan for maintenance and improvement of an agency's service; (2) carefully placing controls where they offer the most prevention for the dollars spent; (3) exerting maximum influence on the planning of others in an effort to make prevention of errors an inherent part of each agency's operation; and (4) periodically reviewing and upgrading quality control systems. Good things happen when planned; bad things happen on their own (see also Chapter 12).

Regional Planning. In recent years, a concern for broader issues—ecology, transportation, urban redevelopment, economic development, water supply, and so on—has fueled an increasing interest in regional (as opposed to city) planning. In places that have substantial growth, it is clearer and clearer that existing governance systems cannot handle the problem.

Strategic Planning. See "Operational Planning."

Transportation Planning. Today there is much less reason to separate business and home than there was when smokestack factories made living near one's work undesirable. Now, in suburbs where service professionals are the new industry, office buildings are being built near stores and houses. Indeed, traffic studies show that more Americans are commuting between suburbs than between suburb and city.

Unfortunately there is little logic to where these suburbs have sprung up. All over the country, one finds office buildings, shopping malls, and housing clusters scat-

These drawings of San Francisco show that a tall building at the top of a hill (left) allows for an unobstructed view down the street and beyond but that a tall building on the slope (right) severely restricts the view from above. In 1984, the city approved one of the toughest plans ever put together for an American downtown area. It strictly limits the height of new buildings and dictates more tapered, graceful designs for them. (Source: Department of City Planning, San Francisco. The Urban Design Plan, *1971, p. 82.)*

tered carelessly along looping roadways near freeway off-ramps. The primary feature of these ubiquitous "centers" is freeway convenience. They create a way of life best seen and understood through the windshield.

Thus, a number of planners have begun to ask how the same basic components of house, workplace, and store can be configured into small, independent towns. The idea is to foster a sense of community and give towns a higher cultural purpose than the efficient flow of traffic.

An example of this new approach to planning for transportation and housing is Phoenix's "urban village concept." Phoenix split into nine separate areas with populations of about 100,000 each, where residents decide the growth patterns of their own "village." Each urban village has a downtown core surrounded by residential areas, with the hopes of keeping workers closer to their homes and off the highways. Although many admit the system does not work as well in reality as it does when theorized on the chalkboard, they credit the system for slowly revitalizing old neighborhoods and unsnarling traffic.

Urban Planning. Although urban planning is not a panacea for all the ills of a city, it is the essential mechanism that a democratic society uses to deal with complex interrelated problems such as suburban sprawl, neighborhood deterioration, visual blight, traffic congestion, air and water pollution, flooding, despoliation of the environment, stable tax base, and economic growth. Urban planning is the basic function of city

Urban planners and government officials in places such as Sacramento, Tampa, and Tacoma would like to see the next generation of suburbs include more of the features of the traditional small town—front porches, long walks, and corner stores. Growing concern over traffic congestion and general living conditions in the suburbs could lead to more projects to develop communities in which life does not revolve around the automobile. (Photo by Ed Kashi)

government that deals with these issues in a comprehensive and coordinated manner. There is no connection between this type of planning and the failed planned economies of Eastern Europe. In fact, Switzerland, the epitome of free enterprise, has perhaps the most vigorous urban planning of any industrialized nation.

The comprehensive plan, the document resulting from the urban planning process, is the means used to forecast and promote more desirable and efficient growth and patterns of development. The planning process should involve all of the "stakeholders" and interest groups—elected officials, business leaders, neighborhood groups, and civic organizations. It should result in a shared vision of the city's future—where it is, where it wants to go from here, what kind of city it will be for future generations, and what means it will use to get there.

More specifically, the comprehensive plan describes future transportation system, general land-use patterns, utilities, parks, and public facilities. It also includes strategies for economic development, neighborhood stabilization, environmental protection, preservation of open space, and urban-design guidelines for important civic places (see "Zoning").

Visionary Planning. Urban planners (see previous item) come in three varieties: incrementalist, deal maker, and visionary (Fulton, 1989). Today comprehensive plans are much more tied to the reality of existing economic conditions and to the nuts and bolts of development deals.

Traditionally, however, urban planning has been distinguished from other public policy professions—city management, for example—by its idealism and breadth of vision. By preparing plans for whole neighborhoods and cities, urban planners provided not just a blueprint for a community's future but also the inspiration for making that future better. As Daniel Burnham, an early planning pioneer, exhorted his colleagues, "Make no little plans; they have no magic to stir men's blood."

The last ten years or so, however, have been difficult times for visionaries. The disappearance of federal renewal funds (Chapter 3) and the increase in neighborhood political power have eliminated some of the freedom a planner like Burnham enjoyed in pursuing his vision. Today's vision planner must increasingly focus on issues related to specific developments. Hence change comes more in increments than in great leaps. Furthermore, the financial crisis in local government has turned urban planners into fiscal deal makers, using land-use regulations as chips in the game of attracting new business to their city and away from someone else's.

Wartime Planning. The experience of World War II left behind changes of thinking about planning that would not entirely disappear. The American economy performed brilliantly during the war. Total output rose about 12 percent a year from 1939 to 1944. Unemployment fell to negligible levels. There was an unprecedented degree of government planning during the war: comprehensive price controls, elaborate mobilization plans, rationing and materials allocation, and so forth. Some drew from that experience the lesson that extensive government planning was feasible and necessary.

Xerox's Planning Sometime around 1969, the golden era of American industry died. And Xerox, which had been a premier American corporation, almost died too. It took more than a decade for top management to realize how good the Japanese competition was. Since that realization, Xerox has done many things to turn itself around. Because the earlier entry, "Business Planning," gave little idea of how a first-rate corporation shapes its destiny and because there might be some lessons here for public administrators, the ten driving forces behind the Xerox turnaround are listed below (adapted from Jacobson & Hillkirk, 1986):

1. Benchmarking: sending investigative teams to see how the best-run organizations in your field do things.
2. Pushing responsibility down (see Chapter 8).
3. Putting more emphasis on market research (see Chapter 4).
4. Locating a rallying point: finding a specific project that might help create fighting spirit in the organization.
5. Capitalizing on state-of-the-art technology.
6. Internationalizing: making your strategy global.

7. Employing just-in-time operations: getting timely deliveries of defect-free supplies from a few local vendors.

8. Employing automation and computerization: (see Chapter 12).

9. Moving faster: U.S. Postal Service, take note!

10. Emphasizing quality (see Chapter 12.)

Zoning. One of the tools cities use to carry out their comprehensive plan (see "Urban Planning") is zoning, that is, regulating land-use patterns and standards. Zoning is not an end in itself but a means of implementing comprehensive planning. Protecting neighborhoods, controlling visual blight and incompatible land uses, and promoting more desirable patterns of regional growth should be the first priorities.

Concepts for Review

- action planning
- crisis planning
- Delphi technique
- developmental planning
- economic planning
- environmental impact statement
- evaluation
- expert forecasting
- exploratory and normative forecasting
- forecasts, predictions
- growth planning
- impact assessment
- implementation
- indicative planning
- leading indicators
- logical incrementalism
- medium-range planning
- operational planning
- planning
- planning premises
- Planning-Programming-Budgeting System (PPBS)
- policy, plan, program
- policy planning
- principles of war
- quality planning
- rational planning model
- regional planning
- technology assessment
- transportation planning
- trend extrapolation
- urban planning
- visionary planning
- zoning

Nailing Down the Main Points

1. The essence of planning is to see future opportunities *and* threats and to exploit or combat them by decisions taken in the present. More rigorously defined, a *policy* is a statement of goals and of the relative importance attached to each

goal. It can be translated into a plan by specifying the objectives to be attained. A proposed set of specific actions intended to implement a plan is called a *program.*

2. The best government agencies devote a great deal of thought to defining their organization's mission. They avoid sweeping statements full of good intentions and focus, instead, on objectives that have clear-cut implications for the work of the organization's members.

3. The rational planning process goes thus: (*a*) Identify the problems to be solved; (*b*) design alternative courses of action to solve the problem and forecast the consequences of each alternative; (*c*) compare and evaluate the alternatives and choose the one whose probable consequences would be preferable; (*d*) design a plan of action for implementing the preferred alternative, and (*e*) keep the plan current through feedback and review.

4. Policy planning, the process of determining goals and their priorities, is often ignored in American government. Too much public policy is defined in terms of program; as such, it seeks to deal only with parts of the system. The influence of political leadership is perhaps greatest at this early stage in the planning process.

5. In the medium-range planning stage, policy begins to be converted into action. Here, in particular, we are concerned with the design of alternatives and the evaluation of each in terms of its consequences. Common errors in this stage: failure to consider enough alternatives and reluctance to question rigorously every alternative (and the assumptions upon which it is founded).

6. Implementation and evaluation are the final two stages in the planning process. They will be discussed more fully in Chapter 9.

7. The model of logical incrementalism can help us to remember the important role that politics, human behavior, and subjective factors play in policy planning.

8. Unlike predictions, which attempt to make absolute statements about what *will* happen, forecasts offer probabilistic statements about what *may* happen. In recent years, the number of forecasting techniques has grown quite rapidly, but most are related to six of the more basic methods: expert forecasting, consensus methods, trend extrapolation, leading indicators, and impact assessment. Properly used, these methods can provide us with a somewhat less murky glimpse of the future of public administration.

9. Besides the general approach to planning discussed in the first half of this chapter, students of public administration should also be conversant with more specialized types of planning. Among the most important of these to a public manager are action planning, crisis planning, and urban planning.

Problems

1. Public officials at all levels of government are frequently criticized for short-sighted decisions. Elected officials may be accused of looking forward only as far as the next election and of placing narrow, parochial interests above the general welfare. To what extent is such criticism justified? Do you see any solution?

2. The anecdote about Kennedy and Goldberg in this chapter illustrates the need for a chief executive to consult widely before making important decisions. Discuss the problems that might arise if this approach to decision making is pushed too far.

3. Unlike several European countries, the United States does not have a full-fledged national planning body. Nonetheless, a number of institutions, such as the Council of Economic Advisors, do have important planning functions. What other institutions would you say contribute to planning at the national level? Should the United States have a central planning body?

4. The EPA routinely disseminates air and water pollution abatement requirements that virtually dictate state and local land use in many situations; this activity reflects a national awareness that, in a complex industrial society, many sorts of public regulation and planning are inescapable. It also poses a national dilemma. On the one hand, the federal government can tamper with a 200-year-old national tradition of land use being determined primarily by private initiative. On the other, it can do nothing. The second option allows communities all over the country, beset by growth troubles, to adopt growth plans. Do you think local governments can effectively influence growth and development? Since the national population is supposed to increase by at least 50 million people in the next 25 years, is *growth control* really just a fancy term for exclusionary policies? Will attempts to manage growth have a negative impact on the local economy?

5. Using back issues of local newspapers, survey the planning process in one urban area for one particular policy problem (e.g., mass transportation). Pay particular attention to when the need was first perceived, who the participants were, what the "leverage points" were, and where the sources of funds were. (The term *leverage points* refers to those participants who, at various times in the entire process, exhibited exceptional power or influence over the course of events.)

6. Some argue that forecasts designed to influence public planners are often so exaggerated and simplified that their effect is the very opposite of what their authors desire. Far from alerting planners to important problems, the doomsday forecast may so condition the planners to disaster that the capacity of the human race to survive is undermined. Discuss.

7. Strategic planning, as discussed in this chapter, implies a comprehensive, systematic scanning of the external environment of an organization. With the basic mission of the organization in mind, administrators try to identify which parts of the environment are relevant for further study. List two to four questions that a college or university might want to consider under each of the following headings:
a. Economic
b. Demographic
c. Sociocultural
d. Political and regulatory
e. Technological

CASE 5.1

★★★★★★★★★★★★★★★★★★★★★★★★★★★★★★★★★★

Robin Hood

It was early in the spring of the second year of his insurrection against the High Sheriff of Nottingham that Robin Hood took a walk in Sherwood forest. As he walked he pondered the progress of the campaign, the disposition of his forces, his opposition's moves, and the options that confronted him.

The revolt against the Sheriff began as a personal crusade. It erupted out of Robin's own conflict with the Sheriff and his administration. Alone, however, he could accomplish little. He therefore sought allies, men with personal grievances, and a deep sense of justice. Later he took all who came without asking too many questions. Strength, he believed, lay in numbers.

The first year was spent in forging the group into a disciplined band—a group united in enmity against the Sheriff, willing to live outside the law as long as it took to accomplish their goals. The band was simply organized. Robin ruled supreme, making all important decisions. Specific tasks were delegated to his lieutenants. Will Scarlett was in charge of intelligence and scouting. His main job was to keep tabs on the movements of the Sheriff's men. He also collected information on the travel plans of rich merchants and abbots. Little John kept discipline among the men, and he saw to it that their archery was at the high peak that their profession demanded. Scarlock took care of the finances, paying shares of the take, bribing officials, converting loot to cash, and finding suitable hiding places for surplus gains. Finally, Much the Miller's Son had the difficult task of provisioning the ever increasing band.

The increasing size of the band was a source of satisfaction for Robin, but also a subject of much concern. The fame of his Merrymen was spreading, and new recruits were pouring in. Yet the number of men was beginning to exceed the food capacity of the forest. Game was becoming scarce, and food had to be transported by cart from outlying villages. The band had always camped together. But now what had been a small gathering had become a major encampment that could be detected miles away. Discipline was also becoming harder to enforce. "Why?" Robin reflected. "I don't know half the men I run into these days."

While the band was getting larger, their main source of revenue was in decline. Travelers, especially the richer variety, began giving the forest a wide berth. This was costly and inconvenient to them, but it was preferable to having all their goods confiscated by Robin's men. Robin was therefore considering changing his past policy to one of a fixed transit tax.

The idea was strongly resisted by his lieutenants who were proud of the Merryman's famous motto: "Rob from the rich and give to the poor." The poor and the townspeople, they argued, were their main source of support and information. If they were antagonized by transit taxes they would abandon the Merrymen to the mercy of the Sheriff.

Robin wondered how long they could go on keeping to the ways and methods of their early days. The Sheriff was growing stronger. He had the money, the men, and the facilities. In the long run he would wear Robin and his men down. Sooner or later, he would find their weaknesses and methodically destroy them. Robin felt that he must bring the campaign to a conclusion. The question was how this could be achieved?

Robin knew that the chances of killing or capturing the Sheriff were remote. Besides, killing the Sheriff might satisfy his personal thirst for revenge, but would not change the basic problem. It was also unlikely that the Sheriff would be removed from office. He had powerful friends at court. On the other hand, Robin reflected, if the district was in a perpetual state of unrest, and the taxes went uncollected, the Sheriff would fall out of favor. But on further thought, Robin reasoned, the Sheriff might shrewdly use the unrest to obtain more reinforcements. The outcome depended on the mood of the regent Prince John. The Prince was known as vicious, volatile and unpredictable. He was obsessed by his unpopularity among the people, who wanted the imprisoned King Richard back. He also lived in constant fear of the barons who were growing daily more hostile to his power. Several of these barons had set out to collect the ransom that would release King Richard the Lionheart from his jail in Austria. Robin had been discreetly asked to join, in return for future amnesty. It was a dangerous proposition. Provincial banditry was one thing, court intrigue another. Prince John was known for his vindictiveness. If the gamble failed he would personally see to it that all involved were crushed.

The sound of the supper horn startled Robin from his thoughts. There was the smell of roasting venison in the air. Nothing had been resolved or settled. Robin headed for camp promising himself that he would give these problems first priority after tomorrow's operation.

Case Questions

1. What are Robin's key problems? How are they related to each other? Trace their emergence.
2. Which problems should Robin tackle first?
3. Develop a new strategy for Robin Hood. Pay close attention to implementation as well as formulation.

Case References

Case copyright © 1985 by Joseph Lampel, New York University. All rights reserved. Reproduced by permission.

CASE 5.2

★★★★★★★★★★★★★★★★★★★★★★★★★★★★★★★★★★

Thinking Strategically at the Veterans Administration

Background

As noted in the beginning of this chapter, planning is the most important management function. Although some organizations hire planning experts, the responsibility for planning rests with public administrators. Essentially, strategic thinking means to take the long-term view and to see the big picture, including the organization and its environment and how they fit together. *Strategic management* is the set of decisions and actions used to formulate and implement strategies that will provide a good fit between the organization and its environment so as to achieve the organization's goals.

The strategic management process helps focus the attention of top management on identifying and resolving key issues. Through this process, they can set a clear organizationwide direction and move the organization toward achieving its goals. Key, or strategic, issues are the most critical questions that affect an organization's future direction, its services, and its basic values. Frequently these issues involve more than one component or function. For example, one strategic issue would be how an organization needs to adjust to serve a dramatically changing population. Another would be how to remedy persistent systemic weaknesses in service quality. A strategic management process, however, does not encompass all the issues an organization faces on a daily basis. Instead, it focuses squarely on the issues that are the most appropriate for the organization's top-management head to address.

The strategic management process will enhance the organization's ability to address the following fundamental topics and questions:

- *Direction:* Where is the department going?
- *Strategy:* How will it get there?
- *Budget:* What is its blueprint for action?
- *Accountability:* How will it know if it is achieving its direction?

Systematically addressing these questions can help the department head proactively manage change and avoid crisis management.

To make these grand abstractions as concrete as possible, let us consider how the strategic management process could help one specific government agency, the Veterans Administration (VA).

Major Management Challenges Facing the VA

The VA is responsible for providing care and services to America's eligible veterans. It currently employs over 219,000 people on a full-time basis, has an annual budget of about $30 billion, and operates three major components—the Veterans Health Services and Research Administration, Veterans Benefits Administration, and National Cemetery System. The VA's mission involves delivering a wide range of services—medical, housing, insurance, education, income, and burial. Its mission also entails using its facilities to educate and train a large portion of the nation's medical practitioners, through affiliations with medical schools, and supporting research that benefits veterans' health care and quality of life. In addition, the VA is responsible for providing medical services in a war or national emergency.

Today the VA faces significant management challenges in effectively fulfilling its mission. Some of the VA's aging medical facilities have not kept pace with changes in patient treatment patterns. Further, weaknesses in certain information and quality assurance management systems have hindered the VA's ability to manage programs and have contributed to delays in service to veterans.

Dramatic changes in the veteran population compound these challenges. This population is aging swiftly (see Exhibit 1A), and the VA will need to make system adjustments to meet the medical and income needs of an older population. Projections show the total number of veterans dropping from 27 million in 1990 to 13 million by 2040 (see Exhibit 1B). This implies the need for well-conceived, long-range, nationwide plans to ensure that the VA can effectively adapt to these population trends. By early in the next decade, most veterans will not have fought in a war, indicating the need to reassess programs and services established primarily for wartime or combat veterans.

To address these challenges, the VA must work with groups affected by and interested in the VA's programs (see Exhibit 2). Groups concerned with the VA's mission are generally any individual, group, or organization that can place a claim on the VA's attention, resources, or output, or that is affected by that output. The administration, the Congress, the veterans' service organizations, and the secretary and key line and staff managers from the Department of Veterans Affairs (all of which are highlighted in the shaded area in Exhibit 2) are concerned with the VA's mission. These entities also represent other concerned groups.

Lessons Learned from Past Strategic Management Efforts

1. The planning process should consider the VA's unique operational, cultural, and environmental circumstances. It also should focus on gaining support from internal managers and key external groups for changes in services by involving them in the process. Most importantly, strong, sustained, and visible secretarial leadership of and commitment to a strategic management process are essential to its success.

2. Key line managers from headquarters and field offices should participate in formulating a strategic direction for the VA. Their participation would enhance the likelihood of congruence between the VA's future direction and the line managers' actions. Past efforts did not involve key line managers from the field in a meaningful dialogue on key issues facing veterans. Without an opportunity to participate in discussions of these issues, these managers did not support the efforts.

3. Because the purpose of the process is to establish a direction for the VA based on the priority needs of the veteran, planned management actions to achieve the VA's direction should shape its budget. In the past, the administrator's staff did not present strategic management as a way to develop a clear future direction. Instead, it used the strategic management process as a budgetary tool to cut costs and implemented it in an abrasive manner, ultimately resulting in active opposition by line and staff managers.

4. The process should elevate only the key issues to the secretary's attention. Line managers criticized past attempts to implement strategic management for creating a "meaningless paperwork exercise." These past efforts required detailed plans that covered too many component objectives and did not focus on the key issues that would have benefited from the administrator's involvement.

5. A strategic management process should foster a shared understanding of the department's future direction among the three components, enhancing consistency between their day-to-day actions and the department's aims. A unified strategic direction for the whole department,

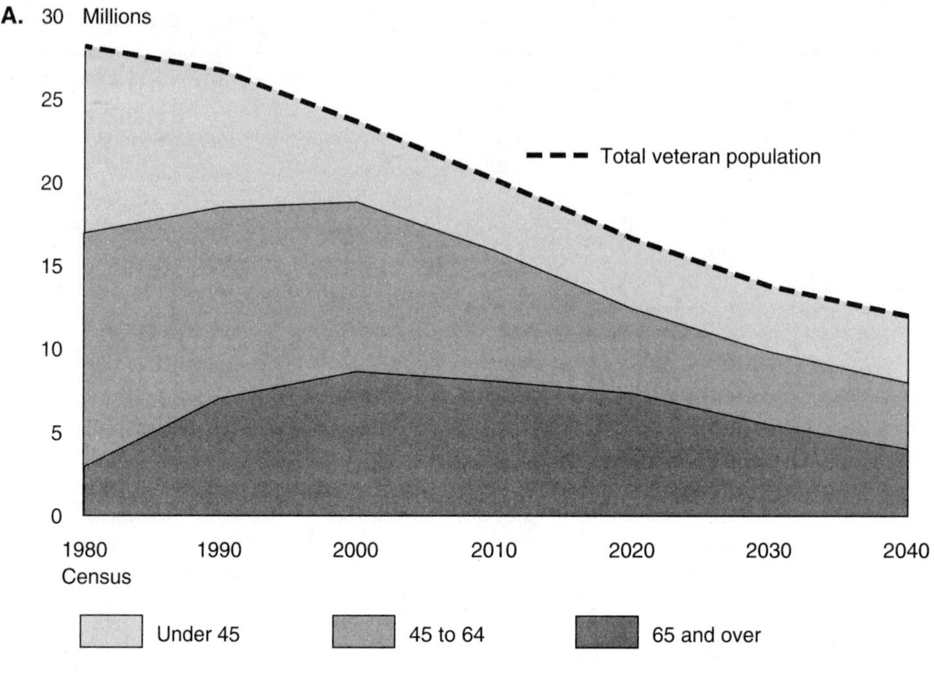

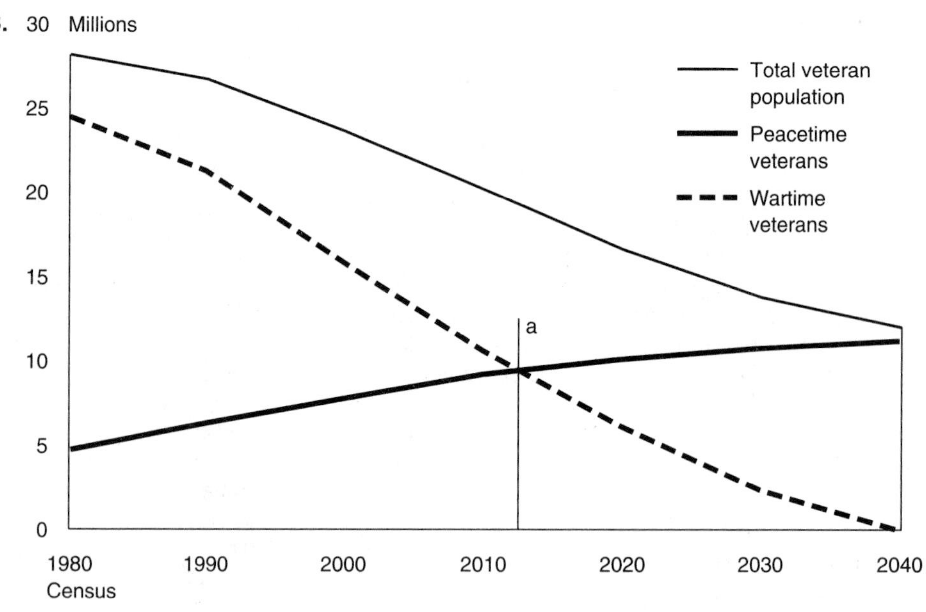

EXHIBIT 1

The Changing Veteran Population Mix

SOURCE: U.S. General Accounting Office, *Management of VA* (Washington, D.C.: U.S. Government Printing Office, 1990), pp. 14 and 15.

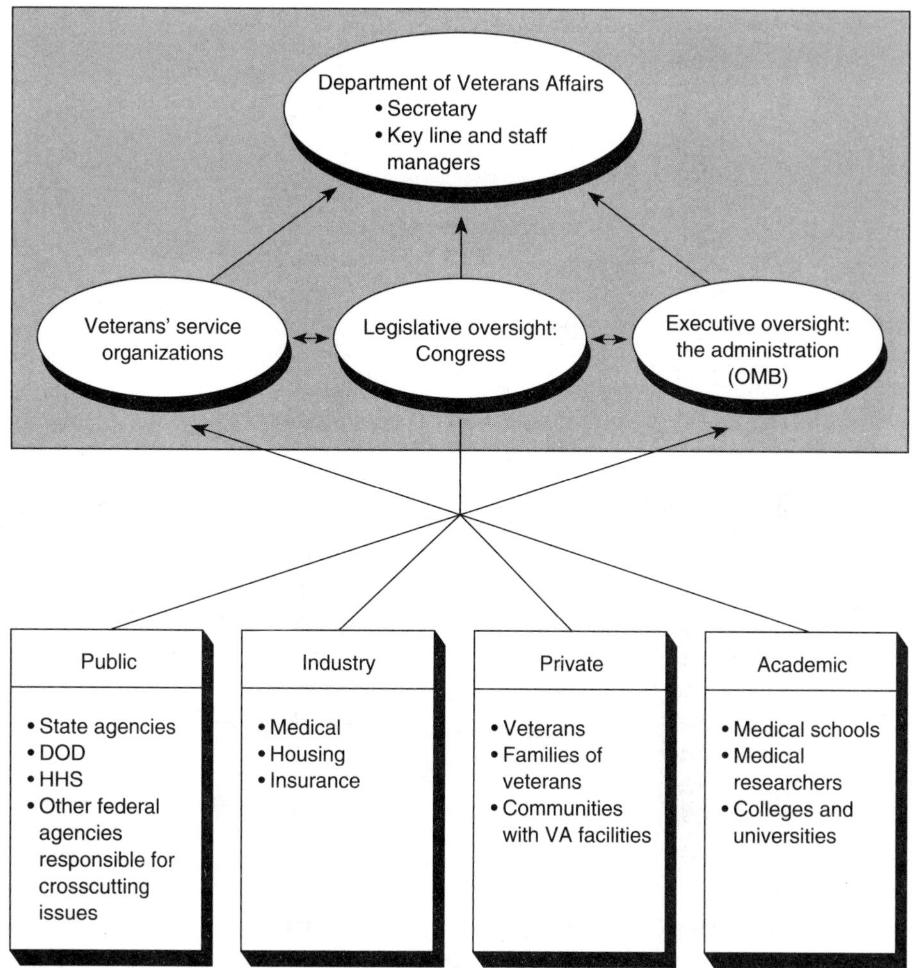

EXHIBIT 2
Groups Concerned with the VA's Mission

SOURCE: U.S. General Accounting Office, *Management of VA* (Washington, D.C.: U.S. Government Printing Office, 1990), p. 17.

based on veterans' priority needs, provides the needed common focus—a shared vision of the future.

6. Early in the strategic management process, the secretary should bring in external groups that influence the VA's policies and operations. Despite the difficulty in bringing together historically disparate interests, their early and active participation should lead to some common ground of understanding and convergence of interests that could permit the VA to advance in new directions. Without the support of these key external groups, the VA's past attempts to plan strategically were not successful.

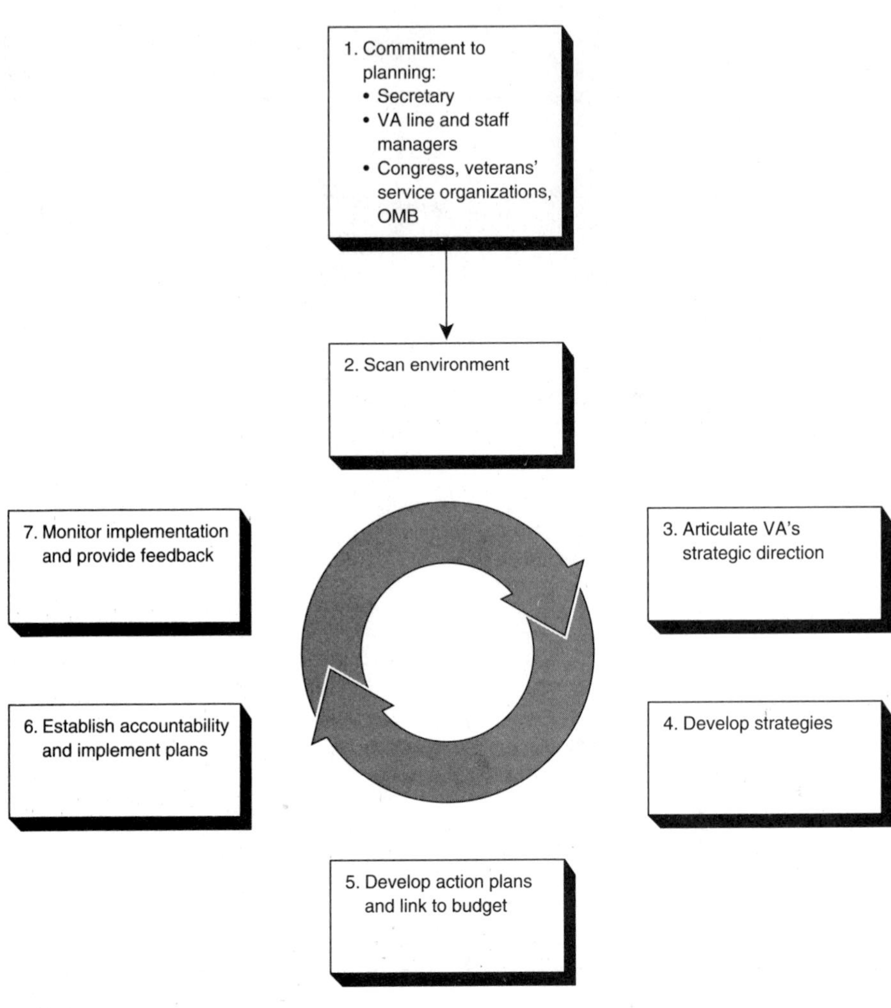
1. Commitment to planning:
• Secretary
• VA line and staff managers
• Congress, veterans' service organizations, OMB
2. Scan environment
3. Articulate VA's strategic direction
4. Develop strategies
5. Develop action plans and link to budget
6. Establish accountability and implement plans
7. Monitor implementation and provide feedback

EXHIBIT 3
A Proposed Strategic Management Process

A Proposed Strategic Management Process

In the light of the foregoing lessons and the VA's needs and environment, Exhibit 3 suggests what a strategic management process might look like. Elements 1 through 5 comprise the strategic planning aspects of the process, while elements 6 and 7 comprise the management functions. Although Exhibit 3 depicts a sequential process, it is iterative—successful problem solving may require that some elements be revisited. Table 1 (pp. 240–241) specifies, for each element, its purpose, participants, and tasks.

Of course, good processes do not ensure good plans. Nor do good plans ensure organizational success. Plans merely set the stage for action. The action, in turn, will only be as good as the ability of the members of the organization to make decisions in a sound and timely manner and to implement plans in a coordinated manner.

Case Questions

1. Conflict often occurs during goal setting because key managers disagree over objectives. Yet in order for goals to be effective, commitment is essential. Two techniques for achieving commitment to goals are coalition building and participation. Discuss how these techniques might be used here. Do managers typically disagree about the direction of their organizations?
2. If the VA's managers develop objectives and a set of actions to attain them, what might they be?
3. Do you think the VA displays effective planning? Would you recommend that the secretary create a planning staff? Encourage more participation from lower- and middle-level managers?
4. Can you think of any ways in which the concerned groups in Exhibit 2 might have objectives that sometimes conflict?

Case Reference

Adapted from U.S. General Accounting Office, *Management of VA* (Washington, D.C.: U.S. General Printing Office, 1990).

CASE 5.3

★★★★★★★★★★★★★★★★★★★★★★★★★★★★★★★★★★★

Peace Corps

Background

In nearly 30 years, the Peace Corps has sent 120,000 volunteers overseas. Born in 1961, during the heady days of John F. Kennedy's New Frontier, the agency got off to a fast start, with more than 15,500 volunteers by 1966. Over the next decade the corps suffered substantial budget cuts and lost some of its identity as it was merged with a new agency, Action (the principal agency for administering volunteer service programs sponsored by the federal government). After Watergate and the war in Vietnam, voluntary service fell out of fashion. By 1970, the number of corps volunteers had dropped below 5,500.

In 1982, President Reagan reestablished the Peace Corps as an independent agency. With a new director, it began to recruit midcareer professionals and slowly regained bipartisan support in Congress. In 1985, Congress mandated that the corps attain 10,000 volunteers.

Today the corps has 6,100 volunteers in 70 countries. Many of them are older and better trained than the early volunteers. The first Peace Corps classes were often dominated by liberal arts majors in their early 20s who worked on community development programs. The average age of today's Peace Corps volunteer is 31. About 60 percent of those accepted for service are trained in specific skills or professions like engineering, veterinary medicine, health and nutrition, computer sciences, forestry, special education, industrial arts, and vocational training. Those who are accepted with bachelors' degrees, but without specialized training or work experience, most commonly teach English. Rural development programs are still relevant, but in developing countries, the Peace Corps is also focusing on urban and environmental programs and on small business ventures.

Goals for the 1990s

As the decade of the 1980s closed, it was apparent that the Peace Corps had been

(text continues on p. 242)

TABLE 1.
Strategic Management Process: Overview of Roles and Responsibilities

	Purpose
Element 1: Commitment to planning	Obtain the support of key groups for the strategic management process.
Element 2: Scan environment	Obtain data to identify and analyze a range of possible strategic issues and support decision making throughout the process.
Element 3: Articulate VA's strategic direction	Envision in broad terms the VA's future direction.
Element 4: Develop strategies	Select the best approaches to address each strategic issue, and achieve the strategic direction.
Element 5: Develop action plans and link to budget	Develop action plans (see p. 219) and obtain resources needed to implement selected strategies.
Element 6: Establish accountability and implement plans	Assure implementation of action plans.
Element 7: Monitor implementation and provide feedback	Evaluate progress in implementing action plans. Ensure that relevant information flows between the components and the office of the secretary.

SOURCE: Adapted from U.S. General Accounting Office, *Management of VA* (Washington, D.C.: U.S. Governmen[t] Printing Office, 1990), pp. 30–37.

Participants	Tasks
Secretary; key VA line (including field) and staff managers; and representatives of external groups concerned with the VA's mission, including the Congress, the veterans' service organizations, and the OMB.	Agree on ground rules for conducting the strategic management process.
Secretary and VA line (including field) and staff managers, with assistance from VA planning staff.	Assess the VA's internal and external environment. Identify a range of possible strategic issues and their implications.
Secretary; key line (including field) and staff managers; and representatives of external groups concerned with the VA's mission, including the Congress, the veterans' service organizations, and the OMB.	Establish a clear direction for the VA's future actions. Select the strategic issues that the process will address.
Key VA line (including field) and staff managers. Key external groups participate as appropriate.	Identify alternate strategies to address each strategic issue. Identify barriers to and consequences of implementing alternatives. Select the alternative with the greatest potential for success and support by external groups.
Primarily component managers (i.e., line managers, not staff).	Develop detailed action plans based on selected strategies. Ensure that action plans shape budget submissions.
VA managers and staff.	Assign responsibility for implementing action plans. Make action plans a reality by incorporating them into operations. Link individual reward system to plan implementation.
Secretary and VA managers.	Monitor progress toward implementing action plans. Periodically report progress and problems to the secretary. Assess adequacy of action plans and take necessary corrective measures. Fine-tune strategic management process as required.

unable to make significant progress toward achieving its congressional mandate to attain 10,000 volunteers. To do so it must overcome a number of problems, which are discussed below.

Providing Trained Manpower. The Peace Corps has not fully implemented mechanisms to attract volunteers with scarce skills, such as doctors, veterinarians, education specialists, and crop extensionists. Instead, it continues to rely heavily on recruitment methods that have been used to attract generalists. The agency also does not provide a career path or adequate incentives to recruiters to seek scarce-skill volunteers. In light of this difficulty, the Peace Corps has instructed its overseas staff to encourage countries not to request volunteers with scarce skills. While the agency meets nearly 100 percent of the requests for generalists, it fills only about 60 percent of requests for individuals with scarce skills with volunteers having those skills. Another 24 percent are filled with "almost match" volunteers who do not fully meet Peace Corps criteria for the assignments.

The Peace Corps does not consistently develop adequate assignments for volunteers. Many volunteers are in assignments that have no specific tasks, objectives, or responsibilities. In some cases, local supervisors are unaware that volunteers are coming and do nothing to prepare for them. Some volunteers spend 6 to 12 months of their two-year tour developing their own assignments. Some volunteers (1) lack adequate language skills; (2) do not have local counterparts to carry on activities once they leave; (3) are in assignments that have little developmental impact; (4) are in positions that could be filled by local nations; or (5) are in assignments that assist wealthy people. These programming difficulties contribute to the relatively high rate of early returns. About 33 percent of Peace Corps volunteers leave before the end of their two-year assignments. A full 50 percent of the older volunteers do not complete their assignments.

Teaching Foreign People About America. In general, the Peace Corps has been successful in achieving its second goal because volunteers work directly on a people-to-people basis in the small towns and rural areas of the countries served. However, it would accurately reflect America's diverse population, and thereby better attain its second goal, by attracting more minorities to serve as volunteers. As of January 1989, only 7 percent of Peace Corps volunteers were minorities. According to Peace Corps officials, attracting minorities is difficult because they sometimes graduate from college with heavy debts and perceive the Peace Corps as a largely white middle-class institution. The Peace Corps has established minority recruitment goals but not has provided recruiters with the incentives or the tools for achieving these goals. Also, until recently, there have been few minorities in the upper levels of Peace Corps management to serve as recruitment role models.

Teaching Americans About Foreign Cultures. The Peace Corps operates a number of programs that seek to give returned Peace Corps volunteers the opportunity to teach Americans about foreign cultures; however, it has not devoted consistent effort or significant resources to this goal. The agency believes that, for the most part, the returned volunteers would perform this function on their own. Recently, returned volunteers formed a national association which seeks, among other things, to perform such "development education" activities. The Peace Corps gave the association grants and assisted in conducting mailings, but it has not made full use of the association and its affiliated groups to attain its third goal.

Case Questions

1. How did the Peace Corps' mission change over the last 20 years? Why?

How might the Peace Corps' mission change in the next 10 years?

2. Which of the Peace Corps' goals would be considered long range? Intermediate?
3. If Peace Corps managers develop plans and objectives to meet these goals, what might they be?
4. What are the strengths and weaknesses of the Peace Corps' current mission and strategy?

Case References

Gerard T. Rice, *The Bold Experiment* (South Bend, Ind.: Notre Dame Press, 1985), Milton Viorst, *Making a Difference: The Peace Corps at Twenty-Five* (New York: Weidenfeld & Nicholson, 1986); Blaine Harden, "The Peace Corps Is Getting Older—And Wiser," *Washington Post National Weekly Edition,* August 17, 1987; Pete Engardio and Steve Askin, "The Peace Corps' New Frontier," *Business Week,* August 22, 1988.

CHAPTER 6

Decision Making

Introduction

Decision making means selecting from various alternatives one course of action. As such, it cannot be divorced from the planning process described in the preceding chapter. Herbert Simon (1957a:1) said that the "task of 'deciding' pervades the entire administrative organization quite as much as does the task of 'doing'—indeed, it is integrally tied up with the latter."

There are at least four steps in decision making:

1. Identifying the problem (or opportunity).
2. Gathering facts.
3. Making the decision.
4. Implementing and evaluating the decision.

We shall explore the first three steps in this chapter, leaving the fourth step for Chapter 9.

Identifying the Problem (or Opportunity)

First, decision makers should establish what kind of problem exists. More specifically, they need to ask if the problem is **generic** or **unique**?

Most of the problems that an administrator faces are generic, that is, they are part of a pattern of problems stemming from one underlying cause (see Figure 6-1). Since this underlying cause is seldom obvious, the tendency of the administrator is to view the problem as a unique, isolated event and to treat it as such. Thus, administrators often find themselves treating symptoms rather than establishing rules or principles that remove the root cause. This is why many administrators make more decisions than they really need to.

Good administrators avoid cosmetic solutions. But the temptation to treat symptoms can be strong, particularly in an age of technology. Consider the concept of the

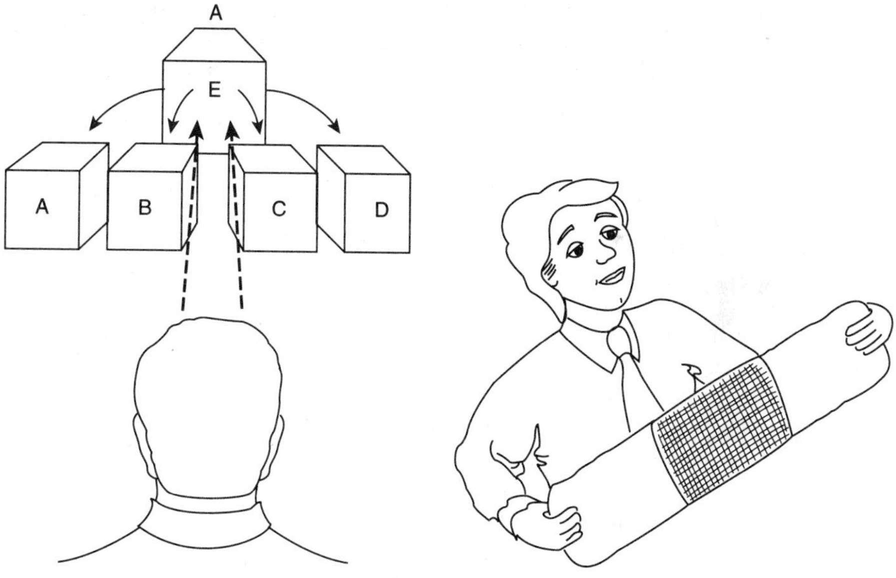

FIGURE 6-1

Generic and Unique Problems, or Why Effective Administrators Make Few Decisions

Effective decision makers know that very few problems or events are unique. Most are manifestations of underlying problems. Therefore, before attempting a quick fix on problems A, B, C, or D, they will try to find the basic problem E. Once E is solved, A, B, C, D, and any future problems stemming from E are eliminated. Thus effective decision makers make few decisions.

Is this not what a good physician does? If a patient complains, on separate visits, of increased thirst, itching, hunger, weight loss, weakness, and nausea, the physician does not simply try to remedy each on an ad hoc basis but rather asks, What might this problem be a symptom of? In contrast, many administrators are forever engaged in quick fixes and cosmetic solutions.

technology fix. The concept was defined by Alvin M. Weinberg (1966) as an innovation devised for the purpose of correcting a social defect. Admittedly, the device has its advantages sometimes; for example, drugs taken orally to prevent unwanted conception as a measure of population control. But quick fixes do not always provide the best solution. Stronger locks, higher (perhaps electrified) fences, and more powerful police weapons can, for example, reduce the *symptoms* of crime without affecting the real causes.

But let us return to the distinction between generic and unique problems and ask, What does the decision maker do about truly unique problems? Peter Drucker (1966) maintains that even events that seem completely isolated turn out to be, upon closer examination, the first manifestations of a new generic problem. Surely this was true of the free speech movement at Berkeley, the 1965 power failure in the whole northeastern North America, and the thalidomide tragedy. These three "isolated" events were actually bellwethers—to the campus turmoil of the late 1960s, the energy squeeze of the early 1970s, and the increased concern over assessing new biomedical technologies of the 1970s and 1980s.

Such events call not for quick fixes but for bold solutions. Drucker (1966:166) argues that a major failure of the Kennedy administration was its tendency to treat generic problems as unique. In the name of pragmatism, its members refused to develop rules and principles and insisted on treating everything "on its own merits."

Gathering Facts

Framing a Decision

With the problem accurately defined, the administrator then turns to framing the response. Here careful attention should be given to what I shall term the upper and lower limits of the decision.

Upper limits refers to the ever-present limitations that determine how far the administrator can go. One former presidential aide (Sorensen, 1963:22–42) notes five:

1. The limits of permissibility (Is it legal? Will others accept it?)
2. The limits of available resources.
3. The limits of available time.
4. The limits of previous commitments.
5. The limits of available information.

The list is self-explanatory, but point 5 merits emphasis simply because administrators rely so much on past experiences in making decisions. The experienced administrator believes, often without realizing it, that past mistakes and accomplishments are an almost infallible guide in decision-making situations. But this is a fallacy. Administrators must try to visualize the world as a whole and as a total system in which their own personal experiences are a very small and inadequate sample. A major corrective to this generalizing from personal experience is statistical analysis. Modern statistics is based on the concept of probability; it deals with the problem of making a probability of judgment about a characteristic of the population (e.g., income) on the basis of information derived from a small sample of that population.

Lower limits refers to what at least must occur for the problem to be solved. For example, Germany knew at the outbreak of World War I that it could win if and only if two minimum conditions were met. Germany would (Condition I) put up weak resistance against Russia thus allowing it to (Condition II) concentrate forces for a knockout blow to France. But as Russia began to penetrate deeper and deeper into East Prussia, the German general staff decided to pull forces from the Western front. Condition II was therefore not met and the chance for victory was lost (Drucker, 1966:132).

Chester I. Barnard (1938:202–5) introduced an idea quite similar to that of lower limits. He calls it the **limiting (strategic) factor** in decision making. It is the factor "whose control, in the right form, at the right place and time, will establish a new system of conditions which meets the purpose. Thus, if we wish to increase the yield of grain in a certain field, and we analyze the soil, it may appear that the soil lacks potash; potash may be said to be the strategic (or limiting) factor." If an administrator can discover the strategic factor—can exercise control at the right times, in the right place, right amount, and right form—then the decision becomes not only simpler (for other factors tend to work themselves out) but also more economical.

Schematically, we can think of every possible solution to a problem as being represented by a point in the box below. Solutions in the top section, however, must be ruled out because they violate the upper limits of a decision. Solutions at the bottom must also be ruled out because they fail to satisfy the lower limits of a successful decision. While this schematic does not directly provide a solution, it does drastically reduce the numbers of possible solutions an administrator might have to consider.

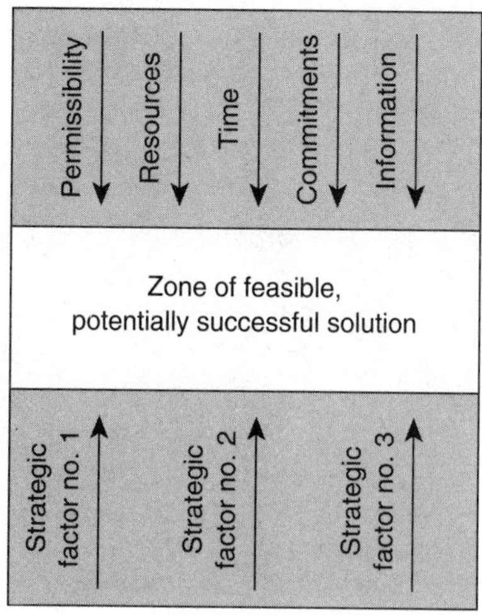

Consulting People

Even kings and queens consulted advisors. Queen Elizabeth did not defeat the Spanish in 1588 by reading *Teach Thyself to Thrash Armadas.* No, she consulted underlings.

It is also generally a good idea to consult those who will be most affected by the decision, checking your facts with theirs and, above all, *listening* to what they have to say (more about this in Chapter 8). The Great Pipeline Fracas of 1982 is a splendid example of what can happen when public executives forget to do this kind of consulting. The problem started when four of America's closest allies—three of them North Atlantic Treaty Organization (NATO) colleagues—arranged for a massive international project with the Soviet Union, a project that was to have been of considerable economic benefit to all parties. The project called for the use of large high-technology components designed and developed by American firms but manufactured by European subsidiaries of those firms, the companies with which the Soviet Union had signed the contracts. Enter Ronald Reagan. Sizing up the situation in a flash, he said "No Way—until the Soviets lift martial law in Poland!"

At first blush, Reagan's seemed a perfectly reasonable position. The project was unquestionably beneficial to the Soviets (the acquisition of badly needed Western currency), and why should America lend a hand to that? The pipeline decision would also be greeted enthusiastically by Polish-Americans. The trouble was that the pipeline decision had not been bounced off the other actors, and it was of considerable impor-

Ever-present limitations determine how far decision making in the White House can go. One of John F. Kennedy's top advisers noted five: permissibility, available resources, available time, previous commitments, and available information (see text). (Paris Match/Carone)

tance to their economies. They had been working on it for a long time; their governments were behind it; scores of companies and subcontractors and scores of thousands of jobs were involved.

Several weeks and many angry allies later, President Reagan lifted his sanctions against the pipeline.

His move had been quietly and persistently pursued by George Shultz, secretary of state. Shultz was, in fact, a man who made consulting with people an art form:

> *For as long as anyone can remember, the Secretary of State's conference room has contained a long mahogany table in two sections, embraced by two dozen or more chairs, with more chairs stacked arm to arm along the wall. Sometime after George P. Shultz's arrival in the building, the furniture was rearranged.*
>
> *Now the conference table is shorter and it is surrounded by only 10 chairs, with a few easy chairs on the periphery.*
>
> *The rearrangement was a signal from the new Secretary that things would be more intimate, more informal and personal than in times past. It was the mark of a man who pays a great deal of attention to dealing with people, a man who has a special way of exercising power.*
>
> *The Shultz approach seems to be, as aides quote it: "Let's get comfortable, talk things over, get everyone's ideas, see what the facts show, see if there isn't some commonsense approach to this problem that we can all feel comfortable with." (*New York Times, *September 7, 1982)*

Making the Decision: Five Analytical Techniques

After gathering facts and suggestions, the decision maker should be ready to begin assessing the various alternatives. In this section, we shall consider five *analytical* techniques that can help the administrator in this critical task:

1. Cost-benefit analysis.
2. Multiobjective models.
3. Decision analysis.
4. Systems analysis.
5. Operations research.

I should emphasize that, in this section, we are examining one particular style of thinking. The analytical method is founded on formal logic; it seeks to break sit-

(text continues on p. 252)

★★★★★★★★★★★★★★★★★★★★★★★★★★★★★★★★★★★

WORKING PROFILE

Herbert A. Simon

(Harry Coughanour, Pittsburgh Post-Gazette*)*

As much as any one person, Herbert A. Simon has shaped the agenda of public administration since 1937. A brilliant polymath, Simon has also won a Nobel Prize in economics, done pioneering work in political science and psychology, and helped lay the foundation for artificial intelligence (the enterprise of trying to build machines that think).

You may recall from our profile of Woodrow Wilson (Chapter 2) that the year 1937 marked the "high noon of orthodoxy." The study of public administration rested then on two great pillars: (1) politics and administration can and should be separated and (2) the principles of administration provided the definitive expression of managerial rationality. But as fate would have it, the very next year a tiny fissure appeared. Chester Barnard, an executive of Bell Telephone, had published *The Functions of the Executive.*

Barnard proposed that executives must perform three key functions: organizational communications, acquisition of essential services from individuals, and formation of purposes and objectives. This emphasis on human, participative, employee-centered executive leadership differs sharply from the cold, abstract principles of administrative orthodoxy. Barnard seemed to be saying that executives cannot apply the principles of administration to an organization in the same way that mathematicians might fit equations to data. Rather, executives must first create and maintain an environment in which effective management can occur and nurture among employees a belief in the purposes of the organization.

When *The Functions of the Executive* appeared, Simon was writing a major part of a volume called *Techniques of Municipal Administration,* which was supposed to inform experienced city managers how to run a city. He was 22 years old and without administrative experience. But aided by Barnard's insights, Simon quickly realized that a little administrative experience goes a long way. As he explains: "Life in organizations is not very different from life elsewhere. Most of the writing on administration, including Barnard's, was based on everyday observation, not on esoteric experimental or observational techniques. . . ." (Simon, 1991:73)

At the same time, Simon also realized that administrative theory could not be built entirely on common sense. "Systematic observation and experimentation were badly needed if the field was ever to become scientific. But until someone built a satisfactory theoretical framework, it would not be clear what kinds of empirical studies were called

★★★★★★★★★★★★★★★★★★★★★★★★★★★★★★★★★★★

★★★★★★★★★★★★★★★★★★★★★★★★★★★★★★★★★★★★★★★

for." (Simon, 1991:74) These reflections planted the seeds for what is generally regarded as the most influential book in public administration ever written: *Administrative Behavior* (1947).

The book contains the foundation of the theory of **bounded rationality** that he says has been his lodestar for nearly 50 years. Bounded rationality, which is a label for the computational constraints on human thinking, had its origins in Simon's study of public recreation in Milwaukee. The question that intrigued Simon was how the decision to divide funds between playground maintenance (administered by one organization) and playground activity (administered by another) was arrived at:

My previous study of economics provided me with a ready hypothesis: Divide the funds so that the next dollar spent for maintenance will produce the same return as the next dollar spent for leaders' salaries. I saw no evidence that anyone was viewing the decision in this way. Was I surprised at their ignoring accepted economic theory? Perhaps, initially, but on reflection, I didn't see how it could be done. How were the values of better activity leadership to be weighed against the values of more attractive and better-maintained playgrounds?

Now I had a new research problem: How do human beings reason when the conditions for rationality postulated by neoclassical economics are not met? (Simon, 1991:370)

In Simon's view, people who behave rationally are not optimizing anything at all; they are simply making decisions based on what their environment tells them they can and cannot do. People do not strive for the best; they look for what is possible within the bounds of their given situation. Instead of satisfying desire, human beings **satisfice,** that is, they search for "good enough" actions rather than optimal ones.

As Simon illustrates in his story "The Apple," which appears in Case 6.2, people torment themselves when they ask too-big questions about their ultimate desires. The proper procedure, according to Simon, is to determine the *boundaries* in which rationality can most constructively operate and then to keep one's sight within them. "Searching for the best can only dissipate scarce cognitive resources."

Administrative Behavior also contained a provocative discussion of the principles of administration. Simon's attack on this pillar of the orthodoxy was derived almost entirely from the logical structure and internal inconsistency of the principles themselves. Chapter 8 discusses the limitations of the principles.

Simon concluded *Administrative Behavior* by suggesting that administrative science may be either theoretical or practical. If it is the former, then propositions about administration may be descriptive of the way in which human beings behave in organized groups. If it is the latter, then propositions about administration would concern how human beings behave if they wish their activity to result in the greatest attainment of administrative objectives with scarce means. Simon urged public administrationists to develop these two forms of administrative science by exploring new fields of inquiry such as sociology, business administration (shades of Woodrow Wilson here), and social psychology.

In many ways, what Simon called for in 1947 was reflected in 1970 when the National Association of Schools of Public Affairs and Administration (NASPAA) was founded. Public administration had clearly become a distinct field of study, blending those practical and theoretical elements Simon had foreshadowed.

★★★★★★★★★★★★★★★★★★★★★★★★★★★★★★★★★★★★★★★

uations down into their component parts and to define problems by isolating them, thus making them more manageable. There are, however, other ways of looking at the world. The last section of this chapter will consider them, pointing out the strengths and weaknesses of each.

Cost-Benefit Analysis (CBA)

In an era of scarcity, interest in weighing cost against benefits rises. Today, the federal government must do more than assess the benefits of goals such as a cleaner environment, safer products, healthier working conditions, and better mass transit—it must also weigh the cost and other side effects of such action.

The methodology for these kinds of assessments has been around at least since 1936. That was the year that CBA became a requirement with the Flood Control Act, which established the policy that "the federal government should improve or participate in the improvement of navigable water . . . for flood-control purposes if the benefits to whomsoever they may accrue are in excess of the estimated costs. . . ."

Most CBA involves familiarity with certain common elements: the measurement of costs and benefits, the distributional impacts, the discount factor, and the decision rules. Let us examine each of these elements.

Measurement of Costs and Benefits. Assume that the U.S. Army Corps of Engineers is about to dig a ditch. Maybe the project is more in the nature of an irrigation system—but I want to keep things simple. To capture all effects, the analyst must proceed systematically, breaking down costs and benefits into major categories.

These categories are shown in Table 6-1 with examples. **Real benefits** are the benefits derived by the final consumer of the public project and, as such, represent an addition to the community's total welfare. They must, however, be balanced against the **real costs** of resources withdrawn from other uses.

Pecuniary benefits and **pecuniary costs** "come about due to changes in relative prices which occur as the economy adjusts itself to the provision of the public service.

Table 6-1.
Major Categories of Costs and Benefits for Irrigation Project

Category	*Costs*	*Benefits*
Real		
Direct		
Tangible	Costs of pipes	Increased farm output
Intangible	Loss of wilderness	Beautification of area
Indirect		
Tangible	Diversion of water	Reduced soil erosion
Intangible	Destruction of wildlife	Preservation of rural society
Pecuniary		Relative improvement in position of farm equipment industry

SOURCE: R. A. Musgrave and P. B. Musgrave, *Public Finance in Theory and Practice* (New York: McGraw-Hill, 1973), p. 142.

As a result, gains accrue to some individuals but are offset by losses which accrue to others. They do not reflect gains to society as a whole" (Musgrave & Musgrave, 1973:141). For example, say that earnings of roadside restaurants increase because of a highway project. Such gains do not reflect a net gain to society, since they are offset by costs to others (i.e., restaurants and grocery stores elsewhere). Consequently, in CBA, we can ignore these benefits.

Real benefits and costs can be either direct or indirect. **Direct benefits and costs** are those closely related to the main project objective. **Indirect benefits and costs**—sometimes called **externalities** or **spillovers**—are more in the nature of by-products. Admittedly, the line between direct and indirect can be fuzzy, requiring a judgment call by the analyst.

The term **tangible** is applied to **benefits** and **costs** that we can measure in dollars; those we cannot—for example, gain in world prestige from space projects—are referred to as **intangible.**

The following items illustrate some of the problems in and techniques for measuring costs and benefits:

- A frequent indirect cost in government programs is compliance costs, or, simply, red tape. For example, a new federal law designed to safeguard employee pension rights can cause small firms to terminate their plans because of paperwork requirements.

"Sure it's unfair to the little guy . . . He's the easiest one to be unfair with."

(From The Wall Street Journal, *with permission of Cartoon Features Syndicate.)*

- It is difficult to measure benefits with rigor. Consider the benefits from air pollution control. Effective pollution control means less damage to health, vegetation, materials, and property. If estimates of these benefits are called "crude approximations," then what would you call estimates for, say, aesthetic benefits (e.g., that the sky is now visible) and human comfort (e.g., that your eyes no longer water)?
- Not all cost-benefit studies reveal benefits exceeding costs. One government study on the benefits and costs of pollution control devices added to autos to comply with federal laws revealed that estimated costs of emission controls exceeded savings from the resulting abatement of pollution caused by auto emissions.

Distributional Impacts of Public Programs. In addition to trying to measure costs and benefits, some thought should be given in CBA in regard to the distribution of the costs and benefits resulting from a public program (Bonnen, 1969:425–26). Who actually benefits? What groups? It is sometimes not easy to identify beneficiary groups clearly. What is the distribution of program benefits among beneficiaries? Who should pay the program costs? Who actually does pay the cost of the program? How are program costs distributed among the burdened groups (see Bonnen, 1969:425–26)?

Discount Factor. Most public projects and programs take place over time, and how the analyst treats this time element is critical.

Again let us keep it simple. Think of time being divided into years and of future benefits and costs accruing in specific years. Table 6-2 shows, in column B, the dollar benefits over an interval of eight years: Since two years are required for construction, no benefits accrue until the third year. Column C shows the costs, which are initially high but then level off. Column D simply shows the net benefits (benefits minus costs) for each year.

Is the $1 million net benefit occurring in the fourth year really worth $1 million in present dollars? No, these future proceeds must be adjusted to allow for the fact that future benefits are less valuable than present ones. The reason is that today's $1 million could be invested and certainly return more than that to the investor four years later. Cost must be adjusted in a like manner. We call making these adjustments—that is, reducing future dollars to be comparable to today's dollars—**discounting.**

To find the value of a dollar in any future year, one need only multiply by a discount factor. The formula is

$$\text{Discount factor} = \frac{1}{(1 + i)^t}$$

where i is the interest rate and t is the number of years. Equipped with this formula (or, more likely, a table of discount factors or a hand-held business calculator), we return to the question posed a moment ago: How much is $1 million four years from today worth today? Assuming a modest interest rate of 10 percent, we first calculate the discount factors and then multiply the $1 million benefit by it. Thus,

Table 6-2.
Hypothetical Cost-Benefit Study (Dollars in millions)

Year	*Benefits**	*Costs**	*Net Benefits*	*Discount Factor (i = 10%)*	*Present Value of Net Benefits*
(A)	*(B)*	*(C)*	*(D)*	*(E)*	*(F)*
1	$ 0	$ 4	−4	.909	$−3.6
2	0	4	−4	.826	−3.3
3	1	1	0	.751	0
4	2	1	1	.683	.7
5	3	1	2	.621	1.2
6	4	1	3	.564	1.7
7	4	1	3	.513	1.1
8	4	1	3	.467	1.4
Total	$18	$14	4		$ −.8

Generally, in cost-benefit computations, only the *direct* costs and benefits are used. The overall study should, however, include a discussion of indirect costs and benefits.

$$\text{Present value} = \frac{1}{(1 + .10)^4} \times \$1{,}000{,}000 = .683 \times \$1{,}000{,}000$$
$$= \$683{,}000$$

Column E in Table 6-2 gives the discount factors for the first eight years of the project. Now we can adjust the net benefits in column D to reflect their present values and show them in column F. If we sum column F, we shall see that by the eighth year the project's costs outweigh its benefits. Clearly, we should not proceed with the project. If we changed the discount rate to 5 percent, however, benefits would outweigh costs by $1.3 million—such is the power of a few percentage points in CBA.

Parenthetically, I cannot help but wonder how many college football players who sign million-dollar professional contracts *to be paid over a five-year period* understand discounting. What is the present value of their income for the fifth year if the discount rate is 15 percent? (Answer on next page.*)

Decision Rules. If we assume that benefits do exceed cost, it does not necessarily follow that we should go ahead with a project. What we do depends on our decision rule.

First, we might be faced with a simple project that involves a yes-no decision; that is, the decision is between doing the project and not doing the project. The criterion we wish to use is the net benefit criterion. Define net benefit (NB) as

$$\text{NB} = \text{B} - \text{C}$$

and use the following decision rule: A simple project should be done if and only if its net benefits exceed zero. Thus, in our example, the net benefit is −$800,000, so

Optimism fills the air when voters are asked to approve construction or enlargement of a lavish public stadium for their communities. New Orleans's Superdome would make Houston's Astrodome "as obsolete as the Roman Coliseum." But soon reality sets in. The costs of remodeling Yankee Stadium (above) escalated from $24 million to $240 million. Because local taxpayers are obligated for such costs, one wonders whether stiffer user fees might not be fairer. What indirect *and* intangible *costs do you think might be involved in such projects? (New York Convention and Visitors Bureau)*

the project should not be undertaken. While this approach might seem obvious, it is an important one since it is frequently used by the Army Corps of Engineers in evaluating whether to approve funds, say for widening a ship channel.

Second, we might be faced with a choice between two mutually exclusive projects. For example, we might have the choice of building four different types of bridges, but we can fund only one. If so, then the general rule is: When choosing one project from a set of mutually exclusive projects, choose the one with the greatest net benefit.

Another criterion, which turns out to be the equivalent of the net benefit criterion mentioned earlier, is the benefit-cost ratio (BCR) criterion. It is defined as

$$BCR = B/C$$

* Answer: $99,400—which, I admit, is still a nice starting salary for a 21 year old. With a discount rate of 5 percent, fifth-year income jumps to $156,800. As I said, how the analyst treats the discount rate is critical.

Is the benefit-cost ratio of any use in choosing among mutually exclusive projects? Unfortunately, the answer is no. In the case of the four bridges, one could be a rather modest footbridge, suitable only for light traffic. Because only a small investment is required, the benefit-cost ratio is likely to be relatively high. But in comparison to a bridge designed for trains and trucks, the net benefits might appear meager indeed.

Third, we might be faced with a case involving nonefficiency objectives. For instance, the distributional consequences of the projects in terms of regional economic development and unemployment might be of central concern; in such cases, pecuniary effects become relevant. Thus, larger contractors, such as the Defense Department and NASA must be concerned, not only with the costs and benefits of a project but also with which state gets the contract, what size business gets the subcontracts, and what kinds of jobs (i.e., skill levels) are involved.

Fourth, we might have to select the *level* at which several projects are to be operated under a budget constraint. In such cases our rule is to push expenditures for each project to that point where the benefit of the last dollar spent is equal to the last dollar spent on any similar project. (As the economists put it, the *marginal* net benefits should be equal.)

Cost-Effectiveness Analysis. One technique closely associated with CBA is cost-effectiveness analysis. This technique attempts to answer the question: How much output do I get for a given expenditure? The advantage of cost-effectiveness analysis is that output or benefits need not be expressed in dollars.

For example, say that we wanted to determine the preferred mix of disease-control programs and that the number of lives saved by expenditures on disease A and disease B are as follows:

	Expenditures	*Lives Saved (Cumulative)*
Disease A	$ 500,000	360
	1,000,000	465
Disease B	$ 500,000	200
	1,000,000	270

"If we only knew the effect of spending $1 million," Robert N. Grosse (1969:1197) explains, "we might opt for a program where all our money was spent on controlling disease A. Similarly, if we only knew the effects of programs of half million dollars, we would probably prefer A, as we'd save 360 rather than only 200 lives. But if we knew the results for expenditures of both half a million and $1 million in each program, we would quickly see that spending half our money in each program was better than putting it all in one assuming we have $1 million available."

The Concept of Opportunity Cost. Related to the foregoing discussion of CBA and cost-effectiveness analysis is an even broader notion about cost. Unlike the person in the street, the analyst looks beyond the actual cash payments in evaluating the costs of public programs and projects. The analyst realizes that some of the most important costs attributable to doing one thing rather than another stem from the foregone opportunities that have to be sacrificed in doing the one thing.

What is the opportunity cost of taking a course in public administration? In addition to the registration fee, one must consider the implicit cost of the highest foregone alternative to the individual. This alternative might be income from a job, or it might be other available opportunities: playing tennis, taking another course, swimming, and so forth. This alternative cost economists term opportunity cost. Since public administrators must operate in a world of continual and eternal scarcity, it is a useful concept—indeed, it pervades the field.

Multiobjective Models

One limitation of CBA is that it accounts for only one objective, usually an aggregate of all accrued benefits in dollar terms. For that reason, the decision maker might want to either replace or supplement it with a newer technique that emphasizes multiple objectives.

Consider a project typical of the ones that spawned CBA: a waste treatment plant. Assuming four sites are under consideration, experts can be asked to rank them on an ordinal scale by five criteria:

1: Effect of project on local transportation (from most positive to most negative):
Project D
Project B
Project C
Project A

2: Effect on land-use planning:
Project B
Project D
Project C
Project A

3: Effect on neighborhood:
Project B
Project D
Project A
Project C

4: Effect on community economy:
Project D
Project A
Project C
Project B

5: Effect on tax base:
Project B
Project D
Project A
Project C

The experts can also be asked to rank the projects on an interval scale ranging, say, from −100 (maximum negative effect) to +100 (maximum positive effect). For the first criteria, the results might look like this:

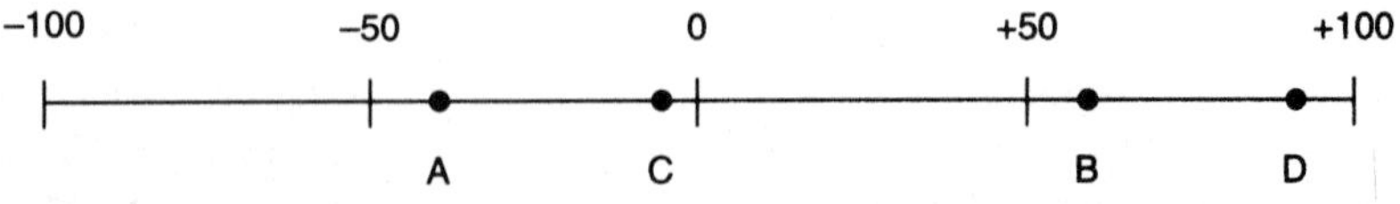

We have said nothing about the relative importance of each criteria. Therefore, decision makers may and probably should assign relative weights to each of the criteria. To see how this process works, consider a second example. How much weight would you accord each of the following criteria in judging a university faculty member?

Teaching effectiveness	?
Professional accomplishment	?
Community service	?
Compatibility with students and faculty	?
	1.00

Note that the sum of your relative weights must be 1.00.

Assume that one university weighted the criteria this way: teaching effectiveness (.40); professional accomplishment (.30); service (.15); and compatibility (.15). Professor Zarkov, who is on the faculty there, has these raw scores: teaching effectiveness (70), professional accomplishment (100), community service (80), and compatibility (60). Zarkov's weighted score would be computed thus:

$$70\ (.40) + 100\ (.30) + 80\ (.15) + 60\ (.15) = 79.$$

The preceding two examples have been highly simplified. In a real application, each criteria would need to be broken down into subfactors, and then weight would need to be assigned to each subfactor. For instance, professional accomplishment in the second example might be broken down into research, consulting, publications, and professional activities.

If the multiobjective model seems tedious, then the reader is invited to consider other methods of making selections . . . .

"Since there are no women or children on board, Mr. Aaron here has suggested that we go in alphabetical order."

(The Saturday Evening Post, *May–June 1982, p. 48. Reprinted with permission from The Saturday Evening Post Society, a division of BFL & MS, Inc. © 1982.)*

Decision Analysis

Suppose a general faces the following situation. According to the general's aides, unless he leads his soldiers to safety, all 600 will die. There are two escape routes. If he takes the first, 200 soldiers will be saved, if he takes the second, there is a one-third chance that 600 soldiers will be saved and a two-thirds chance that none will be saved. Which route should he take? Please pause to consider the question before reading any further.

Because most people reason that it is better to save those lives that can be saved than to gamble when the odds favor even higher losses, they will suggest that the general take the first route.

Now suppose instead that the general's aides tell him that *these* are his two alternatives: If he takes the first route, 400 soldiers will die, if he takes the second, there is a one-third chance that no soldiers will die and a two-thirds chance that 600 soldiers will die. What is your recommendation now?

In this situation, most people will urge the general to take the second route, reasoning that the first involves certain death of 400 soldiers but that the second offers at least a one-third chance that no one will die. What makes this recommendation surprising is that—though both situations are identical—it does not make sense in light of the first recommendation. The only difference between the two situations is that, in the first, the general's aides state the problem in terms of lives saved; in the second, they state it in terms of lives lost (example based on Kahneman & Tversky, 1979).

The point of this exercise is to show you that human reasoning is not always as reliable as we might wish to think. Even when we try to be coldly logical, we give quite different answers to the same problem if it is posed in a slightly different way.

Decision analysis is a technique that can help avoid such mental pitfalls by better structuring complex problems. In this approach, the decision is not viewed as isolated because today's decision depends upon the ones we shall make tomorrow. Thus, the decision problem is examined in terms of a **decision tree.** The tree uses decision forks and chance forks to indicate the interrelationships of choice and possible events.

A typical decision problem that would benefit from this approach is the case of a community threatened with a landslide sometime during the next year, before reforestation is completed (adopted from Public Policy Program, 1972). The basic decision is whether to build a retaining wall. In Figure 6-2, this decision is represented by the small square at the far left. Emanating from the square are two forks—the upper one representing the decision to build; the lower one, the decision not to build.

Regardless of the decision, however, the landslide could occur. This possibility is indicated slightly to the right of the decision square by the two chance nodes. Emanating from each node are two forks—the upper ones representing the actual occurrence of a slide. Based on expert judgment or historical records, a probability is assigned that a slide will occur. In this case the slide probability is 1 in 5 or simply .2. Since retaining walls do not always hold, we must indicate the possibility of failure by yet another chance node even farther to the right. The probability of failure is estimated to be .3.

At the extreme right of Figure 6-2, we have calculated the probabilities of every possible outcome. Once we combine this information with certain costs figures, we

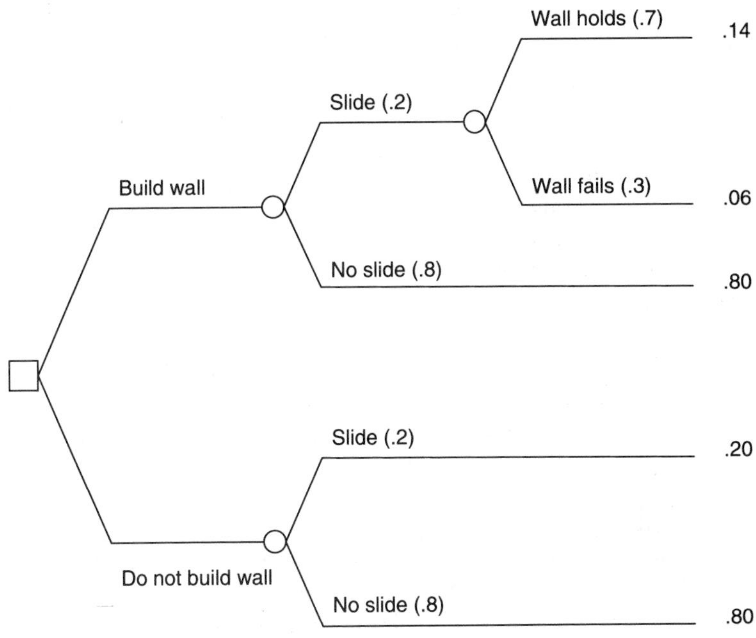

FIGURE 6-2
A Decision Tree

are on the way to knowing whether to build. Basically, we need two costs figures. First, if a landslide occurs, we estimate that the only damages will be to property, valued at $3 million, since population can evacuate. Second, constructing a retaining wall will cost $200,000.

What is the cost of the decision to build? In addition to the outright cost of $200,000, we must figure the benefit from avoiding property damage. This would be .14 x $3 million or $420,000. The net benefit of the decision to build is, therefore, $420,000 minus $200,000, or $220,000.

Systems Analysis

Systems analysis is more a mosaic than a specific analytical technique. And what makes up this mosaic? Bits and pieces from a variety of disciplines—engineering, sociology, biology, philosophy, psychology, economics, and computer science. Very broadly, the systems analysis approach forces us to look at problems as systems; that is, assemblies of interdependent components.

Although this may sound commonsensical—even trite—it is often ignored. Consider this classic example (based on Commoner, 1971:180). A basic problem in sewage treatment is that, when organic sewage is dumped into a river or lake, it generates an inordinate demand for oxygen. But oxygen is needed as well for the bacteria of decay, which use the oxygen-converting organic matter to break down inorganic products.

Consequently, dumping tends to deplete the oxygen supply of surface waters. By killing off the bacteria of decay, it brings to a halt the aquatic cycle of self-purification. Enter now the sanitation engineer. His solution is simply to domesticate the decay bacteria in a treatment plant, artificially supplying them with sufficient oxygen to accommodate the entering organic material. Thus, what is released from the treatment plant is largely inorganic residues. Since these have no oxygen demands, the engineer thinks that he has solved the problem.

Unfortunately, the sanitation engineer did not recognize that he was dealing with a system and that that system includes nature's rivers and streams. The treated sewage is now rich in the inorganic residues of decay—carbon dioxide, nitrate, and phosphate—that support the growth of algae. "Now heavily fertilized, the algae bloom furiously, soon die, releasing organic matter, which generates the oxygen demand that sewage technology had removed."

In order to better appreciate this approach, we will discuss the **four basic steps in systems analysis**: problem formulation, modeling, analysis and optimization, and implementation.

Problem Formulation. Problem formulation is perhaps the most difficult step, sometimes requiring three fourths of the total effort. This step includes the detailed description of the task and identification of important variables and their relationships. Consider an investigation into some observed and perceived difficulties in an urban transportation system. In the systems approach, one begins by deciding whether the prime objective is better service, lower cost, less pollution, or something else. One must also decide what data are necessary: passenger miles by mode of transportation; passenger miles by sex, age, race, and income; passenger miles by time and place; and so forth. Finally, one must identify key decision makers in the urban area and their motivations.

Modeling. The scene changes in the next step: One goes from the real world of the problem to the abstract world of the modeler. The modeler's task is probably more artistic than rigorous, more creative than systematic. He or she must strike a balance between including all relevant aspects of reality and keeping that model simple enough so that it is in line with existing theoretical loads, computation time, and data availability. Ultimately, of course, the test of a model's quality is how effective it is in helping to solve the original problem. Figure 6-3 shows a model for a criminal justice system.

To the uninitiated, a frequent cause of puzzlement is how models such as the one shown in Figure 6-3 can be "quantified." In other words, how can the analyst convert something as physical, as real as police and courts, into something as abstract as a set of mathematical relationships? Although the equations relating the different components in Figure 6-3 probably present a level of sophistication far beyond the scope of this text, the idea behind representing a physical system mathematically involves no chicanery.

Take, for example, a simple inventory system. What would be some important variables in such a system? Among them would probably be:

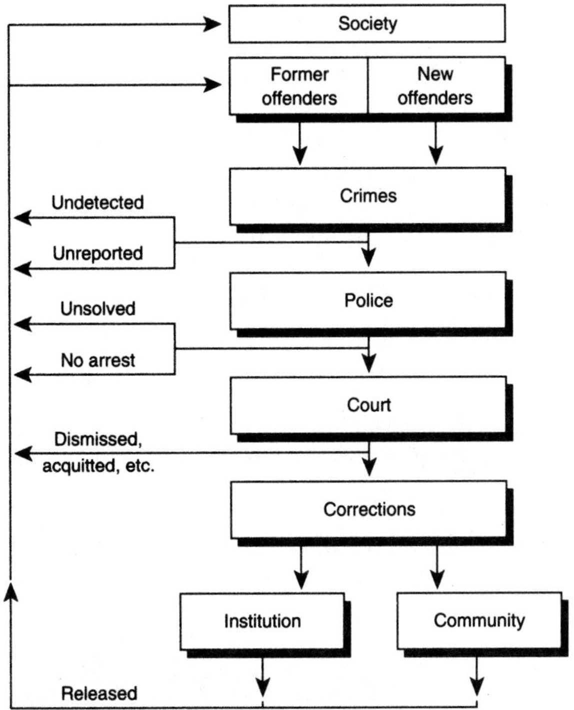

FIGURE 6-3
Model of Criminal Justice System

SOURCE: J.W. Lapatra, *Applying the Systems Approach to Urban Developement* (Strousburg, Penn.: Dowden, Hutchinson, and Ross, 1973), p.154.

C_O = The cost of ordering per unit.
C_H = The cost of holding per unit per time period.
D = The quantity of units used each time period.

A useful model, incorporating these variables, would be:

$$Q = \text{most economical quantity to order} = \sqrt{\frac{2C_O D}{C_H}}$$

Analysis and Optimization. During the analysis and optimization step, the model is studied to find the best strategy for resolving the problem given. Two options might be mentioned: (1) computer simulation and (2) sensitivity analysis.

Simulation models (option 1) allow users to replicate to a great extent the actual dispatch and patrol operations of most urban police departments. Incidents are generated throughout the city and distributed randomly in time and space according to observed statistical patterns. Each incident has an associated priority number, the lower numbers designating the more important incidents. For instance, a priority 1 incident would be an officer in trouble, a felony in progress, or a seriously injured person; a priority 4 incident could be an open fire hydrant, a lockout, or a parking violation. As each incident becomes known, an attempt is made to assign (dispatch) a patrol unit to the scene. In attempting this assignment, the computer is programmed to duplicate as closely as possible the decision-making logic of an actual police dispatcher. In certain cases, this assignment cannot be performed because the congestion level of the accumulated incidents is too high; then, the incident report (which might in actuality be a complaint ticket) joins a queue of waiting reports. The queue is depleted as incidents are assigned to available patrol units. This simulation model is designed to study the patrol deployment strategy and the dispatch and reassignment policy.

The model tabulates several important measures of operational effectiveness. These include statistics on dispatcher queue length, patrol travel times, amount of preventive patrol, work loads of individual patrol units, amount of intersector dispatches, and others.

In sum, simulation provides a tool to assist in answering a wide range of allocation questions. Police administrators should find simulation models valuable for the following purposes:

- They facilitate detailed investigations of operations throughout the city (or part of the city).

Physicists at Canada's National Research Council test model ships, barges, bridges, and drilling platforms in conditions that simulate real oceans—complete with complex wave patterns, underwater currents, high winds, and ice. The scaled-down model ice, made with antifreeze, detergent, and sugar, contains weakened crystals suitable for testing 1/30-scale ships. (Institute for Marine Dynamics)

- They provide a consistent framework for estimating the value of new technologies.
- They serve as training tools to increase awareness of the system interactions and consequences resulting from everyday policy decisions.
- They suggest new criteria for monitoring and evaluating actual operating systems.

The box on pages 266–267 will show you how traffic engineers use simulation models.

One of the advantages of simulation derives from the **counterintuitive nature of public systems.** To call these systems counterintuitive is to say that they do not react in ways we think they should. The reason intuition provides so little guidance in understanding a system's behavior is that the human brain cannot grasp the totality of relationships among all the variables. Thus, common sense tells us that wider highways reduce congestion, but as urban planners have learned, the reverse is often the case.

Not necessarily requiring the assistance of a computer, **sensitivity analysis** (option 2) is available in analyzing the model to find the best strategy for solving the original problem. A sensitivity analysis process consists of making very small changes in the model to show the extent to which results may be importantly altered because of change in one or a few factors. To see how sensitivity analysis might work, let us reexamine Figure 6-3. Assume that the mayor calls for a large reduction in the total operating expenses. Since one does not want to reduce the strength of the police force (the patrol on the line), one looks elsewhere for "fat." Assume, therefore, that the typing pool in the probation division is reduced. As a result, the typing of presentence reports of convicted defendants waiting to be sentenced is delayed. Defendants now must spend even more time in jails, and the system's overall operating costs reach a new high.

Let us try a different tack: Discontinue night courts. But closing these courts adds substantial costs to the police, who will have to house, feed, and guard defendants awaiting court action. Another suggestion might be to reduce the number of judges or prosecutors by 8 percent and the police by 3 percent. What results do you see from such a course of action? Do you see any effects on a city's tax base that might result from cuts in the area of criminal justice?

Implementation. In this subsection, we have discussed the systems approach in terms of four steps, giving particular emphasis to the first three. The last step, implementation, refers to the procedure by which the results determined from the model are translated as a set of actions to the real world. The four steps, however, seldom occur in perfect sequence; indeed, the systems approach is highly iterative. As such, it might easily move through a sequence of steps such as the following: formulating the problem, selecting objectives, designing alternatives, collecting data, building models, weighting cost against effectiveness, testing for sensitivity, questioning assumptions, reexamining objectives, looking at new alternatives, reformulating the problem, selecting different or modified objectives, and so on (Quade, 1966:10).

Simulating Traffic Jams

The Problem

Traffic in the United States has roughly tripled since 1970, whether measured in miles of congestion or in vehicle hours of lost time. Growth of automobile use in the United States exceeds population growth. Peak hours associated with "rush hours" have spread, sometimes turning the daylight hours into one long peak. Average occupancy has fallen to less than one-and-one-sixth persons per car.

Perhaps even more important, travel patterns in the United States have changed. Fewer people now work at home, and far fewer walk to work than did 20 years ago. The central-city-to-suburb pattern of commuting that guided road builders no longer applies. As previously noted, more and more people commute from one suburb to another. Thus America's road networks are radial (from suburbs to downtown), though its travel patterns are more like arcs (from one suburb to another).

Today's grim reality is that freeways work best at a slow 30 to 40 miles per hour. How can that be? When cars can pack more closely together, overall capacity is higher. It is unlikely that things will get better. One recent study forecasts that average speeds in the Los Angeles area will drop by the year 2010 from 31 to 11 miles per hour.

Looking for Solutions

Faced with an increasingly unhappy public, state and local governments are turning to a new generation of technology, in the form of mathematical modeling and increasingly intelligent computer networks. Simulations, available even on desktop computers, are offering surprising new lessons about the dynamics of traffic.

For example, no more than about 9,000 vehicles are in motion at any moment in midtown Manhattan. If a few cars are added to that number, the flow does not just slow, as common sense would suggest. Rather, the immediate result is widespread gridlock. (According to traffic engineers, "gridlock" is not the freezing of a single intersection by traffic coming in from two directions. That is "spillback." Gridlock occurs when traffic jams all the way *around* a block, so that every car is actually blocking itself—the snake biting its own tail, so to speak.)

Simulations can also help us understand the sudden bunching and clustering of traffic—for no apparent reason—that we observe on highways. Traffic might be flowing smoothly, then one or two drivers slow down and everybody behind them starts to slow down, setting off a shock wave. Sometimes congestion is the secondary shock from an accident that

Operations Research (OR)

Preceding the arrival of the systems approach in the decision-making centers of government was the use of OR. The formal inception of OR may, in fact, be traced to World War II. Faced with acute shortages of men and material and working against the clock, the military turned for assistance to the scientific and engineering com-

blocked traffic minutes or hours before. Even after nothing remains for the rubberneckers to stare at, the traffic flow preserves somewhere upstream a kind of memory of the incident.

As traffic engineers study these complex systems, solutions emerge. For example, they find that many towns and cities set their signals running with too long a cycle; flow could be improved simply by changing a 1-minute cycle to a 45-second cycle. Under a system called ramp metering, cars are forced to pause at a red light before they enter; this system holds down the number of cars on the freeway. In many jurisdictions, the system is politically sensitive. When you meter a drive, you penalize an individual who may not see the community benefit. (Los Angeles seems to accept it; San Francisco, equally congested, takes it as a threat to personal liberty.)

More sophisticated computer simulations are required to solve the problem of congestion, however. On a computer screen, tiny red rectangles can be made to move back and forth along tiny streets and clog tiny intersections. They speed up and slow down, change lanes, cut one another off and run red lights (just as in the real world). Modelers can easily rearrange streets and intersections and can even adjust the aggressiveness of the imaginary drivers. Modelers find that simply plugging in average values for drivers is not enough, for exceptionally slow or unresponsive drivers can have a decisive effect on the capacity of a street or an intersection.

If the United States is to avoid becoming a coast-to-coast parking lot, it will need more computer simulation studies of this type. Public administrators from California to New York City, and from Europe to Asia, are setting up ambitious projects that will link computers in traffic centers to sensing devices on the highways. The computers will adjust traffic signals to change the flow. Ultimately this information may be directly beamed to video street maps displayed in every driver's dashboard, showing the sites to avoid.

Although the effects of overexpansion in urban America cannot be controlled without limiting development, many government decision makers think that the new traffic technology can at least hold off the worst consequences.

SOURCE: Based on James Gleick, "National Gridlock," *New York Times Magazine,* May 8, 1989.

munity for help in resolving some knotty operations problems. These problems concerned, for example, the most effective setting of the time fuse of a bomb dropped from an aircraft onto a submarine; the optimal formation of bombers as a function of a target shape; the best bomber-fighter combination to achieve maximum security and still accomplish the mission; the measurement of the effectiveness of arming merchant ships against enemy aircraft; and the optimal location of radar stations. And, due to the revolution that began when electronic computers became commercially available and to the increased demand for greater productivity on a large part of American industry, the use of OR had by the early 1950s spread to industry.

OR (or **management science** as it is increasingly referred to) and the systems approach share many characteristics—for example, use of interdisciplinary teams, modeling, and sophisticated mathematics—but they are not the same. The scope of the former is narrower. It tends to be concerned with problems that can be represented by mathematical models that can be optimized. For example, a typical OR problem would determine (subject to certain constraints) the optimal (i.e., the very best) location in terms of service for a new fire station or a new bus route in a city. OR tends, we might say, to be concerned with problems in the small. Indeed, it was because the World War II teams studied small operational problems that the original (English) name was *operational research;* it was only later modified to *operations research*—with typical American lack of concern for syntax.

The systems approach, on the other hand, is concerned with problems of greater complexity and abstraction (hence: less emphasis on calculation). Actually, OR is one of the most important inputs to the systems approach. Thus, the relationship between the systems approach and OR is much like that between strategy and tactics.

Of all the quantitative techniques that OR emphasizes, **linear programming** is one of the most widely used. Accordingly, we conclude our discussion of OR by considering linear programming.

Linear programming is a mathematical technique for deriving the optimal solutions to linear relationships. Any problem concerned with maximizing or minimizing some economic (e.g., cost) subject to a set of constraints (e.g., human resources, materials, and capital) is a linear programming problem. In general, the technique has been used with enormous success to solve a variety of administrative problems in areas such as the following:

- Determining a product mix that meets certain established specifications at minimum cost. Examples are found in establishing the lowest cost for meeting the standard requirements of adult nutrition. In 1973, one could live on about $95 per year. (But what a product mix this implies: kidneys, cabbage, beans, buckwheat flour, and not much else!)

- Determining optimum product lines and production processes. Examples are found in those situations where capacity limitations exist and decisions must be made as to optimal production of scarce resources.

- Determining optimum transportation routes. For example, a railroad must move a number of freight cars about and wishes to do it at the lowest cost. If there were 3 origins, 10 distributions, and 100 cars to distribute, then the total number of feasible solutions would be in the millions.

- Determining an optimum mix of the number of cattle and elk on the same range to maximize the animal units produced. The U.S. Forest Service faces this type of problem.

- Determining optimal solutions to such problems as stacking aircraft over airports, queueing ships at docks, and easing the congestion of vehicles at toll booths of tunnels and bridges.

The Perry Mason Syndrome, or Why You Need to Understand Analytical Techniques Even If You Do Not Use Them

In recent years, some public administrators and their bright young staffs have displayed a disturbing tendency in their decision making. They try to run the government by poring over the data presented to them from various components in their agency and then subjecting a few experts or senior officials of those components to skeptical questioning. I call this the Perry Mason Syndrome. It is based on the idea that a smart administrator, like a smart lawyer, simply asks the right questions and thereby extracts the truth from the people with the data.

In practice, this approach seldom works. The questioner is helplessly dependent on the official for his or her information. As Henry Kissinger once pointed out, the decision memoranda that lower-level officials hand up tend to contain three alternatives—two ridiculous ones and their preferred one (which is usually listed second). Effective questioners, therefore, ensure that they have independent, firsthand knowledge against which to test alternatives. They are also keenly aware of the First Law of Expert Advice: Don't ask the barber whether you need a haircut. Finally, while they may not have a specialist's understanding of the techniques described earlier in this chapter, effective questioners know that a conceptual understanding is important. Such an understanding helps them ask the right questions about the expert's assumptions, methods, and results.

Putting the Analytical Approach in Perspective

A few years ago, ABC broadcasted on four consecutive nights *The Crisis Game,* a docudrama featuring ten former high government officials acting the unscripted parts of the president and his National Security Council (see photo). Their task was to cope with an imaginary international crisis set a couple of years in the future. The value of this docudrama was that it depicted as never before how presidents and their advisors make decisions. It unfolded spontaneously and impressed many former insiders as being very like the real process. The discussions were often rambling and desultory—in short, quite different from the neat, clear-cut techniques considered in the previous section. There was a stiltedness and pontification by the secretary of defense and showboating by senior advisors. There were also flashes of anger, knowledge tinted by political bias, impatience, and even occasional confusion.

For The Crisis Game, *ABC cast former secretary of state and presidential candidate Edmund Muskie (not shown) as president. Former defense secretary, Clark Clifford (left) played secretary of state, while James Schlesinger (center) had his old title of defense secretary again. (© 1985 American Broadcasting Companies, Inc.)*

The Crisis Game demonstrated that, for better or worse, decision making is a very human affair involving far more than objective analysis. More specifically, the exercise demonstrated things about decision making in the real world. Beginning with the most obvious, it reminded us that most important decisions in government are not rendered by solitary individuals but by groups of people. Second, and this is also fairly obvious, decision making is not an entirely rational process. (Herbert Simon makes this point brilliantly in his story "The Apple," which appears as Case 6.2.) Biases, intuition, rules of thumb, sentiment, experience, and other factors play an important role in determining the outcome of the process. Third, we could see from viewing *The Crisis Game* that some participants were more analytical than others. In other words, there are legitimate alternatives to analytical decision making worth considering. Finally, *The Crisis Game* revealed some real limitations to applying a rigorous analytical approach to every facet of a problem.

To put the analytical approach in better perspective and provide a more accurate picture of decision making as it really is, let us consider each of these four points.

Decision Making in Groups

Because group decision making is so common in public administration, effective managers must be highly skilled in influencing the group process. Here we will systematically consider strengths and weaknesses of groups as decision makers, circumstances in which a group decision-making process should be used, and techniques to help groups arrive at better decisions.

Advantages and Disadvantages. Since managers often have a choice between making a decision by themselves and including others, they should understand the advantages and disadvantages of group decision making.

Groups have an advantage over individuals because they bring together a broader perspective for defining the problem and diagnosing the underlying causes and effects. Most of us tend to develop relatively fixed patterns of thinking, but when people with different styles interact in a group, they can stimulate each other to try new ways of approaching the problem and compensate for the weaknesses in one another's thinking style. (Several of these styles will be identified presently.) Further, groups offer more knowledge and information. Indeed, the diversity of experience and thinking styles present in a group can lead to more innovative solutions than an "expert" could produce working alone. Generally speaking, a group decision is easier to implement because more people feel they had a say in it, and they understand the problem (and exactly what needs to be done) more thoroughly.

Among the most important disadvantages of group problem solving is that it is time-consuming and expensive, which is one reason why groups should not be used for routine or programmed decisions. Moreover, the dynamics of groups can lead to compromise solutions (which satisfy no one) or reduction of valuable dissenting opinions. Finally, there is no clear focus for responsibility if things go wrong.

When to Use a Group. The important task for a manager is to determine when a *specific* group should work on a *particular* problem. Obviously, group members should possess the required knowledge and analytical skills. Beyond that the manager must consider the current work load of potential members (are they overloaded?); the members' expectations about involvement (do they think they have a "right" to participate?); and the group's skills at resolving conflict (is it characterized by open, confronting norms?).

Group decision making is generally called for under the following set of circumstances:

- The problem is relatively uncertain or complex, and has potential for conflict.
- The problem requires interagency or intergroup cooperation and coordination.
- The problem and its solution have important personal and organizational consequences.
- There are significant but not immediate deadline pressures.
- Widespread acceptance and commitment are critical to successful implementation (Ware, 1978).

Improving Group Decision Making. A number of technicians have been developed to help individual managers and groups arrive at better decisions. The **nominal group technique** (NGT), for instance, was developed to ensure that every group member has equal input in the process (Guzzo, 1982:95–126). Because some participants may talk more and dominate group discussions in interactive groups, the nominal group is structured in a series of steps to equalize participation:

1. Working alone, each participant writes down his or her ideas on the problem to be discussed. These ideas usually are suggestions for a solution.
2. A round-robin in which each group member presents his or her ideas to the group is set up. The ideas are written down on a blackboard for all members to see. No discussion of the ideas occur until every person's ideas have been presented and written down for general viewing.
3. After all ideas have been presented, there is an open discussion of the ideas for the purpose of clarification only; evaluative comments are not allowed. This part of the discussion tends to be spontaneous and unstructured.
4. After the discussion, a secret ballot is taken in which each group member votes for preferred solutions. It results in a rank ordering of alternatives in terms of priority.
5. Steps 3 and 4 are repeated as desired to add further clarification to the process.

A **devil's advocate** is assigned the role of challenging the assumptions and assertions made by the group (Schweiger & Finger, 1984). The devil's advocate forces the group to rethink its approach to the problem and to avoid reaching premature consensus or making unreasonable assumptions before proceeding with problem solutions. **Dialectal inquiry** is similar to a devil's advocate except that groups are assigned to challenge the underlying values and assumptions associated with the problem definition. For example, the State Department might form a couple of groups—let us call them the Red Team and the Blue Team—to critically examine prevailing assumptions in the department regarding a particular foreign country.

A fourth technique, perhaps the best known, is *brainstorming.* The key idea here is to increase creative thinking and generation of solutions by prohibiting criticism. Groups of five to ten members meet to generate ideas subject to certain rules. Judgment or evaluation of ideas must be withheld until the idea-generation process has been completed. The wilder or more radical the idea, the better. The greater the number of ideas, the greater the likelihood of obtaining a superior idea. Participants should suggest how ideas of others can be turned into better ideas, or how two or more ideas can be joined into still another idea.

Biases in Human Decision Making

The Working Profile of Herbert A. Simon that appeared earlier in this chapter presented two important concepts that help us appreciate how people really make decisions: bounded rationality and satisficing. The former means simply that people have limits, or boundaries, on how rational they can be. The latter means that decision makers choose the first solution alternative that satisfies minimal decision criteria. Since public administrators lack the time and cognitive ability to process complete information about complex decisions, they must satisfice.

Although administrators can do little to avoid these realities, they can be more aware of certain tendencies in human decision making that lead to mistakes. To make the best decisions, people must understand their own deficiencies. Awareness of the following six biases can help administrators make better choices (based on Schoemaker, 1990; Bazerman, 1986):

1. Seeing only one dimension of uncertainty. In experiments, when subjects are asked to evaluate a venture that carries an 80 percent chance of success, they invariably vote to proceed. But if the problem is reframed and they are told the venture has a 20 percent chance of *failure,* they vote not to proceed. Managers often make a decision after analyzing it from only one or two frames.

2. Giving too much weight to readily available or most recent information. For example, in 1987, Genentech developed a new blood-clot dissolver, and all the company had to do was obtain the FDA's approval to produce it. Genentech executives were so confident of the FDA's approval that they went ahead and invested heavily in the production and marketing of the drug. After all, research showed that, in a test tube, the drug effectively dissolved blood clots, as required by the FDA. But the agency also required "other" information not so readily available—namely, clinical data charting the drug's effect on real people. Since this data was not included, the FDA rejected the application and the company's stock dropped 24 percent (a loss of $1 billion on paper). The company's executives had presumed that the information most readily available constituted all the knowledge needed.

3. Being overconfident. Because they mistakenly equate confidence with competence, managers are forever giving too much weight to self-assured opinions—either their own or those of their subordinates. They often encourage overconfidence by asking their subordinates to come up with the "right" decision all the time. For example, when a group of people was asked to define quantities about which they had little direct knowledge ("What was the dollar value of Canadian lumber exports in 1977?"), they overestimated their accuracy.

4. Ignoring the laws of randomness. Randomness means that the outcome of one event has nothing to do with the outcome of another. Administrators often ignore this principle in making decisions. For example, even though employee performance should be expected to fluctuate each month, an administrator decides that the dip is the beginning of a downward trend and starts an expensive new training program. Trends should not be interpreted from a single, random event. Aristotle said it best: One swallow does not make a summer.

5. Being reluctant to audit and improve decision making. Administrators might require very detailed analysis prior to decision making but be reluc-

tant to analyze their most important decisions retrospectively. Some organizations do prepare from time to time "lessons learned" reports, but few of the organization's members are likely to read them, much less reflect on them.

Alternative Approaches to Thinking

As suggested in the introduction to this section, analysis is not the only approach to decision making. The reality is that administrative decision making is based on the epistemology men and women employ in their search for the truth. By *epistemology,* I mean the thinking and reasoning processes by which truth is reached and understood.

Broadly speaking, there are at least four other epistemological systems besides the analytical that are relevant to managerial decision making (Churchman, 1968, 1971). For simplicity, we can refer to them as **styles of thinking** or approaches to decision making. The four other approaches are as follows:

1. *Empirical,* which builds decisions on the basis of a broad survey of many facts. The Delphi technique, discussed in Chapter 5, the statistical exhibits in Case 9.2, and the examples of bureaucratic malfunctions in Chapter 7 are good illustrations of this approach.
2. *Kantian,* named for the German philosopher Immanuel Kant (1724–1804), which says that neither rational models nor facts alone can lead to the truth; one must have a conceptual framework to make sense of and connect the data one gets through the senses.
3. *Pragmatic,* which says that decisions must be made in accordance with their effects; decisions are not to be judged by theoretical elegance, empirical rigor, or holistic frameworks but by whether they effect a desired result.
4. *Dialectical,* which strives for creative solutions through combining (synthesizing) two or more different ideas into a fresh and useful idea.

It would be beyond the scope of the book to develop these four ideas any further. Thus, it is sufficient to note that (1) each approach has its strengths and weaknesses, and (2) most executives use more than one approach in their day-to-day decision making. Because we have emphasized the analytical approach in this chapter and pointed out its usefulness, we conclude by considering some of its weaknesses. In so doing, I hope to suggest why decision makers need to be aware of—and indeed cultivate—other decision-making skills.

Limitations to Analytical Approach

We begin by considering some specific criticisms of systems analysis and then turn to some more general reflections by one of the foremost intellects in the field of public administration.

Systems analysis begins, it will be recalled, with problem definition. Significantly, one of the most distinguished practitioners of the systems approach, Charles

Hitch (1960:11) maintains that Rand Corporation had never undertaken a major system study where satisfactory objectives could be defined. Where attempts were made, objectivity proved elusive. For example, in a classic systems study on water resources (McKean, 1963), the goals read as follows: *adequate* pollution control; *reasonable* irrigation development; *proper* erosion control and sediment reduction; *suitable* flood control; *optimum* contribution in alleviating the impact of drought; *full* development of the basin's resources for recreational programs. Where did these goals come from? What do the italicized words mean?

Gathering information is also a part of the first step. Writes Ida R. Hoos (1973:162–163):

> *Dear to the hearts of technically oriented analysts is the information-gathering and processing state. In fact, so [agreeable] is the occupation with data that many systems designs, purported to deal with pressing social problems, never progress beyond that point. Displaying the ingestive propensities of a snake, the information system swallows up all the resources allocated to a given project and diverts attention from its larger purpose.*

To buttress her point, Hoos cites the activity of the Bay Area Transportation Study Commission (BATSC), which was instructed to prepare a master regional transportation plan. In the end, the experts "listed as their accomplishments a total of 10 million pieces of information, converted to 1.5 million punch cards, which were recorded on 1,100 reels of magnetic tape which require one and one-half hours of IBM 7094 time to reprocess" (Hoos, 1973:162–63).

In sum, too many analysts apparently think that, if only enough factual research is done, then somehow a valid generalization will automatically emerge. But such is not the case. What do frequently emerge are some very expensive price tags ($3 million in the case of BATSC).

Perhaps the first pitfall to note about the second step, modeling, is that the analyst structures the problem; that is to say, the analyst inevitably must view the problem through his or her own eyes and determine what the relevant variables are. If we assume one wants to wage war against poverty, how does one go about establishing the poverty level? What does one base the calculations on?

The system itself must also be determined. But how inclusive should it be? Clearly, our depicted sanitation engineer (pp. 261–262) was not inclusive enough. Conceivably, the criminal justice system depicted in Figure 6-3 was not inclusive enough. (It had no way of indicating the economic effects of crime rate; e.g., reduced tax base as residents move away from cities due to increase in crime.) "Systems experts have made a great show of addressing totality but have actually dealt with shreds and patches" (Hoos, 1973:161).

The third step in the systems approach is analysis and optimization. Here the analyst runs the risk of becoming locked into attaining the originally stated objectives of the study. This is no paradox, for a good systems study should be **heuristic;** that is, a method to help discover. Obviously, what we need to discover cannot be known in advance. A famous study of the location of military bases conducted by Albert Wohlstetter and his associates at Rand illustrates this nicely (Quade, 1966:125–26).

In 1951, the air force asked Rand to help select locations for new airbases to be built overseas in the 1956 to 1961 period. Wohlstetter's approach was not to try to answer the straightforward request (where should the bases go?) but to examine the assumptions inherent in the question itself. After a year and a half of analysis, he and his staff concluded that adding such bases was too risky, since aircraft positioned overseas closer to the Soviet Union were too vulnerable to surprise attack on the ground. They further concluded that overseas bases were more costly, less of a deterrent, and more of a problem for U.S. foreign policy than an alternative. The alternative was to build more bases in the United States and supplement them with small overseas installations for refueling.

A final pitfall in the systems approach is to let the method supplant the problem. In other words, some experts tend to begin with the question: What problems are available for my techniques? The proper initial question is, of course: What is the problem?

Such experts are not unlike the drunk the police officer finds late at night under a streetlight. When asked what he is doing, the drunk replies that he is looking for his keys.

"Where did you lose the keys?" the officer asks.

"In the alley."

"Then why are you looking for them here?"

"Because," replies the drunk, "this is where the light is."

In spite of such failures as a description of decision making, systems analysis provides a useful framework for categorizing and diagnosing the nature of the departures of actual decisions from the requirements of rationality. In this sense, it provides a useful benchmark.

Concepts for Review

- bounded rationality
- cost-benefit analysis
- cost-effectiveness analysis
- counterintuitive nature of public systems
- decision analysis
- decision making
- decision rules for cost-benefit analysis
- decision tree
- devil's advocate
- dialectal inquiry
- direct and indirect costs and benefits, spillovers, and externalities
- discounting
- four basic steps in systems analysis
- generic and unique problems
- heuristic
- limiting (strategic) factor in decision making
- linear programming
- management science
- multiobjective model
- nominal group technique
- operations research
- opportunity cost
- real and pecuniary costs and benefits, tangible and intangible costs and benefits
- satisfice
- sensitivity analysis
- simulation
- styles of thinking
- systems analysis
- technology fix
- upper and lower limits of decisions

Nailing Down the Main Points

1. Decision making means selecting from various alternatives one course of action. It pervades the entire administrative organization and planning process.

2. Decision making consists of at least four steps: identifying the problem, gathering the facts, making the decision, and communicating and implementing the decision.

3. Recognizing the kind of problem that exists (generic or unique) can significantly improve the quality of decision making.

4. Decision makers should consult other people and consider the upper and lower limits of the decision.

5. In recent years, as the costs of government became a greater concern to the taxpayer and to political leadership, cost-benefit analysis grew in popularity. Now, virtually all costly governmental programs are subjected to some type of cost-benefit analysis.

   This analysis does basically three things. First, it attempts to measure *all* the costs and benefits from a program. Second, since most programs or projects take place over extended periods of time, the flow of future costs and benefits must be converted into their present values. We call making these adjustments *discounting*. Finally, we must decide by one of several decision rules whether the benefits justify the cost.

6. The multiobjective model provides a way of ranking various alternatives according to weighted criteria or objectives. Decision analysis provides a way of choosing courses of action within acceptable limits of risk.

7. The systems approach, or systems analysis, forces us to look at problems as systems, that is, assemblies of interdependent components. The four basic steps in this approach are (*a*) policy formulation, (*b*) modeling, (*c*) analysis and optimization, and (*d*) implementation.

8. While operations research (OR), or management science, shares many characteristics with the systems approach, it is not quite the same thing. The scope of OR is narrower; its nature, more mathematical. Of all the techniques that OR emphasizes, linear programming is one of the most widely used.

9. The analytical approach is only one style of thinking that decision makers use. Others include the empirical, Kantian, pragmatic, and dialectic (synthesis). Each approach, including the analytical approach, has certain strengths and weaknesses. Among the common mistakes in decision making are the following: analyzing the problem from only one or two perspectives; presuming that the information most readily available (or most recently acquired) constitutes all the knowledge needed; failing to calculate a level of confidence for each decision (to avoid overconfidence); and failing to audit and improve decision making. The last mistake helps to explain why some organizations continue to make the same mistakes over and over.

Problems

1. "Decision making is the primary task of the administrator." Discuss.

2. Suppose you were to build a model that would forecast the nationwide demand for nurses 20 years from now. As a start, one must make assumptions about population growth and effects of new drugs. What else? Do you think the list of variables is endless?

3. Are defense and domestic spending really transferable as the concept of opportunity cost may suggest? In other words, do you see any fallacy in comparing a new navy destroyer to so many new hospitals or new schools? What other factors might take a dollar-for-dollar comparison difficult?

4. As the head of a city housing agency, you must decide whether to submit either plan A or plan B (but not both) to the mayor who, in turn, must submit it to the city council. You estimate that there is a 90 percent chance that the mayor would accept A but only a 50 percent chance that the council would accept. The council likes B, indeed, you are certain they would accept it—if, that is, it ever got past the mayor (with only 3-to-1 odds of this happening). You prefer A and evaluate its utility at 1.00. In fact, because you think it the most socially desirable, even if the mayor accepts and has it rejected by the council, you would assign a utility of .40 to these consequences. Of course, if the reject came first from your boss, the mayor, the utility would be somewhat less, say .20. However, Plan B, if accepted by the city council, has a utility of .80 to you. But the worst situation is to have it rejected; there would be no utility in such a case. What should you do?

5. Conduct a systems analysis of your community. This may sound like an overwhelming job. Nevertheless, if you read the proposals Robert K. Lamb makes in "Suggestions for a Study of Your Hometown," *Human Organization,* Summer 1952, you will find ways and means for shortcutting and sampling.

6. Care must be taken in systems analysis to ensure that the measures of effectiveness are appropriate. A classic example of how incorrect measures can throw off the analysis concerns the installation of antiaircraft guns on merchant vessels in World War II. While these guns made the crews feel safer, data on equipped and nonequipped ships showed that only 4 percent of attacking planes were shot down. Because the guns were expensive and needed elsewhere, their removal was proposed. Was the percentage of planes shot down the correct effectiveness measure of the guns? What other criteria might have been used?

7. Use multiobjective criteria to help you decide among four models of automobiles. Using a form similar to the one on page 259, establish criteria and weight it. The final step in your analysis should be to divide the relevance number by the cost of the automobile; this will give you four benefit-to-cost ratios to compare.

8. Give several examples of recent nonincremental decisions in American government.

9. Gotham City has to dispose of 22,000 tons of refuse daily, an amount increasing by 4 percent a year. Currently, it has eight incinerators that have a usable capacity of 6,000 tons a day; residue and nonincinerated refuse must go to sanitary landfills that will be exhausted within five years. Four superincinerators, with a capacity of 20,000 tons a day have been proposed. Unfortunately, they are quite expensive: $1 billion to build and $50 million a year to operate. Moreover, they would add substantially to hazardous air pollution by emitting thousands of tons of soot particulates a year. Outline and discuss an analytical model that could help the mayor of Gotham City decide what to do. What additional information would you need? What are the upper and lower limits of the decision? Is the decision simply one of whether to build the superincinerators, or are alternatives available?

10. The town of Broken Arrow needs a fire department, and you must make recommendations concerning its size and structure. What would be a good rule of thumb for the number of fire engines? (The fire chief of Gotham City suggested that the number of fire engines should be proportional to the number of buildings.) Regarding structure, you have two basic alternatives: (*a*) one central department or (*b*) several decentralized stations. Discuss how you decide between (*a*) and (*b*).

11. Write a paper comparing the decision-making styles of two or more recent presidents. Which style is most effective? Why?

12. "Experience is not only an expensive basis for decision making but also a dangerous one." Discuss.

13. What are the shortcomings in using "lives saved" as a measure of benefit?

14. Use the concept of opportunity cost to explain why lawyers are more likely than physicians to get involved in politics.

15. Given the following data, how would you spend $1 million? What idea is expressed in this exercise?

Disease A		*Disease B*	
Expenditures	*Lives Saved*	*Expenditures*	*Lives Saved*
$ 100,000	100	$ 100,000	50
200,000	180	200,000	50
300,000	250	300,000	135
400,000	310	400,000	170
500,000	360	500,000	200
600,000	400	600,000	225
700,000	430	700,000	240
800,000	450	800,000	255
900,000	460	900,000	265
1,000,000	465	1,000,000	270

CASE 6.1

The Structure of a Government Decision

The Problem

Each year the eastern half of North America is drenched with rain turned acid by waste gases (see Exhibit 1). Some of the acid arises locally but much comes from coal-fired power plants in the Ohio Valley. The power plants' giant smokestacks, located in the valley since passage of the Clean Air Act of 1970, blow sulphur and nitrogen oxides into winds that carry the gases eastward, converting them into sulfuric and nitric acids that wash down in rain.

So far, the chemical and biological resilience of soils and lakes has enabled them to absorb the poison with little visible harm. But as the reserve for neutralizing the acid diminishes, the first signs of widespread damage are beginning to appear.

Utilities, resistant to the heavy costs of emission control, have long disputed almost every link in the argument used by ecologists, which placed the acid rain problem on their doorstep. They urge more study to pinpoint cause and effect. They contend that even if power plants paid to reduce emissions, there would be no guarantee of a corresponding reduction in acid rain.

The Edison Electric Institute forecasted that electricity rates could rise as much as 50 percent if emissions-control legislation was passed. But a major study by the National Academy of Sciences found that—contrary to the utilities' contention—a direct relation holds between the amount of waste gas released and the amount of acid rain or gas deposited. This means that the more the Ohio coal plants cut back, the less acid rain will fall on New York and New England. Thus, control measures would buy something tangible.

The high-level review for the president's advisor confirmed the academy's finding—that acid rain is to blame for major changes in the biology of lakes and for increasing damage to forests. The review also concluded that even without further acid rain, it could take decades for the ecosystems to recover. But its summary stated: "The overall scientific understanding of the various aspects of acidic precipitation is quite incomplete at the present time and will continue to have major uncertainties well into the future."

Options

Three basic approaches to acid deposition and other air pollutants have been put forward:

1. Mandating emission reductions to further control the sources of transported pollutants. Legislated emission reductions could require modest reductions to keep emissions at—or somewhat below—current levels. A previous academy committee concluded that cutting sulfur dioxide by half, or by some 10 million tons a year, would bring acid rain beneath the threshold at which biological systems are damaged. Utilities could approach that target by washing coal before it is burned. They could also switch to low-sulfur coal, particularly in spring when snow melt places an extra acid burden on lakes and streams. But washing and switching would not be enough. Some utilities would also need to install scrubbers, costly equipment that efficiently removes sulfur from emissions. Another potential technology, not yet proven, would be to burn limestone along with the coal.

2. Liming lakes and streams to mitigate some of the effects of acid depositation.

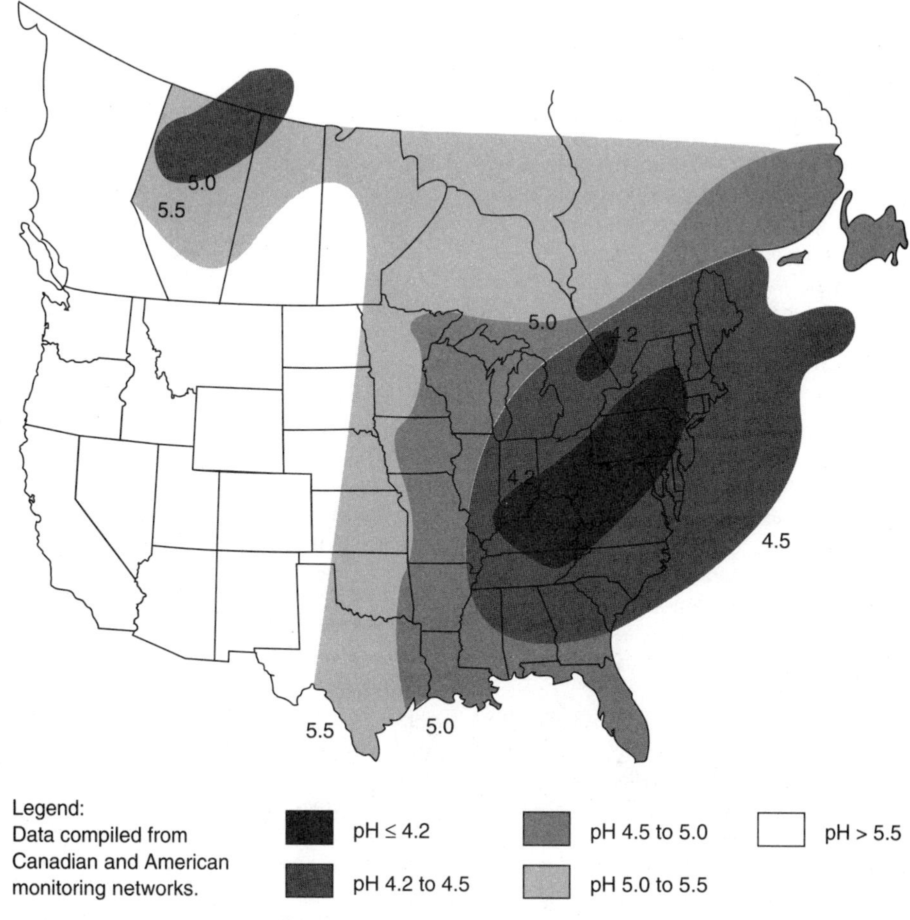

EXHIBIT 1

Precipitation Acidity—Annual Average pH for 1980

SOURCE: U.S. Office of Technology Assessment, *Acid Rain and Transported Air Pollutants* (Washington, D.C.: U.S. Government Printing Office, June 1984), p. 6.

3. Modifying the current research program to provide more timely guidance to Congress.

Case Questions

1. The EPA has to think the options through seriously—but what is it the agency has to think through? What decision is it being asked to make?
2. Where could the decision-making techniques discussed in this chapter help the most?

Case References

U.S. Office of Technology Assessment, *Acid Rain and Transported Air Pollutants* (Washington, D.C.: U.S. Government Printing Office, June 1984); U.S. General Accounting Office, *An Analysis of Issues Concerning "Acid Rain"* RCED-85-13 (Washington, D.C.: U.S. Government Printing Office, December 11, 1984).

CASE 6.2

★★★

The Apple: A Story of a Maze

There once was a man named Hugo who lived in a castle with innumerable rooms. Since the rooms were windowless, and since he had lived there since his birth, the castle was the only world he knew. His mother, who had died when he was very young, had told him of another world "outside," lighted by a single large lamp that was turned on and off at intervals of ten or twelve hours. She had not seen the outside world herself, but stories about it had been handed down from generation to generation. Hugo was never certain whether his ancestors had really lived in, or viewed, this world, or whether the stories had been invented in some remote time to entertain the children of the castle. At any rate, he knew of it only through his mother's tales.

The rooms of the castle were rectangular and very long—it took Hugo almost ten minutes of brisk walking to go from end to end of one of them. The walls at each end of each room were pierced by four or five doors. These doors were provided with locks so that they could be opened from one side, but not the other. The doors on the west end of a room opened into the room, while those on the east end opened out into adjoining rooms. When Hugo entered a room and the door shut behind him, he could not again return on the path along which he had come, but could only go on through one of the eastern doors to other rooms beyond.

At one time, Hugo became curious as to whether the rooms might be arranged in cycles, so that he could return to a room by a circuitous path, if not directly. It was not easy to decide, for many of the rooms looked much alike. For a time, he dropped a few crumbs of bread in each room through which he passed, and watched for evidences of his return to one of these. He never saw any of the bread crumbs again, but he was not certain but what they had been eaten by the mice that lived in the castle with him.

After the death of his mother, Hugo lived alone in the castle. Perhaps it seems strange that he or his ancestors had not long since died of hunger in this isolated life. Most of the rooms were quite bare, containing only a chair or two and a sofa. These Hugo found comfortable enough when he wanted to rest in his wanderings or to sleep. But from time to time, he entered a room where he found, on a small table covered with a white linen cloth, food for a quite adequate and pleasant meal.

Those of us who are accustomed to a wide range of foods, gathered for the pleasure of our table from the whole world, might not have been entirely satisfied with the fare. But for a person of simple tastes—and Hugo had not developed elaborate ones—the fruits and green vegetables, the breads, and the smoked and dried meats that Hugo found in these occasional rooms provided an adequate and satisfying diet. Since Hugo knew no other world, it caused him no surprise that the arrangements of the castle provided for his weariness and hunger. He had never asked his mother who it was that placed the food on the tables.

The rooms stocked with food were not very numerous. Had his education in mathematics not been deficient, Hugo could have estimated their relative number. For the connecting doors between the rooms were of clear glass, and peering through one of them, Hugo could see through a series of five or six doors far beyond. If any of the rooms in this range of vision had dining tables in them, he could see them from where he stood.

When Hugo had not eaten for some time, and was hungry, he would stand, in turn, before each of the four or five exit doors, and peer through them to see if food was visible. If it was not—as usually happened—he would open one of the doors, walk rapidly through the next room and reinspect the situation from the new viewing points now available to him. Usually, within an hour or two of activity, he would finally see on his horizon a room with a table; whereupon he walked rapidly toward it, assured of his dinner within another hour. He had never been in real danger of starvation. Only once had he been forced to continue his explorations as long as four hours before a dining room became visible.

Since life in the castle was not very strenuous, and since the meals that were spread before Hugo from time to time were generous, he seldom took more than two meals a day. If, in the course of a stroll when he was not actually hungry, he came upon a dining room, he simply passed through it, seldom pausing to pick up even a snack. Sometimes he would search for a dining room before retiring, so as to be assured of a prompt breakfast when he awoke.

As a result of this generosity of nature—or of the castle's arrangements, however these were brought about—the search for food occupied only a small part of Hugo's time. The rest he spent in sleep and in idle wandering. The walls of most rooms were lined with attractive murals. Fortunately for him, he found these pictures and his own thoughts sufficiently pleasant and of sufficient interest to guard him from boredom, and he had become so accustomed to his solitary life that he was not bothered by loneliness.

Hugo kept a simple diary. He discovered that his time was spent about as follows: sleep occupied eight or ten hours of each twenty-four; his search for a dining room, about three hours; eating his meals, two hours. The remaining ten hours were devoted to idle wandering, to inspection of the castle's decorations, and to daydreaming in the comfortable chairs with which the rooms were provided.

In this existence, Hugo had little need for personal possessions, other than the clothes he wore. But his mother had given him a small knapsack that he carried with him, containing a comb, a razor and strop, and a few other useful articles—and a single book, the Bible. The Bible, which was the only book he had known or even seen, had been his primer under his mother's tutelage, and continued to provide him with an enjoyable and instructive activity, even though a large part of the "world outside" it talked about was almost meaningless to him.

You might suppose that the murals on the castle's walls would have helped him to understand this world outside, and to learn the meaning of such simple words as "tree." But the pictures were of little help—at least in any ordinary way—for the designs the castle's muralists had painted on its walls were entirely abstract, and no object as prosaic as a tree—or recognizable as such to an inhabitant of the outside world—ever appeared in them.

The murals helped Hugo in another way, however. The long hours spent in examining them developed in him a considerable capacity for understanding and appreciating abstract relations, and it must be supposed that he read the creation myths and parables of the Bible in much the same way—the concrete objects taking on for him an abstract symbolic meaning. That is to say, his way of understanding the Bible was just the reverse of the way in which it was written. The authors of these stories had found in them a means for conveying to humble people in terms of their daily experiences profound truths about the meaning of the world. Hugo, deprived of these experiences, but experienced in abstraction, could usually translate the stories directly back to the propositions they sought to communicate.

I do not mean to imply that Hugo completely understood all that he read. The story of the Garden of Eden was particularly puzzling to him. What attraction did the Tree of Knowledge possess that led Eve to such wanton recklessness—to risk her Edenic existence for an apple? If he did not know what a tree was, he was familiar enough with apples, for he had often found those on the linen-covered dining tables, and his mother had taught him their name. Hugo found apples pleasant enough in taste, but no more so than the many other things that were provided for his hunger. Perhaps in this case, the very fact of his actual experience interfered with his powers of abstraction and made this particular story more difficult to understand than the others. He did, in time, learn the answer, but experience and not abstraction led him to it.

On the afternoon of a winter day—as judged, of course, by the events and calendars of the outside world—Hugo, who had been relaxing in an armchair, felt the initial stirrings of hunger. In his accustomed way, he arose, walked to the east end of the room, and peered through the glass in search of a table. Seeing none, he opened the second door, walked through the next room, and repeated his surveillance. This time he saw, five rooms beyond the fourth door, the table for which he was searching. In less than an hour he had arrived in the dining room ready to enjoy the meal that was waiting for him there.

But on this occasion, Hugo did something he never had done before. Before sitting down to his meal, he scanned the table to see what kind of bread had been provided. He saw in the middle of the table, surrounded with sausages and cheese, a freshly-baked half loaf of dark rye bread. And as this met his eye, there came unaccountably to his nostrils—or more likely to his brain, since his nostrils could have had nothing to do with it—the odor of French bread baked with white flour, and accompanying this imagined odor, he felt a faint distaste for the meal before him.

If Hugo, at this critical moment in his life, had stopped short and pondered, the vague movements of his imagination might have quieted themselves, and his life could have gone on as before. But Hugo, though he had spent much of his life in reflection, had never before had occasion to deliberate deeply about a course of practical conduct, and he did not deliberate now. Without pausing further, he turned from the table, walked around it, and marched on quickly to the next set of doors.

No table was visible through the glass. He pulled open one of the doors, and resumed his rapid walk. At the end of the third room he saw again, through an exit door, a distant table. He peered hard at it to see if he could identify the food that lay on it, but the distance was too great. He walked—almost ran—toward it, and was delighted to find on entering the last room that a loaf of white French bread was included in the collection of items spread before him. He ate his dinner with great gusto, and soon afterward fell asleep.

Hugo's subsequent development—or discovery—of his tastes and preferences was a very gradual matter, and for a time caused him no serious inconvenience. Although not every table was provided with French bread or with ripe olives (he soon began to develop a taste for ripe olives), a great number of them were. Besides, he did not insist on eating these delicacies at every meal. To be sure, the amount of time he spent daily in the search for food increased, but this meant merely that he could substitute a more serious purpose for some of his idle wanderings, which perhaps even increased slightly his pleasure in life.

But several major happenings foretold a more difficult future. On one occasion, Hugo passed by four tables in turn, because the food did not please him, and then, famished with hunger, hurried on for three hours more until he found a fifth—which was no different from the other four except that his hunger was now greater. For several days after this experience, Hugo was less particular in his diet.

At about the same time, Hugo discovered that his preferences were now extending also to the pictures on the castle's walls. Twice, he found himself turning away from a door after a brief inspection of the room beyond, because the colors or designs of the murals did not please him. A few weeks later, he saw a distant dining room at a time when he was moderately hungry, but formed a dislike for the decorations of the rooms through which he must pass to reach it. In the second room he turned aside and peered through the other glass doors—those not leading to the table—to see whether there might be another meal prepared for him that could be reached through more pleasant surroundings. He was disappointed, and proceeded on his original path, but on later occasions he turned aside often with nothing more than a hope that his new path would provide him with a meal.

Now Hugo's diary took on a very different appearance than before. First of all, almost all of his waking time was now occupied in the search for his preferred foods, a search that was further impeded by his distaste for certain rooms. Second, his diary now included more than an enumeration of the paths he took. It was punctuated with the feelings of pleasure and annoyance, of hunger and satiety, that accompanied him on his journeys. If he could have added these feelings together, he could have abbreviated the diary to a simple quarter-hourly log of the level of his satisfaction. This level was certainly now subject to violent fluctuations, and these fluctuations, in turn, sharpened his awareness of it.

Hugo felt himself helpless to blunt these sharpening prongs of perception whose prick he was now beginning to feel. Perhaps it is reading too much into his thoughts to say that "he felt himself helpless." More probably, the idea did not even occur to him that his tastes and preferences might be matters within his control—and who is to say whether in fact they were?

But if Hugo did nothing to curb his desires, he did begin to consider seriously how he was to satisfy them. He began a search for clues that would tell him, when he looked through a series of doors and saw a distant table, what kind of food he would find on it. He developed a theory that rooms decorated in green were more likely to lead to white bread than other rooms, while the color blue was a significant sign that he was approaching some ripe olives.

Hugo even began to keep simple records to test his predictions. He also developed a sort of profit-and-loss statement that told him how much time he was spending searching for food—and with what result—and how much his tastes in decoration were costing him in the efficiency of his search. (In spite of the propitiousness of green and blue for good meals, he really preferred the cheerfulness of red and yellow.)

To a certain extent, these scientific studies were successful, and served to reduce temporarily the increasing pressures on his time. But the trend revealed by the profit-and-loss statements was not reassuring. Each month, the time devoted to finding the best meals increased, and he could not persuade himself that his satisfaction was increasing correspondingly.

As Hugo became gradually more perceptive about his surroundings, and more reflective in his choices, he began also to observe himself—something that he had almost never done in the past. He found that his tastes in decoration were slowly changing, so that he actually began to prefer the green and blue colors that his experience had taught him were most likely to lead him to particularly desired foods. He even thought he detected a reverse effect: that his aversion for highly symmetrical murals, which seemed always to be present in rooms stocked with caviar, was spoiling his taste for that delicacy. But this sentiment was so weak that it might have been merely a construct of his imagination.

This gradual adaptation of his eyes to his stomach served somewhat to quiet Hugo's anxiety, for he realized that it made his task easier. In retrospect, he wondered whether his initial preferences for certain kinds of murals had not developed unconsciously from eating particularly delicious meals in rooms similarly decorated.

Hugo's researches, and the gradual reconciliation of his conflicting tastes, could only have postponed, not prevented, disaster if the growth of his demands had continued. At the time of which we are speaking, he had reached a truly deplorable state. As soon as he awoke each day, he seated himself at the table he had discovered before retiring. But however delicious the meal he had provided himself—even if the eggs were boiled to just the proper firmness, and the bread toasted to an even brown—he was unable to enjoy his meal without distraction. He would open his notebook on the table and proceed to calculate frantically what his objectives should be for the day. How recently had he eaten caviar? Was this a good day to search for peach pie, or, since he had eaten rather well the previous day, should he hold out for fresh strawberries, which were always difficult to find?

Having worked out a tentative menu, he would consult his notebook to see what his past experiences had been as to the time required to find these particular foods. He would often discover that he could not possibly expect to locate the foods he had listed in less than ten or fifteen hours of exploration. On occasions when he was especially keenly driven by search for pleasure, he planned menus that he could not hope to realize unless he were willing to forgo meals for a week. Then he would cross off his list the items, or combinations of items, most difficult to find, but only with a keen feeling of disappointment—even a dull anger at the niggardliness of the castle's arrangements.

Again before he retired, Hugo always opened his notebook and recorded carefully the results of his day's labor. He made careful notes of new clues he had observed that might help him in his future explorations, and he checked the day's experiences against the hypotheses he had already formed. Finally, he made a score-card of the day's success, assigning 10 or 15 points each to the foods he particularly liked (and a bonus of 5 points if he had not eaten them recently), and angrily marking down a large negative score if hunger had forced him to stop before a table that was not particularly appetizing. He compared the day's score with those he had made during the previous week or month.

A period of two or three months followed during which Hugo became almost wild with frustration and rage. His daily scores were actually declining. Fewer and fewer of the relatively abundant items of his diet seemed to him to deserve a high point rating, and negative scores began to appear more and more frequently. The goals he had set himself forced him to walk distances of twenty or thirty miles each day. Although he often found himself exhausted at the end of his travels, his sleep refreshed him very little, for it was disturbed by nightmarish visions of impossible feasts that disappeared before his eyes at the very moment when he picked up knife and fork to enjoy them. He began to lose weight, and because he now begrudged the time required to care for his appearance, his haggardness was further emphasized by a stubbly beard and unkempt hair.

Midway one day that had been particularly unsuccessful, Hugo, almost at the point of physical collapse, stumbled into an armchair in the room through which he was walking, and fell into a light sleep. This time, unaccountably, he was troubled by no dreams of food. But a clear picture came to him of an earlier day—some two years past—when he had been sitting, awake, in a similar chair. Perhaps some resemblance between the sharply angular murals of the room he was in and the designs of that earlier room had brought the memory back to him. Whatever the reason, his recollection was extremely vivid. He even recaptured in this dream the warm feeling of comfort and the pleasant play of his thoughts that had been present on that previous occasion. Nothing of any consequence happened in the dream, but it filled Hugo with a feeling of well-being he had not experienced for many months. An observer would have noticed that the furrows on his forehead, half hidden by scraggly hair, gradually smoothed themselves as he dozed, and that the nervous jerks of his limbs disappeared in a complete relaxation. He slept for nine or ten hours.

When Hugo awoke, the dream was still clear in his mind. For a few moments, indeed, his present worries did not return to him. He remained seated in the chair admiring the designs on the wall opposite—bold, plunging lines of deep orange and sienna, their advance checked by sharp purple angles. Then his eye was caught by the white page of his notebook, lying at his feet where it had slipped from his sleeping fingers. A pain struck deep within him as though a bolt had been hurled from the orange and purple pattern of the wall. Sorrow, equally deep inside him, followed pain, and broke forth in two sobs that echoed down the hall.

For the next few days, Hugo had no heart for the frantic pursuit in which he had been engaged. His life returned very much to its earlier pattern. He rested, and he wandered idly. He accepted whatever food came his way, and indeed, was hardly aware of what he ate. The pain and sorrow he had felt after his dream were diffused to a vague and indefinable sadness—a sadness that was a constant but not harsh reminder of the terror he had passed through.

It was not long, however, before he felt the first stirrings of reviving desire, and began again in a cautious way to choose and select. He could not bear to open the notebook (though he did not discard it), but sometimes found himself thinking at breakfast of delicacies he would like to eat later in the day. One morning, for example, it occurred to him that it had been a long time since he had tasted Camembert. He searched his memory for the kinds of clues that might help him find it, and passed two tables that day because he saw no cheese on them. Although his search was unsuccessful, his disappointment was slight and did not last long.

More and more, he discovered that after he had had a series of successful days, his desires would rise and push him into more careful planning and more energetic activity. But when he failed to carry out his plans, his failure moderated his ambitions and he was satisfied in attaining more modest goals. If Camembert was hard to obtain, at least ripe olives were reasonably plentiful and afforded him some satisfaction.

Only this distinguished his new life from that of his boyhood: then he had never been pressed for time, and his leisure had never been interrupted by thoughts of uncompleted tasks. What he should do from moment to moment had presented no problem. The periodic feelings of hunger and fatigue, and the sight of a distant dining room had been his only guides to purposeful activity.

Now he felt the burden of choice—choice for the present and for the future. While the largest part of his mind was enjoying its leisure—playing with his thoughts or examining the murals—another small part of it was holding the half-suppressed memory of aspirations to be satisfied, of plans to be made, of the need for rationing his leisure to leave time for his work. It would not be fair to call him unhappy, nor accurate to say that he was satisfied, for the rising and falling tides of his aspirations always kept a close synchrony with the level of the attainable and the possible. Above all, he realized that he would never again be free from care.

These thoughts were passing through Hugo's mind one afternoon during a period of leisure he had permitted himself. He now had time again for occasional reading, and he was leafing the pages of his Bible, half reading, half dreaming. As he turned a page, a line of the text called his mind to attention: ". . . and when the woman saw that the tree was good for food, and that it was pleasant to the eyes. . . ."

This time no recollection of apples seen or tasted impeded the abstraction of his thought. The meaning was perfectly clear—no more obscure than in the other stories he enjoyed in this book. The meaning, he knew now, lay not in the apple, but in him.

Case Questions

1. What would you conjecture to be the meaning that Hugo referred to?
2. What concepts presented in this chapter does the above story illustrate?

Case Reference

"The Apple: A Story of A Maze" from *Models of my Life* by Herbert Simon. Copyright © 1991 by Basic Books, Inc. Reprinted by permission of Basic Books, a division of HarperCollins Publishers.

CASE 6.3

★★★★★★★★★★★★★★★★★★★★★★★★★★★★★★★★★★★

Wild Horses

Background

On the western range of the United States roam thousands of wild horses—descendants of those brought to the North American continent by Spanish explorers in the 16th century (see photo). Over time, stray domestic horses belonging to settlers and Native Americans bred with the Spanish mustangs, and at the beginning of the 20th century, an estimated 2 million wild horses roamed America's ranges. For many years, as human settlements and livestock ranching expanded westward, these horses were freely exploited by ranchers, who shot them to make room for cattle and sheep; individuals, who captured them for domestic use and breeding; and by profiteers, who rounded up large herds from the public lands and sold them to slaughterhouses.

In the 1950s, documented abuses suffered by the wild horses led concerned individuals and national humane organizations to push for federal protection. Congress in 1959 responded by passing legislation that prohibited the use of aircraft, motor vehicles, and poisoned water holes to trap or kill wild horses on federal rangelands. Despite the act, wild horse exploitation continued, and by 1971 the reported population of wild horses on federal rangelands declined to about 9,500. Some questioned whether the population might eventually be eradicated. To ensure the survival of the wild horse herds, in 1974 Congress enacted the Wild Free-Roaming Horses and Burros Act.

Soon after the act's passage, more thorough Bureau of Land Management (BLM) censuses revealed that wild horse

Wild Horses in Nevada (Bureau of Land Management)

populations were much higher than the 9,500 previously thought to exist. In the ensuing years, the focus of program debates shifted from ensuring the continued survival of wild horses to determining the number that should remain on the public lands. On the one hand, ranchers (who pay a fee to graze their livestock on public lands) and wildlife conservationists argued that lower population levels should be maintained because horse populations were damaging the range and displacing domestic livestock and various wildlife species also competing for the limited available forage. On the other hand, horse protection groups argued for higher population levels on the basis of their view that horses were not a major cause of the ongoing degradation in public range resources.

Responding to the deteriorating range conditions, Congress enacted the Federal Land Policy and Management Act of 1976 (FLPMA). In the FLPMA, Congress directed the BLM to scientifically manage the rangelands under the principles of multiple use and sustained yield. The act defined multiple use as the management of public lands and their various resource values (fish and wildlife, livestock grazing, mining, recreation, etc.) so that they are used in the combination that best meets the public's present and future needs. The term *sustained yield* means the achievement and maintenance in perpetuity of a high-level annual or regular periodic output of various renewable resources. Under the FLPMA, wild horses and burros are one of the resources that the BLM must balance as it manages the range. In 1978, Congress amended the Wild Horses and Burros Act to require the BLM to maintain a current inventory of wild horses. It also authorized the BLM to remove the number of wild horses deemed to be in excess of what the range can support.

In 1985, Congress directed the BLM to accelerate the removal of wild horses and burros from public rangelands. It took this action in response to information from the BLM that the population of wild horses and burros exceeded the range's carrying capacity and was threatening range resources.

The BLM's Program

Through its land-use planning process, the BLM has determined that a population of about 27,000 wild horses provides the most appropriate level for public lands that the BLM manages in the West. Since the bureau believes that about 42,000 wild horses currently roam the range, it has determined that there is an excess of about 15,000 horses that need to be immediately removed.

Once excess wild horses are rounded up, they are disposed of in various ways. Since program inception, the BLM has removed and disposed of more than 80,000 wild horses from the federal rangelands.

The Adopt-A-Horse program allows individuals to take up to four horses per year for $125 each. Between 1973 and 1990, about 60,000 horses have been adopted through this program. To improve the adoptability of older horses, the BLM has, since 1986, sent these horses to various state prisons so that prison inmates can train and "gentle" them before adoption.

Because of a growing backlog of wild horses in the BLM holding facilities, the bureau initiated the so-called "fee-waiver" adoption program in 1984. This program allowed individuals and Native American tribes to take, free of charge, wild horses that were determined by the BLM to be unadoptable because of age or physical imperfections. After a one-year waiting period, the fee-waiver adopters obtained titles on the horses from the BLM. Under this program, the BLM disposed of about 20,000 horses, surpassing adoptions under the Adopt-A-Horse program in 1987. But the BLM did not always comply with its regulations and internal guidance for approving and monitoring these adoptions. This noncompliance resulted in the inhumane treatment and death of hundreds of horses during the one-year probation period when the horses were still owned by the government. Most adopters sold thousands of wild horses to slaughterhouses.

Continuing Problems for BLM

Although the fee-waiver adoption program was terminated, at least four problems with the BLM's other disposal approaches remain. First, existing information is insufficient to determine the number of wild horses the range can support, the extent of degradation caused by wild horses, or, consequently, the number of wild horses that should appropriately be removed from individual herd areas. For example, the BLM had not assessed the land's carrying capacities in over 20 years in some areas. The one resource area with data less than 10 years old did not use it to set target wild horse population levels and removal objectives. Despite the lack of data, the BLM has proceeded with horse removals using targets based on perceived population levels dating back to 1971 and on recommendations from the BLM advisory groups comprised largely of livestock permittees.

Nor can the BLM provide data demonstrating that federal rangeland conditions have significantly improved because

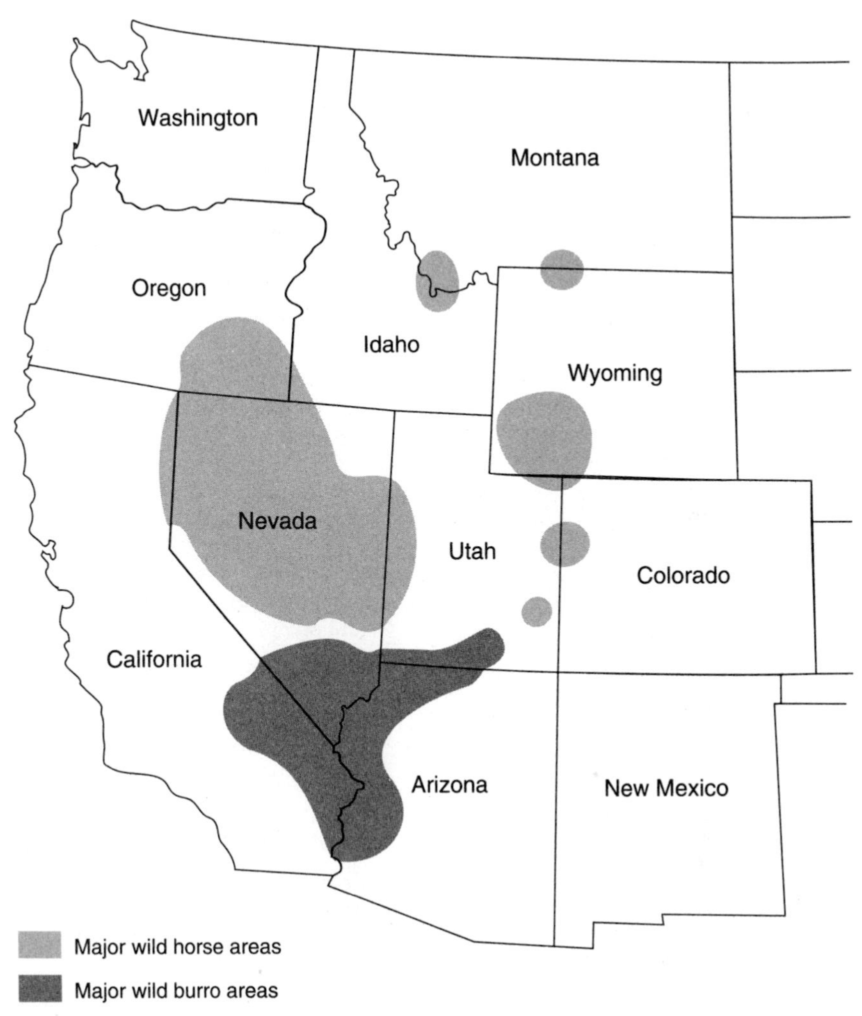

EXHIBIT 1

General Areas of Wild Horse and Burro Herds in the Western States

SOURCE: Bureau of Land Management

of wild horse removals. This lack of impact has occurred largely because the BLM has not reduced authorized grazing by domestic livestock, which, because of their vastly larger numbers, consume 20 times more forage than wild horses. In some areas, the BLM increased authorized livestock grazing levels after it had removed wild horses, thereby negating any reduction in total forage consumption and potential for range improvement.

A second problem is that sanctuaries have proven more costly than originally thought. For example, the BLM agreed to pay the nonprofit Institute of Range and the American Mustang (IRAM) that runs a sanctuary in South Dakota for about $1 a day per horse (or $602,250 yearly for

1,650 horses); but this payment is inadequate. The $1 per day figure was based on the assumption that sanctuary costs would be less than the cost of maintaining a horse on a contract feedlot. This assumption proved incorrect. The BLM may have to routinely pay for supplemental feed, not to mention veterinary treatment and equipment purchases. Moreover, much of the land within the sanctuary is leased from the Rosebud Sioux tribe. IRAM subsequently requested its rate be increased to $1.50.

A third problem is that the halter-training program is not as cost-effective as it could be. Horses remain at prison facilities, where inmates halter train them longer than necessary, increasing costs and resulting in lost adoption opportunities. For example, the BLM's original agreement with New Mexico called for 30 inmates to be available daily to work the horses, but a revised agreement signed in late 1989 stipulated that the state would provide "as many inmates as possible" rather than a mandatory 30. Further, the state is required to "attempt to provide the maximum number of gentled and trained horses as their resources can support." The BLM pays each state on a per-day basis for each horse.

Fourth, the BLM may have to consider other horse disposal options if its horse removals exceed the number that have historically been disposed of through the BLM's Adopt-A-Horse program—about 4,600 horses a year between 1982 and 1989. One alternative would be to hold unadoptable wild horses long enough to sterilize and mark them (so they would not be rounded up in the future) before returning them to their herd areas. Another alternative to protect the range from overgrazing—one authorized by legislation but banned by annual appropriations language and never used—would be euthanasia of healthy wild horses.

Case Questions

1. Which decision-making techniques and concepts described in this chapter are most appropriate to the BLM situation?
2. What suggestions would you make to help the BLM improve its handling of the wild horse problem?
3. How would you model this problem?

Case References

U.S. General Accounting Office, *Improvements Needed in Federal Wild Horse Program* (Washington, D.C.: U.S. Government Printing Office, 1990).

CHAPTER 7 Organizing

Introduction

Planning and decision making, the subjects of the two preceding chapters, cannot be separated from **organizing.** If people are to work together effectively in managing a program, they need to know the part they are to play in the total endeavor and how their roles relate to each other. To design and maintain these systems of roles is basically the managerial function of organization. This definition is a good one. Although many management theorists give loose and woolly definitions, we shall simply try to look at the organization as the practicing manager does. Organizing thus becomes the grouping of activities necessary to attain a program's objectives.

This chapter begins with a survey of the various ways in which people can organize themselves to attain some objective. Particular emphasis is placed on how governments are organized and what problems follow from that type of organization. The chapter concludes by discussing the design and redesign of organizations.

How does our key—namely, looking at organization the way a manager must—differ from the more conventional, more theoretical ones usually encountered in introductory texts? Probably the most obvious difference is simply in appearance, for the latter can often look quite Byzantine—with concepts such as closed model, open model, and model synthesis taking the place of the longitudinal basilicas, circular domes, and large vaults. All in all, a bewildering experience the first time through. But conventional approaches involve more fundamental problems, and we may as well make them explicit if we want to avoid them.

First, conventional approaches to organization tend to ignore external environments such as the political arena. They start from the bogus assumption that managers can simply collect and weigh facts and probabilities, make an optimal decision, and see that it is carried out. Yet in large-scale governmental projects, such a clear sequence of action is seldom possible because of their extended duration, the many technical and social unknowns, the continual discovery of new facts, and the con-

"And so you just threw everything together? Mathews, a posse is something you have to organize."

If people are to work together effectively, they need to know what part they are to play in the total endeavor and how their roles relate to each other. To design and maintain these systems of roles is basically the managerial function of organization.

stantly changing pressures. Given these messy realities, what the manager needs is not an abstract model of other organizations to copy but rather an analytical discussion of the ways to design administrative systems that allow recommitment, reassessment, and redirection.

Second, conventional approaches are unlikely to cover the newer kinds of organizational forms one finds in government and business today. What is sorely needed is a more balanced discussion that covers not only the traditional organizational concepts but also the newer forms of organizations.

Third, and perhaps most importantly, conventional approaches often separate the study of organization from the study of policy planning, even though the two are really quite inseparable. Organization should not be made an end in itself. If anything, the reverse is true: organization should *follow* policy. Otherwise our practicing manager might find himself or herself in a situation similar to that of U.S. military commanders in the Vietnam War. "It was as if someone had ordered the greatest house in the world, using the finest architect, the best stonemason in the world, marble shipped from Italy, choicest redwood for the walls, the best interior decorator, but had by mistake overlooked one little thing: the site chosen was in a bog" (Halberstam, 1969:635).

Four Types of Organizations

Some time ago, Kenneth Boulding (1956) developed a fascinating hierarchy of systems concepts ranging from the simple atom to imponderables beyond the galaxies. We can take this powerful organizing concept, narrow the focus considerably, and construct a comprehensive list of systems of which humans are components. They range from the system most often used in history (leader/follower) to what Alvin Toffler (1970), the futurist, terms "adhocracy"—essentially a selectively decentralized structure that makes heavy use of liaison devices (see Table 7-1).

Leader/Follower Organization

We can begin with the most natural of human relationships, that between leader and followers. The relationship is, however, not as simple as it might appear at first blush.

The leader's authority, for instance, can seldom be satisfied with obedience based merely upon the grounds of common sense or respect. Rather, as Max Weber was to note, authority seeks to arouse something else (love, fear, even awe) in the followers. This line of inquiry led Weber to the conclusion that there are three types of legitimate authority: legal, traditional, and charismatic.

Legal authority we associate with constitutional governments; **traditional authority,** with kings and parents. But it is **charismatic authority** that is most relevant to the leader/follower cluster. It is based on the members' abandonment of themselves to an individual distinguished by holiness, heroism, or exemplariness. The word itself, *charisma,* from the Greek means literally "gift of grace." All charismatic authority implies wholehearted devotion to the person of the leader who feels called to carry out a mission. Examples of this special type of leader/follower relationship

TABLE 7-1.
Four Types of Organizations

	Structure	*Examples*	*Objectives*	*Environment*	*Centralization*
Leader-follower cluster	Leader at center, followers at periphery	Indian tribes, street-corner gangs, military squad, R & D groups, "Kitchen Cabinets"	Survival, innovation	Simple, changing	High
Consortium	Loosely connected assembly of smaller organizations	Delian League, NATO, European Community, public-private partnerships, health maintenance organizations (HMOs), colleges	Critical mass*	Complex, changing	Low to moderate
Pyramid	Hierarchy with single chain of command	U.S. government departments, unions, foundations, school districts, most corporations, organized churches, courts	Efficiency	Stable, certain	High
Adhocracy	Matrix with dual chain of command	NASA, aerospace and electronic industries, R & D firms	Innovation, adaptation	Unstable, uncertain	Low

* That is, an amount necessary to achieve a result. Presumably, subsystems would be unable to achieve this result acting alone.

SOURCE: Adapted from G. J. Skibbins, *Organizational Evolution* (New York: AMACOM, 1974), endpaper.

Sociology in Germany in the late 19th and early 20th century was dominated by one gigantic figure—Max Weber. He exerted a tremendous influence on many of his contemporaries, an influence that increased rather than decreased after his death in 1920. Weber differentiated among three types of authority in terms of legitimacy: traditional, charismatic, and legal-rational. In each case, the basic question can be put as follows: On what basis do those in authority have the right to give orders to their followers? As we will see later in the chapter, Weber also provided the classical description of bureaucracy. (Photo of Max Weber from University of Heidelberg Museum)

would be Hitler's Germany, Castro's Cuba, and the guru/novitiate in arcane religions. We also find charismatic leader/follower relationships among research assistants at the disposal of a scientist who is thought to be a genius or among the aides of a political leader who is thought to represent in his or her person the wishes of the people. Needless to say, the bonds in this relationship are quite strong.

The strengths of this relationship, however, are also its weaknesses. Too often a leader is unwilling to adapt to new challenges. One reason for this low capacity for adaptation is that change could affect the leader's absolute power.

The British historian Arnold J. Toynbee (1946) suggests another reason—the nemesis of creativity. According to Toynbee, it is most uncommon for the creative responses to two or more successive challenges in the history of a group to be achieved by the same individual. Indeed, the party that has distinguished itself in dealing with one challenge—probably an act that brought it to power—is apt to fail conspicuously in attempting to deal with the next. The failures here seem to derive from an overconfidence, an arrogance acquired after the leader's earlier triumphs.

Surely one of the most charismatic leaders the United States ever produced was General Douglas MacArthur. His brilliantly conceived strategy of "island hopping" led to the defeat of Japan during World War II. Rather than follow the conventional doctrine of recapturing, one by one, Pacific islands taken by the Japanese, MacArthur selected only major bases and places located along enemy supply lines. A few years later, during the dark early months of the Korean War, when North Korean forces had almost pushed American troops off the Korean peninsula, MacArthur proposed another bold move: an amphibious landing at the Inchon, deep behind the enemy's front lines. Despite the reservations of many senior officials, the risky landing went ahead and, again, MacArthur proved right. Yet, in the end, his charisma made him so arrogant that he disregarded all the warnings of a Chinese counterattack and blundered into a costly, unnecessary military setback.

Consortium

The consortium organization is actually an association, partnership, or union of two or more institutions brought together for a few particular purposes. One of the earliest examples of this type of organization was the Delian League. In the winter of 478–477 B.C., the Greek city-states in and around the Aegean Sea met on the island of Delos and formed an alliance. The purposes of this early consortium was to free those Greeks who were under Persian rule, to protect all against a Persian return, and to obtain compensation from Persians by attacking their lands and taking booty. League policy was determined by a vote of the assembly, in which early states, including Athens, had one vote. The Delian League was a forerunner of such modern organizations as NATO and the European Community (EC).

Not all consortia are, however, large-scale organizations. Recently, a new coalition was formed in northwest Los Angeles County. It includes private homeless agencies, hospitals, religious organizations, and city agencies from Los Angeles and West Hollywood. The particular purpose for which this consortium was formed was to identify resources for helping the homeless—more shelter space, access to health care and job training, and so on.

Private companies have, in recent years, found this form of organization particularly attractive. To share certain resources and to avoid destructive trade wars, many companies have formed consortia with foreign companies. These loose alliances are premised on the notion that some markets are so large and complex that no single company can hope to control all critical technological elements. Sometimes governments become partners in these consortia.

The Microelectronics and Computer Technology Corporation (MCC) was a precedent-setting, privately funded, for-profit research consortium formed in 1982. Its purpose was to counter Japan's high-tech challenge and to preserve U.S. leadership in electronics. There were 21 members supporting the organization, and though the federal government provided no funding or guidance, it did legislate specific exemptions to antitrust laws without which MCC would have been illegal. By the late 1980s, however, questions were being raised concerning MCC's effectiveness. MCC had difficulty attracting as many first-rate researchers from member companies as planned; apparently, some companies were seeking from MCC a free (or cheap) ride.

Sematech is another consortium composed of 14 companies including such giants as IBM, Hewlett-Packard, Intel, Motorola, NCR, Rockwell, and Texas Instruments. The purpose of Sematech was to develop a "self-sustaining, world-competitive" manufacturing capability for the U.S. semiconductor industry. Unlike MCC, Sematech had federal government participation (see Figure 7-1).

Administrators in consortium type of organizations face three key problems. The first problem stems from the fact that the institutions forming the consortium maintain a certain amount of autonomy. Therefore, a crucial issue becomes, On what basis do those in authority give orders to other members of a consortium? In such a milieu, political and persuasive skills are highly desirable.

Although I would not put all colleges and universities in this category, some I might. As Robert M. Hutchins, who became president of the University of Chicago in 1929 at the age of 30, said of that great institution, the only thing that held it together was the heating system. I shudder to think what he might think of the autonomy—indeed, the raw power—of the athletic departments at some of today's universities.

The second problem stems from the fact that different institutions have different cultures, that is, they share different sets of behavior. Unfortunately, not all administrators are adept at working in different organizational cultures.

The third problem facing the administrator of a consortium is what economists term the free-rider problem. Recall the MCC example. Institutions may attempt to get a free (or cheap) ride on the benefits provided by the consortium by contributing as little as possible to it.

As indicated in the introduction to this chapter, the characteristics of an organization should be determined by the situation. Although we have examined only two types of organization, I do not think it is too early to illustrate the point.

During the late 1980s, the U.S. government and the scientific community had a chance to establish a coordinated national research program to counter AIDS. One of the reasons why they did not do so can be found in the scientific community itself and, in particular, in the way they organize research. Basic biomedical research is a classic example of the leader/follower type of organization. It usually requires only the equipment available in an individual's laboratory and a small group working under the direction of a gifted scientist. Because this type of organization maximizes the scientist's creativity, it has served biomedical research well.

But maximizing individual creativity is not the only way to organize research; and in certain situations, it is not necessarily the best. It could be argued that AIDS research is one area where the consortium-type organization is probably more appropriate than the leader/follower type. According to many experts, when the federal government began dramatically increasing the funding of AIDS research in the mid-1980s, we already had solid information about the virus that causes AIDS. Given this fact, the federal government might have brought together the relevant scientific personnel

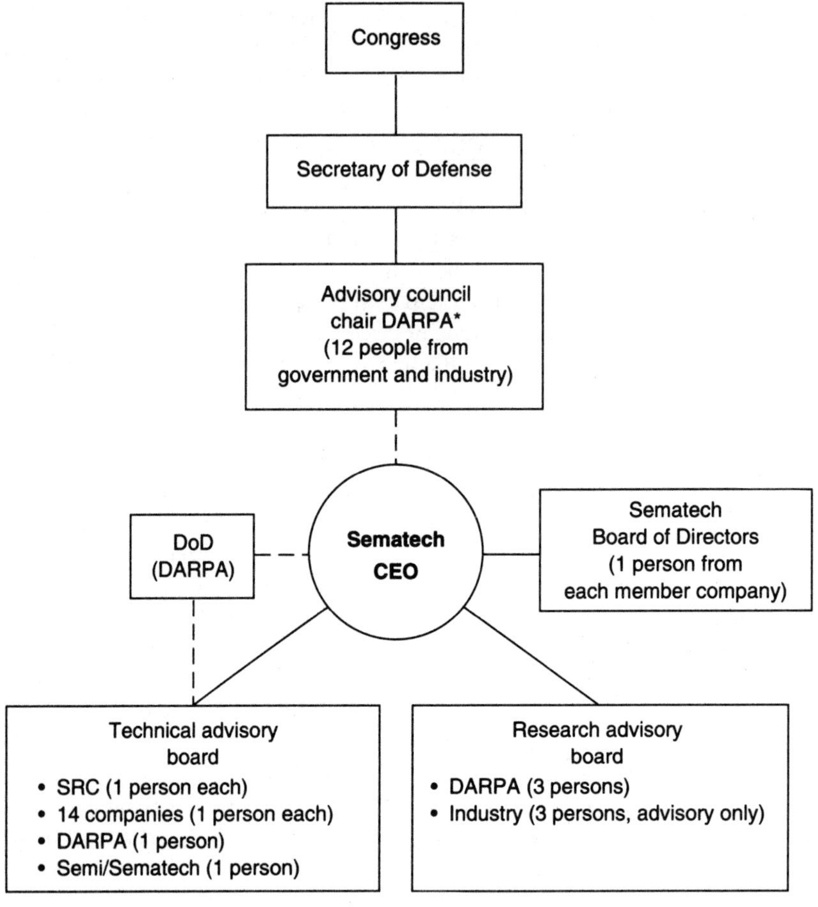

FIGURE 7-1
Sematech Organizational Relationships

* Defense Advanced Research Projects Agency

and research institutes of the country—if not the world—into a consortium with the purpose of producing the needed answers in the shortest possible time. Instead, the NIH chose to create a patchwork of AIDS-related projects with no central coordination.

Pyramidal Organization

The pyramid is a geometric figure, and it symbolizes the structure of the hierarchy. Interaction within a pyramid conforms to the hierarchical structure of the organization and emphasizes superior/subordinate relationships. The concept of hierarchy was defined on page 47.

A closely related concept is that of **bureaucracy.** Most of us have a general idea of what a bureaucracy is, and I have admittedly taken the liberty of using the term in earlier chapters without providing a formal definition. But now I must. Once again, our surest guide is Max Weber (Gerth & Mills, 1946:196–98), who in the early part of this century, spelled out in considerable detail the features of the bureaucratic structure. In simplified terms those features are (1) division of labor based on functional specialization; (2) well-defined hierarchy of authority; (3) system of rules covering the rights and duties of employment; (4) system of procedures for dealing with work situations; (5) impersonality of interpersonal relations; and (6) promotion and selection based on technical competence.

The bureaucratic model was not a description of reality but an *ideal type;* that is, what organizations to varying degrees approximate. Some organizations are more bureaucratic than others, but none are perfect examples of bureaucracy.

Another important thread in the intellectual development of the pyramidal concept begins with the American engineer Frederick W. Taylor (1856–1915) and the scientific management movement and ends with Luther Gulick and Lyndall Urwick and the administrative management movement. Unlike Weber, these three Americans sought to discover principles that would enable the manager to build up and administer an organization in the most efficient manner. Below we discuss four of the more important of these principles.

Division of Labor. Without a doubt, the cornerstone of the four principles is the division of labor into specialized tasks. But how does the administrator do it? Begin by determining the necessary activities for the accomplishment of overall organizational objectives. Then divide these activities on a logical basis into departments that perform the specialized functions. In this way, the organizational structure itself becomes the primary means for achieving the technical and economic advantages of specialization and division of labor.

The procedure is hardly as simple as it sounds, however, for there are many ways by which the administrator can divide and place in separate departments the functions of the organization. The most common, of course, is by objectives. For example, the Department of Health and Human Services organizes in Washington along health and welfare lines; similarly, NASA subdivides into the Office of Manned Space Flight and the Office of Space Science and Applications.

Adam Smith began his classic study of economics, Wealth of Nations *(1976/1776) with a discussion of specialization in pin making. Eight men, each performing a simple task, could turn out far more pins than eight men each performing all required series of tasks.*

Such divisions by use or objective can present problems, however. For example, the interrelationship among components often turns out to be much more complicated than would appear at first. Increasingly, the interfaces become blurred as technology progresses. In nuclear power plants, for instance, one finds no neat dividing lines among the functions of fueling, heating, and power generation.

Another criterion the manager might use in making these structural decisions is geographic. In other words, administrative authority is distributed not by function but by area. In the national government, the Department of State, the TVA, and, to a lesser degree, the Department of the Interior have followed this criterion. In other departments and agencies, division by geography appears in modified form. For example, the secretary of the Department of Health and Human Services also has regional representatives who try to shepherd into one flock the regional commissioner of social security, the regional Public Health Service offices, and the others.

Division of labor might also be based on either process or client. Process-type departments have at their roots either a particular technology or a particular type of equipment, or both. Technology, as used here, refers not only to hardware technology (such as welding in a transportation maintenance work center) but also to software technology (such as accounting or operations research). Obvious examples of client-based agencies include the Bureau of Indian Affairs and the Veterans Administration.

Hierarchy. The second principle of administrative management is hierarchy. It is based on the **scalar principle,** which states that authority and responsibility should flow in a direct line vertically from the highest level of the organization to the lowest level. This flow is commonly referred to as the chain of command. In such an arrangement, a cardinal sin would be to fail to go through channels in trying to get a message to the top.

Span of Control. Closely related to the principles of division of labor and hierarchy is the span of control. This principle concerns the number of subordinates a superior can efficiently supervise. Traditional theory advocates a narrow span to enable the executive to provide adequate integration of all the activities of subordinates. Most federal agencies, apparently mindful of the span of control principle, have kept their principal subordinates to less than 20. But a president without a chief of staff could have more than 200 individuals, commissions, departments, agencies, and other groups reporting directly to him.

Line and Staff. The simplest way to understand the last principle is probably by military analogy. Soldiers with weapons stand in the line, carrying out a military organization's essential functions; meanwhile, usually somewhere behind the front lines, stands (or sits) the staff to investigate, to research, and to advise the commanding officer. Only through the commanding officer can the staff influence line decisions. (What are staff positions in Figure 7-2?)

As any organization—military or otherwise—becomes more complex, managers begin to need advice. Staffs aid managers in many ways. As Anthony Downs (1967:154) points out, a large staff can function as "a control mechanism 'external'

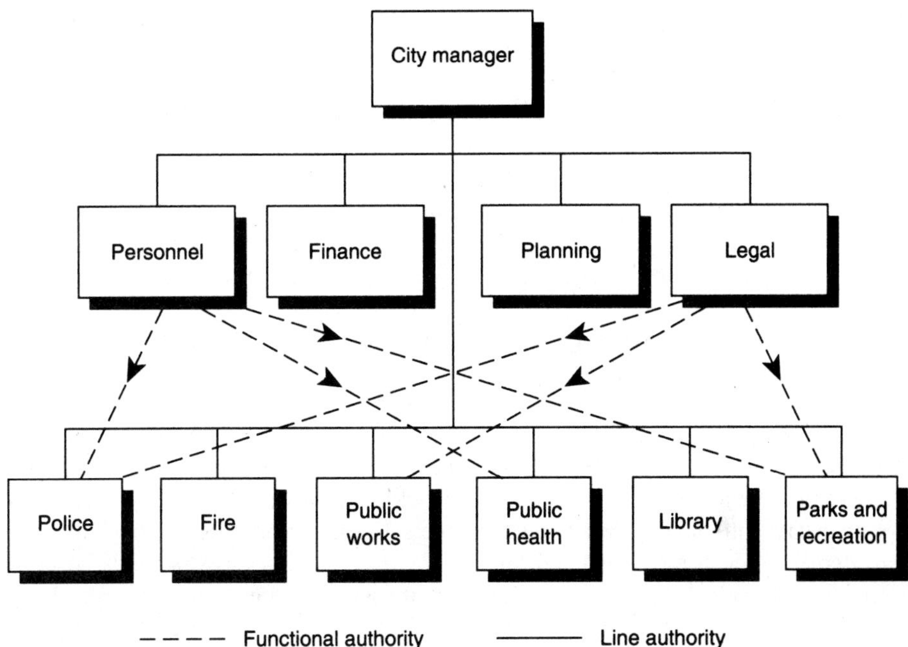

FIGURE 7-2
Line and Functional Authority

to the line hierarchy, promote changes in opposition to the line's inertia, and act as a scapegoat deflecting hostility from its boss." Top executives can use staffs to help bring change to organizations. The innovative capacity of a staff appears to result from (1) the technical orientation of its members, who are younger and better educated; and (2) the incentive structure of the staff, which is to help the top administrator improve the line's performance.

The importance of understanding the line-staff concept cannot be overemphasized. Superior and subordinate alike must know whether they are acting in a staff or line capacity. Lack of clarity on this point often causes friction. And here, the notion of **functional authority** can help. Functional authority is "the right that an individual or department has delegated to it over specified processes, practices, policies, or other matters relating to activities undertaken by personnel in departments other than its own" (Koontz & O'Donnell, 1974:175). Thus, in Figure 7-2, the functional authority of the personnel director might cover and only cover giving competitive examinations and conducting in-service training programs.

The Pathology of the Pyramid

Above we looked at the four principles of management—division of labor (or specialization), hierarchy, span of control, and line and staff—that characterize the pyramidal organization. Now we need to reexamine these principles through a more critical lens. Despite this essentially critical approach, our intent is not to debunk. Rather, we want to point out a few important shortcomings in the pyramidal form of organization.

It also should be kept in mind that, despite its flaws, the pyramidal form of organization and its attendant principles have often served the needs of government well. As a former top administrator of NASA noted, the systematization of these principles resulted in a body of doctrine, which, for all its publicized faults, still provided the building blocks from which parts of a large-scale endeavor could be constructed. The rub, of course, comes when one tries to apply this traditional doctrine too rigorously in large complex undertakings so indicative of all levels of government today.

Division of Labor and Problems of Coordination. Litterer (1973:370–71) notes at least three drawbacks to the division of labor by function. First, a high degree of specialization may tend to make the occupants of these subunits more concerned with their specialty than with the organization's goals. Selznick (in March & Simon, 1958:40–44) refers to this phenomenon as the "internalization of subgoals." Second, because of their interest in their specialty, people may find it increasingly difficult to communicate with other organizational members. Coordination suffers, though its need has increased because of specialization. Third, "in many instances people who have risen through several levels of the organization within a functional specialty have advanced within a very unique professional environment and, consequently, may be poorly equipped eventually to assume overall organization responsibilities." Hence, an agency may have difficulty finding chief administrators within its own ranks.

Sayles and Chandler (1971:15) offer a fourth criticism of specialization. It conflicts with the interdisciplinary efforts required—almost by definition—in large mission or problem-oriented programs:

> *The biologist is asked to conceive of the impact of a hard vacuum on genetics and to work with aerospace engineers on joint endeavors. The project manager is asked to move for six months to a distant location to be closer to a critical development team and to shift both his organizational identity and his family's home every several years. Specialists are asked to give up their specialties in favor of joining multidisciplinary teams and to learn from those whom they would normally ignore or consider beneath their dignity.*

Hitler's master builder, Albert Speer (1970), implies a fifth criticism of specialization—one that surely has some points of reference with Chapter 4. In his memoirs, Speer notes that the ordinary party member was taught that grand policy was much too complex for him to judge. Consequently, one was never called upon to take personal responsibility. Indeed, the whole structure of the system was aimed at preventing conflicts of conscience from even arising. The result was the total sterility of all conversations and discussions among these like-minded persons. Further, the Reich's leaders explicitly demanded that everyone restrict his or her responsibility to his or her own field. "Everyone kept to his own group—architects, physicians, jurists, technicians, soldiers, or farmers. The professional organizations to which everyone had to belong were called chambers (Physicians Chamber, Art Chamber), and this term aptly described the way people were immured in isolated, closed-off areas of life. The longer Hitler's system lasted, the more people's minds moved within such isolated chambers."

Hierarchy and Rigidity. "I used to be in the government service," Dostoyevsky (1960) tells us in *Notes from the Underground.* "I was a spiteful official. I was rude and took pleasure in being so. I did not take bribes, you see, so I was bound to find recompense in that, at least. When petitioners used to come for information to the table at which I sat, I used to grind my teeth at them, and felt intense enjoyment when I succeeded in making anybody unhappy. I almost always did succeed. For the most part they were all timid people—of course, they were petitioners." How do we account for this personal difficulty that clients seem to experience with bureaucracies?

One of America's foremost sociologists, Robert K. Merton (in March & Simon, 1958), in a marvelous, though involved, analysis of bureaucracy, traces it to, among other things, hierarchy. His analysis begins with a demand for control made by the top administrators: more specifically, they are concerned with increasing the reliability of behavior within the organization. Therefore, standard operating procedures (SOPs) are instituted and control consists largely in checking to ensure that these procedures are followed.

Three consequences follow—none of which is good. First, the amount of personalized relationships is reduced. The full human resources of bureaucracy are not being utilized due to mistrust, fear of reprisals, and so on. Second, the participants internalize the rules of the organization; in fact, rules originally devised to achieve organizational goals assume a positive value *independent* of the goals. Third, the categories used in decision making become restricted to a relatively small number. For example, when a specific problem arises, the bureaucrat tends to say that this problem is essentially a certain type of problem. And since the type has been encountered before, one knows exactly how to handle it. Never mind nuances. In this way, an increase in the use of SOPs decreases the search for alternatives.

These three consequences combine to make the behavior of members of the organization highly predictable. This is a nice way of saying that the result is an increase in the *rigidity of behavior* of participants. One of the major costs of rigid behavior is increased difficulty with clients of the organization and with achievements of client satisfaction. Yet client satisfaction is, or should be, a near-universal organizational goal. Another cost of this rigidity in behavior is borne by the organization's own employees in terms of less opportunity for personal growth and development of a mature personality.

Span of Control and Span of Relationships. What really matters in determining the span of control is not how many people report to the manager but how many people *who have to work with each other* report to the manager. For example, the secretary of energy, who has reporting to him a number of top administrators, each concerned with a major function, should indeed keep the number of direct subordinates to a fairly low number—between 8 and 12 is probably the limit. Why? Because these subordinates must work closely with each other. Consider how the secretary attempts

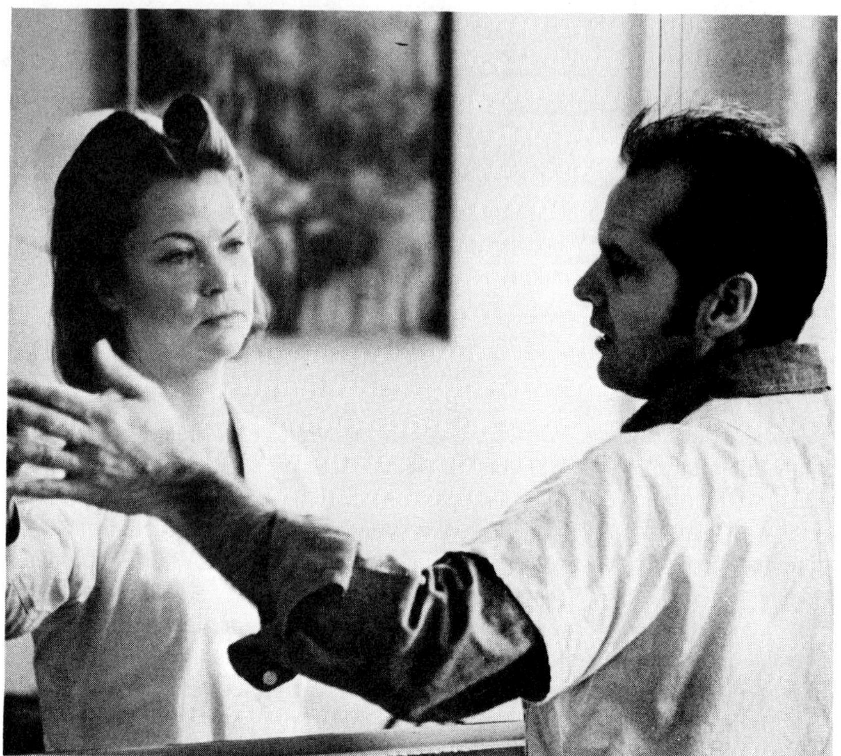

Ken Kesey's One Flew over the Cuckoo's Nest *provides a memorable illustration of how, in bureaucracies, means have a way of displacing the ends they are designed to serve. Although the mission of a mental hospital is to make the sick well, the Big Nurse (portrayed by Louise Fletcher) places so much emphasis on scheduled routines that she will not allow the patients to see the World Series. What makes this refusal so shocking is that the protagonist, Randle Patrick McMurphy (portrayed by Jack Nicholson) has gotten the patients—some catatonic—to organize and vote for the change in schedule. The Big Nurse announces that the vote—which is actually the beginning of a cure—does not count and retreats behind her glassed-in nurse's station. (I am indebted to Howard E. McCurdy for this example.) (Copyright © 1975. Fantasy Films. All rights reserved.*

to exploit solar energy as a potential solution to the energy squeeze. Solar research is assigned to the Office of Research; solar technology to the Office of the Assistant Secretary for Technology; implementation to the Office of the Assistant Secretary for Conservation and Solar Applications; and the Solar Energy Institute conducts and funds activities in all facets of solar energy. Clearly, the heads of these units have to work closely and frequently with each other. Accordingly, a small span of control is called for since the problems of coordination are greater than those of, say, a police sergeant, who supervises several patrols. Each patrol is discrete and relatively autonomous, since there is usually little need for interaction between them; hence, a broader span of control is possible.

A second shortcoming of span of control should be apparent from Figure 2-2. The span of control concept assumes that a manager's main relationship is downward, but this direction, as we saw, is only part of the picture. The upward relationship to overhead authority is at least equal in importance to the downward relationship to the subordinates. Likewise, lateral relations with cognate agencies and interest groups are also important. What is needed, then, is to replace the concept of the span of control with a more relevant concept: the span of managerial relationships. The span of control, in short, is a terribly limited concept in public sector management.

Line and Staff and the Tooth-to-Tail Ratio. What is one to do about the ever-increasing size of staff functions in comparison to line functions? How, in short, can an administrator improve the tooth-to-tail ratio? Why do staff functions seem, inexorably, to grow?

C. Northcote Parkinson (1957), who has a knack for conveying serious thoughts in the form of a joke, provides the most famous answer. He notes that the number of ships and men in the British Navy decreased by 68 percent and 32 percent between 1914 and 1928. Meanwhile, the number of officials in the admiralty *increased* 78 percent. He also notes, for the same period, that the dockworkers increased only 10 percent, while the dockyard officials and clerks increased 40 percent. More recently, Parkinson detected the law at work in sunny California. The Transbay Bridge between San Francisco and Oakland originally had a staff of 12 to keep it repainted. Over the years, the staff grew to 77, even though in the meantime they acquired labor-saving machinery.

Parkinson attributes this kind of growth not to increased work but to the dynamics of staff operations. To begin with, officials tend to multiply subordinates. Thus, if a civil servant—call him A—thinks he is overworked, he will have B and C appointed under him. This act increases his importance and precludes any colleague from taking over some of his work. In time, Parkinson suggests, B will find himself overworked; when A allows him subordinates D and E, he must likewise allow C the same numbers; hence, F and G. (One might wonder why *two* subordinates are necessary in each case. One subordinate would result in a division of work with the original supervisor and, to that extent, the subordinate might assume almost equal status.)

Seven officials are now doing what one did before. How can this be? Parkinson offers another "proposition": Officials make work for each other. For example, an incoming document arrives or comes to D, who decides it really falls within the province of E. A draft reply is then prepared to E and placed before B, who amends it drastically before consulting C, who asks F to deal with it. But F goes on leave at this point, handing the file over to G, who drafts an amendment that is signed by C and returned to B, who revises his draft accordingly and lays the new version before A.

Now, what does A do? This person is beset by many problems created by the new subordinates (e.g., promotions, leaves, domestic problems, raises, transfers, and office affairs). Mr. A could, of course, simply sign it unread. Parkinson (1957:20) thinks not:

A is a conscientious man beset as he is with problems created by his colleagues for themselves and for him—created by the mere fact of these officials' existence—he is not the man to shirk his duty. He reads through the draft with care, deletes the fussy paragraphs by B and G, and restores things back to the form preferred in the first instance by the able (if quarrelsome) E. He corrects the English—none of these young men can write grammatically—and finally produces the same reply he would have written if officials B and G had never been born. Far more people have taken longer to produce the same result. No one has been idle. All have done their best. And it is late in the evening before A finally quits his office and begins the return journey home. The last of the office lights are being turned off in the gathering dusk that marks the end of another day's administrative toil. Among the last to leave, A reflects with bowed shoulders and a wry smile that late hours, like gray hairs, are among the penalties of success.

Before you dismiss Parkinson's little story as mere whimsy, let me give you some actual titles of employees in the District of Columbia School District: community coordinator and community organizer; attendance aide, attendance officer, and attendance counselor; assistant for research and assessment and assistant for research and planning; employee counseling assistant, employee counseling specialist, employee development specialist, employee relations assistant, and employee relations specialist; not to mention interagency liaison and clearly overworked position classification specialist. Let me also suggest that you read the memo in Figure 7-3.

In recent years, several American economists have attempted a more rigorous examination of why bureaucracy continues to grow and grow. These scholars start from the assumption that politicians and bureaucrats behave like consumers and business executives. This assumption allows them to apply conventional economic analysis to the behavior and decisions of actors in the public sector. This field of economics is, accordingly, called **public choice.**

Among the most famous contributors to the field are Anthony Downs (1967), William Niskanen (1971), and Gordon Tullock (1965; 1971). According to Downs, the central problem is that government bureaucracy is not subject to disciplines like those that operate in the private sector. In the public sector, there is little competition and consumer choice to constrain the self-interest of bureaucrats. Because growth is in the self-interest of the bureaucrat (among other things, growth improves chances for promotion), bureaucracies grow far in excess of what the public wants or efficiency justifies. Public bureaucracies, these economists argue, are like private sector monopolies—except that they seek bigger budgets rather than bigger profits.

Personal aggrandizement is not, of course, the only reason for the growth in the tail-to-tooth ratio. New regulations and mandates imposed from the outside can mean more paperwork, and that in turn means more staff. New federal legislation concerning the handicapped, bilingual education, and other matters has certainly contributed to the growth of overhead in our public schools. Similarly, new complex technology has led in many cases to larger staffs. Increasingly, administrators have to rely on the judg-

UNITED STATES GOVERNMENT DEPARTMENT OF HEALTH, EDUCATION, AND WELFARE

Memorandum REGION IV — ATLANTA

TO : Title IX team (Unit II) DATE: November 18, 1977

FROM : Carroll D. Payne REFER TO:
Coordinator, Title IX team

SUBJECT: Routing of completed drafts of Title IX reports and letters.

The above drafts come to me first for review and I then give them to Mr. Gregory for typing. The typist returns them to Mr. Gregory for his record of typing completions. Mr. Gregory will return the typed copies to the originator to review for typing corrections and/or sign off. The originator, after corrections and sign off, will route the typed report or letter to me for sign off and routing to Mr. Clements. Copies of mailed letters come back through Mr. Gregory for recording.

FIGURE 7-3
An Example of Parkinson's Bureaucratic Staff in Operation

SOURCE: *The Washington Monthly,* January 1978.

ment of physicists, microbiologists, software engineers, system designers, operations researchers, and the like in making their decisions.

Adhocracy

The greatest single weakness of the pyramid is that it has a low capability for innovation. The pyramid is a performance, not a problem-solving, structure. It is designed to carry out standard programs, not to invent new ones. Sophisticated innovation requires a fourth and very different structural configuration, one that is able to "fuse experts drawn from different disciplines into smoothly functioning ad hoc project teams" (Mintzberg, 1979:432).

Four characteristics of this newest type of organization are worth noting:

First, adhocracy is a high organic as opposed to a mechanistic structure. Essentially, this means that adhocracies are highly flexible, capable of going from one complex task to another with minimum delay. A human being can do this; a simple machine (say, a lathe) cannot—nor can the pyramid structure.

Second, adhocracy shows little reverence for the four principles of management discussed above. The level of specialization is relatively low; there are fewer different jobs in an adhocracy than in a pyramid. Control is achieved more through a widely shared commitment to the organization's mission than through a hierarchy based on implied contractual relations. Decision-making power is formed wherever there is skill and competence to solve the problem—which may or may not be at the top of the organization. Indeed, the decision may even be made by a nonmanager; it all depends on the nature of the decision.

A third characteristic of adhocracy is a tendency to group the specialists in functional units for housekeeping purposes only. To do their work, however, they are deployed in project teams. The result is a **matrix organization.**

The matrix arrangement gets its name from the fact that a number of project (team) managers exert planning, scheduling, and cost control over people who have been assigned to their projects, while other managers exert more traditional line control (e.g., technical direction, training, and compensation) over the same people. Thus, two administrators share responsibility for the subordinate. The subordinate, in turn, must please two supervisors.

A simple matrix arrangement is shown in Figure 7-4. The five vertical arrows indicate the vertical chain of command for functions; the four horizontal arrows, the lateral chain of command for the projects. The members in the boxes indicate the personnel assigned. Thus, there are 22 people working on Project C, while the public works function has 33 assigned to it. The program manager is essentially a "contractor" who "hires" personnel from the line organization. The project manager is assigned the number of personnel with the essential qualifications from the functional departments for the duration of the project.

Again, the question arises, when should this particular form of organization be used? Let us approach the answer from the opposite direction. A matrix organization

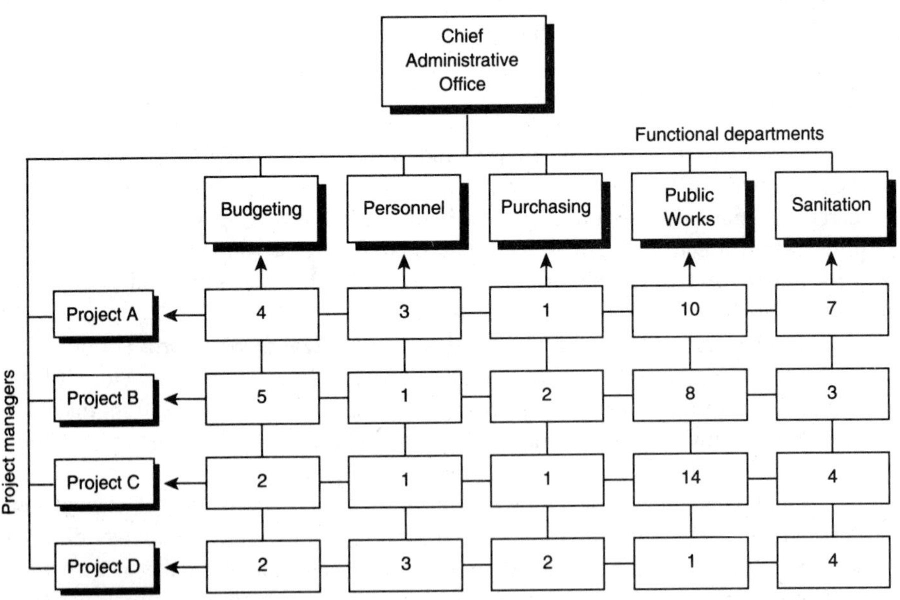

FIGURE 7-4
Matrix Organization

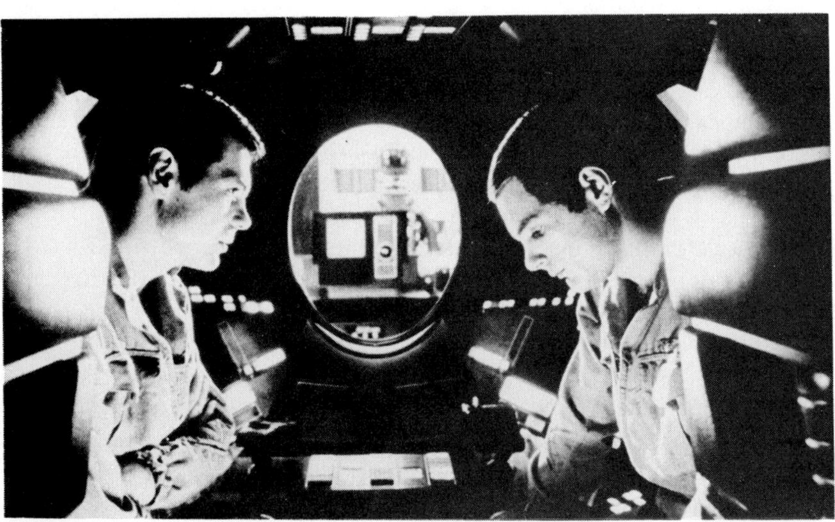

Futuristic models of organization are based on principles fundamentally different from the pyramid model. In Arthur C. Clarke's 2001, *which Stanley Kubrick made into a film, the two astronauts alternated command of the spaceship—clearly violating the principle of hierarchy. Today, fast-growing, high-technology companies are also violating it. Their central management concern is how to stay flexible and nimble in a rapidly changing environment and how to avoid sluggishness as they grow. Intel Corporation has a three-person executive office. One chief executive spends nearly half his time on outside matters (e.g., speaking to the financial and scientific community and government policymakers). A second chief executive does the long-range thinking, and the third runs the company on a day-to-day basis. (From the MGM release,* 2001: A Space Odyssey, *© 1968 Metro-Goldwyn-Mayer Inc.)*

should *not* be used when the work performed by an agency is applied to standardized services with high volumes (e.g., waste disposal), but it can be used effectively when the work performed is for specific, narrowly defined projects (e.g., antitrust cases). As specific projects end, they can be deleted from the organization, for the matrix organization is a fluid organization. A general rule then would be this: When an organization has a large number of specialists—and coordination is therefore difficult—the matrix organization might be a solution.

Project groups do, however, have their problems. They make it difficult for personnel to develop the expertise that they could gain from working in one functional area. Further, technical personnel, who are often shifted back and forth among projects, can feel isolated and rootless. Finally, with personnel constantly shifting from one project to another, an organization can find it difficult to build up a source of accumulated wisdom, such as is possible in functional departments.

To achieve coordination between the various project teams, the adhocracy uses mutual adjustment. Rather than assign the task of coordination to managers, as the pyramid does, the adhocracy leaves it up to most of its members to *assume* that responsibility much in the way members of a well-knit basketball team all work spontaneously to keep its activities focused on the goal of winning. To help foster this process of mutual adjustment, adhocracies are festooned with liaison officials and integration offices.

For example, the space shuttle program has an Orbiter Project Office located at the Johnson Space Center (JSC) in Houston. To help coordinations with Rockwell International, which actually builds the orbiter ("bends the metal" as they say), the project office has a person *permanently* assigned to the Rockwell plant in Downey, California. Because the office must obviously coordinate its design activities with Mission Operation (also located at JSC), a person from the astronauts' office regularly attends project office meetings. To an outsider that person would appear to be a member of the project office; and in a sense, he or she is (see Figure 7-5).

Because the space station program is so incredibly complex, it has more and bigger offices for program integration than did the shuttle program. Personnel assigned to the integrative offices do nothing but examine how all the activities in the program fit together; when the programs do not mesh, these personnel negotiate with the parties involved to get things back on track.

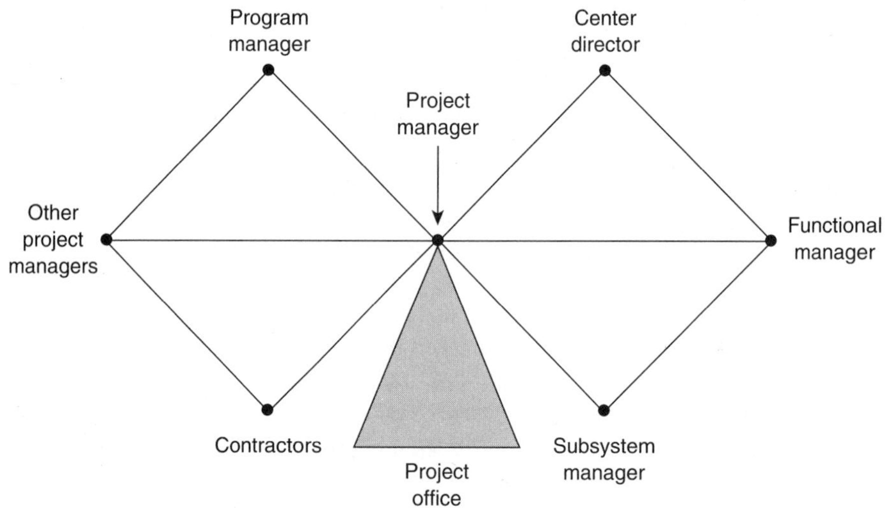

FIGURE 7-5

Simplified Network of a NASA Project Manager

In large-scale, multiorganizational enterprises like NASA, project managers have limited authority over individuals who are outside the project office but who are nevertheless essential to the ultimate success of the project. The situation leads to the familiar pattern of behavior: monitoring, bargaining, cajoling, confrontation, and so on. Fortunately, a project manager can minimize these time-consuming activities by skillfully building and maintaining commitment to the project among these diverse groups.

SOURCE: Grover Starling, "A Framework for Understanding Commitment in the R & D Organization," *Journal of Engineering and Technology Management,* August 1991, p. 253.

The Process of Organizational Design

Limitations to the Organization Chart

Despite the importance of organizational design, most administrators approach it rather informally—indeed, one might almost say the approach amounts to little more than drawing boxes on a page. Eventually, a new organization chart appears, which the administrator can more or less defend.

Organization charts are by no means useless in designing and understanding organizations (see Figures 7-6, 7-7, and 7-8). The organization chart of most agencies shows—indeed is designed to show—at least two things: how work is to be divided into components and who is (supposed to be) whose supervisor. Moreover, it implicitly shows several other things: the nature of the work performed by each component; the grouping of components on a functional, regional, or service basis; and the levels of management in terms of successive layers of superiors and subordinates.

Nevertheless, what the chart does not show is often the most interesting part—at least to someone interested in organization design (Stieglitz, 1969:372–76). In the

(text continues on p. 316)

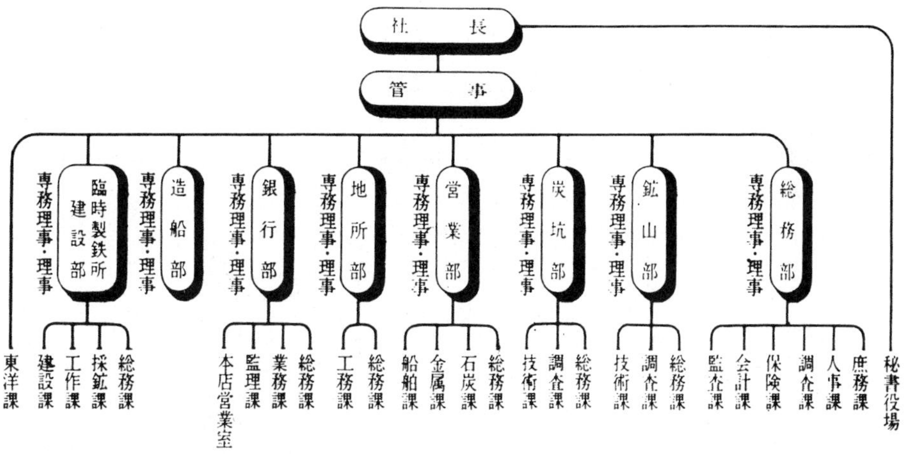

FIGURE 7-6

Organization Chart for Mitsubishi (Circa 1908)

The first organization chart was born in the United States around 1854 when railroad companies began to need maps of their organizations and structures and of the land their trains traveled over. Eventually, the chart migrated from railroads to large industrial and distribution companies and even outside the United States. This chart for the powerful Mitsubishi Group (one of Japan's giant trading companies) shows separate departments for banking, mining, shipbuilding, real estate, and other functions.

SOURCE: *Harvard Business Review,* March–April, 1988, p. 156.

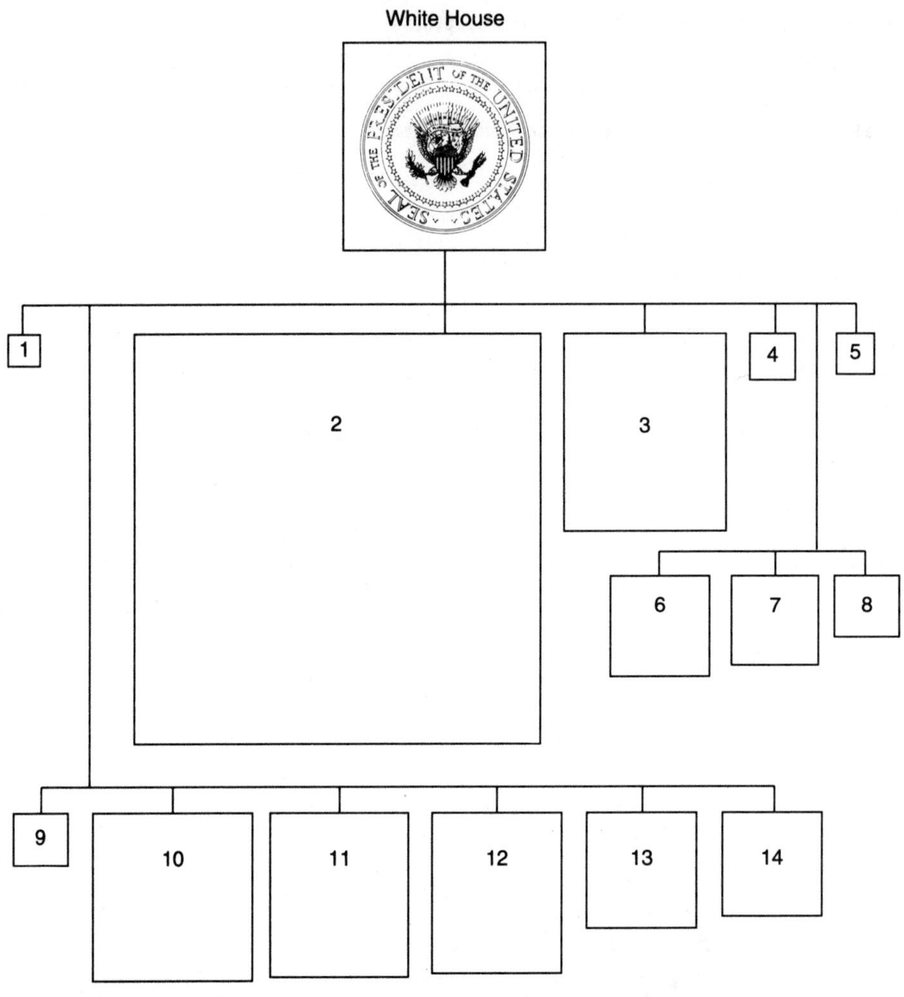

1 Education (121,000)
2 Defense (1,050,000)
3 Veterans Affairs (245,000)
4 Energy (17,000)
5 Housing and Urban Development (13,000)
6 Transportation (64,000)
7 Commerce (53,000)
8 State (26,000)
9 Labor (18,000)
10 Treasury (160,000)
11 Health and Human Services (123,000)
12 Agriculture (121,000)
13 Interior (78,000)
14 Justice (76,000)

FIGURE 7-7

Organization Chart for Federal Government, Showing Departmental Sizes

SOURCE: Based on data in U.S. Office of Personnel Management, *Federal Civilian Workforce Statistics* (Washington, D.C.: U.S. Government Printing Office, 1989).

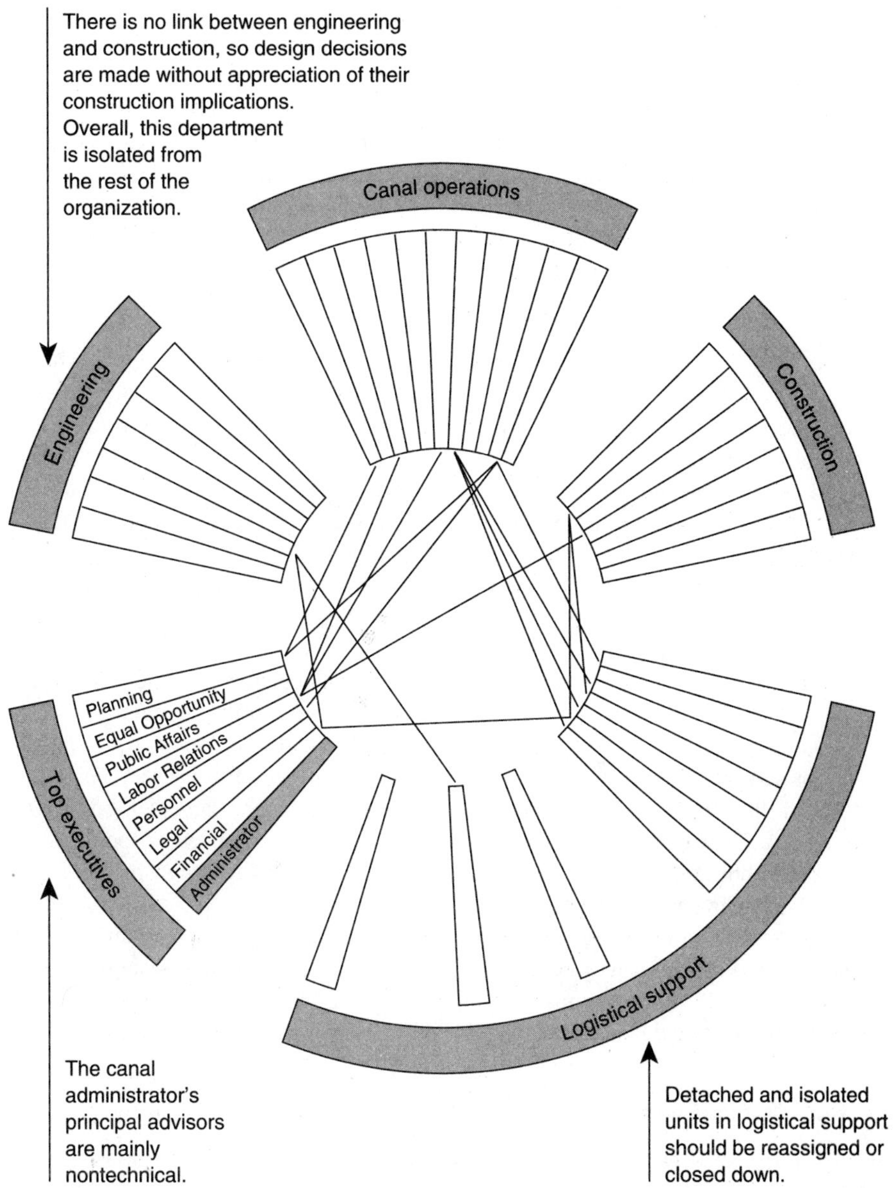

There is no link between engineering and construction, so design decisions are made without appreciation of their construction implications. Overall, this department is isolated from the rest of the organization.
Canal operations
Engineering
Construction
Planning
Equal Opportunity
Public Affairs
Labor Relations
Personnel
Legal
Financial
Administrator
Top executives
Logistical support
The canal administrator's principal advisors are mainly nontechnical.
Detached and isolated units in logistical support should be reassigned or closed down.

FIGURE 7-8
Organization Chart for a Canal Commission
Unlike pyramid charts, which stratify employees along formal lines of command, this circular chart groups them by the significance of their informal communications with others in the organization.

first place, the chart by itself cannot tell us much about the degree of responsibility and authority exercised by positions on the same management level. Two persons on the same management level may have vastly different degrees of authority. In a word, the chart cannot show the degree of decentralization.

Second, attempting to determine line and staff positions from an organization chart is an arduous academic chore. In some agencies, charting methods are used to attempt to make this distinction. For example, the so-called staff units are charted on one horizontal plane, line units on another. Other agencies use skinny lines to connect staff but robust ones to connect line units. To try to interpret these differences in terms of line-staff responsibilities, authorities, and relationships is as difficult as reading the degree of decentralization from the chart.

Third, some people view the linear distance from the chief executive officer as a measure of status or importance. But this interpretation may or may not be correct. It has the same limitations as trying to infer relative importance from size of office, files, parking lot space, and so forth.

Fourth, while the chart shows some major lines of communication, it does not show all. It is axiomatic that every organization is an intricate network of communication; if it were not, then nothing would get done.

Closely related to the preceding limitations to the organization chart is a fifth limitation. The chart fails to show the **informal organization;** that is, "those aspects of the structure which, while not prescribed by formal authority, supplement or modify the formal structure" (Gross, 1968:238). The formal organization, therefore, encompasses all the relationships and channels of communication that people are expected to develop and use in order to meet organizational and, often, personal objectives.

In sum, we would do well to heed the advice of one former secretary of state who said that "organization or reorganization in government can often be a trap for the unwary. The relationships involved in the division of labor and responsibility are far more subtle and complex than the little boxes which the graph drawers put on paper with their perpendicular and horizontal connecting lines" (Acheson, 1959). In an effort to avoid the organization chart pitfall, a process for thinking through a new organizational structure will be given in skeletal form. This process should facilitate the complex task of separating those things that must be taken into account so far as structure is concerned from those that have less bearing on organizational performance.

Three Critical Steps

In designing an organization, we need to address at least three questions: (1) What should the units be? (2) What units should join together, and what units should be kept apart? (3) Where do decisions belong? (The discussion that follows builds around these questions and draws on Drucker, 1973: chapters 42–44.) The analysis suggested by each question should always be kept as simple and brief as possible. In a small agency or office, it can often be done in a matter of hours and on a few pieces of paper. But in a very large and complex enterprise (e.g., Department of Transportation and the executive branch of the state of New Jersey), the job may well require months of study.

Born in Vienna in 1909, Peter F. Drucker was educated as a lawyer. Today, he is probably the world's best-known management consultant. According to Drucker, organizational design must follow organizational purpose. In other words, we cannot properly design an organization until we are clear on its goals. (Irwin Gooden)

What Should the Units Be? Organization design begins not with a consideration of the principles of organization but with a review of the organization's goals. In fact, one could even define organization as the ideal concrete reflection of an agency's goals. A review of goals enables us to begin to determine what are the **key activities.** That is, in what area is excellence required to attain the agency's goals? Conversely, in what areas would lack of performance endanger the results, if not the survival, of the enterprise? Finally, what are the values that are truly important to us?

This line of inquiry puts us in a better position to answer our first question, What should the units be? Clearly, key activities require organizational representation.

Roughly, *all* activities in an organization fall into one of four categories. First are *top-management activities.* These, according to Drucker, include maintaining external relations, thinking through the mission of the agency, making decisions during major crises, and building the human organization. Second are *results-producing activities.* These contribute most directly to the performance of the entire enterprise. While results-producing activities are not hard to discover in the private sector (just look for those directly producing revenue), they are less obvious in the public sector. Third are *results-contributing* or *staff activities;* for example, advising, teaching, legal research, and training. Fourth are the *hygiene and housekeeping activities,* which range from the medical department to the people who clean the floor.

What Should Their Relationship Be? Why go through this exercise in classification? The answer Drucker (1973:534–35) gives is that "Activities that differ in contribution have to be treated differently. Contribution determines ranking and placement." By suggesting a few tentative propositions, perhaps we can begin to see how this classification can help us better answer the question, what units should join together?

- Results-producing activities should never be subordinate to nonresults-producing activities.
- Support activities should never be mixed up with results-producing activities. The split of the Atomic Energy Commission (AEC) into the Energy Research and Development Administration (ERDA) and the Nuclear Regulatory Commission might be viewed, on the other hand, as an effort to follow this proposition. Until this split, the AEC, in effect, combined rather closely a result-producing activity (the development of nuclear energy) with a support activity (the monitoring of safety standards). Today, ERDA activities are part of the Energy Department.
- Top-management activities are incompatible with other activities. One former secretary of housing and urban development argues that, as presidential staff increasingly becomes involved in day-to-day decisions, it spends less and less time on broad, long-range policy issues. (The latter activity is of course what we earlier termed *top-management activity.*) Confusion is created when people at the top try to do too much: "A curious inversion occurs. Operational matters flow to the top, as central staffs become engrossed in subduing outlaying bureaucracies, and policymaking emerges at the bottom" (cited in Otten, 1973).
- Advisory staffs should be few, lean, and nonoperational. Further, advisory work should not be a career; that is, it is work to which career professionals should be exposed in the course of their growth but not work that they should do for long.
- Hygiene and housekeeping activities should be kept separate from other work or else they will not get done. In a hospital where these activities are technically under the upper levels of management, they tend to be neglected. No "respectable" manager in a hospital wants to have anything to do with them. As a result, they are left unmanaged; and this means they are done badly and expensively. But what can be done? One solution is to farm out these activities to somebody whose business is to provide these hotel services.

Where Do Decisions Belong? If we can successfully answer our third question, we achieve two things. We gain a better idea of where the structural units (discussed above) belong, and we reduce the risk that, in a new organization, decision will have to go looking for a home.

The crux of the issue is **delegation of authority;** that is, the determination of the proper level at which a decision should be made. Are any guidelines available? Generally speaking, decisions should be made as low as possible. (The charge of the Light Brigade, one wit reminds us, was ordered by an officer who wasn't there looking at the territory.)

Obviously, the precise level of a decision will depend on the nature of the decision. Specifically, the more a decision is characterized by these four factors, the higher the level at which it must be made:

- *Futurity;* that is, how long into the future the decision commits the organization.
- *Reversibility;* that is, how fast can the decision be reversed if it proves wrong.
- *Impact;* that is, how many other functions in an organization it affects.
- *Rarity;* that is, how distinct the event it.

Now, with some appreciation of the factors that *limit* how low in an organization a decision can be made, our general guideline might be restated as follows: Decisions should be made (1) as close to the scene of action as possible, where the detailed knowledge and firsthand experience is greatest; yet (2) high enough that all affected activities are fully considered. Part 2 simply means that managers who must share in the decision do share and that those who must at least know about it do know. One important aspect of this rule, keeping the boss informed, is described in the Talking Shop.

To the extent that authority to make decisions is not delegated, it is centralized. Absolute centralization in one person is conceivable only in the leader/follower cluster discussed earlier; consequently, for most government organizations, we can safely say that some decentralization is inevitable. On the other hand, if *all* authority was delegated, the position of manager would cease to exist. Indeed, we could hardly say an organization still existed. As I said, the idea is an old one. In *Troilus and Cressida,* Shakespeare puts the following speech in the mouth of Ulysses:

Oh, when rank is shaked
Which is the ladder to all high designs,
The enterprise is sick! How could communities,
Degrees in schools and brotherhoods in cities,
Peaceful commerce from divided shores . . .
Privilege of age, crown, sceptors, laurels
But by rank, stand in authentic place?
Take but rank away, untune that string,
And hark, what discord follows! Each thing meets
In utter conflict.

Design Criteria

Upon completion of the design process, we might reexamine the final product in terms of three standards: clarity, simplicity, and adaptability.

Clarity. Ambiguous relationships can lead to friction, politics, and inefficiencies. Therefore, members of an organization need a clear understanding of the authority and responsibility for action, and they need to understand their assignments and those of their co-workers.

How does the administrator achieve this? One widely used vehicle is, of course, the organization chart. Despite the limitations noted earlier, the chart can, by mapping

(text continues on p. 322)

Talking Shop

The Rewards and Dangers of Overdelegating Authority

Three of my favorite years as an Army officer were spent conducting leadership classes at West Point. One recurring topic was "delegation."

"If you had to choose," I'd ask, "which would you prefer, a boss who overdelegates or one who underdelegates?" Invariably the cadets would opt for the overdelegator. It was understandable. They were young and confident, ready to seize the initiative and to make their individual marks.

"I agree," I'd say. Given a choice, I'd prefer a boss who 'gave me my head,' one like Abraham Lincoln, who showed both character and managerial style when he wrote Grant in the spring of 1864 expressing:

". . . entire satisfaction with what you have done up to this time so far as I understand it. The particulars of your plans I neither know nor seek to know. You are vigilant and self-reliant, and pleased with this, I wish not to obtrude any constraints or restraints upon you. . . . If there is anything wanting which is within my power to give, do not fail to let me know it. And now, with a brave army, and a just cause, may God sustain you."

The cadets, unfortunately, would meet few Lincolns. They might, in fact, encounter "abdicators" rather than "delegators," men like Gen. Henry Halleck, Grant's nominal boss about the time Lincoln was writing the above letter. Grant had told Halleck he wanted to relieve Gen. Nathaniel Banks, a man with strong political support and a personal friend of Lincoln. Halleck replied that relieving such a man would "give offense to a large number of his political friends" and warned: "The administration would be immediately attacked for his removal." Nevertheless, Halleck said: "Do not understand me as advocating his retention in command."

Grant, in other words, was free to act, but if it backfired, he'd be left twisting in the wind with Halleck nowhere in sight. Despite the lack of support, however, we agreed Grant had acted properly by telling his superiors what he intended.

By contrast, Gen. John Charles Fremont, also a man given considerable freedom of action by the administration, had told no one in Washington before issuing his rash 1861 proclamation freeing the slaves of disloyal Missourians, confiscating their property, and under certain conditions even threatening to shoot them. Fremont's impetuous Confiscation Act set in motion a chain of events that led to his removal two months later.

While the above case studies were interesting, cadets seemed to relate more easily to "junior officer" stories than to tales about generals. One such example came from my own experience. At the time, I was a young captain, serving as a regimental Operations and Training Officer. The regimental commander, whom I'll call Col. Higgins, was a passive older man, pondering his retirement and giving the impression that this final assignment didn't do much to arouse his enthusiasm.

That was fine by me. I was enjoying the independence, the responsibility and, to be truthful, the sense of "power." Although I was a junior officer, and in a staff position at that, I had a good bit of "clout." Certain directives might read,

"By order of Col. Higgins," but I was the one writing them. It was a heady feeling.

All was going well. Then a report reached my desk finding fault with a training exercise in the First Battalion, commanded by an officer I'll call Lt. Col. Jack Barnes. Col. Barnes was the regiment's most respected officer, and normally his units performed at a high level. In this case, though, the training inspector had written frankly, and I proceeded to add some sharp words of my own, something to the effect that "These comments are particularly applicable: corrective action should be taken promptly, etc."

Next day I was summoned to Col. Higgins's office. Standing next to his desk was a red-faced lieutenant colonel. Col. Higgins said: "Col. Barnes here was just showing me this inspection report. He feels the tone is much too critical, and I think I agree. Who sent this?"

He handed me the report; I looked at the signature. "Uh, I believe you signed it, colonel."

"Of course I did! But you know I can't read everything that crosses my desk." He glared at me. "You wrote this, didn't you?"

"Yes sir."

"Well, no harm done," said the amiable Col. Higgins. "After this, though, just be more careful how you phrase things."

There'd be no more freewheeling memos; it was obvious I was "on my own."

"Well," I told the cadets, "I think there's a moral there. Freedom of action is fine, and if you're any good you'll fight to gain your boss's confidence so you can have that freedom. The flip side, though, is your responsibility to keep the boss informed, even when he doesn't require it. And if new policy is involved, it means not just informing him, but securing his active approval. Otherwise you've set a trap for both of you, and the jaws of that trap may well snap shut at some awkward moment."

I've remembered those leadership discussions often these past few months. Like millions of others, I've admired the patriotism and "can do" spirit of Ollie North and John Poindexter. Even so, I've wondered. Just as I set a trap for myself years ago back at that training regiment, did they make the same mistake at the NSC?

The confrontation with Col. Barnes taught me a lesson, one that helped me, and I hope helped some of my cadet students. At the time of the incident I placed most of the blame on the unsupportive shoulders of Col. Higgins. It took quite a while for me to realize the blame was shared, and that most of it was probably on my side.

The situations are far from parallel. Covert actions take place in a dangerous, unique arena, and the rules of the game are murky. All the same, the leadership principle of keeping the boss informed, along with the corollary of "whether he likes it or not," still seems axiomatic, whether it be in the military, in business or the highest circles of government.

SOURCE: Harry J. Maihafer, "Manager's Journal," *Wall Street Journal*, September 28, 1987. Reprinted with permission of the *Wall Street Journal* © 1987 Dow Jones & Company, Inc. All rights reserved.

lines of decision-making authority, *sometimes* show inconsistencies and complexities and, thereby, lead to their correction. On the other hand, the administrator who believes that team spirit can be engendered by not clearly spelling out relationships is opening a Pandora's box of organizational ills: intrigue, frustration, lack of coordination, duplication of effort, vague policy, and uncertain decision making. A second vehicle, to be discussed in greater detail in Chapter 10, is position classification, which provides for clear lines of authority and responsibility.

Clarity appears to be especially important in matrix organizations. Thomas J. Peters and Robert H. Waterman, Jr., in their influential *In Search of Excellence,* report that none of the companies they identified as excellent spoke of having formal matrix structures, except for project management companies like Boeing:

> *But in a company like Boeing, where many of the matrix ideas originated, something very different is meant by matrix management. People operate in a binary way: they are either a part of a project team and responsible to that team for getting some task accomplished (almost all the time), or they are part of a technical discipline, in which they spend some time making sure their technical department is keeping up with the state of the art. When they are on a project, there is no day-in, day-out confusion about whether they are really responsible to the project or not. They are. (1982:307)*

The key to making organizations like Boeing and NASA work, Peters and Waterman say, is to make sure that one dimension (e.g., geography or function) has "crystal-clear primacy":

> *The answer is . . . simplicity of form. Underpinning most of the excellent companies we find a fairly stable, unchanging form—perhaps the product division—that provides the essential touchstone which everybody understands, and from which the complexities of day-to-day life can be approached. Clarity on values is also an important part of the underlying touchstone of stability and simplicity as well.*
>
> *Beyond the simplicity around one underlying form, we find the excellent companies quite flexible in responding to fast-changing conditions in the environment. . . . Because of their typically unifying organization theme, they can make better use of small divisions or other small units. They can reorganize more flexibly, frequently, and fluidly. (1982:308)*

Simplicity. "Simplify, simplify, simplify." This might well be the plaint of a modern administrator, as it was of the author of *Walden.* Most overorganization results from failure to realize that an organization is merely a framework for the efficient performance of people.

Narrow spans of control and numerous levels of supervision are two signs that this criterion is probably being ignored. It was not being ignored, however, by Truman when he vetoed an early proposal by scientists for a National Science Foundation. He took particular exception to the provisions insulating the director from the president by two layers of part-time boards and warned that "if the principles of this bill were extended throughout the government, the result would be utter chaos" (quoted in Seidman, 1980:22).

Other signs of overorganization include excessive procedures (red tape), too many committees and meetings, and unnecessary line assistants. The last-named item comes in for especially harsh criticism by one corporate maverick, who said that the only people who thoroughly enjoy being "assistants-to" are vampires: "The assistant-to recommends itself to the weak or lazy manager as a crutch. It helps him where he shouldn't and can't be helped—head-to-head contact with his people" (Townsend, 1970:23). No mercy for the executive assistant to the principal deputy assistant secretary of defense of program analysis!

Adaptability. The basic idea behind the adaptability criterion is that the organization will have a designed-in capacity to change as much as is warranted by its situation. In other words, the organization has flexibility. At one extreme are organizations like NASA, which are constantly being buffeted by technological change. Accordingly, NASA has adopted a complex version of the matrix organization, as we saw in Figure 7-6.

The situation facing the military services (army, navy, marines, and air force) is even more dynamic. They must be able to adapt not only to rapidly changing technology but also to new threats (in the form of potential or real enemies). The need for a modicum of adaptability is not limited, however, to research and development (R & D) organizations and the military. Take the computer. Its use spread quickly to some agencies and was resisted by others.

Adaptability, like clarity and simplicity, is a value that the administrator should want to optimize, not maximize. That is to say, pushing any of these three criteria to their limit would result in an organizational monstrosity. Whatever else it might be, NASA is *not* a simple organization. And, though I am not an expert on the Iraqi military, I suspect that there is greater clarity to be found in the organization chart of an Iraqi heavy armored division than in the one for the U.S. 24th Infantry Division (Mechanized).

Adaptability is a powerful management tool only when it is used to help achieve the organizational goal and fit the organization's contingencies. Consider this case of the Human Services Administration in a large midwestern city:

> In early 1990, the city's welfare operation was totally out of control and heading for certain fiscal disaster. Audits revealed that one third of all recipients were receiving the wrong amount of money and 15 percent were probably ineligible for any assistance. About $50 million of taxpayer's money was being misappropriated through fraud, error, and mismanagement. Welfare rolls and costs were climbing every month. Field operations were chaotic: Unable to handle the crush of clients, welfare centers routinely closed their doors at 11:00 A.M.; police were unable to curb random acts of violence against the welfare workers; employee productivity was less than half of what it should have been; and one third of the employees exceeded their lateness limits and their sick leave allowances. Despite widespread misconduct, the agency fired only a few employees for flagrant abuses.

"Internal redesign" was the watchword at the agency's headquarters, which included few technical people. Top-to-bottom reorganizations had shaken the agency through much of the late 1980s. Headquarters and the center were both realigned at a rate that left veteran caseworkers in a state of mental exhaustion. One center director reported that she had to leave a note behind for her husband each morning. The note consisted of her telephone number for that *day.*

In late 1991 a new city manager resolved to overhaul the welfare system and bring the caseloads under control. She brought in a new management team, got the city council to authorize an additional $3 million for professional staff and computer support. Productivity increased by 20 percent, lines began to disappear at the centers, employee morale rose, and growth in welfare rolls was arrested and then began to decline. Early indications were that the city had achieved a significant cost turnaround.

The point of this story is simple: The initial design of the Human Services Administration was all wrong. In terms of Table 7-1, it was run as a decentralized adhocracy when it should have been designed as a pyramid. Consider the situation. Processing welfare applications is a routine service technology, and mass production techniques are needed to handle thousands of people; a relatively large technical support staff is needed to develop and implement efficient management systems. When the environment is stable, the primary goal of an organization can be efficiency. Just because bureaucracy has been around longer than adhocracy, it should not be dismissed as a less satisfactory solution to a design problem.

The Politics of Reorganization

Rationale

Some (not all) attempts at reorganization are in reality efforts to escape rethinking the principles of sound management outlined above. At the first sign of trouble, the cry goes out for reorganization. As might be expected, the times when this kind of surgery is needed are limited.

Perhaps the most obvious occasion for reorganization is growth. We can illustrate the point with a well-known children's story. If the giant in *Jack the Giant Killer* was to exist many times larger than a normal man, he could not have the same form as a man. In other words, if the giant was to have the same proportions as a normal man but was a hundred times larger in size, his bone structure would be entirely inadequate. Biological design must conform to the square-cube law that says, If a giant was a thousand times the size of a man, his volume would increase (10 x 10 x 10) and so roughly would his weight. But his area would increase only 10 x 10; hence, the cross-sectional area of his bones would increase at a far lower rate than the weight that they had to support. So, when the giant attempts to stand, his leg bone breaks. In short, the *form* of a human is inadequate for a larger being. The square-cube law explains why larger beings walk on four legs like the elephant or float in the ocean like the whale. And the law seems to hold for organizations: Larger organizations require different forms than the smaller ones (Litterer, 1973). For example, if an organization grows significantly, it must provide for additional reporting relationships—otherwise its managers might find themselves with more people reporting to them than they have the time and talent to properly supervise.

A second use of reorganization is to create greater efficiencies and more logical combinations of functions. In 1991, the Texas state legislature began considering a proposal to consolidate several environmental agencies that had been established over the preceding two decades. The arguments for a consolidated environmental agency were the following:

- A consolidated environmental regulatory agency would enhance the ability of the state to deal with multimedia environmental problems. Multimedia refers to the different media (air, land, surface water, groundwater) that constitute the "environment." Sometimes the things that we do to address pollution problems in one medium adversely affect pollution problems in another. A consolidated environmental agency would, presumably, allow the state to solve environmental problems more comprehensively.

- A consolidated agency would allow the state to pool its current agency resources for a more effective and efficient response to environmental problems. This would include resources such as laboratories, regional field offices, field inspectors, and data banks. One prospect would be the ability to use a team approach in conducting inspections of polluting industries. For example, air pollution control, water pollution control, and hazardous- and solid-waste management inspections could be conducted at the same time by a team of inspectors. This would allow the environmental agency to obtain a comprehensive overview of the environmental compliance of a plant.

- A consolidated agency would enhance the coordination of efforts to address different environmental concerns. No matter how great an effort is made to coordinate such activities among different agencies, it is unlikely that that effort will achieve the same degree of coordination possible within one agency.

A third reason for reorganization is to reflect changes in public policy. New programs often require new administrative units. For example, the Strategic Defense Initiative Organization was established in 1984 as a separate agency of the Department of Defense in order to develop technology that would eliminate the threat posed by nuclear ballistic missiles. This adding on of organizational units is actually one of the most common ways in which government agencies adapt. Unable to get each ambassador to accept responsibility for embassy security against terrorism, the State Department simply added a unit designed to do this (Wilson, 1989).

Of course, public policy shift can also lead to the downgrading or outright elimination of certain units. Airline deregulation, which began in the Carter administration, led to the organization death of the Civil Aeronautics Board (CAB).

A fourth reason for reorganization is to make government more politically responsive. To return to a previous example, the consolidation of Texas's environmental agencies would provide greater visibility and accountability to the public than would the current fragmented regulatory structure, which includes the Texas Air Control Board, the Texas Water Commission, and others. Consolidation would also help avoid "buck passing" among agencies when citizens seek answers and responses to their environmental concerns—thus enhancing public accountability of environmental regulators. Accountability would be maximized in an agency with a single, elected head where the person in charge is highly visible to the public and depends upon the voters for his or her job.

Greater accountability also helps explain the trend toward decentralization seen in cities with "little city halls" and neighborhood-based police precincts. But, as the Working Profile of Joe Fernandez suggests, to decentralize, it is sometimes necessary to first centralize. More importantly perhaps, the profile suggests that initial victories form the foundation for other victories. Much of what Fernandez achieved occurred because he had an aura around him that enabled him to make things happen.

Realities

In 1967, Frederick C. Mosher published a careful review of 12 government reorganizations at various levels of government. He found that the reorganizations aimed at changing what agencies did were less successful than those aimed at solving administrative problems. Not surprisingly, he also found that reorganizations imposed from outside an agency tended to be less successful than those generated from within.

If we assume, then, that there are only select instances in which reorganization is called for, what can we say about its effectiveness; that is, does it increase economy and efficiency? At the national level, at least, its track record is poor: Of the 86 reorganization plans transmitted to the Congress between 1949 and 1969, only 3 were supported by precise dollar estimates of savings. No evidence exists that reorganization has ever had much effect on economy and efficiency. Although President Reagan appointed the Grace Commission, or Private Sector Survey on Cost Control, headed by businessman J. Peter Grace, comprehensive reorganization never really became part of the Reagan agenda. The notion of reorganization, that structure makes a difference, seemed to have fallen out of favor.

Reorganization, however, can have significant *political* effects. In one way or another, every reorganization must reflect certain political values and interests. The following examples illustrate what I mean:

- Reorganization can be used to exclude billions in expenditures from the budget and centralize the chief executive's control over the executive branch. President Reagan had his own hit list—the Economic Development Administration, the Synfuels Corporation, and the Departments of Energy and Education. Although he was unsuccessful at reorganizing these out of existence, he did manage to transfer the functions of the Office of Endangered Species to the Ecological Services Division in the Department of Interior. The Office became, in effect, extinct.

- Reorganization can also provide a means for dumping or demoting an unwanted official. An uncooperative bureau chief suddenly becomes someone else's deputy bureau chief.
- Reorganization can be used to bypass troublesome committee or subcommittee chairpersons. Transferring the activities of one office to another can cause a program to fall under the jurisdiction of an unfriendly appropriations subcommittee chairperson.
- Reorganization may be necessary to save a program with little political support in the legislature. This helps explain the frequent reorganization and renaming of the foreign aid agency.
- Reorganization provides a way of rewarding political supporters and providing them with greater access to the chief executive. Hence, Carter created the Department of Education in 1979, and Reagan, the Department of Veterans Affairs in 1988.

The Missing Links in Organizational Design—Managerial Style, Organizational Culture, and Individual Characteristics

When making design decisions, administrators try to simultaneously achieve three things. The first is to create an organizational design that provides a permanent setting in which administrators can influence employees to do their particular jobs. The second is to achieve a pattern of collaborative effort among individual employees. And the third is to create an organization that is cost-effective.

Today we know that there is not one best way to organize; the appropriate structure depends upon the situation facing the agency. While it is easy to dismiss as simplistic the principles of management (span of control between three and seven subordinates; one boss for each person; line does, staff advises; etc.), it is amazing how many administrators, when confronted with an organizational design decision, fall back on these principles. But this practice can be dangerous because these crude principles ignore the great variety of complex situations that an agency might face.

In the last part of this chapter, I have tried to suggest more potent tools for thinking about organizational design issues. The previous discussion introduced four major concepts—clarity, simplicity, adaptability, and reorganization—to help us understand these issues. The focus has been on designing organizations to be consistent with environment, goals, and tasks of the agency. But there are other major factors—about which we know much less—that also must be taken into account if the organizational design variables are to have their intended effect on employee behavior. In a broad sense, the organizational design process must also take into consideration (1) the managerial style of top executives, (2) the organization's culture, and (3) the characteristics of the employees. While these topics will receive extensive treatment in the next chapter, we might briefly highlight their critical relationship to organizational design and redesign.

(text continues on p. 330)

★★★★★★★★★★★★★★★★★★★★★★★★★★★★★★★★★★★

WORKING PROFILE

Joseph A. Fernandez

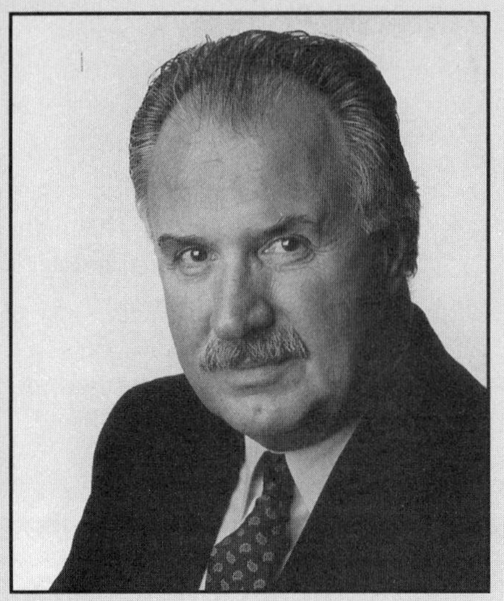

The New York City Schools chancellor ambles into Room 216 and embraces a bubbly teacher who announces to her eight-year-old students, "This is Dr. Joseph Fernandez. He is going to do some great and fantastic things. You'll be seeing him on the news."

Camille Griffin, a shy-looking black girl in the front row, raises her hand and asks which station he will be on. "I'll tell you what, I'll make sure you get in the paper," Fernandez says, hoisting her onto the desk and giving her a hug as the strobe lights flash. The next day, their embrace is on page one of *The New York Times.*

In 1953, Joseph Fernandez was just another 17-year-old dropout on the streets of Harlem. Nearly four decades later, this son of Puerto Rican immigrants would return to New York City to accept one of the toughest jobs in the public sector: chancellor of New York City schools. Upon his arrival, Fernandez announced that he would restructure New York's corrupt, crumbling, and decentralized mess of a school system.

Few doubted that he was serious. Shortly after dropping out of high school, Fernandez joined the U.S. Air Force and later served in Japan and Korea. Back home in 1956, he married, earned a high school equivalence diploma, and used the G.I. Bill to enroll in Columbia University. When a doctor suggested that his young son's breathing difficulties might be helped by a warmer climate, Fernandez and his wife withdrew their savings ($800) and drove to Miami.

After obtaining a degree from the University of Miami, he taught mathematics for awhile. Eventually, he got a master's degree at Florida Atlantic University and became an assistant high school principal in 1971. Fernandez continued to climb the bureaucratic ladder, becoming an assistant superintendent in 1985. Two years later, the Harlem dropout was in charge of the Dade County School District, the fourth largest in the United States. There Fernandez was credited with having transformed public instruction. Could he duplicate the feat in the New York system, with its 1,050 schools, 115,000 employees, 940,000 students, and 27.3 percent dropout rate?

The system was not only big—it was also decentralized. As a result, Fernandez faced several seemingly contradictory problems. First, there was a *decentralized* network of 32 community school boards that ran the elementary and junior high schools. Plagued by cronyism and corruption, a third of the boards was under investigation for charges ranging from selling jobs to dealing drugs. These boards epitomized what Fernandez refused to accept: power without accountability. (Voters rarely bothered to exercise

★★★★★★★★★★★★★★★★★★★★★★★★★★★★★★★★★★★

★★★★★★★★★★★★★★★★★★★★★★★★★★★★★★★★★★

their franchise.) Fernandez wanted more authority over these bodies, including the power to audit their books.

There was also the problem of a huge, paralyzing, and *centralized* bureaucracy that controlled the high schools and the overall budget. Above it all sat the board of education, whose members, appointed by a half-dozen politicians, were answerable to no one.

The signs of neglect were everywhere: schools with shattered windows, broken lights, leaking roofs, no working toilets. Teachers had to spend their own money on pencils, erasers, and chalk. A fifth grader was arrested with 411 vials of crack. A kindergarten student brought a .25-caliber handgun to class. These were the conditions that Joe Fernandez had to change if he was to salvage a system largely abandoned by the white middle class.

The centerpiece of Fernandez's plan to restructure this system was "school-based management," which itself represents a radical form of decentralization. This approach, which he introduced in Dade County, empowers committees of teachers, administrators, and parents at each school to decide everything from class size to the number of Spanish teachers. (The results of this approach in terms of test scores is unclear, but attendance and morale in Dade County did improve.)

Thus Fernandez's aim was to give more power to the schools but not to go so far as to allow a school or a school board to make a decision that interfered with good education. The idea was to give schools the opportunity to make decisions but to maintain an overall standard of performance.

More specific objectives included getting the state legislature to dilute tenure for principals, to abolish the board of examiners (the school system's licensing arm), and to give Fernandez a stronger role in the selection of district superintendents.

As Fernandez recognized, assertiveness over an organization sometimes must be the first step toward decentralization. Decentralization in a school district, or in any large organization, is somewhat like a federal system with checks and balances—and a strong executive is a part of that.

As one might expect, Fernandez's critics complained that he had an authoritarian manner. He admitted his imperviousness to criticism: "One thing I will never have is an ulcer. I get angry and move on." But Joe Fernandez had only one style, and he did not see any problem with it. "It works, I'm telling you!" he fairly shouted to one interviewer. "Do you ever have any doubts about anything?" the interviewer asked. He shot back: "I guess the only doubt I've had since I've been here—and it was only for a fleeting moment, believe me—was whether I was moving too fast. I decided the second I had that doubt that there's a danger in not moving fast enough. Like I said, it was only for a fleeting moment. I quite honestly don't think we're going fast enough."

SOURCES: Howard Kurtz, "The Report Card on Joe Fernandez," *New York Times,* January 22, 1990; Susan Tifft, "Bracing for Perestroika," *Time,* January 8, 1990; James Traub, "Fernandez Takes Charge," *New York Times Magazine,* June 17, 1990; Susan Daley, "Chancellor's Two Approaches to Management," *New York Times,* January 20, 1990; Joseph Berger, "Miami Finds Mixed Results in Fernandez's School Plan," *New York Times,* March 9, 1991.

★★★★★★★★★★★★★★★★★★★★★★★★★★★★★★★★★★

Almost every important study of bureaucratic innovation points to the great importance of top management in explaining change. For example, if Gordon Chase had not been New York's health service administrator or Carl Bianchi Idaho's court system administrator (see Chapter 2), it is unlikely that any significant organizational change would have occurred.

An organization's culture refers to the shared assumptions (implicit and explicit) about what is legitimate behavior. For example, when the Drug Enforcement Agency (DEA) was put under the control of the FBI, DEA agents experienced cultural shock. They had been accustomed to working in a highly decentralized organization, getting cash on short notice to make drug buys and learning their jobs on the street. They suddenly found themselves part of an organization that emphasized centralized decision making, tight control of cash, and elaborate formal training programs: "DEA agents complained that the typical FBI agent would not make a drug arrest for fear of spoiling his clean white shirt; many FBI agents, in turn, could barely conceal their contempt for the casually dressed, fast-moving drug agents" (Wilson, 1989). It was as if Miami Vice had gone to work for IBM.

Today we know that employees' needs at work are too varied and complex to be explained in terms of a paycheck. Thus, to obtain the goals of organizational design given above, administrators must recognize the full range of rewards that motivate people at work. "People are our most valuable resource" is no cliché. It's the new reality.

Concepts for Review

- bureaucracy
- delegation of authority
- design criteria
- division of labor
- four types of organization: leader/follower, consortium, pyramidal, adhocracy
- functional authority
- informal organization
- key activities
- legal, traditional, and charismatic authority
- limitations to the organizational chart
- line and staff
- matrix organization
- organizational design
- organizing
- process of organizational design
- public choice
- rationale for reorganization
- scalar principle, hierarchy
- span of control

Nailing Down the Main Points

1. Organization follows policy. In other words, not until we have decided where we want to go can we know the part people are to play in the total endeavor and how their roles relate to each other.

2. Roughly speaking, people have organized themselves throughout history in one of four ways: leader/follower, consortium pyramid, and adhocracy. The consortium is a mixture of existing conventional organizations (public and private) that have joined to work around strategic problems that no single organization can effectively address. The pyramid especially concerns us, since so many public organizations follow this pattern.

3. Closely related to the pyramidal organization is the concept of bureaucracy, which Max Weber defined in these terms: (*a*) division of labor based on functional specialization, (*b*) well-defined hierarchy of authority, (*c*) system of rules, (*d*) system of procedures, (*e*) impersonality of interpersonal relations, and (*f*) promotion and selection based on technical competence.

4. Also closely associated with the pyramidal organization is the administrative management movement, which sought to discover the "principles" of organization. Among these principles were: (*a*) division of labor, (*b*) hierarchy, (*c*) span of control, and (*d*) line and staff. In certain situations, these principles can be destructive to an organization's mission.

5. Quite unlike the mechanistic pyramidal model of organization is the adhocracy model—less rigid (hence, more flexible), more democratic, less authoritative, more project oriented, and more adaptive. To not a few observers, this organization, because it adapts so well to a rapidly changing environment, might be termed the organization of the future.

6. The essence of the adhocracy is its matrix form: Managers of subunits have two or more bosses and project teams, and functional departments are of equal weight and power.

7. Intelligent organizational design requires more than moving boxes around on an organizational chart; it demands careful attention to four related questions: (*a*) What should the units be? (*b*) What units should join together, and what units should be kept apart? (*c*) What is the appropriate placement and relationship of different units? (*d*) Where do decisions belong?

8. Upon completion of the three-step design process, the results can be reexamined in terms of three standards, which form a kind of design criteria: clarity, simplicity, and adaptability (or flexibility).

9. Reorganization is radical surgery and should be undertaken only when truly warranted. No reorganization can be politically neutral.

Problems

1. Can you think of any examples of consortia in the public sector (other than those mentioned in this book)?

2. Two traditional bases for organizing work are by functional units or by product/

service units. Which of the following units are examples of the former, and which are examples of the latter?

Criminal justice systems	Space shuttle development
Pathology lab	Surgical patient care
Telecommunications	Operations research
Stagehands	Probation department
MPA degree program	Opera production

3. What are the advantages and disadvantages of using charts to illustrate organizational structure?

4. It has been alleged that one of the reasons that the sophistication of organization in government lags behind that of business is due to the lack of competition. Do you agree? If you agree, how might a small dose of competition be introduced?

5. Do you think the presidency is overloaded? Discuss in terms of span of control. What modifications might be made?

6. How might the following institutions look if they were restructured along the lines of a matrix organization: garbage collection service, library, drug treatment clinic, state highway patrol, and university?

7. How can the line-staff concept be viewed as a compromise between hierarchy and division of labor?

8. "In the modern world," wrote Bertrand Russell in *Authority and the Individual,*, "and still more, so far as can be guessed, in the world of the near future, important achievement is and will be almost impossible to an individual if he cannot dominate some vast organization." Do you agree or disagree? Why?

9. Some management theorists say build the organization around people. Quite clearly, this approach was not taken in this chapter. What weaknesses do you see in their approach? What do the most successful football coaches do?

10. Apply the design criteria (clarity, simplicity, and adaptability) to some organization with which you are familiar.

11. Answer the three questions below for a university, a prison, a welfare office, and a church:
    a. Where is excellence required to attain the agency's goals?
    b. In what areas would lack of performance endanger the results?
    c. What are the values that are truly important to us?

    Remember, you will need first to establish goals for each. Do you think you have made the key activities the central, load-carrying elements in your organizational structure? Have the organization's values been organizationally anchored?

12. What do you think the drawbacks are to allowing advisory (staff) work to be a career?

13. Given a choice, should you delegate activities that are familiar to you or those that are not?

14. Some organizations might be termed high reliability organizations (HROs). They operate highly complex technologies in fast-changing, "high-tempo" circumstances and must have remarkably low failure rates. Examples would include nuclear-powered submarines, air traffic control systems, nuclear power plants, and power grids. What special organizational design principles would you suggest for HROs?

CASE 7.1

★ ★

Senator Judson Blair's Office

Judson Blair is a newly elected U.S. senator from a southern state. He is in the process of putting together an office staff and defining its organization. Based on his experience in state government (he had been governor of his home state), familiarity with Washington, D.C., and a conversation with his predecessor, Senator Blair understands that the duties of his office will include:

1. Voting on bills on the Senate floor (which only the senator personally can do). These average about five to six a day when the Senate is in session (approximately ten months a year). Votes are spread out but generally occur in the afternoon and early evening. The senator must go to the Senate floor for each vote, a trip of about seven minutes each way.

2. Monitoring all legislative debate in the Senate and reading all proposed bills.

3. Drafting proposed legislation (mainly amendments; most bills as a whole come from committees).

4. Attending and voting at committee meetings. Anyone can listen to most committee deliberations and hearings, but only the senator member can ask questions, participate in the debate, and vote. Senator Blair expects to be assigned to four committees, which generally meet in the morning (but committees' chairpersons do not coordinate scheduling meetings so conflicts are frequent).

5. Responding to constituent mail. This tends to fall into three categories: (*a*) mail commenting on how the senator votes or expressing criticism or support for his positions; (*b*) requests for assistance on a wide variety of personal matters ranging from social security benefits, to stationing of a child in the military service, to job requests; and (*c*) local governments seeking assistance in dealing with some department of the executive branch of the federal government. Based on the experience of the other senators from similar states, category a should run about 2,000 letters per week; category b, 500 letters per week; and category c, 10 per week.

6. Responding to personal, political, and all other mail (approximately 100 letters per week).

7. Receiving telephone calls and visitors to the office. These include constituents visiting Washington, D.C., and wanting to say hello to their senator and lobbyists wanting to argue for or against proposed legislation. Senator Blair expects about 100 visitors per week.

8. Attending various functions in Washington and the home state as political and social demands arise. Most senators feel this is necessary in order to return favors and keep in touch with home state conditions. Blair expects to return to his home state approximately three times

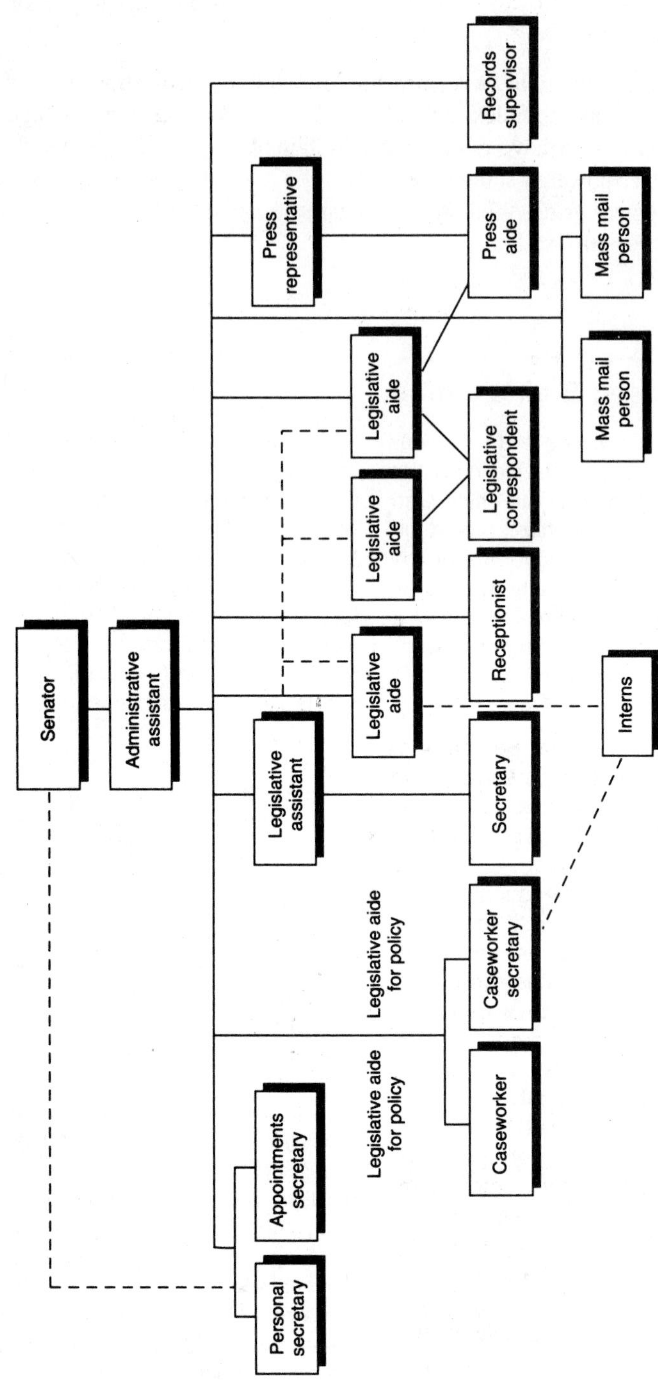

EXHIBIT 1 ....
Organizational Chart for Comparable Senator's Office

a month when Congress is in session and to spend four weeks a year there when not in session.

The Senate offers little guidance on dealing with these duties although there are certain traditional positions across all 100 offices. The title and position of administrative assistant is universal as is that of the principal aide to the senator and general staff administrator. A position of executive, personal, or appointments secretary is also extremely common as is that of press representative, assistant, or secretary. A distinction between professional and nonprofessional staff is common to all officers. Professional staff usually consists of young (under age 35) college graduates, many with masters or law degrees, who are variously termed legislative assistants, legislative aides, or staff assistants. The nonprofessionals are frequently categorized as support staff and include position titles like secretary, support aide, staff aide, typist, and file clerk. Most of them are young college graduates; a few part-timers are current undergraduate, graduate, or law students.

Most offices also have a position called caseworker, which is usually seen as nonprofessional except in a few offices where casework (response to requests for assistance) is assigned to professional staff. About one half of the senators have their caseworkers located in offices in the home state because they feel these people should be close to constituents. This also saves room in the Washington offices, which are very crowded. The other senators have the caseworkers located in their Washington office because they are easier to supervise, and most of their work involves telephone contacts with executive branch officials located in Washington. Exhibit 1 gives the organization chart for one senator's office that is fairly typical. Exhibit 2 summarizes the self-described duties of these personnel.

Senator Blair is both idealistic and pragmatic. He wants to respond to constituents and reflect their views in his voting if they are consistent with his personal views (or not *too* inconsistent), but he also desires to be reelected. The importance of his constituents to him is reflected in his belief that *all* letters should receive replies even if they are just handwritten diatribes against him. And he would like replies back to the writer in a week. He deems it essential that all letters have precisely the correct degree of formality in salutations and closing. That is, if the letter is from someone who knows him personally, he wants the response letter to be headed "Dear (first name)" and signed either "Jud Blair" or "Jud" depending on how close they are. More formal letters should be more conventionally addressed "Dear Mr. (last name)" and signed "Judson Blair." This consistent differentiation is very important to the maintenance of his political relationships and to his image of friendship or approachability.

As a junior senator he realizes that his direct influence as committee member and legislator will be limited unless his legislative initiatives are extremely well researched and drafted.

Blair has been assigned office space in the Dirksen Senate Office Building. It consists of five rooms as indicated in Exhibit 3. He also is allowed a room across the street in an old apartment house the Senate has taken over. Most senators put their part-time mail openers and handlers there. For additional Washington space he would have to pay out of his personal funds. (As far as he knows, only two senators do this—space in the home state in various federal buildings is free and virtually unlimited.) His budget will allow him to hire from 15 to 25 people depending on the relative salaries and proportions of professionals and support staff. Blair has already promised positions to four of his long-term state government staff. They

EXHIBIT 2

Summary of Self-Described Job Duties by Personnel in a Comparable Senator's Office

A. Activities and responsibilities of personal secretary and appointments secretary.
   1. Personal secretary.
      Takes personal dictation.
      Handles office accounts, personal checking account, political account, and charitable account.
      Prepares tax information for accountants.
      Performs personal errands for senator.
   2. Appointments secretary.
      Answers telephone; takes messages.
      Schedules appointments; coordinates office appointments, speeches, and staff.
      Makes travel arrangements.
      Takes and transcribes dictation; types.
      Files.

B. Legislative assistant and legislative aides.
   1. Legislative assistant.
      Has general responsibility for all legislative action.
      Has specific responsibility for matters arising from several committees.
      Writes speeches and floor statements in specific areas.
      Reviews all floor statements prepared by other legislative staff.
      Handles constituent mail in specific area.
      Reviews policy-establishing constituent responses prepared by other legislative staff.
      Oversees Senate floor activities to make sure the senator is prepared for floor action by appropriate staff member.
      Oversees keeping of records of senator's legislative activity.
   2. Legislative aide 1.
      Takes care of all legislation in energy, civil service, and post office.
      Supervises mass mailings with interns.
      Coordinates intern program.
      Performs administrative duties.
   3. Legislative aide 2.
      Follows and initiates legislation in Committees on Human Resources and Finance.
      Writes speeches in specific area.
      Answers constituent mail in specific area.
      Oversees agency in specific area.
   4. Legislative aide 3.
      Covers committees in commerce, judiciary, armed services, banking, housing, urban affairs and related matters.
      Drafts speeches, position papers, and statements in specific areas.
      Drafts legislation in specific areas.
      Advises senator on bills reaching Senate floor from committees.
      Works out approaches to some of the more complex cases arising in home state.
      Drafts responses to legislative mail in specific areas.
      Assists constituents with federal agency problems.

C. Caseworkers.
   1. Caseworker 1.
      Receives, researches, writes, and types answers to constituent inquiries in specific areas.
      Liaisons with federal agencies, state, and local officials.
      Counsels constituents on problems.
      Performs administrative duties.
   2. Caseworker/secretary 2.
      Receives, answers, and types responses to inquiries from constituents.

Does casework for constituents.
Assists legislative aide in supervising interns.
Helps elsewhere in office when needed.
Takes dictation from administrative aide or legislative aide when needed.
Takes over reception desk when receptionist is away.

D. Support staff.
1. Receptionist.
Opens, reads, sorts, and delivers mail.
Answers telephone; takes messages; transfers calls.
Places phone calls for senator.
Handles walk-in constituent requests for information.
Answers some constituent mail.
Meets and greets all incoming people.
Orders office supplies for Washington and home state offices.
2. Secretary to legislative assistant.
Researches, drafts, and types constituent correspondence.
Catalogs *Congressional Record* activities.
Handles Interior Committee for office.
Works on special legislative projects.
Catalogs senator's voting record and voting record scores.
Files legislative records.
3. Press aide (press representative position was vacant).
Writes and processes press releases.
Clips and files news items referring to senator.
Handles legislation and correspondence with regard to agriculture and forestry committees.
Assists legislative aides in their specific areas including doing casework.
Does typing for legislative aides.
Makes up speech scheduling.
Handles press inquiries.
Writes some statements for media.
Lays out and types newsletter.
Produces triweekly TV show for two senators.
4. Legislative correspondent.
Has secretarial responsibility for two legislative aides.
Drafts, types constituent mail in specific areas of people for whom s/he works.
Acts as backup receptionist.
Answers phone; welcomes visitors; makes appointments.
5. Records supervisor.
Classifies all mail done in office.
Sets up files for home states and controls.
Handles all calls and questions with respect to files.
Sets up home state files and control.
Sets up subject files and control.

---

have been approximately equal in terms of past duties, status, and friendship. They include Sylvia Conrath, his personal secretary; Frank Wilson, former state budget director; Samuel Jamison, former state legislative liaison; and Anthony Kingsley, his former state transportation department head and primary political manager. Blair has not yet told them what positions or duties they will have in his Senate office.

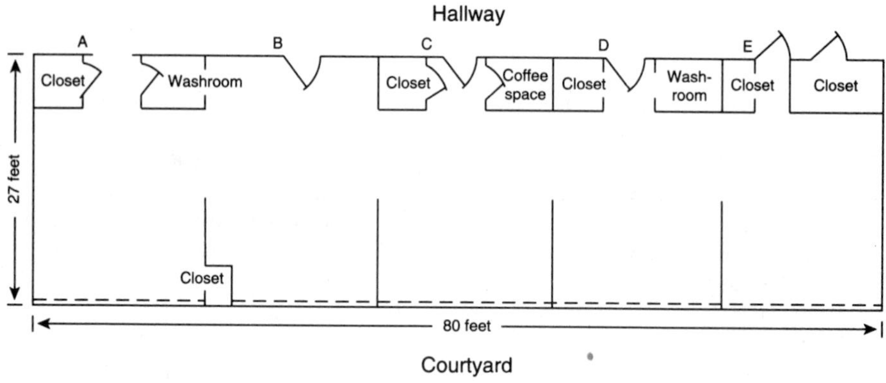

EXHIBIT 3

Plan of Office Rooms

Case Questions

1. What are some possible strategies for Senator Blair in developing an organization chart for his office?
2. What are the criteria for selection?
3. Propose an organization chart defining the duties of each position.
4. Propose an office layout locating the various people in the space. What guided your assignments?

Case Reference

Ross A. Webber, *Management: Basic Elements of Managing Organizations* (Homewood, Ill.: Richard D. Irwin, 1979), pp. 430–38.

CASE 7.2

Chiefland Memorial Hospital

James A. Grover, retired land developer and financier, is president of the Chiefland Memorial Hospital Board of Trustees. Chiefland Memorial is a 200-bed, voluntary, short-term general hospital serving an area of approximately 50,000 persons. Grover has just begun a meeting with the hospital administrator, Edward M. Hoffman. The purpose of the meeting is to seek an acceptable solution to an apparent conflict of authority problem within the hospital between Hoffman and the Chief of Surgery, Lacy Young.

The problem was brought to Grover's attention by Young during a golf match between the two men. Young had challenged Grover to the golf match at the Chiefland Golf and Country Club, but it was only an excuse for Young to discuss a hospital problem with Grover.

The problem that concerned Young involved the operating room supervisor, Geraldine Werther, R.N. Ms. Werther schedules the hospital's operating suite according to policies that she "believes" were established by the hospital's administration. One source of irritation to the surgeons is her attitude of maximum utilization for the hospital's operating rooms to reduce hospital costs. She therefore schedules operations so that idle time is minimized. Surgeons complain that the operative schedule often does not permit them sufficient time to complete a surgical procedure in the manner they think desirable. All too often, there is insufficient time between operations for effective preparation of the operating room for the next procedure. Such scheduling, the surgical staff maintains, contributes to low-quality patient care. Furthermore, some surgeons have complained that Werther shows favoritism in her scheduling, allowing some doctors more use of the operating suite than others.

The situation reached a crisis when Young, following an explosive confrontation with Werther, told her he was firing her. Werther then made an appeal to the hospital administrator, who in turn informed Young that discharge of nurses was an administrative prerogative. In effect, Young was told he did not have the authority to fire Werther. But Young asserted that he did have authority over any issue affecting medical practice and good patient care in Chiefland Hospital. He considered this a medical problem and threatened to take the matter to the hospital's board of trustees.

When Grover and Hoffman met, Hoffman explained his position on the problem. He stressed the point that a hospital administrator is legally responsible for patient care in the hospital. He also contended that quality patient care cannot be achieved unless the board of trustees authorizes the administrator to make decisions, develop programs, formulate policies, and implement procedures. While listening to Hoffman, Grover recalled the belligerent position taken by Young, who contended that surgical and medical doctors holding staff privileges at Chiefland would never allow a "layman" to make decisions impinging on medical practice. Young also had said that Hoffman should be told to restrict his activities to fund-raising, financing, maintenance, and housekeeping—administrative problems rather than medical problems. Young had then requested that Grover clarify in a definitive manner the lines of authority at Chiefland Memorial.

As Grover ended his meeting with Hoffman, the severity of the problem was unmistakably clear to him, but the solution remained quite unclear. Grover knew a decision was required—and soon. He also recognized that the policies Werther professed to follow were only implied policies that had never been fully articulated, formally adopted by board action, or communicated to employees. He also intended to correct that situation.

Case Question

What actions would you recommend to Grover?

Case Reference

John H. Champion and John H. James, *Critical Incidents in Management* (Homewood, Ill.: Richard D. Irvin, 1985), pp. 63–64.

CHAPTER **8**

Leadership in Organizations

Introduction

In order for an organization to be successful in managing programs, administrators must lead and motivate their people. Individuals must relate and communicate effectively; sound decisions must be reached by individuals and groups; and decisions must be implemented in a way that appropriately involves people and obtains their active commitment to a course of action. Thus, effective public administration requires a knowledge of human motivation and behavior (one's own and that of others) and personal skills of working with and for people. Indeed, all of the phases of program management (planning, decision making, organizing, implementing, and evaluating) are performed by people and affect people. The effectiveness with which these tasks are carried out depends on the administrator's skills in diagnosing human problems and taking action to solve them.

The major purpose of this chapter is to develop your skills in diagnosing human problems and taking action to solve them. The chapter is divided into four sections. Each deals with a different class of management problems encountered in organizations. Specifically, this chapter deals with the following fundamentals in managing human behavior in organizations:

1. Understanding what *leadership* styles are effective in different situations and how a manager's style fits the circumstances and resources available.
2. Understanding human *motivation* and harnessing it for group and organizational goals.
3. Understanding and managing *communications* within the organization.
4. Understanding what factors influence the patterns of behavior that emerge over time in a *group* and how these patterns affect the performance of a group.

Leadership

Leadership can be spoken about in at least two ways. The first is sweeping. It conjures up visions of an indefatigable Washington crossing the Delaware and echoes of the message that went out to the fleet in 1939 when Churchill was reappointed to his old post in charge of the Admiralty: "Winston is back." The French critic Henri Peyre (*Time,* July 15, 1974) defined it lucidly:

> *A broad ideal proposed by the culture of a country, instilled into the young through the schools, but also through the family, the intellectual atmosphere, the literature, the history, the ethical teaching of that country. Will power, sensitivity to the age, clear thinking rather than profound thinking, the ability to experience the emotions of a group and to voice their aspirations, joined with control over those emotions in oneself, a sense of the dramatic . . . are among the ingredients of the power to lead men.*

In this section, however, we are concerned more with a second meaning of leadership. While its definition is less sweeping than the first, its presence in administration is more pervasive. Leadership, in this second sense, we define as the process of influencing the activities of a group in efforts toward goal attainment in a given situation. The key elements in this definition are *l*eader, *f*ollowers, and *s*ituation. Leadership, then, is a function of three variables. Symbolically,

$$L = f(l, f, s).$$

For convenience, we term this approach to the study of leadership the contingency approach. But that is not the only way to think about leadership.

Can Leadership Traits Be Identified?

In the past (especially from 1930 to 1950), the most common approach to the study of leadership focused on traits; it sought to determine what makes the successful leader from the leader's own personal characteristics. These inherent characteristics—such as intelligence, maturity, drive, friendliness—were felt to be transferable from one situation to another. The list of traits grew and grew, but no clearcut results appeared. Finally, Eugene E. Jennings (1961) conducted a careful and extensive review of the literature on the trait approach to leadership and concluded: "Fifty years of study have failed to produce one personality trait or set of qualities that can be used to discriminate leaders and nonleaders."

Jennings or no Jennings, the quest for traits—and *the* traits continues. Richard E. Boyatzis (1982) and the staff of McBer and Company in Boston studied over 2,000 managers in 41 different management jobs. He found ten skills relating to managerial effectiveness that stood out:

1. Concern with impact (i.e., concern with symbols of power that have an impact on others).
2. Diagnostic use of concepts (i.e., a way of thinking that recognizes patterns in situations through the use of concepts).
3. Efficiency orientation (i.e., concern with doing something better).
4. Proactivity (i.e., predisposition toward taking action to accomplish something).
5. Conceptualization (i.e., ability to see and identify patterns as concepts when given an assortment of information).
6. Self-confidence (i.e., decisiveness or presence).
7. Use of oral presentations (i.e., effective communication).
8. Managing group process (i.e., stimulating others to work together effectively in group settings).
9. Use of socialized power (i.e., using forms of influence to build alliances, networks, coalitions, or teams).
10. Perceptual objectivity (i.e., ability to be relatively objective; not limited by biases, prejudices, or perspectives).

The model above focuses on middle-level managers. Management knowledge is not stressed because Boyatzis found that such knowledge represents threshold competency and that the successful managers selected were already well grounded.

Harry Levinson (1980) suggests 20 "dimensions of personality" that those responsible for selecting leaders can use to evaluate their behavior. As might be

(text continues on p. 345)

Help Wanted: Leaders

Harry Truman, who turned out to be a much more effective leader than most had expected, defined the concept as well as anyone. Leadership, he said, is "the ability to get other people to do what they don't want to do, and like it." Despite some skepticism about the reality and importance of leadership, all government programs require leaders to see that their objectives are attained. Indeed, leadership is often the single, most critical factor in the success or failure of a program.

For instance, research indicates that the school principal's leadership is the most important factor in determining students' success; the minister's leadership, in determining church attendance and contributions; and the soldiers' confidence in their company, battalion, and division commanders, in determining morale and cohesion. Research also indicates that governors, more than agencies, come up with innovations (55 percent to 36 percent) and that the style and performance of a U.S. president makes a big difference in what happens to legislation, policy, and programs. Similarly, research in the business and industrial sector indicates that leadership is a critical factor in ensuring the survival and prosperity of the firm. Bernard M. Bass documents much of this research in his *Handbook of Leadership: Theory, Research, and Managerial Applications* (New York: Free Press, 1990).

Today an unprecedented array of complex problems in the public sector—toxic wastes, education, AIDS, overseas competition, deregulation, illicit drugs—has greatly increased the need for governments to evolve and adapt. Accordingly, the need for unusually creative leaders to

(continued)

President Harry S Truman at his desk. (The Harry S Truman Library)

propel their organizations through major changes has never been greater. John P. Kotter, a professor at Harvard Business School, contends, "It is not hyperbole to say that there is a leadership crisis in the U.S. today." John W. Gardner, former secretary of HEW and founder of Common Cause, makes this comment: "It becomes harder and harder to believe that we once had a President who, long before coming to office, drafted the Declaration of Independence. And another capable of composing the Gettysburg Address."

One explanation for the dearth of leaders is that schools and colleges, as well as potential employers, tell young people that society needs technicians and professionals, not leaders. Gardner says, "A good many of the young people who come through our graduate and professional schools are well equipped to advise leaders in a technical capacity, but they are not well equipped to lead." Only generalists, Gardner thinks, can cope with the diversity of problems and multiple constituencies that contemporary leaders face.

Another popular explanation for the dearth of leaders is that public officials are frequently exposed to harsh criticism. While external criticism is nothing new, the tendency for employees to speak out against and to even openly oppose a leader's decision is a fairly recent phenomenon. "Who needs this?" some young people might ask. "I'd rather be an accountant, an engineer, or a consultant."

A related explanation for why we do not have more leaders is simple: They shake things up. A lot of top executives do not want to cope with change. The problem can be especially severe in a large government agency, which may have an entrenched bureaucracy with no

*(Bill Day/*Detroit Free Press, *Tribune Media Services)*

recognition of its stake in making change work.

Nevertheless, potential leaders are always present. The crucial question is how schools and organizations can awaken and empower them and then create conditions that allow them to rise to the top.

SOURCES: Kenneth Labich, "The Seven Keys to Business Leadership," *Fortune*, October 24, 1988; *New York Times*, August 18, 1987.

expected, Levinson's and Boyatzis's lists overlap—but a forced comparison of the two reveals the absence of the following items on Boyatzis's list:

1. Tolerance for ambiguity (i.e., can stand confusion until things become clear).
2. Achievement (i.e., is oriented toward organization's success rather than personal aggrandizement).
3. Maturity (i.e., has good relationships with authority figures).
4. Sense of humor (i.e., does not take self too seriously).
5. Vision (i.e., is clear about progression of his or her own life and career, as well as where the organization should go).
6. Perseverance (i.e., is able to stick to a task and see it through regardless of the difficulties encountered).
7. Personal organization (i.e., has good sense of how his or her time is spent).
8. Integrity (i.e., has a well-established value system, which has been tested in various ways in the past).
9. Social responsibility (i.e., appreciates the importance of assuming leadership in the larger community).

A different approach to evaluating traits that enhance executive success was used by Korn/Ferry International and a group of UCLA graduate students (cited in Stone, 1981). The study covered 1,708 senior managers in *Fortune* 500 companies. The respondents were questioned on the traits they thought enhanced their success, and the following picture emerged:

Concern for results (73.7 percent)

Integrity (66.3 percent)

Desire for responsibility (57.8 percent)

Concern for people (49.2 percent)

Creativity (44.7 percent)

Ambition (38.1 percent)

Aggressiveness (36.2 percent)

Loyalty (23.4 percent)

Exceptional intelligence (19.5 percent)

Social adaptability (16.4 percent)

Appearance (14.8 percent)

Using the Contingency Approach

The contingency approach has an important practical advantage over the trait approach. By emphasizing behavior and environment, more encouragement is given to the possibility of training individuals. In other words, people can increase their effectiveness in leadership through training in adapting their leadership style to the situation and the followers. Needless to say, this approach does require that the administrators be good enough diagnosticians to identify clues in an environment and flexible enough to vary their behavior.

Dorwin Cartwright (1962) claims that all group objectives fall into one of two categories: (1) the achievement of some group goal or (2) the maintenance or strengthening of the group itself. The first, which we shall call **task behavior,** refers to "the leader's behavior in delineating the relationship between himself and members of the work group and in endeavoring to establish well-defined patterns of organization, channels of communication, and methods of procedure." When leaders assign group members to a particular task, ask group members to follow the rules, and let group members know what is expected of them, we can say that they are exhibiting task behavior.

The second dimension of leader behavior, which we shall call **relationship behavior,** refers to "behavior indicative of friendship, mutual trust, respect, and warmth in the relationship between the leader and the members of his staff." When the leader finds time to listen to group members, is willing to make changes, and is friendly and approachable, we can say that he or she is exhibiting relationship behavior.

Using only various combinations of these two kinds of behavior, we can plot on Figure 8-1 an infinite number of leadership styles.

Using various combinations of these two kinds of behavior, William Reddin (1970) develops four **basic leadership styles**:

- Quadrant I: Supporting, or human relations, style—This manager has less than average task orientation and more than average relationship orientation.
- Quadrant II: Coaching, or participative, style—This manager has more than average task orientation and more than average relationship orientation.

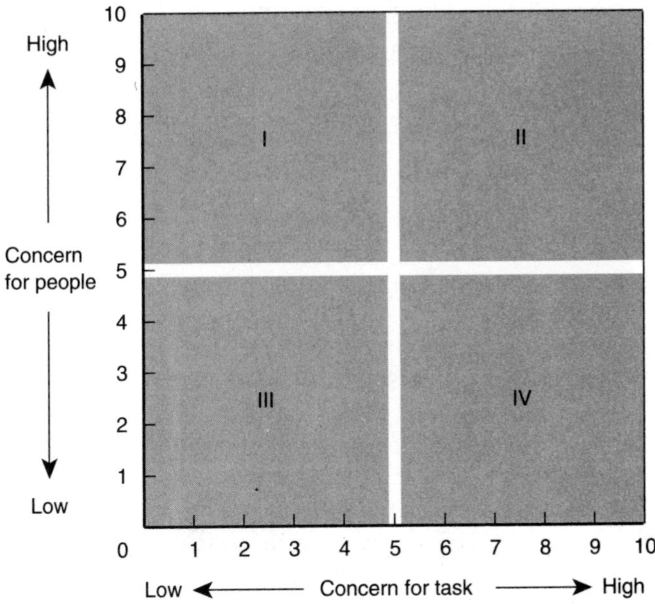

FIGURE 8-1
Leadership Styles

- Quadrant III: Delegating or laissez-faire ("hands off"), style—This manager has less than average task orientation and less than average relationship orientation.
- Quadrant IV: Directing, or autocratic, style—This manager has more than average task orientation and less than average relationship orientation.

The crucial point about these four styles is this: *The effectiveness of managers depends on whether the style they use is appropriate for their situation.* More specifically, to know what is the appropriate style, managers must look to the culture or climate of their organizations; to the nature of the work performed (auditing, street repairs, research and development, and so on); to the styles, expectations, and maturity of their superiors, subordinates, and coworkers. All these factors will help determine which style is effective and which styles are less so.

Because effectiveness results from having a style appropriate to the situation in which it is used, the same basic style can be perceived as being particularly effective or particularly ineffective. Stated differently, a style that works beautifully in one situation might cause a lynch mob to form in another. What is the best management style? It all depends.

Consider the two lists below (from Reddin, 1970:45). Each pair of terms could refer to identical behavior. When that behavior is exhibited in the appropriate situation, everyone nods their heads and mutters the words on the left. But when a manager exhibits the very same pattern of behavior in a different situation, people might shake their heads and mutter the words on the right.

warm-hearted	sentimental
flexible	weak-minded
dignified	pompous
firm	rigid
businesslike	brusque
conservative	reactionary
progressive	left-wing
sensitive	soft
dynamic	overbearing

Based on your own experience, can you think of examples of how a situation has determined the appropriateness of a person's actions?

By now, it should be clear that the effectiveness of an administrator depends to a large degree on his or her ability to size up a situation. To climb outside ourselves, so to speak, and see our situation and study our actions objectively is not easy. Many mechanisms make us insensitive to our situation.

First, we tend to rationalize or kid ourselves. ("I didn't complete the job because other things came up." "I wasn't promoted because my boss is biased.") Second, we see in others what we do not want to see in ourselves. Freud called this tendency projection. So the slacker sees others as lazy; the selfish person complains that others do not share; the administrator with low concern for people complains that no one seems to take an interest in him or her. To maintain projection, administrators must continue to distort reality. Third, we mistake symptoms for cause (this was discussed in Chapter 6). Fourth, we are consumed by a single value—all problems are human ones, all work must be satisfying, or all bigness is bad. Fifth, we may have a high stress level. This is likely to distort our perceptions and feelings about others (Reddin, 1970:141–47).

Now we are in a position to summarize Reddin's theory very briefly. There are four basic styles that an administrator can adopt: supporting, coaching, delegating, and directing. Each of these styles can be either effective or ineffective—depending on the situation. Thus, there are really eight management styles: executive and compromiser; bureaucrat and deserter; benevolent autocrat and autocrat; and developer and missionary (see Table 8-1).

Motivation in Organizations

What is meant by the output of administrators? Not the number of memos they write, phone calls they answer, meetings they attend, or deals they cut. In a fundamental sense, their output is the output of the people over whom they have influence. Management, we must never forget, is a *team* activity.

TABLE 8-1

The Less Effective and More Effective Versions of the Four Basic Management Styles

Basic Style	*When Used in the Appropriate Situation, Effective*	*When Used in the Inappropriate Situation, Ineffective*
Coaching	An *executive* is a good motivating force who sets high standards, treats everyone somewhat differently, and prefers team management.	A *compromiser* is a poor decision maker, one who allows various pressures in the situation to influence him or her too much and avoids or minimizes immediate pressures and problems rather than maximizing long-term production.
Delegating	A *bureaucrat* is primarily interested in rules and procedures for their own sake, wants to control the situation by their use, and is conscientious.	A *deserter* is uninvolved and passive or negative.
Directing	A *benevolent autocrat* knows what he or she wants and how to get it without creating resentment.	An *autocrat* has no confidence in others, is unpleasant, and is interested only in the immediate task.
Supporting	A *developer* has implicit trust in people and is primarily concerned with developing them as individuals.	A *missionary* is primarily interested in harmony.

SOURCE: Based on W. J. Reddin, *Managerial Effectiveness* (New York: McGraw-Hill, 1970).

Administrators have two principal ways to elicit better performance from people: motivation (the subject of this chapter) and training (a topic for consideration in Chapter 10). In his research on motivation, the eminent American psychologist and philosopher William James found that employees can maintain their jobs—that is, avoid being fired—by working at only 20 percent to 30 percent of their ability. But, if highly motivated, employees will work at 80 percent to 90 percent of their ability. The simple equations below illustrate the difference these two factors can make for a hypothetical individual. Let us call him Stakhanov and give him a natural ability of 100.

First assume the employee has a supervisor who neither motivates nor trains Stakhanov:

Performance = 100 x .20 x 1.00 = 20

Now assume he has a supervisor who does motivate and train:

Performance = 100 x .80 x 1.50 = 120

While we probably cannot measure motivation as precisely as our example suggests, we have learned a few things about it in the last 60 or so years. The story itself

(text continues on p. 352)

★★★★★★★★★★★★★★★★★★★★★★★★★★★★★★★★★★★

WORKING PROFILE

Sharpe James

The people of Newark, New Jersey (population 315,000) knew Sharpe James well. From 1970 to 1986, while serving on the city council, he had acquired a reputation for independent ideas and humorous barbs. But could he *lead* the city? In 1986 he and Newark got a chance to find out.

In that year, he defeated the solidly entrenched incumbent, Kenneth A. Gibson, the first black mayor of a major northeastern city. This feat brought James instant national attention as a second-generation black mayor in a city where members of minority groups are no longer satisfied just to have one of their own as mayor.

Having severely criticized Gibson in the campaign, however, James now had to show that he could do more than cast votes or crack jokes. As he explains, "The day I took over, the people wanted to solve all the problems." While he obviously did not solve all Newark's problems in four years, he made commendable progress and was re-elected without opposition in 1990. What can we learn about leadership from James? I would suggest at least four things.

First, he had an agenda, a deep concern for outcome. He was results-oriented and knew that results get attention. Whereas Gibson had focused on direct delivery of social and human services for the people of Newark, it was clear to James that his chief goal for the community should be economic development.

To help him in setting his agenda, James hired a consulting firm to identify the most important management problems on which to concentrate. Their recommendation: Improve the 80 percent rate for collecting taxes, water bills, parking tickets, and other fees. James pursued this goal with a vengeance, putting liens on properties, turning off water, and towing violators' cars. The collection rate rose to 95 percent and revenues, to $30 million.

Mayor Sharpe James of Newark, New Jersey

Agendas should never be written in stone. So, in his second term, James made some subtle shifts in his priorities by focusing more on adding police officers, building rental housing, improving schools, and improving the image of Newark.

Despite the fact that James was mayor, the interaction between him—as leader—and his staff or the city's people—as followers—involved more than simply the giving of commands. His agenda was part of his vision of Newark, and his vision compelled or pulled people—at least some of them—toward him. He did not need to coerce people to pay attention, for he worked on his agenda with such intensity that they were *drawn* in. Thus his leadership was transactional, involving a subtle transaction between leader and follower.

★★★★★★★★★★★★★★★★★★★★★★★★★★★★★★★★★★★

★★★★★★★★★★★★★★★★★★★★★★★★★★★★★★★★★★★

The second thing we can learn from James is that it pays for a leader to be reliable and tirelessly persistent. Residents and community leaders say that the biggest change in the city may be a "can do" attitude personified by James's unstoppable image. "He has uplifted the spirit of the city," one utility executive said.

This persistence is revealed in a variety of ways. In his running battle with the board of education over patronage, accountability, and its $421 million budget (compared to the city's $346 million), he used almost every public appearance to call for the power to appoint board members. In 1990, he finally won control of the housing authority but did not gain authority to demolish most of the ugly high-rise projects, which he considered part of the city's negative image. Still, he fought on.

It seems people tend to trust leaders like Sharpe who are predictable—whose positions are known and who keep at it. As Theodore Friend, III, past president of Swarthmore College, puts it, "Leadership is heading in the wind with such knowledge of oneself and such collaborative energy as to move others to wish to follow. The angle into the wind is less important than choosing one and sticking reasonably to it."

Third, Sharpe knew that leadership depends on shared meanings and interpretations of reality. His actions and symbols framed and mobilized meaning for city hall and for Newark itself. By so doing, he challenged the city's prevailing image of the 1967 riots that scorched the city and left 23 people dead. Indeed, he spent as much time changing that image as he did trying to solve other serious problems.

For example, he installed 775 nylon banners printed with flags or civic messages on downtown lampposts. He knew that the banners might not help the homeless or reduce the high school dropout rate; nevertheless, he considered them absolutely necessary. "What they are is like the eagle somebody puts over a garage," he said. "It just says: 'I live here. I care.' "

Many other initiatives demonstrate his belief in the strength of symbols: a newly organized mounted police, hundreds of new trees, and a new law that requires security gates on downtown stores to be open mesh, so that the city does not appear under siege.

There is substance behind these symbols:

- The state's largest home builder helped put 1,100 residences in the Central Ward.
- For the first time in 20 years, the city's bond rating was upgraded to BBB+ from BBB, saving the city millions in interest payments. Blue Cross and Blue Shield of New Jersey moved 2,500 workers from the suburbs to a new office tower downtown.
- More than $3 billion in commercial development was completed or proposed; and 2,000 houses and apartments were built.
- The city also won state support for a proposed $200 million performing arts center that James hoped would ensure that Newark did not become a reservation for the poor.

Fourth, he knew his worth. That is to say, James had a well-founded confidence in himself without being egoistic, self-centered, or cocky. He recognized his strengths and compensated for his weaknesses. For example, rather than bring into his government cronies and sycophants, he conducted a national search for staff members.

Sharpe also freely concedes his faults—for example, an impatience with the small details of government and a lack of expertise in fiscal affairs: "I'm not a numbers person. I don't sit down and play with calculators. I have a hard time reading my phone bill."

SOURCES: Anthony DePalma, "Newark's New Image Buoys Mayor on Eve of Election," *New York Times*, May 4, 1990; Warren Bennis and Burt Nanus, *Leaders* (New York: Harper & Row, 1985), pp. 44–53.

★★★★★★★★★★★★★★★★★★★★★★★★★★★★★★★★★★★

is fascinating. It begins in the 1920s, when the Harvard Business School, under the supervision of Elton Mayo (1933), conducted a series of experiments in the Hawthorne, Illinois, plant of Western Electric.

Hawthorne Studies

An Experiment—and a Puzzle. In 1924, Western Electric efficiency experts designed a research program to study the effects of illumination on productivity. The assumption was that increased illumination would result in higher output. Two groups of employees were selected: a test group, which worked under varying degrees of light, and a control group, which worked under normal plant illumination. As expected, when lighting increased, the output of the test group went up. But something else happened—and it was entirely unexpected: The output of the control group also went up.

At this point, Western Electric turned for help to Mayo and his associates. Mayo's researchers then began to implement a variety of changes, behavioral as well as physical. Rest periods were scheduled. Work hours were altered. Hot snacks were served. But no matter what was done to the workers, output continued to soar.

Baffled by the results, the researchers took a radical step: They restored the original conditions. This change was expected to have a tremendous negative psychological impact and most certainly reduce output. But output jumped to an all-time high. Why? The answer was fairly simple, but the implications were catastrophic, bringing an almost precise reversal of the whole line of management thought and practice since the Industrial Revolution. In a nutshell, what the Harvard team found—after further investigation, including interviews with over 20,000 employees from every department in the company—was this: The workers' productivity went up because the attention lavished upon them by the experimenters made them feel that they were important to the company. No longer did they view themselves as isolated individuals. Now they were participating members of a congenial cohesive work group.

The general lesson was patent. The significant factor affecting organizational productivity was not the physical conditions or monetary rewards derived from work but the interpersonal relationships developed on the job. Mayo found that when informal groups felt that their own goals were in opposition to those of management and their control over their job or environment was slight, productivity remained low.

In a word, the new goal for management, the golden key, seemed to be *morale.* To maintain a high level of output, the administrator had only to develop ways to satisfy the worker, to make him or her feel good about his or her work, boss, and organization. Dr. Feelgood had replaced the grim efficiency expert.

Behavioral science was making progress. The discovery of the informal group—and, in a larger sense, the humanity of the worker—was, as we said, a real breakthrough in management thought. But the same cannot be said for the concept of morale. As subsequent research began to show, morale was no panacea. Given happy employees, it by no means follows with iron logic that they will feel an urge to work harder and harder. So, disillusionment set in and the scientists began to look for a new tack to improving the effectiveness of organizations.

Why Motivation Should Be Taken Seriously

A major survey (Yankelovich, 1983:6–7) of the American nonmanagerial work force revealed the following disturbing results:

- Fewer than 1 out of every 4 jobholders say that they are currently working at full potential.
- One half said they do not put effort into their job over and above what is required to hold onto it.
- The overwhelming majority, 75 percent, said that they could be significantly more effective than they presently are.
- Close to 6 out of 10 Americans on the job believe that they "do not work as hard as they used to." (This may or may not be true, but it's their perception.)

The Hawthorne Effect Revisited. One of the seminal ideas in contemporary social science is the phenomenon of the "Hawthorne effect"; that is, the tendency of humans to alter their behavior when they are under study by social scientists and thereby jeopardize the accuracy of the study. Using the statistical methods available to them at the time, the Hawthorne researchers found only a small correlation between physical and material factors and output. They concluded that unquantifiable "human relations" accounted for changes in output.

Later research by Parson (1978) and Franke and Kaul (1978) appeared to invalidate much of the Hawthorne study. Parson finds hard evidence that the workers at Western Electric's Hawthorne plant were systematically receiving information feedback, that is, knowledge of results about their output rates. Workers also received a differential monetary award; the faster they worked, the more money they got. The combination of information feedback and differential monetary rewards—not changing environmental conditions—seem to offer the best explanation for the gradually increasing productivity at the Hawthorne plant.

The research of Franke and Kaul is even more surprising. It virtually reverses the original findings of the Hawthorne study. Reanalyzing the raw data using more sophisticated statistical techniques and computers, Franke and Kaul found a significant correlation between output and "managerial discipline." The firing of two workers during the course of the experiments explains most of the changes in output. "Human relations" do partially govern output—not in the sense of "humane treatment" but rather in the sense of simple discipline. Franke and Kaul also concur with Parson that the group pay incentive was of some value in raising output.

The latest episode in this running battle was made by Stephen R. G. Jones (1990), an economist at Canada's McMaster University. Jones argues that his own complex statistical manipulations of the data from the Hawthorne plant's relay assembly test room between 1927 and 1932, where five women worked, show that "interdependence" was crucial after all. "The human relations approach to industrial sociology," he maintains, "is not controverted by the original Hawthorne data from which it began."

Perhaps the main lesson to be drawn from this story is that social science researchers must avoid enthusiastically embracing something scientifically unproven just because it is congenial with their own values.

Maslow's Hierarchy of Needs

The next scene in our story opens with a question, much as the Hawthorne affair did. Money, presumably, was a great incentive to work hard, but when people were asked what was most important to them in their jobs, money often took third, fourth, or even fifth place. Factors like "full appreciation for work done," "feeling in on things," "sympathetic understanding of personal problems," and "job security" ranked higher. Why?

Speaking broadly, we might say that human motives or needs form a more complicated pattern than one is likely to suppose. In the early 1950s, U.S. psychologist Abraham Maslow (1954) did much to describe this pattern by suggesting the existence of a hierarchy of needs. According to Maslow, the behavior of an individual at a particular moment is usually determined by his or her strongest need. If this is so, then it would seem useful for administrators to have some understanding about the needs that are commonly most important to people. Maslow notes five (see Figure 8-2).

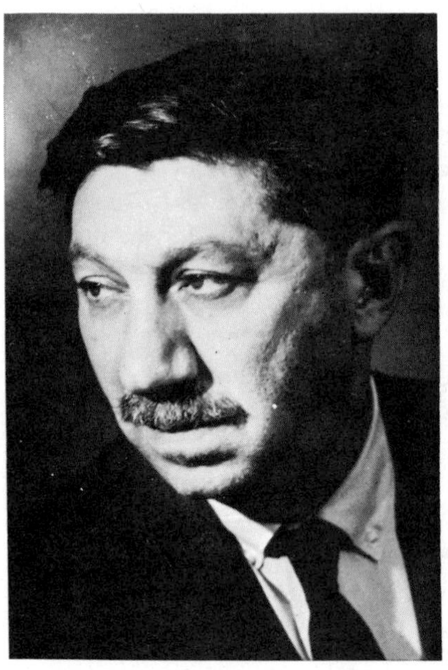

Abraham Maslow (1908–1970). Abraham H. Maslow, who died in 1970, was one of the foremost spokespersons of humanistic psychology. In order to pursue the truth of things, to discover a way of experiencing the highest levels of human awareness, and to research the best social conditions in which people might bring themselves to a "full humanness," he found he could not separate the empirical methods of science from the aesthetics of philosophical inquiry. "Experiencing is only the beginning of knowledge," he said, "necessary, but not sufficient." He introduced the hierarchy of needs, which included self-actualization. In 1965, he described in Eupsychian Management the interrelations between psychological theory and an enlightened modern management. *(Source: The Bettmann Archive Inc.; photography by William Carter)*

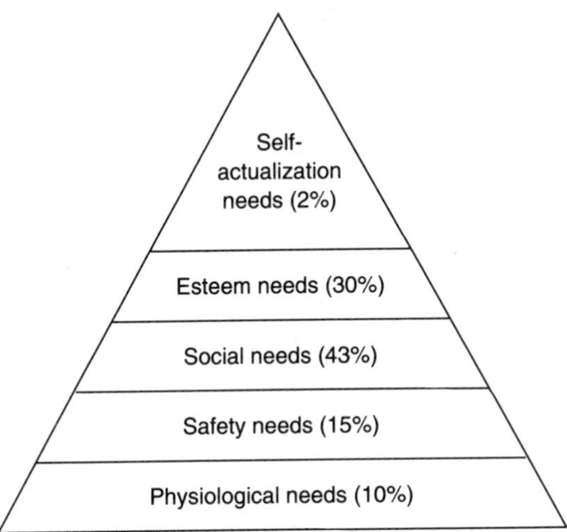

FIGURE 8-2
Maslow's Hierarchy of Needs
NOTE: Several years ago, a group of researchers at the Stanford Research Institute asked what percentage of the U.S. population was living on each of the five levels. These percentages are shown in parentheses.

1. Physiological. In Maslow's formulation, the physiological needs (e.g., food, clothing, and shelter) are at the bottom of the hierarchy. The satisfaction of these needs is usually associated in our society with money. But as these basic needs begin to be fulfilled, other levels of needs become important and motivate and dominate the behavior of the individual.

2. Security. Above physiological needs, Maslow places the need for safety or security. As with other motives, security can be above the surface and apparent to the individual or largely subconscious and not easily identified. The second form can be developed during early childhood through identification with security-minded parents who are willing to accept whatever fate comes along.

Do you want a job that offers a challenge to imagination and ingenuity and that penalizes failure? Or, do you find real satisfaction in the precision, order, and system of a clearly laid out job? (Remember Sinclair Lewis's Babbitt, for whom "a sensational event was changing from the brown suit to the gray the contents of his pockets.") How you answer these questions is a good indication of how important the security motive is to you. Some organizations, it has been suggested (Gellerman, 1963), tend to overemphasize the security motive by providing elaborate fringe benefit programs; for example, medical insurance and retirement plans. While this emphasis can make employees more predictable, it cannot necessarily make them more productive. And if creativity is necessary in their jobs—which is often the case in the public sector where a high percentage of employees are knowledge workers—overemphasis on security can actually thwart creativity.

3. Social. Once physiological and safety needs are fairly well satisfied, social needs become dominant. Considerable sophistication is required to deal effectively with these needs.

In the first place, the administrator needs to recognize that the social needs of decision makers in the organization can lead to **groupthink.** This mode of thinking is regularly encountered in studies of group dynamics when concurrence-seeking becomes so dominant that it tends to override realistic appraisal of alternative courses of action. And no level of decision making is immune to this strain of social conformity.

An important symptom of groupthink is pressure: "Victims of groupthink apply direct pressure to the individual who momentarily expresses doubts about any of the group's shared illusions or who questions the validity of the arguments supporting a policy alternative favored by the minority. This gambit reinforces the concurrence-seeking norm that loyal members are expected to maintain" (Janis, 1971:257). James C. Thompson, Jr., a historian who spent five years as an observing participant in both the State Department and the White House, reports that whenever a member of President Johnson's in-group began to express doubts about Vietnam, the group exerted subtle social pressure to "domesticate" him. The dissenter was made to feel at home provided he did not voice his doubts to outsiders and kept his criticism within the bounds of acceptable deviation. Thompson tells us when one such "domesticated dissenter," Bill Moyers, arrived at a meeting, the president greeted him with, "Well, here comes Mr. Stop-the-Bombing" (cited in Janis, 1971:218).

One behavioral scientist concludes, after poring over hundreds of relevant documents, that social need is the only explanation of why groupthink continues to occur in the corridors of power. Writes Irving L. Janis (1971:174): "My belief is that we can best understand the various symptoms of groupthink as a mental effort among group members to maintain . . . emotional equanimity by providing social support to each other."

A second thing that the administrator needs to recognize about social needs concerns not the corridors of power but the informal work group. Administrators are often suspicious of informal groups that develop in organizations because of the potential power these groups have to lower productivity. But why are such work-restricting groups formed? Studies show that they sometimes form as a reaction to the insignificance and impotence that workers tend to feel when they have no control over their working environment. In fact, the situation is made worse when, at the same time, workers are closely supervised but have no clear channels of communication with the top (see Schachter, 1959). In this type of environment, work restriction becomes a means to preserve the identification of individuals within the group. Yet, informal groups *can* be an asset to administration.

But how? To answer that question we might first note a cardinal insight of recent studies on informal groups: An inherent conflict exists between the social needs of the individual and the requirements of the organization. Social psychologists draw a useful distinction here: The social needs of the individual are called *primary needs* and the requirements of the organization, *secondary needs.* One need not spend much time in public organizations to find out that the vocabulary of bureaucracy abounds with avowals of secondary needs at the expense of primary ones. Consider: "Nothing personal, *but* . . ." or "I'm sorry to have to do this, *but* . . . ."

In contrast, the effective administrator not only tries to avoid this officious approach but also *tries to integrate primary and secondary relationships.* But how does one go about this integration? The successful administrator, according to Katz and Kahn (1966:325–56), "mediates and tempers the organizational requirements to the needs of persons." This mediating, however, is done in ways that are not damaging but actually enhancing to the organization. Further, the administrator "promotes group loyalty and personal ties. He demonstrates care for persons as persons." In trying to influence the people in the organization, the administrator seldom relies on formal powers, such as those found in rules and regulations, but on (1) *referent power*—influence based upon liking or identification with another person; or (2) *expert power*—influence based upon the expertise of the administrator that is relevant to the task.

Write Katz and Kahn (1966:325–66):

> *He encourages the development of positive identification with the organization and creates among his peers and subordinates a degree of personal commitment and identification. He does these things by developing a relationship with others in the organization in which he introduces what might be termed primary variations on the secondary requirements of organization. Within limits he adapts his own interpersonal style to the needs of other persons. In so doing, he generates among members of his group a resultant strength of motivation for the achievement of group and organizational goals which more than compensate for occasional bureaucratic irregularities. The secondary role requirements remain the dominant figure in his behavior, but they appear on a background of, and are embellished by, an attention to primary interpersonal consideration.*

4. Esteem. If we assume then, that the individual social needs are met within the organization, a fourth need comes into prominence: esteem. Failure to understand this need often lies behind the administrator's complaint: "We've given our people everything—good salary, pleasant working conditions, even affection—and yet some are still dissatisfied." In other words, it is precisely because employees have had the three basic needs sufficiently satisfied that a fourth need emerges. And, like social needs, the need for esteem can cause organizational problems unless the administrator finds ways of satisfying it.

Although the need for esteem appears in a variety of forms, we shall discuss only two—recognition and prestige. With each form, however, the message for the public administrator remains the same: Do things to make employees feel important.

*The need for esteem and prestige is fourth on Maslow's hierarchy. The French government distributes a bewildering array of awards each year, which the model displays. According to one sardonic French saying, half the riders in the Paris metro wear the Legion of Honor, while the other half have applied for it. Apparently, Maslow's hierarchy applies cross-nationally. (Picherie/*Paris Match*)*

William James (1952:189) gave an especially gripping explanation of the importance of recognition:

> *We are not only gregarious animals, liking to be in sight of our fellows, but we have an innate propensity to get ourselves noticed, and noticed favorably, by our kind. No more fiendish punishment could be devised, were such a thing physically possible, than that one should be turned loose in society and remain absolutely unnoticed by all the members thereof. If no one turned round when we spoke, or minded what we did, but if every person we met . . . acted as if we were nonexisting things, a kind of rage and impotent despair would be a relief; for these would make us feel that, however bad might be our plight, we had not sunk to such a depth as to be unworthy of attention at all.*

In an organizational setting, what this means is that people look for support from their supervisors. Studies show, for example, a strong relationship between an administrator's supportiveness and the self-esteem of his or her subordinates (see Bowers, 1964). Further, studies by members of the Institute for Social Research at the University of Michigan have shown that supervisors who exert pressure for production *but do not support their people* end up with a low-production organization.

Despite the importance of recognition, most contemporary organizations are deficient in it. This is evident, says Harry Levinson (1968:183) of Harvard Business School, in the repetitive response to a simple question: "If one asks people in almost any organization, 'How do you know how well you are doing?' 90 percent of them are likely to respond, 'If I do something wrong, I'll hear about it.' " According to Levinson, what people are really saying is that they do not feel sufficient support from their supervisors.

The power to gain ascendancy over the minds of men and women and to command their admiration for distinguished performance is prestige. To be sure, some tend to seek only the material symbols of status. Salary, to the extent it carries social value, can certainly be included here as well as under physical needs. Michael Korda's book *Power!* would hardly merit our attention except that its very popularity evidences how widespread (one might say even pathological) the need for people to have their importance clarified has become. In a chapter entitled "Symbols of Power," Korda offers detailed advice on how shoes, typewriters, telephones, office furniture, briefcases, and clocks can all increase status. Here is a sample: "A full calendar is proof of power, and for this reason, the most powerful people prefer small calendars, which are easily filled up, and which give the impression of frenetic activity, particularly if one's writing is fairly large. One of the best power symbols is a desk diary that shows the whole week at a glance, with every available square inch of space filled in or crossed out. It provides visible evidence that one is busy—too busy to see someone who is anxious to discuss a complaint or a burdensome request." The author even suggests, if necessary, filling the diary up with entries such as "gray suit at cleaners" or "Betsy's birthday." "The effect from a distance is awe inspiring" (Korda, 1975:208).

5. Self-Actualization. According to Gellerman (1963), the need for prestige is more or less self-limiting. Once people have gained the level they think they deserve, the strength of this need declines. Prestige now becomes a matter more of maintenance than of further advancement. At this point, too, we witness the emergence of Maslow's fifth and final need: self-actualization.

What exactly is self-actualization? In *The Farther Reaches of Human Nature,* a book light-years removed from Korda's, Maslow (1971:43) provides us an answer:

> *Self-actualizing people are, without one single exception, involved in a cause outside their own skin, in something outside of themselves. They are devoted, working at something, something which is very precious to them—some calling or vocation in the old sense, the priestly sense. They are working at something which fate has called them to somehow and which they work at and which they love, so that the work-joy dichotomy in them disappears.*

Admittedly, this explanation lacks the rigor indicative of good social and behavioral science; and there is no gainsaying the fact that the concept of self-actualization is difficult to pin down. But we must try. (I harbor the belief that the great undiscussed paradox in management literature is that, in discussions of Maslow's hierarchy of needs, the most underdeveloped part, self-actualization, is the most important.)

An especially well-researched motive, closely related to self-actualization, is the urge to achieve. By considering this phenomenon, perhaps we can better understand self-actualization.

Adapting a simple example from David McClelland (1961) can help us distinguish the achievement-motivated person from the socially motivated and esteem-motivated. Given the task of building a boat, the achievement-motivated person would obtain gratification from the making of the boat. This intense interest in the work is, of course, quite consistent with the above quote from Maslow. The socially motivated person would have fun in playing with others and with the boat but would be less concerned about its seaworthiness. Finally, the esteem-motivated person would be concerned with the specific role he or she had in the project and with the rewards of success.

Achievement-motivated persons set moderately difficult but potentially surmountable goals for themselves; they prefer situations where they can obtain tangible information about their performance; and they habitually think about how to do things better. Maslow relates an anecdote about Brahms that illustrates the last point. Somebody had been fiddling around at the piano and was idly playing notes and chords and, in the middle of playing, left the piano. Brahms had to get up and finish the progression. He then said, "We cannot let that chord go unresolved forever."

From the various achievement studies, we have learned that this motive can be taught and developed in people. But how? Levinson (1968:243) provides these guidelines: The administrator "should make demands on people, expect them to achieve reasonable goals, and even some that border on the unreasonable. He should respect their capacity to chart their own course toward those goals if they are adequately protected and supported, acknowledge what they have to contribute toward reaching collective goals, and, following Diogenes's dictum, 'Stand out of their light.' "

To summarize: Maslow contended that human needs could be classified on five levels, with each succeeding need becoming more pressing as the more primitive ones were satisfied. To my mind, this theory was a significant contribution, for Maslow was saying—with far more precision than any of his predecessors—that different people require different treatment by management (in the vernacular: different strokes for different folks). And there is more: The same person may over time require different treatment and management should never expect a cessation of complaints but rather should expect different ones.

This humanistic orientation remains a major influence on how we think about human behavior in organizations. We shall find some implicit criticism of it later in this chapter when we examine contingency approaches to management (see box). But for now, let us pick up the trail and see how Maslow's work influenced the theories of Douglas McGregor and Chris Argyris.

Self-Actualization in Critical Perspective

Maslow would describe himself as an existential psychologist, and this is reflected in the title of one of his most important books, *Toward a Psychology of Being*. Over the last few decades, a worldwide existential psychology movement has developed. One of the leading members of this movement is Viktor E. Frankl (1984), who was confined in a Nazi concentration camp during World War II. The experience gave him deep insight into human nature under pressure. Since all living is a form of pressure, Frankl has extended these insights to apply to what we call ordinary life:

Being human is being always directed, and pointing, to something or someone other than oneself: to a meaning to fulfill or another human being to encounter, a cause to serve or a person to love. Only to the extent that someone is living out this self-transcendence of human existence, is he truly human or does he become his true self. He becomes so, not by concerning himself with his self's actualization, *but by forgetting himself and giving himself, overlooking himself and focusing outward. . . . What is called self-actualization is, and must remain, the unintended effect of self-transcendence; it is ruinous and self-defeating to make it the target of intention. And what is true of self-actualization also holds for identity and happiness. It is the very "pursuit of happiness" that obviates happiness (emphasis added).*

Douglas McGregor: Theory X and Theory Y

Douglas McGregor (1960) was heavily influenced both by the Hawthorne studies and by Maslow's work. His classic book, *The Human Side of Enterprise,* advanced the thesis that managers can benefit greatly by giving more attention to the social and self-actualizing needs of people at work. McGregor felt that managers must shift their view of human nature from a perspective he called Theory X to one called Theory Y. These are important terms in the vocabulary of management.

According to McGregor, managers of the Theory X model view their subordinates as by nature

- Disliking work.
- Lacking ambition.
- Irresponsible.
- Resistant to change.
- Preferring to be led rather than to lead.

Theory Y, by contrast, involves an alternative set of assumptions. A manager operating under a Theory Y perspective views subordinates as naturally

- Willing to work.
- Willing to accept responsibility.
- Capable of self-direction and self-control.
- Capable of creativity.

Theory Y is not just Theory X's opposite (although that is what many observers conclude). McGregor did not intend that the two sets of assumptions be forced into the hard versus soft mold. Rather, he meant Theory Y to be an integrative set of assumptions. As McGregor (1960:49) notes in describing the paradoxical qualities of Theory Y:

> *The central principle of Theory Y is that of integration; the creation of conditions such that the members of the organization can achieve their own goals best by directing their goals toward the success of the enterprise . . . . The concept of integration and self-control (also) carries the implication that the organization will be more effective in achieving its economic objectives if adjustments are made in significant ways to the needs and goals of its members.*

Chris Argyris: Personality and Organization

Argyris argues that the management principles discussed in the last chapter are in conflict with the view of human nature advanced by Maslow and McGregor. For example, the principle of specialization assumes people will behave more efficiently as tasks become specialized—but specialization inhibits self-actualization. The principle of chain of command assumes efficiency is increased by a clear-cut hierarchy in which the top controls the bottom—but hierarchy creates dependent, passive, and subordinate workers with little control over their work environments. Span of control assumes efficiency will increase when a supervisor's responsibility is limited to seven employees—but span of control also creates dependent, passive, and subordinate workers with little control over their work environments.

Argyris predicts that when people suffer incongruence between their mature personalities and management practices, they will be prone to absenteeism, turnover, aggression toward higher levels of authority, apathy, and alienation, and to a focus on compensation as the ever-increasing trade-off for their unhappiness. Argyris is fairly specific in what he means by "mature personalities." He maintains that seven changes (see Figure 8-3) take place in the personalities of individuals *if* they are to develop into mature people over the years. I emphasize the word *if* because the correlation

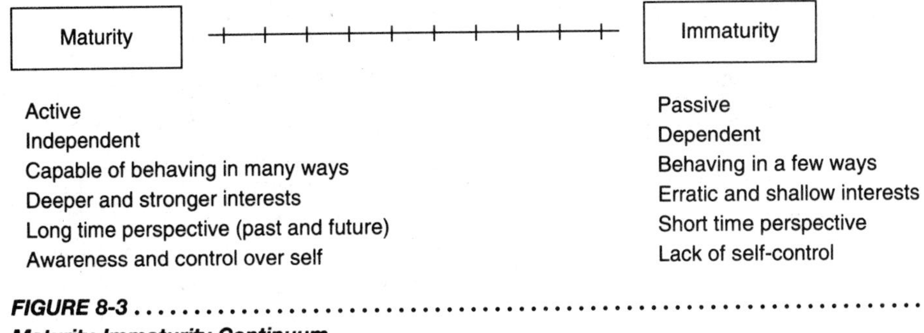

FIGURE 8-3
Maturity-Immaturity Continuum

between longevity and maturity is not a perfect one. Some men and women never grow up, while some 12 year olds might exhibit a remarkable degree of maturity. But Argyris's crucial point is that the percentage of the adult population that does not grow up is much smaller than would be suggested by the bureaucratic-pyramidal values dominating many organizations.

His advice to administrators is to accommodate the mature personality by (1) *expanding job requirements* to include *more task variety and responsibility* and (2) adjusting supervisory styles to include *more participation.* In sum, Argyris suggests that managers who respond to "mature" personalities will achieve productivity. Psychological success, Argyris says, requires that individuals define their own goals.

In light of the remarkable productivity gains in Japanese companies that practice techniques like job design and participation, there is more reason than ever to believe Argyris.

Frederick Herzberg: Satisfiers and Dissatisfiers

In his groundbreaking *The Motivation to Work* (1959), Frederick Herzberg reports on the results of his and his associates' empirical investigation of motivation. Essentially, they found five factors that determined job satisfaction: achievement, recognition, work itself, responsibility, and advancement (Figure 8-4). In addition, they found five factors that were associated with job dissatisfaction: company policy and administration, supervision, salary, interpersonal relations, and working conditions. Significantly, the satisfying factors were all related to job content.

These findings are most suggestive. They tell us that jobs should be designed to be challenging and should provide ample opportunity for worker recognition. They tell us that employees should be given as much discretion as possible. They tell us that employees should be able to diversify activities, which is not the same thing as merely taking on more work. And finally they tell us that employees should be able to witness some of the result of their output.

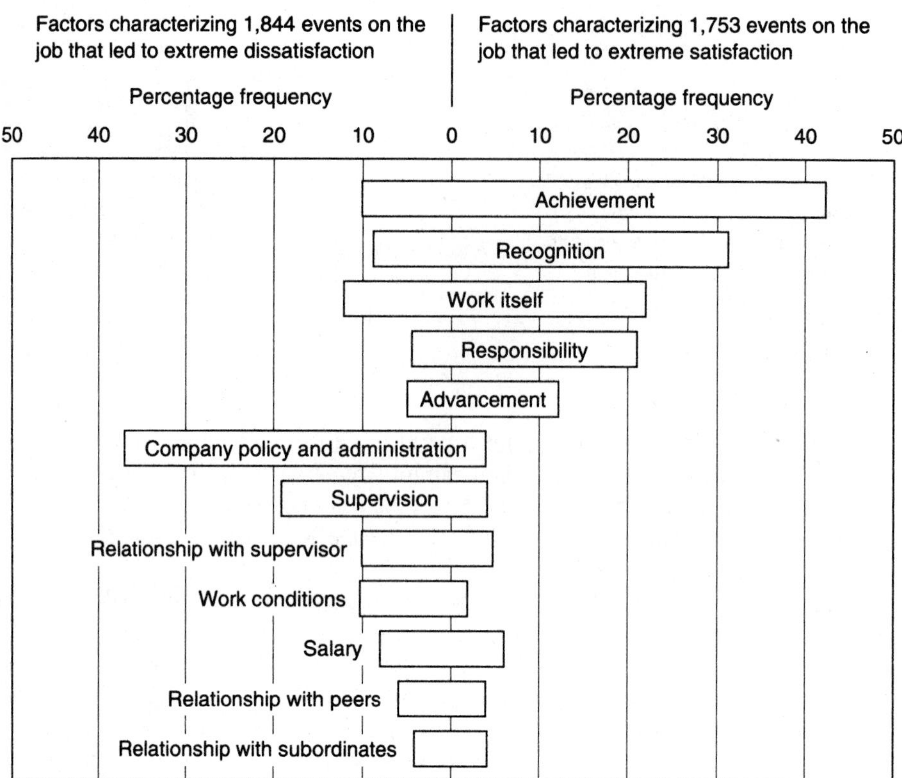

FIGURE 8-4

Comparison of Satisfiers and Dissatisfiers

SOURCE: F. Herzberg, et al. 1959. *The Motivation to Work* (New York: John Wiley & Sons).

How well does job enrichment work? According to Roy W. Walters (1972):

The best proof of any theory is the hard, fast results which occur when the theory becomes practice. Job enrichment efforts in a number of cases over the last few years have produced excellent results, both for the companies and for the individual workers. In one organization, job enrichment saved $300,000 for the company by increasing production per employee. This was done by expanding job responsibilities and by reducing verification of the work. In another organization, the savings were $100,000, realized through increased production and reduction in the number of employees. In still another company, quality of output improved 35 percent.

But effective job design does not apply solely to workers. Drucker (1966:78–92) offers these guidelines for designing executive and professional jobs:

- Do not start out with the assumption that jobs are created by nature or God. Know they have been designed by highly fallible people. Therefore, guard against the "impossible" job, the job that simply is not for normal human beings. "Any job that has defeated two or three men in succession, even though each had performed well in his previous assignment, must be assumed unfit for human beings." Examples of such "undoable," people-killer jobs include the presidency of a large university and the ambassadorship of a major power.
- Make each job demanding and big. "It should have challenge to bring out whatever strength a man may have. It should have scope so that any strength that is relevant to the task can produce significant results." Surveys of physicians in the Army Medical Corps, chemists in the research lab, nurses in the hospital produce the same results: "The ones who are enthusiastic and who, in turn, have results to show for their work, are the ones whose abilities are being challenged and used."

Significantly, many of the nation's largest and most successful corporations—AT&T, Texas Instruments, General Foods, Monsanto, Polaroid, and so forth—have long had vigorous job-design programs. The public sector, some charge, has been guilty of trailing far behind. In this area, however, the consequences are especially costly. Albert Camus put it accurately and briefly when he wrote: "Without work all life goes rotten; but when work is soulless, life stifles and dies."

Summing Up

The number of scholars who have tried to answer the question of what motivates employees is quite staggering. Thus far in this chapter, you have been introduced to only a tiny fraction.

While these scholars put their theories and findings in different bottles, the contents are pretty much the same. I do not think that many of them could argue with or greatly add to the following statement by Fritz J. Roethlisberger, one of the pioneers in the study of human behavior and an early chronicler of the Hawthorne studies:

> *People at work are not so different from people in other aspects of life. They are not entirely creatures of logic. They have feelings. They like to feel important and to have their work recognized as important. Although they are interested in the size of their pay envelopes, this is not the matter of their first concern. Sometimes they are more interested in having their pay reflect accu-*

rately the relative social importance to them of the different jobs they do. Sometimes even still more important to them than maintenance of socially accepted wage differentials is the way their superiors treat them.

They like to work in an atmosphere of approval. They like to be praised rather than blamed. They do not like to have to admit their mistakes—at least, not publicly. They like to know what is expected of them and where they stand in relation to their boss's expectations. They like to have some warning of the changes that may affect them.

They like to feel independent in their relations to their supervisors. They like to be able to express their feelings to them without being misunderstood. They like to be listened to and have their feelings and points of view taken into account. They like to be consulted about and participate in the actions that will personally affect them. In short, employees, like most people, want to be treated as belonging to and being an integral part of some group. (Quoted in McNair, 1957)

We might also do well to remind ourselves that, despite all the studies and all the theories, no equation can ever tell us quite all we need to know about leading people. While theory can help guide us and can conveniently encapsulate complex truths, leadership remains, at least in part, an art. The Talking Shop will, I hope, give you a deeper appreciation of this very important idea.

Communicating in Organizations

"If the oldest complaint is nobody asked us," Churchill once observed, "the next oldest is nobody ever told us." Churchill, who knew a thing or two about leadership in organizations, is suggesting here that we carefully consider communication. Indeed, we should. The sheer mass of communication that occurs in running a government program is overwhelming. Consider this: Managers spend over 80 percent of every working day communicating. How do they communicate? One survey broke down managers' communication time as follows (Mintzberg, 1973):

- Face-to-face meetings (69 percent)
- Telephone calls (6 percent)
- Walk-around tours (3 percent)
- Reading and writing at desk (22 percent)

In the public sector, the problem of communication is compounded by the fact that the public is often closely involved in program planning and operations. For example, when Massachusetts's controversial bottle bill became law a few years ago, amid turmoil created by uncertainty as to when, exactly, the law would go into effect, state agencies were deluged with calls about the law. As a result, a statewide toll-free telephone hot line was installed. The hot line quickly became not only an educational tool but also the critical link between the public officials and the state officials and the statewide focal point for questions and complaints about the law.

What Communication Is—and Is Not

The essence of communication is not speaking and writing; rather, it is *sharing*. Communication thus can be defined as the process by which information and ideas travel from A to B and are then understood by B. Communication is not just sending information, for often A intends to motivate or influence the behavior of B. Once B perceives what A is trying to communicate—is "with" A, so to speak—A has successfully communicated with B. The managers who fail to keep these distinctions in mind, who continue to view communication simply in terms of speaking and writing, run the risk of making the following types of mistakes.

Using Gobbledygook. The first mistake is the use of language characterized by circumlocution and jargon, which is usually hard to understand. This practice is so prevalent in bureaucracy that there is even a special term for it: *gobbledygook.* (The term originated during World War II when someone fancifully reformed the word *gobble*—the throaty cry of a male turkey.)

Consider the final paragraph of a letter I have on my desk regarding OMB Circular A-21, a compilation of regulations governing reimbursement to universities that conduct federally financed research: "Since data is central to the issue of refined implementation guidance and legislation defers implementation, we believe it is advisable to examine the data that your organization is assembling to preclude any such unintended effects." What could this possibly mean? Never mind, the author obviously was not thinking of communication in terms of the reader's understanding. Communication for him was simply writing. Period.

There is an old axiom that should be carved on the desk of every public administrator: An order that can be misunderstood will be misunderstood. A desperate measure, defacing government property, but how else can the administrator be forced to write in a clear, straightforward manner?

Rather than struggle with that question, let us turn to a more answerable one: Why do administrators engage in gobbledygook? One reason, I think, is to avoid unpleasantness: We do not fire incompetent employees; we "select them out" or "nonretain them." (Note too the use of the collective pronoun *we*.) Nor do we ever, ever cut the budget; we make "advance downward adjustments." Unions do not strike; they engage in a "job action." Prisons are "correctional facilities."

Because of gobbledygook in the corridors of bureaucracies, the ability to read between the lines becomes almost a job requirement. Here is a primer (from the *Empire State Dispatch,* reprinted in the *Wharton Magazine*):

(text continues on p. 372)

Talking Shop ....

Leadership as a Liberal Art

While we usually associate the word *art* with beauty, with things we hang on walls or put on pedestals, it can also connote utility and knowledge. We are familiar with the concepts of teaching and medicine as arts. Phrases such as "arts and crafts" and "industrial arts" refer primarily to the production of useful things. And it is in this context that the term *liberal arts* should be understood. It refers to skills of the mind.

Thus art is distinct from science in that the former aims at the production of some desired effect. Art is knowledge of *how* to make something happen. Science is knowledge *that* something is the case. Because leadership is preeminently concerned with making things happen, effecting change, leadership is closer to art than science. Moreover, when talking about leadership, our knowledge that something is the case is much more modest than, say, in physics. For example how does job satisfaction relate to productivity? Despite thousands of studies, we really do not know. Some researchers find positive correlations; some, negative correlations; and others, no correlation at all.

While leadership may be based in large measure on behavioral science (as medicine is based on biological science), it must go beyond science in formulating general rules for the guidance in particular situations. Much of the knowledge on which the performance of a leader is based is *tacit knowledge:* knowledge that is not openly expressed or stated. Tacit knowledge is considered to be practical rather than scientific, informal rather than formal—and usually not easily taught. Here are 21 prime types of such knowledge:

1. When to be tough.
2. How to organize meaning for members of the organization.
3. How to listen.
4. When to micromanage (i.e., get deeply involved in the unit's operations).
5. How to determine the difference between what you need to know and what you do not need to know.
6. When and how to criticize.
7. How to balance short-term losses against long-term gains, and vice versa.
8. When to take a second look at first impressions.
9. How to understand things from other points of view.
10. When to let others off the hook.
11. How to learn from one's mistakes.
12. When to use humor.
13. How to admit mistakes or ignorance.
14. How to know the abilities and values of those with whom you work.
15. How to turn crises into opportunities.
16. When to wait and when to act.
17. How to accept criticism nondefensively.
18. When to seek help.
19. How to know who to trust.
20. How to know what people expect of you.
21. When to cut your losses.

By using the word *tacit,* I do not wish to imply that such knowledge is completely inaccessible to conscious awareness. Certainly Jefferson recognized and appreciated Washington's mastery of item 16 above: "Perhaps the strongest feature of his character was prudence, never acting until every circumstance, every consideration was maturely weighed; refraining when he saw doubt, but, when once decided, going through with his purpose whatever obstacles opposed." Nor do I wish to imply that such knowledge is unteachable, merely that it is usually not taught directly as a scientific law or mathematical operation might be. As Robert J. Sternberg of Yale University puts it, "much tacit knowledge may be disorganized and relatively inaccessible, making it potentially ill-suited for direct instruction."

Keeping that proviso in mind, let us see what we can learn about just the first four items on the list. (Item 6 will receive special attention in Chapter 10.) But remember: The balance of this knowledge must be acquired through experience. Good luck!

When to Be Tough

Few job specifications for management positions fail to include the word *aggressive* along with *bright* and *articulate,* and no one wants to work for a wimp. Yet serious students of contemporary organizations report almost invariably that displays of screaming, table-pounding pushiness are no longer deemed acceptable behavior. Indeed, some of today's most successful leaders seldom even give orders—rather they ask questions, make requests, and allow themselves occasional observations.

Leaders must know the difference between being tough and being mean. There are situations in which people have to be pushed, but if it is done on the wrong issue, at the wrong time, or in the wrong way, the leader loses credibility. Morale will sag, resentment will build, the flow of information will cease, and productivity will drop.

Mortimer R. Feinberg, chairman of BFS Psychological Associates in New York, notes three situations in which a leader might want to be tough or engender fear or at least a high degree of anxiety among subordinates:

- To enhance performance in an emergency. "When you're under pressure, when you don't want innovative give and take, but rather concentration on detail and thorough execution of routine, use a jolt of fear."
- To clinch a performance review. If the real purpose of a performance review is improvement and performance has been substandard, then managers should not be reluctant to give an objective assessment. But they should also give the employee a way to dispel his or her fear—namely, a plan for improvement.
- To move an employee to seek help with a personal problem. For example, "The fear of getting fired is often the only stimulus that will break through the wall of self-justification the drinker or drug-abuser builds

(continued)

around his problem." The manager who fails to use fear in such a situation, who raises the issue as gently as possible, is not being kind—quite the opposite.

The leader should minimize the negative effects of being tough in two ways. The first is to make the fear situational, not personal, by emphasizing that the employee should be afraid of the consequences of his or her own actions, not of the leader as a person. The second is to offer praise on a job well done when the emergency injection of fear has done its work and the emergency is over.

How to Organize Meaning

When volunteers at the 1984 Olympics revolted over their garish uniforms, Peter Ueberroth, a master of the symbolic jester, rallied the troops by wearing a different uniform each day. When Labor Secretary Elizabeth Dole was featured speaker at the 1990 meeting of the Labor Policy Association, she insisted that the group furnish her with a lectern. At speech time, she walked up to the lectern and asked her hosts to remove it so she could talk to the gathering more personally.

Such actions as these have a particularly startling property: Although they may be the most effective way for changing organizational attitudes in today's environment, they are too trivial to be seriously considered by many managers—one reason, perhaps, why they have not been explored. Furthermore, such symbolic actions carry no guarantee that they will work; they are experimental and imprecise tools at best.

Nonetheless, the capacity to influence and organize meaning through symbols is an essential factor in leadership. Because all organizations depend on the existence of shared meanings and interpretations of reality to facilitate coordinated action, leaders articulate and define what was previously implicit or unsaid. They invent images, metaphors, and models that provide a focus for new attention.

In a basic sense, symbols are the very stuff of leadership. Thomas J. Peters explains:

Executives, after all, do not synthesize chemicals or operate lift trucks; they deal in symbols. And their overt verbal communications are only part of the story. Consciously or unconsciously, the senior executive is constantly acting out the vision and goals he is trying to realize in an organization that is typically far too vast and complex for him to control directly.

What mundane tools might best aid the executive interested in effecting change through symbol manipulation? To signal watchers, which includes nearly everyone in his organization, there is no truer test of what he really thinks is important than the way he spends his time. As Eli Ginsberg and Ewing W. Reilley have noted: "Those a few echelons from the top are always alert to the chief executive. Although they attach importance to what he says, they will be truly impressed only by what he does."

As reported in Chapter 3, Lilienthal created a myth for the TVA around the ideal of grass-roots democracy, which not only rallied the organization's supporters and fended off its opponents but also provided a sense of purpose for those within the organization and gave guidance for the conduct of TVA programs.

How to Listen

The higher one advances in management, the more critical listening abilities become. Poor listeners tend to be poor negotiators because they cannot tune in to what the other person truly wants or might settle for. They leave themselves open to unpleasant surprises. They are poor in crises because, under high stress, even a good listener's system will shut out incoming signals. Yet it is in a crisis that information is most needed.

Listening carefully to subordinates with special expertise—what we termed the monitoring role in Chapter 1—becomes more important the higher the manager rises in the organization simply because there is a wider range of information to be absorbed. To expedite this role, managers should put the subordinate at ease and avoid turning the conversation into an inquisition. Managers should also avoid the tendency to filter information, that is, to hear only what they want to hear. Rather, they should listen carefully, take notes, and try to read between the lines.

Here are additional points that can help one master the art of listening:

- Ask questions—carefully timed, neutral in tone, unloaded—the more open-ended the better. Use questions to draw out the speaker's feelings ("You're pretty upset about this, aren't you?"), though an observation ("I noticed that you're livid with rage") or a reference to your own experience ("Something like that happened to me once.") will serve as well.
- Probe the areas you should be hearing about but are not. Is your subordinate perhaps tiptoeing around an incipient problem? The bad listener assumes that if it is not mentioned, it must be okay. The good listener, sometimes sadder but wiser, knows better.
- Toward the end of the conversation, rehearse for the speaker what you understand him or her to have been saying: "All right, what I hear from you is that . . . ." Rehearse not just the words, but also the emotions behind them. This will provide a check on your internal paraphrase, and a final assurance to the speaker that you really were paying attention. Be open to corrections. Then, once the two of you have got the gist straight, give the listener your considered response.

When to Micromanage

The American culture model of a leader is someone who is really involved, in control. But that type does not always get the most productivity and initiative out of people. President Jimmy Carter would certainly fit this model—his micromanagement extended at one point to scheduling the White House tennis court—but he was not regarded as a particularly effective leader.

The style of Carter's successor, Ronald Reagan, was quite the opposite. Reagan once summed it up this way: "Surround yourself with the best people you can find, delegate authority and don't interfere as long as the overall policy you've set is being carried out." But after the Iran-contra scandal, some might say that the first nine words of that advice should be in italics.

For leaders in important positions, the debate over delegating versus hands-on

(continued)

management is nonsense: They must delegate. Delegating frees them to communicate direction, goals, and enthusiasm. So, the real question is not whether to delegate but *how.*

A leader who delegates as much as Reagan did rises or falls on the quality of the people to whom he or she delegates and on the extent to which he or she holds them accountable. When something does not feel right, the leader must investigate. Thus, leaders need personal ways of staying in touch with their organizations and the outside world. No chain of command can do this for a leader because hierarchies tend to filter out information.

A leader who delegates must insist on accountability and performance review. Some successful delegates rely on tracking systems to follow major initiatives on a regular basis. They also set "boundary conditions," or limits of authority beyond which employees may not go. Reagan created, however, a confusing climate so that his subordinates did not really know what was intended.

Leaders must delegate, but there are situations that require them to get personally and even deeply involved. Such involvement can be the critical factor that gets a reluctant staff moving, or it may be required until subordinates can do the job the way the leader wants it done. But, alas, there is no scientific formula to tell leaders when they are in such situations.

SOURCES: Mortimer R. Feinberg, "When to Engender Fear . . . or at Least a High Degree of Anxiety," *Wall Street Journal,* October 24, 1988; Walter Kiechell, III, "Getting Aggressiveness Right," *Fortune,* May 27, 1985; Paula Bern, "The Art of Listening," *New Woman,* May 1988; Walter Kiechell, III, "Learn How to Listen," *Fortune,* August 17, 1987; Karl E. Weick, *The Social Psychology of Organizing* (Reading, Mass.: Addison-Wesley, 1979); Thomas J. Peters, "Symbols, Patterns, and Settings," *Organizational Dynamics,* Autumn 1978; Tower Commission, *Report of the President's Special Review Board,* February 26, 1987; Robert H. Waterman, *The Renewal Factor* (New York: Bantam Books, 1988); Steven V. Roberts, "Did the Reagan Style of Management Fail Him?" *New York Times,* March 6, 1987; Robert J. Sternberg, *The Triarchic Mind: A New Theory of Human Intelligence* (New York: Viking, 1988), pp. 209–29.

It's in the process: We forgot about it until now.
We'll look into it: Meanwhile you may forget it, too.
Take this up at our next meeting: That will give you time to forget.
Project: A word that makes a minor job seem major.
Under consideration: Never heard about it until now.
Under active consideration: We're trying to locate the correspondence.
We're making a survey: We need more time to think up an answer.
Let's get together on this: You're probably as mixed up as I am.
Note and initial: Let's spread the responsibility.
Forwarded for your consideration: You hold the bag for a while.

(text continues on p. 374)

What Is a Great Communicator?

Early in his administration, the media dubbed Ronald Reagan "the Great Communicator," which suggested a special category of human skill. For Reagan was no *orator;* nor was he a *rhetorician, elocutionist, raconteur, sermonizer,* or *lecturer.* As suggested earlier in this chapter, the term *communication* places more stress on its effect on the listener than do the previous six italicized words and less on just what the speaker is doing. By referring to a "great communicator," we stress the fact that listeners are not just hearing words but appreciating and comprehending them.

Well, even the great communicators misfire sometimes. *The Capitol Hill Weekly* diagrammed the following explanation given by President Reagan when he was asked about his knowledge of certain details of the Iran-contra affair: "Since I was not informed—as a matter of fact, since I did not know that there were any excess funds until we, ourselves, in that checkup after the whole thing blew up, and that was, if you'll remember, that was the incident in which the Attorney General came to me and told me that he had seen a memo that indicated there were more funds." For those who might like to see that sentence diagramed, here is what the rhetoricians at *The Capitol Hill Weekly* came up with:

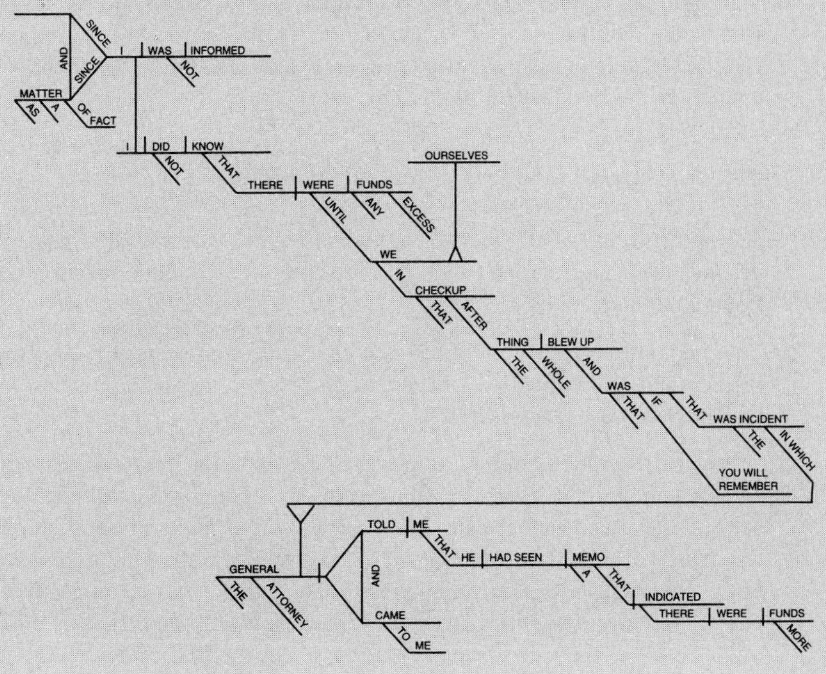

Another reason for gobbledygook is the desire to dress up petty thoughts and make them sound impressive. Since the 1960s, the most popular way of doing this is to use computer jargon. It is really quite easy to do: "Based on integral subsystem considerations, a large portion of the interface coordination communication effects a significant implementation of the preliminary qualification limit."

Missing Opportunity: The Power of Words. The real tragedy of using gobbledygook is the missed opportunity. The right words can spur others to action. An impressive body of research supports the thesis that the quality of one's talk does make a difference in one's success in emerging as a leader (Bass, 1990). This research suggests the following:

1. Getting across the meaning of a message may require the development of innovative approaches. Not only do feelings and ideas need to be communicated, but messages have to be remembered. Memorable messages tend to be brief.
2. Contrary to what one might think, consistency of messages by leaders is not crucial. Their influence depends on their status rather than on the consistency of their statements. Changing opinions several times during a discussion does not appear to harm a leader's influence.
3. The timing of a statement makes a difference in a leader's influence. Those who stated their opinions either early in a discussion or late in a discussion were better able to have their opinion accepted than those who stated their opinion in the middle of a discussion.
4. Style also influences the effectiveness of managers. It is particularly important for managers to be seen as trustworthy and highly informative. Trustworthiness or credibility, in turn, depends on being a careful listener and on being informal and open in two-way conversations. Informativeness depends on being seen as a careful transmitter of information and on using frank communications.
5. The medium affects the message. Stationery and signatures still have more impact than electronic mail and faxes. Who would frame a computer-mailed printout (Falvey, 1989)?
6. Linguistic *form* may be more important than linguistic substance in influencing a subordinate's behavior. For example, some forms can suppress the subordinate's tendency to calculate the costs and benefits of carrying out the request. He or she may comply without thinking about the cost when told, "We've just got a last-minute rush report that needs to be completed before we leave tonight." (The semantically direct, "Complete this report," might result in the subordinate's thinking about the cost of compliance and desiring an inducement for doing so.) The leader's language can also be

palliative. For example, a staff manager, with no way of rewarding line employees for information she requires, may get the information by putting her request in this form: "This won't take long, but can you locate some good cost estimates for . . .?"

7. Electronic mail and other modern communications technology, which provide every employee instant communication with every other employee's personal computer terminal, suggest to some that the quality of writing will regain the status it had before the telephone. (Thomas Jefferson is reported to have written more than 55,000 letters during his presidency.) But others fear that this impressive technology may, in the long run, cripple the ability of modern managers to communicate directly, clearly, and truthfully their thoughts to employees.

The spreadsheet has replaced the well-reasoned report as the medium of communication. Instead of conclusions and support reasoning, we get data. To be able to write down an idea in a couple of complete sentences is a dying art. To be able to illustrate that idea with some easily understood examples is beyond most managers. To be able to make step-by-step recommendations as to how to implement the idea is rarer yet. Taking the charts and graphs generated on a computer and printing them in a report is no substitute for the text they have replaced. (Falvey, 1989)

Making Wrong Assumptions. Another communication mistake is to assume that only words convey messages. Most managers are astonished to learn just how much communication is not verbal; major parts of the shared understanding come from the nonverbal messages of facial expression, voice, manner, posture, and dress. One study found the relative weights of spoken words, voice (pitch, tone, and timbre), and facial expressions to be 7 percent, 38 percent, and 55 percent, respectively (Mehrabian, 1971).

The implications of this research are obvious when a manager must decide whether to send a written or oral message. Both types of messages have their advantages and disadvantages. Written messages, for example, can be retained as permanent references to work from and guide action during implementation. Additionally, they have the advantage of providing a legal record, although, over time, the retention of voluminous written communications can be very expensive. As a general rule, memos should be used as seldom as possible and then only to remind, clarify, or confirm.

Of paramount importance in the use of the written message are clarity and simplicity. To ensure that messages leaving his headquarters met this dual standard, Napoleon, it is said, kept on his staff an exceptionally ungifted captain. The officer's responsibility was to read all outgoing messages; if he was able to understand them, then presumably no officer in the Grande Armée would have any difficulty. While it is unlikely that any agency head today could get such a position authorized, one can at least try to keep the reader in mind when drafting a memorandum.

Even then, the reader may still be uncertain as to the writer's fine meaning. Tone and nuance are not easily put into words. Accordingly, in certain instances, oral communication is preferable.

The biggest advantage of oral over written communication, at least during implementation, is that it is two-way. When the speaker's message creates ambiguity, the listener can ask follow-up questions (such as, "As I understand it, you mean so and so?"). At the same time the supervisor has the opportunity to *receive* as well as impart information.

One final point is closely related to oral communication: The importance of on-site inspections by top management during the management of a program is hard to overemphasize. If we suffer from armchair generals, then surely we can suffer too from armchair administrators. People in top positions tend to forget Gray's Law of Bilateral Asymmetry in Networks: "Information flows efficiently through organizations, except that bad news encounters high impedance in flowing upward" (quoted in Dickinson, 1978:74).

The role of the supervisor during one-on-one conversations is to facilitate the subordinate's expression of the situation or problem. One way to accomplish this is to always *ask one more question:* "When the supervisor thinks the subordinate has said all he wants to about a subject, he should ask another question. He should try to keep the flow of thoughts coming by prompting the subordinate with queries until *both* feel satisfied that they have gotten to the bottom of a problem" (Grove, 1983:76).

During face-to-face encounters, the listener must resist the tendency to evaluate communication prematurely. According to Rogers and Roethlisberger (1952), those who would communicate should be listened to in noncommittal, unprejudiced fashion and thus be encouraged to state their full position before response is generated. Halberstam (1969:305–6) reports that this dictum was repeatedly ignored during the American involvement in Vietnam. For example, during his on-site visit, McNamara, then secretary of defense, tended to look for the war

> *to fit his criteria, his definitions. He went to Danang in 1965 to check on the marine progress there. A marine colonel in I Corps had a sand table showing the terrain and patiently gave the briefing: friendly situation, enemy situation, main problem. McNamara watched it, not really taking it in, his hands folded, frowning a little, finally interrupting. "Now, let me see," McNamara said, "if I have it right, this is your situation," and then he spouted his own version, all in numbers and statistics. The colonel, who was very bright, read him immediately like a man breaking a code, and without changing stride, went on with the briefing, simply switching his terms, quantifying everything, giving everything in numbers and percentages, percentages up, percentages down, so blatant a performance that it was like a satire. Jack Raymond of the* New York Times *began to laugh and had to leave the tent. Later that day Raymond went up to McNamara and commented on how tough the situation was in Danang, but McNamara wasn't interested in the Vietcong, he wanted to talk about the colonel, he liked him, that colonel had caught his eye. "That colonel is one of the finest officers I've met," he said.*

Open Communication and Organizational Innovation

Another aspect of management communication concerns the organization as a whole. Organizationwide communications typically flow in three dimensions—downward, upward, and horizontally. Innovative managers agree that the most common roadblock they have to overcome is poor communication with other departments on whom they depend for information. A communication system, depending on the kind adopted by a given organization, can either constrain or empower the effort to innovate. (The following discussion is based on Kanter, 1989.)

The most innovative organizations generally encourage face-to-face information sharing in real time (i.e., at the moment the issue comes up). Open communication systems in these organizations stress *access across segments.* Open-door policies mean that all levels can, theoretically, have access to anyone to ask questions and even to criticize. Some organizations even have a policy that all meetings are open, that anyone may attend any meeting. Such norms acknowledge the extent of interdependence—that people in all areas need information from each other.

Physical arrangements in such organizations also reflect openness. There are few private offices, and those that do exist are not very private. Indeed, employees often go to the library or conference room to hide to get things done, especially sensitive matters like budgets. Lack of reliance on support staffs for message taking and typing also facilitate open organization.

Open communication may also mean that public punishments occur when people *fail* to communicate or when they hoard information. For example, a manager might create brochures for his unit and produce them without consulting other members of the agency. The brochure might be beautiful but out of sync with agency standards. As a warning to others, the agency head might then call the manager to account in front of his peers and upper-level managers and freeze his resources.

There are two problems with open communication that middle managers frequently encounter. The first is obvious: overload. Inessential communication is simply cast upon the organization rather than targeted only to people who should get it; meetings are held when memos would do; and so forth. The other problem is less obvious: underload. The very existence of an open communication system can encourage people to think that everyone knows everything. So people will either fail to pass something on (on the assumption it is known already) or take as truth authoritative-sounding misinformation passed on through informal channels.

Managing Organizational Groups

This final section looks at groups from a managerial point of view. It focuses on the features of group behavior important to the manager who wants to understand how to manage a group for increased effectiveness. It considers what factors influence the patterns of behavior in a group and how these patterns affect the performance of a group.

Work groups can be a crucial link between the individual and the larger organization—the place where the individual finds fulfillment and friendship and protection from the uncertainty and impersonality of the organization. Yet complaints like the following are common: "What a day I had . . . a complete waste of time. I spent three hours with the Community Mental Health Board and then two hours with the assistant commissioner of hospitals and her staff trying to decide what to do about our affiliation contract. Then I spent the lunch hour with the site visit team . . . then an hour mediating between the service group and the teaching group about a program,

"Mr. Smith's office doesn't have a door. You have to batter your way through the wall."

According to Kanter (1989), the most innovative organizations encourage face-to-face information sharing in real time. Open communication systems allow all levels to have access to anyone to ask questions. Less innovative organizations may have different norms. (Drawing by Gahan Wilson; © 1991 The New Yorker Magazine, Inc.)

and on, and on, and on." Therefore, throughout this section, we will be concerned with what managers need to know in order to avoid this kind of trap and to participate effectively in, as well as lead, work groups.

Stages of Group Development

A group can be defined as two or more people who interact regularly to accomplish some goal. Typically, groups go through a period of evolution or development. Although there is no rigid pattern that all groups follow, they usually go through four stages:

1. The first stage is **forming.** As the term itself suggests, members of the group get acquainted and begin to test which behaviors are acceptable and which are unacceptable to other members of the group.
2. During the **storming** stage, members begin to disagree about what needs to be done and how best to do it. Conflict and hostility characterize this stage. Unless the group moves beyond this stage, and some do not, it will never become a high-performance team. The leader should encourage participation by each member.
3. During the **norming** stage, conflict is resolved and harmony emerges. Each member takes on certain responsibilities, and everyone develops a common vision of how the group will function. During this period, the leader should emphasize oneness within the group and help clarify group norms and values.
4. Finally, the group begins **performing;** that is, moving toward the accomplishment of its goals. Group members confront and resolve problems in the interest of task accomplishment.

One of the most famous and powerful working groups in government today is the seven-member Federal Reserve Board, which controls the nation's money supply. What happened there in 1986 nicely illustrates our four-stage model. Paul Volcker, chairman of the group from 1979 to 1987, had a single goal: to stop inflation. Group members agreed with Volcker's direction until four new members were appointed by President Reagan. The new members believed that faster growth in the economy was possible without reviving inflation and that money was too tight and interest rates must be reduced. Volcker, who had had his way on almost every decision up until this time, now found himself with what was, essentially, a new group.

During the forming stage, Chairman Volcker failed to detect the intense concerns of his new colleagues on the board. The world economy was slowing down and, if the board did not act quickly to stimulate the U.S. economy, continued high interest rates could push it into recession. It was clear at the board's meeting on February 24, that the group had entered its storming stage. After heated debate, Volcker was handed his first recorded defeat as chairman, 4 to 3. Obviously, he had lost control of the group.

Volcker was furious afterwards. He talked about resigning immediately. Still upset, he went to a scheduled luncheon with then–treasury secretary, James Baker. Counseling compromise, Baker discreetly persuaded Volcker to remain as chairman. Volcker did, but the norms of the group had changed from what they had been for almost seven years. "Instead of being the dominating authority, he was now compelled to be more collegial. Instead of the 'System men' who had surrounded him at the board table, . . . he now faced colleagues who were outsiders—less in awe of the institution's folklore and also decidedly different in their perspective on political economy" (Greider, 1989:701).

As the members continued to work together, conflict receded and mutual understanding grew. Volcker found that establishing a good working relationship with the new members needed just a little time. He showed more tolerance for dissent, and his former opponents began to appreciate his view.

Since all organizations contain groups, managers need to learn, as Volcker certainly did, how groups should be managed. Below we will consider the management of four types of groups: functional group, task force, committee, and decision-making group.

Functional Groups

We begin with the most obvious of groups: the manager and his or her subordinates in the formal chain of command. Thus, a functional group represents a specific department or work unit in the organization. The second shift nursing group on the third floor of Jackson County Hospital is a functional group working under a nursing supervisor. Since virtually all aspects of interaction between a formal leader and his and her work group are related to the management of functional groups, all areas of management covered in this chapter are pertinent. Several specific implications can be drawn, however, from our earlier discussion of the stages of group development.

Managers should work to establish high-performance **norms,** that is, the expectations and guidelines that are shared by group members for how members should behave. Norms serve an important function for group members in stabilizing their interactions along predictable paths. So when a manager decides that some norms are blocking group effectiveness, he or she must examine the purpose the norms serve before attempting to change them.

Managers should also recognize the potential problems associated with **roles;** that is, the characteristics and expected social behavior of an individual. Roles may develop so that in addition to the formally appointed leader of a group, one or more *informal leaders* may arise as well. Recall the revolt Volcker faced at the Federal Reserve. The informal leader of that 1986 revolt was Wayne Angell, a Kansas banker and wheat farmer. Another role is *social deviant*—a person unwilling to follow an important norm of the group. Carried further, a member who fails to follow several norms of a group where other members are less tolerant, may become a *social isolate.* Roles such as these are often helpful in defining what the norms are in a group. At one end of the continuum, formal leaders are likely to adhere closely to group norms; at the other extreme, social isolates violate some and perhaps many of the group norms.

People in a group develop patterns of behavior that contribute to or detract from the functional group's ability to achieve its mission. You have probably been in a group where one person consistently cracked jokes to break tensions and reharmonize relationships, or where someone supplied technical information, or where someone kept an eye on the clock or calendar and made sure the group stuck to its agenda and made its deadline.

Finally, the manager needs to realize the importance of **group cohesiveness;** that is, the extent to which group members are attracted to the group and its mission and motivated to remain in it. At least five factors foster cohesiveness:

1. *Interaction:* The more people are together, the more cohesive will be the group.
2. *Shared goals:* If the group members agree on goals, the group will be more cohesive.
3. *Personal attraction:* When members have similar attitudes and values, they enjoy being together.
4. *Competition:* Competing with other groups helps cohesiveness.
5. *Success:* Winning and praise from outsiders builds cohesiveness.

Task Forces

Not long ago U.S. Customs Service agents seized a fishing boat returning to Miami from the Bahamas. The "fishermen" seemed unusual: One wore a Pierre Cardin pullover, and the other, a Sassoon jacket. Under a concealed floor the agents found 1,000 pounds of marijuana. The agents were part of the South Florida Task Force, a group made up of elements not only from the Customs Service (drawn from cities across the country) but also from the army, the navy, the air force, the coast guard, the FBI, and the DEA.

Now let us travel northeast from the sunny shores of Miami to the wild lands of the Northern Rockies, where more than 15,000 people from the Forest Service, the Bureau of Land Management, the National Park Service, the Bureau of Indian Affairs, the army, and numerous state and local agencies have formed a task force to battle fires. In the past, the Forest Service had one person in charge, a fire boss, whose single task was to put out the blaze. Other tasks, such as conducting evacuations, repairing environmental damage, or even protecting homes (instead of trees) from fire, fell haphazardly to other agencies and people. Under the new arrangement, the people in charge are called the incident commanders.

The responsibility of the incident commanders extends to such detailed questions as whether fire-fighting teams are draining local supermarkets of hand soap so that residents cannot buy any. To handle such tasks, each commander is assigned a team that stays together throughout the fire season. Each team has members in charge of specialties such as managing aircraft, figuring payrolls, or devising firefighting strat-

Talking Shop

How to Manage a Task Force

Starting Up the Task Force

The task force leader should meet as early as practicable with the upper-level management group that established the task force. The purpose of this critical, early meeting is to discuss the group's objectives. Is the objective to investigate a poorly understood problem or to recommend a solution to an obvious one? Or is the objective to respond to a crisis caused by a sudden change in the organization's environment?

In recent years we have had a Needs Analysis Task Force, a Tylenol Task Force, a Task Force on Inflation, and an Emergency Task Force on Utility Shutoffs. Some are getting quite specialized: the United Methodist Task Force on Language Guidelines, for instance, or the Milwaukee Common Council Task Force on Sexual Assault and Domestic Violence.

As the two examples given in the text (involving drug interdiction and fire fighting) illustrate, however, not all task forces are grimly determined groups blasting away with a 131-page report; the mission of many can be *action-oriented.* Perhaps the task force also has secondary objectives such as gaining commitment to a decision by involving the people who will be affected by its implementation or developing managers by exposing them to people from other functional areas of the organization. The task force leader may, at this time, wish to define alternative purposes. It may help for the leader to write out a statement of what he or she perceives to be the group's mission; this statement can then serve as the basis for discussion with senior officials.

The mission, however, is not the only thing that calls for early clarification. General operating procedures regarding deadlines, budgeting, personnel (full- or part-time?), information flows, and decision-making authority should also be clarified.

Finally, the leaders should speak with, preferably face-to-face, the individuals who might serve on the task force. Do they have the necessary knowledge, interest, time, and interpersonal skills to make the task force a success?

Conducting the First Meeting

Once mission, procedures, and personnel have been clarified, the leader should begin to prepare for the first meeting. It is important to keep three objectives in mind. First, because it is probably the first time all members will be together, the pattern of interaction begun here will set the tone for all subsequent encounters. Second, and most important, is to reach a common understanding of the group's mission. Everyone must be "reading from the same sheet of music." Third, explicit

egies. The team's members are drawn from state, local, and federal agencies (Manning, 1989).

Governments establish task forces like the two just cited to work on problems and projects that cannot be easily handled by a regular functional organization that attention should be given to the group's working procedures and relationships. How often will it meet? Is it big enough to organize into subgroups? How do members communicate between meetings? What will be the ground rules (norms) for making decisions, resolving conflicts, and handling sensitive issues (e.g., turf)? How will progress be monitored and reported?

Running the Task Force

Although specific circumstances will vary, here are some general principles to keep the project moving forward. The leader should do the following:

- Hold full task force meetings frequently enough to keep all members informed about group progress.
- Avoid aligning himself or herself too closely with one position or subgroup too early.
- Recognize the conflicting loyalties created by the members participating in the task force while they are still connected to their "home" departments.
- Communicate information among task force members and between the task force and the rest of the organization.

Completing the Project

As suggested earlier, the work of many task forces culminates with a written report. But the report's importance lies in the decision-making process it generates.

A tentative outline of this report should be prepared as early as practicable and circulated among group members. This outline can serve as a guide to the development of drafts of specific recommendations. These drafts, in turn, become the basis for working out differences among members.

Before the formal presentation of the report, the leader should brief key executives. In preparing the formal presentation at which the report is released, careful attention should be given to speakers, to their sequence, to audiovisual aids, and to other such details. For example, when the McDonald's Corporation released in 1991 its task force report on waste reduction, it made sure that the report was printed on recycled paper.

At the end of the formal presentation, it might be a good idea to schedule a second, *decision-making,* meeting. Executives can use the time between these two meetings to read the report, consider its implications, and solicit further classification from task force members.

SOURCE: For a fuller discussion of these suggestions, see James Ware, *Some Aspects of Problem Solving and Conflict Resolution in Management Groups,* 9-479-003 (Cambridge, Mass.: Harvard Business School, 1977).

might be found in the Customs Service and the Forest Service. A task force can be a powerful management tool for resolving complex and challenging problems such as international drug traffic or raging forest fires. It is equally effective for dealing with more mundane problems such as overhead cost reduction.

Several factors contribute to the strength of this type of group: It is task oriented; it possesses a diversity of skills; and it rarely contains any "deadwood" because group members are selected on the basis of competence relative to the problem.

Having opted for the task force device, the administrator should be aware of the special sources of trouble associated with this organizational form. Many task force leaders find that their working relationships with other agency heads have not been clearly defined by the top-level political executives. Although political executives can seldom give the leader as much guidance and support as he or she might wish, they can easily jeopardize the task force's success by lack of awareness, ill-advised intervention, or personal whim. Further, there are innumerable possibilities for interagency conflict. Finally, the severe penalties of delay in resolving the problem often compel the task force leaders to base their decisions on relatively few data, analyzed in haste.

These problems, however, are hardly insurmountable. Moreover, as long as administrators must face unfamiliar and complex problems, it seems safe to say that the task force form of organization will be a part of public administration for some time to come.

Clearly, the success of a task force's effort depends heavily on the way its activities are managed. The Talking Shop suggests a number of useful operating guidelines for increasing the effectiveness of this type of group.

Meetings

Compared to the term *task force,* the word *committee* sounds dull. Most managers make it a point of honor to dislike meetings. Some would probably agree with Henrik Ibsen's observation that "when the devil decided that nothing should be done, he decided to create the first committee."

Yet the cold reality is that managers live in a swirl of meetings. According to one survey, the average manager spends the equivalent of 21 work weeks in meetings inside and outside the office (Hymowitz, 1989). Some spend up to 70 percent of their time in meetings. Unfortunately, most public administrators have no formal training in how to plan, run, or participate in a meeting, which probably helps explain why so many view meetings as unnecessary or unproductive. Handled properly, meetings represent probably the single most efficient mechanism to solve a problem or make a decision, when information on the matter at hand exists here and there throughout the organization and everyone will have to get behind the outcome. For the savvy subordinate, meetings also provide an uncommon chance to demonstrate one's talents to more senior officials. Let us look first at how to run a meeting and then at how to participate in one.

Wisdom in this sphere begins with asking a simple question: Is this gathering really necessary? If, as suggested above, the aim is to decide something beyond the capacity or authority of any one person, then the answer is in the affirmative. But if the reason is simply to disseminate information ("All right, you people, listen up"), and there is no serious need for questions afterwards, then the meeting is probably unnecessary. Use the phone or a memo.

The catchy term "task force" was born with the dramatic success of the U.S. Navy in World War II. Because it suggested bold action—producing visions of mighty aircraft carriers and supporting flotillas splashing through seas in pursuit of some challenging objective—it was not surprising that bureaucrats and politicians would soon adopt it. The current popularity of "task forces" may have even contributed to the faded (perhaps tarnished) reputation of "committees." (Photo by AP/Wide World)

When a meeting is necessary, the convener should draw up an agenda and circulate it well in advance—two days beforehand, at a minimum. A list of attendees should accompany the agenda; it may affect how people prepare. ("Them again? Uh oh. I better have all my ducks in a row for this meeting.")

Having the right people present does not mean just including those who are needed but also excluding those who are deadweight. A study by Robert Sternberg (1988) shows that the most effective groups have a balance among group members of intelligence, on the one hand, and social abilities, on the other. A group strong in either intelligence alone or affability alone, Sternberg finds, is handicapped.

Ideally, the meeting itself begins with a three- to five-minute orientation speech. The convener covers the following: goal of the meeting and procedures to follow; history of the problem and its likely consequences; range of possible solutions and constraints that any solution must fit; addition or deletion to agenda (if any); and appointment of a recorder. Then the convener says as little as possible for the rest of the meeting—intervening only to keep the discussion on track and as intelligent as possible.

Rather than vote for a formal ratification, the convener might say something like, "We seem to have agreed on this, this, and this. Is everyone on the bus?" Then the convener looks for nodding heads. In wrapping up, the convener states who specifically will do what and confirms that a report of the meeting will be circulated.

Participants, too, need to do their homework before the meeting, think of the points they wish to make, and gather evidence to support them. Participants are also advised to arrive a few minutes early. According to social psychologists, the more time a groups' members spend getting comfortable with each other (joking, etc.), the more likely the meeting is to be productive and the members, as individuals, to be effective.

Once the meeting begins, participants should listen carefully and then pick the right moment to make their points. This is a little like jumping aboard a moving train. Jump too soon, and the train may run over you; jump too late, and you will miss it. When effective participants do present their ideas, they tend to do it in crisp, declarative sentences that quickly summarize their evidence. The more they present their solutions as an outgrowth of the discussion—as something the others have helped them see and may now help refine, rather than as a stroke of solitary genius—the more likely they are to persuade.

The Enduring Importance of Leaders and Leadership

Critics complain that leadership is fundamentally antidemocratic. Nonetheless, throughout history, few subjects have proven more fascinating than leadership. As James MacGregor Burns (1978:2) wrote, "Leadership is one of the most observed . . . phenomena on earth." The reason is clear. In every time and place, leaders have made a difference—they have had an impact on public affairs. The men and women who seek to lead—and not just administer—do not shrink from the problems, failures, and battles that they surely will face. As Theodore Roosevelt put it in a speech at the Sorbonne in 1910, leaders are the ones who are willing to enter the arena:

It is not the critic who counts; not the man who points out how the strong man stumbles, or where the doer of deeds could have done them better. The credit belongs to the man who is actually in the arena, whose face is marred by dust and sweat and blood; who strives valiantly; who errs, and comes short again and again; because there is not effort without error and short-coming; but who does actually strive to do the deeds; who knows the great enthusiasms, the great devotions; who spends himself in a worthy cause, who at the best knows in the end the triumphs of high achievement and who at the worst, if he fails, at least fails while daring greatly, so that his place shall never be with those cold and timid souls who know neither victory nor defeat.

Concepts for Review

- basic leadership styles
- communication
- contingency approach
- forming, storming, norming, performing
- functional groups
- gobbledygook
- group cohesiveness
- groupthink
- Hawthorne studies
- job satisfiers and dissatisfiers
- leadership
- Maslow's hierarchy of needs
- motivation
- norms
- organizational development (see problem 6)
- roles
- stages of group development
- task behavior, relationship behavior
- task force
- Theory X and Theory Y
- trait approach to leadership

Nailing Down the Main Points

1. Management is a team activity. The performance of an administrator is inextricably linked to the output of his or her employees.

2. In the past, a popular approach to the study of leadership was to list traits. Unfortunately, this approach leaves little room for considering such important variables as the maturity of the followers and the nature of the situation.

   Thus, the contingency approach to leadership tells us that the appropriate style will depend on the personality of the leader, the maturity of the followers, and the nature of the situation. A useful way of classifying leadership styles is in terms of the relative emphasis the leader places on tasks and on people.

3. Because of its profound influence on employee performance, motivation is a subject that no manager can afford to ignore. In this century, the behavioral sciences have helped to expand the manager's understanding of motivation. First,

the Hawthorne studies revealed that organizational productivity was the result not only of physical condition or monetary rewards (as perhaps Frederick Taylor would have it) but also of interpersonal relationships developed on the job. In particular, the researchers found that when informal groups felt their own goals were in opposition to those of management and their control over their job or environment was slight, productivity remained low. In short, morale affects productivity.

4. In the early 1950s, Abraham Maslow suggested that human motives or needs formed a more complicated pattern than generally thought. Behavior of an individual is actually determined by his or her strongest need; that is, by the need in Maslow's hierarchy that has not been, as yet, satisfied. The managerial implications of Maslow's theory should be made explicit: Determine the employee's strongest need, and design motivational strategies for him or her with that need in mind. Different strokes for different folks, as the colloquial expression has it.

5. According to McGregor, Theory X managers believe that subordinates are uninspired workers who seek to avoid responsibility and work assignments. By contrast, Theory Y managers hold that all subordinates view work as rewarding, if given a chance by management. McGregor thought that management's perception of subordinate behavior played a significant part in determining leadership style.

6. Argyris believes that many modern organizations keep their employees in a dependent state, thus preventing individuals from achieving their full potential.

7. Frederick Herzberg developed another popular theory of motivation called the two-factor theory. His findings suggest that the work characteristics associated with dissatisfaction are quite different from those pertaining to satisfaction.

8. The figure on page 389 shows the relationship between contingency leadership (as discussed in point 2 above) and Maslow's hierarchy of needs (as discussed in point 4), McGregor's Theory X and Theory Y (point 5), Argyris's theory on mature personality and organization (point 6), and Herzberg's motivation-hygiene theory (point 7).

9. Communication takes up 80 percent of a manager's time. Perceptions, communication channels, nonverbal organization, and language and listening skills all affect communications among people in the organization. Innovative organization in particular requires open communication.

10. Organizations use groups (or teams) as part of the formal structure and to encourage employee involvement. Most teams go through systematic stages of development: forming, storming, norming, and performing. Advantages of using teams include increased motivation, diverse knowledge and skills, satisfaction of team members, and organizational flexibility.

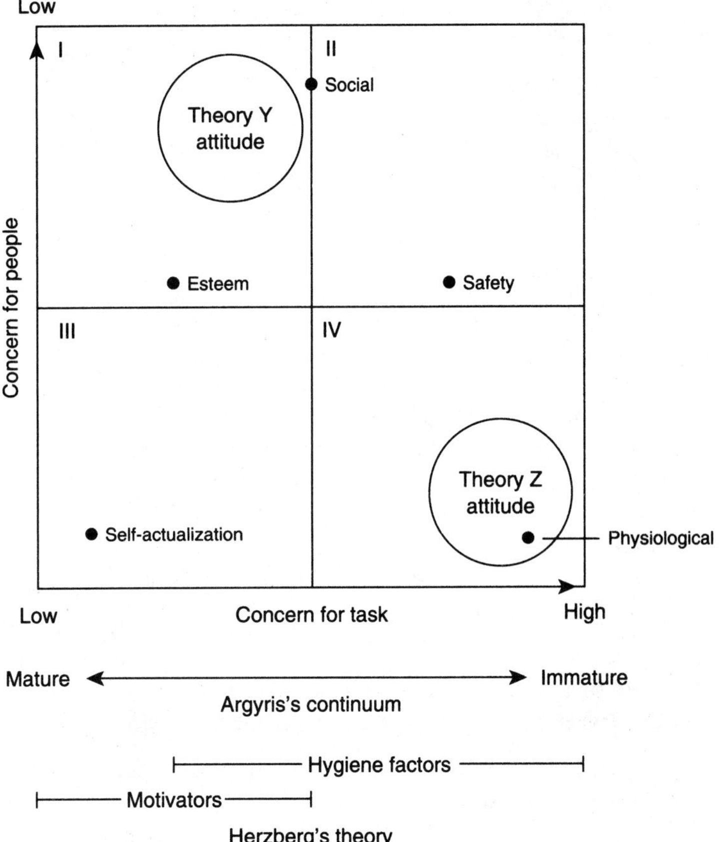

Problems

1. "Most theories about human behavior in organizations say the same thing only with different language." Using only the ideas in this chapter, can you support this assertion?

2. Think of specific ways in which a supervisor could motivate through the prestige needs of employees. Are they meaningful?

3. In terms of Maslow's hierarchy, what motivates you? How would you determine what motivates employees?

4. John Gardner says that when people in even a democratic organization develop sacrosanct rights, the organization itself rigidifies. Indeed, the more democratic an organization is, the more the vested interests of its members will be reflected in its policies. Thus a democratic organization may be especially resistant to

change. Do you agree with this analysis? Can you think of any examples that either prove it or disprove it?

5. Katz and Kahn (1966:302) consider the essence of organizational leadership to be the "influential increment over and above mechanical compliance with the routine directives of the organization." Despite the fact that all supervisors at a given level in the hierarchy are created equal, they do not remain equal. Why? (In thinking through this question, the various sources of power noted at the end of Chapter 2 might prove useful.)

6. In management literature, *organizational change* is defined as change involving some modification in the goals, structure, tasks, people, and technology that constitute the essence of the organization. *Organizational development* is defined as the application of behavioral science knowledge in a long-range effort to improve an organization's ability to cope with change in its external environment and increase its internal problem-solving capabilities.

   Discuss the relevance of Figure 5-3 to these two concepts. How does logical incrementalism help an administrator cope with potential sources of resistance to change such as fear of the unknown, need for security, no felt need to change, vested interests threatened, and contrasting interpretation?

7. A study shows that more than 50 percent of a city's bills are not being paid within 30 days, and some are not being paid within 18 months. As a consequence, most first-rate suppliers do not want to do business with the city. As city manager what do you tell your ten department heads?

8. What, if anything, in this chapter might help to explain the following statement about the boxer Joe Frazier:

   It astounds Joe Frazier that anyone has to ask why he fights. "This is what I do. I am a fighter," he says. "It's my job. I'm just doing my job." Joe doesn't deny the attractiveness of money. "Who wants to work for nothing?" But there are things more important than money. "I don't need to be a star because I don't need to shine. But I do need to be a boxer because that's what I am. It's as simple as that." (Quoted in Grove, 1983:169)

9. For years the performance of a state's facilities maintenance group, which is responsible for keeping government buildings in the state capital clean and neat, was mediocre. No amount of pressure or inducement from the secretary of state, who had ultimate responsibility, seemed to do any good. What recommendations would you make?

10. You receive a rush assignment late on Friday afternoon, requiring that certain difficult engineering drawings be completed as soon as possible. The only employee you feel can do this complex task is independent, outspoken, and adverse to overtime. How do you get this employee to do something above and beyond the explicit duties of the job?

11. Translate the following examples of bureaucratese into plain English. Use no more than seven words for each. (Answers are printed upside down at bottom of page.) The first example is an actual National Park Service regulation; the second is provided by John O. Morris, a Huntford lawyer.

*a. "No person shall prune, cut, carry away, pull up, dig, fell, bore, chop, saw, chip, pick, move, sever, climb, molest, take, break, deface, destroy, set fire to, burn, scorch, carve, paint, mark, or in any manner interfere with, tamper, mutilate, misuse, disturb, or damage any tree, shrub, plant, grass, flower, or any part thereof, nor shall any person permit any chemical, whether solid, fluid or gaseous, to seep, drip, drain, or be emptied, sprayed, dusted on, injected upon, about or into any tree, shrub, plant, grass, flower."

*b. "We respectfully petition, request, and entreat that due and adequate provision be made, this day and the date hereinafter subscribed, for the satisfying of these petitioners' nutritional requirements and for the organizing of such methods of allocation and distribution as may be deemed necessary and proper to assure the reception by and for said petitioners of such quantities of baked cereal products as shall, in the judgment of the aforesaid petitioners, constitute a sufficient supply thereof."

12. Here is another translation exercise. Find respectable substitutes for this jargon that often clutters up writing and conversation in the administrative world.

ballpark	optimize
bottom line	at this point in time
game plan	due to the fact that
interface	parameter

Two of these terms, *optimize* and *parameter,* are correct under certain circumstances. What are they?

13. "I am a great believer, if you have a meeting, in knowing where you want to come out before you start the meeting." Discuss.

* Answers: (a) Do not hurt the plants, and (b) Give us this day our daily bread.

CASE 8.1

★★★★★★★★★★★★★★★★★★★★★★★★★★★★★★★★★★★★

Sanitation Workers at the Gate

Centerville is a beautiful, peaceful, but rapidly growing town in the heart of the Sun Belt. One winter day, Roland Jackson, B.S. (psychology), M.P.A., an assistant city manager of a large midwestern town, decided he would answer an ad for a new city manager in Centerville. The city council liked him, and he liked what he saw of the town.

At 8:10 A.M. on his tenth day at the helm, his intercom bleeped. In hushed tones, his secretary said, "Mr. Jackson, there are five garbage collectors here demanding to see you. They seem angry."

Jackson had a crowded schedule that day and was six organizational levels removed from a sanitation worker, but he told his secretary to send them in. He believed in an open-door policy.

Sanitation workers were the lowest-paid and least-skilled workers on the city's payroll. Their occupation, as most people know, involves hard, dirty work in all kinds of weather. The five, who were all black, wished to complain that their supervisor, who was white, always assigned them to the toughest routes and never allowed them to drive the truck. They wanted that changed, pronto.

Jackson was obviously in a tough position. The grievance had clear racial overtones and could escalate. Yet he did not want to undermine the authority of all those managers and supervisors that stood between him and the five angry men seated across from him. Nor could he afford to offend the union that purported to represent these workers. These workers had gone out of channels in more ways than one.

Case Question

You are Jackson. It is now 8:12 A.M. How do you play it?

CASE 8.2

★★★★★★★★★★★★★★★★★★★★★★★★★★★★★★★★★★★★

Fred the Great

Fred Pfeifer has planned a special meeting with Dan Rodriguez, director of the Bureau of Intelligence and Research. The bureau, which Dan heads, coordinates programs of intelligence, research, and analysis for the U.S. Department of State and other federal agencies. It also produces intelligence studies and current intelligence analyses essential to foreign policy determination and execution.

Dan seldom deals directly with Fred Pfeifer, who is two levels below him on the bureau's organization chart. Fred's immediate supervisor is Lloyd Briggs. In Fred's view, Lloyd fits the image of the State Department well: clubby, establishmentarian, all-white, all-male. Fred is convinced there still exists an "old-boy" network within the department, spawned in upper-crust universities and maintained in mahogany-paneled men's clubs along the East Coast.

Fred believes that Dan respects him. They are, after all, very much alike: hard-driving young men, endowed with quicksilver minds, and outside the "network."

What motivates Fred? Like other public administrators, he wants a good income and job security; but unlike some, he is motivated by work itself. Unless there is a challenge, a variety of problems, he gets too relaxed. He played football in high school and intramural sports in college; he likes to take risks and is fascinated by new techniques and methods.

Fred is also a highly paradoxical man: cooperative but competitive; detached and playful but compulsively driven to succeed; a team player who would be a superstar; a team leader but a rebel against bureaucracy; fair but contemptuous of "losers" (his term). He does not want to build an empire, but he does enjoy running things well. He was the driving force in getting a state-of-the-art decision support system installed in the bureau. As Lloyd once joked, "There are two kinds of people in my shop—first are those who do not understand that damn system, and then there is Fred Pfeifer."

Because of an exceptionally high score on the foreign service examination, Fred was pretty much able to choose his field of work. Thus, he avoided the consular career path; stamping foreigners' visas and listening to the complaints of distraught American travelers would have been a dispiriting grind for him. He likes to be where the action is, at the center.

Even a person as gifted as Fred imagines himself in an unreal, romantic fantasy. Ignoring the fact that he seldom leaves the comfortable surroundings of Washington, D.C., he once told a colleague that he is like "the cowboy entering a village alone on his horse. Without even a pistol—just armed with his machete of wit." Although that quip got around the office and caused much laughter, Fred did not bother to take down the Clint Eastwood poster some wiseacre had hung on his office door.

Some of the people on his staff have trouble making sense of Fred's metaphors. He speaks of the "game plan," of making "the big play," of "going to have to punt," and of "trying an end around." His staff meetings have a locker-room atmosphere, where discussion of operations is punctuated with detached, mildly sadistic humor. As he once told Lloyd, "The superior has to keep the inferior in his place." He is neither bigoted nor hostile—just insensitive.

Today, as his meeting with Dan Rodriguez begins, Fred is the steely-eyed cowboy, playing for high stakes. As always his approach is direct.

"Dan, I've been here two years, and I think you know what I can do." He pauses momentarily, allowing for an obligatory nod. "Well, I've also had a chance to observe Lloyd closely. It is my considered opinion that he does nothing for the bureau. If this were the Bureau of Pinecones and Squirrels, or something like that, it wouldn't matter, but as you well know, we are involved here in deadly serious business. Lloyd is a likable loser and ought to go."

Not allowing Dan to respond, Fred reveals his plan. "I think it is time that the performers were recognized and the deadwood eliminated. I've always felt I must either move up the ladder or quit. I hope you agree."

Case Questions

1. What is the problem here?
2. What are Dan's options?
3. What course of action would you recommend Dan take?

CASE 8.3

★★★★★★★★★★★★★★★★★★★★★★★★★★★★★★★★★★★

Diane Wilson and Steve Carmichael

Diane Wilson is an Office of Economic Opportunity clerk who processes grants to organizations for the poor. She speaks: "Life is a funny thing. We had this boss come in from Internal Revenue. He wanted to be very, very strict. He used to have meetings every Friday—about people comin' in late, people leavin' early, people abusin' lunch time. Everyone was used to this relaxed attitude. You kind of went overtime. No one bothered you. The old boss went along. You did your work.

"Every Friday, everyone would sit there and listen to this man. And we'd all go out and do the same thing again. Next Friday he'd have another meeting and he would tell us the same thing. (Laughs.) We'd all go out and do the same thing again. (Laughs.) He would try to talk to one and see what they'd say about the other. But we'd been working all together for quite a while. You know how the game is played. Tomorrow you might need a favor. So nobody would say anything. If he'd want to find out what time someone come in, who's gonna tell 'em? He'd want to find out where someone was, we'd always say, 'They're at the Xerox.' Just anywhere. He couldn't get through. Now, lo and behold! We can't find him anywhere. He's got into this nice, relaxed atmosphere. . . . (Laughs.) He leaves early, he takes long lunch hours. We've converted him. (Laughs.)

"We had another boss, he would walk around and he wouldn't want to see you idle at all. Sometimes you're gonna have a lag in your work, you're all caught up. This had gotten on his nerves. We got promotion and we weren't continually busy. Anytime they see black women idle, that irks 'em. I'm talkin' about black men as well as whites . . .

"One day I'd gotten a call to go to his office and do some typing. He'd given me this handwritten script. I don't know to this day what all that stuff was. I asked him 'Why was I picked for this job?' He said his secretary was out and he needs this done by noon. I said, 'I can't read this stuff.' He tells me he'll read it. I said, 'Okay, I'll write it out as you read it.' There's his hand going all over the script, busy. He doesn't know what he's readin'. I could tell. I know why he's doing it. He just wants to see me busy.

"So we finished the first long sheet. He wants to continue. I said, No, I can only do one sheet at a time. I'll go over and type this up. So what I did, I would type a paragraph and wait five or ten minutes. I made sure I made all the mistakes I could. . . .

"I took him back this first sheet and, of course, I had left out a line or two. I told him it made me nervous to have this typed by a certain time, and I didn't have time to proofread it, 'but I'm ready for you to read the other sheet to me.' He started to proofread. I deliberately misspelled some words. Oh, I did it up beautifully. (Laughs.) He got the dictionary out and he looked up the words for me. I took it back and crossed out the words and squeezed the new ones in there. He started on the next sheet. I did the same thing all over again.

"I'm gonna see what he does if I don't finish it on time. Oh, it was imperative! I knew the world's not gonna change that quickly. It was nice outside. If it gets to be a problem, I'll go home. It's a beautiful day, the heck with it. So 12:30 comes and the work just looks awful. (Laughs.) I typed on all the lines, I continued it anywhere. One of the girls comes over, she says, 'You're goin' off the line.' I said, 'Oh, be quiet. I know what I'm doin'. (Laughs.) 'Just go away.' I put the four sheets together. I never saw anything as horrible in my life. (Laughs.)

"I decided I'd write him a note. 'Dear Mr. Roberts: You've been so much help. You proofread, you look up words for your secretary. It must be marvelous working for you. I hope this has met with your approval. Please call on me again.' I never heard from him." (A long laugh.)

Steve Carmichael is a twenty-five year old project manager for the Neighborhood Youth Corps. "I doubt seriously if three years from now I'll be involved in public administration. One reason is each day I find myself more and more like unto the people I wanted to replace.

"I'll run into one administrator and try to institute a change and then I'll go to someone else and connive to get the change. Gradually your effectiveness wears down. Pretty soon you no longer identify as the bright guy with the ideas. You become the fly in the ointment. You're criticized by your superiors and subordinates. Not in a direct manner. Indirectly, by being ignored. They say I'm unrealistic.

"The most frustrating thing for me is to know that what I'm doing does not have a positive impact on others. I don't see this work as meaning anything. I now treat my job disdainfully. The status of my job is totally internal: Who's your friend? Can you walk into this person's office and call him by his first name? It carries very little status to strangers who don't understand the job. People within the agency don't understand it. (Laughs.)

"Success is to be in a position where I can make a decision. Now I have to wait around and see that what I say or do has any impact. I wonder how I'd function where people would say, 'There's hotshot. He knows what he's talking about.' And what I said became golden. I don't know if it would be satisfying for me. (Laughs.) That might be more frustrating than fighting for everything you want. Right now I feel very unimportant."

Case Questions

1. What is the problem in this case?
2. How would you motivate Wilson and Carmichael?
3. Which techniques discussed in the chapter do you find most useful in answering the last question?

Case Reference

Studs Terkel, *Working* (New York: Pantheon Books, 1972), pp. 448, 450, 458, and 460–61.

CASE 8.4

★★★★★★★★★★★★★★★★★★★★★★★★★★★★★★★★★★★★★

When a Peer Steps on Your Toes

Elaine runs the travel office of a midwestern state. She is a devoted employee and prefers written communications because they are precise, a quality that she feels is necessary for making travel arrangements.

April is the new chief of staff for the state's secretary of Health and Human Services. April has not had time to meet other office heads, for she travels extensively. In her previous job, she made all her own travel arrangements, since a travel office was not available.

When April's bills arrived at the accounting department the other day, they were forwarded to Elaine for approval and explanation. State policy requires that travel requests be made in writing two weeks in advance and that all travel be scheduled through the travel office. Realizing that April had not read the travel policy given to her when she was hired, Elaine wrote her a terse note: "I am enclosing another copy of the state's travel policy. I am sure this will help us handle your travel needs more efficiently." Elaine also sent a copy of the note to April's boss.

For April's next trip, the travel office made the arrangements and delivered the tickets to April's department. But on the morning of the trip, April's secretary called to request a different time, a different airline, and a limo at the airport—to take her to a different hotel. These last-minute changes doubled the price of the trip.

Elaine asked one of her reservationists to talk to April's secretary and explain the policy. This did little good, and the problems continued.

Finally, Elaine calls April and tells her bluntly that the confusion must stop. When Elaine tries to explain state policy, April responds with her need for flexibility. When Elaine reminds her that the state wants to save money, April suggests that Elaine read the recent infant mortality statistics. After a few more minutes of this kind of exchange, the two hang up angrily.

Case Questions

1. What went wrong? What mistakes have Elaine and April made with respect to their communications?
2. Are last minute changes in travel arrangements to be expected in public health work? If so, how might communication be structured differently between the public health department and the travel office?
3. If you were Elaine, how would you handle this problem?

Case Reference

Based on Mary Jean Parson, "When a Peer Steps on Your Toes," *Savvy,* April 1986, pp. 16–17.

CHAPTER 9

Implementation and Evaluation

Introduction

Half the business of thinking is knowing what one is after in the first place. Before launching into this chapter, we might pause to review the structure of program management. The key is Figure 5-1, which showed policy planning as a dynamic process. Good program management begins with careful attention to goals and to the objectives for attaining goals. Careful attention to objectives, in turn, means considering alternative strategies for the attainment of each objective. In particular, the policy planner wants to ask what the likely effects of each alternative will be. Decision making pervades the entire process of program management. Based on the assumption that today's administrator should be acquainted with the tools and techniques of rational decision making, most of Chapter 6 was devoted to exploring this approach to decision making.

The story does not end here, however.

Four vitally important, exceedingly difficult, and frequently exciting tasks remain—organizing, leading, implementing, and evaluating. Once it is clear what needs to be done, the agency does not just throw everything together as did the hapless deputy in the cartoon appearing at the beginning of Chapter 7. Programs and policies, like a sheriff's posse, require a degree of *organization*—and, as we saw in the last chapter, *leadership.*

Now to the subject of this chapter. Again, let us be crystal clear about what we are after. First, we want to know the potential problems the administrator faces when attempting to implement a program; then, too, we want to know the strategies available for overcoming such problems. Second, regarding evaluation, we need to know what it is and how it works. But this will not be easy, for few areas in the field of public administration are more neglected than evaluation.

The combination of two major subjects within one chapter can be, I think, justified to the extent they are closely related. Indeed, without decent evaluation, the administrator has little way of knowing how well implementation is going. A former cabinet secretary put it well: "Evaluation is a necessary foundation for effective implementation and judicious modification of our existing programs. At this point, evaluation is probably more important than the addition of new laws to an already extensive list of educational statutes. . . . Evaluation will provide the information we require to strengthen weak programs, fully support effective programs, and drop those which simply are not fulfilling the objectives intended by the Congress when the programs were originally enacted" (cited in Wholey et al., 1970:19).

Because we are dealing with two major subjects, I have split the chapter into Parts A and B.

Part A will begin by clarifying what implementation is and why it is a vital concern of the administrator. Then a number of techniques are discussed that, in combination, should improve the chances of success in program implementation.

In Part B, we shall begin by posing the same question about evaluation that we did about implementation—namely, why is it so important to the public administrator? The remainder of Part B examines evaluation as an aid to better decision making.

A. Implementation

Understanding the Process

We shall let implementation mean just what the dictionary says it means: to carry out, accomplish, fulfill, produce, complete. But what is it that is being implemented? A policy, yes; but more exactly, that part of a policy that we defined in Chapter 5 as a program.

The distinction between policy and program is an important one when speaking of implementation. The great difficulty in government today is not so much determining what appear to be reasonable policies on paper as it is "finding the means for converting these policies into viable field operations" (Williams, 1975:453). In short, we have more good solutions (i.e., policies) than appropriate actions (i.e., programs).

We may view the implementation process from a variety of perspectives. Because the process entails so much bargaining and maneuvering, the political perspective sketched in Chapter 2 can be quite useful in understanding it. Because the process often involves intergovernmental relations, the discussion of grants found in Chapter 3 is also useful. Indeed, it could be argued that the division of authority among governments in the American federal system explains more than anything else the failure of certain programs. Because the process invariably generates value questions concerning who should benefit, what actions are fair, and so forth, the discussion of administrative responsibility and personal ethics found in Chapter 4 is relevant. Finally, because implementation occurs in organizational settings, the planning and decision-making perspectives adopted in the last two chapters are also relevant.

There are, however, two other useful perspectives on implementation not analyzed elsewhere in the book: implementation as the complexity of joint action and implementation as a system of games.

Perspective 1: Complexity of Joint Action

Pressman and Wildavsky (1973) note among the major difficulties in implementing new social programs or program modifications, two in particular: multiplicity of participants and multiplicity of perspectives. These two factors converge to delay—and, in many instances, stifle—administrative efforts to secure the joint action required in program implementation. Let us consider their analysis of the Economic Development Administration's (EDA) efforts in Oakland.

On the face of things, the effort to help the black unemployed of Oakland, California, began brilliantly. There were dedicated and powerful officials in Washington who were concerned that, if the city did not receive meaningful help quickly, it might be torn apart by riots. The officials were able to get a multimillion-dollar congressional appropriation to finance a program to provide jobs, while also enlisting Oakland businesspeople and governmental officials in the effort. And many of the usual bureaucratic barriers to action were struck down. It would be hard to think of a more propitious beginning for a government program—yet within three short years, the program was essentially a failure. Not very much money had been spent, and the number of new jobs obtained for the hard-core unemployed was ridiculously small. Why?

One answer is that governmental programs, even when designed to be carried out in a direct and simple manner, eventually come to involve a large number of governmental and nongovernmental organizations and individuals. In the case of the EDA's employment effort in Oakland, the authors admit to oversimplifying the situation by restricting the participants to only the EDA, the rest of the federal government, and the city of Oakland, each with its constituent elements. The EDA consisted of the initial task force, the EDA operating departments in Washington, the agency's leadership, the regional office in Seattle, and the field office in Oakland. Other federal government agencies that became involved included the GAO, HEW, the Department of Labor and the navy. Participants in Oakland were the mayor, city administrators, the Port of Oakland, World Airways, and several of the city's black leaders, conservative groups, and tenants of the Port of Oakland.

Some of these participants (such as the Department of Labor) became involved because they possessed jurisdictional authority over important parts of the project; others (like the navy) entered the process when they felt their interest being impinged on; and still others (such as black people in Oakland) were intentionally brought into the program by the EDA in order to build local support for the projects.

Each participating group had a distinctive perspective and therefore a different sense of urgency—though they still agreed on the ends of policy (developing jobs for unemployed minorities) and the means of achieving it (creating jobs through grants for public works). But different perspectives make or break a program. Several reasons why participants can agree on the ends of a program and still oppose (or merely fail to facilitate) the means for effecting those ends might be given (Pressman & Wildavsky, 1973:99–102).

1. Direct incompatibility with other commitments. Thus, HEW came to view one of EDA's training proposals as competing for scarce funds with one of its own training institutions in the area.
2. No direct incompatibility but a preference for other programs. Many EDA employees viewed rural areas and small towns—not urban areas—as the proper focus of the agency.
3. Simultaneous commitments to other projects. The Port of Oakland's architect/engineer delayed his work on plans for the marine terminal because his staff was busy on other port projects.
4. Dependence on others who lack a sense of urgency.
5. Differences of opinion on leadership and the proper organizational role.
6. Legal and procedural differences. For example, regarding the quality of landfill, at every point, the Port of Oakland and the EDA had their own engineering opinions.

Perspective 2: A System of Games

Eugene Bardach (1977) uses the ***metaphor of "games"*** to analyze the implementation process. He argues that the game framework illuminates the process by directing our attention onto the players, their stakes, their strategies and tactics, their resources, the rules of play (which stipulate the conditions for winning), the rules of fair play, the nature of communication among the players, and the degree of uncertainty surrounding the outcome.

This leads us to an insightful definition of implementation: a process of assembling the elements required to produce a particular programmatic outcome and the playing out of a number of loosely interrelated games whereby these elements are withheld from or delivered to the program. The list below identifies some of the most common implementation games.

- The management game—The view that a constellation of troubles inherent in the process of implementation in a democratic society "can be solved by designing better management tools and procedures and by giving more power to institutions specializing in management, like the personnel department or the auditor's office."

- Tokenism—The "attempt to appear to be contributing to a program element publicly while privately conceding only a small ('token') contribution."
- Massive resistance—A means of obstructing program implementation by withholding critical program elements or by overwhelming the capacity of the administrative agency to enforce punishment for noncompliance.
- Easy money—A game played by parties in the private sector who wish to make off with government money in exchange for program elements of too little value. (Around Washington, consultants are called the Beltway Bandits, because many of them have offices along I-495, a highway that loops downtown.)
- Budget—As we will see in Chapter 11, heads of bureaus tend to be budget maximizers. "As part of their budget game, moving money somehow, somewhere, and fast, even at the price of programmatic objectives, is the characteristic strategy of virtually every governmental agency that channels grants to other levels of government or to nonprofit institutions."
- Funding—Bureaus that receive grants try "to rescue not only money but flexibility in regard to its use."
- Up for grabs—Often the mandate for a program will identify a lead agency and provide a modest budget but fail to clearly prescribe what other element might be involved and for what expected purpose. "In this confused situation, the few unambiguously mandated elements are up for grabs by a number of potential clientele groups to be converted into political resources."
- Piling on—As onlookers see a program moving successfully in its intended direction, "some see it as a new political resource, an opportunity to throw their own goals and objectives onto the heap." The net effect of a large number of additional objectives added to the program is that the program may triple.
- Keeping the peace—Quite a few programs originate with the desire to eliminate real or imagined evil. When activists or zealots run these programs, a backlash can form among other political interests.
- Tenacity—This game can be played by anyone; all it requires is the ability and will to stymie the progress of a program until one's own terms are satisfied. While no one player may want to kill the program, the net effect of many actors' playing tenacity may be just that.
- Territory—All bureaucratic organizations struggle to ensure that some other organization is not given a program element that is perceived to be in "their" jurisdiction.

- Not our problem—While bureaus may try to expand their territories, "this drive normally evaporates as soon as the bureau recognizes that the program will impose a heavy work load or that it will take the bureau into an area of controversy."

Toward More Effective Implementation

Early Planning

Implementation needs more careful attention during the policy development. That is to say, when the broad objective of policy is being set, efforts should be made to keep the number of participants and decision points small. Policy statements should contain action commitments and answer several distinct questions: What action has to be taken? Who is to take it? Do these people have the capacity to do it?

Given the psychological makeup of policymakers, however, this lesson might not be an easy one to put into practice. Write Pressman and Wildavsky (1973:136–37): "The view from the top is exhilarating. Divorced from problems of implementation, federal bureau heads . . . think great thoughts together. But they have trouble imagining the sequence of events that will bring their ideas to fruition. Other men, they believe, will tread the path once they have so brightly lit the way. Few officials down below where the action is feel able to ask whether there is more than a rhetorical connection between the word and the deed."

The most successful coach in the history of college football (323 victories), Paul Bryant, used to gesture from the sidelines with rolled-up sheets of paper that contained his carefully constructed game plan as well as a scribbled reminder not to forget "the itty-bitty, teeny-tiny things" that lose football games. Bryant would rehearse problems that might arise in a game over and over. In the language of management theory, we would call this not watching out for the itty-bitty things but contingency planning or scenario writing. (University of Alabama)

One good antidote for this psychological tendency to discount what could go wrong in the future is ***scenario writing.*** This method, Bardach (1977:254) writes,

> *simply involves an imaginative construction of future sequences of actions→consequent conditions→actions→consequent conditions. It is inventing a plausible story about "what will happen if . . ." or, more precisely, inventing several such stories. Telling these stories to oneself and one's professional peers helps to illuminate some of the implementation paths that the designer does not want taken. He or she is then in a position to redesign some features of the system of implementation games that permit him or her and his or her colleagues to tell stories with happier endings. Trial and error through successive interactions produce better and better endings.*

Perhaps the late Paul Bryant, former University of Alabama football coach, said it even better: "It's the itty-bitty, teeny-tiny things that beat you."

In addition to paying closer attention to implementation during policymaking, there are other ways of improving the effectiveness of implementation. One is to pay as much attention to the creation of organizational machinery for *executing* a program as for launching one. Again, Pressman and Wildavsky (1973:145–46):

> *EDA leaders took great pains to design the best organization they could think of for approving applications, committing funds, and negotiating initial agreements. But in most of the projects they did not spend as much time* ensuring that the initial commitment would be followed up *by the agency; in fact, the EDA itself seemed to lose its own intense interest in the program after 1966. Although those who design programs might not generally enjoy the less exciting work of directing their implementation, a realization of the extent to which policy depends on implementation could lead such people to alter their own time perspectives and* stay around for the technical details of executing a program *(emphasis added).*

Scheduling Models

Scheduling models, another implementation technique, facilitate the coordination of activities of an enterprise and help achieve a better utilization of resources. These models are useful for a wide range of activities, from a seemingly trivial task of scheduling a field office tour for a high-ranking official to a very complex job of scheduling activities in the space program. While a wide variety of such scheduling models are in use, we shall mention only three: **Gantt chart,** Critical Path Method (**CPM**), and Program Evaluation Review Technique (**PERT**).

In 1917, Henry L. Gantt developed the bar chart. Essentially, the bar chart describes progress by comparing work done against planned objectives. Figure 9-1 shows the application of the basic Gantt charting technique to a generalized project.

The Gantt chart might be redesigned as a CPM chart. This would have several advantages. First, because bars are replaced by a network of flow plan, the network

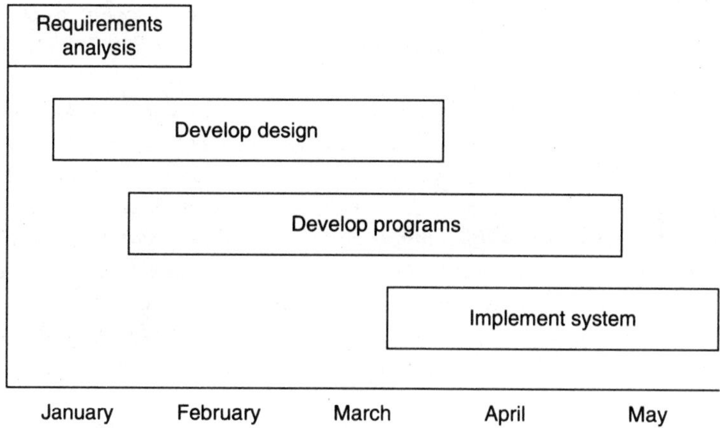

FIGURE 9-1
Gantt Bar Chart

shows how events and activities are related. In CPM and PERT charts, events (e.g., "start testing") are often shown as circles. Activities are the time-consuming elements of the program and are used to connect the various events; they are shown as arrows. Thus, the CPM chart reflects all significant program accomplishments and better approximates the complexity of the program.

Since most events depend on one or more prior events, the charts show the interrelationship of events leading to the accomplishment of the ultimate objective. Within the project is a ***critical path;*** that is, the longest possible time span along the system flow plan. To determine the critical path, events are organized in sequence. The starting point for plotting the critical paths is the final event in the total network. From the final event, related events are placed sequentially backwards, until the starting point is reached. Next, all the expected elapsed times (t_e) are summed throughout the network paths to determine the total expected elapsed time for every path of the network. The completion date of the project is dependent on the path that takes the longest time. Because this path has the highest total elapsed time, it is called the critical path. (In Figure 9-2 the critical path is indicated by heavy arrows.)

Knowing the critical path can be very useful to the decision maker. If an activity is on the critical path, any slippage or delay for the activity will delay the completion of the entire project. Conversely, slippage in an activity not on the critical path will not normally affect the project deadline since the difference between the lengths of time along the critical path and the noncritical paths is slack.

To determine the elapsed time between events, one must make estimates. When the decision makers have had some experience with the various activities in the project, they can use estimates based on this experience. This approach might be fine for public works projects such as street construction and repair, but when confronted with a nonregular project—for example, the space station—estimation would be more difficult. In such cases, decision makers need a more systematic approach to estimation. PERT provides it.

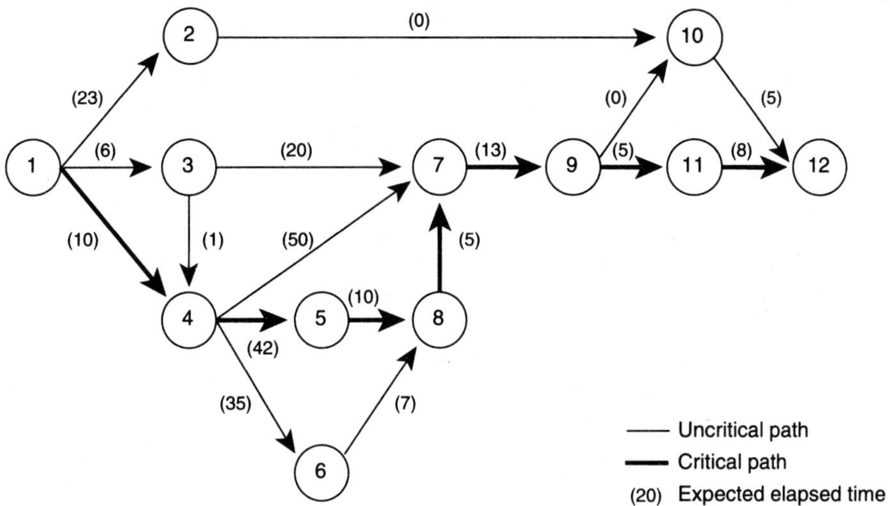

FIGURE 9-2
PERT Network
SOURCE: Adapted from U.S. Air Force Systems Command, *PERT-Time System Description Manual* (Washington, D.C.: Headquarters AFSC).

With PERT, the expected elapsed time between events is based on three possible completion assumptions: optimistic completion time (O); most likely completion time (M); and pessimistic completion time (P). Based on these three time estimates, a simple formula can be derived that will give an estimation of how long the activity will take. Assuming O = 6 weeks, M = 8 weeks, and P = 16 weeks, the expected elapsed time can be computed using the formula:

$$\frac{O + 4M + P}{6} = t_e = \frac{6 + 32 + 16}{6} = 9$$

The estimation is then used in the flow diagram.

While PERT has obvious strengths—it forces careful planning, permits experimentation, encourages participation in the planning process, permits effective control, and so on—it is not without its limitations. Many capable administrators insist that one cannot wait for a problem to make itself known through such schedule control techniques: Anticipating trouble requires closer observation.

In his account of the development of the Polaris submarine (where PERT and a dozen other management techniques originated), Sapololsky (1972) suggests that PERT might have a political rather than management function:

> *Whenever there was a question on Polaris's development status or the like, program officials always had a colored chart, a slide, or a computer printout which would demonstrate the effectiveness of the management team. Actually, this strategy might well be labeled the "Slight of Hand Strategy" since few of*

these management techniques were ever used to manage the Polaris development. The use of PERT in the program, for example, was strongly opposed by those technical officers who were in charge of the development effort and there never was a complete application of the technique in the program, but the illusion of PERT's use was carefully cultivated. During most critical stages of the Polaris development when PERT's role was minimal, the program held hundreds of briefings and prepared thousands of booklets describing how PERT was guiding the missile's progress. The message was that no one need be concerned about the quality of the program's development decisions as the program itself was the pioneer in perfecting management systems for complex projects. And since enough people who could influence policy believed this to be the case, the program was able to gain the independence and flexibility it needed to deal effectively with the missile's technological uncertainties.

Expediters, Incentives, and Participation

Another implementation technique is the use of an expediter. The expediter is employed to ensure that others have the materials and equipment needed to accomplish their tasks and also to coordinate and accelerate the flow of information among the program's participants. Expediters can be units within a larger organization, or they can be individuals. The Program Coordination Division of the OMB is a case in point. But whether the expediter is a single individual or an organizational unit, the position is a means by which presidents, governors, city managers, department heads, and other top executives demonstrate that things can work, that there is someone who can jump into the breach, representing their office and getting things done. In the final analysis, however, administrators must be their own expediters, which is a way of saying that they must **follow up** (see box).

Governments have, of course, a wide range of mechanisms for encouraging proper behavior among those involved in a program. Proper behavior simply means behavior that leads to attainment of the program's objectives. These mechanisms range from political techniques such as persuading (discussed in Chapter 2) to former mechanisms such as those shown in Table 9-1. As indicated, the formal mechanisms are not without drawbacks when applied to an area of policy such as pollution control.

In addition to fully recognizing the drawbacks summarized in Table 9-1, the administrator should strive to build *incentives* into the program. One notorious example of ignoring the incentive question might be a social welfare program in which the combined benefits to recipients make it extraordinarily unprofitable to work.

The problem of incentives, however, applies to the administrator as well as to the client. Consider the Small Business Administration: "Measures have not been developed which can be used to judge the performance of various regional loan offices in terms of overall program objectives. Defaulted loans, on the other hand, are easily identified, and a significant default rate is sure to invite congressional questions. Loan

(text continues on p. 409)

The Art of Follow-Up

Writing a sharp note in the margin of a memo will hardly ensure that something will or will not be done. Administrators must constantly check to see if their orders are being carried out.

Follow-up is hard but necessary work. As an aide to Franklin Roosevelt wrote (quoted in Edwards, 1980:155): "Half of a president's suggestions, which theoretically carry the weight of orders, can be safely forgotten by a cabinet member. And if the president asks about a suggestion a second time, he can be told that it is being investigated. If he asks a third time a wise cabinet officer will give him at least part of what he suggests. But only occasionally, except about the most important matters, do presidents ever get around to asking three times."

If follow-up is necessary for the chief executive, surrounded by a huge and competent staff, then it must be even more critical at less exalted levels of administration. For instance, Carl Officer (second from right), when mayor of East St. Louis, Illinois, did not spend Monday through Friday in his office jotting memos and greeting visitors. Rather, he played troubleshooter—inspecting buildings, seeing that fire crews are at their stations on time, and jumping into city police cars unannounced to ride along on the graveyard shift. (Photo courtesy City of East St. Louis, Illinois)

TABLE 9-1
Alternative Governmental Mechanisms for Pollution Control

Mechanism	*Example*	*Difficulties*
1. Prohibition	Full treatment of effluents and sewage required of all businesses and municipalities.	An optimal solution to pollution does not require full treatment, only "right amount," since the natural biological processes in lakes and streams give them a certain capability of cleansing themselves.
2. Directive	Government determines the *extent* to which municipalities bordering Lake Erie treat sewage.	It is very difficult to determine just what percentage of organic matter and phosphorus to remove. And even if a standard could be set, it must be translated into directives for each of the entities that emit pollutants.
3. Taxes and subsidies	Tax polluters give subsidies to businesses that hire hard-core unemployed.	Immense information requirements are necessary for the implementation of these schemes. Government must know the effect of pollution and unemployment so that a tax or subsidy could result in just the right amount of waste discharge or hiring.
4. Regulation	Require that all new cars be equipped with devices designed to reduce the level of pollutants in the exhaust.	Regulation, to be effective, must be accompanied by the practice of periodically inspecting all cars. Expensive. Inflexible.
5. Payment	Federal subsidy for capital costs of improving regional sewage facilities.	Crude: Does not easily provide proper coordination for all the relevant units in the system. Limited to problems where capital costs—rather than, say, operating expenses—are the block to improvement of the situation.
6. Action	Where the fish population of a lake is endangered by overfishing, the government continually stocks the lake.	Limited applicability.

SOURCE: Adapted from O. A. Davis and M. I. Kamien, "Externalities, Information, and Alternative Action," in Joint Economic Committee, *Analysis and Evaluation Expenditures* (Washington, D.C.: U.S. Government Printing Office, 1969).

officials, therefore, tend to avoid risky loans. As a consequence, far from meeting their original objectives, the programs end up, in many cases, simply in making loans of commercial quality at less than commercial rates" (Schultze, 1969:208). Similarly, federal reimbursement formulas contribute to hospital inefficiency. "Essentially each hospital is reimbursed by the federal government for the 'reasonable costs' of delivering services to patients under Medicare and Medicaid programs. Payment is matched to the individual costs of each hospital. There are virtually no incentives for efficiency. Any savings from more efficient operations result in lower federal payments; any increased costs are fully passed on. To the extent that larger staffs bring prestige and promotion, there are positive incentives for inefficiency" (Schultze, 1969:213).

Another way of improving implementation is **participative decision making.** To see it in practice, we turn neither to Washington nor to Oakland but to Japan. When faced with a policy decision, the top management in a Japanese organization refers it to a committee of "appropriate people." The decision-making process now becomes—to some Americans at least—excruciatingly slow. But finally a consensus is reached. What makes the resulting policy a good one is that the people who must participate in the implementation phase have participated in the policymaking phase; they are already presold. Moreover, this process "makes it clear where in the organization a certain answer to a question will be welcomed and when it will be resisted. Therefore, there is plenty of time to work on persuading the dissenters, or making small concessions to them which will win them over without destroying the integrity of the decision" (Drucker, 1973:470).

Case Management Systems

Much of the resources of a public sector organization is devoted to processing cases: patients in hospitals, welfare clients in a department of human resources, labor disputes in a labor relations board, apartment buildings for an office of housing code enforcement, grant proposals for a foundation, and so on. While these organizations may be involved in very different enterprises, when the particular jargon of each organization is stripped away, we see that their basic processing stages are similar and can be discussed in terms of the **case-procession pipeline** shown in Figure 9-3. (The following discussion draws on Rosenthal and Levine, 1980.)

Acquisition. New York City's child protection system investigates about 60,000 complaints of abuse and neglect a year, yet officials believe that as many as 120 children die of abuse or neglect (*New York Times,* January 6, 1989). Clearly, the process by which cases enter the pipeline is vital to any case-processing program.

There are other ways besides complaints by which cases arrive. For an authorization organization (i.e., one that issues licenses or grants awards), applicants themselves bring their requests to the pipeline. A more aggressive method of case acquisition than waiting for complaints or requests to arrive is search, or outreach, activities. This method requires the staff to seek new cases. An example of this would be periodic on-site plant visits by inspectors from the Occupational Safety and Health Administration (OSHA).

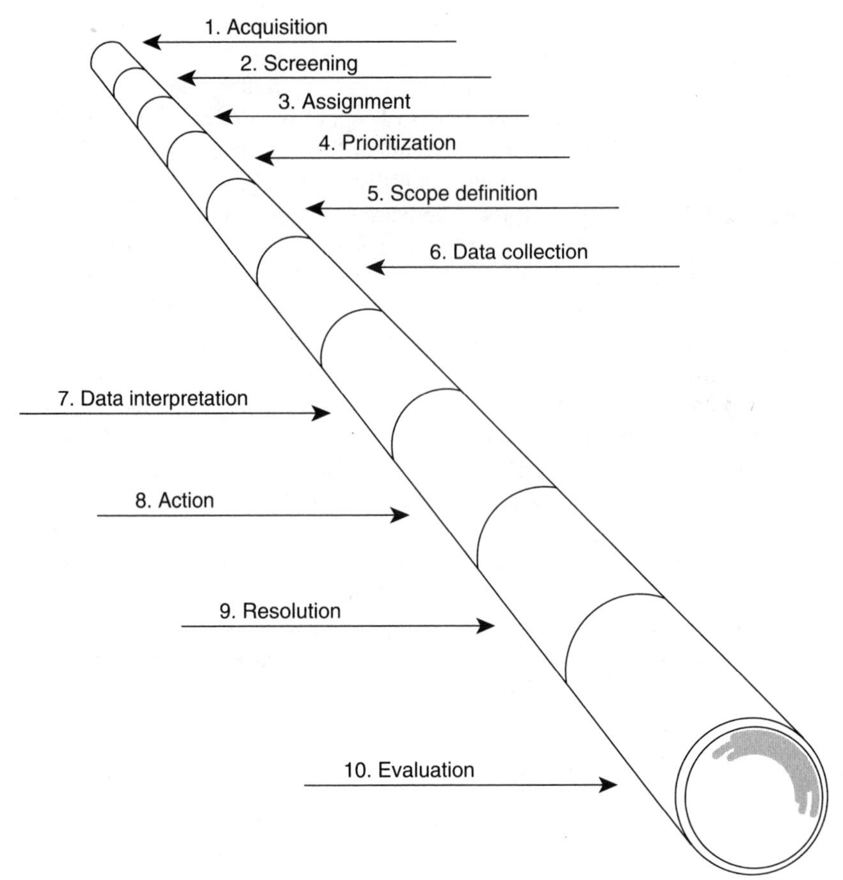

FIGURE 9-3
The Case-Processing Pipeline

The acquisition stage entails at least two other considerations. Will case identification be centralized or decentralized? Will it involve only its staff or will it depend on other agencies for referrals?

Screening. The screening stage of case management involves determining the eligibility of potential cases. Sometimes the potential case fails to meet statutory specifications or eligibility requirements. Fortunately, not all of the 60,000 complaints of child abuse turn out to be serious enough to warrant being logged in and referred for subsequent analysis and response.

The more precise the criteria, the more consistent the screening process:

> *. . . when case screening criteria are not sufficiently refined, when staff training is inadequate, or when management is not effective at monitoring the intake activity, inconsistencies will result. An intake clerk in a housing code*

> *enforcement program may refuse to accept one case because the tenant's tone of voice makes the condition seem not to be "very important." A short time later, another intake clerk, hearing a more emphatic plea for the same type of assistance from another tenant, may decide that the program ought to respond with an inspection. A similar kind of inconsistency may be found in the behavior of intake clerks in local welfare offices. Such inconsistencies can occur frequently and may be particularly costly when emergencies are not adequately identified. Until intake activities are sufficiently controlled, an agency can never be sure that its established policies are being followed. (Rosenthal & Levine, 1980:393)*

Yet the criteria should not be so rigid that the agency finds itself violating an important principle of administrative responsibility we discussed in Chapter 4: flexibility.

Essentially, there are two errors to avoid in the screening process. One is the acceptance of an inappropriate case. Made frequently enough, it can prove quite expensive. The other is the incorrect rejection of a potential case. Made in programs such as child protection, it can be fatal.

Assignment and Prioritization. Once in the pipeline, the case becomes part of the active caseload. It is assigned to a processing unit where either one caseworker is designated to handle it or several caseworkers from a pool may handle parts of it.

It is management's responsibility to ensure that this takes place as expeditiously as possible and that no case falls between the cracks. A New York State investigation, for example, found serious deficiencies in this aspect of New York City's child protection program. It found that when cases were transferred to workers who were supposed to monitor troubled families over the long term, the cases went unassigned for an average of 13 weeks. At least one case was not assigned to a caseworker for 44 weeks. The report also noted that the whereabouts of the files on 15 cases was "not known." (*New York Times,* May 4, 1989)

Whatever the caseworker's title—investigator, inspector, hearing officer, social worker, attorney, adjustor, or something else—he or she will need to decide on the case's urgency. Because it is usually impossible for a public sector case-processing program to satisfy promptly all the demand for its service, priorities must be set. Table 9-2 outlines a variety of potential priorities for processing cases and identifies the methods of implementing them and the potential side effects.

Essentially, a case-progressing program can be viewed as a complex queuing system. A case initially takes its place at the end of a line, or queue; a service is delivered that permits the case to move to the next queue; when that step is completed, it moves to the next queue; and so on, until the case is finally discharged. Management must determine the most efficient sequence for the separate steps or services performed.

Scope Definition. In a child protection case, a common question is whether to include the entire family or just the child who is the focus of attention. An agency

TABLE 9-2.
Examples of Priorities for Handling Cases

Goal	*Method*	*Side Effects*
1. Close as many cases as possible, quickly.	Locate potentially simple cases regardless of age and process only these.	Will develop major backlog of complex cases and less ability to juggle slack time.
2. Close all cases opened prior to *X* date.	Use a great percentage of investigator time on old cases.	May waste time on irrelevant cases and lose momentum on important ones.
3. Affect the lives of as many citizens as possible.	Select cases based on size of jurisdiction or organization and/or number of employees, constituents, or members affected.	Fewer cases will be closed because larger more complex cases take much longer to investigate.
4. Make some significant response to every new case within *Y* days.	Assign *all* cases to investigators regardless of work load and require that they collect applicable data immediately even if they can't begin analysis for months.	Expectations may be raised then reduced because it will take longer to complete analysis.
5. Process the most important cases quickly.	Screen incoming cases to identify those that are most important and give them top processing priority.	Some cases will take longer to process than otherwise but targeted processing may make greater impact.
6. Process cases equitably (if slowly).	Assign priority based on data case opened. Always handle oldest case first (first-in first-out).	May waste time on irrelevant cases and lose momentum on important ones; gain equal treatment under law.
7. Process *all* cases as quickly as possible.	Close trivial or simple cases as soon as possible. Avoid expanding scope of other cases; interpret scope as narrowly as possible.	Quality of case analyses will be reduced; cases may be prepared so simplistically that compliance will be minimal.

SOURCE: Stephen R. Rosenthal and Edith S. Levin, "Case Management and Policy Implementation," *Public Policy,* Fall 1980, p. 394

might, if it chooses, define the case quite broadly and offer families far more in the way of counseling, day care, and services like teaching mothers budgeting skills, hygiene, and how to send their children to school on time. In New York City, caseworkers are supposed to make sure that *all* the children in a household that has been reported as abusive or neglectful are doing well, but in a third of the cases, this is not done.

In an enforcement case, such as OSHA might handle, the range of charges to pursue is often a matter of discretion. So, again, the scope of a case has to be defined.

Data Collection and Interpretation. Data collection refers to issuing subpoenas, administering tests, conducting interviews, and performing any other information-gathering activity that will help the worker decide how to handle the case. Sound dull? Then consider the case of Jessica Cortez, a five-year-old Brooklyn girl who was beaten to death in December 1988. A state investigation of this case revealed it had been handled extremely poorly. Caseworkers had been confused over the identity of various Cortez children and repeatedly failed to look up records that might have triggered more serious concern about the situation. Indeed, the investigation found that, in 57 percent of the 240 cases received, caseworkers did not look up past records even though they knew such records existed. The report also found that the city frequently did not complete the most basic elements of data collection—seeing a child's home and meeting with the individuals named in the allegation of abuse.

Data interpretation refers to the review and analysis of these materials. In the social services agencies, this process is called "assessment"; in law enforcement agencies, "determination of probable cause"; and in medical and public health agencies, "diagnosis." According to experts, here are some of the factors that could signal to a caseworker that a child like Jessica might be in a fatal situation: absence of a grandmother, a mother living with a boyfriend, and a history of drug abuse.

Action. In a social service agency, the action stage of case management will usually involve a service or a treatment plan designed to achieve some beneficial effect on the client. Management must ensure that the caseworkers' guidelines are clear in this vital stage of the process.

Consider this situation. Children are sent on a trial visitation to their mother who has seriously abused them. They come back with immersion burns. One might say that suggests the mother should not have her children. But that action might not be in the decision-making rules of the system. The manual might say something like this: "If you determine the child is in imminent danger, take him or her out of the household."

In enforcement or authorization organizations, action will usually mean holding a hearing or a trial and then reaching a finding or a verdict.

Resolution. Sometimes, in licensing or child protection situations, the action stage requires continual monitoring or inspection rather than a single decision. In such instances, it might be a long while before the case is closed or resolved.

Depending on the organization, resolution can take many forms—a fine, a sentence, a plea bargain, a consent decree, a release, an agreement, and so on. Resolution may also mean that the case has simply been passed to another agency or jurisdiction. In any event, resolution means that a case is no longer considered active.

Evaluation. Because all nine of the preceding stages must be selectively monitored, the ultimate stage of the case-processing pipeline is evaluation. Unfortunately, finding good performance measures is exceedingly difficult. When a worker might be sharing a case with other workers or, even more likely, working on several cases—of varying levels of difficulty—each day, measuring that worker's performance obviously becomes difficult. Processing time, a concern of both management and client, can be measured in at least two ways. **Throughput time** is the period from the initial acceptance of the case until its ultimate resolution. **Direct handling time** is the total time that various employees actually spend on the activities associated with handling a particular case.

Management should also try to set appropriate quality standards, which requires thinking through the final output of the program. In the context of a particular case management program, what does "adequate" mean? Benchmarking (that is, making comparisons to similar programs elsewhere) is of only limited help because no two programs are identical. For example, while many experts say that New York City is far from doing all that it could with regard to child abuse, direct comparisons between that city and other communities are hard to make. Some are run by states and others, by counties and municipalities. The state of Illinois, which has a larger population than New York City—11 million compared to 7.5 million—had 97 deaths from child abuse the same year New York City had 126. But we cannot say one system is better than the other until we have controlled for certain variables outside the system, such as numbers of drug addicts per 100,000 and heterogeneity of the population.

Although management might not be able to find a good benchmark, it still should, as part of its evaluation process, consider what innovative programs are doing. For example, New Jersey, just across the Hudson River from New York City, leads the nation in use of parent aides—community volunteers who visit troubled homes in addition to regular caseworkers—to offer help, advice, and friendship.

This might be a good place to repeat an earlier point. Public policy statements tend to be quite general—but implementation issues are considered to be "operational details" to be worked out by program managers and their staff. Yet, for case-processing systems, the resolution of many of these mere "details" will largely determine whether Jessica Cortez and others like her live or die. Since these systems are complex and poorly understood, public administration might pay more attention to them.

Management by Objectives (MBO)

MBO has four features that make it especially well suited for contributing to program implementation. First, those accountable for directing the organization determine what they want to achieve during a particular period; that is, they establish overall objectives and priorities. Second, all key management people are encouraged to contribute their maximum efforts to attaining these overall objectives. Third, the planned achievement of all key management people is coordinated to promote greater total results for the organization as a whole. Fourth, a control mechanism is established to monitor progress compared to objectives and feed the results back to higher levels (McConkey, 1975).

The system has been applied successfully in a variety of organizations. Among the nonprofit-type organizations are hospitals, schools, police departments, nursing homes, defense departments, municipal governments, and federal agencies. Stripped of its business school jargon, the system works as follows (Brady, 1973):

1. The annual MBO cycle begins when the department formulates its budget. Program managers are urged to accompany each request for funds with a list of measurable, specific, results-oriented objectives. Secretaries (or city managers) then compare these initial proposals with what they want the department to accomplish during the coming year. During this stage, they work closely with the agency heads.

Here is a typical dialogue between former HEW secretary Elliot L. Richardson and an agency head as they formulated an objective (quoted in Brady, 1973):

> AGENCY HEAD: One of our agency's most important initiatives this year will be to focus our efforts in the area of alcoholism and to treat an additional 10,000 alcoholics. Given last year's funding of 41 alcoholic treatment centers and the direction of other resources at the state and local level, we feel that this is an achievable objective.
>
> SECRETARY: Are these 41 centers operating independently or are they linked to other service organizations in their communities? In other words are we treating the whole problem of alcoholism, including its employment, mental health, and welfare aspects, or are we just treating the symptoms of alcoholism?
>
> AGENCY HEAD: A program requirement for getting funds is that the services involved must be linked in an integrated fashion with these other resources.
>
> SECRETARY: I am not interested in just looking at the number of alcoholics that are treated. Our goal ought to be the actual rehabilitation of these patients. Do you have data to enable you to restate the objective in terms of that goal?
>
> AGENCY HEAD: As a matter of fact, Mr. Secretary, we have developed a management information and evaluation system in which each grantee will be providing quarterly data on the number of alcoholics treated, as well as on the number of alcoholics who are actually rehabilitated.
>
> SECRETARY: How do you define *rehabilitated?*
>
> AGENCY HEAD: If they are gainfully employed one year after treatment, we regard them as being rehabilitated.
>
> SECRETARY: Please revise this objective, then, to enable us to track progress on how effective these programs really are in treating the disease of alcoholism and in rehabilitating alcoholics.

2. The staff of the secretary draws up the department's budget and forwards it to the president for action.

3. The secretary then prepares for his agency heads and regional managers a list of the priorities determined during the budget preparation. In light of these priorities, the executives review and alter as necessary their preliminary objectives. Typically, they will select eight to ten objectives that represent the most important results expected of their programs. Just prior to the start of the fiscal year, they submit these objectives—along with milestones that must be reached (e.g., expand OEO projects to increase capacity by 25,000 patients by September) and resources that must be expended for their accomplishment—to the secretary.
4. The office of the secretary and his staff workers in each agency monitor progress in meeting the objectives. The success of the entire MBO system depends largely on the bimonthly management conferences attended by principal staff aids. Here managers seek advice or assistance in meeting their objectives. Prior to the conference, managers must submit an evaluation of the status of each objective.

The preceding four steps centered on the relationship between a secretary and agency heads. With only minor modifications, the system could, and should, be spread throughout the hierarchy. In other words, for MBO to work properly, managers at all levels should have objectives and milestones.

MBO delivers many benefits to the managers: a greater voice in determining his or her job; agreement on what is expected and appraisal based on results (not busyness or personality); better management of time by focusing on the priorities; and fewer surprises through continual monitoring (McConkey, 1975:chapter 9).

The road to developing an effective MBO system, however, is not without pitfalls. Some organizations might be tempted to adopt the system without really understanding it. Or, organizations can overlook the fact that MBO takes time (three to five years) before it can reach an effective level of operation. As should have been apparent from the dialogue between Richardson and the agency head, setting good, measurable objectives is no easy task. Finally, MBO can be dealt a lethal blow by omitting periodic reviews (such as the previously mentioned management conference) or failing to reward managers who achieve high performance levels.

In summing up the first half of this chapter, I am reminded of a cartoon that appeared in *The Wall Street Journal* a few years ago. A baby bird, ready to dive from the edge of the nest, asks its mother, "Any instructions, or shall I just wing it?" What marvelous commentary on the typical approach to teaching implementation in many management courses. Of course, most public administrators know that winging it sometimes is unavoidable, that they have to learn from their own mistakes. But at the same time, the implementation process can be made a little smoother by paying attention to the concepts and techniques outlined above.

Implementation is closely connected to evaluation, the subject to which we now turn. Indeed it is hard to name any two subjects in the field of public administration more closely related. Until a program has been properly implemented, administrators cannot reasonably evaluate it. Unless we have information on implementation, we do not know how to interpret results of evaluation studies. A program may have failed because the original design was poor *or* because the design was never implemented. Therefore, information on implementation is critical for making sense of evaluative studies (see Edwards, 1980:8–9).

B. Evaluation

Why Evaluation?

Program evaluation is the systematic examination of a program to provide information on the full range of its short- and long-term effects on citizens. Put simply, it asks: Is this program delivering?

The answer to that question should be of considerable interest to the administrator. It provides a sound basis for deciding whether "to continue or discontinue the program; . . . improve its practices and procedures; . . . add or drop specific program strategies and techniques; . . . institute similar programs elsewhere; . . . allocate resources among competing programs; and . . . accept or reject a program approach (Weiss, 1972:16–17).

Evaluation thus forces decision makers to take a closer look at their programs. While this seems only fitting and proper, it is not a popular notion; the practice of evaluation remains very much the neglected stepchild of program administration. Some think that top administrators lack incentive to take evaluation more seriously:

> *The political appointees find they can score more points with the public by proposing new ways to do things rather than finding what went wrong in the past. Bureaucrats have a vested interest in protecting their empires and will not welcome meddlesome reviews by outsiders. Interest groups only reinforce these bureaucratic tendencies. The only one who really cares is the taxpayer, but until the problem is forcefully brought to his attention, he is blissfully ignorant of program performance. (Malek, 1978:212–13)*

Gloomy though these ruminations may be, responsible administrators and elected officials *should* take evaluation seriously. In what follows, we certainly will. The discussion builds around three topics:

1. The major types of evaluation used by policymakers and program managers.
2. The general procedure for evaluation research.
3. The termination of government activity (when an evaluation's findings are purely negative).

Types of Evaluation

Evaluation for Policymakers

Three major types of evaluation are of interest to policymakers: national program impact evaluation, demonstration projects, and field experiments.

National Program Impact Evaluation. Programs for disadvantaged preschool children that attempt to overcome the handicaps of poverty began over two decades ago. Head Start was the largest of these.

Early reports on the programs concluded that the preschool intervention did little to improve the academic performance of disadvantaged children. But such early evaluations could follow the progress of the children for only a few years.

By the early 1980s, it was possible to ascertain how children who were in the programs in the 1960s were doing as teenagers and young adults. Two longitudinal studies (i.e., measured over a certain period of time) found that the preschool programs were beneficial.

One report is *Young Children Grow Up* by Lawrence J. Schweinhart and David P. Weikart (1980). The project started in 1962 among preschool children at an elementary school in Ypsilanti, Michigan. The 123 children included in the study were black and from low-income families. Over a period of four years, 58 of the children attended (for either one or two years) a preschool program that emphasized active learning, problem solving, motivation, and communication. The remaining 65 children received no special attention.

Tracing these children in recent years, Schweinhart and Weikart found several differences between the two groups. By age 15 the children who had attended the preschool program scored 8 percent higher than the children of the control group on tests of reading, mathematics, and language. The preschool students required and received fewer years of special education as they progressed through school. Preliminary data indicate they were completing high school at a higher rate and were showing more interest in attending college. They also had better employment records and lower rates of arrest than the members of the control group.

A 1979 cost-benefit analysis (see Chapter 6) done by Schweinhart and Weikart found that two years of preschool education for one child cost $5,984, whereas the benefits have a value of $14,819. These benefits include the reduced need for special education, an increase in the projected earnings of the students, and the value of the mother's time as a wage earner when the child attended the preschool program.

The second report, *Head Start: A Successful Experiment,* is by Bernard Brown and Edith H. Grotberg (1980) of the U.S. Department of Health and Human Services. They found that Head Start, which enrolled some 430,000 children in 1979, provided not only education but also assistance in health and nutrition. Parents were encouraged to participate, and social services were made available to the family. Brown and Grotberg summarize the conclusions of more than 700 studies of Head Start published between 1969 and 1977: "Head Start has brought about a quiet revolution in children's institutions. . . . Early childhood programs are now accepted and functioning. The

One major type of evaluation of interest to policymakers is national program impact evaluation. Two major reports issued in the early 1980s measured the long-term impact of preschool training and concluded that such preparation does *provide a head start. Thanks in part to such analysis, Head Start escaped deep budget cuts.* (Wisconsin State Journal)

acceptance can be seen not only in support for Head Start but also in the phenomenal rise in nursery schools, preschool programs in the public schools, and quality day care for middle-class children. It is evidenced in the large numbers of books, records, toys, and television programs for preschool children."

Demonstration Projects. The philosophy of the demonstration project is quite simple: Before we launch a program nationwide, let us try it in a few selected cities or regions.

A good, straightforward example of evaluation by a demonstration project is the Police Fleet Plan. According to this plan, police are allowed to take their police cars home with them for their private use in off-duty hours—thus putting a lot more police cars on the city streets. A city that had some interest in the possibility of adopting the Police Fleet Plan might try it first in a few precincts before adopting it citywide. The evaluation results were quite positive in the Urban Institute's study of the Indianapolis Police Fleet Plan: auto thefts went down, auto accidents went down, outdoor crime, purse snatching, and robbery went down.

Field Experiments. One of the best ways to evaluate a program is to use a randomized, controlled field trial. This means, first, that individuals or groups are selected to be included in the new program entirely by chance and, second, that the program is observed under actual operating conditions ("in the field"). Finally, the results obtained from the participating individuals or groups are compared with results from a similar randomly selected **control group.**

Unlike program impact evaluations, which tend to be retrospective, the demonstration project and field trial may be introduced into public programs either before a major operating program is started or simultaneously with a major operating program. But the principal difference between the field trial and the demonstration project

Encourage Pilots of Everything

With the problems facing public administrators becoming evermore complex, it might be a good idea to replace some of the talk and analysis with text. More specifically, Tom Peters suggests that managers (1) substitute pilots and prototypes for proposals; and (2) find trial sites and field champions for new programs, projects, and products as far from headquarters as possible. "Piloting," rather than constant rehashing of abstract proposals, must become a way of life.

This prescription is even more applicable to the public than to the private sector. I remember chiding a city's middle managers. Most were spending the majority of their time floating proposals for this or that, trying to stretch an already badly stretched budget.

"But why," I said, "should anyone support this or that new program? You have no evidence that it works." "Precisely" was the reply. "We need demonstration money to try it." In one case, demonstration money meant $250,000 for a nine-month test, with a formal evaluation due six months later. After some heated debate, we came to agree that a "quick and dirty" test could be performed in 90 days in the field (out of sight of top management) for $5,000 to $20,000; moreover, there was a champion already out there, a person who'd wanted to have a go at it for years.

In fact, there is always someone "out there" ready to take a whack at it, whether we're talking about a school district or a complex military technology project. Furthermore, almost anything can be subjected to a partial test in 90 days for $25,000 or less. (This is not speculation. I've repeatedly seen it done in supercomputers and financial services alike.)

"Devote 100 percent of your time (or 50 percent, to be realistic) to getting that one, real, first piece of test-generated evidence," I counsel public managers. "Then float the $250,000 proposal." Even better, try several partial pilots before going to the trough to try to pry loose the scarce resources.

Another part of the conversation goes like this: "But what if the little one blows up? The whole deal will be scotched before we've even tried to get the money." You can probably guess my answer: "Better to know now, and get a little egg on your face, than to find out later, at great expense, and get the frying pan thrown at you too."

SOURCE: From *Thriving on Chaos* by Tom Peters Copyright © 1987 by Excel, a California Limited Partnership. Reprinted by permission of Alfred A. Knopf, Inc.

is that in the field trial those responsible for the evaluation exercise have control over input variables (e.g., purpose, staffing, clients, length of service, location, size of program, auspices, and management) and carefully measure outputs to determine the extent to which the project reaches its objectives. In short, the conditions are a little closer to those of the laboratory. An outstanding example of a field experiment is the OEO's negative income tax experiment (see Case 9.2).

Evaluation for Program Managers

Evaluative research is also useful to program managers at federal, state, or local levels who have responsibility for operating programs. According to Wholey (1972:365), "The primary evaluation payoff (in terms of decisions actually influenced) may be in evaluation that is done in enough detail to get at the effects of operational changes within operating programs. Many program managers really want to know what works best under what conditions." Here are two examples of evaluation systems designed to help program managers:

- In 1971 the District of Columbia Sanitation Department, in conjunction with the Urban Institute, developed a monitoring system for solid-waste collection activities. Inspectors, armed with reference photographs and a tape recorder, drove along city streets and alleys rating the cleanliness of the block (by comparison with reference photograph). Writes Wholey (1972): "This system . . . produces data on the *outputs* of services not simply inputs or estimates of outputs. One can imagine this system being used to assess the results of operational changes in sanitation department activities or to justify budget requests." In sum, the system helps the managers determine whether particular additional inputs (e.g., increased services) do in fact produce differences in outputs (e.g., moving a neighborhood's streets and alleys from an average rating of four to a rating of two).

- Public school personnel are rarely provided with data relevant to decision making. The Urban Institute, therefore, attempted to develop a system for estimating the relative effectiveness of different public schools in Atlanta. In this project, schools were classified by the economic level of the students and by the amount of pupil turnover. The institute tested the notion that information on the relative effectiveness of schools running comparable student populations could be useful to the superintendent and staff (Wholey, 1972).

How to Evaluate

In the preceding section, we noted several types of evaluation. To set down a general procedure for carrying out each type is not easy. Perhaps the best approach to such a formulation is to say that evaluation research follows, ideally, a procedure reminiscent of the classical research experiment. The **steps in an evaluation** are (1) find out the goals of the program; (2) translate the goals into measurable indicators of goal achievement; (3) collect data on the indicators for those who have been exposed to the program and for those who have not (i.e., the control group); and (4) compare the data on program participants and controls in terms of goal criteria.

Find Goals

There are three points to keep in mind about goals. First, programs are likely to have multiple goals: To evaluate only one is to evaluate partially. A program to reduce air pollution, for example, might be concerned with the reduction of several types of air pollution at several sources. For purposes of evaluation, the sweeping goal of "reduce air pollution" might be broken into components, represented by this matrix (adapted from Cook & Scioli, 1972):

	B_1	B_2	B_3	B_4	B_5
A_1					
A_2					
A_3					
A_4					
A_5					

where the *A*s represent pollution types (viz., carbon monoxide, sulfur oxides, hydrocarbons, nitrogen oxides, and particles) and the *B*s, pollution sources (viz., automobiles, industry, electric power plants, space heating, and refuse disposal). Thus, rather than consider air pollution in terms of one composite figure, the evaluator considers it in terms of several separate measures.

Second, many areas of public policy lack standards (or benchmarks) by which a goal can be established. The Schlitz Brewing Company may have as its goal for next year to increase sales more than Coors increases its sales. But how does the public decision maker know the proper goals for reduction of poverty and illiteracy in the year ahead?

Third, programs do not only move toward official goals. They accomplish other things, sometimes in addition to and sometimes instead of, as Weiss (1972:25) puts it. For example, programs that may increase the supply of workers in a particular occupation (intended consequence) may result in the exertion of downward pressures on the wages of existing workers in the occupation (unintended consequence). A good evaluator tries to look at all possible effects of program activity.

Translate Goals into Measurable Indicators

Program goals tend to be ambiguous, hazy. Consider this one for an urban transportation program: "To provide access to community services, facilities, and employment in a safe, quick, comfortable, and convenient manner for all segments of the community without causing harmful side effects." How would you translate these goals into measurable indicators of achievement?

Winnie and Hatry (in Hatry et al., 1973:27) suggest the following criteria:

- For accessibility and convenience: (1) percentage of residents not within *x* distance of public transit service and more than one hour from key destinations; and (2) citizen perception of travel convenience.
- For travel time: (3) time required to travel between key origin and destination points; and (4) congestion—duration and severity of delay.
- For comfort: (5) road surface quality ("bumpiness") index; and (6) citizen perception of travel comfort.
- For safety: (7) rate of transportation-related deaths, injuries, and incidents or property damage; and (8) number of transportation crime incidents.
- For minimum cost to users: (9) costs per trip.
- For maintenance of environmental quality: (10) noise level along transportation corridors and number of persons at risk; and (11) air pollution attributable to transportation sources and number of persons at risk.
- For general public satisfaction: (12) citizen perception of adequacy of transportation services.
- For monetary costs: (13) program costs.

Some experts distinguish different classes of program effects. **Output** is the service rendered—for example, number of children finishing a Head Start program. **Outcome** is the effect in more subtle terms—for example, reading levels and study habits. Finally, **impacts** are the long-term effects on society—for example, a literate population.

For another interesting example of how to measure impacts we might turn to the work in the area of **social indicators.** In a seminal work on this subject, Professor Raymond A. Bauer (1966:1) described social indicators operationally as "statistics, statistical series, and all other forms of evidence that enable us to assess where we stand and are going with respect to our values and goals."

The social indicator movement has developed concurrently with evaluation research. And, given the dearth of respectable evaluation studies, some have argued for social indicators as a substitute for experimental evaluations. In my opinion, this substitution would be unfortunate because social indicators cannot tell why a program succeeds or fails. Yet the *why* is often as important as the *how well.*

Suppose we wanted to measure the quality of life in 18 cities. The most desirable rating is numbered 1 and the least favorable is 18. The social indications are described as follows:

- Unemployment: in percentage of labor force out of work.
- Poverty: in percentage of households with cash incomes under $3,000 a year.

Talking Shop

The Courage to Evaluate

Evaluation of programs in the public sector is probably more important than in the private sector, because it has to do with accountability. The public pays for programs and deserves to know how its money is being spent. Nevertheless, it is rarely done in the public sector, partly because it is scary to know how you are doing and partly because it looks "unproductive." There *appears* to be greater payoff in putting resources directly into programs than in using them for evaluation. As the press and the politicians might phrase it, "Look at that staff of 30 people who don't produce a single service for the tax dollars they are consuming. They just go around 'evaluating.' We know what that means—they don't do anything!" The manager has to fight this skepticism with good, useful evaluation.

1. *Know the difference between the wrong program and poor management of the right program.* We frequently assume that when a program goes wrong, it is because we are doing the wrong thing, when in fact it is that we are not doing very well what we set out to do. As a result of this mentality, there are probably more shifts from program to program (to deal with the same problem) then there need to be. An evaluation should discern the difference. Do not throw out the baby with the bath water unless necessary.
2. *Be in control of your evaluation effort.* Evaluations invariably produce at least some bad news, and you can bet it will find its way into the newspapers or some other public record. You can try to instill in your staff the confidential nature of their work, but it will not prevent leaks. Be prepared to get ahead of the problem, perhaps by announcing a plan of corrective action.

- Income: in terms of money income per person, adjusted for cost-of-living differences.
- Housing: in costs for a moderate-income family of four, using 75 percent renters, 75 percent homeowners.
- Health: based on deaths of infants under one year of age per 1,000 live births.
- Mental health: in terms of the rate of reported suicides per 100,000 population.
- Public order: in terms of rate of reported robberies per 100,000 population.
- Racial equality: comparing white and minority unemployment rates.
- Community concern: measured by individual contributions to United Fund charitable appeals.

3. *Make your evaluators produce.* Because there is a tendency to think evaluators are good for nothing, it is important that they work very hard to prove their worth to the organization. Oftentimes, showing you are doing evaluation is just as important as the evaluation itself.
4. *Use the evaluation results.* Nothing makes evaluators more discouraged than seeing their work sit on the shelf. When a study is completed, become informed of its major findings and assign program staff to follow through on the recommendations. If a study is no good, let the project leader know why, so he or she can improve next time.
5. *Use different sources of information for evaluation.* Use a first-rate reporting system. Have on-site inspections by internal evaluators. Also, have on-site visits by outsiders, because these can be more objective—at least they appear more objective, which may be important for the audience (e.g., press, legislature). Perform objective studies using hard data; for example, police records to determine the effect of methadone treatment on the crime rate. Objective studies have the advantage of keeping the on-site evaluators honest because they know that data exist to verify their own findings and perceptions. They cannot blast a program irresponsibly.

Evaluations can be misleading because evaluators are judged by what they find wrong. This is why you rarely find a positive report by the GAO. Insist that your evaluators include the positive aspects of a program as well as its deficiencies.

SOURCE: Gordon Chase, *Bromides for Public Managers*, Case N16-84-586 (Cambridge, Mass.: Kennedy School of Government, 1984), pp. 33–34.

- Citizen participation: in terms of percentage of voting-age population that cast votes in presidential elections.
- Educational attainment: measured by median school years completed by persons 25 years old or older.
- Transportation: in terms of costs for a moderate-income family of four.
- Air quality: measuring concentration of suspended particulates.
- Social disintegration: in terms of estimated narcotics addiction rates per 10,000 population.

Collect Data

Data for evaluation research can come from a variety of sources and research techniques. To name but a few: interviews, questionnaires, observation, ratings, institu-

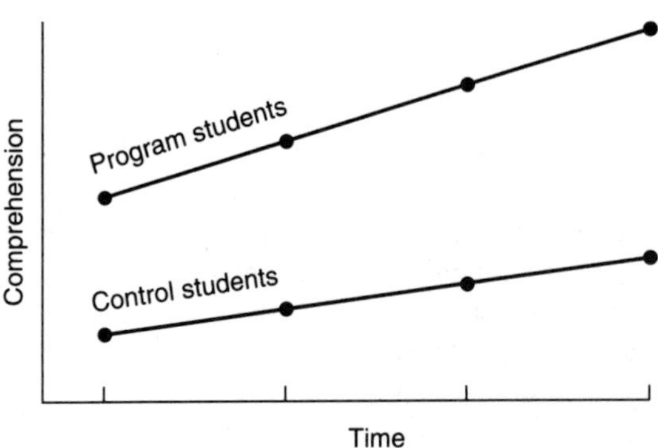

FIGURE 9-4
Quasi-Experimental Analysis for the Effect of Specific Course Work, Including Control Series Design

tional records, government statistics, diary records, physical evidence, clinical examinations, financial records, and documents (e.g., minutes of board meetings, newspaper accounts of policy actions, and transcripts of trials).

Data must be collected not only for those who participated in the program but also for those who did not; the latter is termed the *control group.* Figure 9-4 shows the measurable effect (comprehension scores) of a program involving new foreign language teaching methods on the program participants in comparison to a control group of similar students studying under traditional methods.

Compare Data

The classic design for evaluation is the experimental model that uses experimental and control groups. Out of the target population, units (e.g., people, precincts, or cities) are randomly chosen to be in either the group that gets the program or the control group. Measures are taken of the relevant criterion variable (e.g., vocabulary scores) before the program starts and after it ends. Differences are computed, and the program is deemed a success if the experimental group has improved more than the control (Weiss, 1972:60–61). Or, in terms of the model below, the program is a success if $(b - a)$ is greater than $(d - c)$.

	Before	After
Experimental	*a*	*b*
Control	*c*	*d*

The model is deceptively simple. How can the evaluator always ensure that nothing else caused the change but the program? For example, suppose a city reports a healthy drop in its crime rate. To attribute this drop solely to the effects of one program would be difficult. During the period of improvement, several major program actions may have occurred—for example, expansion of police force, buildup of a drug treat-

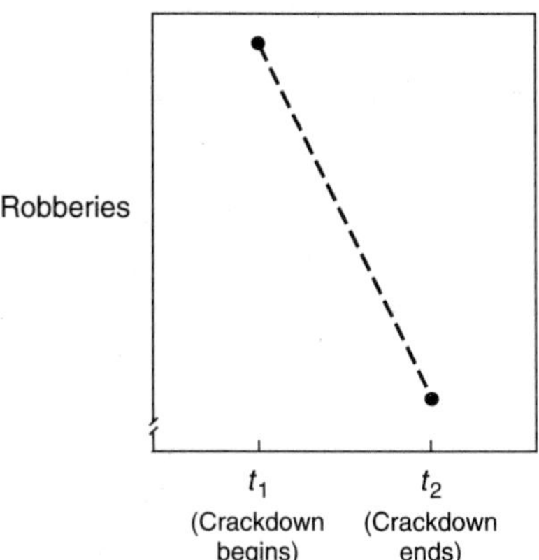

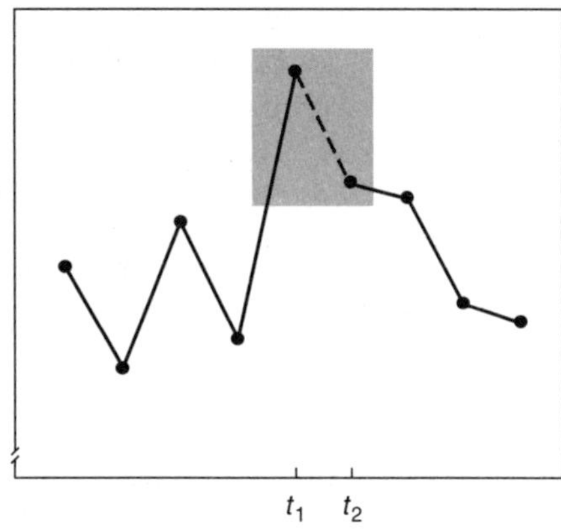

FIGURE 9-5
Evaluation and Fluctuations of Time Series Data

ment program, and installation of new street lighting. In addition, social conditions may have changed—for example, the population became older and the unemployment rate dropped (see Figure 9-5).

Regardless of the specific approach taken to evaluation, two final points need to be kept in mind. First, to be useful, evaluation must be viewed as a tool of management. Ideally, evaluators and the administrator cooperate. When the policy decisions about program design are to be made, the evaluator should ask the manager to specify the objectives of the program. The evaluator also determines the administrator's set of assumptions about what is believed to happen when money is spent and the intervention is made—tests cannot be designed for people who are unable to state their assumptions. Finally, the evaluator determines what kind of data would cause the administrator to act (i.e., make adjustments in the management of the program) and the kinds of action the administrator has the authority and willingness to implement (see Horst et al., 1974:300–8).

Second, since most programs that work well usually produce only relatively small gains in their early stages, evaluation should be built into the new program, its strengths and weaknesses being examined while it goes forward.

The Ordeal of Termination

The major deficiency in most discussions of evaluation is not hard to pinpoint. Such discussions tend to overlook the question of what to do when the findings are purely negative. After all, the whole justification for evaluative studies is to discover programs that are not working and then either to fix them or to stop them. But termination of a governmental activity does not follow automatically from a study's conclusion. In one 50-year period, only 27 organizations in the federal government were terminated, while the number of organizations increased from 175 to 394 (Kaufman, 1976).

Assuming one has the courage to actually try to eliminate a program that comes up over and over with failing marks in its evaluations, how does the would-be terminator proceed? Robert D. Behn (in Levine, 1980) offers several hints. First, do *not* float a trial balloon (i.e., testing public reaction to a proposal by having another person suggest it, thereby avoiding embarrassment to the author if reaction is strongly negative). Such action will give the opposition time to mobilize. Second, enlarge the policy's constituency. To close the Massachusetts public training schools, the Department of Youth Services' commissioner "recruited a number of liberal interest groups that were upset with the treatment of juveniles at the institutions. This new constituency broadened the scope of the conflict." Third, focus attention on the policy's harm to *particular* groups and individuals. Fourth, preclude compromise; this puts the supporters of the policy on the defensive. "A stand-up fight ensues, and the terminator has a chance for a clean knockout."

Fifth, recruit an outsider as terminator, such as Howard J. Phillips, who became acting director of the OEO for the sole purpose of dismantling that agency. Sixth, accept short-term cost increases, since terminating a policy often costs more in the short run than continuing it. Seventh, buy off the beneficiaries. Attempting to mollify those opposed to termination is one source of the short-term increases in costs. Eighth, advocate not "termination," with all its strong negative connotations, but "adoption," with the connotation of something new and better. "Consequently, the termination of policy A may best be realized through the adoption of policy B, when the selection of B necessitates the elimination of A."

Finally, terminate only what is necessary. "The distinction between a policy and the agency that administers it is important. Is the policy to be terminated because it is too expensive? The policy can be terminated and the agency maintained, or the agency can be terminated and the policy transferred to another department. To concentrate their energies, terminators must understand precisely what is their target."

Concepts for Review

- case management systems
- case-processing pipeline
- complexity of joint action
- control group
- CPM, PERT
- critical path
- demonstration projects
- direct handling time
- evaluation
- expediter
- field experiments
- follow-up
- Gantt chart
- impacts
- implementation
- incentives in public policy
- management by objectives
- metaphor of "games"
- national program impact evaluation
- outcome
- output
- participative decision making

- scenario writing
- scheduling models
- social indicators
- steps in an evaluation
- throughput time

Nailing Down the Main Points

1. With the organizational structure decided upon, the process of carrying out, accomplishing, or fulfilling the objectives of a program can begin. In short, we say implementation can begin. In the public sector, however, this task can be exceedingly difficult. Chances are the participants are heterogeneous and many. Chances are their perspectives on and priorities for a given program or project vary.
2. Given these difficulties, it becomes especially important to consider implementation at the start of the planning process—and that means during the policy planning stage (see Figure 5-1). Additionally, certain management techniques can increase the probability of success. Among these are scheduling models, expediters, incentives, and management by objectives.
3. Scheduling models facilitate the coordination of the activities of an enterprise. Among the leading types are Gantt chart, Critical Path Method (CPM), and Program Evaluation Review Technique (PERT). Regarding PERT, some authorities have suggested that it might be as much window dressing as a real control technique.
4. Because public administration often involves processing cases, careful attention should be given to the design and operation of a case management system.
5. Program evaluation is the systematic examination of activities to provide information on the full range of the program's short- and long-term effects. Based on this information, the decision maker can know whether to continue the program, to modify its procedures, or to expand its application. In short, evaluation forces managers to take closer looks at their programs. While evaluative activity today remains a much underdeveloped activity, it is at least receiving increasing attention.
6. Three major types of evaluation in particular concern policymakers: national program impact evaluation, demonstration projects, and field experiments (using a control group). It appears that the second and third types of evaluation have the best chance of influencing policymakers. The principal difference between the field trial and the demonstration project is that in the former those responsible for evaluation exercise greater control; conditions, in other words, are closer to those of a laboratory. One advantage of the field trial is accuracy: It measures what it is supposed to.
7. Evaluative research is useful to middle-level program managers as well as to the policymakers at the top. Wholey thinks, in fact, that the primary evaluation, pay-

off—in terms of decision actually influenced—is evaluation that is done in enough detail to get at the effects of operational changes within operating programs. Performance auditing can also be quite important at this level.

8. One of the best approaches to carry out an evaluation is reminiscent of the classical research experiment: (*a*) Find out the goals of the program; (*b*) translate the goals into measurable indicators of goal achievement; (*c*) collect data on the indicators for those who have been exposed to the program and for the control group; and (*d*) compare the data on the program participants and controls in terms of goal criteria.

9. Evaluators must remember that, above all, evaluation is a management tool. At the same time, managers need to remember that evaluation should not be a "go or no-go" proposition, with one test determining whether a major social program is to be launched; rather, evaluation should be built into the new program, examining its strengths and its weaknesses while it goes forward.

Problems

1. Crucial to the success of an MBO system is the writing of objectives. The objectives should tell *what* (the end result), *when* (a target date or period), and *who* (who is accountable for the objectives). Further, objectives should meet several criteria: cover only priority matters; be specific (no weasel words like *reasonable* or *highest*); be realistic yet set a level of difficulty that stretches the manager; and be supportive of the objectives of other departments (McConkey, 1975:52–59). Now, in light of this criteria, develop several objectives for a specific administrative position (e.g., director, division of criminal investigation; executive director of mental health center; and training director).

2. What weaknesses can you find in each of the measures of quality of life on pp. 266–267? Can you think of better measures? How would you weigh each aspect to get an overall figure for the quality of a city?

3. Discuss the advantages and disadvantages of setting up a new agency to carry out a program.

4. The objectives of a city's recreation program are these: "To provide all citizens, to the extent practicable, with a variety of leisure opportunities that are accessible, safe, physically attractive, and enjoyable. They should contribute to the mental and physical health of the community, to its economic and social well-being and permit outlets that will help decrease incidents of antisocial behavior such as crime and delinquency." Establish some measurable evaluation criteria for these objectives.

5. Prepare a paper on recent evaluative research on the U.S. criminal justice system. You may want a narrower topic: "Does punishment cut down on crime?" "Do work-release programs boost a convict's chance of getting a job?" and so on.

6. Social researchers say that when the results of the experiment accurately reflect the effect the program had on the participants, the study has *internal validity.* When the results of the experiment can be generalized to a broader population, they say it has *external validity.* How do you think field trials, national program impact evaluation, and demonstration projects compare in terms of these two types of validity?

7. Find the critical path in the following network. (Hint: Begin by working backward, assigning cumulative numbers to each mode. You do not need to test all possible paths. Follow this principle: If the optimal path from X to F passes through Y, and if the optimal path from T to F passes through X, then the optimal path from T to F passes through Y.).

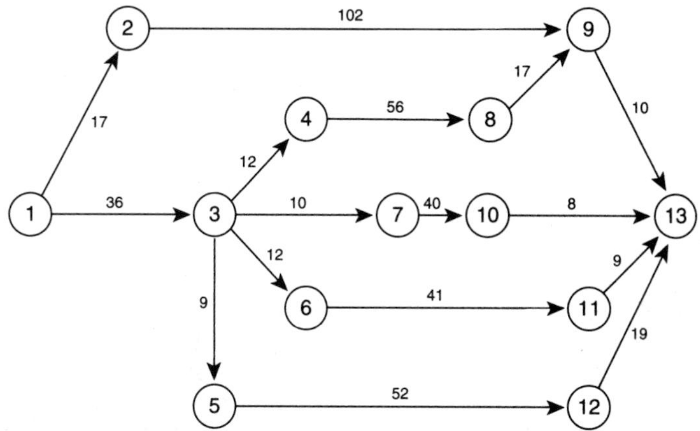

8. Your spouse has decided that you will build a patio and barbecue grill during your vacation. Since your annual vacation starts next week, you must have a plan in order to complete the patio on time. And because your spouse wants an enclosed patio, you will have to hire some help. Listed below are the activities and events involved. Prepare a PERT network for the patio project, including any additional events and activities you deem necessary to portray your plan adequately.

Events	*Activities*
Spouse's approval of design	
Building permit applied for	Apply for building permit
Building materials ordered	Order building materials
Ground leveled	Level ground
Help hired	Hire help
Concrete forms laid out	Lay out concrete forms
Structure fabricated	Fabricate structure
Building inspection approved	Receive building permit
Lighting installed	Install lighting
Concrete work finished	Finish concrete
Project completed	Receive materials
Materials received	Pay help

Help paid	Order concrete
Ready-mix concrete ordered	Build barbecue
Barbecue completed	Paint
Painting completed	Building inspection
Building permit received	Receive concrete

CASE 9.1

★★★★★★★★★★★★★★★★★★★★★★★★★★★★★★★★★★★★★

Slime in the Ice Machine

The director of the city health department is putting increased pressure on his food and restaurant division to improve its performance. And well he might. Every Thursday evening the director must listen to a five-minute exposé on filth in the city's restaurants. These exposés are delivered by a flamboyant local television reporter, Marvin Zinger. Citing one of the city's most popular restaurants, this was his report last Thursday: "Food was left *uncovered* over night; meat was kept at *improper* temperatures; *rodent* droppings were found in storage area; and *slime* was found in the ice machine!" Now local newspapers have picked up the drumbeat and have begun to run editorials criticizing the health department for infrequent inspections and long delays in responding to complaints about certain restaurants.

The food and restaurant division consists of 7 inspectors, 28 clerical employees, and 7 managerial and supervisory employees. The division head claims that he does not have enough staff and budget to be thorough and quick to respond and to make frequent visits—all at the same time.

Case Question

Improving the level of operation in the division might entail several different principles discussed in this chapter. As a recently hired consultant, you have been asked by the harried director to prepare a memo discussing, in general terms, possible changes.

CASE 9.2

★★★★★★★★★★★★★★★★★★★★★★★★★★★★★★★★★★★★★

American Social Policy, 1965–1985: Losing Ground?

Unintended Consequences of Government Programs

After 20 years and hundreds of billions of dollars spent on attempting to banish poverty in the United States, most scholars are not quite sure what to make of the effort. But Charles Murray, a senior fellow at the Manhattan Institute for Policy Research, is not one of them. In his book *Losing Ground,* Murray argues that the assessment of this problem should not be so murky.

Why is it, he asks, that poverty declined impressively from 1950 until 1968, only to begin growing and finally to stall while the greatest expenditure in U.S. history was being funneled toward the disadvantaged (see Exhibit 1)? Why has

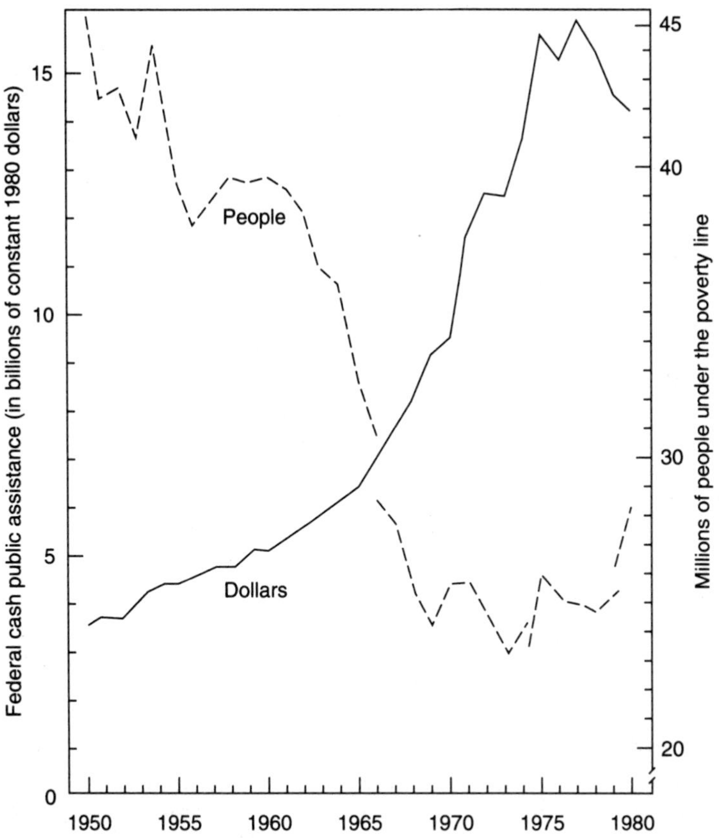

EXHIBIT 1
The Poverty/Spending Paradox

SOURCE: Charles Murray, *Losing Ground: American Social Policy, 1950–80* (New York: Basic Books, 1984), p. 57.

the number of people living in "latent poverty"—those actually in need or those who would be in need without government assistance—risen almost steadily since shortly after Great Society programs began in earnest (see Exhibit 2)? For years, latent poverty had declined. Why did the participation of young black males in the labor force (that is, those who had jobs or were looking for them) begin to fall sharply just when job-training programs began to spread?

The Labor department spent little on job training during the 1950s. From 1962 through 1980, however, nearly 33 million people enrolled in some kind of job-training program. Yet the performance of the very groups most targeted steadily worsened. Finally—to cite just one more of Murray's queries—why did the birthrate among unmarried teenagers rise during a period when the birthrates of virtually every other category of women, white and black, married and single, declined? Although the sexual revolution affected almost everyone, only single teenagers went counter to the general fertility trend, with one well-known result being the fem-

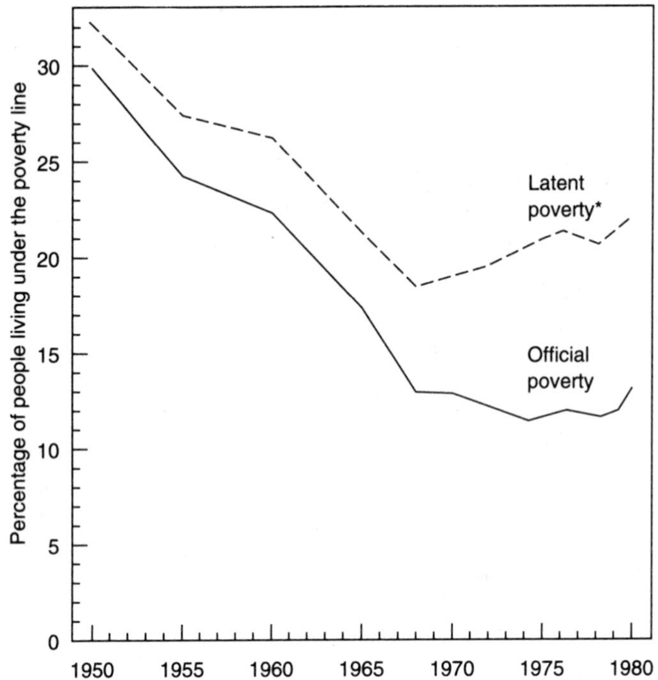

EXHIBIT 2
Two Views of Poverty, 1950–1980

* *Latent poverty* is a term that applies to everyone who would be poor without government help. In 1964, when the War on Poverty began, almost all emphasis was on eliminating poverty in this more fundamental sense. In other words, the goal was to eliminate altogether the need for "a dole." The "official poverty" measure has nothing to do with people's ability to make a living for themselves.

SOURCE: Charles Murray, *Losing Ground: American Social Policy, 1950–80* (New York: Basic Books, 1984), p. 65.

inization of poverty. (In 1980, more than half of 5.3 million poor families were headed by women with no husband in the home, versus less than one quarter of that number in 1959. In 1980, female-headed families accounted for more than half of the 11 million children living in poverty, versus less than 25 percent two decades earlier.)

Murray gives a disturbing answer to these puzzling questions. He maintains that government programs, which changed incentives and thus behavior, are themselves the explanation. More specifically, Murray argues that these programs made it less likely that energetic, talented men and women living in poverty would work their way out because the short-term benefits of doing so had diminished. Antipoverty programs even altered people's decisions about when and under what circumstances to bear children. In part, this phenomenon simply had to do with money, Murray thinks. Government programs narrowed the gap between the minimum wage and nonworking income, and in some states, the gap occasionally vanished. Moreover, the psychic rewards for escaping poverty also contracted as the notion took hold that society's flaws, and not individual behavior, explained everyone's plight.

Murray reminds us that historically the only path out of poverty has been long tedious hours of usually unpleasant, hard-to-get work; that is the way immigrants today still succeed. Contrary to conventional wisdom, education is not the normal ticket to prosperity for those at the lowest social levels. And, because the effort requires an unremitting commitment, it is not easily begun if short-term options make life tolerable.

The Social Scientists and the Great Experiment

What most clearly helps to establish these cause-effect relationships, Murray argues, is an ambitious attempt to evaluate the effect a guaranteed income would have on people's work effort. Briefly defined, a negative income tax provides payments to individuals whose income falls below a certain "floor," thereby guaranteeing, in effect, a minimum income.

The OEO vehicle for providing the proof took the form of the most ambitious social science experiment in American history. Known as the negative income tax (NIT) experiment, it began in 1968, ultimately used 8,700 people as subjects, and lasted for ten years.

The federally financed NIT experiment was launched at sites in New Jersey and Pennsylvania, then extended to Iowa, North Carolina, Indiana, Washington, and Colorado. At each site, a sample of low-income individuals was selected by researchers and was randomly split into two groups: the experimental group and the control group. Members of the experimental group were told that for a specified number of years (usually three) they would have a floor put under their incomes, whether they worked or not. The benefits to participants were varied in order to test their reactions to the gradations of generosity of the guaranteed income. Members of the control group received no benefits.

During the next decade, the results dribbled in. Finally, by the end of the 1970s, the social scientists had enough information to begin drawing some conclusions.

The key question was whether the NIT would reduce work effort among the poor. The answer was yes, and the reduction was substantial. In Seattle and Denver, for example, the NIT trimmed "desired hours of work" by 9 percent for husbands and by 20 percent for wives. ("Desired hours of work" was measured by actual employment after factoring involuntary work reductions, such as layoffs, out of the calculation.) Young males who were not yet heads of families—"nonheads" in the jargon—were especially affected. They were at a critical age in their lives—about to assume the responsibilities of marriage and just establishing themselves in the labor force. If they were going to escape from poverty, now was the time to start. The NIT had a disastrous impact on the number of hours they worked weekly—down 43 percent for those who remained nonheads throughout the experiment, down 33 percent for those who married. The NIT also produced a striking increase in the duration of unemployment after a participant in the experiment lost his or her job.

What about the impact of welfare on the family? Looking again at the Seattle and Denver experiments, the marriage dissolution rate was 36 percent higher for whites who received NIT payments than for those who did not and 42 percent higher for blacks. Interestingly, no such effect was observed among participants in Indiana because in that state couples were under the impression that they would lose their NIT payments if they split up.

Criticisms of Murray's Thesis

Murray naturally has many critics. They make the following points:

- Progress stopped in the 1970s because the economy began to slow.

Things would have been worse without the poverty programs.

- Overall progress seemed to stop because of the growing number of old people in the population. But progress really did not stop; blacks kept gaining.
- Progress did not really stop. The poverty measure is misleading because it is based on gross cash income. If one considers the dollar value of "in-kind" assistance (food stamps, Medicaid, housing benefits), one gets a different picture.
- It would have been worse without the War on Poverty.

Case Questions

1. Assume Murray has just briefed you. What questions might you ask or what criticisms might you make about Exhibit 1?
2. What biases, if any, do you see in the NIT experiment? Do you see any ethical problems in the experiment?
3. How would you test the objections Murray's critics raise? What data would you want, and what would you do with it?
4. Must final judgments in social science often rest on faith?

Case References

Charles Murray, *Losing Ground: American Social Policy, 1950–80* (New York: Basic Books, 1984); Martin Anderson, *Welfare* (Stanford, Calif.: Hoover Institution, 1978); Robert H. Haverman, *A Decade of Federal Antipoverty Programs* (New York: Academic Press, 1977); Blanche Bernstein, *Politics of Welfare* (Boston: Abt Books, 1982); John F. Schwarz, *America's Hidden Success: A Reassessment of Twenty Years of Public Policy* (New York: W. W. Norton, 1983.)

CASE 9.3

★★★★★★★★★★★★★★★★★★★★★★★★★★★★★★★★★★★

The China Lake Experiment

The Problem

The China Lake Naval Weapons Center (NWC) is located far from China and far from any lakes—150 miles north of Los Angeles, California, in the Mojave Desert. At that location, personnel officials cited problems in (1) recruiting the numbers of qualified personnel needed because starting salaries were not competitive with private industry and (2) retaining qualified senior personnel because of limited promotional opportunities above certain levels.

At the Naval Ocean Systems Center (NOSC), located near downtown San Diego, personnel officials described a different set of problems. Line managers at NOSC lacked flexibility when assigning work to their employees because the General Schedule (GS) position classification process required too much paperwork and time. Indeed, the GS provides rank designation (ranging from GS-1 to GS-18) and salary designation for each position in the civil service. Clerks and typists are appointed at GS-1 through GS-4 levels; key management personnel typically rise to GS-13 to GS-15. Moreover, the classification process was in the hands of personnel specialists rather than those of the line managers. NOSC officials thought that this situation made managers' jobs more difficult because it hindered their ability to effectively administer personnel resources.

Tampering With the System

Could the effectiveness of federal laboratories like the NWC and the NOSC really be enhanced if line managers had more control over personnel functions and employees' expanded opportunities through a more flexible personnel system? To learn the answer to these questions, the Office of Personnel Management (OPM) began a demonstration project in the 1980s, involving 3,076 employees at NOSC and 4,579 at NWC. It would change the GS system in three fundamental areas: classification, performance appraisal, and pay.

The changes in the classification system primarily involved combining the 18 separate GS grade classifications into broad pay bands and streamlining the classification process. In lieu of GS grades, the project established five separate career paths, and within each path employees were placed into one of several broad pay bands. Under this system, the process of classifying a position is greatly simplified and is now carried out by line managers using basic descriptions of positions within each career path. This gives managers more control of their staff and can speed up the process of hiring new employees.

The demonstration project featured a performance appraisal process, which consisted of three phases—development of a performance plan, interim reviews, and final appraisal at the end of the appraisal period (usually one year). The performance plan establishes the expectations of employee performance during the upcoming appraisal period. The expectations are written as objectives that employees are to accomplish. At least one interim review is required during the appraisal period. During the interim review, employees and their supervisors discuss how the employee is performing in relation to the performance plan and whether changes to the plan are needed. At the end of the rating period, the employee's performance is evaluated in relation to the objectives contained in the plan.

An analysis of this information was also affected by the project's establishment of five performance levels in the NOSC and NWC performance appraisal systems. Before the project, three performance levels were used—outstanding, satisfactory, and unacceptable. Thus, it was not possible to determine how many employees who were rated as satisfactory performers under the previous three-level system would have been placed in the levels directly above and below satisfactory in the new five-level system.

Because the pay bands incorporate at least two GS grades, adopting this system gave the NOSC and the NWC more discretion in determining the starting salary to be offered to new employees than previously existed. Subsequently, employees' pay levels are adjusted annually on the basis of performance and can include a salary increase within the same band, a one-time bonus or performance award, or a combination of both. Also, employees can receive pay increases through promotions to a higher band. In addition to performance-based pay increases and bonuses, employees in the two laboratories are also eligible for the same general pay adjustments (comparability) granted to employees under the GS system. Employees with ratings of fully successful or higher receive a full general increase, and employees with below fully successful ratings receive either one half or none of the general increase.

Was the Experiment Successful?

The project's original goal—improved laboratory effectiveness—could not be demonstrated primarily because of the inherent difficulty in defining and measuring such effectiveness. Instead, the true measure of the project's success was that it showed that the revised personnel management procedures could be implemented and that these procedures were superior to the procedures the NOSC and the NWC used before the project was established. The use of simplified classification, the establishment of a more direct link between performance and pay, and the increased managerial control over personnel functions appeared to help the NOSC and the NWC to achieve improve-

TABLE 1.
Views of Supervisors at Demonstration and Control Labs

I have enough authority to determine my employees' pay.

	Demonstration Labs			*Control Labs*		
	Disagree	*Undecided*	*Agree*	*Disagree*	*Undecided*	*Agree*
1979	83.4%	6.4%	10.1%	76.0%	9.1%	15.0%
	(272)	(21)	(33)	(218)	(26)	(43)
1981	62.5%	19.2%	18.3%	70.8%	13.9%	15.3%
	(212)	(65)	(62)	(194)	(38)	(42)
1982	54.8%	16.5%	28.7%	75.6%	10.6%	13.9%
	(206)	(62)	(108)	(136)	(19)	(25)
1983	48.8%	14.1%	37.1%	80.8%	10.1%	9.1%
	(201)	(58)	(153)	(168)	(21)	(19)
1984	40.5%	12.3%	47.2	75.4%	13.6%	11.0%
	(145)	(44)	(169)	(144)	(26)	(21)
1987	30.2%	16.1%	53.9%	71.7%	11.0%	17.3%
	(197)	(105)	(352)	(353)	(54)	(85)

I have enough authority to influence classification decisions.

	Demonstration Labs			*Control Labs*		
	Disagree	*Undecided*	*Agree*	*Disagree*	*Undecided*	*Agree*
1981	35.2%	42.4%	22.4%			
	(102)	(123)	(65)			
1982	47.3%	29.5%	23.2%			
	(157)	(98)	(77)			
1983	56.2%	25.2%	18.6%			
	(221)	(99)	(73)		No Data*	
1984	63.2%	20.1%	16.7%			
	(204)	(65)	(54)			
1987	18.8%	23.1%	58.1%	38.0%	21.1%	40.8%
	(123)	(151)	(380)	(187)	(104)	(201)

*Between 1981 and 1984 this question was asked of demonstration supervisors only.

SOURCE: U.S. Office of Personnel Management, *Effects of Performance-Based Pay on Employees in the Navy Demonstration Project: An Analysis of Survey Responses 1979 to 1987* (Washington, D.C.: U.S. Office of Personnel Management, 1988).

ments in managerial flexibility over work load assignments, recruitment of employees, and retention of quality employees.

To test the effects of the new personnel processes, a nonequivalent control group evaluation design was used. The objective of this design was to determine project impacts by making before and after comparisons between sites participating in the demonstration project and similar nonparticipating sites. If demonstration and nonequivalent control groups have sufficiently similar characteristics and the required data are collected, this is one of the stronger evaluation designs for ruling out external events as explanations of study findings (see Table 1).

Given the inherent difficulties of doing a rigorous, controlled evaluation of a complex program in a dynamic environment, it is probably not reasonable to expect the OPM's evaluation of this one project to have fully answered all questions. But it did represent an important step in building a knowledge base on systemic methods of improving personnel management and performance. By conducting more small-scale projects of this nature and constantly improving evaluations of them, the weaknesses of individual studies will become less prominent and the applicability of findings to other settings will be enhanced.

Case Questions

1. Discuss the strengths and weaknesses of this evaluative study. Be sure to address the issue of causation and the problems of measurement and generalizability.
2. Assuming that the new system is proven superior to the old, why might it still not be adopted throughout the federal government?

Case References

U.S. Office of Personnel Management, *A Summary Assessment of the Navy Demonstration Project* (Washington, D.C.: U.S. Office of Personnel Management, 1986); U.S. General Accounting Office, *Observations on the Navy's Personnel Management Demonstration Project* (Washington, D.C.: U.S. Government Printing Office, 1988); Carolyn Ban, "The Navy Demonstration Project: An Experiment 'in Experimentation,'" in Carolyn Ban and Norma Riccucci, eds., *Public Personnel Management* (New York: Longman, 1991), pp. 31–41.

CASE 9.4

★ ★

The Politics of Getting an Idea Adopted: The Inchon Decision

Preliminaries

When the Korean War began in 1950, Douglas MacArthur—the most brilliant and among the most flamboyant American generals of the 20th century—was soon selected to command United Nations forces there. Only five days after North Korea began the war by invading South Korea, MacArthur seized on a concept for winning the war. Afterward he would write in his *Reminiscences:* "I was now ready for the last great stroke to bring my plan to fruition . . . a turning movement deep into the flank and rear of the enemy that would sever his supply lines and encircle all his forces south of Seoul" (see Exhibit 1).

Upon returning to his headquarters in Tokyo on July 4, 1950, he ordered his staff to prepare plans for such an operation. Six days later they had developed Operation Blueheart, which called for a landing on July 22. The plan was, however, absurd; it did not allow sufficient time for preparation, and MacArthur did not have enough troops.

So MacArthur was forced to abandon Blueheart but not the idea. He turned his energies toward getting the troops he would need—no small task. As J. Lawton

EXHIBIT 1

The North Korean Invasion—June 25, 1950

The North Korean invasion on June 25, 1950, headed by seven infantry divisions and a tank brigade, spilled across the 38th parallel and shattered the beach that had existed. The four poorly equipped South Korean divisions could offer little opposition. Seoul, the South Korean capital, fell in three days and the Allied forces retreated to the Pusan perimeter (shaded area). The United Nations Command offensive of September 1950 was the dramatic counterstroke devised by MacArthur. The crux of the operation was the landing at Inchon (arrow). The successful landing turned the tide of the war.

Collins, the army chief of staff told him: "General, you are going to have to win the war out there with the troops available to you in Japan and Korea." MacArthur replied: "Joe, you are going to have to change your mind."

Among his first steps was to get the marines on board. In explaining his bold idea of a landing at Inchon, he held out to General Lemuel C. Shepherd, Jr., commander of the Fleet Marine Force, Pacific, the opportunity for the marines to grab a significant role in the Korean War and then induced Shepherd himself to request from the joint chiefs of staff (JCS) that more marines be sent from the United States.

The navy also had to be won over. During a visit to MacArthur in July, General Collins had spoken privately to Admiral James Doyle, the naval commander. He found the admiral unenthusiastic about the Inchon invasion. When Collins asked him about landing in an area with 35-foot tides, Doyle replied, "It will be extremely difficult . . . but it can be done." Collins had been in the military long enough to recognize a hedge when he heard one. Doyle was, in effect, saying: "The plan is foolhardy, but I'm not going to argue it with MacArthur. If ordered, I'll undertake it."

Before returning to Washington, Collins met once more with MacArthur. Although Collins remained skeptical about an Inchon landing, he felt a marine division could be sent. This implied promise was good enough for now, MacArthur thought; when he got the marines under his control, he would deal with the Pentagon's worries about Inchon.

During the last part of July, MacArthur continued to send message after message explaining his reasons for wanting an amphibious assault. He also had the opportunity to argue this case directly to a White House emissary, effectively bypassing the JCS. Truman had sent advisor W. Averell Harriman to Tokyo to protest MacArthur's public statements in support of Chiang Kai-shek. Ironically, MacArthur was able to turn Harriman's remonstration into a successful opportunity to lobby for his Inchon plan.

On July 23, he cabled the JCS that plans for the operation, now renamed "Chromite," were ready. Two days later, he received word that he would get his cutting edge: The marines would be sent.

"A Masterful Exposition"

Yet the JCS remained wary. In August, having received little additional information from MacArthur about Operation Chromite, the chairman of the JCS, Omar Bradley, sent General Collins along with chief of naval operations, Admiral Forrest Sherman, across the Pacific—perhaps as much to dissuade as to discuss.

Collins, Sherman, MacArthur, and various staff personnel met in Tokyo at 5:30 on the afternoon of August 23 in a paneled six-floor conference room in the Dai Ichi Building; it was the most impressive assemblage of military leadership since the war had begun.

It was not hard to see why the JCS and others were having second thoughts. MacArthur had chosen the unlikeliest harbor on the peninsula: Inchon, on the Yellow Sea, 150 miles north of Pusan, had no beaches, only piers and seawalls. The attack would have to be launched in the heart of the city. The waters approaching the harbor could easily be mined; currents there ran as high as eight knots. In any one of a hundred turns, a sunken or disabled ship could block the little bay. Worst of all were the tides, among the highest in the world. The only dates when the surf would be high enough to accommodate amphibious ships and landing craft in 1950 were September 15, September 27, and October 11. September 15 was best, but high tide then crested first at dawn, too early for awkward troop transports to maneuver beforehand in the narrow passage, and again a half hour after sundown, too late for a daylight attack. Therefore, as many marines as possible would have to be put ashore during the 2 hours of the first flood tide; 12 hours would pass before the second flood tide would permit reinforcement. As one naval officer said afterward: "We drew up a list of every natural and geographic handicap—and Inchon had 'em all. . . . Make up a list of amphibious 'don'ts' and you have an exact description of the Inchon operation."

Not surprisingly, every flag and general officer in Tokyo—including General Walker whose Eighth Army would be freed from the Pusan Perimeter (see Exhibit 1) by a successful drive against the North Koreans—tried to talk MacArthur out of the operation. Even MacArthur's own staff was unconvinced, but he turned a deaf ear to all.

For 80 minutes these objections were heard in the conference room that Wednesday afternoon in Tokyo. MacArthur sat silently, impassively, puffing on his pipe. When everyone finished, he remained silent a few more moments, possibly for dramatic effect: MacArthur enjoyed the suspense. He wrote later: "I waited a moment or so to collect my thoughts. I could feel the tension rising in the room. [General] Almond shifted uneasily in his chair. If ever a silence was pregnant, this one was. I could almost hear my father's voice telling me as he had so many years before, 'Doug, councils of war breed timidity and defeatism.' "

Then he spoke for 45 minutes without notes, quietly at first, then gradually "building up emphasis with consummate skill." Collins commented later: "Even discounting the obvious dramatics, this was a masterful exposition of the argument for the daring risk he was determined to take."

MacArthur began by telling them that "the very arguments you have made as to the impracticabilities involved" confirmed his faith in the plan, "for the enemy commander will reason that no one would be so brash as to make such an attempt." Surprise, he said, "is the most vital element for success in war." Suddenly he was reminding them of a lesson they had all learned in grammar school: the surprise British raid on Quebec in 1759, when a small force scaled supposedly impossible heights and caught the French totally unprepared.

The amphibious landing, he said, "is the most powerful tool we have." To employ it properly, "we must strike hard and deep." Inchon's hurdles were real, "but they are not insuperable." And he had another history lesson that they may not have learned: In 1894 and 1904, the Japanese had landed at Inchon and seized all Korea. He said: "My confidence in the navy is complete, and in fact I seem to have more confidence in the navy than the navy has in itself." Looking at Sherman, he said: "The navy has never let me down in the past, and it will not let me down this time." As to a Kunsan landing, farther south, he believed it would be ineffective. "It would be an attempted envelopment," and therefore futile. "Better no flank movement than one such as this. The only result would be a hookup with Walker's troops. . . . This would simply be sending more troops to help Walker 'hang on,' and hanging on is not good enough. . . . The enemy will merely roll back on his lines of supply and communication." Kunsan, the "only alternative" to Inchon, would be "the continuation of the savage sacrifice we are making at Pusan, with no hope of relief in sight."

He paused dramatically. Then: "Are you content to let our troops stay in that bloody perimeter like beef cattle in the slaughterhouse? Who will take the responsibility for such a tragedy? Certainly, I will not."

Pouncing on Inchon and then Seoul, he said, he would "cut the enemy's supply line and seal off the entire southern peninsula. . . . By seizing Seoul I would completely paralyze the enemy's supply system—coming and going. This in turn will paralyze the fighting power of the troops that now face Walker."

If he was wrong about the landing, "I will be there personally and will immediately withdraw our forces." Doyle, stirred, spoke up: "No, General, we don't know how to do that. Once we start ashore we'll keep going." MacArthur had reached them. When another man pointed out that enemy batteries could command the dead-end channel, Sherman, intractable till then, sniffed and said, "I wouldn't hesitate to take a ship in there." MacArthur snapped back: "Spoken like a Farragut!" He concluded in a hushed voice: "I can almost hear the ticking of the second hand of destiny. We must act now or we will die. . . . Inchon will succeed. And it will save 100,000 lives."

The following Monday, four days later, the Supreme Commander of Allied Powers received approval from Washington for Operation Chromite.

The "Promptitude to Act"

MacArthur had little doubt about his ability to move his men rapidly, to display, in Churchill's words, "that intense clarity of view and promptitude to act which are the qualities of great commanders." Two days after the cable from Washington, MacArthur's staff had issued bulk operation plans; none were sent, however, to the JCS.

In fact, the JCS were kept in the dark regarding the details until the last minute. MacArthur did send a young lieutenant

General Douglas MacArthur congratulates General Oliver P. Smith, commanding general of the First Marine Division, for the successful Inchon invasion. (Signal Corps photo/Sgt. Herbert Nutter)

colonel to Washington, who managed to arrive the night before the landing and briefed the JCS only six hours before it took place.

Early on the morning of September 15, the invasion armada, a total of 19 ships, approached their target under cover of darkness. MacArthur, age 70, came onto the flag bridge of the *McKinley* to watch the bombardment. As usual he wore his battered, salt-stained garrison cap.

The last bombs hit at 6:20 A.M.; four minutes later seven landing craft touched shore. At 6:55 A.M., Sergeant Alvin E. Smith tied an American flag on a shell-torn tree on the crest of Radio Hill. MacArthur, binoculars focused on the island, nodded approval. He told Admiral Doyle, "Say to the fleet, 'The navy and marines have never shone more brightly than this morning.' " He arose. "That's it," he said, "let's get a cup of coffee."

Epilogue

At the end of D-day all objectives had been taken, with 20 men killed, 1 missing and 174 wounded. The surprise had been total. By the end of D + 1, the First and Fifth Marines had linked up and advanced to secure and establish a perimeter six miles inland from the landing sites. MacArthur's bold stroke paid off fully when Seoul was captured on September 22, and the demoralized remnants of the North Korean army fell backward after the Inchon landing forces linked up with the Eighth Army four days later.

Case Questions

1. What are the main lessons in this case about the practical politics of getting an idea adopted?
2. What do you think of the way in which MacArthur failed to keep the JCS informed?
3. What other important ideas presented in Part II of this book do you see illustrated by this case?

Case References

Douglas MacArthur, *Reminiscences* (New York: McGraw-Hill, 1964); Joseph C. Goulden, *Korea: The Untold Story* (New York: McGraw-Hill, 1982); William Manchester, *American Caesar* (New York: Dell, 1978).

PART III

Resources Management

CHAPTER 10 Human Resources Management

Introduction

The public administrator can and should turn to others for help with certain people-related activities. What kind of help might this be? Some managerial concerns that might require expert assistance are basic. For example, the work to be performed in the organization must be broken down into jobs; each job in turn should have a clear description of the work it entails. At the same time, a plan must be developed to assure equal pay for equal work; that is, the compensation scale should be based on the skills required by the job. These two areas of concern, **position classification** and **compensation,** provide the basis for effective recruitment.

Recruitment, or **staffing,** is the process of matching individual skills and aptitudes with job specifications. It is another area of managerial concern in which help might be desirable. Too often administrators agonize over termination decisions when a wiser investment of time would have been in the selection decision. Closely associated with the staffing concern are the procedures used to recognize accomplishment and to take optimal advantage of individual abilities. In particular, the public executive frequently needs assistance in such critical areas as examination, performance evaluation, and promotion.

For help in the never-ending task of motivating employees, the administrator might turn to others for help with training and counseling. Similarly, in those difficult cases of individual suspension and dismissal, the prudent administrator might seek assistance.

The foregoing concerns—classification and compensation, staffing, training, and separation—are the traditional concerns of **public personnel management** (PPM). They form the core of this chapter.

But to these traditional concerns we must add a second layer, which can be called the "new concerns" of PPM. One of the better publicized of these concerns is **organizational culture;** that is, the shared values of an organization. Because some climates are more conducive to productivity than others, this idea is an important one.

Another layer to consider is the legal environment of PPM. Of particular importance are laws and court cases involving labor relations and affirmative action.

Figure 10-1 illustrates how the various aspects of human resources management fit together. People enter public service through one of the four personnel systems. These four systems appear at the top of the model as inputs to the model.

At a bare minimum, human resources management consists of the five functions shown in the middle box: staffing; classification and compensation; training and management development; advancement; and discipline and grievances. These five functions affect employees at many junctures in their careers. More pervasive in influence are the culture (or shared values) of the organization and the laws affecting personnel practice. A human resources management system that neglects the former misses an opportunity to enhance the productivity of employees; but one that neglects the latter risks protracted legal battles and adverse publicity.

Even Methuselahs must sooner or later depart the system. As indicated at the bottom of the model, exit occurs in three ways: dismissal, retirement, or resignation.

The remainder of this chapter will be an explication of Figure 10-1.

The Structure of Public Personnel

Framing a satisfactory typology of personnel systems is, as Frederick C. Mosher (1968:135–75) correctly notes, a challenge: "American governments have displayed almost unlimited ingenuity in developing different kinds of arrangements for the employment of personal services, ranging from compulsion (selective service) to volunteers (Peace Corps, Vista, etc.) and without compensation (WOC), with a great variety of categories in between." Nevertheless, for purposes of description, analysis, and comparison, Mosher is able to classify the public service into **four main types of**

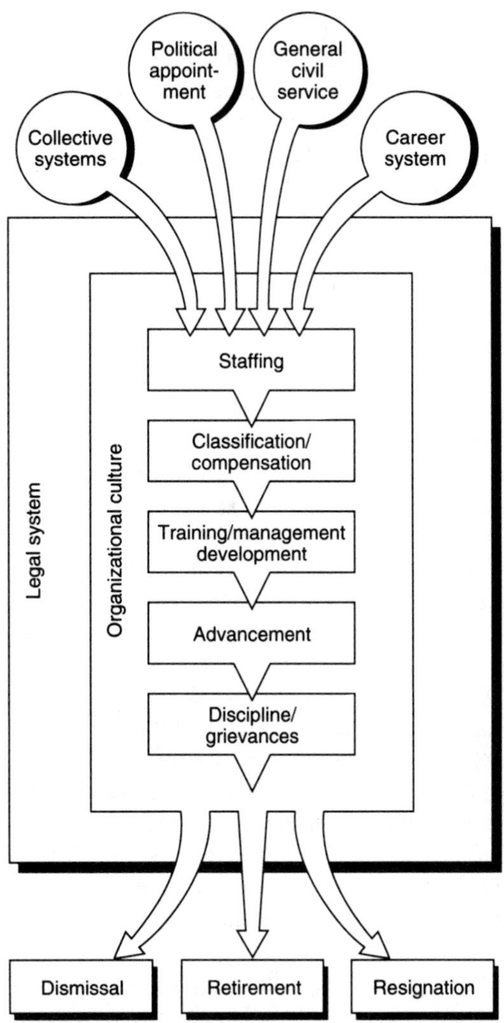

FIGURE 10-1
Framework for Analyzing Human Resources Management

personnel systems: political appointees, general civil service, career systems, and collective system.

Political Appointees

Political appointees are those public officials appointed to an office without tenure who have policymaking powers and are outside the civil service system. Presidents are allowed to make about 5,000 political appointments to top positions within the executive branch. These jobs range from cabinet officials to confidential secretaries. At the state and local level, civil service law and practice vary so widely that generalization is hazardous; but as Mosher (1968:166) notes: "It is safe to assume that most of the larger governments in industrialized areas have political executives in approximately parallel capacities and roles. Some have a great many more proportionately than the federal government; some have many fewer."

General Civil Service

In the federal government, the general civil service system is composed of white-collar personnel, mostly nonprofessional, who have tenure. Their employment is administered in keeping with traditional civil service practices.

That tradition is easily traced back to the 1870s, when the obvious abuses of the **spoils system** (i.e., the right of elected officials to reward their friends and supporters with government jobs) had produced demands for reform that could not be ignored. By 1883, the first civil service law, the **Pendleton Act,** passed. This legislation, also known as the **Civil Service Reform Act** of 1978, established the bipartisan Civil Service Commission to choose federal employees from lists of those who had passed competitive examinations (the so-called merit system).

The examinations under the civil service system are practical rather than scholarly. Each available position is described in detail, and the examinations are geared to the needs of each. After passing a written test, the candidate might take an oral examination if the job warrants it. If successful with both, the person's name is placed on an eligibility list, which is set up on the basis of examination scores. Federal law requires that the agency choose from among the top three to five scores on the list, without passing over veterans. In many merit systems there are further job requirements, such as height and weight requirements for police officers, high school or college graduation for particular occupations, and certifications or licenses for many civil service positions (e.g., for the position of attorney or physician). Such requirements, however, must be clearly job related.

Merit systems can be organized in many ways. In many jurisdictions, a nonpartisan or bipartisan commission or board is charged with general program direction and appellate functions, leaving to a personnel director (appointed by the board or the chief executive) the responsibility for day-to-day program administration. In others, a personnel director reporting to the chief executive is responsible for general program direction, with a civil service commission or board serving in a watchdog, advisory, or appellate role (or all three).

Career Systems

Government jobs outside the civil service system are not necessarily appointive, for many agencies have developed their own career systems. These systems are composed of white-collar personnel, generally professionals and paraprofessionals, who are tenured in the agency and occupation though not in the position. Their employment is administered as a progressive, preferably planned development. In such a system,

The job of surgeon general of the United States carries with it very little official authority. Its holder performs no surgery. The formal duties are modest: to issue reports on public health issues, to advise on federal health policy, and to provide leadership for the 5,300 officers in the Commissioned Corps of the United States Public Health Service. He or she is a political appointee, but in the political hierarchy, the position's power is limited—the surgeon general reports to the assistant secretary for health, placing him or her three levels below cabinet ranking. In fact, most surgeons general of the past have been obscure figures.

One of the most visible members of the Reagan Administration, however, was Surgeon General C. Everett Koop. That visibility allowed him to parlay his job into a position of far greater power than the title officially provides, as he dealt forthrightly with the AIDS crisis and championed a smoke-free society. His strong point was to say things as honestly as he could, in a strong and authoritative voice, for the benefit of the public's health. (Photo by Linda L. Creighton—USN&WR)

repeated failure to attain promotion—being "passed over" too many times—can result in dismissal; hence, the expression "up or out."

The model of the career system is that of military officers. In fact, the military system has been copied in or adopted to a number of other federal activities—for example, the Foreign Service, the Public Health Service (see photo), the FBI, the CIA, and the TVA. In varying degrees, it has also been a model for state and local police systems and local fire departments.

Unlike the civil service system, a career system emphasizes the individual rather than the position. Thus, as Mosher (1968) points out, a "nonprofessional civil servant working in the Department of the Navy is most likely to respond, 'I work for the Navy Department'; an officer, 'I am an officer (or an admiral or captain) in the navy.' "

Career systems possess several challenges to the manager. For example, members of a career personnel system, such as the naval officer above, must work with other personnel within the organization who lack comparable career status. Obviously, when personnel are working together on the same project but under two distinct employment systems, the possibility of friction is great.

Collective System

The collective system is composed of blue-collar workers whose employment is governed primarily through bargaining between union or association and governmental jurisdiction. But these blue-collar, low-skilled jobs in the federal government are disappearing, while the need for highly skilled and technically trained workers is soaring (see box).

Basic Functions of a Public Personnel System

Staffing

The term *staffing* refers to the process of recruiting, selecting, and advancing employees on the basis of their relative ability, knowledge, and skill.

Recruiting and Testing. Merit recruiting means more than just posting an examination announcement on a bulletin board. Every possible source of qualified candidates within the appropriate labor market must be reached in a positive way. A program of positive recruitment includes elements such as the following (U.S. Civil Service Commission, 1974):

- Writing examination announcements in clear, understandable language.
- Advertising in publications that circulate to the various segments of the population, and using other media such as radio and television.
- Establishing easy-to-reach job-information centers.
- Visiting colleges, high schools, and community organizations.
- Using mobile or storefront recruiting centers.
- Developing continuing contacts with minority and women's organizations.

Selection on the basis of "relative ability" presumes being able to draw distinctions among the qualifications of competing candidates fairly and objectively.

(text continues on p. 454)

Civil Service 2000

After the budget cuts and reductions in force that marked the 1980s, the United States will be in a hiring mode for the 1990s and beyond. Like employers in the private sector, the federal government is projected to have more openings in the next 20 years than there are skilled, trained, and qualified people to fill them. Nationally, only a quarter of the jobs are professional, technical, and managerial, but in the federal government, the figure is twice as high and expected to grow. Experts predict a 17 percent increase in engineers, a 15 percent increase in lawyers, and a 10 percent increase in management-related federal workers during the next 12 years.

Three million Americans work for the federal government in nonmilitary jobs, almost 98 percent in the executive branch. States that have more than 100,000 federal civilian employees include California, Florida, Illinois, Maryland, New York, Pennsylvania, and Texas.

Just to keep a stable work force, the federal government hires about 300,000 people a year for about 200 occupations. Of that number, 135,000 of the new hires are career civil servants.

One of the biggest hurdles, if not the biggest, to bringing talented people into government has been pay. Most federal jobs, given general service (GS) grades from 1 to 18, pay 22 to 40 percent less than comparable ones in the private sector, according to an annual Labor Department survey. To help bridge the gap, the Office of Personnel Management (OPM), which sets hiring policies, has approved raises of up to 30 percent for some critically scarce employees, including scientists, engineers, doctors, nurses, mathematicians, accountants, and computer specialists. In addition, the Senior Executive Service (SES) of top federal executives and political appointees offers salaries of up to $108,300 (as of 1992).

As Congress and the president work to close these gaps, OPM continues its war against red tape by reducing the multiple forms and reviews once synonymous with a federal job hunt. Most agencies now have "direct-hire authority" for hard-to-fill spots. This means qualified applicants can submit their Form 171, the government's official resume, directly to an agency's personnel office, bypassing the OPM and saving considerable time.

While government may never entirely catch up with the private sector in monetary rewards, it has always been quite competitive in rewards for the psyche. For example, Karen Tenke-White made a smooth jump in 1989 from private industry to a GS-13 civil engineering job with the Army Corps of Engineers in Chicago, lured by a "marvelous" training program and her perception that the government treats women fairly. "These people are interested," she says of her new employers. "They want you."

Promotion to positions of real responsibility generally come much quicker in government. Furthermore, there is the opportunity to work on problems of national importance. After all, there's only one NASA and one Center for Communicable Diseases. The variety of jobs and locations is also appealing. For example, David Lilly, an investigator with the Labor Department's mine safety and

(continued)

health administration, is based in Juneau, Alaska. He helped rescue baby Jessica McClure from a well in Midland, Texas. Teresa Moreno-Fullerton, a special agent in Los Angeles with the Treasury's Bureau of Alcohol, Tobacco, and Firearms, has helped uncover drug and money-laundering operations. Intangible rewards such as these must be weighed against monetary rewards that come from a career of, say, producing purple bowling balls or deciding whether dancing bears should go around the cereal bowl clockwise or counter-clockwise.

How does one find the best job when there are some 175 agencies to choose from? Privately published vacancy listings like *Federal Career Opportunities,* at (803) 281–0200, or *Federal Jobs Digest,* at (914) 762–5111, can help. For 40 cents a minute, you can dial (900) 990–9200 and get a recorded message on federal job opportunities. You can also leave a request for exam applications to be mailed. Applications for fall exams are accepted in early fall. The *Federal Careers Directory* explains the types of jobs offered in all major agencies and includes educational requirements and contact names. Individuals can order the book (stock number 006-000-01339-2) through the Government Printing Office at (202) 783–3238.

SOURCES: U.S. General Accounting Office, *The Public Service* (Washington, D.C.: U.S. Government Printing Office, September 1990); Hudson Institute, *Civil Service 2000* (Washington, D.C.: U.S. Government Printing Office, 1990); *U.S. News & World Report,* September 17, 1990; *Chicago Tribune,* May 13, 1990.

Recent court decisions have made it clear that all selection tools must be valid and job related. In other words, performance on a test has to match performance on the job.

Employers have, of course, other methods besides written tests to evaluate candidates for initial employment or advancement: performance tests, panel interviews, ratings of relevant training, and experience, or any combination of these with other tests. For most jobs, a combination of job-related testing devices, rather than any single one, provides a better measure of the knowledge, skills, and abilities needed for successful job performance.

David McClelland (1973) proposes testing for competence rather than intelligence. He attacked the circular reasoning that links psychological tests to our credential-happy society. The basic problem with many proficiency measures for validating ability tests is that they depend heavily on the credentials—habits, values, accents, interests, and so on—that people bring to the job and that makes them acceptable to management and to clients. Employers have a right to select people who have gone to the right schools because they do better on the job, but psychologists do not have a right to argue that it is the intelligence of these people that makes them more proficient in their jobs.

McClelland is also interested in getting away from multiple-choice tests. A. N. Whitehead once wrote that these tests require only one level of mental activity beyond being awake: recognition. In any event, according to McClelland, sorting out the trivial from the absurd is hardly a good way for a person to prove his or her capabilities. For example, McClelland set up for the U.S. Information Agency a screening program that used the PONS (profile of nonverbal sensitivity) test. McClelland played short tape segments to job applicants and then asked them what emotion was being expressed. Presumably, this kind of sensitivity would be important to diplomats. (The State Department, however, vetoed the program: "Too experimental.")

Selection. Once a competitive examination is completed, an employment list based on the examination results is established and the names of the highest ranking eligibles are certified to the appointing official for selection. The process itself is called **certification.** According to merit concept, only a limited number of qualified eligibles should be certified. To do otherwise, such as certifying a whole list of eligibles, for example, would change the basis for hiring from competitive merit to a "pass-fail" system.

Personnel systems usually follow the **rule of three,** which permits the appointing official to choose among the top three individuals certified to him or her, without passing over veterans. Why have a rule of three? The first reason is to overcome the objection that written tests cannot appraise personality factors adequately, that the examining process can produce individuals who may qualify intellectually but have serious personal problems. The second reason is to appease appointing officers by bringing them more into the process.

Significantly, the Hoover Commission recommended instead that applicants be grouped into several categories such as "outstanding," "well qualified," and "unqualified," and that appointing officials select individuals from the higher categories, moving down as each list was exhausted. Today, as the crucial issues in public administration become productivity and efficiency—not patronage, which the civil service system was designed to eliminate—these recommendations are more acceptable than ever.

An increasing number of critics claim that state and local civil service commissions—usually appointed by successive mayors or governors and removable only for cause—cannot easily be controlled by a single, elected executive. Because elected officials have little control over the selection of their employees, they are obviously hampered in instituting the programs they were elected to carry out.

In short, critics maintain that civil service commissions are archaic and inflexible. Denver police officers, for example, are still required to have a minimum of four molar teeth, an apparent holdover of "bite the bullet" to remove the wax that bullets used to be encased in. And until only recently, Denver police regulations stipulated that Civil War veterans be given preference for job vacancies (Laing, 1975).

Regardless of the process by which candidates are certified, the managers eventually face the decision of selecting one individual to fill the vacancies. This decision is perhaps the heart of staffing. But what should the manager look for?

In a word, strength. Writes Drucker (1966:Chapter 4):

> *Whoever tries to place a man . . . in an organization to avoid weakness will end up at best with mediocrity. The idea that there are well-rounded people, people who have only strengths and no weaknesses . . . is a prescription for mediocrity . . . strong people always have strong weaknesses, too. Where there are peaks, there are valleys. And no one is strong in many areas. There is no such thing as a "good man." Good for what? is the question.*

Drucker relates the familiar story of how Lincoln learned this lesson the hard way. Before Grant came a string of generals whose main qualifications were their lack of major weaknesses.

> *In sharp contrast, Lee . . . had staffed from strength. Every one of Lee's generals, from Stonewall Jackson on, was a man of obvious and monumental weaknesses. Each of them had, however, one area of strength, and only this strength, that Lee utilized and made effective.*
>
> *One story about Lee captures especially well the meaning of making strength productive. After learning that one of his generals had, again, disregarded his orders, Lee, who normally controlled his temper, became furious. Finally, an aide asked, "Why not relieve him?" Lee turned in complete amazement, looked at the aide, and said, "What an absurd question—he performs."*

Classification and Compensation

At all levels of government, the basis of the civil service is the position classification system. Simply stated, **position classification** involves identifying the duties and responsibilities of each position in an organization and then grouping the positions according to their similarities. A good system can help the administrator make better decisions regarding the relationship of duties and responsibilities to the other concerns of personnel administration. After all, a fair compensation plan does require an understanding of the duties and responsibilities of each position ("equal pay for equal work"); effective examination and recruiting do require knowledge of what the agency is examining and recruiting for; and determining the qualifications necessary for performing the job does require an understanding of what the job entails.

Although position classification evolved as a convenient and useful tool, today the concept is frequently under attack. First, the procedures for classification can be a paperwork maze in which job incumbents have considerable influence, though they often view the process with trepidation: "For all practical purposes, the technicians evaluate the jobs in the government system, and the line or functional management must accept their judgments. Industry reverses the process. The line or functional managers—who certainly know the jobs best—evaluate the various positions and tell the technicians in personnel where they should be valued in the structure'' (Patton, 1974:34).

While evaluating the difficulty of duties may not cause too many problems, evaluating and comparing *responsibilities* often does. How many subordinates are supervised? How much time is spent in actual supervision? Who is supervised? How much innovation is expected? To attempt to weigh these factors objectively is no easy task.

Some attack position classification as being obsolete. Although it once provided a way of treating people equitably and eliminating spoils, position classification is not always relevant to activities performed by the more sophisticated organizations discussed in Chapter 7. In such organizations, the work situation becomes too collegial, too free-form for rigid position classifications. In such an organization, position classification (or rank-in-job approach) might be replaced with the **rank-in-person-approach,** which uses the abilities and experience of the individual as the basis for making various personnel decisions (e.g., setting of compensation). Examples of this kind of system include the military and college faculties. The rank-in-person concept, therefore, means that a person carries a rank regardless of the duties performed at a particular time.

Like position classification, compensation of public employees is a very important and often a very controversial part of public personnel administration. Based on our discussion of motivation in Chapter 8, the importance to the employee of an adequate and equitable compensation schedule should be apparent. If the employee perceives that the plan is unfair, conflict is likely.

But how does one establish a good pay plan? The general rule is this: Pay according to differences in levels of duties and responsibilities.

The expert who has probably thought the most about this question is Elliott Jacques (1970, 1979) at England's Brunel University. At the heart of Jacques's findings is a concept that he calls the time frame of the individual. His research indicates that individuals vary radically in terms of the time periods they need to think out, organize, and work through tasks. What makes this research relevant to compensation is his finding that there is a sort of natural structure to organizations engaged in work wherein most jobs can be classified according to the time frame required of the incumbent. Jacques thinks that the best organizations, in terms of morale and productivity, are those whose structure follows what might be called the natural hierarchy. That is, one-day time-frame workers report to a supervisor who can organize at least the next three months; that supervisor, in turn, follows the directions of a manager who can plan a year or longer; that manager reports to an executive with a two-year time frame; and so on.

The federal government pays its employees at salary levels that are generally comparable to those in the private sector (see box on pp. 453–454). However, the government provides fringe benefits that are 76 percent higher than those in the private sector. Why is this the case? In the 1920s, it was felt that neither civil service pay nor military pay was competitive with salaries in private business. Rather than simply raise pay, Congress decided to push costs far into the future (where current taxpayers and voters would not notice them) by setting up an exceedingly generous pension system.

Talking Shop

Picking Talent

Selecting talented people is a managerial art that public administrators should be trained in but seldom are. The reason for the importance of selection is simple: Hiring mistakes can be extremely expensive. Not only does it take time and money to get rid of and replace the person, but it also takes time and money to repair the damage he or she did.

Experts point to four major mistakes managers can make in selecting a job applicant. One is to hire everyone in their own image when, like orchestra leaders, they actually need a wide array of talents to produce the right sound. Another mistake is doing all the talking during the interview. A third mistake is not to prepare for the interview. As a result, the right questions do not get asked; or if they do, managers do not hear the answers because they are too busy thinking about their next brilliant question. The fourth mistake is to ask the *wrong* question. In these litigious times, managers should probably check with the agency's legal staff or human resource department to find out what they should not say in the interview. In California, for example, you may not inquire about the applicant's age, birthplace, nationality, sex, marital status, family or plans for a family, race, height, weight, general health, religion, arrest record, military record, credit rating, or name and address of a relative to be notified in case of an emergency.

When the time comes for the interview, managers should begin by putting the candidate at ease. Managers can learn more from relaxed candidates than from tense ones. After *briefly* explaining the nature of the job, managers should plunge into the heart of the interview—and ask questions.

Essentially managers are trying to answer three basic questions:

Training and Management Development

How important is training? A number of headlines help answer that question. The headline, "FEDERAL AVIATION ADMINISTRATION'S TRAINING COURSES FOR INSPECTORS APPALLINGLY OBSOLETE," appeared after a Delta Air Lines crash in Texas killed 14. When the headline, "FEDERAL NARCOTICS AGENTS RAID THE WRONG HOUSE," appeared, Justice Department officials were forced to admit that many drug enforcement agents had had little enforcement experience and had been hired by agencies right after college. "CITIES MAY BE LIABLE FOR POOR TRAINING," appeared after the Supreme Court ruled in *City of Canton* v. *Harris* that cities and counties may have to pay damages if their employees are not trained properly. "RECRUITS IN POLICE ACADEMY RECEIVE 12-LESSON PROGRAM ON RACIAL SENSITIVITY," appeared a few months after charges of racial biases by community groups.

1. Can the candidate do the job?
2. *Will* the candidate do the job (i.e., is he or she motivated enough)?
3. Will the candidate fit into the organization?

Here are some more specific questions worth asking:

- On your last job, what was it that you most wanted to accomplish but didn't? Why not?
- What was the best job you ever had? Worst job? Best boss? Worst boss? Why?
- What do you pride yourself on?
- You don't have to answer this: Tell me about some important event in your childhood. How did it shape you?
- Why are you interested in changing jobs?

What makes questions like these effective is that they are open-ended and not susceptible to brief yes or no answers. Nor do they telegraph the desired response, as these questions do: Would you say you work well with people? Was getting your MPA a positive experience for you?

After the interview managers should compare notes with others who may have interviewed the candidate. The references of the winner should be thoroughly checked. These references might be asked to suggest others who might be consulted regarding the candidate. But the best person to hire is someone who worked for you before and did a good job or someone who worked for a person you know and whose judgment you trust.

SOURCES: Jim Kennedy, "Job Interviews: Getting Beyond the Fluff," *U.S. News & World Report,* September 13, 1987; Walter Kiechell, III, "How to Pick Talent," *Fortune,* December 8, 1986.

Proper training can, of course, do much more than reduce the possibility of such indelicacies as midnight raids in the bedrooms of innocent citizens. In the first place, by providing employees with the opportunity to improve themselves, specific training and development programs help to reduce the number of dead-end jobs in an agency. Reducing such jobs and providing opportunity for advancement can, in many instances, increase motivation. Further, training programs can help to remedy a situation faced by many minority groups, namely, the difficulty of attaining a government position because of skill deficiencies.

Finally, training helps prepare employees for certain jobs that are unique to the public sector. As government continues to serve as the armature of technological progress and the champion of social progress, the number of these unique jobs will, very likely, increase.

For these reasons, then, managers should not prejudge training programs as time-consuming frills. On the contrary, they should look to their agency's employee devel-

An aerial view of the Federal Executive Institute reveals the attractiveness of the setting.

opment branch as a key ally in their own tasks of employee motivation and program management.

A manager should also be aware of the types of training programs available. The orientation program is perhaps the most elementary, but it is not unimportant. When well conceived, an orientation program can make employees more productive more quickly. **On-the-job training** (OJT) is a second type. Basically, an individual without all the needed skills or experience is hired and then learns the job from another employee.

For administrative, professional, and technical (APT) personnel, a wide variety of development programs are available, inside and outside the organization. For example, there are workshops and institutes (such as the Federal Executive Institute at Charlottesville, Virginia); professional conferences; university and college programs; management development programs; internships; and sabbaticals. **The Intergovernmental Personnel Act of 1970** opened up federal in-service training programs to state and local employees and authorized grants to them. Similarly, the Labor Department's Public Service Careers Program and the Justice Department's Law Enforcement Assistance Administration also attempt to foster state and local programs. Since the development of in-service training programs at these levels has lagged behind that of the federal government, these trends are to be applauded.

Nor should **job rotation**—that is, transfer from unit to unit—be neglected as a method of providing for employee development. Herbert Kaufman (1960) furnishes an excellent example of how this type of training works. Transfers in the U.S. Forest Service, he found, do not wait for vacancies; rather, they are made every three or four years to acquaint employees with the various perspectives of duties of employees at all job levels and with a variety of specialties. According to the service, such a practice seeks "the development, adjustment, and broadening of personnel." The advantages of such a program for developing a pool from which top management can be drawn

What Is Going on Here?

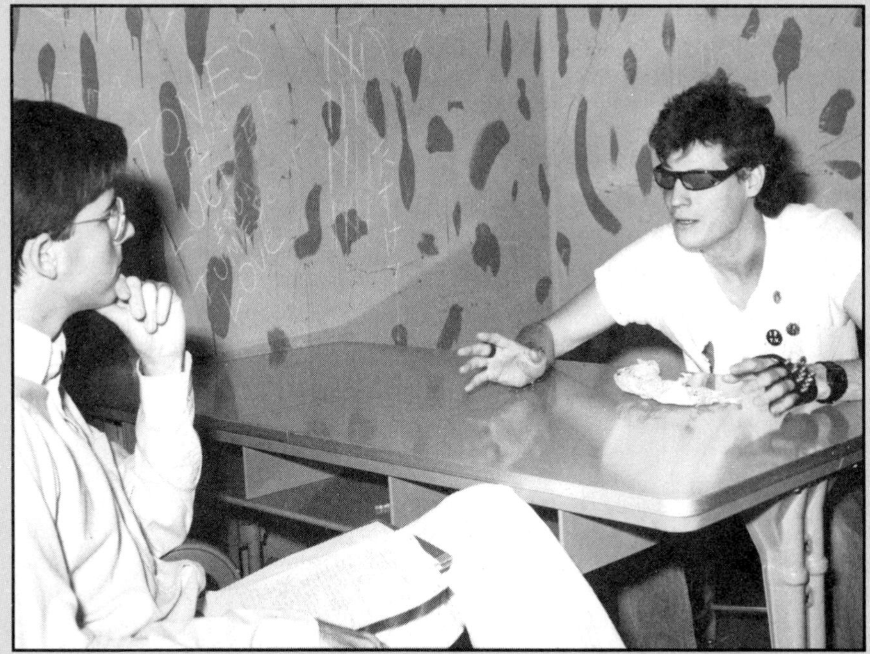

Answer: Training in a mock jail cell at the Foreign Service Institute, two trainees enact an embassy official counseling an American tourist imprisoned in the hostile country of Z. (U.S. State Department)

are obvious. Compare it to an agency that allows its top management to progress up the ranks within one functional specialty.

In general, the purpose of a management development program in the public sector is to extend the years of usefulness of those administrators who may be confronted with premature obsolescence and to prepare high-potential middle managers, whose past performance has been outstanding, for assuming higher managerial functions (Pomerleau, 1974). Because management development is a way of increasing the supply of managerial talent, it is at the heart of PPM today.

What criteria should an organization use in selecting relatively inexperienced managers in whom to invest its management development resources? The use of the **assessment center** method is one answer. This method involves multiple evaluation techniques (see Table 10-1) selected to bring out behavior related to the qualities identified by research as important to job success in the jobs for which the participants are under consideration. By observing, over a one- to three-day period, a participant's handling of the simulated problems and challenges of higher-level jobs, assessors are

TABLE 10-1.
Description of Exercises Used at the Assessment Center

Assigned Role Group Discussion
In this leaderless group discussion, participants, acting as a city council of a hypothetical city, must allocate a $1 million federal grant in the time allotted to make other judgments on the varying proposals offered. Each participant is assigned a point of view to sell to the other team members and is provided with a choice of projects to back and the opportunity to bargain and trade off projects for support.

Nonassigned Role Group Discussion
This exercise is a cooperative, leaderless group discussion in which four short case studies dealing with problems faced by executives working in state government agencies are presented to a group of six participants. The participants act as consultants who must make group recommendations on each of the problems. Assessors observe the participant's role in the group and the handling of the content of the discussion.

In-Basket Exercise
Problems that challenge middle- and upper-level executives in state government are simulated in the in-basket exercise. These include relationships with departmental superiors, subordinates and peers, representatives of other departments, representatives of executive and legislative branches, the public, and the news media. Taking over a new job, the participants must deal with memos, letters, policies, bills, and so on, found in the in-basket. After the in-basket has been completed, the participant is interviewed by an assessor concerning his or her handling of the various in-basket items.

Speech and Writing Exercises
Each participant is given a written, narrative description of a policy, event, situation, and so on, and three specific situational problems related to the narrative, each requiring a written response. The participant is also required to make a formal oral presentation, based upon the background narrative description, before a simulated news conference attended by the Capitol Press Corps and interested government officials and citizens (assessors).

Analysis Problem
The analysis problem is an individual analysis exercise. The participant is given a considerable amount of data regarding a state agency's field operations, which he or she must analyze and about which he or she must make a number of management recommendations. The exercise is designed to elicit behaviors related to various dimensions of managerial effectiveness. The primary area of behavior evaluated in this exercise is the ability to sift through data and find pertinent information to reach a logical and practical conclusion.

Paper and Pencil Tests
Three different commercially available, objectively scoreable tests are included in the assessment: a reading test used for self-development purposes, a reasoning ability test, and a personality test. The latter two are being used experimentally at present, and as with the reading test, are not made available during assessor discussions.

SOURCE: W. C. Byham and C. Wettengel, "Assessment Centers for Supervisors and Managers," *Public Personnel Management,* September–October 1974. Reprinted by permission of the International Personnel Management Association, 1313 East 60th Street, Chicago, Illinois 60637.

able to get a feeling for a participant's ability before the promotion (Byham & Wettengal, 1974).

The first recorded use of assessment procedures was by the German army to help select officers during World War I; the first major use of it in the federal government was by the IRS in 1969. The last few years, however, have witnessed increasing application by government jurisdictions in the United States and Canada.

The current curriculum of the State Department's orientation course uses simulated situations and crises, such as trying to negotiate freedom for an American tourist jailed in the unfriendly land of Z (see photograph). The diplomats in training also attend seminars at centers where, for two-and-a-half days they simulate every aspect of an embassy's operation. Their instructors, all veteran Foreign Service officers, alternately praise and goad, pushing and stretching to get the maximum performance. James H. Morton, who runs some of the seminars, says: "The tougher and more realistic the training is back here in the States, the fewer surprises the new guys are going to run into overseas" (quoted in Ayres, 1983).

Advancement

Most jurisdictions provide that a new employee must serve a probation period for a limited time, usually six months. During this period, the manager should give him or her special attention in matters of instruction, indoctrination, and general adjustment to the job. In theory, probation is the last phase of the testing process, for at this time the individual may be discharged without the right of appeal and reinstatement. Unfortunately, very few dismissals occur during probation. Apparently, few managers have the fortitude to judge others when careers are at stake.

A career service must provide opportunity for advancement. But this does not preclude filling positions from outside as well as from within the service to keep an organization from becoming too inbred or to obtain especially outstanding persons for positions above the entry level. To maintain an organization's vitality and competence without harming employee morale, many jurisdictions provide for filling positions from within unless a better-qualified person is available from outside. Using the same approach, some jurisdictions turn to the outside only when there is an insufficient number of well-qualified persons for consideration within the organization.

In state and local jurisdictions, a competitive promotional examination—covering general administration, psychology, personnel, and so on—is often required of employees. Supporters maintain that the open competitive promotion helps motivation and combats inertia. But most federal agencies have avoided competitive promotion by examination.

In addition to examination, performance ratings can take the form of measurement of output (such as in the management by objectives system discussed in Chapter 9), rating characteristics, or narratives. The checkoff or objective evaluation consists of rating employees on a scale concerning such qualities as writing ability, initiative, and promptness. The narrative approach allows managers to be more flexible in discussing the good and bad points of subordinates; but because they are difficult to compare and more time-consuming, they are less popular than the objective form.

One criticism of **performance appraisal** as practiced in government might be cited. The process is periodic rather than continuous. But the manager should not wait until, say, the end of the year to tell an employee he or she is not performing. The good and bad aspects of performance should be discussed as they occur.

An excellent vehicle for the latter is the conventional interview. If an administrator is squeamish about expressing judgments regarding subordinates, then he or she should at least stay away from managing large nonroutine public programs. On this point James Webb (1969:166), former NASA administrator, deserves a careful hearing:

> *As NASA administrator it became my practice to meet privately once each week with each of NASA's eight top executives for an hour of face-to-face, structured discussion that amplified and expanded the feedback process that had been continually going on between us. Inputs from all sources were brought into focus in these meetings, where no holds were barred. There were no intermediaries and no agreed ground rules. There were just two men, each charged with heavy responsibilities and vested with substantial powers, sitting face-to-face, probing each other's minds on problems, possible solutions, and how we and our other associates were doing our jobs. These were not staff meetings; we had staff meetings, too. The face-to-face evaluation and discussion meeting was a penetratingly personal confrontation on many matters that neither would have wanted to bring up in meetings with broader attendance.*

Discipline and Grievances

Two of the more sensitive concerns of PPM are disciplining employees and listening to their complaints. Reprimands, suspensions, demotions, reassignments, and dismissals can obviously have an adverse effect on the career of an employee; accordingly, few managers enjoy situations that call for such forms of discipline. And yet, the public expects, quite rightly, efficient service from those paid by its taxes.

Nor do managers usually enjoy the complaints of subordinates. Even administrators who pride themselves on their open-door policy usually become unhappy when an employee begins to complain. The complaint seems to indicate that somehow they have failed to a degree as a manager. Whether an administrator finds discipline and grievances sensitive matters or not, he or she needs to keep several points in mind about each.

In disciplinary matters, the administrator should strive for improvement in employee performance. This improvement is only possible if disciplinary policy and standards of performance are clearly understood by all and are impartially applied. Further, disciplinary actions should always be based on a careful assessment of the facts. Failure to do so can result in considerable embarrassment for the administrator if the employee decides to refute the charges and have the disciplinary action reviewed by an impartial body.

Discipline in an organization takes many forms, oral and written reprimands being the most common. And if the administrator can make it clear (1) that the objective of the reprimand is solely to correct employee action, and (2) that mutual respect exists between the two, then these forms should work. Still, the administrator should not turn to them too readily. Is the employee's action sufficiently important to require a reprimand? If the answer is yes, then are more indirect, less formal approaches available? A well-thought-out hint or joke might suffice for the moderately perceptive employee.

If reprimands continue to prove ineffective, then more severe forms of discipline need to be considered: suspension, demotion, reassignment, and dismissal. In such cases, the administrator will probably need to turn to the personnel office for assistance.

Suspension and demotion are less than satisfactory, except when an employee has demonstrated lack of ability in a particular position. Suspension often creates hostility. Demotion, or reassignment, by reducing motivation, can hamper agency performance, as the following interview by Terkel (1972:454) indicates:

> *When management wants to get rid of you, they don't fire you. What they do is take your work away. That's what happened to me. They sent somebody down to go through my personnel file. "My God, what can we do with her?" They had a problem because I'm a high-grade employee. I'm grade 14. The regional director's a 17. One of the deputy directors told me, "You're going to be an economic development specialist." (Laughs.)*
>
> *I'm very discouraged about my job right now. I have nothing to do. For the last four or five weeks I haven't been doing any official work, because they really don't expect anything. They just want me to be quiet. What they've said it's a 60-day detail. I'm to come up with some kind of paper on economic development. It won't be very hard because there's little that can be done. At the end of 60 days I'll present the paper. But because of the reorganization that's come up I'll probably never be asked about the paper.*

Dismissal means being fired for cause; it does not refer to those employees who must leave government because of economic measures.

Public administrators, like their counterparts in industry, avoid dismissal as long as possible. And this is for good reason: The process is unpleasant and difficult—especially when the administrator has failed to fully document the case against the employee. Even when the dismissed employee has no right of appeal for reinstatement, the administrator may suddenly face strong external pressure from legislators, influential friends, and professional groups. Internally, he or she might face displeasure from other employees.

To guarantee fair play in personnel actions, most agencies provide for appeals. What this statement does not convey is how grueling a hearing can be for the administrator. The employee's lawyer naturally tries to discredit the administrator's motives. At times, an observer might wonder whether the administrator is on trial. Yet, much can be said in favor of the hearing procedure: It helps forward not only individual rights but also administrative responsibility.

In contrast to appeals, grievance procedures are designed more for hearing employee complaints about working conditions and other aspects of employment (e.g.,

Talking Shop

Good and Bad Criticism

In modern management theory, with all its talk about empowering employees, the word *criticism* has fallen out of favor. And yet what *does* the manager do when Roberta arrives at around 10:30 A.M. every Monday; when six of seven clerks in the license bureau stand around chatting while the line of citizens becomes longer and more irate; when George continues to smoke after the practice was banned from all state buildings; or when Richard pounds a broken photocopy machine and then shouts abuse at the company representative? What is an enlightened manager to do?

According to management consultants, the following simple points, if remembered, will help you to handle employees who have grievances or require discipline:

1. *Watch for signs of dissatisfaction and act before the problem becomes too serious.* Maintain open lines of communication and be accessible.
2. *Get all the facts.* Give the employee a chance to present his or her side fully. Try to see the employee's side.
3. *Remain calm and courteous.* Grievances and disciplinary matters can be very emotional experiences. Recognize this from the start and resolve to remain in control no matter how loud and angry the other party may be.
4. *Be positive not punitive.* Rather than treat employees harshly (e.g., making threats) and expect them to "shape up," stress why certain rules must be enforced. Express confidence that the employee can improve. Research has shown that people respond well to criticisms that are specific, prompt, and delivered in a considerate manner. A mark of well-honed criticism is that it focuses on what a person has done rather than on seeing poor work as a mark of character. Another mark is its specificity. It is such precise information that turns a critique into an opportunity for improvement. Constructive criticism tells the employee exactly what he or she did wrong and does not make a cryptic and vague attack. Robert Baron (1990) of Rensselaer Polytechnic University reports that the poor use of criticism was among the top five most often-mentioned causes of conflict at work, ahead of mistrust,

job evaluation) and resolving them. While such procedures obviously benefit the employee, they also promote better management. Most administrators think they are fair, equitable, considerate, and sensitive to their employees. And perhaps they are, but the power and authority of their position can keep employee grievances from surfacing directly. Consequently, the effects of unresolved grievances begin to surface in other, more indirect ways such as higher turnover figures, reduced motivation, and more union organizing.

conflicting personalities, and disputes over power and pay.

5. *Be firm when necessary.* After every effort has been made to change an employee's behavior, discharge might be the only permanent solution.
6. *Be consistent.* Anytime there is a significant infraction of a standard, managers should act. Managers should be impersonal when enforcing rules.

The best approach to discipline, however, is to avoid situations in which its use is called for. True believers in participatory management should institute team discipline where each work area sets up its own standards and rules and enforces them. Such an approach can be remarkably effective because it replaces hierarchical control with something even stronger—social or group control. ("Boy, did you ever let us down." Ouch!)

Whatever approach a manager chooses, the following strategies can help keep things from reaching a boiling point at which some form of discipline might be necessary:

- Keep workers informed regarding the quality of their work.
- Correct minor irritations promptly.
- Encourage constructive suggestions.
- Keep promises.
- Assign work impartially to employees with equal skill and ability.
- Explain your orders unless they are obvious.
- Be consistent unless there's an obvious reason for change.
- Explain change, even when the change doesn't require negotiation.
- Act as soon as possible on requests.
- Avoid showing favoritism.
- If you must take corrective action, do not make it a public display.

In short, use common sense and assume that fair treatment will pay off in cooperation. When a dispute does arise, resolve it (if possible) before it becomes a formal grievance. Personnel or labor relations officers can help prevent an issue from escalating into a grievance.

SOURCES: "How to Discipline in the Modern Age," *Fortune,* May 7, 1990; Terry L. Leap and Michael D. Crino, "How to Deal with Bizarre Employee Behavior," *Harvard Business Review,* May–June 1986; Daniel Goleman, "Why Job Criticism Fails," *New York Times,* July 26, 1988.

Grievance procedures are generally prescribed in civil service rules or regulations rather than in laws; but regardless of jurisdiction, for a grievance to work, certain elements are essential. First, the procedures should specify the steps to be followed by employees and supervisors to resolve differences. Established lines of authority should normally be followed—the immediate supervisor first and then up the line. Some jurisdictions provide a final avenue of review to an impartial panel when all else fails. Finally, employees filing grievances must be protected from reprisal.

Organizational Culture

As indicated in Figure 10-1, these five functions—staffing, classification and compensation, training and management development, advancement, and discipline and grievances—are embedded in something called organizational culture, which can have a powerful influence on performance.

Organizational culture can be defined as the predominant value system of an organization. When an organization's underlying values and beliefs are internalized by its members, several benefits ensue: The culture eases and economizes communications, facilitates organizational decision making and control, and may generate higher levels of cooperation and commitment. In short, organizational culture helps to overcome the centrifugal tendencies of a large bureaucracy by instilling in its members a sense of unity and common purpose.

This process can be encouraged through selection—people are hired because their personal values are already consistent with the organizational culture. It can also be encouraged through socialization—newcomers learn values and ways of behaving that are consistent with those of the organization. And, if you will recall the example from Chapter 1, of Peter Ueberroth and the Los Angeles Olympic Organizing Committee, organizational cultures can even operate in temporary organizations.

Two organizations in the public sector have been particularly successful in matching culture and goals: The U.S. Forest Service and the U.S. Marine Corps.

The U.S. Forest Service

Herbert Kaufman describes how the Forest Service selects people "who fit." Weakly motivated people are advised to turn to other pursuits: "To a considerable extent, those who persisted were self-selected, a rather dedicated group prepared to accept whatever the profession had to offer" (1960:163). "Recruiting publicity tends to deter the impatiently ambitious, the seekers after the easy job and comfortable and stable life" (1960:164). Almost all the professional employees of the Forest Service are educated in forestry, which leads to widespread consensus on technical matters within the organization: "Appropriate behaviors, receptivity to agency directives are in this sense 'built into' them. Postentry training is designed to intensify in the rangers the capacity and willingness to adhere to the service's goals."

But the Forest Service also makes an effort to ensure an environment that promotes its members' identification with the well-being of the organization. For example, a policy of rapid transfer builds identification with the Forest Service as a whole. "Whenever a younger man severs his ties in a location to which he has just become adjusted and takes a new place, an experienced Forest Service officer—a mentor—is there to receive him, support him, guide him" (Kaufman, 1960:178). Promotion is relatively slow and, for senior-level positions, is always *from within* the Forest Service. This practice ensures that top administrators absorb many of the prevailing values, assumptions, and customary modes of operation.

(Used by permission of the USDA Forest Service)

Identification is heightened by the use of symbols. The Forest Service insignia—the shield-shaped badge with the agency name and a tree emblazoned on it—is a familiar and respected one the country over. In Washington, the agency uses distinctive wooden plaques rather than the standard signs to identify its offices, while rustic signs bearing its emblem appear on almost all the properties it manages. Indeed, it has been said the adoption of the designation "service"—now a fairly commonplace term, but a novelty when it was originally selected—instead of the more common "bureau," helped set it in a class by itself, accentuating its self-consciousness and corporate spirit. These are all small things, but they do set the agency apart. Many public servants, asked who their employer is, are likely to name "the government," or perhaps their department. Forest officers will almost invariably respond, "the Forest Service." (Kaufman, 1960:185)

To understand why the Forest Service has placed such emphasis on developing a strong culture, we must understand the fundamental principle upon which it was founded, namely, that resource management begins and belongs on the ground. It follows then that the ranger district, and *not* the headquarters in Washington, D.C., must be the backbone of the organization. But given that principle, how can one delegate great responsibility and authority to the men on the ground, pursue a unified policy direction, maintain high morale, and avoid any trace of scandal—all at the same time? So far, the only explanation the Forest Service has been able to come up with is to build and maintain a strong organizational culture.

Strong organizational cultures have strong traditions. Many of the Forest Service's values and beliefs can be traced back to the creed of Gifford Pinchot (the service's first chief), which was proclaimed in 1905.

The U.S. Marine Corps

The traditions of the Marine Corps go back much farther than those of the Forest Service—to the battle honors it earned from its inception in 1775. Alan Ned Sabrosky

An organization's culture may not always be in alignment with its needs and environment. The difference between desired cultural norms and values and actual norms and values is called the culture gap. *Culture gaps can be immense, as was brutally demonstrated late on the evening of Saturday, March 2, 1991.*

After leading Los Angeles police on a high-speed car chase, Rodney King, a 25-year-old unemployed black construction worker recently paroled on a robbery charge, was clubbed and stomped by three white officers while a dozen other white officers watched. To some people the beating was remarkable only in one respect: It was videotaped by a bystander who happened to be trying out his new camera.

People both inside and outside the Los Angeles Police Department (LAPD) were forced to conclude that the police were wed to a paramilitaristic, us-against-them culture that was at odds with the more community-oriented norms many big-city departments adopted after the urban riots of the 1960s. The following excerpt is from the Report of the Independent Commission of the Los Angeles Police Department, *which was issued four months after the Rodney King incident:*

> *The L.A.P.D. has an organizational culture that emphasizes crime control over crime prevention and that isolates the police from the communities and the people they serve. With the full support of many, the L.A.P.D. insists on aggressive detection of major crimes and a rapid, seven-minute response time to calls for service. Patrol officers are evaluated by statistical measures (for example, the number of calls handled and arrests made) and are rewarded for being "hard-nosed." This style of policing produces results, but it does so at the risk of creating a siege mentality that alienates the officer from the community. . . .*
>
> *Graphic confirmation of improper attitudes and practices is provided by the brazen and extensive references to beatings and other excessive uses of force in the M.D.T.'s [Mobile Digital Terminals]. The commission also found that the problem of excessive force is aggravated by racism and bias, again strikingly revealed in the M.D.T.'s.*
>
> *The failure to control these officers is a management issue that is at the heart of the problem. . . . The L.A.P.D.'s failure to analyze and act upon these revealing data evidences a significant breakdown in the management and leadership of the department.*

(Photograph © Ted Soqui/Impact Visuals)

(in Bonds, 1983:206) of the Center for Strategic and International Studies explains how the Marine Corps uses this tradition to strengthen its organizational culture and how the values of that culture manifest themselves:

> *As with any military establishment, the U.S. Marine Corps has its own set of traditions, reflecting an institutional interpretation of the corps' past performance. In part, of course, such traditions are self-serving, highlighting only that which is worthy of emulation and ignoring or discarding anything that is not. Yet traditions cannot be dismissed lightly, especially in the case of a military institution. For such traditions not only influence the way in which the corps sees itself, and how others view the corps. They also shape the missions assigned to the corps, and the way in which it organizes itself for battle.*
>
> *Over the years, the Marine Corps has traditionally viewed itself as an elite force of infantry, highly disciplined and reliable (its motto is* Semper Fidelis, *or "Always Faithful"), which constituted the "cutting edge" of American diplomacy and power. The dictum that "every Marine was first and foremost a rifleman," while often only nominally accurate, reflected this perception. Even today, the fact that Marine ground combat formations are relatively large units with a high proportion of infantry is evidence of its continued significance.*

To summarize, organizational cultures can have an important effect on the success of an organization. By codifying and symbolizing so that everyone can see "the way we do things here," organizational culture can have a positive influence on the behaviors and working environments of all employees. In organizations with strong cultures, everyone knows and supports the organization's objectives; in those with weak cultures—perhaps the Peace Corps (Case 5.3) can serve as an example—no clear purpose exists. Thus, organizational culture complements not only human resources management but also the sense of mission, the process of strategy formulation discussed in Chapter 5.

Organizational culture is not, of course, without liabilities. Important shared beliefs and values can interfere with the needs of the organization, the people who work in it, or the public. To the extent that the content of an organization's culture leads its people to think and act in inappropriate ways (e.g., police being too aggressive), the culture will retard the attainment of positive results. Because cultures are not easily or quickly changed, this condition should not be dismissed lightly.

The logical next question is this: How do public managers actually change the culture? The organization's underlying value system cannot be managed in traditional ways using conventional techniques. To effect cultural change, managers must adopt a "symbolic manager" approach. The Working Profile shows how one symbolic manager defined and used signs and symbols to influence the culture of the Tactical Air Command.

(text continues on p. 474)

★ ★

WORKING PROFILE

William Creech

The Tactical Air Command (TAC) is the arm of the U.S. Air Force that provides quick-reaction air reinforcements for use overseas. When General William Creech arrived at TAC in 1978, he found that its chief peacetime performance measure, the sortie rate, had been falling for ten years at an annual rate of nearly 8 percent per year. (A sortie is an exercise in which aircraft, pilot, and support group are tested as a unit in simulated combat conditions.)

This disturbing fact led Creech to begin reshaping the culture at TAC—an organization of 113,000 people. He realized that the centralization that had occurred during the previous decade had resulted in an organization that devalued competition among subunits. Furthermore, emphasis was on the higher-level unit, the wing, rather than on the lower-level (output-oriented) unit, the squadron. (Between 18 and 24 aircraft make up a squadron.) Although the air force always deploys or fights as a squadron, the centralization logic that prevailed before Creech took command had led to squadrons literally being abolished. Colorful aircraft tail markings were not allowed. Squadron patches were forbidden. Even the fabled 94th—the squadron in which Eddie Rickenbacker, the leading U.S. ace of World War I served—disappeared with all its history and unit pride.

Creech brought back all the colorful pennants, tail markings, and arm patches (along with mugs, ties, tie tacks, T-shirts, and other paraphernalia). Each squadron was told to do its own scheduling and was given its own decentralized computers—much to the dismay of the central MIS (management information system) people.

Creech effected many other changes. Previously, sergeants "had evaluated themselves by the thickness of their carpets." Creech insisted that specialists of all skills get out of their offices and back to the flight line and that everyone cross-train. Everyone was given broader and deeper jobs. A job's breadth is measured by the number of physical (operating) tasks a person performs. Its depth is measured by the number of thinking (managerial) tasks performed. These include troubleshooting, problem solving, and planning. Making a job broader is often called *job enlargement;* making it deeper is *job enrichment.* While Creech thought a lot about leadership, he also believed that leadership—at least, top leadership—cannot do it all. His aim therefore was to create leaders at many levels.

★ ★

Creech singled out his maintenance and supply people for special recognition. The sergeant in charge of an aircraft was now called a "dedicated crew chief"; highly visible bulletin boards inside and outside an aircraft maintenance unit (AMU) facility included pictures of that AMU's dedicated crew chiefs—always next to their planes. The AMUs outputs were made highly visible. Walls were dotted with sizable charts showing trend lines with key readiness and quality-improvement indicators. The most vital indicators were posted on big boards outside the unit, visible to all who drove by (i.e., all one's competitive peers). Competitions among supply and maintenance units were introduced. Regular award banquets for supply and maintenance people became commonplace.

But Creech's superb appreciation of the power of symbols in an organization manifested itself in more dramatic ways than bulletin boards:

On an inspection visit soon after he took over he came across a supply office in disrepair, the epitome of the second-class status to which supply people had been relegated (and the issue toward which he was directing so much energy). The supply sergeant, a fifteen-year veteran, occupied a government-gray chair with a torn back (mended with electrical tape) and only three casters—the fourth leg was propped up on a block of wood. Creech ordered his aide to have the chair boxed and sent to TAC's Langley, Virginia, headquarters. Soon thereafter the general held a major ceremony. The three-star general—Creech has four stars—who headed logistics was "awarded" the chair, and told that it was now his *chair, until the supply operation was cleaned up.*

In 1984, when Creech turned over his command, he published a set of principles. Among them were the following:

- *Create a climate of pride:* "Instill individual dignity. Provide challenge and opportunity to each. Intangibles matter."
- *Create a climate of professionalism:* "Esprit is the critical measure."
- *Educate, educate, educate:* Do this by means, first and foremost, of regular feedback.
- *Make it better:* Create a sense of individual and organizational worth. Create an "optimistic organization." Provide a climate for continuous change: "The leader is not just a scorekeeper and steward. He is responsible for creating something new and better."

How effective were the changes Creech made at TAC? During his five years as commander, the sortie rate rose at an annual rate of over 11 percent. Although it used to take four *hours* on average to get a part to a temporarily inoperable plane, the average was now eight *minutes.* What makes these reversals all the more remarkable is that they occurred without any increase in budget, any improvement in technology, or any expansion of work force. (Creech's work force was actually less experienced, on the average, than his predecessor's.)

SOURCE: Based on Tom Peters and Nancy Austin, *A Passion for Excellence* (New York: Warner Books, 1986), pp. 56–57, 278–84, and 323.

The Legal Environment's Top Ten List

In attempting to survey the legal environment of human resources management, the mind risks being swept away, whatever the motivation, into confusion or dullness. Consider this: The legislative history stretches back to the days when Chester A. Arthur resided in the White House, and the case law applicable to human resources management is vast, contradictory, and ever-changing. The prudent thing to do here is to focus only on the most important laws and cases currently in effect.

1. Civil Service Reform Act of 1978

Critics had long argued that personnel practices made it difficult for presidents to assemble teams of highly competent officials to implement new programs. To overcome this problem, President Jimmy Carter and the head of the Civil Service Commission, Alan K. Campbell, developed a package of reform proposals. After a major struggle in Congress and Carter's spending of large amounts of political capital, the Civil Service Reform Act passed in 1978.

The most visible reform in the new law was an organizational one. The Civil Service Commission split into two units: the **Office of Personnel Management** (OPM) and the **Merit Systems Protection Board** (MSPB). Although a number of personnel functions are decentralized to line agencies, the OPM has general responsibility for recruitment, training, performance appraisal, and policy leadership in the federal government. MSPB safeguards employees' rights to due process and equitable treatment and protects whistle-blowers against unfair reprisals.

In addition to these structural changes, the act created a separate personnel system for the highest-ranking civil service officials. This **Senior Executive Service** (SES) encompasses nearly 7,000 executives. About 10 percent of SES personnel are political appointees, selected outside ordinary merit channels and loyal to the president; the remainder are of course career executives, committed more to the federal service than to any particular president to further enhance responsiveness. The act makes it easier to transfer these executives from one position to another.

The third important thing that the act did was to restate and elaborate one of the fundamental themes of public personnel administration in the United States: the **merit principle.** Simply put, staffing (recruitment), compensation, advancement, and retention should be based on merit; that is, the employee's ability, education, experience, and job performance. The merit principle rejects criteria such as patronage (political payoffs), friendship, kinship, race, and religion.

During most of the 19th century, federal, state, and local governments operated on what was known as a **spoils system** ("to the victor go the spoils"). Politicians who won handed out government positions to their supporters as rewards. In 1883, Congress passed the **Pendleton Act,** which made the principle law. State and local governments also adopted the merit system—either on their own or in response to federal laws requiring such systems.

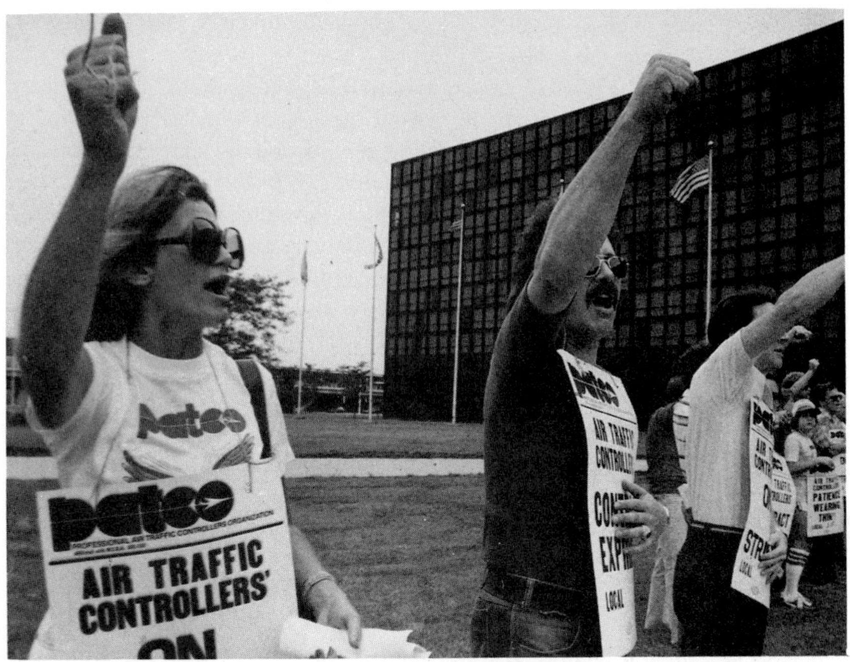

When 11,400 U.S. government air traffic controllers went on strike during a contract dispute with the Federal Aviation Administration (FAA) in 1981, President Reagan fired them en masse. Then, four months after the strike, he signed an executive order barring the strikers from reemployment in FAA facilities. It was the strongest action ever taken against striking federal workers by a U.S. president, and its legacy still ripples through American society. Reagan's decision to fire the controllers quickly and decertify their union rather than attempt to negotiate an end to the strike, is regarded by labor analysts as a catalyst in American management's increasingly aggressive tactics against unions. (AP/Wide World Photos)

Unfortunately, merit systems have a downside. Critics charge that an emphasis on objective testing and job security can lead to mediocre, unresponsive government. The Civil Service Reform Act therefore tried to provide a merit system that still allowed managers some discretion in recruiting, compensating, and firing employees.

Finally, the Reform Act brought federal labor relations under one comprehensive act. It also established an independent Federal Labor Relations Authority (FLRA), giving collective bargaining for federal employees a firm legal foundation. While scholars and practitioners may debate how much difference the establishment of the OPM, the MSPB, and the SES and the reinstatement of the merit system have made, no one can doubt the importance of this aspect of the act. The numbers tell why.

While union membership has declined in the private sector, the numbers show one area in which organized labor has enjoyed robust health. The average pay increase in contracts negotiated by unions representing government workers between 1983 and 1988 was 27 percent. The average increase for private sector workers was 22 percent. In 1960, 5 percent of state and local workers were unionized; in 1988, nearly 37 percent were. Some labor analysts predict that government workers will outnumber private sector workers among the rank and file.

What accounts for the relative prosperity of public sector unions? For one thing, over the past 20 years or so, the once-controversial question of whether public employees should be allowed to join unions has been largely resolved. Today only 15 states, all in the southwest and southeast, discourage it; only two of them—Texas and North Carolina—prohibit it. Then, too, public sector unions have considerable political leverage. Political leaders cannot with impunity allow the city government or transit systems to shut down. Nor do political leaders bargain as competitively as business executives, who have more incentive to maintain labor costs.

Labor relations will undoubtedly remain an issue of special interest to students of public administration. The accompanying Talking Shop discusses how managers handle the issue of collective bargaining.

2. Civil Rights Act of 1964

The key provision of the Civil Rights Act is **Title VII,** Section 703(a). Please read the following excerpt carefully because I wish to refer back to it later:

> *It shall be an unlawful employment practice for an employer—(1) to fail or refuse to hire or to discharge any individual, or otherwise to discriminate against any individual with respect to his compensation, terms, conditions or privileges of employment, because of such individual's race, color, religion, sex, or national origin; or (2) to limit, segregate, or classify his employees or applicants for employment in any way which would deprive or tend to deprive any individual of employment opportunities or otherwise adversely affect his status as an employee, because of such individual's race, color, sex, or national origin. . . . Nothing contained in this title shall be interpreted to require any employer . . . to grant preferential treatment to any individual or to any group because of the race, color, religion, sex, or national origin of such individual or group on account of an imbalance which may exist with respect to the total number or percentage of persons of any race, color, religion, sex, or national origin employed by any employer.*

Thus, the emphasis of the 1964 act was on **equal opportunity** for the individual. Preferential treatment, including, it would appear, such devices as quotas, was not only not required, but expressly forbidden. In addition, discrimination was seen as an intentional, calculated act to exclude some people from work.

From Equal Opportunity to Affirmative Action. No sooner had the Civil Rights Act seemed to fulfill old promises at last than President Johnson was observing at his historic commencement address at Howard University in June 1965:

> *But freedom is not enough. You do not take a person who, for years, has been hobbled by chains and liberate him, bring him up to the starting line of a*

(text continues on p. 480)

Talking Shop

Labor-Management Relations

The Collective Bargaining Process
The process by which an employer and employee representatives attempt to arrive at agreements governing compensation and working conditions is shown in the diagram below.

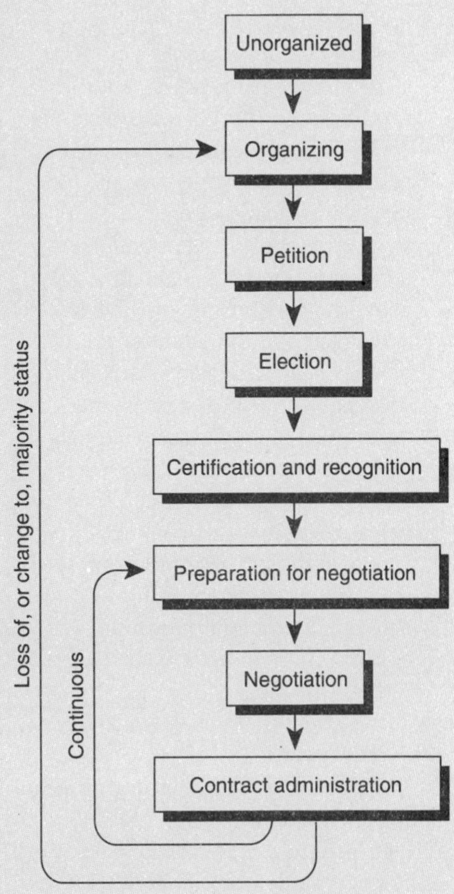

1. *Organizing.* At this beginning stage, the employees try either to create an organization or to select one from those already existing outside organizations that want to represent them. These organizations will try to win the support of the employees by an organizing campaign. They will use such techniques as distributing literature, soliciting membership, and holding discussion meetings.
2. *Election.* Two fundamental issues must be resolved at this second stage. First, the bargaining unit must be determined. This means it must be decided which employees in the political jurisdiction will be grouped together for collective bargaining purposes. Second, the bargaining agent must be named. In other words, it should be decided what organization, if any, will represent the employees within the **bargaining unit** for the purpose of labor relations activities.
3. *Negotiation.* This is when the actual process of collective bargaining begins. The main intention of these negotiations is to reach an agreement between the public employer and the employee representative. The agreement should be one they both can "live with" concerning the job terms and the conditions of those employees involved.

   This step also includes impacts resolution or dispute settlement. Although it is not a true stage of labor relations, it is a situation that sometimes arises when the parties are unable to reach an agreement by themselves. An outside party intervenes to settle the impasse (see below). Types of dispute settlement

(continued)

vary, ranging from limited intervention to a type in which the outside neutral person imposes an agreement upon the parties.

4. *Contract administration.* This final stage is the very heart of labor relations because it involves putting the collective bargaining agreement into practice on a day-to-day basis. No matter how hard negotiators work to write a clear and understandable agreement, disputes inevitably arise about the true meaning of the written agreement and the intent of the parties when they agreed to particular provisions. These disagreements occur even among reasonable and well-intentioned people. They are handled through grievance procedures, a vital part of contract administration. These procedures resemble impasse procedures because here again a neutral person is often called in to help resolve the dispute.

What Happens When the Process Breaks Down?

An **impasse** is a condition during negotiations when either party feels that no further progress can be made toward reaching a settlement. If collective bargaining is to work, provisions must be made for the resolution of such conditions in a manner that recognizes rights, legitimate interests, and power of both labor and management as representatives of the public. The most desirable way to resolve impasses is for both sides to reopen negotiations and bargain until they reach an agreement or to employ neutral third parties to help break the deadlock. If such efforts do not succeed, more formal steps are required. The responsibility for resolving, or facilitating the resolution of, impasses in collective bargaining should be given to a neutral agency that is professionally staffed, adequately compensated, and equipped with a range of procedures for settling, or facilitating the settlement of, public sector labor disputes. Such responsibility might be given to the public-employee relations board or lodged in a separate agency committed exclusively to dispute resolution. Creation of a separate agency may enhance the perception of neutrality, although public-employee relations boards might accomplish the same purpose by establishing a separate division for providing mediators, fact finders, and arbitrators or lists of professionals experienced in public sector dispute resolution.

The dispute-resolution procedures for which the agency should be equipped include the following:

- **Mediation.** A mediator is a neutral third party who attempts to conciliate disputes between labor and management but does not have the power to enforce a settlement.
- **Fact-finding.** A fact finder (or panel of fact finders) is a neutral third party who hears the cases presented by each side, often in a formal proceeding, and generally makes specific recommendations for resolving the dispute. Fact-finding is typically the second step after mediation has failed.
- **Arbitration.** An arbitrator is a neutral third party who goes beyond fact-finding to decide in favor of one side or the other. In binding arbitration, the decision of the arbitrator is final. ("Interest arbitration" refers to resolution of impasses arising in bargaining;

"Another setback—the mediators just went out on strike."
(From The Wall Street Journal, *with permission of Cartoon Features Syndicate.)*

"grievance arbitration" refers to the settlement of disputes in interpretation of a contract that has already been executed.) In last-offer arbitration, the arbitrator must find in favor of the last offer (or separable items in the last offer) presented by each of the parties; this presumably encourages each side to bargain seriously and to be reasonable in their positions in the knowledge that an unreasonable offer will result in the adoption of the other side's proposal. Seventeen states now provide for arbitration of collective bargaining impasses. However, compulsory and binding arbitration is typically opposed by managers who fear that these mechanisms provide a third party who is unfamiliar with local conditions and unaccountable to local authority with the power to bind government to costly settlements. In 1978, Dayton, Ohio, voters rejected a proposal to submit future impasses in bargaining with fire fighters to arbitration even though the city had recently suffered a strike by fire fighters.

Preoccupation with the techniques of resolving bargaining impasses or other labor disputes should not divert attention from a more fundamental source of labor peace; that is, mutual respect between employees and management based on good day-to-day working relationships and concern for the legitimate interests of both sides. (Chapter 8 suggested points to consider in establishing such a relationship.) Nevertheless, building a tradition of harmonious employee relations

(continued)

depends upon the existence of fair and workable arrangements for resolving disputes.

Similarly, preoccupation with the issue of public-employee strikes should not divert attention from the task of establishing workable mechanisms for dispute resolution. However, achieving peaceful dispute resolution depends in part upon how the issue of strikes is handled.

What It All Means

To generalize, labor laws impose several duties on public administrators:

- To bargain in **"good faith."** This means that the parties make an earnest effort and act meaningfully to help bring an agreement into being. For example, the parties should be willing to sit down at reasonable times and exchange nonconfidential information, views, and proposals on subjects that are within the scope of bargaining. Both sides should be represented by duly authorized spokespersons. When bargaining fails to bring agreement, differences should be justified with reasons. The parties must be ready to put into writing whatever agreement they arrive at. Most important, they must be willing to consider compromise solutions to their differences with an open mind and to make an effort to find a mutually satisfactory basis for agreement.
- To work with an employee organization that is the exclusive representative of the employees in the bargaining unit.
- To bargain over wages, hours, and other terms and conditions of employment.
- To commit to writing the agreement that is reached on the subjects of negotiation—if the employee organization requests it.
- To abide by that agreement day by day in those departments and agencies covered by the agreement within a given jurisdiction.

The laws also impose several restrictions on public administrators:

- Interference, intentional or unintentional, with the employee's right to (1) organize or join organizations for collective bargaining purposes; (2) participate in collective bargaining through representatives; or (3) engage in other legal activities, alone or in a group, designed to affect the terms and conditions of employment, is prohibited.
- Interference in any way with the formation or administration of any employees' organization, or contribution of financial or other support to that organization is prohibited.
- Discrimination, direct or indirect, for or against employees to discourage or encourage membership in any employees' organization is prohibited.

race and then say, "You are free to compete with all the others" and still justly believe that you have been completely fair.

Thus it is not enough just to open the gates of opportunity. All our citizens must have the ability to walk through those gates.

> *This is the next and the more profound stage of the battle for civil rights. We seek not just freedom but opportunity. We seek not just legal equality but human ability, not just equality as a right and a theory but equality as a fact and equality as a result.*

The outgrowth of that promise for positive approaches is that *affirmative action* efforts have been developed at all levels of government. Affirmative action plans require employees to demonstrate good faith in their efforts to increase opportunities for *deprived groups*—a term inclusive of blacks, Chicanos, Native Americans, Asian-Americans, and women. The Equal Employment Opportunity Commission (EEOC) is only one of many federal agencies administering the Civil Rights Act in general or the affirmative action programs in particular. There are overlapping jurisdictions of the Labor Department; the Department of Health and Human Resources; Department of Education; the Justice Department; the EEOC; and the federal courts. When one federal agency approves or requires a given practice, this in no way protects an employer from being sued. Indeed, federal agencies have sued one another under this act.

An effective **affirmative action plan** (AAP) need not require quotas (e.g., "23.7 percent of employees will be black, Hispanic, Asian, Indian, Eskimo, or Aleut"). I think that the following list of recommendations, which was gleaned from actual AAPs, illustrates the point:

- Offer preferential treatment to disadvantaged persons and minority group members. This recommendation means that a jurisdiction will take affirmative action to remedy the results of past discrimination and increase its employment of minorities. Specifically, preferential treatment includes aggressive recruiting for minorities, selective certification for certain positions, and training programs to allow the disadvantaged to become fit for merit system jobs.
- Establish selection systems based on job-related, culture-fair evaluations. The essential point is that we need not find coal shovelers who can scan Virgil correctly, but coal shovelers who are properly qualified for shoveling. Likewise, the examination should not be culturally biased. An obvious example of cultural bias is an overly sophisticated English vocabulary on a written test for a Chicano. Similarly, individuals that have spent the majority of their lives in a low-income urban setting might find that some examinations favor a more middle-class suburban background.
- Initiate measures designed to assure that members of the affected group who are qualified to perform the job are included within the pool of persons from which the selecting official makes the selection.
- Make a systematic effort to provide career-advancement training, both in the classroom and on the job, to employees locked into dead-end jobs.
- Establish long-term goals and short-range, interim goals and timetables for the specific job classifications, all of which should take into account the availability of basically qualified persons in the relevant job market.

- Appoint a top official with responsibility and authority to direct and implement your program: (1) Specify responsibilities of program manager; and (2) specify responsibilities and accountability of all managers and supervisors.
- Publicize, internally and externally, your policy and affirmative action commitment.
- Survey present minority and female employment by department and job classification: (1) Identify present areas and levels of employment; (2) identify areas of concentration and underutilization; and (3) determine extent of underutilization.
- Establish internal audit and reporting systems to monitor and evaluate progress in each aspect of the program.

Court Interpretations. The Supreme Court began to transform Title VII of the Civil Rights Act in **Griggs** v. **Duke Power Co.** (1973). A group of black employees challenged the company's requirement of a high school diploma and satisfactory intelligence test score for certain jobs previously given only to white employees. While it was quite obvious that the company had discriminated in the past, the trial court found that such practice had ended. The real issue was, however, that the job requirements did not seem to "bear a demonstrable relationship to successful performance of the jobs for which it was used" and that both requirements had a disparate racial impact. Though Duke Power had no discriminatory intent, the fact that both requirements disqualified more blacks than whites served to show a violation of the law. The upshot of the decision was this: In order to avoid incessant litigation trying to prove that their requirement predicted job performance, employers would be more inclined to adopt a quota system.

Six years later, in **United Steelworkers of America** v. **Weber,** the court decided unequivocally that racial preferences were allowed by the Civil Rights Act. Kaiser Aluminum and Chemical Corporation entered into a collective bargaining agreement with its union that set racial hiring goals for its plants. At the plant in Gramercy, Louisiana, 13 trainees were selected from the production work force for an in-house training program that would end in a better-paying job. Because of the plan, the most senior black selected had less seniority than several white workers who were rejected. One of the latter, Brian Weber, sued under the 1964 act.

A majority of the Supreme Court held that the purpose of the act was to break down barriers to black employment, and therefore an employer could give preference to blacks. Chief Justice Burger, who had agreed with the *Griggs* decision, dissented, saying that the majority's decision was "contrary to the explicit language of the statute." Moreover, the court's decision accomplished "precisely what both its sponsors and its opponents [in Congress] agreed the statute was *not* intended to do."

In **Johnson** v. **Transportation Agency, Santa Clara County** (1987), the Court appeared to move Title VII even closer to being a group entitlement law rather than an antidiscrimination law. The transportation agency adopted an AAP that permitted its managers to consider, when making a promotion, whether an employee was a minority, a woman, or a handicapped person.

When an opening for road dispatcher occurred, seven applicants were found qualified and received scores of above 70 on an interview, which meant they were eligible for selection. Paul Johnson received a score of 75, and Diane Joyce scored 73. Three supervisors conducted a second interview and then recommended that Johnson be promoted. But Joyce had gone to the county's affirmative action coordinator, who afterwards spoke with the agency's affirmative action coordinator, who in turn recommended to the agency's director that Joyce receive the promotion. Because there had not been a female road dispatcher and the agency wanted a "balanced" work force, Joyce got the job.

The court majority did not support Johnson's objection: "The Agency appropriately took into account as one factor the sex of Diane Johnson. . . . The decision to do so was made pursuant to an affirmative action plan that represents a moderate, flexible, case-by-case approach to effecting a gradual improvement in the representation of minorities and women. . . . Such a plan is fully consistent with Title VII, for it embodies the contribution that voluntary employer action can make in eliminating the vestiges of discrimination in the workplace."

Now compare this passage with the actual language of the Title VII, Section 703(a) quoted earlier. Critics of the decision argue that what happened to Johnson violated the statute, that the agency actually discriminated against him because of his sex. "It makes little sense, or justice," one critic wrote, "to sacrifice a white or a male who did inflict discrimination to advance the interests of a black or a female who did not suffer discrimination. No old injustice is undone, but a new injustice is inflicted" (Bork, 1990:106). Dissenting opinion on the court itself has pointed out that, at the time Title VII was debated, proponents of the law emphatically denied that such reverse discrimination would be legal.

In **Richmond** v. **J. A. Croson Co.** (1989), the court made some moderate adjustment to civil rights doctrine. Richmond, Virginia required prime contractors who were given city construction contracts to subcontract at least 30 percent of the dollar amount to businesses to minority businesses. The court found the city's set-aside program to be a violation of the equal protection clause in the 14th Amendment (no state shall "deny to any person . . . the equal protection of the laws"). The 30 percent quota therefore was not an allowable remedy since there was no evidence that the city or anyone in the Richmond construction industry had illegally discriminated against anyone.

What is going on here? As public administrators and their brothers and sisters in the private sector sit on the sidelines wondering where an increasingly conservative court will move next—quotas, affirmative action, or equal opportunity—they might ponder the following pair of propositions:

1. Whether the Supreme Court has correctly interpreted the Civil Rights Act will probably never be answered to everyone's satisfaction. But this much is clear: The court has operated in a policy vacuum, so to speak. At any time from 1964 to the *Croson* decision, a span of a quarter century, the

Congress could have clarified its position on these nettlesome issues, but it chose not to. In 1991, Congress did debate a civil rights bill that opponents called a "quota bill" because it encouraged discrimination lawsuits based on statistical disparities and shifted the burden of proof to the defendant. After much debate and compromise, it was eventually signed into law by President Bush.

2. While it is probably true that the strongest proponents of the Civil Rights Act in the 1964 Congress did not expect what happened to Misters Weber and Johnson to happen and that the idea of quotas is repugnant to many blacks and whites, there *is* a case for quotas. And it should be heard. Americans set quotas all the time. Universities with national reputations seek regional diversification in the student body—not to mention diversification in extra-curricular talent. ("We want her because she's a first-rate oboe player." "We want him because he can run 40 yards in 4.6 seconds and can catch in traffic.") Then there is the matter of subjectivity. What does it mean to say that Paul is 2 points more qualified than Diane? Moreover, it is at least conceivable that the member of the transportation agency's panel had a subconscious bias toward men. Research shows that we tend to regard people like ourselves more highly than those less like us.

Sexual Harassment. One final aspect of the Civil Rights Act remains to be discussed. Under Title VII, sexual harassment in the workplace is a form of discrimination, and the usual remedies apply—back pay, reinstatement, and attorney's fees.

Sexual harassment refers to unwelcomed advances, requests for sexual favors, and other verbal conduct (e.g., sexual jokes) or physical conduct (e.g., pinching, arms wrapped around the shoulder) of a sexual nature when submission to such conduct is made either explicitly or implicitly a condition of employment. Sexual harassment can also occur when such conduct interferes with an individual's work performance; in fact, in recent years a greater proportion of cases involves co-worker rather than boss-subordinate incidents.

To protect itself from cases of sexual harassment, an organization should have a strict policy banning it in all forms. While policies make employees more aware, this policy may need to be reinforced with an education program that outlines examples, subtle and not so subtle, of sexual harassment. Further, there should be a mechanism for sexually harassed people to file complaints, and, once management becomes aware of the allegation, it should investigate—thoroughly and promptly. Sexual harassment is no joke, even though many harassers see it that way.

3. The Hatch Act

One of the oldest concerns in PPM is that public employees should be removed from partisan politics. This notion was embodied in the Political Activities Act of 1939, commonly referred to as the Hatch Act. Over time, the act was broadened to cover state and local employees working on federally funded projects. Several states have enacted similar legislation.

The Hatch Act was provoked in 1939 by rampant corruption and by party pressures on jobholders. During the depression, some Works Progress Administration (WPA) officials used their positions to win votes for the Democratic party among the legion of WPA workers. Therefore, Democrat Senator Carl Hatch of New Mexico introduced the bill to end such corrupt practices in national elections.

The Hatch Act today forbids bribery or intimidation of voters and limits political campaign activities among federal employees—no ringing doorbells in someone's election campaign, running a political fund-raising operation, and so forth. Such activities on behalf of an incumbent legislator or a winning challenger would presumably magnify that civil servant's political influence and make Congress more beholden to him or her.

Have another example. Assume the Hatch Act is abolished. An auditor for the IRS is a good stout Republican. While off duty on a Monday evening, she takes advantage of her new freedom by taking an active part in managing a Republican campaign. Her picture is in the papers. She appears on television. And on Tuesday morning she audits the income tax returns of a prominent Democrat.

Elimination of the Hatch Act, therefore, could be bad for employees and bad for the public. As I argued in Chapter 2, politics can never be wholly divorced from public administration. There ought to be no divorce. The old spoils system had its merits in that it provided a degree of responsiveness. But at the working, career level of the civil service, allowing *partisan* political activity, on duty or off duty, is an idea fraught with trouble.

4. *Garcia* v. *San Antonio* (1985)

Today few people question the constitutionality of minimum-wage and maximum-hours legislation for private industry. But may Congress impose the same economic rules on state and local government?

This question arose in 1974 when Congress applied the provisions of the Fair Labor Standards Act to employees of state and local governments. Two years later the Supreme Court decided in *National League of Cities* v. *Usery* that states were constitutionally insulated from interference by Congress in determining the wages paid to employees carrying out government functions. The Tenth Amendment, which reserved to the states and the people powers not delegated to the national government, blocked any such attempt. What Congress could require of General Electric, it could not require of West Virginia.

But the concept of constitutional insulation for state and local government collapse would not last long. In a close vote, the Supreme Court ruled in *Garcia* v. *San Antonio Metropolitan Transit Authority* (1985) that state and local governments should not rely on the court to referee a struggle between them. Instead local officials would have to ask Congress to change the wage and hour laws.

Note that the *Usery* decision allows the court to set aside federal laws that interfere too heavily with governance at the state and local levels. But *Garcia* leaves such interference entirely in the hands of Congress. In the earlier ruling, the court held that the Constitution did not permit Congress to "directly replace the state's freedom to structure integral operations in areas of traditional government function." In *Garcia* the Court said that 13 million state and local government employees are subject to federal wage and hour standards.

5. Americans with Disabilities Act of 1989

The Americans with Disabilities Act bars discrimination against the disabled in workplaces, public accommodations, transportation, and communication services. Its coverage extends to Congress—but not to the rest of the federal government. State and local governments *are* covered, however.

This sweeping antidiscrimination measure affects 43 million Americans with physical and mental disabilities. It also bars discrimination by private business against people with AIDS or its virus. (Senate conservatives made sure that its protections do not cover such groups as drug users, pedophiliacs, transvestites, and kleptomaniacs.)

The bill requires nearly every kind of retail establishment, from barbershops to banks, to be accessible to the disabled and to be usable by them. While the legislation does not spell out precisely what changes would be necessary, in some cases this means installing access ramps, widening doorways, and modifying restrooms. The transportation industry is required to make new buses and trains accessible to people in wheelchairs.

The measure mandates elevators in new commercial and public buildings of more than two stories and calls for employers to provide special devices and services for those with impaired hearing or vision.

Another provision bars an employer from discriminating against a job applicant who is disabled. The bill requires firms to make "reasonable accommodations" for disabled employees, unless that obligation places an "undue hardship" on an organization.

Representatives of trade and industry groups say that the law is likely to cost businesses hundreds of millions of dollars a year. Some of its chief sponsors in Congress minimized the issue of cost, saying that it is overestimated and shortsighted. They cite studies of accommodations made by employers affected under a 1973 act covering federal structures that indicate that simple devices costing as little as $35 to $50 were sufficient to assist a disabled person in performing a regular job (*New York Times,* August 14, 1989).

In sum, the law is well intended, addresses a legitimate and serious national problem, and sets goals with which few people can disagree. But its broad prescriptions are so ambiguous and potentially overreaching that federal judges quite likely will struggle for years to define what the law means and how to enforce it.

6. Intergovernmental Personnel Act of 1970

The Intergovernmental Personnel Act (IPA) seeks to improve state and local management practices through the sharing of personnel for fixed periods of time among levels of government. Although the original intent was to allow state and local governments to tap the expertise that might exist in federal agencies and universities, the IPA has helped to develop a broader perspective and to encourage innovation at the federal level as well.

The law also provides federal grants to assist state and local governments that are willing to upgrade their personnel systems. Thirty-five states do not have central personnel agencies employing merit standards that generally conform with IPA principles.

Actually, the impetus for reform came at the local level before it did at the federal. In 1877, the New York Civil Service Reform Association was pushing hard for the elimination of patronage and the establishment of merit principles for the public service in New York City, New York State, and the federal government. Similar organizations were soon formed in other cities, and in 1881, they merged to create the National Civil Service Reform League (the forerunner of the present National Civil Service League). It was this movement that formulated and lobbied for the passage of the Pendleton Act of 1883, which established the federal civil service system.

In 1883, New York State also passed a civil service law that applied to county and city as well as state employees. Massachusetts followed suit in 1884. Several big cities subsequently passed their own civil service laws.

7. *O'Conner* v. *Ortega* (1987)

O'Conner v. *Ortega* deals with employee privacy. While looking into charges of sexual harassment and malfeasance at a state hospital, investigators conducted a search of Dr. Dennis M. O'Conner's office. O'Conner sued. The Court ruled, however, in the government's favor because its investigators had applied a standard of reasonableness when they conducted the search. Lower federal courts have also upheld use of polygraph tests by police and prison officials for preemployment screening.

Another important aspect of the privacy issue for public employees is drug testing. And, again, the operative standard for management seems to be one of reasonableness. Are there reasonable grounds for believing an employee was impaired (i.e., stoned) on the job? Can the agency demonstrate that an employee represents a clear and present danger to other workers or to the general public? For example, the Supreme Court has held that government regulations requiring drug and alcohol testing of railroad crew members involved in serious accidents are constitutional, because such tests are a reasonable and effective way to serve the government's interest in promoting the public safety (*New York Times,* March 22, 1989).

8. Age Discrimination Act of 1975

By the year 2000, the median age for employed Americans will reach 39. Between 1986 and 2000, the number of people between ages 48 to 53 will leap a staggering 67 percent (U.S. Department of Labor, 1988:5). Moreover, older Americans are politically active.

Mindful of all this, Congress passed the Age Discrimination Act of 1975, which made illegal most discrimination based on age in the workplace against people aged

40 to 70. Unless age is essential to the performance of a certain job, employers may not give preference to younger workers in hiring, firing, or granting of benefits. Furthermore, in 1986 Congress eliminated mandatory retirement ages in most occupations, meaning that a worker is no longer obliged to retire by age 70. These are substantial protections for older Americans, but the legal right to work longer has obvious effects on the job opportunities of younger Americans just entering the work force.

9. Equal Pay Act of 1963

Responding to inequities that were becoming obvious, Congress passed the Equal Pay Act, which ensured the principle of "equal pay for equal work." That means that men and women working in the same establishment under similar conditions must receive the same pay if their jobs required equal (similar) skill, effort, and responsibility. In paying *its* staff, Congress exempted itself from this law. (In fact, in hiring staff, Congress has exempted itself from all major civil rights and labor laws.)

Given the fact that about 46 percent of the current work force is female, one might wonder why the Equal Pay Act appears so low on our list. Soon after its passage, it became apparent that equal pay for equal work reached only a small fraction—perhaps less than one fifth—of the labor force. For example, it was now illegal to pay a male telephone operator more than a female operator—but how many male telephone operators were there in 1963? Therefore, some began to call for a new approach to deal with the traditionally low wages for work in female-dominated occupations.

The new approach might be called equal pay for work of equal value or, simply, **comparable worth.** Studies show that jobs traditionally held by women and demanding the same level of skills, responsibility, and effort tend to pay less than jobs traditionally held by men. This is a major reason why working women, despite equal pay laws, still earn in hourly pay only about 70 cents for every dollar earned by men.*

The crucial question is whether courts and the government have the right or the practical ability to calculate the relative worth of disparate jobs (say, librarian and plumber) and then to mandate that wages be adjusted accordingly. Normally, pay levels are and should be determined by supply and demand in the job market. But women's wages have been depressed because of the work they do.

Over the years, localities have studied and implemented comparable worth. Implementation has now gone forward in 20 states and nearly 1,000 local agencies (Evans & Nelson, 1989). Federal courts have, on the whole, been unwilling to deal with the issue directly.

Whatever the future of this doctrine, the male-female pay gap will probably continue to narrow perceptibly. As women catch up to men in years of schooling and

* It is sometimes difficult to pinpoint whether such differences can be justified by ability and experience or whether subtle discrimination is involved. According to one study, women earn 80 percent as much as males with equivalent schooling, work experience, and type of job (O'Neill, 1983). Unquantifiable differences, such as degree of job commitment or the marketability of one's education (not all college degrees are created equal), may provide part of the explanation. On the other hand, some discrimination may have escaped measurement—for example, employers could be denying women on-the-job training.

TABLE 10-2.
Federal Employment by Sex and Grade

Grade	*Percentage Women*		
	(1970)	*(1987)*	*Percentage Change*
1–6	72.2	74.9	+3.7
7–10	33.4	51.4	+53.9
11–12	9.5	30.0	+315.8
13–15	3.0	14.2	+473.3
16–18	1.4	6.9	+492.8

SOURCE: Based on U.S. Office of Personnel Management, *Occupations of Federal White-Collar and Blue-Collar Workers* (Washington D.C.: U.S. Office of Personnel Management, 1988).

TABLE 10-3.
Top Municipal Jobs by Sex

Job	*Percentage Women*
Fire chief	0.1
Police chief	0.5
Director of public works	1.2
Superintendent of parks	3.5
Mayor	10.5
City manager	11.7
Chief health officer	19.2
Director of recreation	22.5
Controller	23.9
Purchasing director	27.3
Personnel director	32.3
Chief financial officer	34.4
Director of data processing	36.0
Treasurer	49.7
Clerk	73.7
Librarian	79.2

SOURCE: International City Management Association, *Municipal Year Book,* 1988.

work experience, disparities such as those in Tables 10-2 and 10-3 are likely to become much less.

10. *Elrod* v. *Burns* (1976)

In this case, the Supreme Court finally did what local law enforcement agencies, state attorneys, and community reform groups could not. It managed to drive a stake through the heart of the patronage system at the grass roots. Successful sheriffs, county treasurers, and so forth could no longer use the system to appoint their partisan supporters if the appointment required removal of otherwise satisfactory employees not loyal to the incoming party. To do so is to violate the incumbent's First Amendment right regarding freedom of association. The court did allow, however, for the removal of confidential employees (e.g., personal secretary) and policymaking employees.

With this loss of the job-reappointment advantage, it makes little sense to continue a patronage system. Furthermore, moving to a merit system has significant advantages in light of the trends shaping the future of public administration. As we will see in the next chapter, that future will definitely be inhospitable to inefficiency, corruption, and cronyism.

Concepts for Review

- affirmative action plan
- Age Discrimination Act of 1975
- Americans with Disabilities Act of 1989
- arbitration
- assessment center
- bargaining unit
- certification
- Civil Rights Act of 1964
- Civil Service Reform Act of 1978
- the collective bargaining process
- comparable worth
- compensation
- culture gap
- equal opportunity, affirmative action
- Equal Pay Act of 1963
- fact finding
- four main types of public personnel systems
- *Garcia* v. *San Antonio*
- "good faith"
- *Griggs* v. *Duke Power Co.*
- Hatch Act
- impasse
- Intergovernmental Personnel Act of 1970
- job rotation
- *Johnson* v. *Transportation Agency, Santa Clara County*
- management development
- mediation
- merit principle
- merit system, merit recruiting
- Merit Systems Protection Board (MSPB)
- *O'Conner* v. *Ortega*
- Office of Personnel Management
- on-the-job training
- organizational culture
- Pendleton Act
- performance appraisal
- position classification
- public personnel management
- rank-in-person approach
- *Richmond* v. *J. A. Croson Co.*
- rule of three
- Senior Executive Service (SES)
- sexual harassment
- spoils system
- staffing
- Title VII
- *United Steelworkers of America* v. *Weber*

Nailing Down the Main Points

1. The term *human resources management* refers to activities undertaken to attract, develop, and maintain an effective work force within an organization. Human resources management builds on three fundamental assumptions. First, every

manager—and not just people in the personnel office—should pay attention to the development and satisfaction of the employee. Second, employees are assets. People, not buildings and computers, allow organizations to accomplish their missions. Third, human resources management is a matching process, integrating the organization's goals with employees' needs.

2. Frederick C. Mosher classifies personnel systems into four main types: (*a*) political appointees, (*b*) general civil service, (*c*) career systems, and (*d*) collective system.

3. Staffing refers to the process of recruiting, selecting, and advancing employees on the basis of their relative ability, knowledge, and skill. Drucker says staff for strength.

4. At all levels of government, the basis of the civil service is position classification; that is, identifying the duties and responsibilities of each position in an organization and then grouping the positions according to their similarities. Nevertheless, today the concept is frequently under attack. Like position classification, compensation is a very important and controversial part of public personnel administration. The general rule for establishing a good pay plan is to pay according to differences in levels of duties and responsibilities.

5. In disciplinary matters, the administrator should strive for improvement in employee performance.

6. Organizational culture, the shared values of an organization, exercises a powerful influence on performance in the area of public personnel management.

7. One of the most visible concerns of public personnel management is labor relations. The growth in public sector employee unions really got underway in 1962 when President Kennedy guaranteed them recognition and bargaining rights by executive order. The collective bargaining process provides systematic procedures for the resolution of management-labor conflict. It consists of four major steps: organizing, election, negotiation, and contract administration.

8. One of the most important laws in the legal environment of a federal agency is the Civil Service Reform Act of 1978, which divided the old U.S. Civil Service Commission into two new agencies: the Office of Personnel Management (OPM), to serve as the personnel arm of the president, and an independent Merit Systems Protection Board (MSPB) to provide recourse for employees with complaints.

9. The Civil Service Reform Act also created the Federal Labor Relations Authority to oversee federal labor-management policies.

10. In 1965, President Johnson said that it is not enough just to open the gates of opportunity: "All our citizens must have the ability to walk through those gates." The outgrowth of that pronouncement was that affirmative action efforts developed at all levels of government. Affirmative action plans require employers to demonstrate good faith in their efforts to increase employment oppor-

tunities for deprived groups in accordance with Title VII of the Civil Rights Act of 1964.

11. Recent Supreme Court rulings and executive branch efforts have refocused anti-discrimination law on equal opportunity rather than affirmative action.

Problems

1. Select a public sector job and then decide from among the following what the examination used to determine the fitness and ability of the applicants should consist of: (*a*) written test, (*b*) performance test, (*c*) evaluation of education and experience as shown on the application, (*d*) oral examination, (*e*) interview, (*f*) physical test, and (*g*) health examination. How would you weigh each part? Be prepared to defend your choices.
2. Write a paper comparing the British, French, and American public personnel systems.
3. Do you agree with Peter Drucker's statement on the primary importance of job skill in hiring? Can you think of any other traits that might be at least equally important?
4. "Thanks to machinery, air conditioning, and noise control, work has become much less nasty—only in the civil services, the police and fire departments, and the imagination of sociologists has work become more degrading and unpleasant in recent years" (Mayer, 1976:55). Discuss.
5. Take an administrative position in the public sector and, using Table 10-1, design your own assessment center exercise. Be prepared to defend your design.
6. Write a paper on the right to strike in the public sector. Be sure to address pros and cons.
7. The public sector is becoming increasingly co-ed, particularly at the higher administrative levels. This generates dilemmas for both men and women in an organization. Some are trivial, but others are quite serious, affecting both careers and agency operations. Slowly, case by case, pragmatic solutions are evolving. In a sense, they constitute a series of do's and don'ts. The following series was suggested for corporate women and their male associates (*Business Week,* March 22, 1976). Which do you find appropriate? Inappropriate? What would you add?

For Men Executives	*For Women Executives*
Do:	**Do:**
Be as supportive or critical of a woman as of a man.	Plan your career and take risks.
Practice talking to her if you are self-conscious.	Stress your ambition. Ask "What can I do to get ahead?"
Let her open the door if she gets there first.	Speak at least once in every 10-minute meeting.

Tell your wife casually about a woman peer.

Don't:

Make a fuss when appointing the first women.

Tune her out at meetings.

Say "Good morning, gentlemen—and lady."

Apologize for swearing.

Take the chip off your shoulder.

Don't:

Say "I worked on . . ." when you wrote the entire report.

Imitate male mannerisms—or do needlepoint at meetings.

Hang on to the man who trained you.

Leap to serve coffee when someone suggests it's time for a break.

8. Identify some organization with which you are reasonably familiar. Then design a performance appraisal form for managers. (Hint: The three lists of leadership traits on pp. 342 and 345–346 might be a good place to start.) Would you weight the traits in order to determine a raw score? Why or why not?

9. Develop a set of questions that you would ask a job candidate. (Specify the position.) With one of your classmates playing the role of candidate, conduct your interview before the class. Have the class critique your performance.

CASE 10.1

★★★★★★★★★★★★★★★★★★★★★★★★★★★★★★★★★★★

Patricia Delacruz

After 13 years of working in a social service agency in her hometown, Patricia Delacruz stepped into a rare vacancy: provisional supervising clerk in charge of a typing room, mail room, and security area. For 3 years she worked hard, motivating and developing the 20 employees under her and introducing many modern management techniques. But today finds Patricia wondering whether her efforts had been a complete waste.

Here is why. Recently, in the name of fairness, the state civil service board began requiring that a promotional exam be required to find a permanent placement for the supervising clerk position. Everyone—even an entry-level clerk—was eligible to take it.

Now the results are in. Patricia placed 12th, and one of her own clerks, 1st. Patricia was devastated: She must forfeit her job to a person with considerably less experience. "I *proved* myself in the provisional position. Shouldn't that count for something?"

Case Questions

1. Was the procedure fair?
2. What management perspective is reflected in the way the civil service board selected people for supervisory jobs? Would another perspective be better for this type of organization?
3. What would you do if you were Delacruz?

Case Reference

Based on Betty Lehan Harragan, "Career Advice," *Working Woman* (July 1986), pp. 22–24.

CASE 10.2

★★★★★★★★★★★★★★★★★★★★★★★★★★★★★★★★★★

Gardner City Police Department

In 1967 officers of the Gardner City Police Department became affiliated with the American Federation of State, County, and Municipal Employees (AFSCME). At this time, the middle-management ranks of the Gardner City Police Department, especially sergeants, lieutenants, and captains, decided not to be represented by the union.

At the beginning, the benefits AFSCME gained through the collective bargaining process were small and automatically given to middle management. AFSCME has now been in operation for six years, and during the last two years has won some very good fringe benefits and wage increases for its members.

In 1973 AFSCME invited middle management to join the union. The middle-management echelon of the police department was the only group in Gardner City not affiliated with a union. The fire department had been totally organized since the inception of the firemen's union. The police middle management met and discussed the offer to join AFSCME. They decided not to join since it would be detrimental to the mission of the officers. They also felt that their affiliation with a union would cast a shadow of doubt as to where their loyalty rested. This decision on the part of middle management left them without any representation in regard to benefits and wages.

Up until this time, the city manager, through the city council, had immediately passed on all union gains to middle management without a request from them.

One of the issues included in the 1971 contract was a 10-cent night-shift differential. This benefit, however, was not passed on to middle management.

In the 1975 negotiations, more new benefits were gained for union members. Middle management, once again, did not receive any of these new benefits. As a result of this action, middle management decided it was time to bring these inequities to the attention of the city manager. A formal letter (see Exhibit 1) was drafted and sent to the city manager. All middle-management members of the Gardner City Police Department signed the letter. The city manager then wrote a reply (see Exhibit 2) to their letter, responding to their expressed inequities.

EXHIBIT 1

Letter to City Manager of Gardner City

February 14, 1975

Dear Sir:

We, the members of the supervisory and management echelon of the Gardner City Police Department, would like to take this opportunity, with all due respect, to voice our collective opinions regarding several inequities which we believe may develop from the ranks which are not included in the bargaining unit.

We consider our echelon, supervision and management, as an extension or arm of the city manager and the chief of police, and as such our loyalty must and does in fact remain with these administrators. We have vividly demonstrated this loyalty in the past by voting against our inclusion in the bargaining unit representing the operational echelon of the department.

Recently, in what appeared to be a job action by members of the department bargaining unit, the responsibility for providing police protection fell on the shoulders of supervisory personnel whose loyalty was demonstrated by reporting for duty and performing all required services for the citizens of Gardner City. We feel that in order to prevent a conflict of interests and perpetuate the strong loyalty to the administration, we cannot and should not become affiliated with a bargaining unit. No man can serve two masters and be equally loyal to each.

However, self-preservation and self-esteem are two most intense behavioral drives possessed by man and to these ends we have composed this communication.

First and of long-standing concern to our numbers is the inequity which exists between bargaining-unit members and our ranks with respect to the night-shift differential. The night-shift differential has been in existence for several years and was not initially offered to nonunion employees nor has it ever been discussed with our numbers. Currently, only eight supervisors would be concerned with this pay differential, but it is an inequity to the supervisory ranks of the department.

The next area of concern to nonunion personnel was the apparent fact that the bargaining unit has obtained an additional $35 uniform allowance. No additional allowances were forthcoming to supervisors which was embarrassing and thought provoking. Embarrassing since it was apparent on that payday when two checks were received by union-employees and none by supervisors that "you guys don't rate,"—a somewhat grating statement heard by most supervisors upon reporting for pay.

Thought-provoking in that if initially we were not included in the night-shift differential then not included in the allocation of funds for additional uniform allowance, it is apparent that the future is not getting brighter for supervisors who are loyal nonunion members.

These inequities should not have accrued initially. To allow the initial oversight to carry over from year to year and to overlook the appropriation of funds to guarantee those additional benefits to supervisors is most detrimental to the morale of the supervisory echelon.

We respectfully request that the nonunion supervisors of the police department be placed on parity with other city employees and that this be standard for each subsequent contractual agreement. This would eliminate the annual apprehension and the requirement that we must communicate inequities on a yearly basis.

We request these aforementioned conditions be considered in the light of fairness, equality, and an opportunity to provide a prideful environment for supervisors who are not union-affiliated.

Respectfully,

Supervisors of the
Gardner City Police Department

EXHIBIT 2 . . . .

Letter to Chief of Police of Gardner City

February 27, 1975

Dear Chief:

This is in reply to the letter dated February 14, 1975, signed by all sergeants, lieutenants, and captains, in which they set forth certain alleged inequities in the benefits offered to nonunion personnel.

I would point out that, with the exception of the chief and assistant chief, all other supervisors receive overtime pay at the rate of one and one-half times regular pay. This benefit is not extended to any other supervisor in Gardner.

In addition, I must remind you that last year the classification for chief and assistant chief was upgraded in order to compensate for the lack of time-and-one-half provision in these two positions.

In order for me to secure money to implement the requests contained in their letter, it will be necessary for me to request an additional appropriation from the city council. If you will provide me with the cost figures to cover the numerous requests made, I will present this to the city council.

Very truly yours,

City Manager

Case Questions

1. What is the problem?
2. How do you think middle management will respond to Exhibit 2?
3. Should the city council automatically pass on to middle management benefits that police officers gained through contract negotiations?
4. What problems can you foresee as a result of permitting supervisory personnel to be members of a police officer's union?

Case Reference

Prepared by Richard M. Ayers, FBI Academy, and Thomas L. Wheelen, College of Business Administration, University of South Florida, as the basis for class discussion. Copyright © 1975 by Thomas L. Wheelen and Richard M. Ayres.

Presented at a case workshop and distributed by Intercollegiate Case Clearing House, Soldiers Field, Boston, Massachusetts 02163. All rights reserved to the contributors. Printed in the U.S.A.

CASE 10.3

★★★★★★★★★★★★★★★★★★★★★★★★★★★★★★★★★★★

Society of Equals

Ted Shelby doesn't make very many mistakes, but . . .

"Hey, Stanley," said Ted Shelby, leaning in through the door, "you got a minute? I've just restructured my office. Come on and take a look. I've been implementing some great new concepts!"

Stanley is always interested in Ted Shelby's new ideas. For if there is anyone Stanley wants to do as well as, it is Edward W. Shelby IV. Stanley follows Ed back to his office and stops, nonplussed.

Restructured is right! Gone are Ted's size B (Junior Exec.) walnut veneer desk and furniture, and his telephone table. In fact, the room is practically empty save for a large, round, stark white cafeteria table and the half-dozen padded vinyl swivel chairs that surround it.

"Isn't it a beauty! As far as I know, I'm the first executive in the plant to innovate this. The shape is the crucial factor here—no front or rear, no status problems. We can all sit there and communicate more effectively."

We? Communicate? Effectively? Well, it seems that Ted has been attending a series of Executive Development Seminars given by Dr. Faust. The theme of the seminars was—you guessed it—"participative management." Edward W. Shelby IV has always liked to think of himself as a truly democratic person.

"You see, Stanley," says Ted, managing his best sincere/intense attitude, "the main thing wrong with current mainstream management practice is that the principal communication channel is down-the-line oriented. We on the top send our messages down to you people, but we neglect the feedback potential. But just because we have more status and responsibility doesn't mean that we are necessarily (Stanley duly noted the word, "necessarily") better than the people below us. So, as I see the situation, what is needed is a two-way communication network: down-the-line and up-the-line.

"That's what the cafeteria table is for?" Stanley says.

"Yes!" says Ted. "We management people don't have all the answers, and I don't know why I never realized it before that seminar. Why . . . let's take an extreme example . . . the folks who run those machines out there. I'll bet that any one of them knows a thing or two that I've never thought of. So I've transformed my office into a full-feedback communication net."

"That certainly is an innovation around here," says Stanley.

A few days later Stanley passed by Ted Shelby's office and was surprised that Ted's desk, furniture, and telephone table were back where they used to be.

Stanley, curious about the unrestructuring, went to Bonnie for enlightenment. "What," he asked, "happened to Shelby's round table?"

"That table we were supposed to sit around and input things?" she said. "All I know is, about two days after he had it put in, Mr. Drake came walking through here. He looked in that office, and then he sort of stopped and went back—and he looked in there for a long time. Then he came over to me, and you know how his face sort of gets red when he's really mad? Well, this time he was so mad that his face was absolutely white. And when he talked to me, I don't think he actually opened his mouth; and I could barely hear him, he was talking so low. And he said, 'Have that removed. Now. Have Mr. Shelby's furniture put back in his office. Have Mr. Shelby see me."

My, my. You would think Ted would have known better, wouldn't you? But then, by now you should have a pretty firm idea of just why it is those offices are set up as they are.

Case Questions

1. Why did Shelby's new idea fail?
2. What could he have done?

Case Reference

R. Richard Ritti and G. Ray Funkhouser, *The Ropes to Skip & The Ropes to Know* (New York: John Wiley & Sons, 1982), pp. 21–22. Reprinted by permission of John Wiley & Sons, Inc.

CASE 10.4

★ ★

Choosing a Manager

The director of human resources for the Pearson Construction Company had to recommend someone for a high-level management position in the company. Careful screening of all employees narrowed the selection to two men: John Jarvis and Bill Franklin. After lengthy interviews, the following information was accumulated.

Jarvis had a company tenure of three years. He was seldom absent from work, had obtained a college degree in business administration by taking evening courses, and his superiors rated his management potential as promising. The one factor against him was that he appeared impatient and overly ambitious. During his interview with the director of human resources, Jarvis indicated that promotions had not occurred fast enough and that unless he received this promotion, he would seek employment elsewhere.

Franklin was several years older than Jarvis. He had been with the company since graduation from a nearby university six years ago. He was rated by superiors as a steady, dependable, intelligent employee, who had little opportunity to display his talent. Three years ago, he turned down a more responsible position in another city. The reason he gave for not accepting the position was that it involved relocating and required some traveling. Since then, he had not been given another opportunity to move upward in the organization.

Case Questions

1. How important is seniority?
2. Who would you advise the director to select?

Case Reference

John M. Champion and John H. James, *Critical Incidents in Management* (Homewood, Ill.: Richard D. Irwin, 1985), p. 290.

CHAPTER 11 Budgeting

Introduction

Central to the management of government's financial resources is the budget. Administrators devote much time and energy to preparing it. Its adoption represents a critical juncture in the policy-planning process, for few major programs are conceivable without the expenditure of money.

Budgeting, however, is important for other reasons as well. Because it is the means by which public officials allocate and raise resources to achieve social objectives, budgeting answers the bedrock question of politics: Who gets how much for what purpose, and who pays for it? In this sense, the budget provides an X ray of the values and priorities of a free people. And because values and priorities vary from person to person, we may safely assume the budget process often involves ferocious political battles. In recent years, these battles have become, if anything, even more fero-

Budgeting is a common practice to the extent that everybody—households, corporations, clubs, agencies, and so on—must anticipate income and expenses. Historically, the word budget *referred to a leather bag in which England's chancellor of the exchequer carried the statement of the government's needs and resources to Parliament. In time, however, the budget came to refer to the papers within the bag rather than to the bag itself. The photo above shows recent chancellor, Nigel Lawson, carrying the traditional budget "bag" (which is now really a box) before speaking in the House of Commons.*

Across the Atlantic, in the United States, budgets are carried in neither bags nor boxes but are bound in volumes that, for at least the major units of government, contain an extensive array of data in standardized formats. The massiveness and complexity of major budgets are generally so intimidating that one wonders whether those responsible have purposefully made budget reading unappetizing. In any case, public administrators must be able to understand the development and functioning of budgets if they are to perform effectively. (Photo by AP/Wide World)

cious. The explanation for this intensification has its roots in the inexorable climb of public expenditures and taxes at all levels of government. In 1951, federal expenditures were 14.4 percent of the gross national product (GNP); by 1987 they had grown to 22.8 percent of the GNP. State and local expenditures rose from 6.1 percent to 9.3 percent during the same period.

The nub of the problem is not just the spending; rather, it is the fact that governments, whose finances started sliding in the late 1980s, are not taking in enough revenue to pay for all the services that citizens, corporations, courts, and elected officials demand. When that happens, you get deficits.

Given their size and complexity, government budgets can, at times, seem almost beyond comprehension (see box). But much of this difficulty can be avoided by focusing on the **four basic phases of the federal budget cycle.** These are shown in the following schematic:

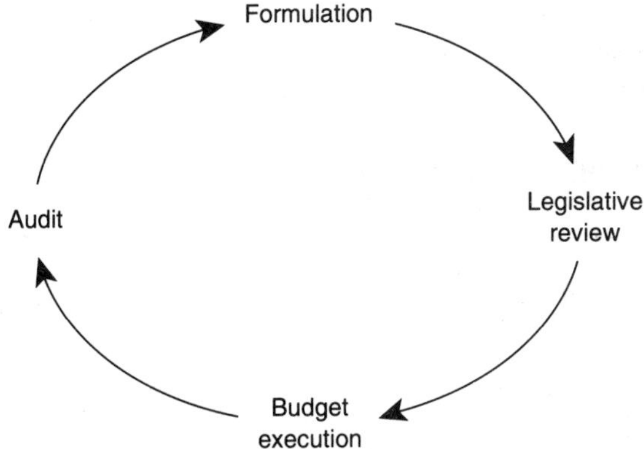

We illustrate this four-phase process first by looking at the federal budget cycle and then by considering budgeting in state and local governments.

Following that, we consider the dreaded "T" word—*taxation.* I do not think I exaggerate the fear that politicians have of this word. They avoid its use at all costs, and when they absolutely must use it, they use weasel words like "revenue enhancement." The fourth and final section makes two predictions (fairly safe ones, I must admit) about the future of budgeting in the United States.

The Federal Budget Cycle

The connection between governmental plans, the focus of Chapter 5, and the budget, the subject at hand, is strong. Strictly speaking, a plan is really no more than a statement of purpose, a piece of paper, a mere shadow. Not until it appears in the budget does it take on life and begin to matter. In this sense, the budget animates a plan.

And there is more. Because the budget must reveal how funds are allocated among many and varied programs, it provides us with probably the most clear-cut way of determining national priorities.

Remember the concept of opportunity cost introduced in Chapter 6? This concept can help us see more clearly what we mean by choice of priorities. Opportunity cost represents the implicit cost of the highest foregone alternative to an individual or group; in short, it is the true cost of choosing one alternative over another. The president each year is confronted with a multiplicity of such choices. He soon learns that spending in one area is viewed by certain groups as money not spent in their areas of special interest.

There is no universally acceptable fair way to cut a budget. Speaking of his plan to cut all mass transit operation subsidies, a president might explain his approach with

(text continues on p. 504)

Can the Budget Be Understood?

In early 1990, President Bush proposed to Congress a budget of $1.23 trillion. When the budget went from $990 billion to $1.23 trillion, it almost seemed to go down, because we have little experience dealing in millions, billions, and trillions.

To begin to appreciate the size of this number, consider a stack of new $1,000 bills. One hundred of these, or $100,000, would make a stack about one-half-inch high. A stack of $1,000 bills the height of the Empire State Building would be worth $6 billion. If Bush's budget was presented in $1,000 bills, it would make nearly 206 stacks, each the height of the Empire State Building.

Another reason the budget cannot be easily comprehended is that it consists of 190,000 accounts. If you wanted to reach each of the account names (and many have long titles) to get a slight idea of the disposal of *your* money (I assume you pay taxes), how long do you think that would take? Now imagine that you want to find out what is actually in the accounts and whether the money is well spent. How long do you think that would take for just 190 of them?

Removing our green eyeshades, we find that, even at a more general level of analysis, budgeting remains a complex affair. Consider, for example, its major functions. Besides the two obvious ones—allocating resources to programs and raising funds through taxes and loans—at least six others can be identified:

1. Stabilizing the economy through fiscal policy. Let us define our terms. **Stabilization** refers to policies instituted by the federal government to achieve national economic goals of steady growth, full employment, and low inflation. Essentially, two types of policies are used to achieve stabilization: **fiscal policy** (the mix of expenditures, taxes, and debt financing) and **monetary policy** (the control over the money supply and interest rates).
2. Holding operating agencies accountable for the efficient use of resources provided in the budget.
3. Controlling expenditures to ensure that they are legal and compatible with policies of elected officials.
4. Providing a mechanism for transferring funds from one level of government to another.
5. Serving as a mechanism for achieving planned social and economic goals.
6. Providing leverage through the power of the purse to pressure agencies to manage their programs in a prescribed way.

Given, then, the size, complexity, and multiple functions of budgets, one may wonder how they ever get prepared. Well, they do, and part of the reason is that policymakers simplify the process in a variety of ways. For example, the system does not start from scratch each year but from a base budget that is carried over from the previous year. The starting point for each year's budget battle is a calculation of the cost of continuing existing programs without change and an adjustment of the costs merely to reflect shifts in work load (e.g., increase in number of clients) and effects of inflation. This estimate is variously termed the base budget,

"Sayyyyy . . . do you know anything about budgets?"
(© 1991 by Mort Gerberg. Reprinted from Harvard Business Review, *April–May, 1991.)*

the **current services budget,** the continuing services budget, and recurrent budget.

While measuring all budget changes against this baseline does simplify things politically, it greatly complicates the political debate for the average citizen. For example, if last year Congress determined that a program would be cut by 20% this year, then a budget consistent with that cut may not be a cut at all, according to the current services concept. Say that an agency with a $100-million budget would need $125 million just to stand still. A twenty percent *cut* would leave them with a budget of $100 million. The average citizen might wonder *where's the cut.*

Another "simplifying" device is **incrementalism.** For the most part, the budget process concentrates on marginal adjustments of the budget base. Increase 6 percent here, cut 4 percent there, and so forth.

A third factor that helps simplify the budget process is that many significant government functions are **off-budget items;** that is, they do not appear in budget totals. Included here would be public enterprises, public authorities, government corporations, and other business-type organizations that have the power to raise their own revenue. Special funds like the Highway Trust Fund, which can be used solely for special pur-

(continued)

poses and cannot be transferred to any other program, also help simplify the process.

A final factor that helps to simplify the budget process is the cold fact that about three fourths of the federal budget consists of so-called **uncontrollables.** Statutes mandate Medicare, Medicaid, food stamps, unemployment insurance, pensions, and farm price supports. Interest on the national debt (about 15 percent of the budget) is also uncontrollable; it must be paid this year if the government hopes to borrow next year. Given these uncontrollables, and the legislature's reluctance to tamper with the original statutes, budget negotiations begin by taking three fourths of the pie off the table. Trying to decide how to divide one fourth a pie is presumably less complicated than deciding on the whole thing. Of course, simpler budgeting is not necessarily *better* budgeting.

a rhetorical question: Is it fair to ask people in Omaha and Des Moines to get the people in Chicago and New York to work on time? But New Yorkers and Chicagoans would probably find that philosophy hard to buy since they help the farmers of Omaha and Des Moines with water projects and agricultural subsidies. Nevertheless, the reordering of priorities does go on. During the defense buildup of the 1980s, the $55 million in the Pentagon budget for military bands went untouched while funds for children with learning disabilities were cut 25 percent.

Space programs come in for similar questioning—not only by groups of urban activists but also by groups of certain scientists. A case in point is the American Miscellaneous Society, a group, which, despite its whimsical title, is composed of quite serious oceanographers and other less space-oriented scientists. Their slogan: "The ocean's bottom is at least as important as the moon's behind."

Keeping these ideas in mind, we now turn to the four overlapping phases of the budget process: formulation, legislative review, budget execution, and audit.

Formulation

The president's transmittal of his budget proposals to the Congress early in January climaxes many months of planning and analysis throughout the executive branch. Formulation of the budget for **fiscal year** 1992, for example, began in the spring of 1990 (see Figure 11-1).

This is the way it works. In the spring, agency programs are evaluated, policy issues are identified, and budgetary projections are made, giving attention both to important modifications and innovations in programs and to alternative long-range program plans. In early June, preliminary plans are presented to the president for his consideration. At about the same time, the president receives projections of estimated receipts, prepared by the Treasury Department, and projections of the economic outlook, prepared jointly by the Council of Economic Advisors, the Treasury Department, and the OMB. As one might gather from the title of the last-named agency, its director is a particularly important player in the process (see Working Profile).

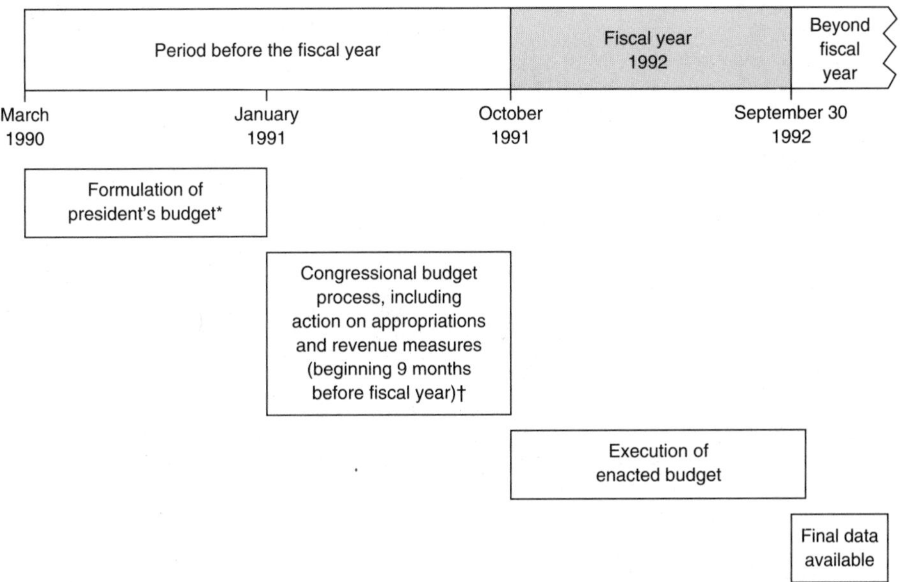

FIGURE 11-1
Major Steps in the Budget Process

* The President's budget is transmitted to the Congress within 15 days after the Congress convenes.

† If appropriation action is not completed by September 30, the Congress enacts temporary appropriations (i.e., a continuing resolution).

Following a review of both sets of projections—that is, of expenditures and receipts—the president establishes general budget and fiscal policy guidelines for the fiscal year that will begin about 15 months later. Tentative policy determinations and planning **ceilings** are then given to the agencies as guidelines for the preparation of their final budget requests during the summer.

Agency budget requests are reviewed *in detail* by the OMB throughout the fall and are presented, along with OMB recommendations, to the president for decision. Overall fiscal policy issues—relating to total budget receipts and outlays—are again examined. The actual budget data from the most recently completed fiscal year provide an essential reference base in this review and decision process.

Legislative Review

The Budget Act of 1974. For decades, the president's budget was the only comprehensive statement of priorities and revenue and spending recommendations. But in 1974 Congress, seeking a greater role in managing the government, passed the **Congressional Budget and Impounding Control Act,** which requires it to adopt an annual budget.

(text continues on p. 509)

★★★★★★★★★★★★★★★★★★★★★★★★★★★★★★★★★★

WORKING PROFILE

Richard G. Darman

Perhaps the most influential budget director ever, Richard G. Darman is regarded by many as a man who approaches every task with a scheme, an angle. Nevertheless, he is admired by both his political foes and his friends for his intelligence, capacity for work, analytical ability, and mastery of government programs.

Commitment to Service

Born into a family of wealthy New England mill owners, Darman rejected the idea of taking over the family business. He was more attracted to his mother's notion of social obligation: She did volunteer work for terminal cancer patients and the needy.

At Harvard in the early 1960s, Darman was influenced by President John F. Kennedy's soaring rhetoric:

Now the trumpet summons us again—not as a call to bear arms, though arms we need; not as a call to battle, though embattled we are; but a call to bear the burden of a long twilight struggle, year in and year out, "rejoicing in hope, patient in tribulation," a struggle against the common enemies of man: tyranny, poverty, disease, and war itself.

And so, my fellow Americans, ask not what your country can do for you; ask what you can do for your country.

It is our task in our time and in our generation to hand down undiminished to those who come after us, as was handed down to us by those who went before, the natural wealth and beauty which is ours.

Since his days as a romantic undergraduate, Darman has—to his credit—consistently urged citizens to abjure what he calls "nowism," the temptation to live for today, not the future.

Although Kennedy's call to public service struck Darman, he did not react, as some of his classmates did, by joining the Peace Corps in Peru. Instead, he went to Harvard Business School to learn how to get things done (not how to make money).

After earning his MBA, he worked briefly as a management consultant but said it was little more than "designing boxes without a lot of thought about what goes into them." But working for a Washington bureaucracy would be something else. Darman therefore went to work for Elliot L. Richardson in HEW. Secretary Richardson embodied Darman's public service ideal, and Darman soon became his protegé, following him through HEW, the Defense Department, and the Justice Department in the Nixon administration.

Joining the White House staff in 1981, Darman served as the deputy to President Reagan's chief of staff, James A. Baker, III. Four years later, Darman followed Baker to the Treasury Department, where he served as deputy secretary. He left the Treasury Department in 1987 to be a managing director of Shearson Lehman Hutton and held that position until he became the Bush Administration's budget chief, the man with a trillion-dollar checkbook.

Darman at OMB

The OMB is technically a branch of the White House, but it offers the potential of immense power to a skillful director. The way government decision making has evolved over the last decade has probably made the OMB job as important as any domestic cabinet job. Everything comes down to the budget, and someone who understands how to use that job is going to be powerful.

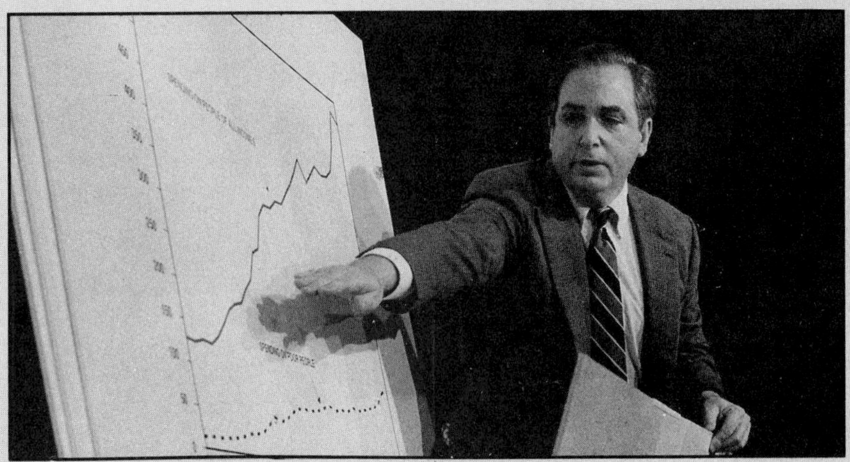

Richard G. Darman, director of the OMB, briefing reporters on the Bush Administration's budget.

When word spread in early 1990 that the administration's budget would be presented that year in one large book instead of the usual collection of smaller volumes, the response around Washington, from Congress and bureaucracy, from lobbyists and reporters, was the same: What is Darman up to now?

Politicians and scholars disagree whether his reputation for always having something up his sleeve makes him less effective as one of the president's chief budget negotiators. Perhaps there's a fine line between having an angle, a strategy, and being improperly devious. Some members of Congress who think him devious may simply resent him because he is hard to second-guess, outwin, or outplan.

And Darman certainly knows how to do those things. Even David Stockman, who was OMB director when Darman was a White House aide, marveled at his political skills. "At first, I had not liked him that much," Stockman wrote in his book, *The Triumph of Politics.* "He was always asking inconvenient questions or seemingly preoccupied with the process-tactics, trades, players, deals, winning. I later realized he saw these as inextricably linked with substance. . . . I came to admire his hard-headed, cogent, and zestful approach to political strategy."

Foresight

Darman is much more farseeing than most people in government. That was apparent from an introduction he wrote to the budget for fiscal year 1991. The tone of this introduction might have irked some members of Congress; but Darman wanted to remind them of a fact that they often neglect: Enormous future expenses (like medical care for an aging population) flow inexorably from obligations that Congress enters into today. Here are excerpts from Darman's introduction:

One curious thing about future Federal lia-

(continued)

bilities is that many of them are not yet fully visible. Their particular nature varies. But each is like a hidden Pacman, waiting to spring forward and consume another line of resource dots in the budget maze. . . . A few introductory points may help outline the problem:

Rising Costs of Health Care. A quarter of a century ago, health care expenditures consumed about 6 percent of America's gross national product. Now, that share has almost doubled, to 12 percent. . . . There are, nonetheless, increasing demands to assure health insurance coverage for those not now covered, and to provide better financing for long term care. Each of these could entail an additional multi-billion dollar annual bill. Yet the projected health expenditure obligations of current law are not fully covered by projected future receipts. The estimated present value of unfunded liabilities (the actuarial deficiency) for Medicare hospital insurance alone would be over $250 billion. . . .

Rising Claims of Mandatory Programs. In President Kennedy's administration transfer payments to individuals comprised about a quarter of the Federal budget. Now they consume almost half. . . . (Mandatory programs plus net interest expenditures account for almost 62 percent of the budget.) Since these programs generally have broad-based and well-represented beneficiary populations, they tend to have a powerful claim on resources and grow faster than the economy as a whole. Yet again: It would seem obvious that this pattern of more rapid growth cannot be extended indefinitely. . . .

Unfunded Retirement Program Liabilities. There are clearly identifiable major shortfalls in unfunded Federal employee retirement programs—although these should be serviced by future contributions. . . .

Obligations to Clean Up Federal Facilities. The present-value cost of already-identified future clean-up obligations and waste management improvements at Federal facilities over the next 30 years is on the order of $140–200 billion. . . .

Contingent Risks of Federal Credit Programs and Government-Sponsored Enterprises. There can be no denying that there is an enormous and increasing Federal exposure—approaching one trillion dollars in direct and federally guaranteed loans alone.

Contingent Risks of Federal Insurance Programs. These formal insurance programs cover bank deposits, pensions, veterans' life insurance, crops, floods, overseas private investment, nuclear risks, and war risks. The total face value of this insurance coverage (excluding Medicare) exceeds four trillion dollars. . . . The likely future claims are virtually certain to be in the tens of billions of dollars.

Darman gave special emphasis in the introduction to "investing in the future," that is, pursuing growth-oriented economic policies so that future economic productivity and federal receipts are higher than they would have been without those policies in place. This emphasis on investing in the future, Darman writes,

is consistent with three fundamental points: First, a budget must be viewed as more than a static snapshot; it necessarily influences the future, and the nature of that influence must be examined. Second, there is a generally accepted moral obligation to try to leave future generations in a better position than their predecessors. Third, the obligations for future expenditures and debt service are more manageable insofar as current expenditures and tax policy contribute to increased growth. Together, these three points argue compellingly for attention to the extent to which a budget (and its associated economic policy) encourage investment—investment in the future.

SOURCES: U.S. Office of Management and Budget, *Budget FY1991* (Washington, D.C.: U.S.

Government Printing Office, 1990); Lawrence J. Haas, "Budget Guru," *National Journal*, January 20, 1990; David E. Rosenbaum, "Budget Director's Deeds Obscured by Reputation," *New York Times*, January 29, 1990; Howard Gleckman, "The Trillion Dollar Man," *Business Week*, March 13, 1989; Steven V. Roberts, "From Charmin' Darman to Tricky Dick," *U.S. News & World Report*, January 22, 1990; David A. Stockman, *The Triumph of Politics* (New York: Harper & Row, 1987).

★★★★★★★★★★★★★★★★★★★★★★★★★★★★★★★★★★

The Budget Act attempted to control **impoundment**—the refusal of the executive branch to spend money appropriated by Congress—and required Congress to adopt a resolution that sets a floor under revenue and a ceiling on spending. The resolution also includes categories of spending limits for 13 major federal functions such as the military, agriculture, and transportation.

The law is also intended to force Congress, after it completes work on the separate appropriations and authorizations it customarily enacts each year, to fit them into an overall framework by passing a second resolution setting final, binding targets.

The Budget Act sets up a timetable for Congress to make its major fiscal decisions. All measures are to be in place by the beginning of the government's budget year, October 1, but these deadlines are often not met.

As the first step in the budget process, the president is required to submit his budget 15 days after Congress convenes in January. For the next several weeks, both House and Senate Budget Committees conduct hearings to examine the president's estimates and projections.

By April 15 the budget committees are scheduled to report the first budget resolution, which sets overall goals for tax and spending broken down among major budget categories. Congress is supposed to complete action on the first budget resolution by May 15, but it has often been adopted later in the session.

On the basis of the guidelines set in the first budget resolution, Congress is supposed to approve the individual authorization and appropriation bills. The second budget resolution, due September 15, establishes firm ceilings on spending categories. But Congress has found the budget debate so contentious and time-consuming that it has been writing into the first budget solution language that automatically readopts it as the second.

On September 25 Congress is scheduled to complete action on the reconciliation bill, and by October 1, to complete action of all 13 appropriation bills.

How Well Has the Budget Act Worked? In recent years Congress has found it impossible to pass all the appropriation bills before the start of the fiscal year. So it has resorted to a device known as a continuing resolution, which authorizes money for departments and agencies that have not received their regular appropriations. More and more, the continuing resolutions have become omnibus appropriations bills, wrapping several measures into one package and in principle conforming to the spending levels set in the overall budget resolutions. But perhaps the most damaging criticism that can be made of the Budget Act is not that members of Congress have failed to follow procedures but that the act itself has failed to control rising federal deficits.

Such concerns led Senators Gramm, Rudman, and Hollings to introduce a bill to "mandate" deficit ceilings each year. The most striking feature of the plan, which became law in 1985, was that it authorized the president, when Congress exceeded its own limits, to cut spending "across the board" (except for social security). In theory, Congress appeared to cancel in one stroke the Budget Act of 1974, which had attempted to prevent presidents from *not* spending (i.e., impounding) money it had authorized. In reality, the law tended to reduce the significance of presidents' budgets, because it set deficit ceilings too low for serious policy proposals to meet. As a result, presidents and lawmakers resort to accounting tricks like moving paydays from one year to another and leaving out of the budget much of the money being spent to rescue savings and loan institutions.

Whatever the effects of this law are, it marks another fascinating episode in the story of Congress's effort to achieve fiscal self-discipline. Yet such an assessment might be too harsh. As Alice M. Rivlin, the first director of the **Congressional Budget Office** (an analytical staff set up by the act itself), has correctly observed: "We want more government than we can pay for, and no process can help solve that problem."

One final observation regarding the first and second phases of the budget process needs underscoring. To be effective in the budgetary process, the administrator should understand the various **political strategies in the budget process** (see box).

Budget Execution

Once approved—whether by salesmanship, analysis, or a little of both—the budget eventually is passed and becomes the financial basis for the operations of the agency during the fiscal year.

Under the law, most budget authority and other budgetary resources are made available to the executive branch through an apportionment system. Under authority delegated by the president, the director of the OMB apportions (distributes) appropriations and other budgetary resources to each agency by time periods (usually quarterly) or by activities. **Obligations** may not be incurred in excess of the amount apportioned.

Obligations refer to the amount of orders placed, contracts awarded, services rendered, or other commitments made by an agency during a given period. Sometime during this period, payment will have to be made, probably by check.

The objective of the apportionment system is to assure the effective and orderly use of available authority and to reduce the need for requesting additional or supplemental authority.

What happens if an agency has funds that are not obligated by the end of the year? The general view among all bureaucrats—whether they are providing services to Eskimos in the frozen tundra of Alaska or pursuing drug traffic in the Florida Keys—is that the cash turns into pumpkins on September 30. At the very least, they

(text continues on p. 515)

Talking Shop ....

The Politics of Budgeting

Aaron Wildavsky has identified group strategies employed within the roles pursued in the budget process on the basis of an analysis of the United States Congress. Many of these strategies—"links between intentions and perceptions of budget officials and the political system that imposes restraints and creates opportunities for them"—are transferable to other governments. Two agency strategies are *ubiquitous.* The first is cultivation of an active clientele for help in dealing with both the legislature and the chief executive. The clientele may be those directly served (as with farmers in particular programs provided by the Department of Agriculture) or those selling services to the particular agency (as with highway contractors doing business with a state department of highways). Agencies unable to identify and cultivate such clientele will find budget hearings difficult because active support may be difficult to mobilize.

A second ubiquitous strategy is the development of confidence of other government officials. Agency administrators must avoid being surprised in hearings or by requests for information. Officials must show results in the reports they make and must tailor their message's complexity to their audience. If results are not directly available, agencies may report internal process activities, such as files managed or surveys taken. Confidence is critical because, in the budget process, many elements of program defense must derive from the judgments of the administrators, not from hard evidence. If confidence has been developed, those judgments will be trusted; if not, those judgments will be suspect.

Another group of strategies—*contingent* strategies—depends on the budget circumstances, and particularly on whether discussion concerns (1) a reduction in agency programs below the present level of expenditures (the budget base), (2) an increase in the scope of agency programs, or (3) an expansion of agency programs to new areas. Some strategies seem strange or even preposterous; they are used, however, and should be recognized because the budget choices involved are vital parts of government action. It cannot be emphasized enough, however, that strategy and clever rhetoric alone are not sufficient; they matter not at all if basics of the budget—its logic, justifications, mathematics, and internal consistency—are faulty.

Several strategies are applied as a program administrator responds to proposals for reduction in base (if a program may be terminated or reduced from its existing level of operation). These include the following:

1. *Propose a study.* Agency administrators argue that rash actions (such as cutting his or her program) should not be taken until all consequences have been completely considered. A study would delay action, possibly long enough for those proposing cuts to lose interest and certainly long enough for the program administrator to develop other arguments for the program.
2. *Cut the popular programs.* The administrator responds to the pro-

(continued)

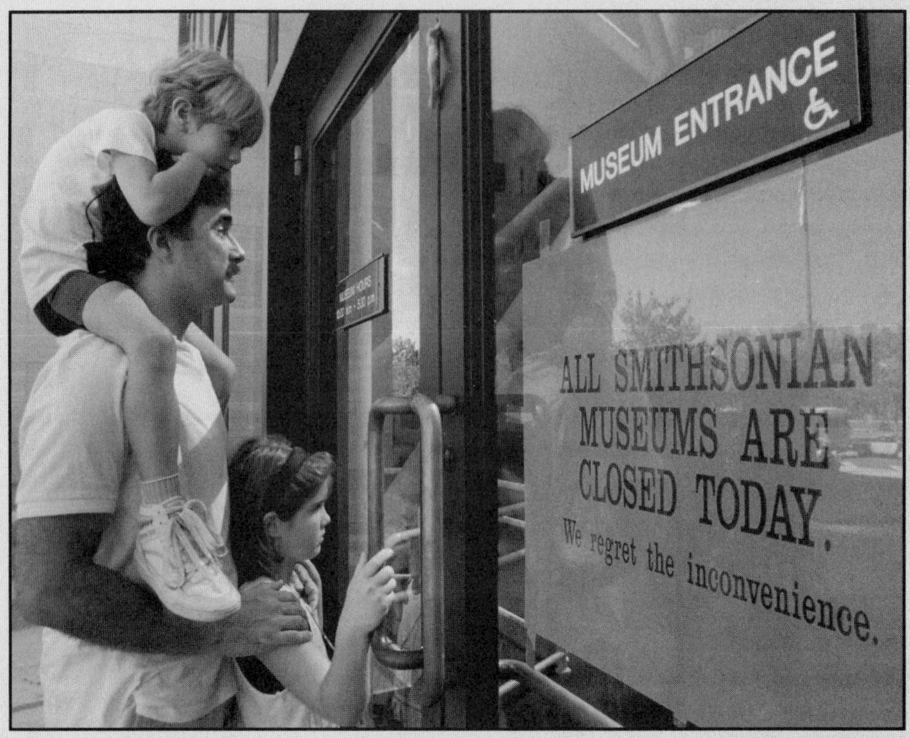

One strategy available to administrators faced with a proposed reduction in funding is to cut or eliminate popular programs. This father and his children peer mournfully into the window of the Smithsonian's Air and Space Museum—closed on a Columbus Day weekend because of a budget crisis. (Photo by AP/Wide World)

posed reduction by cutting or eliminating (or at least releasing to the news media plans for such action) programs with strong public support (see photo). By proposing that the school band or athletic programs be eliminated, for instance, the administrator hopes to mobilize sufficient outcry to ensure no budget cuts. The careful reviewer will have other activities that are particularly ripe for reduction, so that the political horrors painted by the administrator do not dominate discussion.

3. *Dire consequences.* The administrator outlines the tragic events—shattered lives of those served, supplier businesses closed, and so on—that would accompany the reductions.
4. *All or nothing.* Any reduction would make the program impossible, so it might as well be eliminated.
5. *You pick.* The administrator responds that all agency activities are so vital that agency directors are unable to choose which would be reduced or eliminated if agency funds are cut. Therefore, those proposing the cut

should identify the targets, thereby clearly tracking the political blame for the cut and, hopefully, scaring away the reduction. Anyone proposing a reduction for an agency needs a definite package proposal, in case such a strategy unfolds.

6. *We are the experts.* The agency argues that is has expertise that the budget cutter lacks. The reduction is shortsighted, based on ignorance, and, thus, should not occur.

A different group of strategies applies when the agency seeks to continue or augment operations of its existing program:

1. *Round up.* Rounding program estimates—work load, prices, costs, and so on—upward to the next-highest hundred, thousand, or million creates substantial slack.
2. *"If it don't run, chrome it."* The budget presentation sparkles with data, charts, graphs, and other state-of-the-art management trappings. While much of the material may not relate directly to the decision at hand and the base data may not be particularly accurate, the quality of the show is intended to overpower its weak substance.
3. *Sprinkling.* Budget items are slightly increased, either in hard-to-detect general categories or across the board, after the basic request has been prepared. The thin layer of excess is spread so thin that it cannot be clearly identified as padding. If enacted in full, the budget would allow the agency a significant operating cushion. Such a practice may leave no traces at all; however, surpluses might emerge during budget execution.
4. *Numbers game.* Agency administrators may discuss physical units—facilities operated, grants initiated, acres maintained, and so on—rather than the funds requested and spent. The intent is to divert attention from substantially increased spending for each unit.
5. *Work load or backlog.* Administrators often base their request on greater client demands or a backlog of unfilled requests. The argument is frequently reasonable, especially if the work load measure is germane to the agency function, if the agency is doing something that needs to be done, and if the backlogs are not simply residuals of poor management of existing resources.
6. *The accounting system trap.* Either side of the budget process may argue that a proposed expenditure must be made (or is forbidden) because the accounting system controls such transactions. The argument can be politically important. However, accounting systems exist to help management implement policy and to provide information for policy decisions. Policy choices should not be made difficult by the accounting system.

Programs and agencies develop an institutional momentum. To propose a new program, a program that expands the scope of agency operations, entails special challenges because the new program lacks any such momentum. Some budget processes even place new programs in a

(continued)

separate decision structure. The new program is considered only after available revenues have covered requests from existing activities. Other processes cause trouble for proposed programs simply because clients and constituents to provide political support have not yet developed. Some strategies are characteristic of the new proposal:

1. *Old stuff.* Administrators may disguise new programs as simple extensions of existing operations, as growth and nothing new for the agency. When the new operation has developed an institutional foundation (directors, clients, and political allies), it can be spun off into an independent life, having been nurtured through early development by existing agency operations.
2. *Foot-in-the-door financing.* A project starts with a small amount of funding, possibly under the guise of a pilot or demonstration program or as a feasibility study. Modest amounts build each year until the program is operational and has developed a constituency. By the time full costs are identified, it may be more economical to spend more money to finish the task rather than to irretrievably abandon the costs sunk into the project.
3. *It pays for itself.* Supporters of new programs sometimes argue that the program will produce more revenue than it will cost. Although many revenue department activities may well do just that, the case is made in other areas as well. Examples include arguments made by law enforcement agencies concerning collections of fines and, with growing frequency, by economic development departments concerning induced tax collections from economic activity lured by the project.
4. *Spend to save.* Expenditure on the proposal would cause cost reduction somewhere else in the government. The net budget impact would be nil, or even positive, if spending one dollar in agency A would allow spending to be reduced by one dollar or more either in that agency or somewhere else in government. Whether that claimed spending reduction actually would occur is another argument.
5. *Crisis.* The proposal may be linked to a catastrophe or overwhelming problem—AIDS, economic development, homelessness, energy crisis, and so on—even though the link may be tenuous, simply because the agency perceives that such proposals are less likely to be reduced. But an agency must use caution. Skeptics are apt to question why it did not foresee and deal with the problem before it reached crisis proportions.
6. *Mislabeling.* The actual nature of a program may be hidden by mixing it with another, more politically attractive program. Examples abound: military installations may have blast-suppression areas that look strangely like golf courses; university dormitories or office buildings may have roofs that have seats convenient for viewing events on the football field; the rigid upper

surface covers for the new sewers may support vehicular traffic; and so on. But these strategies require an essentially supportive environment; the key participants in the budget process all need to be in agreement on the proposal because budget people remember and make allowances in later years.

7. *What they did makes us do it.* An action taken by another entity may place demands on the agency beyond what could be accommodated by normal management of existing programs. If school libraries were to be closed and teachers continued to assign reference work, local public libraries might argue for new programs to accommodate student requests for assistance.
8. *Mandates.* Some external entity (courts, a federal agency, the state, etc.) may legally require an agency action that would entail greater expenditure. Rather than rearrange operations to accommodate the new requirement, an agency may seek new funds to meet the requirement. The agency may, in fact, have requested that the external entity issue the mandate as a budget strategy. The approach can be compelling, but analysts need to determine the grounds and authority of the mandate and the extent to which revised operations can accommodate the mandate before simply accepting the budget consequences. The approach also has applications for base expansion and, if the time frame is sufficient, for defense against cuts.
9. *Matching the competition.* Agencies often compare their programs with those operated by others and use the comparison as a basis for adding new programs. (Seldom does the comparison lead to a proposal that some programs be eliminated because similar agencies do not have them.) The argument is also used to expand existing programs.
10. *It's so small.* Program proponents may argue that a request is not large enough to require full review, that its trivial budgetary consequences do not make the review a reasonable use of time. Those understanding foot-in-the-door financing are naturally wary of such arguments and generally respond that smallness makes activities natural candidates for absorption by the agency without extra funds.

SOURCE: John L. Mikesell, *Fiscal Administration: Analysis and Applications for the Public Sector,* 3d ed. (Pacific Grove, Calif.: Brooks/Cole, 1991), pp. 53–57.

had better have a good story for Congress, the OMB, and even their bosses if they expect the same level of funding the following year.

The result of this view is the bureaucratic phenomenon of the year-end spending spree. Fourth-quarter obligations of the federal government tend to run about 30 percent higher than those obligated in the second quarter.

Audit

This step is the final one in the budget process. The individual agencies are responsible for assuring—through their own review and control systems—that the obligations they incur and the resulting **outlays** are in accordance with the provisions of the authorizing and appropriating legislation and with other laws and regulations relating to the obligation and expenditure of funds. (Outlays are the values of checks issued, interest accrued on the public debt, or other payments made, *minus* all refunds and reimbursements to the government.) The OMB reviews program and financial reports and keeps abreast of agency programs in attainment of program objectives. In addition, the comptroller general, as agent of the Congress, regularly audits, examines, and evaluates government programs. His findings and recommendations for corrective action are made to the Congress, to the OMB, and to the agencies concerned.

Why audit? One audit, conducted by the Defense Department in May 1984, found that more than half the spare parts the department purchased were "unreasonably" priced. The auditors estimated that the Pentagon was probably paying about 13 percent more than it showed. With a $22-billion spare parts budget, that amounts to a tidy sum (Bernstein, 1984). According to the GAO, lax auditing resulted in the Medicaid program spending $500 million to over $1 billion unnecessarily (*New York Times,* February 12, 1985). Much of the fraud occurs in programs designed to provide services, training, and aid to the disadvantaged. But it is not the recipients of the services who are doing most of the cheating but those relatively well-to-do individuals who contract with government to provide their services. They include a former employee of the Department of Transportation who embezzled some $856,000 by putting his name on checks intended for an Atlanta subway. They include the officials of a health plan in California who persuaded some people to sign enrollment forms by telling them that it was a petition to impeach then-governor, Ronald Reagan. And they include the case of the dentist who extracted healthy teeth from poor children so that he could collect fees from a Medicaid dental plan. "It was just awful," said Joel W. Collins, the assistant United States attorney who prosecuted that case. He said the dentist had been found to have billed the government for thousands of dollars worth of work not actually performed as well as for work that was not required. "There was one girl about 13 years old who only had about three teeth left in her mouth," Collins said. "Looking at her just broke your heart" (Marro, 1978). Why audit, indeed!

State and Local Budget Process

While the federal budget process might appear mind-boggling—with its extended cycle, series of deadline dates, multiyear outlook, and intermittent congressional involvement—state, local, and institutional budgeting is relatively simple to comprehend. It will be even easier if, at the outset, we clear away some features that are peculiar to certain governments, leaving a common-core budgeting process to describe. (With certain modifications, much that follows applies equally to service institutions such as universities and hospitals.)

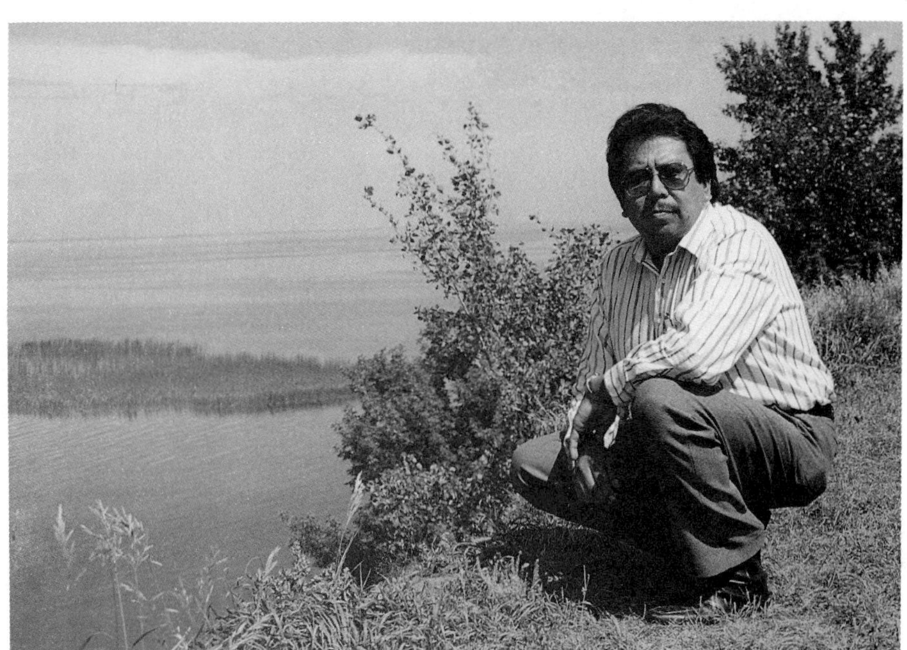

The Red Lake band of Chippewa Indians and the tribe's secretary, Bobby Whitefeather (above), thought they were doing well financially until an audit uncovered decades of sloppy accounting by the Bureau of Indian Affairs (BIA). The tribe thought that timber, mineral, and fishing royalties from their Minnesota reservation were pouring into a trust fund managed by the BIA, but the audit found the fund $800,000 short. The bureau was doing many questionable things with the tribe's money without the tribe's knowledge. Like many federal agencies, the BIA often does not know where its money comes from or where it goes.

*This was not always the case. In the 1950s, many federal agencies were on the cutting edge of financial management; but today, in part because of budget cutting, they lack up-to-date systems. The GAO found the records of the air force in such disarray in 1990, that it gave up trying to reconcile its book. Obviously, such financial mismanagement of financial resources costs taxpayers dearly. (Photo by Monte Draper/*Business Week*)*

Most states place budgeting responsibility solely with the executive, but some establish a budget commission that has legislative representation. In one state, Arkansas, budgeting is entirely a legislative function. Virtually all local budgets are prepared by the executive, although this distinction is blurred under the commission form of municipal government.

The federal budget cycle, as we saw, begins in October. But this is not the case with most other jurisdictions in the United States. Many local governments have fiscal years beginning in January. All state governments (except Alabama, Michigan, New York, and Texas) start their fiscal years in July. The fiscal year in Alabama and Mich-

(text continues on p. 520)

Help Strikes Again—The Auditors Have Landed

The base newspaper of a military installation in Texas which had been beleaguered by a streak of bad luck once headlined, "Inspector General and other problems arrive."

Joe Sherick, the Defense Department's very dedicated and able Inspector General, speaking of his boss Caspar Weinberger, once said: "My good news is his bad news." At very best, in the world of audits the good news is that there is no bad news. That's as good as it gets.

Auditors, reviewers, inspectors, and other forms of overseers perform a truly important role, but that role can be beneficial only when applied *constructively* and with considerable moderation. The prevailing trend would suggest the existence of an explosion in the overseer business, with an ominous threat approaching that there will soon be no one left for the auditors to audit. When this day of an infinite watcher-to-worker ratio arrives, it will presumably be necessary to focus audits on the mistakes which would have been made had in fact there been anyone doing anything. . . . The increase in magnitude of the oversight effort by the federal government alone is on the order of 200 percent per decade, possibly making it America's fastest growing industry. . . .

There are fully tens of thousands of federal auditors of one type or another at large today, of whom a disproportionately large 20,000 are assigned to ferret out the Department of Defense's transgressions—via both internal and external audits. No matter whether the production rate in the factory is one per month or 1000 per month, the grandstand is always full. Chuck Mills, a former football coach at Wake Forest, reminds us that a spectator is a person "who sits forty rows up in the stands and wonders why a seventeen-year-old kid can't hit another seventeen-year-old kid with a ball from forty yards away . . . and then he goes out to the parking lot and can't find his car."

An auditor, like any good Monday-morning quarterback, endowed with the 20-20 hindsight of his profession, can never be wrong. . . .

Lord Barnetson, chairman of the *London Observer,* has had attributed to him the following anecdote about how a management critic would review Schubert's *Unfinished Symphony:*

It appears that for a considerable period of time the four oboe players had nothing to do. The number should be reduced, and their work spread over the whole orchestra, thus eliminating peaks of activity.

All twelve violins were playing identical notes. This seems unnecessary duplication and the staff of the section should be drastically cut. If a large volume of sound is really required, this could be obtained through an electric amplifier.

Much effort was absorbed in the play-

ing of demisemiquavers. This seems an excessive refinement, and it is recommended that all notes be rounded up to the nearest semiquaver. If this is done, it would be possible to use trainees and lower grade operators.

No useful purpose is served by repeating with horns the passage that has already been handled by the strings. If all such redundant passages were eliminated, the concert could be reduced from two hours to twenty minutes. If Shubert had attended to these matters, he would probably have been able to finish his symphony after all.

Any bureaucrat worthy of the name will soon strategize that a fail-safe way to guard against criticism is *never* to take risk, even when that risk may be very prudent and may have significant probable payoff. Extrapolating the theory that the only people who never make bad decisions are those who never make any decisions, we can logically conclude that the only people whose work cannot be criticized are those who produce no work. Managers thus quickly learn to fear bad news with even greater fervor than they covet good news. We are inevitably led to the observation by Meg Greenfield of *The Washington Post* that "there is a profound commitment in this country today to not letting anything happen."

Or, as Bum Phillips [former] coach of the New Orleans Saints and the Houston Oilers, stated with equal profundity but perhaps less eloquence, "You gotta have rules, but you also gotta allow for a fella to mess up once in a while." Like the time the Denver Broncos' celebrated rookie quarterback, suffering a difficult first season, inadvertently lined up for the snap, in full view of 70,000 people, not behind the center but behind a *guard*—to the enormous surprise and consternation of *at least* one person in the stadium.

As the old saying goes, "There is a difference between giving and handing people their head." In Woodrow Wilson's words, "If there is one principle clearer than any other, it is this—that in any business, whether of government or mere merchandising, somebody must be trusted."

SOURCE: From *Augustine's Laws* by Norman R. Augustine. Copyright © 1983, 1986 by Norman R. Augustine. Used by permission of Viking Penguin, a division of Penguin Books USA Inc.

igan coincides with the federal fiscal year, but New York has an April start and Texas, a September start.

One can sense quite different priorities for spending among the various U.S. cities. Minneapolis, for example, spends significant sums on snow removal (as could be expected), and also, perhaps not as predictably, has a relatively large traditional commitment to the park board. Houston, on the other hand, must spend considerable amounts on storm drainage due to its low topography, but it spends nothing on municipal zoning because, uniquely among large U.S. cities, it does not have a zoning code.

Leaving aside peculiarities in budget responsibility and reporting cycles, the state and local budgeting process can be readily conceptualized in terms of our four-phase cycle.

Formulation

For the executive to begin to prepare the executive budget, several streams of information must come together. The discussion that follows elaborates on Figure 11-2, which portrays those streams.

Perception of public needs should begin any governmental budgeting process. Public perceptions are almost always felt, at least implicitly, through election results or annual surveys. If the government's job is to maximize public benefits using available resources, then public needs and priorities must be the starting point for budgeting.

Next, preliminary estimates are made for each category of revenue (tax proceeds, fees and user charges, and intergovernmental transfers). The resultant gross revenue projection is compared against the current year budget level to see what kind of growth in public services can be sustained.

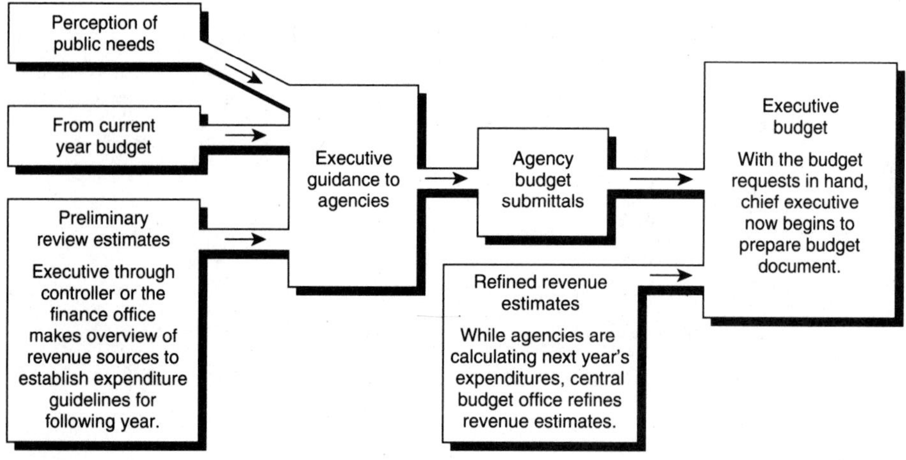

FIGURE 11-2
Formulating the Executive Budget

With a perception of public needs and preliminary revenue estimates, the public executive is prepared to offer guidance to executive agencies in its budget preparation. Usually, this guidance is incremental—a certain percentage of change in expenditure from the previous year is specified. Sometimes, the executive may require an agency to prepare a zero-based budget, providing justification for both existing elements and new elements of the program.

Four basic categories of expenditure in agency budget submittals must be forecasted: personnel, materials, service contracts, and direct client payments. Of these, personnel is the most important.

The Central Budget Office must prepare refined revenue estimates for those revenues that come directly to the government's general fund. Not all revenues, however, are under the purview of the central office. User charges, which derive from the performance of a public service (e.g., transit fares, university tuition, and public hospital payments), are generally budgeted by the agency responsible for the service.

The purpose of the **executive budget** is to present to the legislative body a comprehensive picture of proposed operations for the budget year, expressed both verbally and statistically. The term **budget document** refers either to a single document or—as in the case of larger local governments and states—to several documents. Regardless of its size, the important elements of the budget document generally include the following: the budget message of the chief executive officer (which sets forth in broad outline the aims of the proposed budget); the official estimate of revenue; a summary of the proposed expenditures for the budget year; and detailed expenditure estimates (which present and justify overall expenditure needs in terms of perceived requirements).

Legislative Review

The budget is now ready for presentation for legislative review and approval and, through the mass media, to the people. In local governments, initial consideration of the budget by the legislative body ordinarily takes place in public session. Heads of departments and agencies are invited to defend their requests for funds, and the finance officer is asked to explain the revenue measures called for to balance the budget. At this time, citizens are offered an opportunity to present their views on any aspect of the budget that interests them.

Some cities and states provide for the possibility of executive veto and legislative reconsideration of the budget as adopted. The veto comes in several varieties: the entire budget, an entire item, and the reduction of an item.

In government organizations and in some other nonprofit organizations, there are actually two budgets. One which may be referred to as the **legislative budget,** is essentially a request for funds. Most of the media reports about government budgets relate to the legislative budget, and many textbook descriptions of government budgeting focus exclusively on this budget. The second budget, the **management budget,** is especially important during the execution phase of the process. It is prepared after the legislature has decided on the amount of funds to be provided. This budget corresponds to the budget prepared in a profit-oriented company; specially, it is a plan

What Are Finance Officers and What Do They Do?

Scene: City Hall, City Council meeting.

Time: Hours before the legal deadline for the council to adopt the budget.

Problem: Balance the fine-tuned, long-fought-out budget, and come up with another $10 million for a last-minute project desperately needed to satisfy the council member whose vote is needed to approve the budget.

Action: Everyone (including the mayor, whose fat-cutting, no-taxing lips were read just last fall) turns to the finance officer, who then recites possible stratagems: sell bonds instead of paying for improvements out of current revenues (too visible); increase revenue assumptions (not credible); move the last pay period into the next fiscal year (cute, but too tricky); revise investment earnings assumptions to decrease the city contribution to the employee retirement fund (getting better); lease equipment instead of buying it outright (terrific!).

Financial wizardry is not the finance officer's primary calling. Most are less concerned with policy dazzlers than with keeping the finances in solid shape. But governmental financial management today includes a wide range of activities and requires an ever-deepening set of skills which in combination begin to resemble a wizard's repertoire.

Government finance officials may have any of a mind-boggling array of titles. While "governor" or "mayor" conjures up a clear notion of what that person does, just what a finance director does is less sharply defined.

The Government Finance Officers Association has compiled a list of twenty-two finance functions including: assessments, auditing/pre-audit, auditing/post-audit, budget, cash management, central accounting, debt administration, debt issuance, disbursements, fixed asset management, grants management, internal

showing the amount of spending that each responsibility center is authorized to undertake.

Budget Execution

During this phase, just as in the federal cycle, administrators try to attain program goals within monetary limitations. The steps they follow cover the entire fiscal year.

Whatever the particular politics of the jurisdiction or the peculiar structural impediments, state and local finance officers have the same mission. They must plan, manage, and account for the public's money. For most finance officers (see box), this means overseeing the accounting system, managing cash flows, keeping an eye on spending decisions, and tapping from time to time the capital markets.

Accounting. All phases of the budget process require recordkeeping. **Accounting** is the system of recording, classifying, and reporting financial transactions in an orderly way.

audit, investment management, inventory, pension administration, policy analysis and research, purchasing, payroll, revenue collection, risk management, tax billing and utility billing.

It is not unusual for these functions to be divided among several offices, some elected and others appointed and integrated into the administration. About two of every three local governments have an official with the title "finance director" or a similar title inferring broad duties.

The most common configuration, especially for smaller governments, is to have a finance director and an independent assessor. Almost as common is for there to be a controller (responsible for accounting and financial reporting) or a treasurer (responsible for collections and cash management) thrown into the mix. As jurisdiction size increases, so does complexity. Budget directors, collector/assessors, and separate purchasing, data processing and risk management departments frequently appear on the scene, with an auditor tossed in for good measure to make sure everyone else is doing things legally. The larger and older the city, the more likely that finance activities are strewn over the governmental landscape.

This often-frustrating complexity is borne out of the historical fact that managing public money has traditionally been a responsibility viewed with concern. By and large, those designing the governmental system have cared far more about maintaining control, accountability and diffusion of power than about efficiency and coordination. It's that way throughout most of the rest of our democratic government and it should not be surprising to find that in finance as well.

SOURCE: John E. Petersen, "Managing Public Money," *Governing*, June 1991, p. 56.

The oldest type of accounting is cash accounting. Receipt transactions are recorded at the time funds are received, and disbursements are recorded when checks are issued. Other types of accounting are accrual and cost. **Accrual accounting** records expenditures when an obligation is incurred (as you record a check when written, not when your bank actually makes payment) and records revenues when earned (for example, when taxes are due, not when the taxpayer actually pays). **Cost accounting** concentrates on reporting the cost of providing goods and services (for example, how much did it cost to repair one mile of city streets last year?)

While there are many similarities between government accounting and business accounting, one difference is worth noting. In business accounting all the available resources are, in effect, in one cookie jar. But, in a public sector organization, the resources may be accounted for in several separate cookie jars, each of which is called a **fund.** Each fund has its own set of accounts, and each fund is therefore a separate entity, almost as if it was a separate business. The purpose of this device is to ensure that the organization uses the resources made available to each fund only for the purpose designated by that fund. And that is why a university president may not use the scholarship fund to expand the faculty club.

The following discussion of cash management, purchasing, and debt administration draws heavily from Peterson (1991).

Cash Management. The cash flow of state and local governments, taken as a whole, is close to a trillion dollars a year—and it has got to be managed. The money comes sloshing in as taxes and charges. Then, it is shifted among governments as grants and reimbursements (as discussed in Chapter 3) or stored somewhere—in checking accounts, in short-term investments, or in long-term investments. Where the money is stored depends, of course, on when government needs it. Finally, it is paid out to employees, contractors, vendors, bondholders, pensioners, and grant recipients.

The distinction between short-term investments and long-term investments is important: The former is typically carried on as part of the daily operations of government; the latter finances trust fund activities. Public-employee retirement systems, with assets of $800 billion, which must be invested, are the most significant example of a trust fund for state and local governments. Contributions to these funds have risen from 3.2 percent of expenditures in 1980 to 3.8 percent in 1987.

Government investment policies usually require managers to maximize the safety of funds and investment returns. The problem for the manager is determining where to trade off the safety for return, for the safest securities are invariably those that bring the lowest returns. In the past, government cash managers were often restricted to a short list of acceptable investments (e.g., U.S. Treasury bonds). But in recent years the menu of acceptable investments has grown longer, and the manner in which investments can be made has become more varied. The upshot of these changes is that cash management has become a more sophisticated operation. John E. Peterson (1991:54), senior director of the Government Finance Research Center of the Government Finance Officers Association, writes:

> *The routine call to the local bank to pick up some U.S. notes at the next auction was replaced by the frazzled finance officer fielding inquiries from a legion of brokers, securities dealers and bankers attempting to market the latest in repurchase agreements, government security mutual funds, and other newfangled devices. And, of course, the current concern over the safety of funds in even the tried and true financial institutions, banks and thrifts makes none of this easier.*

Purchasing. To attain the objectives of their programs, state and local governments spent $653.6 billion in 1987. About 42 percent of this was for salaries and wages; the remainder went to purchase structures, equipment, supplies, and services of all kinds. The list of items purchased ranges from power plants to paper clips.

We can also break down expenditure by function as follows:

Education	(29.3 percent)
Health and welfare	(17.8 percent)
Highways	(6.8 percent)
Utilities	(8.7 percent)
Police and fire protection	(4.6 percent)
Other	(33.8 percent)

Essentially, public purchasing officers operate like their private sector counterparts, seeking the greatest *quantity* of the best *quality* at the lowest *price*. But, again, difficult trade-offs must be made. Decisions must also be made about privatizing and contracting, two topics discussed in Chapter 3.

One area of steady progress in government procurement has been group buying, where numbers of cooperating governments make their purchases together:

> *Large-scale purchasing generates definite economies of scale as well as economic leverage in dealing with sellers. Another derivative of this approach has been the development of standard specifications and the use of uniform procurement systems. The computerization of government in general and of finance in particular has had major implications for the way in which procurement is carried out. Government purchasing agents are able to maintain large files of products and vendors, "canned" bidding forms and contracts, and other data management and processing procedures that allow them to access broader markets more efficiently in their eternal quest for the best bid. (Peterson, 1991:56)*

Debt Administration. Because the largest cities and counties are financial grants and even small governments are multimillion-dollar enterprises, it is fair to say that government finance is "high finance." The municipal bond market is large and sprawling. In 1990, about 9,000 new issues of long- and short-term debt were sold, totaling $160 billion.

When raising capital, state and local governments have their own market, that for tax-exempt securities. Tax exempt means that the interest income on these securities is not subject to federal (nor, frequently, to state or local) income tax. As a result, the interest rates that governments pay are the lowest in the financial markets.

However, financing a large-scale project is not a daily occurrence for most, any more than buying a house or sending a child to college is for a family. Not surprisingly, many finance officers rely on advisors to assist them in the process of designing and issuing debt.

Audit

Audits take different forms. Financial audits determine whether funds were spent legally and whether financial records are complete and reliable. Management or operations audits focus on efficiency of operations. Program audits examine the extent to which desired results are being achieved. And performance audits assess the total operations of an agency.

The "T" Word

The subject of this section is taxes. And the problem it presents to the administrator and legislator, as the French finance minister J. B. Colbert once said, resembles the problem of plucking a goose: how to get the largest amount of feathers with the fewest squawks. For other equally cynical views about this necessary evil of governance, see the box on the following page.

Attitudes About Taxes Through History

1620 "Neither will it be that a people overlaid with taxes should ever become valiant."
—Francis Bacon

1774 "To tax and to please, no more than to love and be wise, is not given to men."
—Edmund Burke

1789 "In this world nothing can be said to be certain, except death and taxes."
—Benjamin Franklin

1819 "The power to tax involves the power to destroy."
—John Marshall

1872 "Government is the great fiction, through which everybody endeavours to live at the expense of everybody else."
—Frederic Bastiat

1888 "Taxed on the coffin, taxed on the crib,
On the old man's shroud, on the young babe's bib,
To fatten the bigot and pamper the knave
We are taxed from the cradle plumb into the grave."
—Representative Thomas R. Hudd of Wisconsin

1894 "What is the difference between a taxidermist and a tax collector? The taxidermist takes only your skin."
—Mark Twain

1935 "How much money did you make last year? Mail it in."
—Simplified tax form suggested by Stanton Delaplane

1938 "We will spend and spend, and tax and tax, and elect and elect."
—Harry Hopkins

1950 "There is no such thing as a good tax."
—Winston Churchill

1987 "Once even the suggestion of a state income tax would fell a legislator here like a .44 magnum at two feet."
—Mark W. Stiles, Texas state legislator

Tax Structures

Figure 11-3 summarizes not only the size of the revenues generated by the federal, state, and local governments in the United States but also the distribution of sources at both levels. Before considering the individual merits of these sources, let us note three pragmatic concepts with which a financial manager in the public sector should be acquainted when developing a tax system: tax equity, tax efficiency, and tax overlapping. (The following discussion of these three concepts draws on Slinger, Sharp, & Sandmeyer, 1975.)

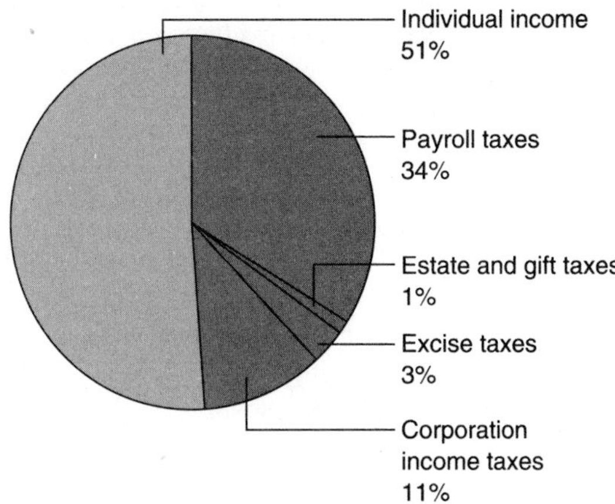

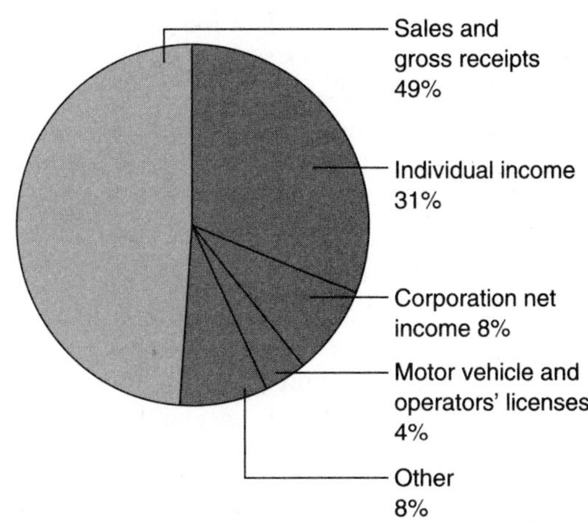

FIGURE 11-3

Total Revenue by Major Financial Sectors for the Federal Government and for State and Local Governments: 1989

SOURCE: Adapted from *Statistical Abstract of the United States 1991,* pp. 276 and 324.

Tax Equity. A fair tax would be, first, one that treated equally people in equal economic circumstances. A tax distribution that adheres to this principle provides for what is technically known as **horizontal equity.**

A fair tax should also treat unequals unequally; this principle is called **vertical equity.** What is its justification? First, that taxes should be distributed among taxpayers in relation to their ability to pay. For example, those with higher incomes should pay a higher proportion of their income in taxes. If they do, then the tax is progressive. However, some American conservatives have advocated an income tax that takes the *same* proportion of taxes at each income level. For example, everyone pays 30 percent of their income in taxes, regardless of what the income might be; this kind of tax we call, for obvious reasons, *proportional.* A **regressive tax** means that the ratio of tax payments to income *declines* as income rises: The more you earn, the less you pay proportionally. An excellent example of this kind of tax is a sales tax on food. Consider a family of four with an annual income of $10,000. Assuming they spend $4,000 on food and that the sales tax on it is 5 percent, they are paying $200 per year on food, or 2 percent of their annual income. Now contrast this hypothetical family with a professional couple (no children) making $60,000 a year. They eat well, spending $4,000 a year. But what percentage of their income goes to taxes on food? Obviously far less than that for our family of four. Of these three kinds of taxes, therefore, we generally say that the ability-to-pay principle is most closely associated with **progressive taxation.**

The second justification for the concept of tax equity is the "benefit received principle." In a sense, the principle attempts to apply a free-market approach to the distribution of taxes. Direct charges or *user fees* for government goods force individuals to reveal their willingness to pay for these goods. Noting that it costs $1.3 billion a year to run the U.S. Coast Guard, President Reagan in 1981 proposed that American boat and yacht owners pay a user fee for the services they receive. While this principle faces many practical limitations at national level (how do you apply it to a social good such as national defense?), local governments are able to apply it to many services—parking, recreation, garbage collection, libraries, utilities, and so on. Yet, even at the local level, there are limitations to the application of this principle. Many benefits, such as fire and police, accrue collectively and are difficult to measure. Or, sometimes the objectives of government are in direct opposition to the principle, public assistance being a case in point. "In spite of these limitations, in those cases where it is possible to measure individual benefits with reasonable accuracy and where the purpose of the government service is not to redistribute income, many economists hold that taxes should be selected in such a fashion that they can be defended by reference to the benefit received principle. Such procedure, it is held, is more likely to result in an equitable and efficient distribution of taxes" (Slinger, Sharp, & Sandmeyer, 1975:44).

Tax Efficiency. Another useful concept in developing a tax system is tax efficiency. This concept involves basically two things: economic efficiency and administrative efficiency. Economic efficiency concerns the effect the tax has on the private sector; that is, does it disturb the relative prices of private goods, the pattern of consumption and saving, and the pattern of leisure? Ideally, all these effects would be minimal.

Administrative efficiency concerns how easy the tax is to collect. In some cities, for example, it is necessary for city agents to raid those businesses that have been remiss in paying the selected sales tax. The efforts feature unveiling photographic blowups of prominent citizens who owe taxes, publishing past-due tax rolls, and locking doors of businesses that have not paid their taxes.

The costs of compliance to the taxpayer should not be overlooked. From the standpoint of efficiency, a flat rate national income tax would appear superior to a progressive tax with multitudinous loopholes and exemptions.

Tax Overlapping. The concepts of tax overlapping and **tax coordination** are not difficult. In a federal system like that of the United States, two or more levels of government frequently use the same tax base. In New York City, for example, all three levels tax personal income. At the same time, in a relatively mobile society like that of the United States, it is not uncommon for businesses and individuals to carry out economic activities that make them liable to taxes in many different taxing jurisdictions at the same level of government; for example, in different cities.

While total elimination of these types of overlap is probably impossible, the administrator, if concerned with economic efficiency and taxpayer inequities, cannot ignore them. It is therefore necessary to try to coordinate taxing efforts at one level of government with those at the other two. Fortunately, each level tends to rely mainly on one type of tax.

Coordination between jurisdictions at the same levels can also be important. For example, different tax rates on cigarettes sometimes result in wholesale smuggling of cigarettes across state lines.

Sources of Revenue

Knowledge of these three concepts—tax equity, tax efficiency, and tax overlapping—can help an administrator and legislator appreciate the advantages and disadvantages of selecting different sources of taxes. But they must also know the characteristics of each source (see Table 11-1).

Taxes are not the only source of revenue. Actually, nontax revenue of cities in recent years increased in relative importance, reaching close to one half the general revenue of cities by the end of the 1960s. In general, municipal nontax revenue is composed of user charges and state and federal aid. Since the latter was discussed in Chapter 3, we limit our remarks below to user charges.

The use of the price system offers significant advantages in terms of both resource allocation and equity. As William Vickrey (in Mushkin, 1972) notes, if prices are closely related to costs, there are "substantial possibilities for better utilization of resources, reduced levels of charges on the average, and improved service, all of which are inherent in pricing policies that are imaginatively concerned in terms of economic efficiency." A few examples should serve to make concrete Vickrey's remark:

- Imposition of user charges can prevent excessive wasteful use of electric power or water within an urban area.
- Imposition of a price charge can ration facilities among users. A park or outdoor concert has a limited capacity; excessive demand, therefore, can bring demand into line with supply.
- Imposition of fees and charges can help control activities that damage air and landscape or cause pollution or congestion. This is the rationale for

TABLE 11-1.
Comparison of Revenue Sources

Type	*Pro*	*Con*
1. Personal income tax	1. Ease of collection (withheld) 2. Progressive 3. Stable source of revenue	1. Unpopular with public 2. Difficult to collect if not withheld 3. Tends to be borne more by middle-income groups due to law loopholes for higher-income groups 4. Reduces monetary rewards of greater effort and risk taking
2. Corporate income tax	1. Ease of collection 2. Popular with general public 3. Progressive 4. Tends to redistribute wealth	1. Depresses rate of return on invested capital 2. Is displaced to consumers of corporate products or services 3. Reduces capital available for reinvestment 4. Double taxation—shareholder's dividends are taxed after corporation is taxed
3. Property tax	1. Very stable source of revenue 2. Revenue increases as value of property and improvements increase 3. Constantly expanding tax base	1. Difficult to collect delinquent amounts except by foreclosure 2. Are very regressive at low-income level 3. Resources and needs are unequally distributed through society (e.g., some communities have high public needs but little taxable property) 4. Difficult to assess property
4. Estate, inheritance, and gift tax	1. Progressive 2. Burden not easily displaced 3. Tends to redistribute wealth and create equality of opportunity among new generation	1. Difficult to collect 2. Unpopular with general public 3. Tends to reduce large family fortunes that might be used for capital investments

TABLE 11-1.
Comparison of Revenue Sources

Type	*Pro*	*Con*
		4. Double taxation from federal and state levels
5. Sales tax	1. Ease of collection 2. Relatively stable source of revenue 3. Less visible—paid pennies at a time 4. Reaches nonresidents	1. Regressive 2. Difficult to enforce
6. User charges	1. Efficient 2. Improved equity from direct pricing 3. Registers public demand for a service	1. Most government services do not fit requirement for finance by price (e.g., fire protection) 2. Some beneficiaries (e.g., poor) ought not pay

what some think are excessive taxes on downtown parking lots. User charges also have advantages in terms of equity. Due and Friedlaender (1973:100) put the case in a nutshell: "Except where special circumstances dictate otherwise, usual standards of equity dictate that persons pay for what they get."

Thinking Ahead

Not all prophesy is hazardous, and with respect to budgeting in the 1990s, we can say with a high degree of certainty at least two things. One is that dissatisfaction with the budget process—its politics, its incrementalism, its smoke and mirrors—will continue to generate efforts to reform it. The other thing is that spending and revenue and spending projections will ensure that the deficit remains a major issue in public finance.

The Quest for Budget Reform

What should the purpose of a budget be? Different generations have answered that question differently. The generally accepted purposes of budgeting are, according to Allen Schick (1966), control, management, and planning. *Control* he identifies as legislative concern for tight control over executive expenditures. The most prevalent means of exerting this type of expenditure control has been to appropriate by object

Adam Smith's Criteria for Judging Economic Systems . . . . .

In *Wealth of Nations* (1776), the Scottish economist Adam Smith proposed four standards that should be followed in taxation. While the language of the standards has changed somewhat over the years and the emphasis has shifted somewhat to accommodate the demands of a more complex economy, modern reformers are still concerned with issues of tax-bearing ability (equity), collection costs (efficiency), and disruptions of the economy.

I. The subjects of every state ought to contribute towards the support of the government, as nearly as possible, in proportion to their respective abilities; that is, in proportion to the revenue which they respectively enjoy under the protection of the state.

II. The tax which each individual is bound to pay ought to be certain and not arbitrary. The time of payment, the quantity to be paid, ought all to be clear and plain to the contributor, and to every other person.

III. Every tax ought to be levied at the time, or in the manner, in which it is most likely to be convenient for the contributor to pay it.

IV. Every tax ought to be so contrived as both to take out and to keep out of the pockets of the people as little as possible, over and above what it brings into the public treasury of the state. A tax may either take out or keep out of the pockets of people a great deal more than it brings into the public treasury. . . .

(Portrait: Mary Evans Picture Library)

of expenditure—for example, felt-tip pens, half-ton trucks, salaries, and no-lead gasoline. Financial audits then are used to ensure that money has in fact been spent for the items authorized for purchase. This focuses information for budgetary decision making upon the things government buys, such as personnel, travel, and supplies, rather than upon the accomplishments of governmental activities. In other words, responsibility is achieved by controlling the input side.

The *management* orientation emphasizes the efficiency with which ongoing activities are conducted. Emphasis is placed upon holding administrators accountable for the efficiency of their activities through such methods as work performance measurement (e.g., how many forms typed do we get for *X* dollars spent).

Finally, *planning* is reflected in the budget message for fiscal 1968: "A federal budget lays out a two-part plan of action: It proposes particular programs, military and

What Is a Snack?

One of the problems of the sales tax is knowing what to tax. Under California law, snacks are not really considered food and therefore are subject to sales tax. Officially speaking, the items on the left are snacks; those on the right, food. Really.

Snack	Food
Ritz crackers	Soda crackers
Popped popcorn	Unpopped popcorn
Ding Dongs	Doughnuts
Granola bars	Granola cereal
Imitation pork rinds	Pork rinds
Chocolate bars	Chocolate chips
Thin matzoh crackers	Thin matzohs
Screaming Yellow Zonkers	Muffins
Slice of pie (wrapped)	Whole pie, pie slice on plate
Candy bars with nuts	Nuts

civilian, designed to promote national security, international cooperation, and domestic progress. It proposes total expenditures and revenues designed to help maintain stable economic prosperity and growth" (Schick, 1966:243). Here we see an obvious emphasis on programs and the relationship between revenues and expenditures to accomplish objectives.

The overall development just outlined should be viewed, however, not in terms of three separate phases but in terms of accretion. Thus, the function of the budget today is really a combination of all three purposes. Now let us consider how the purpose of a budget shapes its format.

Line-Item Budgeting. The first image that generally comes to mind with the utterance of the word *budget* is a list of items and their associated costs. Indeed, a line-item budget used for projection and control of expenses remains at the heart of the budgeting process.The line-item budget is designed to keep spending within the limits set by the legislative body. Cost categories are established for the recording of all expenditures, and backup bookkeeping systems contain sufficient detail to ensure that all disbursements (i.e., expenditures) are made in accordance with the law. The makers and keepers of line-item budgets rely on accounting skills—the ability to keep track of revenues and expenses in a systematic way. They focus on answering the question: "How was the money spent?" While tabulations of line-item costs are still fundamental to any budgeting process, the concept of budgeting has generally been extended beyond the strict definition of expenditure control.

Performance Budgeting. Oscar Wilde once defined a cynic as "a man who knows the price of everything and the value of nothing." Perhaps, then, President Franklin Roosevelt was trying to battle cynicism in government when his second administration introduced the concept of performance budgeting. In 1939, the Bureau of the Budget was transferred from the Treasury Department to the newly formed Executive Office of the President with the directive to "keep the president informed of the progress of activities by agencies of the government with respect to work proposed, work actually initiated, and work completed." The idea was that the work programs of the several agencies could be coordinated and that the monies appropriated by the Congress could be expended in the most economical manner possible. The bureau would prevent overlapping and duplication of effort.

Thus began the search at the federal level for an answer to the question that, over 40 years later, still haunts government at all levels: Is the public getting its money's worth? As the end result of line-item budgeting, government should be able to tell the public that an agency spent, say, $19,872,403.91, with so much going to salaries and wages and fringe benefits, so much spent on various materials and supplies, and so much paid out under each of numerous contracts. But with performance budgeting, government should be able to tell the public how much public service was delivered for this $19,872,403.91. If the agency is a city sanitation department, performance measures could be given to show how many tons of trash were collected; the cost per ton and the cost per pickup; and comparative unit costs to indicate efficiency of the department against previous years, comparable departments in other cities, and comparable services provided by private sanitation companies.

The development of valid performance measures for public agencies ranges from the difficult to the impossible. Unique problems are encountered in each field of public endeavor at each level of government. Currently, most government budgets include an aspect of performance budgeting, often in the form of a narrative describing the accomplishments and work in progress of the agency or department. But objective, quantitative evaluations of governmental units—evaluations that attempt to answer the question, Is the public getting its money's worth?—are rarely done either within the budgetary process or outside of it.

As noted in Chapter 1, a basic difference between business and government concerns the way they are paid. The former is paid for satisfying customers; the latter, out of a budget allocation. "Being paid out of a budget allocation changes what is meant by performance. Results . . . mean a larger budget. Performance is the ability to maintain or increase one's budget. Results . . . that is . . . achievement toward goals and objectives, are, in effect, secondary." Hence efficiency becomes sin. "The importance of a budget-based institution is measured essentially by the size of its budget and the size of its staff. To achieve results with a smaller budget or a smaller staff is, therefore, not performance" (Drucker, 1973:141–47).

Can anything be done? Consider how hypothetical university president Albert James might conduct his annual planning session. Due to a mandate from the governor, he announces that the total budget for all units under his direction will be reduced by 10 percent from the previous year's level.

Further, James gives the following ground rules to his vice presidents: (1) Emphasis is to be placed on increased productivity; (2) standards of quality are to be maintained; (3) budgetary allocations, both in total and by individual units, are fixed; and (4) final budgets are due on September 1.

Each of the vice presidents submits his or her budget when the deadline falls. Not surprisingly, it reflects exactly what the president had called for; he is ebullient in commending his staff for their planning expertise.

Is anything wrong in this approach? Certainly, on the surface at least, the president's desire to cut old programs is not wrong. But what is questionable is his approach. First, this approach precludes real participation by the managers; he deliberately refuses to establish any competition among his managers for the available capital. In contrast, the Department of Defense has five committee members on a resource-allocation committee, each of whom heads units competing for the same resources.

Second, the inefficient as well as the efficient are rewarded (or penalized) with equal severity. The most efficient unit is cut by precisely the same percentage as the least efficient—namely 10 percent.

Third, the president puts the budget at the wrong end of the planning process; he should consider his priorities first, and then make cost allowances.

The lesson is this. Top administrators, as well as members of Congress, can cut programs, but they need, as far as possible, to establish competition *within* the organizational units for the resources.

Program Budgeting. Without ever having really mastered performance budgeting, the federal government proceeded to develop an even broader view of budgeting in the early 1960s. Robert McNamara, as secretary of defense in the Kennedy administration, introduced the Planning-Programming-Budgeting System (PPBS) into the Defense Department. Where line-item budgeting is limited to *accountability* and performance budgeting extends only to the realm of *efficiency,* program budgeting attempts to stretch the process into issues of *allocation* among various competing agencies and programs. It was not as if funding allocation had never before taken place—legislative bodies had historically performed this function based on inputs from constituents and from affected agencies. What the proponents of program budgeting hoped to accomplish was the injection of greater rationality into the process, by first planning *goals* and *objectives,* then developing *programs* to achieve these goals, and finally budgeting for projects within each program.

In 1965, President Johnson began requiring other federal agencies to implement PPBS. But nondefense agencies found their domains far less quantifiable; goals and objectives did not easily translate into programs and projects. Meanwhile, some state governments switched to program budgeting but did not find the system workable. Many state and local governments, after a review of the system, decided to keep what they had. While much of the terminology of program budgeting remains at the federal level, the program-budgeting process is more honored in the breach than in the observance.

Zero-Based Budgeting. Much of the decision making in the budgetary process is incremental, that is, involving minimal increases or decreases from last year's budget. Not so with zero-based budgeting—a recent variation of PPBS. Here the basic objectives of a program are examined by taking an if-we-are-to-start-all-over-again look; that is to say, each program is challenged for its very existence each budget cycle. In 1962, at the same time the Defense Department was developing and refining PPBS, the U.S. Department of Agriculture engaged in a zero-based budget experiment. In 1971, Georgia (under Jimmy Carter) and, in 1977, the United States (also under Carter) attempted to use it.

Zero-based budgeting (ZBB) involves three basic steps. First, all current and proposed programs must be described and analyzed in documents called decision packages. These documents are designed to help top management evaluate the programs in terms of purpose, consequences, measures of performance, alternatives, and costs and benefits. Next, the program packages are ranked through cost-benefit analysis (see Chapter 6). Finally, resources are allocated in accordance with this ranking.

Now that at least 20 states along with the national government have tried incorporating ZBB into their budgeting procedures, we should be able to draw some conclusions about the effectiveness of this technique.

In general, ZBB does not substantially reduce state or federal expenditure growth. This should not be surprising. Many programs in a state's budget (e.g., statutory entitlements, federal grant policies, and court rulings) are excluded from ZBB guidelines. Similarly, a large part of the federal budget is uncontrollable in the short run. Budgeters are wasting their time if they try to apply the techniques to entitlement programs like social security. The chances for ZBB to reduce budgetary growth for cities appear brighter, however. The reason is that the majority of city budgets are mostly salary expenses—which are relatively controllable (see Draper & Pitsvada, 1981).

In general, ZBB does not appear to aid in the identification of program initiatives and improvements. While a number of state officials say that the technique facilitates the elimination of unproductive programs, few report substantial reductions in these programs (*P.A. Times,* March 1, 1980).

On the positive side, ZBB does force top managers to pay more attention to everyday operations, because they must rank specific expenditure items. But it is too burdensome and detailed for normal budgeting purposes. In any event, good managers should be well acquainted with the programs in their organizations. ZBB can be useful as a resource allocation device to flag programs needing particularly close attention. The remaining activities can be budgeted for in an incremental fashion or, as is done in the province of Ontario in Canada, through the use of the following format (Herzlinger, 1979:67):

Last year's budget	Changes caused by change in			This year's budget
	Quantity	Quality	Inflation	

To summarize the discussion thus far, Figure 11-4 suggests how one government bureau might arrange the same budgetary information in four different ways: line-item, program, performance, and zero-based.

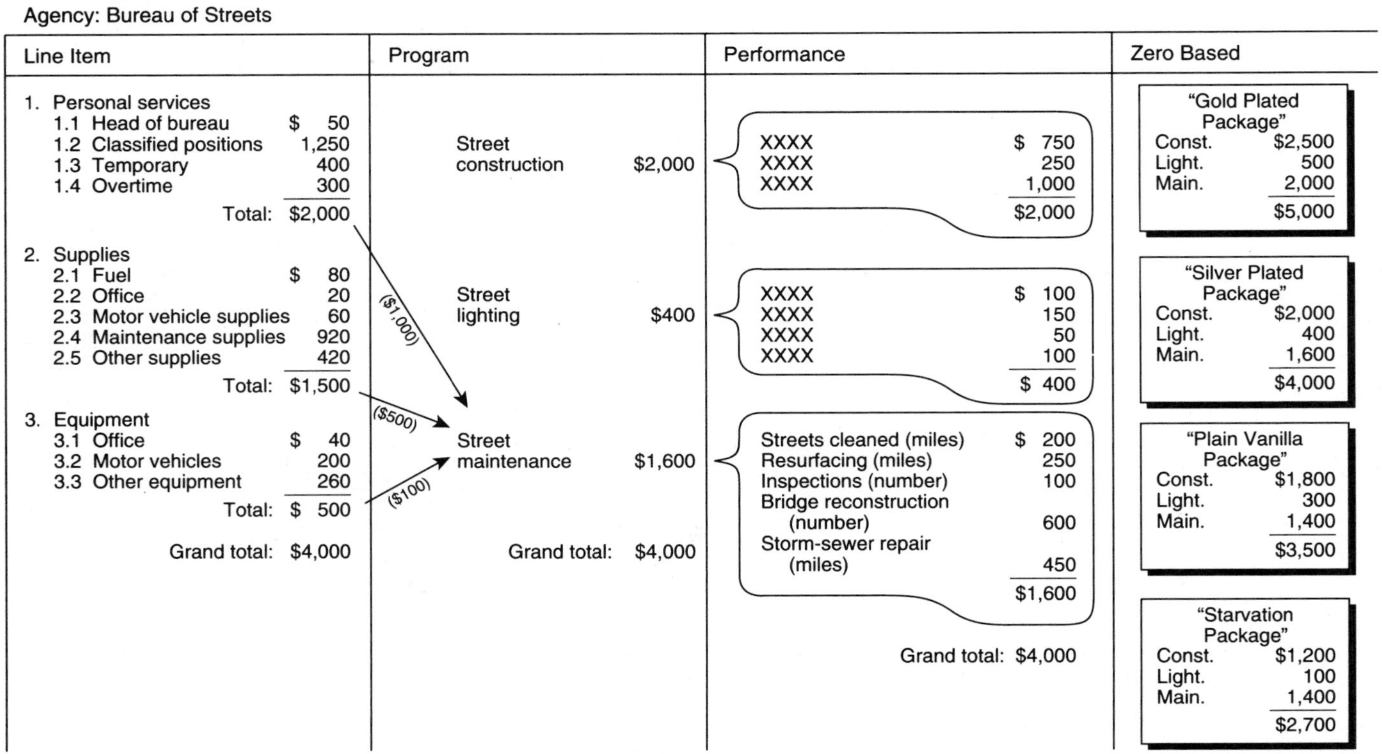

Agency: Bureau of Streets

Line Item

Line Item	
1. Personal services	
1.1 Head of bureau	$ 50
1.2 Classified positions	1,250
1.3 Temporary	400
1.4 Overtime	300
Total:	$2,000
2. Supplies	
2.1 Fuel	$ 80
2.2 Office	20
2.3 Motor vehicle supplies	60
2.4 Maintenance supplies	920
2.5 Other supplies	420
Total:	$1,500
3. Equipment	
3.1 Office	$ 40
3.2 Motor vehicles	200
3.3 Other equipment	260
Total:	$ 500
Grand total:	$4,000

($1,000) ($500) ($100)

Program

Program	
Street construction	$2,000
Street lighting	$400
Street maintenance	$1,600
Grand total:	$4,000

Performance

Performance	
XXXX	$ 750
XXXX	250
XXXX	1,000
	$2,000
XXXX	$ 100
XXXX	150
XXXX	50
XXXX	100
	$ 400
Streets cleaned (miles)	$ 200
Resurfacing (miles)	250
Inspections (number)	100
Bridge reconstruction (number)	600
Storm-sewer repair (miles)	450
	$1,600
Grand total:	$4,000

Zero Based

"Gold Plated Package"	
Const.	$2,500
Light.	500
Main.	2,000
	$5,000

"Silver Plated Package"	
Const.	$2,000
Light.	400
Main.	1,600
	$4,000

"Plain Vanilla Package"	
Const.	$1,800
Light.	300
Main.	1,400
	$3,500

"Starvation Package"	
Const.	$1,200
Light.	100
Main.	1,400
	$2,700

FIGURE 11-4

Four Ways to Prepare a Budget (Dollars in thousands)

Capital Budgeting. Should the federal government have a capital budget like state and local governments, foreign governments, and corporations? Some economists say yes; others disagree.

A capital budget separates long-term investments in buildings, bridges, roads, vehicles, computers, and the like from current operating expenses. Although the federal government separates budget items by categories (such as defense, energy, and income security programs), it combines all capital and operating expenses; therefore, the construction of a new dam is treated the same way as, for example, a purchase of potatoes for the White House kitchen.

Cities manage their resources differently. They have an operating budget intended for day-to-day expenses (such as payment of salaries) and financed through revenues. But they also have a capital budget intended for changes in the physical plant of the city (such as new schools and mass transit systems). It is financed through borrowing. Although important relationships exist between the two types of budgets, there are special characteristics of capital projects that justify their separation from operating expenses. The following characteristics of capital projects have contributed to the segregation (Moak & Hillhouse, 1975:98–99):

- Because of their life span, capital projects have a long-range effect upon the community; therefore, they need to be planned within a long-range perspective (of five or six years).
- Since capital projects affect land use, traffic circulation, density of population, and future physical look of the municipality, they require a special expertise, namely, that of the architect–city planner. When applying the principle of a division of labor, the programming of capital improvements has been assigned to those especially equipped to do the job.
- Many current operating decisions are subject to reversal, in whole or in part, at the end of (or even during) the current budget. New York City's budget is changed about 5,000 times during its July 1 to June 30 lifetime, as funds are shifted about through "budget modifications." In contrast, capital decisions are irreversible for an extended period; mistakes last longer and are apt to be more costly.
- The ability to postpone more capital projects (usually much more easily than current services) means that, without a separate budget, important capital expenditures would often be neglected by cities.

Some opponents, however, are concerned that a capital budget for the federal government would serve as an excuse for more, not less, deficit spending by inviting more spending on public-works projects. They fear that a capital account could open the United States to what some call "the New York City syndrome," making it all too easy to disguise unbudgeted operating expenses as long-term capital outlays.

Other opponents are concerned about the *negative* impact a capital budget could have on social welfare programs. Because it is far easier to value such tangible assets as roads and public buildings, the argument goes, a capital budget would make it increasingly difficult to justify spending to feed the hungry or to send a young person to college on a government loan.

Finally, there is a fear that trying to run the United States by business standards could blur the role the federal government plays in stabilizing the economy. The overall fiscal policy ought to be related to the needs of the economy as a whole; for example, it may sometimes be appropriate for the government to run a deficit during a recession.

But any accounting system is open to abuse, especially when, like the U.S. budget, it serves as a political document. A more businesslike budget would be neither a panacea for past ills nor a threat to the nation's fiscal priorities. The key reason for changing the way the budget is drawn would be to improve the information it offers about the country's true financial condition.

The Outlook for Deficits

The View from Washington. Not so long ago, one journalist reported that the federal deficit was causing about as much hysteria in Washington as when Confederate general Jubal A. Early threatened to capture the city in 1864—and maybe as much as when the British burned it in 1814. While the hysteria may have lessened, the issue has not gone away and probably will not for some time. To understand the issue, we need to ask three questions: (1) Why does the deficit matter? (2) How do we measure it? and (3) What might government do about it?

(1) With the economy running close to full capacity, large and persistent budget deficits undermine the future well-being of the country by consuming savings that would otherwise be available to finance investment supporting long-term economic growth. Numerous studies, statistical indicators, and everyday observations all strongly suggest that America has not been saving and investing enough to achieve the related goals of assuring future living standards and preserving a degree of influence in the world adequate for the protection of our basic interests. Long-term improvements in living standards and other aspects of economic strength depend on growth in productivity. A nation will likely suffer diminished productivity growth if it saves too little and is unable to invest adequately. The international comparisons shown in Figure 11-5 make this point dramatically; those who grow are those who save.

The effects of an investment shortfall are cumulative. An interruption of a few years in a generally high level of investment is no cause for alarm. But the implications for the future are increasingly ominous when, year after year, the nation

- Skimps on investing in plant and equipment, education and training, and research and development.
- Allows environmental hazards to accumulate by declining to invest in preventive measures.
- Subjects highways, airports, and other public facilities to increasingly intensive use, but fails to make adequate provision for orderly maintenance and expansion.

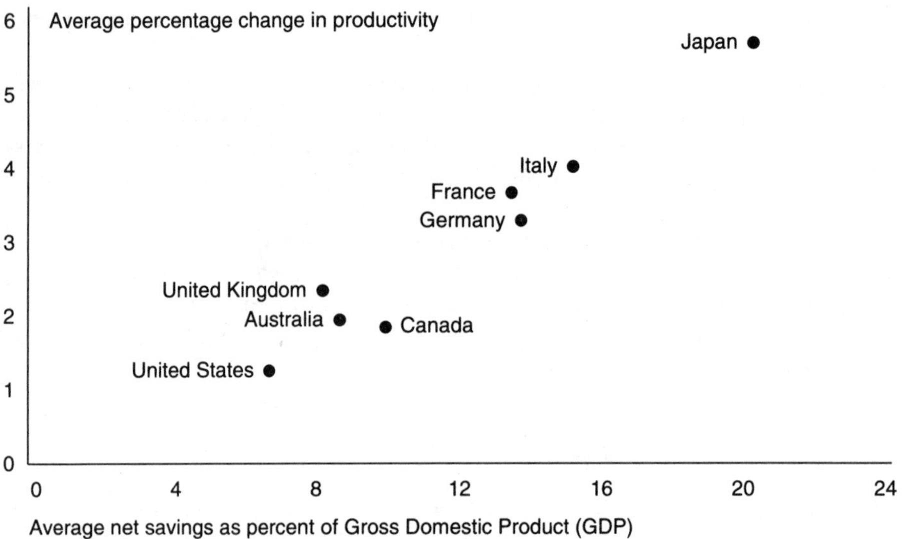

FIGURE 11-5
Countries with High Net Savings Experience High Productivity Growth (1960–1987)
SOURCE: U.S. General Accounting Office, *The Budget Deficit* (Washington, D.C.: U.S. Government Printing Office, 1990), p. 47.

- Finances a major proportion of its domestic investment by borrowing abroad and selling off assets to foreign investors.

The budget deficit is not the only reason for this underinvestment, but it has been a major contributor to the problem by absorbing between one half and three fourths of the net savings generated by the private sector and by the accumulating pension funds of state and local governments. (The foregoing analysis is from the U.S. General Accounting Office, 1990c.)

(2) While the federal deficit is a serious matter requiring serious thought, we must keep it in perspective. One way to measure it is in absolute terms: $220 billion in fiscal year 1990. Another way to look at it is on a comparative basis. The U.S. budget deficit as percentage of GNP is smaller than that of France, for example, and falls in the middle of the range for all industrialized democracies. Today the ratio of net government debt (federal, state, and local) as computed by the Organization for Economic Cooperation and Development is about 30 percent of our GNP, about the same general range as Japan, Canada, and West Germany, and much lower than Italy or Britain. Levels of saving appear lower in the United States, and this is thought to make public deficits less tolerable here, but in an age of global capital markets, capital goes where it is wanted and stays where it is well treated.

Compared to the GNP, the deficit at about 5 percent does not appear overwhelming. Private corporate debt is far larger. And remember, as discussed earlier in this chapter, everything the federal government buys is "expensed"—from the space shuttle to a ten-cent pencil. By contrast, a family buys a home with the help of a mortgage, since it is a capital asset, and balances its budget not against a one-time capital cost, but on a cash-flow, debt-service basis. All businesses are run on the same principle—but not the federal government. Capital expenditures for the latter total about 13 percent of total expenditures. If funded in a capital budget, the operating budget would be nearly balanced.

It is worth bearing in mind that when the government runs a deficit, it is putting more money into citizens' hands than it is taking away in taxes. Few think that will cause a recession (i.e., zero or negative growth for two consecutive quarters). Nor are deficits necessarily inflationary, provided the Federal Reserve Board does not permit the money supply to grow too quickly. Nor must deficits cause interest rates to rise; indeed, throughout the 1980s, as deficits rose, interest rates and inflation fell.

(3) There are really only three ways to do this. Perhaps the single, most important variable affecting the size of the deficit in the 1990s will be the economic growth rate. But maintaining that rate at a sufficiently high level, not to mention avoiding recessions, involves luck and economic wizardry.

The other two options—cutting spending and raising taxes—require neither luck nor wizardry, but they do require considerable political will. To see why spending cuts are difficult to make, you need only break the budget into four parts. Using approximate figures, here is what you get:

Defense	$300 billion
Entitlements and other mandatory spending	$525 billion
Interest payments	$180 billion
Everything else	$205 billion

For defense, there is rough agreement that not much can be cut immediately—maybe $20 billion. And even this number, while politically popular in the abstract, will not be politically popular in all its particulars. Few members of Congress let *their* bases be closed without a murmur. Presidents do not want to see U.S. troops strength abroad reduced at a more rapid rate—that is, a more rapid rate than is consistent with preserving strong alliances and negotiating equitable and enforceable agreements with potentially hostile countries.

Turning to entitlements, we must ask, How many are prepared to make a good case for reducing programs like social security ($250 billion), Medicare ($100 billion), or Medicaid ($40 billion)? Programs such as these are often called **entitlement programs** because one becomes "entitled" to payments if one meets criteria established by legislation—not because one provides some good or service in return. Because these **transfer payments** have large constituencies, politicians are reluctant to reduce them.

In addition, you obviously cannot reduce the interest payments on the debt, and the $205 billion left for everything else now totals just 6.7 percent of GNP—down from 9.5 percent in 1980. In short, there is not much left in the turnip to squeeze.

That leaves us with the revenue option. Here are three strategies to look for in the 1990s:

- Raising consumption taxes—especially on alcoholic beverages, tobacco, and gasoline. A less likely possibility is a value-added tax (VAT). Unlike a sales tax, which is paid only by the purchaser of the finished product, a VAT would tax a product at every stage in the product's development where value has been added.
- Improving tax compliance. Audits by the IRS indicate that the government loses about $80 billion a year because of tax cheating on legally earned income. Although only 6 percent of wage income goes unreported, almost one sixth of dividend and interest income and one half of capital gains income is not reported to the IRS. Tax cheating erodes the fairness of the tax system and redistributes income from honest to dishonest taxpayers. Although no one knows for sure how much revenues could be increased through improved enforcement, this much is clear: In the 1960s 5 percent of all returns were audited; today, only about 1 percent.
- Close loopholes. There are many tax-subsidy provisions in the present federal income tax. Eliminating all of them would yield about $250 billion. Eliminating just the following top five would yield about $150 billion: (1) exclusion of pension fund contributions; (2) deductibility of mortgage interest on homes; (3) exclusion of employer contribution for medical expenses; (4) deductibility of state and local taxes; and (5) exclusion of social security benefits.

The View from the State House. At 50 state capitols, the ebullient era of the 1980s has come to an end. In the 1990s, it seems unlikely that state officials will have year-in, year-out revenue increases fueled by a strongly expanding economy. (In three years of the 1980s, the U.S. economy grew more rapidly than Japan's.) It was revenue growth that allowed the states to take over certain social programs from the federal government and launch new programs in education, housing, and economic development.

In 1991, 30 states faced potential deficits. For example:

- California's combined budget for 1991–1992 was nearly $13 billion. If the governor laid off every state employee and shut down universities and prisons, the budget still would not have balanced.
- Texas faced a deficit of $4.6 billion, but Connecticut's $2.4 billion was proportionally even greater—37 percent of the state's general fund budget.
- To fill a $6 billion deficit, Governor Mario Cuomo suggested the biggest spending cuts in New York history, including $3.3 billion in aid to local governments (see photo).

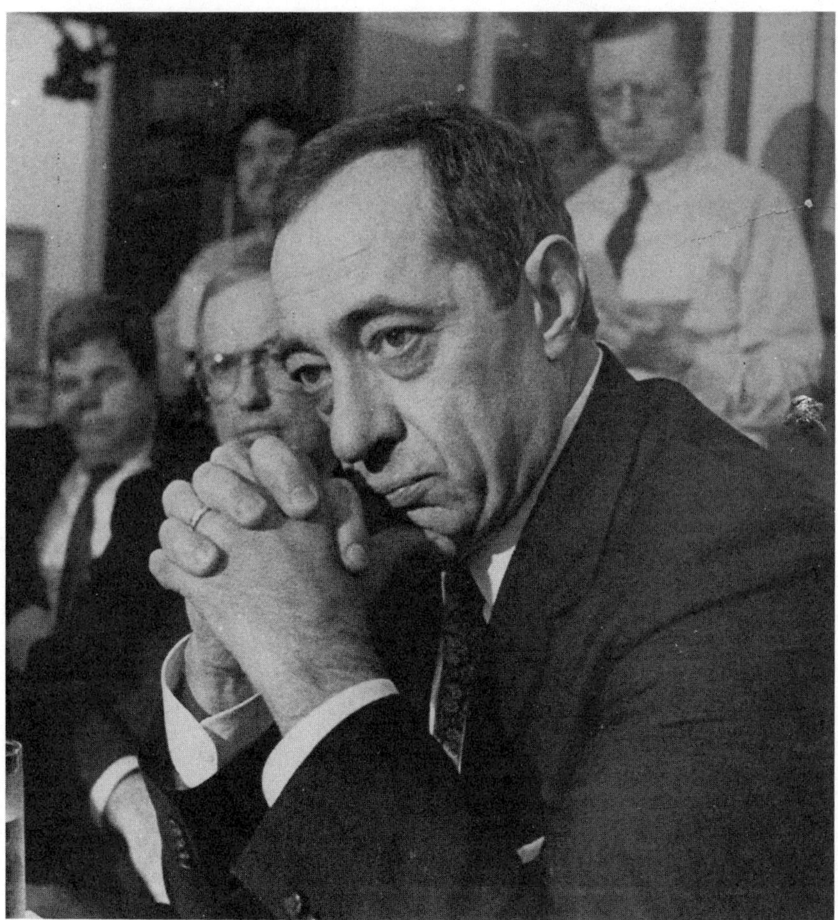

Governor Mario Cuomo at a news conference on New York budget in 1990. His budget plan revealed a basic problem with many state budget processes: There is no direct relation between what the state takes in and what it gives out. And whatever budget a governor presents, the legislature generally transforms it in ways that cost more money but produce no more revenues. (The New York Times/*David Jennings*)

Unfortunately, there are reasons to believe that the deficit problem will probably continue to plague the states through the 1990s. In the first place, the U.S. economy seems to have entered an era of "rolling recessions" from region to region. Second, as previously indicated, states are assuming more of the burden of federal programs. Third, they face major increases in the costs of Medicaid (18.4 percent in 1990 alone), bridge and highway maintenance, prison construction, and new schoolrooms.

Fourth are court-ordered mandates, which lead to more spending. Take Texas. Federal courts have ordered multimillion-dollar improvements in the state's overcrowded prison system and the mental health system. And a state district judge has

How Good Are Lotteries?

Lotteries are a relatively painless way of raising new revenues in an era when voters are demanding no tax hikes and no cuts in services. Since New Hampshire inaugurated the first modern state lottery in 1964, 31 other states have followed suit. By 1988, ticket sales reached $17 billion annually—about $250 per household in the lottery states—and supplied only about 4 percent of state revenues.

Lotteries are probably here to stay. But there are lotteries and then there are lotteries. Until the mid-1970s, most state operations were old-fashioned raffles, but revenues were disappointing. In an effort to boost sales, the states invented exciting new contests—"instant winner" games, computerized numbers games, and lotto contests with huge jackpots. Now under development are games that bear an uncanny resemblance to slot machines. At the same time, the states began using print and television advertising to promote gambling as a way of getting rich quick.

Is this what government ought to be doing? Neal R. Peirce, a syndicated columnist who specializes in city and state affairs, thinks not:

Lotteries have become a massive, regressive, debilitating tax—especially on lower-income people. Statewide sales of over $100 per adult per year are commonplace, meaning that hundreds of thousands of people are spending over $1,000 on the tickets. A study in New Jersey found that over one-third of families that live in poverty at under $10,000 a year spend over one-fifth of their income on lotteries.

SOURCES: Charles T. Clotfelter and Philip J. Cook, "Redefining 'Success' in the State Lottery Business," *Journal of Policy Analysis and Management*, Winter 1990; Neil R. Peirce, "Lottery Blight Keeps Spreading," *Houston Chronicle*, May 9, 1989.

ruled the school finance system unconstitutional—a situation that will cost between $1.6 billion and $5 billion to fix.

Fifth are the demographics. Take California. In 1990, it experienced a 235,000-student increase, fed by the state's vast immigration. This will likely be repeated in the 1990s. Meanwhile, welfare rolls rise by about 40,000 each year. Prisons add over 10,000 inmates a year. Thus, Texas and California, like many other states, face structural deficits that every economic expansion will probably not cure.

Given this set of circumstances, states are beginning to do what the federal government did in the 1980s—shove responsibilities to the next level down. In about half the states, aid to counties, cities, and towns is being trimmed. Local officials have to decide whether to increase taxes or cut critical local services, or both. These decisions will be particularly difficult because localities have neither the broad taxing authority nor the diversified tax base of states. They can, say, run a lottery as states have done (see box). Moreover, for both state and local officials, most of the "easy" savings have been made: shedding luxury services, forcing layoffs of excess personnel, tightening accounting practices, and so on.

Residential property tax revenue has traditionally represented the majority of income for most U.S. cities and counties. But people dislike the property tax so much that it is an unlikely future source of increasing revenue for local governments. Property taxes are always hot-button issues because they are ratcheted up automatically in most places as assessments rise, and homeowners believe they do not have control over them. To offset expected loss of income, farsighted local governments increasingly turn to new sources of revenue. In many fast-growing suburban areas, builders are being told that if they want permission to construct housing subdivisions or commercial complexes, they must absorb the expenses that once had been the province of the public sector.

Whatever new revenues states and local governments generate in the 1990s, it is unlikely that they will be applied to innovative new programs in criminal justice, child care, infrastructure replacement, or any other area; rather, they will be used to reduce the deficit. The worst-case scenario for the 1990s is higher taxes for less service. This could translate into a lower quality of life for millions of Americans. The possibility, which is real enough, should lead to some hard thinking about what the public sector does and how it does it. Budget woes will never end unless we find more efficient, economical ways to do business. Perhaps the next chapter will supply some answers.

Concepts for Review

- accounting
- audit
- budget document
- budgeting
- capital budgeting
- cash management
- ceilings
- Congressional Budget and Impoundment Control Act of 1974
- Congressional Budget Office
- cost accounting, accrual accounting
- current services budget (base budget)
- debt administration
- deficits
- entitlement programs
- executive budget
- fiscal policy, monetary policy
- fiscal year
- fund
- four phases of federal budget cycle
- horizontal and vertical equity
- impoundment
- incrementalism
- legislative budget
- line-item budgeting
- management budget
- obligations
- off-budget items
- outlays
- performance budgeting
- political strategies in the budget process
- program budgeting
- progressive and regressive taxation
- purposes of budgeting
- sources of revenue
- stabilization
- state/local budget process
- tax efficiency
- tax equity
- tax overlapping, tax coordination
- transfer payments
- "uncontrollables" in federal budget
- user fees
- zero-based budgeting

Nailing Down the Main Points

1. Chapter 5 introduced the concept of planning. In this chapter, we have seen how fiscal resources are marshaled to attain the goals of those plans. More specifically, administrators use budgets to establish executive branch plans, to provide a means for approval of those plans by the legislative branch, and to control and review the implementation of approved plans. The language of budgeting and spending includes a number of concepts that often get confused, but at least keep this in mind: Budgets are simply plans translated into their financial implications.

2. The federal budget cycle, which was changed considerably by the Congressional Budget Act of 1974, consists of four phases: (*a*) executive formulation, (*b*) congressional authorization and appropriation, (*c*) budget execution and control, and (*d*) review and audit. The Congressional Budget Act of 1974, which established the Congressional Budget Office to serve both houses and a committee on the budget in each house, substantially changes item b. In the past the president would send his budget to Congress each January and then Congress would pass a series of bills authorizing various programs and appropriating the money to pay for them. But these bills were enacted on a *piecemeal* basis. Under the new act, however, overall targets are set on income and expenditures (in broad categories); how one spending bill relates to another is emphasized. The new Congressional Budget Office, meanwhile, helps analyze the president's budget and suggests alternatives.

3. State, local, and institutional budget processes vary considerably. Nevertheless, we can generally characterize such budgeting as a nine-step process: (*a*) perception of public needs, (*b*) preliminary revenue estimates, (*c*) executive guidance to agencies, (*d*) agency budget submittals, (*e*) refined revenue estimates, (*f*) executive budget, (*g*) legislative review, (*h*) execution of budget, and (*i*) audit and evaluation.

4. The first step in execution of state, local, and institutional budgets is the allocation of elements of the appropriation. The most common and systematic scheme by which money is allocated is a numerical one in which a number is assigned to every fund; each fund, in turn, is divided into accounts. The next step in the execution of the budget is to allot the money for a specified period of time.

   Accounting plays a major role in both these steps. Indeed, no organization—public or private—can function effectively without a good accounting system. Why? Because expenditures must be kept within the approved budget totals; because what has been paid must be available to legislative audit; and because accounting systems (such as cost and accrual) serve as excellent management tools.

5. Although the box on p. 526 had a number of negative things to say about taxes, we might also note what the American jurist Oliver Wendell Holmes, Jr. (1841–1935) had to say on the subject: "Taxes are what we pay for civilized

society." Because most Americans today would reply that they are paying quite enough and not getting the civilization they contracted for, public administrators and elected officials face a real challenge in the fiscal arena. Money always matters, and those who collect it, invest it, plan to use, and keep track of it are invariably important players. But the skills and concerns of money managers become critical in times of fiscal stress.

6. Three important concepts that a financial manager ought to keep in mind when developing a tax structure are tax equity, tax efficiency, and tax overlapping. A fair or equitable tax would (*a*) treat equally people in equal economic circumstances and (*b*) treat unequally people in unequal economic circumstances. Tax equity further implies that, when feasible, people will be charged according to benefit received.

   Tax efficiency means that the tax will neither disturb the public sector too much nor prove difficult to collect. Last, tax overlapping refers to the coordination of taxing efforts by various levels of government.

7. To achieve stability and autonomy of financial resources, administrators should develop a diverse mix of income sources. Among the leading sources of revenue for governments are personal income tax; corporate income tax; property tax; estate, inheritance, and gift tax; and sales tax.

8. Personal income tax, the leading source of federal revenue, is a function of the definition of income, allowable deductions, exemptions, and tax rates. Given the numerous exclusions and deductions, the income tax in the United States is "eroded" at upper levels. In a sense, these exclusions and deductions are examples of a larger phenomenon: tax expenditures. Some experts and government analysts think these tax preferences really should be viewed as subsidy *payments* to preferred taxpayers.

9. The generally accepted purposes of budgeting are control, management, and planning. Significantly, emphasis on each purpose has shifted over the years, but today the function of the budget is really a combination of all three.

10. Associated with each purpose or function are certain specific types of budgets. For example line-item and performance budgeting go with the control and management functions; planning-programming and zero-based budgeting, with the planning function. A capital budget is a plan for investment in capital assets (e.g., buildings and bridges) separate from current or operating expenditures.

11. The question remains: Why do sophisticated techniques like PPBS and ZBB keep coming and going? Or, to put the same question differently, why does the traditional budget continue to last? The short answer, as Aaron Wildavsky (1978:508) has put it, is that the traditional budget has the "virtue of its defects." It makes calculations easy because it is not comprehensive. History provides a stronger base on which to make current budgetary decisions than the future provides. The future is the more logical base, of course. But because it is largely unknowable, it offers a weaker base. The traditional budget allows one

to change the objectives of a program without attacking the entire policy or agency. Its year-by-year budgeting, though not too good for long-range planning, does allow for adjustment, accountability, and price changes. In sum, Wildavsky writes, "Traditional budgeting lasts . . . because it is simpler, easier, more controllable, more flexible than modern alternatives."

Problems

1. The following two statements illustrate what principle discussed in this chapter?

"The average cost of tax collection is 4.4 percent of the local income tax revenue in Pennsylvania local governments."

"With the progress of industrial society and the development of a pecuniary economy, there followed a successive shift in emphasis to income rather than property as an index of ability to pay. Today, wealth is reflected in the person's income—earned and unearned—not real property," (*P.A. Times,* November 1, 1980).

2. One response to revenue-raising limitations being placed on local government is to delete exemptions. For example: "Welfare and charitable groups enjoying property tax exemption include a diverse group of organizations such as the YMCA, fraternal clubs, chambers of commerce, labor unions, the American Legion, Masonic Lodges, orphanages, humane societies, hospitals, and retirement and nursing homes" (Florestano, 1981:124). Which exemptions would you delete? How would you justify it?

3. An interesting ethical question arises when the rules under which an agency is forced to operate are such that effective and efficient operations are inhibited. Should managers get the job done and cover up the fact that in order to do the job they had to break rules, or should they use the existence of the rule as an excuse for not getting the job done? Managers with different temperaments answer this question in different ways. For example, in a certain state, the legislature has set maximum rates at which part-time psychiatrists can be employed by state mental health institutions. These rates are about one half the going rate for psychiatrists, so at these rates few psychiatrists would work for the state. Administrators therefore hire psychiatrists for half a day and pay them for a full day. This is the only way they can hire psychiatrists. On balance, have they done wrong (Anthony & Herzlinger, 1980:446)?

4. How would you interpret the following figures? Good news or bad?

- When Ronald Reagan was elected president, the richest 1 percent of taxpayers were paying 18 percent of all income taxes. When he left office, they were paying 27 percent.
- When Reagan was elected, the wealthiest 5 percent were paying 38 percent of all income taxes. In 1988 they were paying 46 percent.
- The wealthier 50 percent of Americans pay 94.5 percent of all federal income taxes.

5. Two kinds of taxes not explicitly mentioned in Table 11-1 are the luxury taxes (e.g., taxes on furs, jewelry, Jaguars, boats, and airplanes) and the sin taxes (e.g., taxes on alcohol, tobacco, oil, gasoline, and firearms). What impacts—secondary as well as immediate—do you think each kind of tax has?

CASE 11.1

★★★★★★★★★★★★★★★★★★★★★★★★★★★★★★★★★★★

City of Houston

When oil prices began to collapse in the early 1980s, Houston collapsed with them. But by late 1988, the signs showed that the economy of America's fourth-largest city was picking up. This pleased the mayor, Kathy Whitmire, whose ability to cope with recession had carried her into her fourth (two-year) term of office. But not all the news that year was good. By late February it appeared that the city budget was in deficit by as much as $11 million. That estimate would grow to $14 million, then reach $20 million. The law required that it be balanced by July 1.

Whitmire was adamantly opposed to any tax increase. Yet the scope for savings and spending cuts had been narrowed by years of cost-cutting. The police, fire, waste-collection, and library services had all been cut in recent years. City employees had not received a pay raise in four years. Against this backdrop, Whitmire told her 16 department heads on Wednesday, March 2, that they should submit to her by Monday their plans to cut spending to help close the revenue gap within four months (see Exhibit 1).

They dutifully made their submissions on Monday, and city hall was in an uproar on Tuesday as city council members digested reports that as many as 1,129 layoffs—the most drastic cutbacks in city history—might be required.

In his memo, Police Chief Lee P. Brown said 287 police officers would have to lose their jobs:

We are running the department with an insufficient number of civilian personnel. Further cuts would mean that police officers would have to be removed from patrol duties to perform tasks that they are not trained to perform.

Obviously, this would decrease our effectiveness in policing the communities. Consequently, it would be counterproductive to reduce civilian personnel.

Brown said the first targets would be such programs as the popular storefront police stations and the downtown mounted patrol, because "our first priority, now as always, is to put officers in cars on the streets."

Health Department officials said the mayor's goals would necessitate laying off 208 employees, curtailing AIDS education efforts, closing kennel operations at the animal control center, closing one health facility, and eliminating preventable and communicable disease services at one center. The department's rodent control program would also be eliminated.

The parks and recreation director said it would take 96 layoffs in his department to meet Whitmire's goals. He said eight to ten city pools and the same number of recreation centers could not open in the summer under this scenario.

How could Whitmire, who had a reputation as a good manager, have gotten herself into these dire straits? The budget deficit appeared because revenue fell short of expectations. Whitmire had expected the $1.3 billion budget to be balanced with the help of increased contributions from the fines levied by the municipal courts, particularly for traffic

EXHIBIT 1
Whitmire's Requested Spending Cuts

Department	*Current Estimated Spending Level for 1988 (In millions)*	*Requested Cut*	*Percentage Change*
Courts, Justice Division	$1.7	$45,000	2.6
Police	$171	$1 million	.58
Fire	$110	$1 million	.9
Traffic and Transportation	$7.8	$145,000	1.8
Public Works	$32.8	$1.239 million	3.8
Library	$15.5	$1.158 million	7.4
Parks and Recreation	$19.7	$1.358 million	6.9
Health and Human Services	$28.1	$1.793 million	6.4
Mayor's Office	$2.2	$22,000	1
Planning and Development	$1.8	$140,000	7.7
Personnel	$2.3	$51,000	2.2
Real Estate	$1.4	$129,000	9.2
Legal	$4.6	$500,000	10.8
General Services	$25.5	$2.058 million	8
Finance and Administration	$4.3	$43,000	1
Solid Waste	$32	$500,000	1.5

SOURCE: *Houston Chronicle,* March 3, 1988.

offenses. But they failed to materialize. Embarrassed, the mayor responded by dismissing the courts' administrator and dozens of his staff.

To make matters worse, by March 1988 it was apparent to everyone that the city's health insurance fund for its employees had run up huge losses. In fact, it had been losing more than $1 million a month since early 1987. The reserves in that fund were now depleted. An extra $17 million would be needed to pay health claims and to return the reserve to a healthy level. Whitmire said that she had learned that the fund was losing money only within the last three months. She criticized the company that administered employee health claims for not alerting the city to the seriousness of the problem sooner.

The president of Health Economic Corporation, Stephen Coady, countered that his company had been working with the city's risk management division as far back as July 1987 to redesign the health plan to cover costs that he realized were getting out of control. Coady said his company sent the risk manager of the city reports on a regular basis that allowed the city to estimate annual expenses. But according to a Whitmire aide, the mayor was never briefed on the situation. The deputy director of Finance and Administration, Cheryl Dotson, thought that Health Economic Corporation should have brought its concerns directly to the attention of the city finance director. Part of the problem, Dotson said, was that June 1987 was a period of transition for the city's Finance and Administration Department: The old director was being replaced with a new one. Moreover, the risk manager "was far enough down in the department that there may have been a communications problem."

The most lucrative expedient for Whitmire seemed to be the enforcement of a long-standing, long-ignored, $10-a-year license fee for cats and dogs. While she considered other changes, she knew there were only two certain ways to bring order to the budget. One option was to cancel or delay some large municipal projects. Delaying the city's aggressive building program might save the city as much as $6 million in debt service over the next year, but it could also generate a loss of $669 million to the local economy. Another option was a tax increase.

Case Questions

1. Discuss the Houston situation in terms of the budget and finance concepts described in this chapter. Which concepts seem most relevant for suggesting a course of action to Whitmire?
2. Based on the information available in this case, would you say that Whitmire's approach was appropriate?
3. If you were a member of the city council, what changes in Houston's budgeting system would you suggest?
4. Police Chief Brown said that his memo is simply an analysis showing where he believes the ax should fall in a worst-case scenario. Do you agree or disagree?

Case Reference

Houston Chronicle, March 3, 9, 12, 13, and 27, 1988.

CHAPTER 12 The Information Revolution

If you think someone in the computer room manages your information, you're not a manager. It's integral to what you do. You manage your budget and your people, and you need to manage your information.

Sharon Dawes, director of the New York Forum for Information and Resources Management

Introduction

An information revolution is sweeping through the public sector, and no public administrator can escape its effects. The thesis of this chapter is that dramatic reductions in the cost of obtaining, processing, and transmitting information are changing the theory and practice of public administration.

At the heart of this revolution are accelerating and compounding trends in computer technology and communications technology. Since the first computer was built in 1942, technological developments have been breathtaking. Had the automobile industry experienced a similar rate of development, one could buy a Rolls Royce for $280 and drive it a million miles on a gallon of gas. Within the next decade or so, according to many experts, the cost-effectiveness of computer technology will increase at least a millionfold. Using techniques already demonstrated in the laboratory, it should be possible to put a billion transistors on a single chip, excelling the computing power of 20 Cray 2 supercomputers, which sell today for up to $20 million apiece. But this single chip would work much faster and more reliably than 20 Crays, and it would cost under $100 to manufacture.

Information technology, however, consists of more than just computers. Managers must conceive of it broadly in order to encompass a wide spectrum of increasingly linked technologies. Take for instance the spreading use of glass fibers, or fiber optics (see photo). Today AT&T runs a fiber-optic line between Chicago and the East Coast that can transmit information at a rate of about 500 Bibles a second. (Transmitting the entire Library of Congress would take eight hours.) By the end of the decade, this fiber-optic technology could be available in most homes and offices in the United States. (Leebaert, 1991; Davidson & Davis, 1991)

Most public administrators know that this revolution is under way, and few dispute its importance. As the quote opening this chapter suggests, administrators have a growing awareness that these technologies can no longer be the exclusive territory of the data processing department and that they, as administrators, need to become directly involved in the management of this resource—just as they have done with human and fiscal resources.

While technological trends may be making the need for the management of information more acute, the need itself is not new. That information has value is a commonplace notion in government. "Information," as anyone who deals with politicians will hear over and over, "is power." As Herbert Kaufman (1981) observed in the *Administrative Behavior of Federal Bureau Chiefs,* public managers spend most of their time accumulating and assimilating information. They need information about their environment—present *and* future. They also need information about the problems that their agencies face, the available alternatives, the probable effects of those alternatives, the internal actions required for implementation, the outputs produced, and the expenditures required.

Moreover, because public organizations tend to face more complex problems than do private ones, the information needs of the former are probably greater:

> *Addressing the acid rain problem is more difficult than solving ring around the collar. . . . Issues do not enter the public sphere unless they are too complex or too difficult to be addressed by the private market. Therefore, the need for information in the public sector tends to be greater than in the private sector. Accordingly, the probability of achieving managerial control tends to be lower in the public sector than in the private sector. The greater complexity and resultant information requirements for public management account for some of the caution and slow pace of public programs. For this reason, successful information management is absolutely essential for the public entrepreneur. The public sector's greater information needs tend to increase the cost of having too much of the wrong information and not enough of the right information. Sufficient information can reduce risks and increase the probability of successful entrepreneurship. (Cohen, 1988:78)*

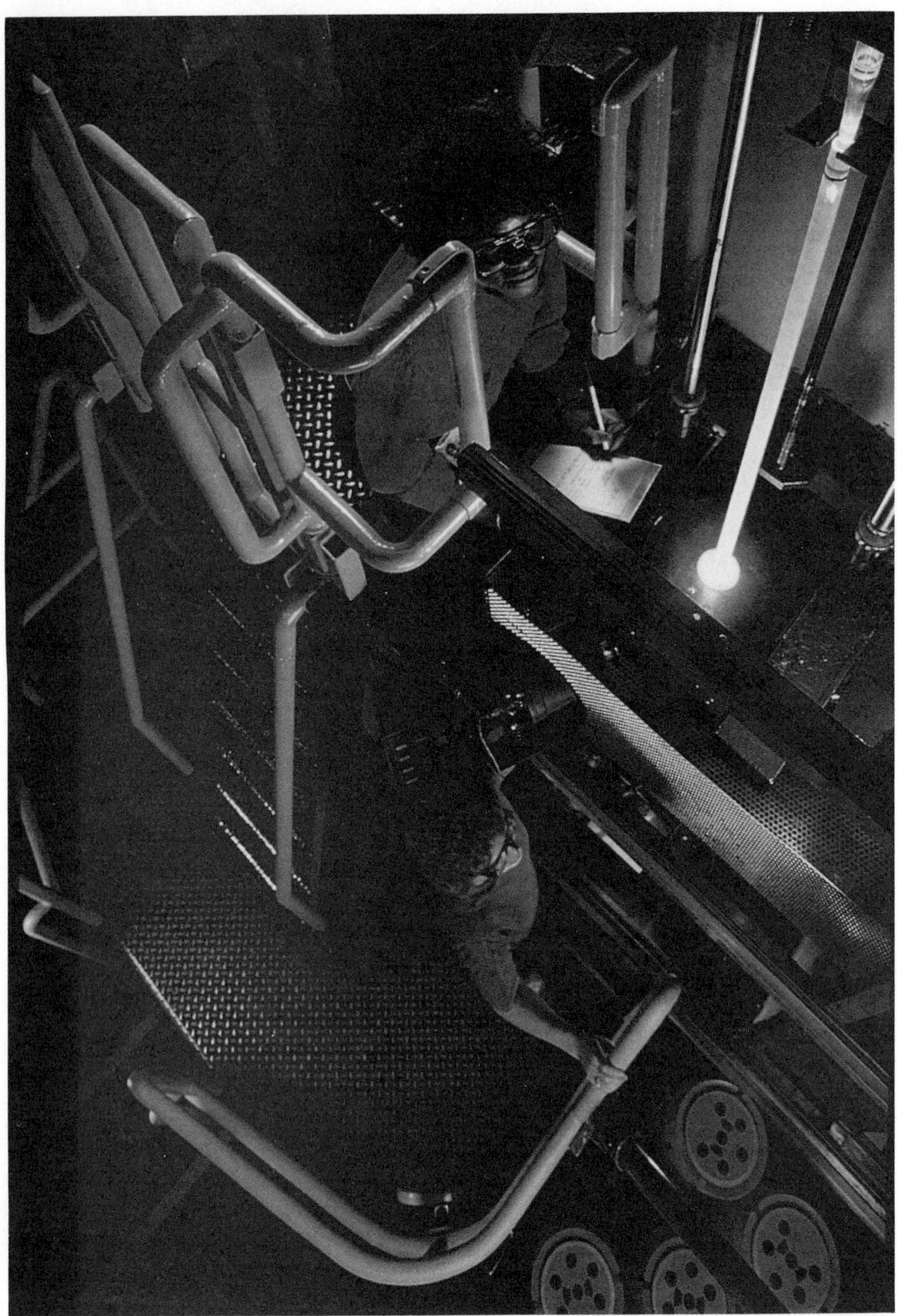

A fiber draw tower in AT&T's Atlanta factory heats a glass rod until thin strands can be pulled from it like taffy. These optical fibers—glass threads that carry information as pulses of light—have supplanted copper in long-distance cables. By one estimate, 17 million homes and small businesses will be "glass houses" by 1999.

To appreciate how managers use information in control and decision making, we must distinguish data from information. **Data** are raw, unsummarized, and unanalyzed facts. **Information** is data that are meaningful and that alter the receiver's understanding. Information is the data that managers actually use to interpret and understand events in the organization and the environment. David Morgan, head of Dallas's data processing department, explains the distinction this way: "I can tell you at any time of the day where a squad car was. What I can't tell you is where it was needed. We've got data; we don't have information." Information, Morgan argues, is what you get when you take useful data and manipulate it in a way that makes sense for program management (quoted in Gurwitt, 1991:51).

To effectively manage and control organizations in an information-dominated world, public administrators must understand the technology of the information revolution. That is where we begin—with a survey of this technology and its uses. Next, we examine the effects that this technology is having on the conduct of work and the structure of organizations in the public sector. (Case 12.1 provides a practical example of how placing vast amounts of useful information before all kinds of people allows them and hence the agency to perform better.) The fourth section, the heart of the chapter, lays out a framework for thinking about how this resource can be better managed.

Information Technologies

Information Systems: The Fundamentals

An **information system** is any mechanism for collecting, organizing, and distributing data to organizational personnel. Any such system must have five basic components:

1. *Inputs* are the raw data that enter the information system. There are data about demographics, land use, finances, economics, poverty rates, and criminal practices; there are data for breakdowns of soil types and stream flows, sales tax receipt figures, and purchase outlay totals; and there are data for statistics on murder rates, jail population studies, welfare recipients, and driver's license holders.

2. *Processing* involves the ability to manipulate, organize, sort, and perform calculations on the data. Processing transforms the data into a form useful for administrators. Los Angeles, for instance, uses a sophisticated computer model that combines meteorological and geographic data to tell air quality officials what levels of particular raw pollutants they can allow to be put into the air if they are to meet federal and state standards.

3. *Storage* is the system function in which data are stored in an organized manner for future processing or until needed by system users. A simple example will show how important the storage function is. Over the next few years, Massachusetts will spend billions of dollars on three major pub-

lic works projects in the Boston area. In the process, the state will be paying an enormous amount of money for its contractors to develop information necessary to complete the projects—hydrologic data, engineering data, and information about an estimated 5,000 utility lines that will have to be relocated. If that information is not stored in a form that is retrievable, then 5, 10, or 15 years down the road, the state will have to buy it back from the companies it is paying to develop it (Gurwitt, 1991).

4. *Control* is a device for determining whether the information system is delivering information of sufficient quality, timeliness, completeness, and relevance for users. The control function must also have the capability to change the output.

5. *Output* includes reports and other organized information produced by the information system for users. A major problem in public administration is that much of the information generated is the result of mandated requirements by legislatures and that this information may be entirely unsuited to what managers actually need to know. For example, the data universities keep on travel focus on types of travel (in-state, out-of-state, and international), but say nothing about whether the money was spent for research, faculty recruitment, and so on. The latter is, of course, the kind of information a manager could really use when assessing the value of travel.

These five components must be part of every information system—whether manual or computer based. However, in this section, we focus chiefly on systems that use electronic computing technology to create the five system components. (Readers who do not know the difference between hardware and software might find the accompanying box helpful.)

Computerized Information Systems

Transaction Processing Systems. The initial purpose of computing in the 1960s was to reduce clerical costs by computerizing the flow of day-to-day transactions. The transaction processing system (TPS) performs the agency's routine, recurring transactions. A ticket issued for a violation, the amount of overtime recorded for an employee, a payment made to a client, and the disbursements made to a vendor are all transaction items that government organizations must follow and record. TPSs are designed to capture and store these transactions accurately.

Management Information Systems. As information systems evolved, management information systems (MISs) were the next stage beyond TPSs. Essentially, an MIS is a mechanism that collects, organizes, and distributes the data used by managers in performing their various tasks. MISs provide information in summary that pertains to specific management problems, whereas lists of thousands of daily organizational transactions are virtually useless for planning, decision making, and implementing. Administrators can use MISs to summarize and check the status of programs, projects, and personnel.

Hardware and Software—and Other Bits of Computer Jargon

Hardware refers to the physical machinery that makes up a computer system, as opposed to software, or programs that make the hardware do useful things. Hardware is useless without software to make it work.

The fundamental working parts of the hardware are the *chips.* These are small slivers of silicon with tiny electric circuits etched onto them; these circuits process and store data. Chips, also called semiconductors, are packaged in small blocks of plastic; the whole package also is referred to as a chip.

The brains of the computer—where it does its computing—is the **central processing unit** (CPU). In a microcomputer, the CPU is a single chip, the microprocessor. The box that holds the CPU also may contain other electronic parts, but they are only depots and conduits for information flowing to and from the CPU. The whole box is often called the CPU for convenience.

Let us return for a moment to **software.** Software contains the coded instructions, or programs, that make a computer do its job. When you "run" a program, you are turning control of the computer over to the set of instructions in that program. A simple program may do nothing more than flash "Hi, Mom!" on the screen; a sophisticated program may be able to run a space station.

A special kind of software, called an **operating system,** makes the computer do basic housekeeping chores, such as passing information to peripheral equipment like printers. It is different from "applications software," which makes the computer do specific things such as manage the payroll, maintain a database, or draw graphs. Most applications software cannot work unless the operating system is also running, ready to do the housekeeping for it. Operating systems for different computers are usually so different that an applications program written for one computer will not run on any other. Computers that cannot run the same software are said to be "incompatible."

Back to the hardware. Where does a computer store information internally for immediate use? The answer is, in its **memory.** Programs do not function unless they are placed in memory. The more complicated the program, the more memory it requires.

For example, a fire and rescue agency might use an MIS to track training records, which are especially important in this type of organization. In fire and rescue agencies and other such units involved in public safety, employees often cannot take part in a particular operation unless the appropriate training has been received and all requisites of certification have been met. Mistakes in sending uncertified personnel to do a job invite poor performance and lawsuits. Thus, the objective of this MIS is clear: to provide quick and accurate information on the status of training and certification. Who has it? What kind? When is recertification necessary? What requirements remain before certification is reached (Sacco & Ostrowski, 1991:299–318)?

Electronic data processing began in the public sector. In 1880, it took officials carrying out the 1880 census eight years to complete the count, and continued immigration would only make the job worse in the future. To solve the problem, Herman Hollerith, a young engineer attached to the health statistics division of the surgeon general's office, took cards the size of dollar bills and punched holes in the cards in predetermined positions relating to the type of data being recorded: sex, age, size of family, location, date of birth, nationality, and so on. The number of separate bits of data thus recorded on the card was extremely large. When the 1890 census was taken, the machines Hollerith had designed to go with his cards were used for the first time. The census was completed at twice the speed of the previous one, at an estimated saving of a half-million 1890 dollars. Hollerith's tabulator was the genesis of the modern computer. (The Bettmann Archive)

Although expectations ran high when MISs were first introduced, they have often proven disappointing in use. Many reasons might be given. Because of the variety and fragmentation that characterize a public administrator's job, many tasks are simply unsuitable for computers. Out of fear, ignorance, or a little of both, employees sometimes sabotage or underuse the system. Improper implementation (e.g., moving too fast, before all the "bugs" are out of the system) is another cause for failure. One of the biggest problems with information systems is that the information is not what the manager really needs for decision making. But perhaps the heart of the matter is this: "The problem with MIS is more with the 'M' than the 'IS.' Information systems technology has improved tremendously since the first glow of MIS in the 1960s. MIS is better used to enhance good management than to improve bad management" (Bozeman & Straussman, 1990:113).

Richard L. Van Horn (1982), former head of management systems for Rand Corporation, makes a similar point: "A computerized inventory system with poor ordering rules will reorder the wrong quantities of the wrong parts faster and more consistently than its manual counterpart. The computer's outstanding attributes of speed, large memory, consistency, and the ability to follow complex logical instructions are of value *only to the extent that they are applied within a good management process.* Computers are a complement to, not a substitute for, careful management" (emphasis added). Van Horn also issues a warning against "computational fundamentalism": "Computer users must remember that precision is not accuracy. Without question, computers operate with great precision. They can perform long and complex processing of instruction, text, and numbers without introducing any new errors. As a result, computer output neatly printed on display screen or paper is often treated like pages from Holy Writ. This computational fundamentalism is, as many managers have found through costly experience, a dangerous assumption."

Thus, we come back to Herbert Simon's point (noted in Chapter 6): Human judgment and intuition are still required elements in any complex, unstructured situation. Information needs of organizations are much broader than what the computer alone can supply. This is particularly true with respect to planning. Computers can help government do things right—as all taxpayers want—but they can never ensure that it will do the right things.

Decision Support Systems. The DSS concept, which is closely related to the MIS concept, began to emerge in the 1970s. Decision support systems (DSSs) represent the final and most sophisticated computer-based information support developed for managers. These systems were specifically developed to help managers with **unstructured** and **semistructured problems** that MISs were not flexible enough to handle. The fundamental difference between these two types of problems and **structured problems** lies in the amount of complexity, uncertainty, political influence, novelty, and conflict inherent in the problem. Unstructured problems are inherently complex, uncertain, and conflictual and subject to extensive political influence. Structured problems are more likely to be routine and organized and subject to rational solutions. Semistructured problems fall between these two extremes. Another way of saying all this is that structured problems can be programmed and unstructured and semistructured ones cannot.

DSSs exhibit several characteristics that make them appropriate for unstructured and semistructured problems. DDSs retrieve, manipulate, and display information needed for making specific decisions. They are interactive; that is, managers can make inquiries about pressing questions and receive answers rather than just periodic reports. Moreover, they have access to multiple databases, with information from both inside the organization and outside the organization.

For an example of a DSS, let us consider a capital construction project. As discussed in the previous chapter, capital projects can be recreational parks, school buildings, irrigation facilities, communication towers—or any other undertaking that requires considerable time to plan, fund, and construct. Typically, governments authorize large bond issues to fund these projects. One aspect of capital project planning is laying out a plan so that public officials can see how much to pay for the construction. In other words, the timing of the sale of bonds must be such that money is available when needed. A DSS can lay out options and help managers decide on the timing of bond sales to provide and replenish cash for a set of capital projects. The DSS can give managers an idea of what period-by-period borrowing demands they will likely face and how to meet those demands:

> *This is a complex situation that exhibits some of the characteristics of semi-structured and unstructured problems. Individuals planning the cash flow and the timing of bond sales face numerous uncertainties. The rate at which cash is used can veer sharply from the expectation. A project may move faster or slower than anticipated and thus throw off the plans set in the original budget. Interest rates can turn up or down very quickly, nullifying the best of schemes. Debt limits can be severe. As a result of the many factors involved and the uncertainty associated with each, the DSS can only act as a decision aid. It cannot substitute totally for the judgment of expert decision makers. (Sacco & Ostrowski, 1991:215)*

For capital project planning, when the manager wants to ask a number of "what if" questions, the **spreadsheet** is an invaluable tool. What is a spreadsheet? It is a type of software that closely resembles an accountant's worksheet; divided into rows and columns, the spreadsheet facilitates analysis.

Artificial Intelligence. Unlike MISs and DSSs, which support the manager who makes decisions, artificial intelligence (AI) operates as an advisor to, or even a replacement for, the human decision maker. The term *AI* covers a wide range of computer programs that mimic human behavior, such as the ability to learn from experience, understand normal written and spoken language, and see and make inferences. For example, HAL, the supercomputer in the movie *2001* (see photograph on p. 311), was the ideal result of AI technology; it had a whole range of emotions and thought processes, including psychosis. It could simultaneously hold intelligent conversations, maintain radio contact with Earth, beat its crewmates at complex games, and control every circuit aboard the Jupiter-bound spaceship.

With 2001 less than ten years away, we do not have anything like the fictional HAL 9000. At this point, the most practical application of AI in public administration is the **expert system,** a computer program that duplicates the thinking process that professionals and managers use when making decisions. For example, in Baltimore County, when detectives are faced with a case they cannot solve, they turn to REBES (Residential Burglary Expert System). This sophisticated computer program applies the experience of dozens of veteran burglary detectives to the circumstances of a particular break-in and shifts through a database of thousands of solved and unsolved burglary cases (discussion based on Martin, 1991).

The system can provide a list of other burglaries that might have been committed by the same person. It can draw a profile of the likely perpetrator; for example, "A male youth who is a drug user, lives near scene of crime in the southwest precinct, is an amateur, and had accomplices." It can then give the names of those in the database who fit that profile ranked by the probability that any of them might have committed the crime. REBES performs in seconds what might have taken several detectives weeks to do.

Expert systems are not just for law enforcement. Montgomery County, Maryland, has expert systems for helping county workers quickly determine their retirement benefits and for guiding caseworkers who take adult crisis calls. Austin, Texas, has an expert system to help property developers through the maze of local zoning and building regulations. Merced County, California, has an expert system to help welfare workers know what questions to ask applicants. The system then tells the worker what programs the applicant is eligible for and what amount of benefits the applicant is entitled to. While it may look simple, behind the screen the computer is churning through more than 5,000 rules of eligibility.

Because the government is full of experts—masters of tax auditing, building inspections, fleet maintenance, and so on—there are many potential applications of expert systems. The question is, How does one get this expertise from the heads of experts into a computer program? The answer is that they are asked, in excruciating detail, how the experts do what they do. What does a smashed window, as opposed to a picked lock mean? (The burglar is probably an amateur.) What is the significance of the fact that a medicine cabinet was ransacked? (The burglar may be an addict.) The result is a set of several-hundred rules expressed in a format of "if *X*, then *Y*" statements.

Expert systems are not, however, substitutes for humans but rather are highly capable consultants. In the case of REBES, police officers must still apply the detective's traditional tools and intuition to investigate a case. For one thing, machines do not have hunches (e.g., on whether an amateur burglar might have learned some professional techniques in prison). Nor do they have common sense. Unless they are told, computers do not know that if you do not drink water for several days you will get thirsty; if you go to work in a car, you typically get home by car. Nor do they understand the subtleties of human language. If I say, "I saw a bicycle through the window and wanted it," you would know *it* meant the bicycle, not the window. A computer would not.

Networking. Information technology not only affects how individual activities are best performed; through new information flows, it also greatly enhances an organization's ability to exploit linkages between activities, both within the organization and outside the organization. **Networking** is the linking together of groups and departments within or among organizations to share information resources such as databases. Thus networking increases the computer resources available to each manager and improves interdepartmental coordination.

The U.S. Department of Transportation (DOT) has been a pioneer among agencies using networking. Emphasizing the use of micros and portables in its field offices, especially for auditing, DOT has netted millions of dollars in fines for bid rigging on federally financed transportation projects. Unfortunately, DOT is somewhat the exception. For the most part, the government's computers cannot talk to each other; most are simply incompatible. For instance, the New York regional office of the Department of Health and Human Services alone uses ten different brands of incompatible computers.

Interorganizational networks can link the information systems of two or more organizations. Organizations that regularly do business with one another can now do so more efficiently and with less paperwork by communicating with computers. One example of an interorganizational network involves electronic tax filing. The IRS claimed that the benefit of filing tax returns electronically is that people can get their refunds three weeks sooner. And since about 75 percent of all taxpayers receive a refund that averages approximately $900 per person, the IRS felt the market for such a service would be large. The benefit to the IRS is that electronic filing is less expensive to process.

But the IRS does not allow filing from home, because it wants some kind of professional authorization. This opened an opportunity for banks, which were soon asking themselves, Why not let customers get the refund the same day? That notion spawned instant-refund services that cost customers about $40 if they want to get their refund checks back the same day they file. American Express has also gotten into the refund network. What was important to this company was not the amount of the refund but the *information* on the tax form. Therefore, American Express began offering electronic preparation service, saying to the consumer, "If you file it using our services, and if you also allow us to take a look at your form, we will come back and give you advice as to how much you could have saved if you had bought some of the American Express products" (Venkatraman, 1990). This is an excellent example of how information can be used to gain competitive advantage.

Over the past decade, computer networks have quietly spun a communications web across the globe, transmitting everything from electronic memos to the results of particle-physics experiments. The **High Performance Computing Act of 1991** creates a National Research and Education Network (NREN) that will link millions of people in a unique way only now being envisioned. The NREN (pronounced "en-ren") is expected to evolve from a prototype research and education network called the Internet, which already links some three-million researchers, educators, and others around the world. Indeed, monthly Internet growth in excess of 30 percent was cited as one proof that the high-capacity NREN is needed. Proponents say the NREN will engender laboratories without walls, new business possibilities, global electronic mail, and interactive "textbooks," in which arcane mathematical and scientific concepts spring visually to life.

In making the case for the NREN, Senator Albert Gore (1991:152) draws an interesting analogy:

> *Our current national information policy resembles the worst aspects of our old agricultural policy, which left grain rotting in thousands of storage silos while people were starving. We have warehouses of unused information "rotting," while critical questions are left unanswered and critical problems are left unsolved. For example, the* Landsat *satellite is capable of taking a complete photograph of the entire earth's surface every two weeks. It has been operating for nearly 20 years. Yet more than 95 percent of those images, which might be invaluable to farmers, environmental scientists, geologists, educators, city planners and businesses, have never been seen by human eyes.*

Telecommunications

As the preceding discussion of networking suggests, the last few decades have witnessed remarkable advances in our capacity to transmit information, as words, sounds, or images, over great distances in the form of electromagnetic signals. The basis of these advances is, of course, technological developments such as fiber optics, noted earlier in the chapter. Let us take a look at five of these new communication and conferencing devices.

Electronic Mail. Few people remember it, but Oliver North was tripped up partly because he did not understand a piece of software. When he tried to destroy all the messages he had sent about the Iran-contra affair (p. 144), he did not realize that IBM's PROFs electronic mail system made an automatic backup, so he left an easy trail for investigators to follow.

Electronic mail simply entails sending messages to another person's computer and "parking" them there. The message sits in the receiver's terminal and is read when the computer is turned on. Though this process is basically a form of one-to-one communication, it is also effective for mass communication, because a message can be sent to several people on a mailing list. Electronic mail is a convenient, economical way to bridge geographic distance and save the time of mailing a letter.

An extension of electronic mail is **computer conferencing,** which links managers and professionals in a computer network that allows ongoing dialogue, electronic meetings, and rapid communication.

The Facsimile Machine. The fax machine can send and reproduce copies of documents over telephone lines. Invented in 1850 in London, the technology has grown vastly more sophisticated in recent years; it began its latest boom in Japan where modern times demanded quick visual reproduction of a language with thousands of characters.

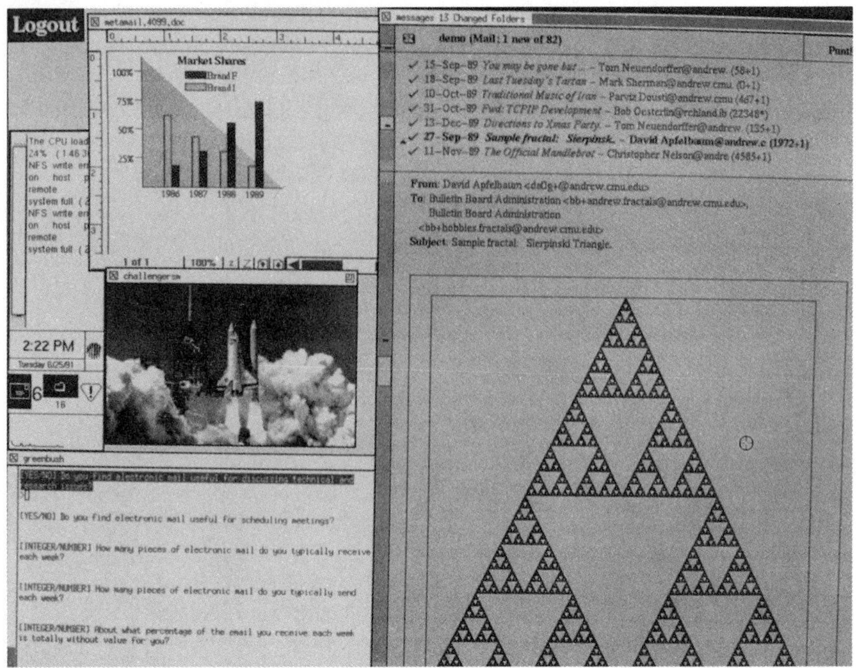

Advanced electronic mail, such as this experimental setup at Bellcore, will make it possible to transmit graphics, animation, self-contained computer programs, and audio recordings. Such features will broaden the applications for networked communications. They may also restore some of the social cues now absent from electronic mail and thereby modify the behavior of its users. (Photo by Marc Skinner)

The fax machine subtly changes how people communicate. It has, for instance, reduced the breathing room that mailing allows. When sending something by mail or even overnight express, one gets it off one's desk and does not have to deal with it for another two or three days; now it is back in ten minutes. On the other hand, faxing allows one to complete papers much closer to deadlines. Faxing may be helping to increase the impatience that comes with automation. When Federal Express appeared on the business scene, many began to think that they had to have things by 10:30 the next morning; now they have reached a level where even that seems like an intolerable delay.

One advantage of faxing is that it combines speed with useful visual cues. Like a letter—and unlike the electronic mail sent by computers—fax lets the sender signal different levels of formality by choosing between typing and handwriting and between agency letterhead or sheets from a memo pad. Another advantage involves international communications. Besides offering the comfort of having everything spelled out in a document and the freedom to communicate despite time differences, faxing promotes a much more direct exchange. Whereas letters from abroad often include formal circumlocutions, faxing encourages a straightforward memorandum style (Solomon, 1988).

Voice Message Systems. Essentially, in voice messaging, the computer acts as a giant answering machine because the computer answers a manager's phone, relays memos, gives out information, and takes messages. Like any new technology, it has advantages and disadvantages:

> *A voice message system can be a wonderful resource to staff people with inadequate clerical support. It allows a staff person to temporarily turn off a phone and remain in touch with the work environment. It greatly encourages oral communication because you are guaranteed at least indirect access to the person you are trying to reach. The disadvantages of this system are not intrinsic to its use but arise when it is misused. At a certain organizational level, a senior manager will receive so many voice messages that he could spend his entire day listening to them. Unlike a human secretary, a voice message system cannot prioritize messages. It cannot be scanned visually in a few seconds. It cannot interpret the urgency of a message, ask questions, or call a manager out of a meeting. (Cohen, 1988:91)*

Videoconferencing. Videoconferencing is the immediate exchange of information via cameras and audio equipment—regardless of where in the state or municipality individuals happen to be located. This technology has been around since at least 1964, when AT&T unveiled its Picturephone at the New York World's Fair. From its inception, it has been touted as an effective way to cut employee travel costs. Nevertheless, it did not catch on until recently because any travel savings were more than offset by unwieldy and expensive equipment; complicated heating, cooling, and lighting requirements; and prohibitive transmission expenses.

Given the budgetary squeezes (Chapter 11) that deprive governments of critical resources and the drop in the cost of meeting screen to screen, the 1990s might prove an ideal time for many agencies to adopt videoconferencing technology. Depending on what the purpose of the meeting is, a videoconference can be up to 90 percent as effective as being there in person; if the purpose is merely to communicate information, the videoconference may be 100 percent effective. It is, however, less effective when the purpose for being there is a brainstorming, creative purpose.

Electronic Bulletin Boards. This technology is used to disseminate routine information on fringe benefits, job openings, and various events through the organization's computer system. To reduce paperwork, the technology can be expanded to store policy manuals, job descriptions, telephone numbers, and other documents.

One does not need to be within an organization to take advantage of this technology. Acting on his own, one man in Colorado Springs, for example, led a successful campaign to block a local ordinance placing restrictions on home-based entrepreneurial activities. Surprised that he was the only citizen to attend the first hearing on the ordinance, he brought the issue to the community's attention by publishing it, together with a list of his concerns, on his computer bulletin board. A small notice in the local newspaper helped to advertise his plan. A number of people contributed their comments via the computer bulletin board. When a second hearing was held several weeks later, 175 people appeared at the meeting to defeat the ordinance.

To provide citizens with a new means of learning about government activities, some electronic bulletin boards have been established by state or local governments. In May 1987, for example, the Utilities and Commerce Committee of the California State Assembly set up an electronic bulletin board system, "The Capitol Connection," which enabled participants to learn about legislative and regulatory issues and to engage in debate with other participants on these issues. Accessible via four telephone lines, forums were set up to comment on various pieces of legislation. Although this bulletin board had about 1,000 registered users, it was recently discontinued for lack of funding (U.S. Office of Technology Assessment, 1990).

The Effect of Information on the Conduct of Work and the Structure of Organizations

Costs and Benefits

A computer system represents an expensive, high-technology capital investment, and such investments often promise high savings only for high risks. For instance, some estimate that county and city governments alone are spending about $1 billion a year on computer systems. At a minimum, such investments demand thoughtful and continuing attention from administrators (see box).

There are several reasons why computers do not always live up to their promise. Computers can motivate government employees to accumulate a lot of unnecessary data, and these systems do not always generate better information for making decisions. Danziger (1977) gives two good reasons why computers often fail to generate personnel savings: "Staff reductions are the exception on most of the more complex tasks which have been computerized. . . . [And] data coding and entry often involve more staff time per transaction than did the manual system." Furthermore, in the political areas of government, there is a reluctance to eliminate jobs that might be affected by automation, and other jobs are protected by civil service.

Notwithstanding such concerns, computers and telecommunications can help to streamline the management of government programs. Consider the following two examples:

- *Automated financial transaction systems.* Today, more than 70 different federal benefit programs provide care, goods, and services to people who meet eligibility requirements based on income level or needs. Although the processes by which these programs are administered can vary significantly, there are five steps that are more or less common to them all. These are as follows: (1) determining eligibility and benefits; (2) verifying the eligibility of recipients; (3) issuing benefits; (4) verifying the receipt of benefits; and, in some cases, (5) redeeming benefits. Because these steps all entail the storage, retrieval, and exchange of information, each could be automated

(text continues on p. 568)

Talking Shop

Asking Hard Questions When Introducing New Technology

Do computers cut costs? Former mayor Dianne Feinstein of San Francisco says that she has "always been suspicious of the golden glow of technology." In 1983, she tightened considerably the city's computer-buying policies. Afterward the city bought from 4 suppliers rather than 44, thus ensuring compatibility.

In 1985, she took a much more dramatic step by freezing expenditures for new computers and forming a committee of senior city managers to see how much computers actually raise productivity. She wanted to know, in short, how much computers are really worth. "If we're saving millions of dollars, I want to be able to keep the libraries open longer, have better park maintenance, or put more police on the street."

Former San Francisco mayor Dianne Feinstein (City of San Francisco)

A busy senior executive in a state agency, county courthouse or city hall may find it difficult to manage the increasingly complex environments that computers have created. Yet his or her participation is crucial if the new technology is going to work as hoped. To help this executive, here is a "crib sheet" of 12 basic questions that should be discussed with the staffers in charge of introducing the technology.

1. Does our approach to information technology fit within our overall corporate strategy for our government?
2. Do we leverage technology and information to more people within our organization?
3. What new services will we be able to implement through cost savings derived from effective information technology?
4. How long do I have to wait until results begin showing up?
5. How have we prepared our organization to assimilate this new technology?
6. Have we considered fundamental changes to the way we do business to take advantage of the opportunities this new technology offers?
7. Are we in danger of stopping something that is working quite well, simply because we're introducing a new technology?

(continued)

8. What are the *real* costs including future upgrades, transition costs, training and operation?
9. Is this a customized application? Are we the only ones for whom the provider is creating this system?
10. How does this application fit our strategic database and applications environment?
11. Does it improve services to the citizens?
12. Does it bring our governments closer to the citizens?

SOURCES: The discussion about Feinstein is based on *Business Week*, June 24, 1986; the questions appeared in *Governing*, February 1989.

using state-of-the-art communication and information technologies. With automation, for example, tax authorities could electronically collect financial records from banks, employers, investment houses, and mortgage lenders; determine a person's tax assessment; and then electronically credit or debit that person's account. In similar fashion, government agencies could employ new technologies to electronically deliver public assistance benefits such as cash, food stamps, and Medicaid (U.S. Office of Technology Assessment, 1990).

- *Advanced training technology.* Over the next ten years, the Federal Aviation Administration (FAA) will use computer-based instruction to train engineers, electronics technicians, air traffic controllers, and other technical personnel; these people represent a major portion of the FAA's approximately 46,000 employees. The FAA estimates that it has avoided $10 million in prior training costs through use of this form of training. Recent cost-benefit analyses indicate this training could reduce future expenditures for training air traffic controllers, who represent about 45 percent of the FAA's work force, by about $14 million between 1988 and 1993. According to the FAA, computer-based instruction results in avoiding some training costs because it reduces the time students and instructors must spend in the classroom. It also enables employee training to be scheduled around the existing work load and according to employee-supervisor needs. The FAA believes students using this training retain more material than they do through classroom instruction (U.S. General Accounting Office, 1987).

Benefits, however, should not be measured solely in terms of productivity gains. The faster and more efficient delivery of services also can help governments do even more important things: save human lives and enhance democratic processes (see box).

(text continues on p. 570)

Using Information Technology for Competitive Advantage: A Public Sector Perspective

It is hard to underestimate the strategic significance of the new information technology. In the private sector, this technology is transforming the nature of products, processes, companies, industries, and even competition itself. The importance of this technology to the public sector is not in dispute. The question is only when and how public administrators exploit it. Those who anticipate the power of the information technology will be in control of events; those who do not respond will be forced to accept mounting criticisms from a disgruntled citizenry. The following two examples clearly illustrate the preferable approach to the new information technology.

Responding to Emergencies

An increasing number of governments, especially municipalities and counties, are using map-based, computer-aided dispatching systems to accelerate and improve their responses to emergency situations. Suppose a huge dry-cleaning plant at the edge of a city is shattered by an explosion. A citizen uses a nearby public phone to dial the city's "enhanced 911" (E911) services. The call automatically passes through the telephone company's automatic number identification computer, which supplies the exact location of the public phone. As the E911 center answers the call, the location of the public phone, as defined by both street address and latitude-longitude coordinates, is automatically extracted from the dispatching system's database and displayed on the call taker's screen. A second screen displays a map showing the location of the public phone. The call taker then routes the information to the appropriate dispatcher. At the dispatcher's computer, the receipt of the emergency information triggers the dispatch system to search its database for fire, police, and ambulance stations closest to the dry-cleaning plant. If police, fire, and medical vehicles are equipped with mobile data terminals, personnel will have used them to enter the types of equipment available in each vehicle, and the database will display that information on the dispatcher's screen as well. Automatic vehicle-location devices beam the location of each police car, fire engine, and ambulance in the vicinity onto the dispatcher's computerized map screen. Finally, the database displays for the dispatcher the types and locations of any hazardous materials, such as chemicals, that are used at the dry-cleaning plant. The dispatcher then contacts the relevant stations and vehicles. The emergency vehicles' mobile data terminal screens also show the fastest route from the vehicles' respective locations to the site of the emergency. Since the explosion at the plant, fewer than 30 seconds have elapsed between the citizen's E911 call and the dispatch of response units.

Public Electronic Network

A few years ago, a Santa Monica, California, survey found widespread interest on the part of residents in using computers to communicate with their local government. As a result, the city set up the Public Electronic Network, or PEN, a

(continued)

videotex system that offers residents, businesses, and schools free on-line access to Santa Monica officials and services. Based on privately owned personal computers and public terminals located throughout the city, PEN provides residents access to a variety of information databases, including notices of government meetings; city council agendas and minutes; officials' voting records; public library card catalogues; guides to Santa Monica social services; and information on recycling, rent control ordinances, schools, and local transportation. Citizens can communicate directly with any department in the Santa Monica government. They can get library references, find out where to pay parking fines, and ask questions of council members. City staff members are required to respond to each request within 24 hours. PEN also permits citizens to communicate among themselves and to participate in public-policy discussions.

SOURCE: Based on M. J. Richter, "High-Tech Dispatch System Can Save Lives—and Money," *Governing*, August 1991; and "The Real Advantages of Putting Government on Line," *Governing*, May 1991.

Decision Making

What effect does information technology have on group decision making? Early researchers thought that it would improve it because computer messages were plain text; that is, electronic discussions would presumably be more rational, more logical than face-to-face discussions in which social skills, personalities, and status become factors.

But the issue proved more complicated than that. In a fascinating series of experiments, Lee Sproull and Sara Kiester (1991) compared how small groups make decisions using computer conferences, electronic mail, and face-to-face discussion. The results confirmed the notion that an electronic network induces people to talk more frankly and equally. Furthermore, such groups generated more proposals for action than did face-to-face discussions. But the increased democracy associated with electronic interactions also has disadvantages. For example, when it is impossible for people to interrupt one another, as in face-to-face discussions, the time to reach a decision increases fourfold.

And that is not all. Conflict becomes more likely, especially when a few people try to dominate control of the network. Subtle cues, like tone of voice and eye contact, are missing when people sit at separate terminals to communicate. Because electronic messages lack information regarding job titles, social importance, hierarchical position, race, age, and appearance, people feel less bound by status and norms. Their behavior may be impulsive and self-centered. They may feel less concern for others, express extreme opinions, and vent their anger more readily than if they were face-to-face. Computer scientists already have a term for the emotional outbursts that can have an adverse effect on the group—**flaming.**

Organizational Structure

Information technology is beginning to affect the structure of public organizations, though most organizations still reflect the constraints of a nonelectronic era when interdependent employees had to be close physically and the chain of command dictated who reported to whom. Modern information technology allows, however, for much more flexibility and much less hierarchy.

The speed with which information technology transforms the public sector will depend in part on how quickly schools and government agencies can transform the workers themselves. Indeed, because computers place a premium on an ability to deal with abstract thought, the concept of the subordinate may need redefining. At the same time, computers transform relations between managers and workers. What happens to the chain of command when workers can access all sorts of databases, gaining their own understanding of the organization and forming their own ideas of how it should operate? The result can be unprecedented anxiety, tension, and ambivalence.

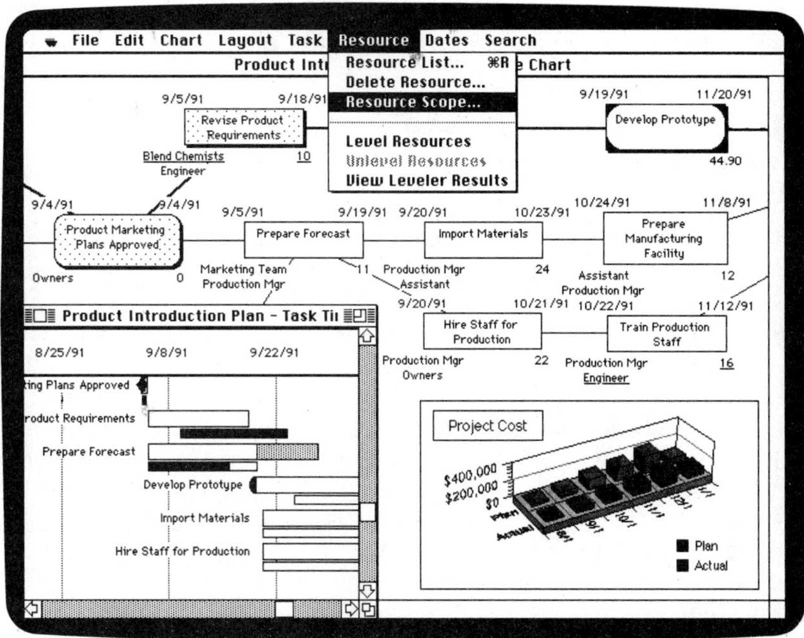

While information technology has certain disadvantages for group decision making (see text), there is little doubt that the personal computer has enhanced the ability of the individual decision maker to make complex decisions in a much shorter time and with less guesswork. For example, Breakthrough Software's Project Manager, like most project management packages, produces Gantt charts that indicate what tasks must occur when. It also graphs the level of specific resources required each day and juxtaposes this information with the relevant Gantt chart tasks. Compare this screen shot to Figure 9-1. (Courtesy Breakthrough Software)

Managers want and need control, but the new technology enables workers to improve their performances on their own. What will managers do? They may end up using the technology mainly to routinize, subdivide, and control jobs. Using it this way would likely be a mistake for organizations; it would mean sacrificing the potential that information technology offers for improving the services of those organizations. To fulfill that potential, jobs will have to be redesigned to give employees the opportunity for more, not less, initiative—to allow them to interpret information and make decisions based on it. This idea of putting useful information before all kinds of employees, allowing them to do their jobs better, is at the heart of **total quality management** (TQM). Under TQM, employees are encouraged to strive to improve quality and productivity in all of the organization's processes. (For more information on TQM and an illustration of how one city successfully used it, see Case 12.1.)

To be sure, this approach strikes at the very heart of traditional concepts of managerial authority. In the hierarchical organization, where managers are paid to think and workers, to do, the idea that learning and free inquiry by the entire work force is crucial to performance can be extremely threatening to some managers. The new technology challenges the control that management has traditionally had over information and hence over an important source of managerial power and privilege.

Strategic Management in the Information Revolution

From the Bronze Age to the Gulf War, information has provided leaders with a competitive advantage. Just as knowledge of how to use metals in the manufacturing of tools and weapons gave the ancient civilizations of Mesopotamia and Sumer advantage over their rivals, the U.S.-led victory over Iraq was the direct result of the intellectual supremacy of allied arms (e.g., smart bombs) and military doctrine rather than big battalions and big guns.

It is unlikely, however, that information has ever been as critical a resource as it is today. Every public administrator, whether running a 6-person shop in a medium-size city or a 300,000-person department in Washington, needs to have an information strategy. To develop such a strategy, he or she will need to think through at least three key questions:

1. What information do I need to perform and accomplish my unit's mission?
2. How can I generate more and better information within my unit?
3. What information do I have that should be disseminated to others, and what is the best way to package it?

Information Acquisition

Managers should constantly ask themselves what information they need to accomplish their unit's mission. As the accompanying cartoon might suggest, a more prevalent attitude in many of today's organizations is, The more data the better. Indeed, as Russell Ackoff (1967) has suggested, the less a manager understands a problem, the more likely he or she is to play it safe and, with respect to information, ask for everything. Specialists in information technology, who understand even less about the problem than the manager, oblige by providing ever more of everything. The result is an overload of irrelevant information. The cure involves managers thinking through the kinds of information they need. To accomplish this task properly requires that the top management establish clear, simple objectives that can be translated into particular actions with specific information requirements.

Formal Reporting Systems. Without clear-cut objectives, managers might become preoccupied with the details of operation—administrative issues, salaries, square footage of office space, and supplies—and neglect the purposes for operation. Besides being output-oriented, a good reporting system for a program has the following characteristics (Chase, 1984):

- *Timeliness.* Receiving a report at the end of the month for the previous month does managers little good.
- *Specificity.* People should be identified by name. Quality should be quantified whenever possible. For example, to measure the quality of a field investigator, one could use the number of times his or her reports were rejected as inadequate.
- *Honesty.* Any reporting system sets up incentives; avoid perverse ones that allow for cheating.

More data is not necessarily better . . .

"Feeding time . . . "
(From The Wall Street Journal, *with permission of Cartoon Features Syndicate.)*

- *Relevancy.* Most importantly, reports should be used. Senders should receive feedback. Do not ask for so much information that staff does not have time to complete its work. Cohen (1988) reminds us that, when a manager requires the staff to report one particular bit of information rather than another, the manager is signaling priorities. If the manager asks for information that matches actual priorities, the reporting system can serve management.

A good example of a large and successful formal reporting system was that of the British-run civil service in India. As the accompanying box indicates, that organization had virtually no middle management. Do you think that this might be indicative of information-based organizations of the future?

In addition to information about immediate concerns, managers must plan. What information might be needed in the future? In the early 1970s most of the environmental concern was focused on air and water pollution, and until the late 1970s, very little information was collected about landfills. Many landfills were no more than open dumps, where nearly anything, including hazardous materials produced by industry, could be disposed of. Few were equipped with the means to monitor potential groundwater pollution. Although many of these landfills were owned or operated by local governments, few officials thought to ask what information might be needed in the future.

Informal Networks. Because managers' views on issues are shaped to a certain degree by the positions they hold, experienced managers correct for such bias by filtering information according to its source. In Anthony Downs's (1967) classic work, *Inside Bureaucracy,* the author identifies a number of **antidistortion factors in the communication system.** These factors include the following: (1) multiple internal information sources and overlapping responsibilities; (2) direct communication through hierarchical levels or elimination of such levels; (3) distortion-proof messages (e.g., summarization of details in nontechnical language with little jargon); and (4) external sources of information.

Few presidents followed Downs's four recommendations more faithfully than Eisenhower. While his aides thought that his eagerness to hear all sides before making a decision was a source of weakness and that his sensitivity to external voices led him to mediocre decisions, Eisenhower thought this trait a strength:

> *He wanted to hear every legitimate point of view, to take all possible repercussions into account, before acting. Among other things, this meant he abhorred yes-men. During a Cabinet discussion over ways to cut spending, for example, [Henry Cabot Lodge, Jr., ambassador to the United Nations] suggested reducing grants to the states for highway programs. Eisenhower replied that "my personal opinion is that we should spend more for highways." Lodge mumbled, "I withdraw." Eisenhower wanted none of that. "It's open to discussion," he told Lodge, and reminded him that "I've given way on a number of personal opinions to this gang."*

Eisenhower actively sought conflicting views. When he took office, the Canadians were threatening to build the St. Lawrence Seaway on their own if the United States would not join them in the project. Eisenhower wanted to participate, but he knew there was strong opposition, because Milton Eisenhower and George Humphrey were leading spokesmen for the Pennsylvania and Ohio railroad and coal companies that opposed the project. Eisenhower thought the Pennsylvania and Ohio crowd were putting their selfish interests ahead of the obvious long-term good of the United States, but he insisted on hearing their point of view. In late April, he told Milton he realized he was "hearing only the pro side of the argument," so he invited a group of railroad presidents to the White House, and for three hours listened to their side. They claimed that the seaway would cost the United States more than $2 billion; proponents were suggesting that the cost would be less than $500 million. "In such a confused situation," Eisenhower told Milton, "you have to dig pretty deep to find out what the facts really are because each allegation is presented with a very large share of emotionalism and prejudice." (Ambrose, 1984:79–80)

The point is this: Managers cannot afford to wait behind their desks for the formal reporting system to supply them with all the information they need. They must aggressively seek information by using internal networks ("grapevines") and external networks, and they must assiduously cultivate the latter over years:

Sometimes in the crush of day-to-day business it is easy to neglect human relationships. In the long run, such neglect can be costly. Social interaction makes work life more interesting and can also provide you with channels often needed to accomplish important tasks. . . . External contacts are important reality checks. If too much of your professional or social network is within a single organization, your information base is likely to be quite limited. (Cohen, 1988:86)

Human Biases in Interpreting Information. Whether information arrives through a formal reporting system or an informal network, a manager must be aware of certain human weaknesses in interpreting information. Here we can mention only a few. The aim is simply to make the point that managers, being human, are not nearly as objective as they might think themselves.

- People think that the more accurate the information is, the more informative it is. Not necessarily. Weather announcers invariably give barometric pressure to the hundredths of an inch. Who does this help?
- People seldom think straight about very unlikely events, which explains the popularity of lotteries and the fear of being struck by lightning.
- People are influenced by how the information *looks.* Information on a computer printout might carry more credibility than the *same information*

Back to the Future: The British Civil Service in India

The British ran the Indian subcontinent for two hundred years, from the middle of the eighteenth century through World War II, without making fundamental changes in organization structure or administrative policy. The Indian Civil Service never had more than one thousand members to administer a vast and densely populated subcontinent—a tiny fraction (at most 1 percent) of the legions of Confucian mandarins and palace eunuchs employed to administer a not-much-more populous China (and an even tinier fraction of the 22 million civil servants an independent India now employs). Most of the Britishers were quite young; a thirty-year-old was a survivor, especially in the early years. Most lived alone in isolated outposts with the nearest countryman a day or two of travel away. And for the first hundred years there was neither telegraph nor railroad.

The organization structure was totally flat. Each district officer reported directly to the "Chief Operating Officer," the provincial Political Secretary. Since there were nine provinces, each Political Secretary had about one hundred people reporting directly to him, many times what the doctrine of span of control would allow. Nevertheless, the system worked remarkably well for a long time, in large part because it was designed to ensure that each of its members had the information he needed to do his job. Each month the district officer spent a whole day writing a full report to the Political Secretary in the provincial capital. He discussed his principal tasks—there were only four, each clearly delineated: prevent the natives from killing each other in racial and religious conflicts; keep down banditry; dispense justice impartially and honestly; assess and collect taxes. He put down in detail what he had expected would happen with respect to each of these tasks, what actually did happen, and why the two differed if there was a discrepancy. Then he wrote down what he expected would happen in the ensuing month with respect to each key task and what he was going to do about it, asked questions about policy, and commented on long-term opportunities, threats, and needs. In turn, the Political Secretary "minuted" every one of those reports, writing back a full commentary.

SOURCE: Peter F. Drucker, *The New Realities* (New York: Harper & Row, 1989), pp. 212–13.

acquired over lunch. By emphasizing the benefits of a project over its risks, a briefer can help ensure its acceptance. If the briefer does not wish for the project to be adopted, she can merely emphasize the risks. In both cases, the exact same information is given, only with different emphases.

- People tend to anchor their judgments on some initial point of reference—whether relevant to the task or not. This may be the initial piece of information presented in a long series, the "expertise" of the speaker, or any number of things.
- People do not like to appear ignorant. It requires courage and self-confidence to say things like, "I don't understand that. Would you please go

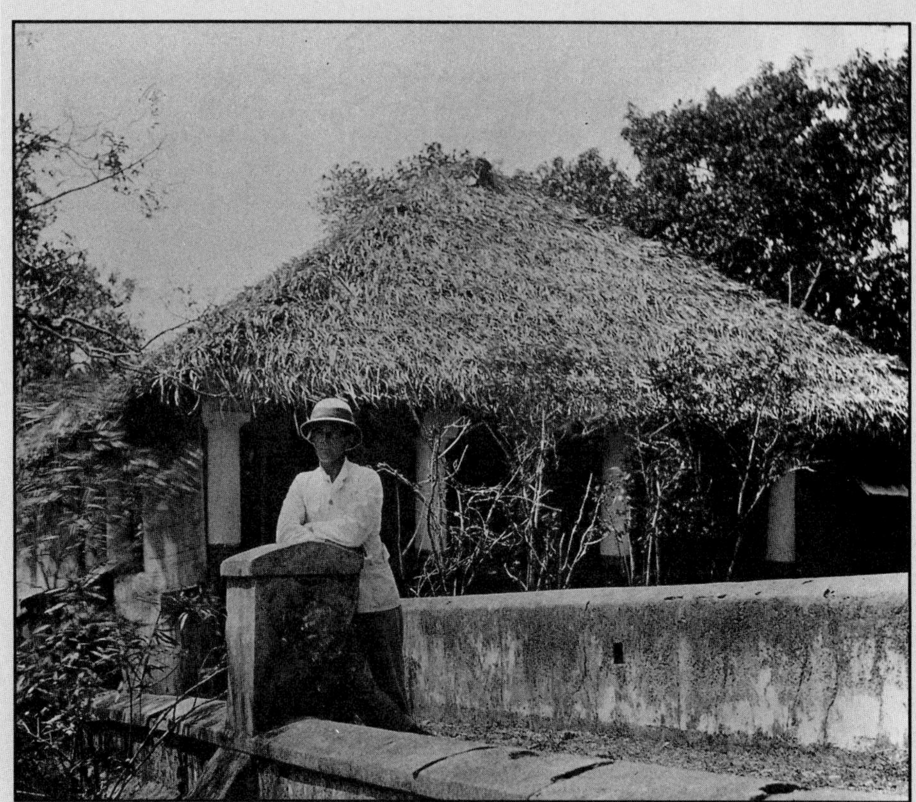

District officer in a small station. This photograph from 1898 suggests something of the loneliness that often faced a district officer. (Photo from Men Who Ruled India*)*

over it again?" or "Draw me a picture," or "What does that mean?" Instead we find ourselves uttering a series of "Uh-huhs," while involuntarily nodding our heads and pretending to a knowledge we do not have.

Creating Information

Information has a peculiar property not shared by human resources and fiscal resources: It is not used up by being used. Indeed, the more it is used, the more there is, since new insights and new information are likely to accumulate. The notion of scarcity is turned inside out, and the central task of public executives becomes not only the efficient use of resources but also (1) the encouragement of cooperation across boundaries and (2) the establishment of a learning system in order to generate new information.

While it may be too early to specify exactly what a true information-creating organization would look like, we have clues.

Finding Information Resources Within the Organization. Perhaps the first step in getting more from an organization's information assets is to find them. Ask a city manager what funds she has left for the last quarter of the fiscal year, and she probably will not even have to put you on hold to get the answer. But probably no one on her staff has a handle on the information capital in the organization; that is, on the value of the intellectual skills of the city's employees.

Let me illustrate the problem. Scientific Generics is a management consulting firm that helps organizations map their technological assets; that is, locate them, define them, and establish routes for getting them to other parts of the organization. Often its clients are startled to learn how much intellectual capital they have—just as was President Kennedy after the Bay of Pigs fiasco when his attorney general informed him that he (the attorney general) and the secretary of agriculture probably knew more about such an operation than anyone else in the cabinet. (The story appears on page 196.) One of Scientific Generics's clients had a division that knew how to drill minuscule holes to make connectors for fiber-optic cables. Its drillers were the best in the world. Yet it was not until the company—working with the consulting firm—mapped its technology assets that it was able to transfer its drilling skill to another division that made connectors for copper wiring systems (*Fortune,* June 3, 1991).

Establishing a Learning Environment. According to Richard Pascale (1990), eight specific factors influence an organization's capacity to learn:

1. The absence of an elite group or a single viewpoint that dominates decision making. If this group or viewpoint exists, then top management can spin off groups as separate units, unaffected and insulated from the dominant viewpoint.

2. The extent to which employees are encouraged to challenge existing ways of doing things. This encouragement must not be part of a double bind in which managers feel they are simultaneously exhorted to exercise initiative and then undermined for doing so.

3. The use of external data (benchmarks) on agency performance. For example, how does a state agency's turnover rate compare to that of similar agencies in other states? What is the ratio of administrative costs to revenue collected in your state as compared to that of other states? External benchmarks can shake up internal complacency and expose problems.

4. The equity of the reward system for breakthrough ideas and the distribution of status and privilege.

5. The historical legacy and folklore of the organization extolling learning and new ideas.

6. The degree of **empowerment** of employees at all levels. Learning depends on a sense of initiative and commitment, an eagerness for inquiry and the consideration of options, and an active participation in a collective process of discussion and problem solving. Pascale (1990:249) writes: "Values and trust establish the preconditions that encourage individuals to think, experiment, and improve. It follows that learning organizations share, above all else, an abiding commitment to people and a faith in the human capacity to find a better way. Once employees know what an organization stands for, and believe that it is sufficiently trustworthy to warrant their commitment and effort, they begin to truly extend themselves." In nonlearning organizations, when a malfunction occurs, someone goes out and kicks something; in a learning organization, people have a meeting. According to Masaaki Imai (1976), most problems are rooted in the system. Because the employees most intimately involved with the system are best able to spot its flaws, they need to be empowered to initiate fixes. This means more than doing one's job better; it means looking at the system that affects how the job is done. In such an environment, it is quite clear that every manager's job is to free his or her subordinates.

In sum, systematically encouraging employees to learn requires fairly radical organizational strategies. The centerpiece of such a strategy must be a redefinition of the authority that is dominant in most government agencies today. It means increased equality, broad access to information, and conception of work as a professional career. What it does not mean is a two-class system marked by a Berlin Wall between the employers and the managers. Some argue that women managers may have a particular advantage in this new type of work environment (see box).

Capturing, Capitalizing, and Leveraging. First, here is a horror story. The U.S. Postal Service has often introduced automation at the expense of the valuable information that its workers accumulate. In the last decade, the Postal Service has transferred responsibility for changes of address from letter carriers to clerks in a central mail facility who collect all change-of-address forms and then activate a computerized system that forwards the mail. Letter carriers on a route can tell whether a name is merely misspelled or a letter is really intended for a different person; and they often know when a son or daughter rather than a whole family has moved. But under the new regulations, the carriers are forbidden any role in adjusting address changes. If two letter carriers are sorting their mail and one spots a letter that, because of a change of address, should go to the other's route, he or she is not allowed to give the letter to the other carrier. Instead, it must be rerouted back through the main mail facility. This makes it difficult to spot even the most egregious errors. Management has also ignored the encyclopedic knowledge of addresses and ZIP codes that letter sorters

(text continues on p. 582)

Women and the Information Revolution

(The New York Times/*Michael Geissinger*)

Information-based organizations require a somewhat different organizing principle than that developed in the industrial era. To be a leader in these organizations, it is no longer an advantage to have been socialized as a male.

What might be termed the "military management model" served well after World War II. The work comprised tasks that were outer-directed, mechanical, and easy to supervise. Power was centralized in the hands of managers who told workers with high school educations or less what to do.

But with the coming of the information revolution, the dominant principle of organization has begun to shift from management *in order to control people* to leadership *in order to bring out the best in people.* "This is not," John Naisbitt and Patricia Aburdene write, "the 'leadership' individuals and groups so often call for when they really want a father figure to take care of all their problems. It is a democratic yet demanding leadership that respects people and encourages self-management, autonomous teams, and entrepreneurial units." It seeks to move people in some direction mostly through noncoercive means. "Outside the military management model, men and women are equally capable of inspiring commitment and bringing out the best in people. . . . Women might even hold a slight advantage since they need not 'unlearn' old authoritarian behavior to run their departments. . . . Like their male colleagues, . . . they must learn to coach, inspire, and gain people's commitment." They gain commitment by sharing authority and empowering people.

Naisbitt and Aburdene argue further that, if the prototypical industrial worker was male, then the prototypical information worker is surely a woman. Eighty-four percent of working women are part of the information/service sector. According to the Bureau of Labor Statistics, they hold nearly 40 percent of the 14 million executive, administrative, and managerial jobs—nearly double the 1972 figure.

In the opening paragraph of a recent *Fortune* article, Jaclyn Fierman (1990:115) writes:

Suddenly men *have to worry about gender equality. A cadre of consultants, academics, and executives say Mr. Hard-charging Manager could soon be out of a job. In his place they see a more nurturing, empathic sort, a born consensus builder. She—emphatically she—shuns the trappings of power and prefers "centrarchies" to hierarchies. Best of all, she is simply being herself. Sally Helgesen's recent book,* The Female Advantage, *claims that with their superior management instincts, women "may be the new Japanese."*

Judy B. Rosener maintains the following:

Women are far more likely than men to describe themselves as transforming subordinates' self-interest into concern for the whole organization and as using personal traits like charisma, work record, and interpersonal skills to motivate others. . . . Women leaders practice . . . "interactive leadership"—trying to make every interaction with coworkers positive for all involved by encouraging participation, sharing power and information, *making people feel important, and energizing them. (Quoted in Fierman, 1990; emphasis added)*

But Rosener, who is a faculty member at the School of Management at the University of California, Irvine, thinks that interactive leadership should not be linked too directly to being female, since some men use that style and some women prefer the command-and-control style.

Women have achieved, if not a majority, a substantial proportion of the previously male-dominated careers in an increasingly information-based public sector. Consider the case of Christina Lund (opposite, right), a U.S. trade negotiator, and Amelia A. Porges (left), associate general counsel in the office of the U.S. trade representative. *The New York Times* reports American officials and students of trade negotiations as saying that foreign officials, who are not used to dealing with career women in their own countries, often feel awkward when face-to-face at a negotiating table with American lawyers, economists, and other professionals who happen to be women. This is a situation that tends to favor the United States. It provokes uncertainty about how the negotiations will be conducted, and that uncertainty can be used effectively on the U.S. side, which remains on a steady course though the other side may be thrown off balance. Balance is a critical element in any negotiation.

accumulate. Operators on the letter-sorting machines are not allowed to take the initiative to key in the right ZIP code when, for instance, they see a Chicago letter with a Cleveland ZIP code (Judis, 1988).

Notwithstanding the Postal Service, new technology may be changing information sharing in organizations for the better. Some of the most important information—personal experiences, war stories, folklore about what works and what does not work, gossip about how workers really should behave, and so on—never appears in traditional distribution systems.

In the past, the spread of such personal information has been strongly determined by physical proximity and social acquaintance. As a result, distant or poorly connected employees have lacked access to local expertise, even though this untapped knowledge often represented an important informational resource for the organization. This is no longer true. Today electronic groups can provide a forum for sharing such expertise independent of spatial and social constraints. This is the way it works. A significant information flow might begin with the "Does anybody know . . .?" message appearing on the computer networks. A sender might broadcast an electronic request for information to an entire organization, to a particular distribution list, or to a bulletin board. Anyone who sees the message can reply (Sproull & Kiester, 1991:121).

The answers received can be electronically redistributed by putting them in a public computer file on the network. Thus, the organization has created a repository of information that is working and accessible even when an employee is out of the office or leaves the organization.

These so-called electronic bulletin boards are not the only way to capture information in an organization. A study by Xerox revealed that repairpersons learn the most about fixing copiers not from manuals but from swapping stories. Instead of viewing this activity as a waste of time, Xerox managers provide opportunities for storytelling at informal get-togethers and loosely organized off-site meetings (*Fortune,* June 3, 1991).

Information Dissemination

Perhaps the first rule of effective information dissemination within an organization is for everyone to constantly ask himself or herself, who depends on me for what information? While information inventories and electronic bulletin boards can help enormously, ultimately, dissemination requires that each person take the fullest responsibility for information.

The rule is particularly applicable to bad news. It is *always* better to be the bearer of your own bad news. Christopher J. Matthews (1988) even advises to "hang a lantern on your problem." To illustrate the point, he reminds us of Ronald Reagan's first presidential debate with Walter Mondale in 1984. His overall performance was, as *Newsweek* put it, "shaky." Speculation was rampant that the 73-year-old president might finally be showing his age. The stage was set for the second debate, and there would be only one issue: Reagan's age. An early question cut to the heart of the issue. Would he be able to function in high-pressure situations like the Cuban missile crisis?

Reagan was ready. In a tone of mock seriousness, he replied, "I will not make

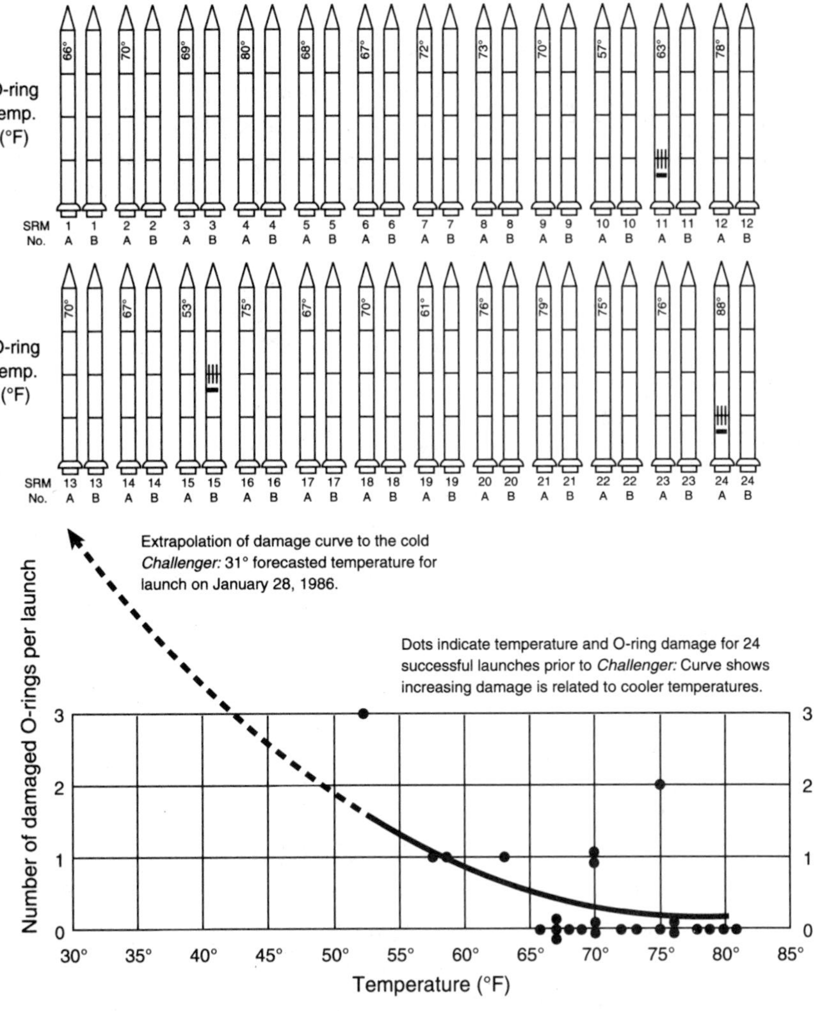

As these two diagrams demonstrate, how information is presented sometimes can be a matter of life and death. Morton-Thiokol, the maker of the space shuttle's solid-fuel rocket boosters, prepared the top chart, which attempts to relate damage to the boosters to the temperature at launch time. But clutter and confusion hide the fact that might have saved the Challenger *astronauts. Edward R. Tufte has redrawn the chart to make crystal clear that fact—damage had most often occurred before at low temperatures, and no launch day had been nearly as cold as the 31 degrees predicted for* Challenger. *[Source: Report of the Presidential Commission of the Space Shuttle Challenger Accident and Edward R. Tufte,* Visual Explanations *(Cheshire, Conn.: Graphics Press, forthcoming)]*

my age an issue in this campaign. I am not going to exploit, for political purposes, my opponent's youth and inexperience." Matthews (1988:159) comments:

> *"Hang a lantern on your problem" applies with equal force to cases where you're selling yourself one-to-one and when you're targeting a broader audience. Retail or wholesale, the one durable truth obtains: when in doubt, get it*

out. If you've done something your boss is not going to like, it is far better that you yourself bring him the bad news. It gives him a perfect opportunity to let his steam off. It shows that you are not trying to put one past him. Most important, it protects him from being surprised and embarrassed by hearing it from someone outside.

Effective information dissemination within an organization also means that managers consider carefully *how* to present it. This is not as straightforward an affair as it may seem. Experts in particular tend to get bogged down by their own knowledge and regularly miss key points when they try to convey what they know. Richard Saul Wurman (1989:125) puts it succinctly: "Familiarity breeds confusion." Ask an expert the time, and he will tell you how to build a clock. The solution is for the expert to provide the doorknob into each thought so the receiver "can grapple with the learning connections along the journey."

Now let us consider the dissemination of information *outside* the organization—from government to citizens. Informational programs in government generally take the form of (1) a campaign on particular topics—for example, environmental consequences of product packaging or revision of the state's deer season law; (2) steady play on a central theme for a long period of time—for example, conservation of natural resources; or (3) the issuance of news without any specific objectives—for example, personnel change.

Typical of a fairly sophisticated information-dissemination program is that of the Oklahoma State Department of Health. It has these three objectives:

1. To establish a system whereby newsworthy information on public health may be disseminated through all appropriate channels of communication.
2. To develop a capability for technical assistance, advice, and consultation to line programs within the State Department of Health and to local health units on informational materials, public relations, and other appropriate aspects of informational activities.
3. To provide a focal point, or clearinghouse, for both the mass media and the departmental staff on consistency of information to be released and policy statements representing the department's overall posture and attitude.

At the local level, information dissemination is particularly important. Consider the aggressive multimedia approach that was taken by Lake County, Florida, to inform and educate the public about recycling (*P.A. Times,* July 1, 1991):

- Public service announcements on local cable television, door hangers, and buttons are used to make large numbers of people aware of the program.
- County staff members give speeches that provide detailed information about recycling.

- The county distributes a pamphlet describing businesses and nonprofit groups that accept recyclable materials. Highlights of the Florida Solid Waste Management Act are also included. Another pamphlet lists the materials that are collected, including specific instructions for disposal.
- County staff also prepares a newsletter titled *Recycling Report.* The Fall 1990 issue featured questions and answers about recycling and facts and figures about materials and suggestions for reuse of products. The "Rappin' Recycler" character helps with program publicity.
- The newsletter also includes a telephone number for a recycling hot line. Callers can obtain information about public and private recycling activities in the county.

Generally speaking, public administrators place too much stress on formalized communications and not enough on actual face-to-face communications. For example, one state highway commission takes great effort to prepare an attractive, readable annual report but does nothing about a red-tape licensing procedure that irritates large numbers of citizens (Cutlip & Center, 1982).

Another common problem in conveying ideas getting bogged down in introductions. "An audience," Wurman (1989:129) writes, "will be more receptive to new information if they aren't kept in suspense, made anxious trying to guess where someone is going. Many people can't really listen to an idea until key questions about it have been answered in their minds."

Yet another problem concerns what to do when the listener simply refuses to listen (see box on page 586).

Finally, one of the most effective ways for government to convey information to its citizens is through the news media. Unfortunately, many local officials do not know how news media representatives operate, how to work with them, or how important good press-government relations are. Compounding the problem is the fact that, because of limited staff and limited space and time, the news media cannot fully perform government's information function—especially at the local level:

> *Information regarding the time and location of 35 animal vaccination clinics throughout a 4,000-square mile county will wind up in agate type near the classifieds in the daily newspaper, and won't be carried at all by either radio or TV. One county practitioner comments, "More and more, it is becoming essential to government to aim its message at a specific audience carefully and precisely. Messages sent through the media get filtered, filtered by the reporter's experience and knowledge, filtered by the rewrite man, by the copydesk and headline writer." (Cutlip & Center, 1982:520)*

A solution to this problem is suggested by the previously cited Lake County experience: Develop alternative channels for information dissemination.

Presenting Information Creatively

Imagine that you are director of the OMB, and one day the president's deputy chief says to you, "Don't get offended now, but you might as well know it. When you sit there with the president going over how hard spending cuts are, the man's eyes glaze over. He tunes out completely." Well, that is fairly close to the situation David A. Stockman (shown conferring with Reagan) faced in 1982. In his book *The Triumph of Politics,* he explains how he met the challenge and *did* get his message across.

"To convince the President it really was as bad as I was saying, I invented a multiple-choice budget quiz. The regular budget briefs weren't doing the job. I thought this might be the way.

"The quiz divided the entire budget up into about 50 spending components and gave him three spending-cut choices on each, ranging from a nick to a heavy whack. Next to each choice was a description of what the impact of the cut would be (how many people would be thrown out into the snow), and of its political prospects (e.g., "previously defeated 27–2 in committee").

"The President took the quiz in November 1982. During several long sessions in the Cabinet Room we had gone through all 50 budget components. The allowed him systematically to look at the whole $900 billion budget, to see it brick-by-brick. It also allowed him to get his hands dirty, maybe even bloody, with the practical chore of nitty-gritty cutting. Once the President went through it, he would understand that the budget was not a matter of too many bureaucrats and filing cabinets, but a politically explosive, vast, complex network of subsidies, grants, and entitlements. He would see that to cut COLAs by $14 billion meant taking $1,263 a year out of the pockets of 36 million Social Security recipients and several million more military and civilian retirees.

"The President enjoyed the quiz immensely. He sat there day after day with his pencil. He listened to his senior staff and the economic team discuss the relevant policy and political ramifications, then announced his choice and marked the appropriate box.

"And rarely chose to make a whack. They were mostly nicks. 'Yes,' he would say, 'we can't go that far.' Or, 'No, we better go for the moderate option or there will be a drumbeat from the opposition.'

"The last session was on a Friday afternoon. I could tell the President was delighted about having endured the

Concluding Observations

The contemporary language of public administration is inadequate to fully express the implications of the information revolution. As Shoshana Zuboff (1988:394) has written:

> *We remain, in the final years of the twentieth century, prisoners of a vocabulary in which managers require employees; superiors have subordinates; jobs*

(White House photo)

ordeal. It had occasioned a number of anecdotes about the federal monster and he had happily dispensed them to the group assembled at the cabinet table.

"When we told him what his grade was early the next week, he was not so pleased. He had flunked the exam. After making all his cuts the five-year deficit remained at a staggering $800 billion."

SOURCE: Excerpt from *The Triumph of Politics* by David A. Stockman. Copyright © 1986 by David A. Stockman. Reprinted by permission of Harper-Collins Publishers.

are defined to be specific, detailed, narrow, and task-related; and organizations have levels that in turn make possible chains of command and spans of control. The guiding metaphors are military; relationships are thought of as contractual and often adversarial. The foundational image of work is still one of a manufacturing enterprise where raw materials are transformed by physical labor and machine power into finished goods.

But the images associated with physical labor, with the picture of the pin factory on p. 301 can no longer guide our conception of management in the public sector. The jobs of people there are not performed on an assembly line and cannot be managed as though they were. It is almost impossible to "supervise" information work because invisible mental tasks have replaced visible physical ones. Work is how they communicate with citizens and elected officials; work is what they write in memos; work is what they say at meetings. How does one "manage" these things?

As we have repeatedly seen in this chapter, the information-based organization is an arena through which information circulates, information to which human creativity is applied. I will let Zuboff (1988:395) have the last word:

> *The quality, rather than the quantity, of effort will be the source from which added value is derived. Economists may continue to measure labor productivity as if the entire world of work could be represented adequately by the assembly line, but their measures will be systematically indifferent to what is most valuable in the [information-based] organization. A new division of learning requires another vocabulary—one of colleagues and co-learners, of exploration, experimentation, and innovation. Jobs are comprehensive, tasks are abstractions that depend upon insight and synthesis, and power is a roving force that comes to rest as dictated by function and need. A new vocabulary cannot be invented all at once—it will emerge from the practical action of people struggling to make sense in a new "place" and driven to sever their ties with an industrial logic that has ruled the imaginative life of our century.*

Concepts for Review

- antidistortion factors in the communication system
- artificial intelligence (AI)
- biases in interpreting information
- central processing unit
- computer conferencing
- data
- decision support system (DSS)
- electronic bulletin boards
- electronic mail
- empowerment
- expert system
- flaming
- hardware
- High Performance Computing Act of 1991
- information
- information system
- learning environment
- management information system (MIS)
- memory
- networking
- operating system
- software
- spreadsheet
- total quality management (TQM)
- transaction processing system (TPS)
- unstructured, semistructured, and structured problems
- video conferencing
- voice message systems

Problems

1. "The new information technology makes the behavior of employees much more visible." Explain this statement and discuss its implications for employees and their bosses.
2. How do information needs for control and decision making differ by hierarchical level?
3. If you were asked to help design and implement an information system for a department at your university, how would you proceed? How would you overcome resistance?
4. "The greatest threat the personal computer poses is that managers will take it seriously and come to believe that they can manage by remaining in their offices and looking at displays of digital characters." Discuss.
5. Research and then outline an information strategy for a child protection system for a large city, the war on drugs, the management of hazardous waste by the EPA, or the role of the FCC in the 1990s. Remember the three key questions you need to think through.
6. How does a DDS differ from an MIS?
7. "Managers need more ways to convey the images and impressions they carry inside of them. This explains the renewed interest in strategic vision, in culture, and in the roles of intuition and insight in management." Explain and discuss.
8. This chapter suggested that the computer revolution tends to make decision making more democratic. Is this a good state of affairs?
9. Do women really manage differently than men?

Nailing Down the Main Points

1. What really makes an agency successful probably has nothing to do with information technology (IT). Rather, organization and management are the decisive factors that determine success. Public administrators of course understand this. What they do not always understand is how information technology can significantly improve their agency's performance. IT allows us to do things that we could not have thought about a few years ago. Public administrators must translate this technological capability into value to the client, value to the citizen. Public administrators must move beyond looking at IT merely as a means to collect data on a historical basis, and they must understand information so that they can *act* on it for the present and the future.
2. Information systems process huge amounts of data and quickly transform them into high-quality information that is relevant to the needs of the administrator.

Computer-based information systems include transaction processing systems (TPSs), management information systems (MISs), and decision support systems (DSSs). TPSs are used at lower organizational levels; MISs provide information for middle managers; and DSSs help senior managers address more strategic questions.

3. Other new technologies being adopted by public organizations include artificial intelligence, electronic mail, facsimile machine, voice message systems, videoconferencing, electronic bulletin boards, and networking. Managers are often attracted to the latter technology by the promise of faster communication and greater efficiency. But, as suggested in point 1 above, the real potential of network communications has more to do with influencing the overall work environment and the capabilities of employees. Managers can use networks to foster *new* kinds of task structures and reporting relationships. They can use networks to change the old patterns of who talks to whom and who knows what. They can use this IT to empower employees.

4. Because we are becoming an information society, it is unlikely that information has ever been as critical a resource as it is today. The following simple diagram can help a public administrator who heads a subunit (SU) within an agency (A) manage his or her information more strategically:

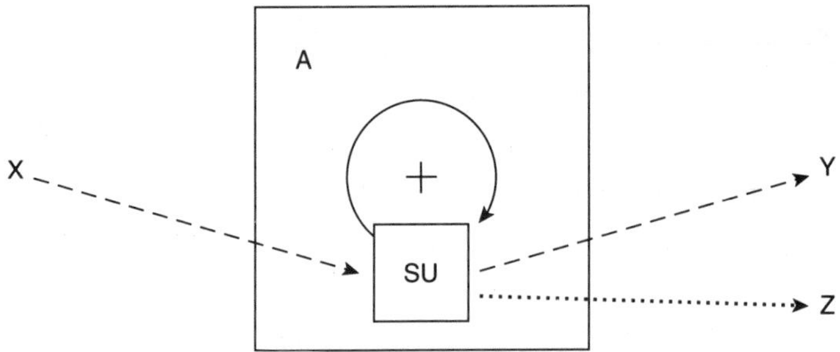

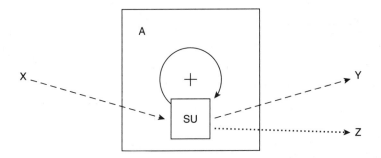

The first question to ask is, What information do I need to perform and accomplish my unit's mission? Some of that information might be external, as suggested by the dashed arrow from source X; but some information might be available within the agency untapped. The positive feedback loop represents an important aspect about information as a resource: Unlike other resources, it does not get used up; rather, it can grow—if properly managed—at an exponential rate. For example, if one combines certain information about metallurgy with information about wine presses, inks, and devices for stamping, one then knows how to build the printing press. If those four bits of information remain separate, however, the printing press remains a mystery. Finally, the two arrows going to X and Y suggest two questions for the manager of the subunit: What information do I have that should be disseminated to others, and What is the best way to package it?

5. Managers cannot just take a stodgy organization, hire smart people, buy shiny new IT, and expect good things to happen. Harnessing information capability requires managers to think hard about what kind of organization they want to lead and maybe even change significantly.

6. The choice facing tomorrow's public administrators is straightforward. They can retain the traditional preoccupation with authority and use IT to replace or control people. Or, they can put the role of authority in proper perspective and begin to provide their organizations with clear simple objectives that employees at all levels can translate into specific actions. They can then compare the results of these actions with expectations and provide feedback. They can acknowledge the power of this new technology to place vast amounts of useful information before all kinds of employees, allowing them to do their jobs better.

CASE 12.1

★★★★★★★★★★★★★★★★★★★★★★★★★★★★★★★★★★★

Madison's Quality and Productivity Campaign

Long appreciated in Japan but ignored in his own country, W. Edward Deming visited Madison, Wisconsin, in 1983, about the time his precepts about statistical process control and worker empowerment (see Exhibit 1) were being adopted at Ford and other U.S. companies. One of Deming's seminars so impressed then-mayor Joe Sensenbrener that he resolved to bring quality management to city government.

The city garage seemed a likely place to start, given a recent audit disclosing long delays in repair and major pieces of equipment unavailable for the many agencies that used the garage's fleet of cars and trucks. When Sensenbrener and his assistant arrived at the First Street Garage to investigate its problems, the manager and mechanics were surprised and doubtful. But by pledging his personal involvement and confirming the worker's critical role, the mayor got them to agree to form a team and gather data.

The team found that not having the right parts in stock caused many of their delays. The problem with stocking parts was that the city purchased many different makes and models of equipment each year. The reason for this bewildering variety of types, makes, and models of equipment was a policy that required the city to buy whatever vehicle had the lowest price on the day of the purchase. As one mechanic said:

It doesn't make any sense. When you look at all the equipment downtime, the warranty work that weak suppliers don't cover, the unreliability of cheaper machines, and the lower resale value, buying what's cheapest doesn't save us anything.

After checking with the city attorney, Sensenbrener and the team decided to rewrite the specifications so they included not only price but also warranty, ease of maintenance, availability of parts, and resale value. The new purchasing policy replaced a 24-step process with multiple levels of control with a 3-step process.

Employees were so delighted with this success that they began to research the possible savings of a preventive mainte-

EXHIBIT 1

Deming's 14 Points

1. *Create constancy of purpose for improvement of product and service.* Management must change from a preoccupation with the short run to building for the long run. This requires dedication to innovation in all areas to best meet the needs of citizens/clients.
2. *Adopt the new philosophy.* Americans have been too tolerant of poor performance and sullen service. We need a new philosophy in which mistakes and negativism are unacceptable.
3. *Cease dependence on mass inspection.* Inspection is equivalent to planning for defects; it comes too late, and it is ineffective and costly. Instead, processes must be improved.
4. *End the practice of awarding contracts on price tag alone.* Purchasing departments customarily operate on orders to seek the lowest-priced vendor. Frequently, this leads to supplies or services of low quality. Instead, they should seek the best quality and work to achieve it with a single supplier for any one item in a long-term relationship.
5. *Improve constantly and forever the system of operations and service.* Improvement is not a one-time effort. Management and employees are obligated to continually look for ways to reduce waste and improve quality.
6. *Institute modern methods of training on the job.* Too often, employees learn their jobs from other employees who were never trained properly. They are forced to follow unintelligible instructions. They cannot do their jobs because no one tells them how.
7. *Institute modern methods of leadership.* Lower-level managers must be empowered to inform upper management about conditions that need correction; once informed, management must take action. Barriers (such as reserved parking places for top management) that prevent employees from doing their jobs with pride must be removed.
8. *Drive out fear.* Many employees are afraid to ask questions or to take a position, even when they do not understand what the job is or what is right or wrong. People will continue to do things the wrong way or to not do them at all. The economic loss from fear is appalling. It is necessary for better quality and productivity that people feel secure.
9. *Break down barriers between staff areas.* Often staff areas—departments, units, and so on—are competing with each other or have goals that conflict. They do not work as a team so they can solve or foresee problems. Worse, one department's goals may cause trouble for another. Each discipline must stop optimizing its own work and instead work together as a team for the company as a whole. Multidisciplinary quality control circles can help improve design, service, quality, and costs.
10. *Eliminate slogans, exhortations, numerical goals, and targets for the work force.* These never helped anybody do a good job. Let people put up their own slogans. Although workers should not be given numerical goals, the organization itself must have a goal: never-ending improvement.
11. *Eliminate work standards and quotas.* Quotas focus on quantity, not quality. They are usually a guarantee of inefficiency and high cost. To hold a job, a person meets quotas at any cost, without regard to damage to the organization.
12. *Remove barriers to pride of workmanship.* People are eager to do a good job and distressed when they cannot. Too often, misguided managers, faulty equipment, and defective materials stand in the way. These barriers must be removed.
13. *Institute a vigorous program of education and training.* Because quality and productivity improvements change the number of people needed in some areas and the jobs required, people must be continually trained and retrained. All training must include basic statistical techniques.
14. *Create a structure in top management that will push every day on the above 13 points.*

NOTE: Deming's words, with minor modifications, are in italicized headings. The remainder of each paragraph paraphrases his discussions.

nance program. By riding with police on patrol, mechanics learned that the squad cars spent much more time at idling speeds than in the high-speed emergencies they had assumed and planned for in tuning the engines. In cooperation with other city departments, the mechanics developed new driver checklists for vehicle condition, maintenance schedules for each piece of equipment, and an overtime budget to cut downtime and ensure that preventive maintenance work was done. Average vehicle turnaround time dropped from nine days to three. For every $1.00 invested in preventive maintenance, Madison saved $7.15 in downtime.

These results encouraged Sensenbrener to look for managers and employees in other departments who had the imagination and motivation to be pioneers. Sensenbrener recalls:

Their most important characteristic, I found, regardless of political philosophy or training, was a strong ego: the capacity to take responsibility for risks, share credit for success, and keep one eye on the prize. We found enough of these people to begin a new round of experiments like our successful First Street prototype.

Among other things, workers began to get directly involved in choosing the most cost-effective tools and materials for their jobs. For example, city painters picked the most durable, long-lasting paints for city housing projects, and police officers chose the equipment they would be using every day in their patrol car "offices." But all selections had to be made on the basis of hard data.

The health department faced a different problem: how to give citizens quicker, better answers to their questions about clinics and programs. Employees began to sample and analyze the questions that were coming in; then, on the basis of that data, they set up briefings for phone receptionists so they could answer most questions directly. They also created a clear system of referrals for more complicated requests.

Madison's energy-resource recovery plant also formed a QP team (for quality and productivity). The plant converts solid waste into a fuel suitable for generating electricity. The mission of the team, which consisted of three workers and three managers, was to discover why it was taking garbage truck drivers up to one-and-one-half hours to enter the plant, dump their loads, complete their paperwork, and get back out again.

The solution seemed obvious: expand the plant's tipping platform (at a cost of several million dollars) to allow more than one truck at a time to empty its contents. But after attending eight full-day sessions on the mechanics of quality—including group dynamics, consensus decision making, and basic statistics—the team members wanted to base their decision on hard data. They spent four weeks logging drivers' activities. Their conclusion: Bottlenecks could be reduced if the plant cut down on inspections and paperwork and if half the trucks started work an hour earlier. These recommendations cut the average waiting time to 15 minutes. The city now picks up trash with 23 trucks, down from 26.

Perhaps the most celebrated example from Madison's QP campaign was the creation of an experimental police district. The police chief, David Couper, identified progressive officers interested in transforming the department and rebuilding community confidence. Together they created a police mission statement that made peacekeeping the department's primary role and put law enforcement second. In other words, the department deployed more of its resources to underlying causes of crime, interacted with schools and neighborhood organizations, developed relationships with minority and student leaders, and put a higher priority on outreach.

Couper and 50 police volunteers who

helped implement the mission statement believed that a decentralized police district with a neighborhood headquarters would lead to more effective peacekeeping by giving better service to residents and by encouraging officers to "adopt" the neighborhood and vice versa. Officers in the district elected their own captains and lieutenants, determined their own staffing and work schedules as a team, and networked with neighborhood associations to set law-enforcement priorities.

Soon residents in the Madison Experimental Police District were seeing their police on the streets, at neighborhood meetings, and at their doorsteps to interview them about their concerns. Home burglaries decreased 28 percent between 1986 and 1989, while the rest of the city saw a 15 percent increase.

Overtime in the experimental district was reduced to 200 hours, while overtime in other districts of comparable size was nearly 1000 hours. This savings was achieved after officers in the district ran a study of the kinds of calls that kept police on duty beyond their regular shifts. They discovered that a high percentage of such calls were not urgent, so they arranged with dispatchers to put these calls on a "B" list if they came in less than 45 minutes before the end of a shift. When new officers came on, they would take those calls first and attend to them at regular pay.

Eight years after Sensenbrener began his QP campaign, Madison still has an entrenched bureaucracy and much remains to be done. But his campaign did prove that quality management applies to the public sector as well as to the private sector.

Case Questions

1. Which of Deming's 14 points (Exhibit 1) do you see illustrated in this case?
2. What factors might make total quality management (TQM) harder to achieve in the public sector than in the private sector?
3. Why do you think the manager and the mechanics were "surprised and doubtful"?
4. What political or behavior factors are involved in successfully implementing a TQM program in an organization?
5. A term that appears several times in the exhibit is *productivity.* Earlier in this book, we defined productivity as the ratio of output to input. We also noted that it was synonymous with efficiency. How does the concept of quality relate to productivity?
6. What risks do you see in the police department's QP program that were not apparent in the other programs?

Case References

Ronald Henkoff, "Some Hope for Troubled Cities," *Fortune,* September 9, 1991; Joseph Sensenbrener, "Quality Comes to City Hall," *Harvard Business Review,* March–April 1991.

CASE 12.2

★★★★★★★★★★★★★★★★★★★★★★★★★★★★★★★★★★★★★★

A Call for Help

In September 1966, Mark Mechanic, the director of a university computer center in upstate New York, was working at his desk when the phone rang. On the other end was Paul Powers, an executive in charge of evaluation at the local United Way. After some initial pleasantries, Paul began to describe a problem he was facing.

Mark, I just came from a meeting with the directors of the various neighborhood agencies that we fund. They really unloaded on me. Paul Williams started complaining about the number of forms he has to fill out. He says he has to do ours, then fill out different forms for the Office of Economic Opportunity (OEO) and still different forms for his other funding sources. Some of the agencies have money from the Federation of Settlements and Neighborhood centers and some even have private sources. Anyway, once he started it, the thing really began to snowball. Everyone in the place jumped on the bandwagon. The only way I could restore order was to promise them that I would look into a consolidated information system.

At first the whole thing seemed like just another problem. But after thinking about it, I decided that they have given me a real opportunity. For years we have been trying to get good performance data. Here is a chance to do some real evaluation. The thought of comparing every center on the same set of objective measures interests me. It would finally be possible to base funding on performance. We would have the capacity to compile longitudinal data and measure changes over time. Everyone wins: they cut out paperwork, and we get real control.

I checked with OEO and some of the others. They know it will be expensive, but they all are interested. The question is how to develop a system? We figured you are the best man we could contact for advice. You know some of their problems. What do you say? Can you help us out?

Mark Mechanic indicated that he was very interested. A week later, he had his first meeting with the directors of eight neighborhood centers and executives from three funding agencies. The directors all had similar problems. Most of their agencies had evolved from local settlement houses to neighborhood centers that provided a number of services to local residents. Services varied widely but usually included housing, employment, recreation, food, clothing, child care, health services, and referrals and transportation to other agencies. Some centers had as few as five caseworkers; other centers had as many as 30. Each had its own unique variety of funding sources, and each was inundated with paperwork.

During the discussion of a potential information system, Mechanic explained what might be done to reduce the paperwork. He pointed out that the current narrative reports written by the caseworkers and the wide variety of forms could be reduced to several standardized forms. From the information on the standardized forms, the computer could produce summaries that would eliminate 80 percent of the paperwork that the directors were doing. The presentation generated considerable enthusiasm, and it was agreed that Mechanic's staff would begin to wade through the numerous forms used in each of the agencies.

After three months, the computer staff had conducted over 100 interviews with people from all levels of the eight agencies and had gathered 190 forms that were currently in use. For the next two months, they sorted and analyzed the forms. By the end of five months, the computer staff members felt that they had a rough understanding of information needs and were ready to begin designing a basic set of forms. In order to start that process, they scheduled interviews with each of the eight directors. The purpose of the interviews was to present their initial conclusions and to determine the exact information needs of the directors. By the end of another month, the directors each had been interviewed at least twice. Shortly thereafter, Mechanic met with the members of his staff. At one point in the meeting, the following discussion took place.

MECHANIC: *"Up until now you have all been enthusiastic. All of a sudden you seem discouraged. What happened?"*

BILL MEADOWS (project director): *"Mark, the directors of the centers are idiots. They don't understand the first thing about information systems."*

MECHANIC *"Idiots! What do you mean?"*

MEADOWS *"We go in and ask them what information they need. They get a shocked look on their face, like they never had thought of such a question. They hem and haw. We try a different tack and ask them what decisions they have to make. Again they are shocked. They can't even tell us what decisions they have to make. They have no vision of what an information system is or what it might do for them. No matter how many times we go back, they still cannot deal with the questions we need answered. Whenever we are around the directors disappear."*

MECHANIC: *"If they disappear, what do you do?"*

MEADOWS: *"Well, it is sort of a tacit agreement. We don't bother them with questions and they don't bother us with objections. We show them the forms and they look at them and say O.K."*

Case Questions

1. Do the United Way agencies really need a computer-based information system? Of the various types of information technology discussed in this chapter, what would you recommend?
2. What suggestions would you make to Bill Meadows regarding the design and implementation of the information system?

Case Reference

Robert E. Quinn, "Computers, People, and the Delivery of Services: How to Manage the Information System," in John E. Dittrich and Robert A. Zawacki, eds., *People & Organizations* (Plano, Texas: Business Publications, 1985), pp. 226–28.

CASE 12.3

★★★★★★★★★★★★★★★★★★★★★★★★★★★★★★★★★★★

Using Tacit Knowledge

It is your second year as a mid-level manager in a state agency for transportation. You head a department of about thirty people. The evaluation of your first year on the job has been generally favorable. Performance ratings for your department are at least as good as they were before you took over, perhaps even a little better. You have two assistants. One is quite capable; the other just seems to go through the motions and is of little real help.

Although you are well liked, you believe that in the eyes of your superiors there is little to distinguish you from the nine other managers at a comparable level in the company.

Your goal is rapid promotion to the top of the agency.

Case Questions

1. The following is a list of things you are considering doing in the next two months. You obviously cannot do them all. Rate the importance of each by its priority as a means of reaching your goal:
    - ____ a. Participate in a series of panel discussions to be shown on the local public television station.
    - ____ b. Find ways to make sure your superiors are aware of your important accomplishments.

____ c. As a means of being noticed, propose a solution to a problem outside the scope of your immediate department that you would be willing to take charge of.

____ d. When making decisions, give a great deal of weight to the way your superior likes things to be done.

____ e. Accept a friend's invitation to join the exclusive country club that many higher-level executives belong to.

2. The agency has sent you to a university to recruit and interview potential trainees for management positions. Rate the importance of the following student characteristics by the extent to which they lead to later success in business:

____ a. ability to set priorities according to the importance of your task

____ b. motivation

____ c. ability to follow through and bring tasks to completion

____ d. ability to promote your ideas and to convince others of the worth of your work

____ e. the need to win at everything, no matter what the cost.

3. A number of factors enter into the establishment of a good reputation in government as a manager. Consider the following factors and rate their importance:

____ a. critical thinking ability

____ b. speaking ability

____ c. extent of college education and the prestige of the school attended

____ d. no hesitancy to take extraordinarily risky courses of action

____ e. a keen sense of what superiors can be sold on.

4. Rate the following strategies of working according to how important you believe them to be for doing well at the day-to-day work of a business manager:

____ a. Think in terms of tasks accomplished rather than hours spent working.

____ b. Be in charge of all phases of every task or project you are involved with.

____ c. Use a daily list of goals arranged according to your priorities.

____ d. Carefully consider the optimal strategy before beginning a task.

____ e. Reward yourself upon completion of important tasks.

5. You are looking for several new projects to tackle. You have a list of possible projects and desire to pick the best two or three. Rate the importance of the following considerations when selecting projects:

____ a. The project should prove to be fun.

____ b. The project should attract the attention of the local media.

____ c. The project is of special importance to me personally.

____ d. The risk of making a mistake is virtually nonexistent.

____ e. The project will require working directly with several senior executives.

Case Reference

Adapted with minor modifications from *The Triarchic Mind* by Robert J. Sternberg. Copyright © 1988 by Robert J. Sternberg. Used by permission of Viking Penguin, a division of Penguin Books USA Inc.

APPENDIX

Career Management

The literature of public administration gives much attention to motivating employees in order that they might achieve higher levels of performance. The literature also gives some attention to allocating monetary resources in an efficient, effective, and responsible manner. But on the question of how the administrator should manage himself or herself, the literature is as silent as snow.

One of the keys to increasing one's present performance and developing one's future career is knowing how to best utilize one's time. Therefore, this section examines both short-term and long-term problems of time management. It will discuss short-run causes of time waste and methods for effective time utilization. It will also discuss a longer-term condition that can waste time. That condition is stress. Finally, it will discuss how public administrators can become architects of their own achievements, provided that they have a time perspective that allows for maturation and growth.

Managing Short-Term Time

Categorizing Time Usage

A number of management advisors recommend that their clients keep a log of how they spend their time. After a week or so, one can then draw a profile of how his or her time has been spent. Invariably, the exercise provides a mild shock. Most administrators find that they spend far more time on trivialities or, at least, peripheral activities than they imagined. Conversely, they spend far *less* time on the truly important activities—that is, on the activities that are *directly* related to the accomplishment of the organization's prime mission.

The effective administrators will therefore group their daily and weekly activities according to importance. Here is one possible categorization:

Important and urgent.

Important but not urgent.

Urgent but not important.

Busywork.

Wasted time.

Needless to say, these administrators try to work on the things that matter most.

Effective administrators, in fact, almost define a good year, week, or day in terms of the objectives they want to accomplish, and they allocate their time accordingly.

In doing this, they try to work on the most difficult or unpleasant tasks at the time of the day when they are freshest and most creative. For many people, this period is in the early morning. As Benjamin Franklin put it, "Plough deep while sluggards sleep."

In allocating their time, effective administrators try to bear in mind the principle of concentration. This principle says that similar activities should be grouped together (e.g., make all your phone calls at the same time). It further says that progress on difficult tasks requires uninterrupted chunks of time.

How does a lower-level administrator avoid interruptions for one- or two-hour periods? Well, arriving early at the office is one way. While not ideal, it is probably better than carrying work home at night and on weekends. Spending the lunch hour in the office is another tactic that can be used on occasion. Arranging with the supervisor to work one afternoon a week at home is also a possibility. Perhaps the most basic tactic is simply to know how to handle interruptions. Phone calls can be screened. (For example: "Ms. Peterson is busy right now, but I can interrupt her if you wish.") If one does not have the luxury of a secretary or an answering machine to do the screening, then one can at least minimize the length of the interruption. (For example, begin by cordially asking the caller, "What can I do for you?") Of course, administrators should also try to develop nonintrusive methods for dealing with others.

Closely linked to the principle of concentration is the so-called Pareto rule: Significant items in a group constitute a small part of the total group.* Schematically the rule looks like this:

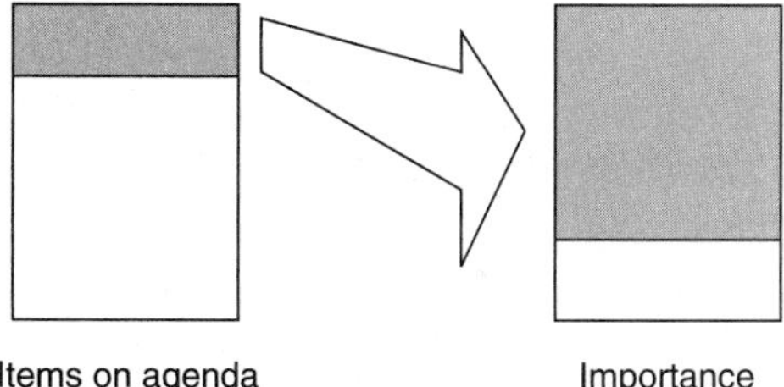

The rule tells us that, on any list of items, the "vital few," which are seldom more than 20 percent of the total number, can account for 80 percent of the total value or cost. The rule seems to apply (and do not ask me why) across a wide range of phenomena. Twenty percent of an agency's clients account for 80 percent of the agency

* Named after Vilfredo Pareto (1848–1923), the Italian economist and sociologist.

work hours. Twenty percent of an agency's programs account for 80 percent of its revenue. Twenty percent of an agency's employees account for 80 percent of total sick time. Twenty percent of all callers account for 80 percent of total phone calls. Twenty percent of a political candidate's speaking engagements account for 80 percent of his or her public exposure.

Handling Correspondence and Meetings

Incoming mail should be screened and sorted. Some can be thrown away unopened; second- and third-class mail can be dumped in a pouch for opening and reading when one's energy level is low; the rest should be opened and handled immediately. (A good rule is to handle each letter only once.) If possible, write a reply on the letter itself, making a copy for your files and returning the original with your note at the bottom.

For administrators who must answer each letter every day, two items are extremely valuable. One is a dictating machine. While a dictated message may lack some of the polish of a drafted reply, the time saved in most cases is well justified.

On longer terms, the administrator may want to jot down an outline to dictate from. Like the dictating machine, boilerplates or model letters are useful. For example, many agencies find that the vast majority of inquiries they receive fall into a dozen or so categories. Having a set of boilerplate letters handy can help the administrator avoid drafting new replies each time.

Meetings are a necessary part of public administration. But if allowed to grow unattended, they can spread like crabgrass and choke an agency. A good way to combat that danger is to write out notes on the purpose of the meeting, on what is to be accomplished, on what each attendant might contribute, and on whether other alternatives for communication are possible.

Joseph D. Cooper (1971:279–80) recommends the following list of legitimate reasons for calling a meeting:

1. *The matter concerns some important change from existing practice. It should have an important bearing on operations or require* collective *judgments in reaching a position.*

2. *A variety of* interacting *knowledges, opinions, and judgments must be brought to bear, especially when new ideas, solutions, and approaches are needed.*

3. *Time is not available for the handling of the matter step by step, referral by referral, through ordinary administrative channels. The meeting is expected to bring all relevant interests together at the same time to permit a timely decision to be made.*

4. *An excuse is needed to take a matter out of ordinary administrative channels where it has languished.*

5. *The decisions reached are more likely to be carried out if those affected participate in making them.*

(From The Wall Street Journal, *with permission of Cartoon Features Syndicate.)*

6. *The matter calls for judgment of a collective nature in an area in which the group called together has had prior experience, especially when intangibles are involved.*
7. *Action assignments on decisions to be reached must be clarified for the benefit of each participant to assure properly coordinated action.*
8. *The discussions have a training value for some participants in terms of subject matter or opportunities to observe how people interact and reach judgments.*

Before the meeting, the convenors should publish an agenda of the issues to be dealt with and distribute any relevant printed matter in advance. The meeting should be started on time, unless the convenor wants to punish those who came on time and reward those who came late. Group members will work more efficiently if the ending time is stated clearly at the outset. At the end of the meeting, the convenors should summarize what was covered and agreed to; then they should follow up with a memo.

Delegation

While there are certain duties that should not be delegated, many can be; for example, fact-finding prior to a decision, finding someone to represent you at meetings, and doing tasks that will help develop subordinates through exposure to new problems. Administrators should delegate anything another can do better, sooner, or cheaper—and reward subordinates for taking initiative.

Administrators must also learn to say no: They must avoid taking on so many extra tasks that they become too bogged down to have time left for the truly important tasks. Similarly, they must avoid letting certain subordinates bring them into the solution of a problem or the performance of a task that is quite properly the province of the subordinate. (In other words, do not let subordinates put the monkey on your back.)

The Habit of Work

The work *habit* has a generally bad connotation. This is unfortunate, for it blinds us to the fact that there are good habits. Effective administrators develop the habit of making themselves work. Each time they take on an unpleasant task first, avoid detours, or decide a trifle quickly, they are reinforcing good work habits. They learned through experience the Virgilian motto: "Things live by moving, and gain strength as they go."

Like world-class runners, effective administrators know that hitting one's stride is important. However, tempo and pace do not mean driving yourself beyond your capacities. To be sure, under the stress of external conditions, you may be compelled to overextend yourself. But it is doubtful that the result will be optimal performance. In any event it is certainly not a level of performance that can be maintained over a lifetime.

Managing Long-Term Conditions That Waste Time

Running a small city in the United States consists not only of attending Rotary luncheons and Boy Scout weiner roasts. In fact, small town mayors or city managers face many of the crises that their big city counterparts have: threatened nuclear disaster for the mayor of Harrisburg, Pennsylvania; armed Ku Klux Klan on the rampage in Decatur, Alabama; and serious flooding in Meridian, Mississippi. So it is not surprising that when they attend the annual meeting of the U.S. Conference of Mayors, in addition to sharing wisdom on drafting municipal budgets and motivating employees, they also want to learn how to cope with stress.

What Is Stress?

Technically speaking, stress is the body's response to any demand made on it. Psychologists call the demand the "stressor." A stressor can take many forms—dealing with red tape; negotiating with a union; meeting a project deadline; getting a promotion, a demotion, a transfer, or a divorce; and so on.

These stressors affect the body's chemistry and its nervous and hormonal systems. If unchecked, the pressures can lead to some real time wastes such as heart attacks, high blood pressure, strokes, neuroses, depression, backaches, headaches, and ulcers. Stress and its related disorders probably cost the government several million dollars a year by cutting productivity, ending careers early, causing absenteeism, and

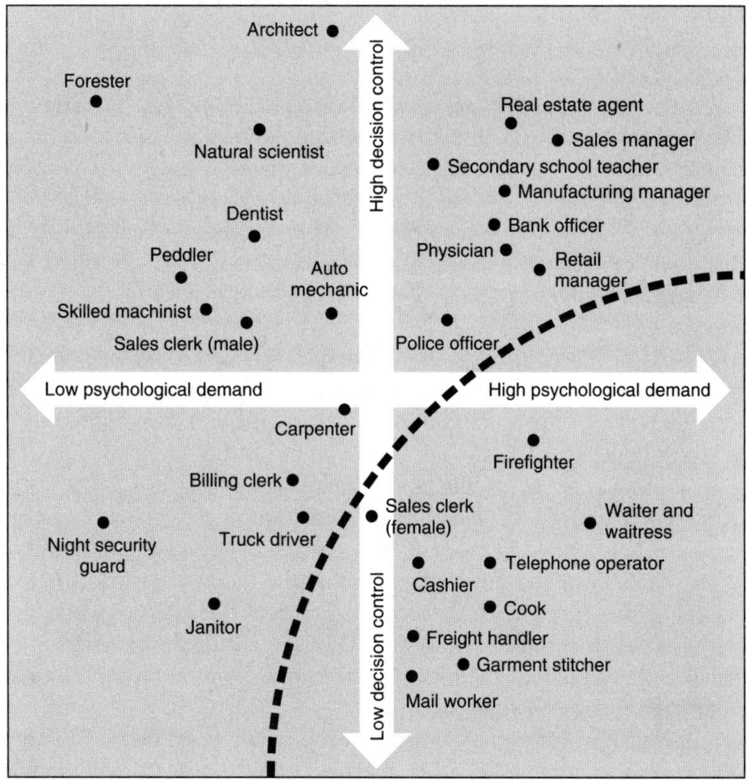

FIGURE A-1
Stress at Work
SOURCE: R. A. Karasek et al., *Social Science Medicine,* March 1982.

prompting alcohol and drug abuse. Of course, some jobs tend to be more stressful than others.

Recent research suggests that workers whose jobs involve high stress but little decision making are more subject to cardiovascular illness. Jobs to the right of the curve in Figure A-1 are among the top 25 percent in risk. Machine-paced assembly line workers were from 70 percent to 200 percent more likely to develop heart disease than were low-level managerial personnel.

Methods for Coping with Stress

A number of techniques are available to break the pattern of tension. Each administrator must pick his or her own method or combination of methods.

Many experts think that transcendental meditation, a simplification of yoga, is the best technique with which to begin. One chooses a target for concentration known as a mantra (usually a word) and meditates sitting in a relaxed position with eyes closed. This quietude allows the mind to rest and clear itself of fears and anxieties.

According to Barrie Greiff, a psychiatrist on the staff of Harvard Business School, "The trick is to do TM consistently and learn to enjoy it" (quoted in *Business Week,* August 23, 1976).

Herbert Benson in his *Relaxation Response* (1975) suggests a variation of the TM technique that requires no formal instruction. According to Benson, a professor of medicine at Harvard, one can use "a word, a sound, a prayer, or an object as a focal point for concentration" to evoke a quieting effect.

One of the newer routes is biofeedback. This technique attempts to enhance an individual's voluntary control over significant bodily functions with the aid of an electronic instrument. Biofeedback has been reported effective in the treatment of migraines.

Finally, physical exercise—from walking to marathon running—can provide some release from tension. Because the mind and body are interrelated, plain physical work affects the state of the mind and lowers heart rate and blood pressure.

The preceding techniques all concentrate on increasing one's tolerance for stress. But one may also need to change the circumstances causing stress. Thus, if something at work does not work, fix it. Time management, such as discussed earlier in this section, can also help one gain inner control on the job. Focusing only on what one can do, doing one's best, and not worrying about the outcome (when it is too late to matter) can all help reduce stress. Of course, if none of these tactics work, the easiest thing to do is avoid the problem altogether: Quit the job or go on vacation.

Whatever the technique employed, the objective is not to totally eliminate stress but to optimize it.

Medical research finds stress productive up to a certain point. This holds true not only for administrators but also for managers of all kinds. "It's important to me to be in a high-pressure environment," Thomas W. Landry, the Dallas Cowboys coach, says. When the pressure is off, "I'm already looking forward to the next time" (quoted in *Business Week,* April 30, 1979). Landry has flourished under the stress of professional football coaching for more than 20 years.

The lesson is clear: Each administrator needs to balance the value and the dangers of stress for himself or herself (see Figure A-2).

Transcending Time and Moving Up the Career Ladder

Few people who spend any time in the world of administration hold the belief that promotion always goes to the best and the brightest. Other variables are also involved—especially a clear sense of where one wants to go, a capacity to learn from mistakes (while not worrying about them), and an ability to grow and broaden oneself intellectually.

Several brilliant professors were surprised to learn that a less talented colleague had been made assistant president of their university. The man was not especially gifted or even well liked, but he had a clear sense of where he wanted to go (namely,

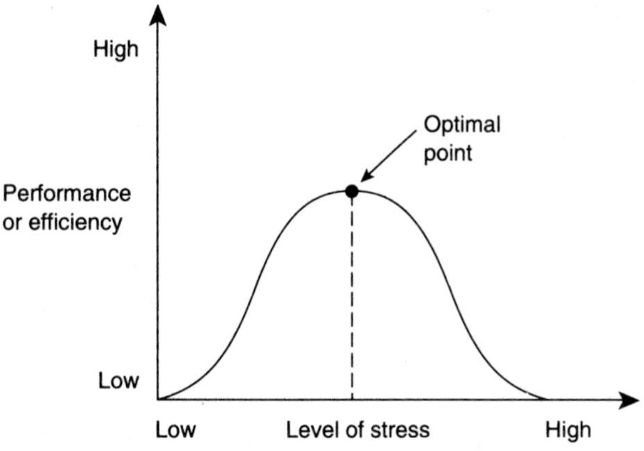

FIGURE A-2

Yerkes-Dodson Law

In 1908, Robert M. Yerkes and John D. Dodson demonstrated that as stress increases, so do efficiency and performance. But this relationship persists only to a certain level, then deleterious effects begin to appear.

SOURCE: Adapted from H. Benson and R. L. Allen, How Much Stress Is Too Much? *Harvard Business Review,* September–October, 1980.

high in academic administration). Consequently he devoted much of his free time to work on committees chaired by the president, to observe and read about how a university president's job was handled, and to help the president whenever he could. In time, he became a sort of unofficial aide to the president. So when the board of trustees created the new position of assistant president, he was the obvious choice.

In addition to knowing where one wants to go, moving up the career ladder involves several other things.

Avoiding Obsolescence

Elsewhere I have written about the accelerating obsolescence of a master's degree in business administration (see Starling, 1988:4–7). This point is equally valid for a degree in public administration. Some of what a student is taught today will not be taught five years from today. Throughout this century, and especially since World War II, the rate at which knowledge of administration becomes obsolete has increased. Thus, the pressure on today's student to stay current after leaving the university is greater than ever. In my estimation, an administrator who tries to operate only on the skills developed at school will cease to advance in about 12 years.

To combat this creeping obsolescence, several strategies are available. One can read broadly as well as stay up with one's own specialty. One can seek new experiences and assignments within the organization. One can list his or her assumptions about the best way a certain task should be performed. And, of course, one should take advantage of the organizational training programs.

Developing an Executive Attitude

The best executives, public and private, all share certain characteristics: a strong desire for personal achievement; a respect for authority (which is just a way of saying that they are good followers); a decisiveness (which means they are not afraid to make decisions); courage of their convictions; an ability to view critically their own accomplishments; and maturity (which means they realize that the world was not put here solely for the purpose of making them happy).

To this list of characteristics others might be added: Throughout their careers, the best executives learn from their own supervisors. They do this by observation, but they also do it by asking questions, since most top managers are delighted and even flattered to talk about how they got where they are and how they operate. And the best executives are aware that, for better or worse, politics *does* matter (see box).

For women who enter the administrative world, this learning process is especially important. Because that world is still governed by the male lifestyle, career-oriented women need to learn the subliminal rules of the game. Margaret Hennig and Anne Jardim (1977) offer some advice that amounts to learning to play the game the way men do:

- Define your goals: Analyze the costs and rewards of a management career. What do you really want 5, 10, and 20 years from now? Set specific targets.
- Acquire technical competence, but beware of overinvesting in a specialty: Be ready for a broader perspective.
- Look for someone in a higher management position who will act as your mentor and coach. Expand your horizons and make yourself visible to other departments.
- Be prepared to take risks and sometimes to fail, but stay on the lookout for opportunities to prove your managerial skills.

To summarize this appendix is a difficult but necessary task. When pressed to nail their subject down to its quintessence, some economists have been known to reply, "TINSTAAFL" (there is no such thing as a free lunch). Can students of organizational behavior do the same? I know of no instances. But I think if I were so pressed, and free to let my bias come into play, I would look to leadership as the key to motivation. Now, by leadership I do not necessarily mean the kind of star quality recorded in the mass media, though it certainly has a measure of greatness in it. And, while I cannot describe it in eight words, I can come close by quoting the sixth century B.C. Chinese philosopher Lao-tzu: "Of a good leader . . . When his work is done . . . They will all say, 'We did this ourselves.' "

Political Dos and Don'ts for Moving Up the Career Ladder

Do

- Look at the downside of linking up with powerful factions.
- Let friends offer advice about political problems.
- Speak up to your boss if it means keeping peer respect.
- Discern what your boss wants in return for a raise or promotion.
- Establish your walkaway point—and stick to it.
- Admit your mistakes before the boss discovers them himself.

Don't

- Assume your boss always has your best interests at heart.
- Get involved in a showdown you are pretty sure to lose.
- Try to imitate the social graces of a smooth rival.
- Accept blindly anyone's claim that he or she is the boss's friend.
- Talk about things you are not officially supposed to know.
- Respond in kind to smear campaigns—they can backfire.
- Be a corporate loner. You do need friends to get ahead.

SOURCE: R. Bell, *You Can Win at Office Politics (New York: Times Books, 1984).*

Bibliography

Acheson, D. 1959. Thoughts about thoughts in high places. *New York Times Magazine,* October 11.

Ackoff, R. 1967. *Art of problem solving* (New York: John Wiley & Sons).

Agranoff, R. 1989. Managing intergovernmental process. In J. L. Perry (Ed.), *Handbook of public administration.* San Francisco: Jossey-Bass.

Allison, G. 1971. *Essence of decision.* Boston: Little, Brown.

Ambrose, S. E. 1984. *Eisenhower: The president.* New York: Simon & Schuster.

Anderson, J. E. 1990. *Public policy making.* New York: Houghton Mifflin.

Anthony, R. N., and Herzlinger, R. E. 1980. *Management control in nonprofit organizations.* Homewood, Ill.: Richard D. Irwin.

Austern, D. T., et al. 1978. *Maintaining municipal integrity.* Washington, D.C.: U.S. Department of Justice.

Ayres, B. D. 1983. A new breed of diplomat. *New York Times Magazine,* September 11.

Baker, R. J. S. 1972. *Administrative theory and public administration.* London: Hutchinson University Library.

Bardach, E. 1977. *The implementation game.* Cambridge, Mass.: MIT Press.

Barnard, C. I. 1938. *The function of the executive.* Cambridge, Mass.: Harvard University Press.

Baron, R. 1990. Countering the Effects of Destructive Criticism. *Journal of Applied Psychology,* 235–247.

Bass, B. M. 1990. *Handbook of leadership.* New York: Free Press.

Bauer, R. A. (Ed.). 1966. *Social indicators.* Cambridge, Mass.: MIT Press.

Bazerman, M. H. 1986. *Judgment in managerial decision making.* New York: John Wiley & Sons.

Behn, R. D. 1978. Terminating public policies. *The Wall Street Journal,* October 16.

Benson, H. 1975. *The relaxation response.* New York: Morrow.

Bernstein, P. W. 1984. What's behind the spare parts follies? *Fortune,* October 29.

Bok, S. 1978. *Lying: moral choice in public and private life.* New York: Pantheon.

Bolt, R. 1962. *A man for all seasons.* New York: Vintage Books.

Bonds, R. 1983. *The U.S. war machine: An encyclopedia of American military equipment and strategy.* New York: Crown.

Bonnen, J. T. 1969. The absence of knowledge of distributional impacts. In Joint Economic Committee, *The analysis and evaluation of public expenditure.* Washington, D.C.: U.S. GPO.

Bork, R. H. 1990. *The tempting of America: The political seduction of the law.* New York: Simon & Schuster.

Boulding, K. E. 1950. General systems theory: The skeleton of a science. *Management Science,* vol 2.

Bowers, D. G. 1964. Self-esteem and supervision. *Personnel Administration,* July–August.

Boyatzis, R. 1982. *The competent manager: A model of effective performance.* New York: John Wiley & Sons.

Boyer, W. W. 1964. *Bureaucracy on trial: Policy making by government agencies.* Indianapolis: Bobbs-Merrill.

Bozeman, B., and Straussman, J. D. 1990. *Public management strategies.* San Francisco: Jossey-Bass.

Brady, R. 1973. MBO goes to work in the public sector. *Harvard Business Review,* March–April.

Brown, B., and Grotberg, E. 1980. *Head Start.* Washington, D.C.: U.S. GPO.

Burns, J. M. 1978. *Leadership* (New York: Harper & Row).

Byham, W. C., and Wettengel, C. 1974. Assessment centers for supervisors and managers. *Public Personnel Management,* September–October.

Caldwell, L. K. 1972. Environmental quality as an administrative problem. In *The Annals.* Philadelphia: American Academy of Political and Social Science.

Cartwright, D. (Ed.). 1962. *Group dynamics: Research and theory.* Evanston, Ill.: Row & Peterson.

Cervantes, A. J. 1973. Memories of a businessman-mayor. *Business Week,* December 8.

Cetron, M., and Davies, O. 1991. *Crystal globe.* New York: St. Martin's Press.

Chase, G. 1984. *Bromides for public managers,* Case N16-84-586. Cambridge, Mass.: Kennedy School of Government.

Christensen, C. M. 1983. "Bureaucrat" need not be a dirty word. *The Wall Street Journal,* November 7.

Churchill, W. S. 1959. *Memoirs.* Boston: Houghton-Mifflin.

Churchman, C. W. 1968. *Challenge to reason.* New York: McGraw-Hill.

———. 1971. *The design of inquiring systems.* New York: Basic Books.

Clarke, A. C. 1963. *Profiles of the future.* New York: Harper & Row.

Cleveland, H. 1972. *The future executive.* New York: Harper & Row.

———. 1975. How do you get everybody in on the act and still get some action? *Public Management,* June.

Coates, J. F. 1971. Technology assessment. *Futurist,* December.

Cohen, S. 1988. *The effective public manager.* San Francisco: Jossey-Bass.

Commoner, B. 1971. *The closing circle.* New York: Alfred A. Knopf.

Cook, T. J., and Scioli, F. P. 1972. A research strategy for analyzing the impact of public policy. *Administrative Science Quarterly,* September.

Cooper, J. D. 1971. *How to get more done in less time.* New York: Doubleday.

Cutlip, S. M., and Center, A. H. 1982. *Effective public relations.* Englewood Cliffs, N.J.: Prentice-Hall.

Danziger, J. N. 1977. Computers, local governments, and the litany of EDP. *Public Administration Review,* January–February.

Davidson, B., and Davies, S. 1991. *2020 vision: Winning in the information economy.* New York: Simon & Schuster.

Dickinson, P. 1978. *The official rules.* New York: Dell.

Doig, J. W., and Hargrove, E. C. 1990. *Leadership and innovation: Entrepreneurs in government.* Baltimore, Md.: Johns Hopkins University Press.

Dostoyevsky, F. 1960. Notes from the underground. In *Three short novels of Dostoyevsky.* Translated by Constance Garnett. New York: Doubleday.

Downs, A. 1967. *Inside bureaucracy.* Boston: Little, Brown.

Draper, F. D., and Pitsvada, B. T. 1981. ZBB—looking back after ten years. *Public Administration Review,* January–February.

Drucker, P. F. 1966. *The effective executive.* New York: Harper & Row.

———. 1973. *Management: tasks, responsibilities, practices.* New York: Harper & Row.

———. 1989. *The new realities.* New York: Harper & Row.

Due, J. F., and Friedlaender, A. F. 1973.

Government finance. Homewood, Ill.: Richard D. Irwin.

Edwards, II, G. C. 1980. *Implementary public policy.* Washington, D.C.: Congressional Quarterly Press.

Evans, S. M., and Nelson, B. J. 1989. *Wage justice: Comparable worth and the paradox of technocratic reform.* Chicago: University of Chicago Press.

Falvey, J. 1989. Deaf, dumb and blind at the helm. *The Wall Street Journal,* April 10.

Fein, B. 1986. What ever became of the new federalism? *Houston Chronicle,* February 26.

Fierman, J. 1990. Do women manage differently? *Fortune,* December 17.

Fink, T. 1989. Need neighborhood services? Try hiring the neighbors. *Governing,* October.

Fitch, L. G. 1974. Increasing the role of the private sector in providing public services. In W. D. Hawley and D. Rogers (Eds.). *Improving the quality of urban management.* Beverly Hills, Calif.: Sage Publications.

Florestano, P. S. 1981. Revenue-raising limitations on local government. *Public Administration Review,* 1981.

Fowles, A. M. 1974. Public information. In S. P. Powers et al. (Eds.). *Developing the municipal organization.* Washington, D.C.: ICMA.

Franke, R. H., and Kaul, J. D. 1978. Hawthorne experiment—First statistical interpretation. *American Sociological Review,* October.

Frankl, V. 1984. *The unheard cry for meaning.* New York: Washington Square.

Fulton, W. 1989. Visionaries, deal makers, incrementalists: The divided world of urban planning. *Governing,* June.

Garreau, J. 1991. *Edge City.* New York: Doubleday.

Gellerman, S. W. 1963. *Motivation and productivity.* New York: American Management Association.

Gerth, H. H., and Mills, C. W. (Eds.). 1946. *From Max Weber: Essays in sociology.* New York: Oxford University Press.

Gieringer, D. H. 1985. The FDA's bad medicine. *Policy Review,* Winter.

Gilbert, C. E. 1959. The framework of administrative responsibility. *Journal of Politics,* May.

Gilder, G. 1981. *Wealth and poverty.* New York: Basic Books.

Ginzberg, E., and Vojta, G. J. 1981. The service economy in the U.S. economy. *Scientific American,* March.

Gore, A. 1991. Infrastructure for the global village. *Scientific American,* September.

Greenberg, D. S. 1967. *The politics of pure science.* New York: New American Library.

Greider, W. 1989. *Secrets of the temple: How the federal reserve runs the country.* New York: Touchstone Books.

Grodzins, M., and Elazar, D. J. 1966. *The American system.* Chicago: Rand McNally.

Gross, B. M. 1968. *Organizations and their managing.* New York: Free Press.

Grosse, R. N. 1969. Problems of resource allocation in health. In U.S. Congress, Joint Economic Committee, *The analysis and evaluation of public expenditures.* Washington, D.C.: U.S. GPO.

Grove, A. 1983. *High-output management.* New York: Random House.

Gurwitt, R. 1991. The decision machine. *Governing,* May.

Guzzo, R. A. 1982. *Improving group decision making in organizations.* New York: Academic Press.

Gwertzman, B. 1983. The Shultz method. *New York Times Magazine,* January 2.

Halberstam, D. 1969. *The best and the brightest.* Greenwich, Conn.: Fawcett Crest Books.

Hales, C. P. 1986. What do managers do? A critical review of the evidence. *Journal of Management Studies,* 23.

Hall, T. 1976. How cultures collide. *Psychology Today,* July.

Hatry, H. P., Winnie, R. E., and Fisk, D. M. 1973. *Practical program evaluation for state and local government officials.* Washington, D.C.: Urban Institute.

Helmer, O. 1968. *Report on the future of the future—state-of-the-union reports,* Report R-14. Middleton, Conn.: Institute for the Future.

Hennig, M., and Jardim, A. 1977. *Managerial woman.* New York: Anchor.

Herbers, J. 1989. 17th-century counties struggle to cope with 20th-century problems. *Governing,* May.

Herzberg, F., et al. 1959. *The motivation to work.* New York: John Wiley & Sons.

Herzlinger, R. E. 1979. Managing the finances of nonprofit organization. *California Management Review,* Spring.

Hitch, C. J. 1960. *On the choice of objectives in systems studies.* Santa Monica, Calif.: Rand.

Hofstadter, R. 1948. *The American political tradition.* New York: Alfred A. Knopf.

Hoos, I. R. 1973. Systems technique for managing society: A critique. *Public Administration Review,* March–April.

Howitt, H. M. 1984. *Managing federalism: Studies in intergovernmental relations.* Washington, D.C.: CQ Press.

Huntington, S. P. 1952. The marasmus of the ICC: The commission, the railroads, and the public interest. *The Yale Law Journal,* April.

Hymowitz, C. 1989. Day in the life of tomorrow's manager. *The Wall Street Journal,* March 20.

Imai, M. 1988. *Kaizen.* New York: Random House.

Jacobson, G., and Hillkirk, J. 1986. *Xerox: American samurai.* New York: Macmillan.

Jacques, E. 1970. *Work, creativity, and social justice.* New York: International University Press.

———. 1979. Taking time seriously in evaluating jobs. *Harvard Business Review,* September–October.

James, W. 1952. *Principles of psychology.* Chicago: Encyclopaedia Britannica.

Janis, I. L. 1971. Groupthink. *Psychology Today.* November.

Jantsch, E. 1967. *Technology forecasting in perspective.* Paris: OECD.

Jennings, E. E. 1961. The anatomy of leadership. *Management of Personnel Quarterly,* Autumn.

Jones, S. R. G. 1990. Worker interdependence and output: The Hawthorne studies reevaluated. *American Sociological Review,* April.

Judis, J. B. 1988. Mission impossible: The postal service struggles with old problems, new competition—and the public. *New York Times Magazine,* September 25.

Kahneman, D., and Tversky, A. 1979. Intuitive prediction: Biases and corrective procedures. *Management Science,* 12.

Kanter, R. M. 1989. *When giants learn to dance.* New York: Simon & Schuster.

Karasek, R. A., et al. 1982. *Social Science Medicine,* March.

Karr, A. 1975. The "wild man" of transportation. *The Wall Street Journal,* October 27.

Katz, D., and Kahn, R. L. 1966. *The social psychology of organizations.* New York: John Wiley & Sons.

Kaufman, H. 1960. *The forest ranger: A study of administrative behavior.* Baltimore, Md.: Johns Hopkins University Press.

———. 1981. *Administrative behavior of federal bureau chiefs.* Washington, D.C.: Brookings Institution.

Kaufmann, W. 1973. *Without guilt and justice.* New York: Peter H. Wyden.

Kennedy, J. F. 1956. *Profiles in courage.* New York: Harper & Row.

Kissinger, H. 1979. *White House years.* Boston: Little, Brown.

Koontz, H., and O'Donnell, C. 1974. *Essentials of management.* New York: McGraw-Hill.

Korda, M. 1975. *Power!* New York: Random House.

Kotler, P., and Andreasen, A. 1991. *Strategic management of nonprofit organizations.* Englewood Cliffs, N.J.: Prentice-Hall.

Kotz, N. 1969. *Let them eat promises: The politics of hunger in America.* Englewood Cliffs, N.J.: Prentice-Hall.

Krauthammer, C. 1984. The moral equivalent of . . . . *Time,* July 9.

Laing, J. R. 1975. Civil service setup: Born as a reform idea, now hit by reformers. *The Wall Street Journal,* December 22.

Lambright, W. H. 1976. *Governing science and technology.* New York: Oxford University Press.

Lasswell, H. 1951. The policy orientation. In H. Lasswell and D. Lerner (Eds.). *The policy science.* Stanford, Calif.: Stanford University Press.

Lax, D. A., and Sebenius, J. K. 1986. *The manager as negotiator.* New York: Free Press.

Leebaert, D. 1991. *Technology 2001: The future of computing and communications.* Cambridge, Mass.: MIT Press.

Levine, C. H. 1980. *Managing fiscal stress.* Chatham, N.J.: Chatham House.

Levinson, H. 1968. *The exceptional executive.* Cambridge, Mass.: Harvard University Press.

Lewis, A. 1975. When government works. *New York Times,* October 27.

Likert, R. 1961. *New patterns of management.* New York: McGraw-Hill.

Lindblom, C. E. 1959. The science of muddling through. *Public Administration Review,* Spring.

———. 1968. *The policy making process.* Englewood Cliffs, N.J.: Prentice-Hall.

Lindblom, C. E., and Braybrook, D. 1963. *A strategy of decision.* New York: Free Press.

Lippmann, W. 1955. *The public philosophy.* Boston: Little, Brown.

Litterer, J. A. 1973. *The analysis of organization.* New York: John Wiley & Sons.

Long, N. 1949. Powers and administration. *Public Administration Review,* Autumn.

MacIntyre, A. 1984. *After virtue: A study in moral theory.* Notre Dame, Ind.: University of Notre Dame Press.

Malek, F. V. 1978. *Washington's hidden tragedy: The failure to make government work.* New York: Free Press.

Manning, R. D. How to fight wildfires. 1989. *Governing,* February.

March, J. G., and Simon, H. A. 1958. *Organizations.* New York: John Wiley & Sons.

Marro, A. 1978. Fraud in federal aid may exceed $12 billion annually, experts say. *New York Times,* April 16.

Martin, J. 1991. The computer is an expert. *Governing,* July.

Maslow, A. H. 1954. *Motivation and personality.* New York: Harper & Row.

———. 1971. *The farther reaches of human nature.* New York: Viking.

Matthews, C. 1988. *Hardball.* New York: Summit Books.

Mayer, M. 1976. *Today and tomorrow in America.* New York: Harper & Row.

McClelland, D. 1961. *The achieving society.* Princeton, N.J.: Van Nostrand Reinhold.

———. 1973. Testing for competence rather than for "intelligence." *The American Psychologist,* January.

McConkey, D. D. 1975. *MBO for nonprofit organizations.* New York: AMACOM.

McGregor, D. 1960. *The human side of enterprise.* New York: McGraw-Hill.

McKean, R. H. 1963. *Efficiency in government through systems analysis.* New York: John Wiley & Sons.

McNair, M. P. 1957. What price human relations? *Harvard Business Review,* March–April.

Mehrabian, A. 1971. *Silent messages.* Belmont, Calif.: Wadsworth.

Milgram, S. 1974. *Obedience to authority: An experimental view.* New York: Harper & Row.

Mintzberg, H. 1973. *The nature of managerial work.* New York: Harper & Row.

———. 1975. The manager's job: Folklore and fact. *Harvard Business Review,* July–August.

———. 1979. *The structuring of organization: A synthesis of research.* Englewood Cliffs, N.J.: Prentice-Hall.

Mitoff, I. I. 1988. Crises management: Cutting through the confusion. *Sloan Management Review,* Winter.

Moak, L. L., and Hillhouse, A. M. 1975. *Concepts and practices in local government finance.* Chicago: MFOA.

Molitor, G. T. T. 1975. Schema for forecasting public policy change. In A. A. Spekke (Ed.), *The next 25 years.* Washington, D.C.: World Future Society.

Morstein-Marx, F. (Ed.). 1946. *The elements of public administration.* Englewood Cliffs, N.J.: Prentice-Hall.

Mosher, F. C. (Ed.). 1968. *Governmental reorganization: Cases and commentary.* Indianapolis: Bobbs-Merrill.

———. 1968. *Democracy and the public service.* New York: Oxford University Press.

Moynihan, D. P. 1973. *Coping: Essays on the practice of government.* New York: Random House.

Muller, R. 1980. *Revitalizing America: Politics for prosperity.* New York: Simon & Schuster.

Musgrave, R. A., and Musgrave, P. B. 1973. *Public finance in theory and practice.* New York: McGraw-Hill.

Mushkin, S. (Ed.). 1972. *Public prices for public products.* Washington: Urban Institute.

Naisbitt, J. 1980. The new economic and political order in the 1980s. Paper delivered to The Foresight Group, Stockholm, Sweden, April 17.

National Academy of Public Administration. 1989. *Privatization: The challenge to public management.* Washington, D.C.: National Academy of Public Administration.

Neustadt, R. D. 1960. *Presidential power.* New York: John Wiley & Sons.

Newfield, J., and Barrett, W. 1988. *City for sale: Ed Koch and the betrayal of New York.* New York: Harper & Row.

Niskanen, Jr., W. A. 1971. *Bureaucracy and representative government.* Chicago: Aldine-Atherton.

Nozick, R. 1974. *Anarchy, state, and utopia.* New York: Basic Books.

O'Neill, J. 1983. The change in women's economic status. Paper presented before U.S. Congress Joint Economic Committee, November 9.

Osborne, D. 1989. The Kemp cure-all. *New Republic,* April 3.

Osborne, D., and Gaebler, T. 1992. *Reinventing Government.* Reading, Mass.: Addison-Wesley.

Otten, A. L. 1973. Bureaucracy in the White House. *The Wall Street Journal,* August 23.

Palumbo, D., and Maynard-Moody, S. 1991. *Contemporary public administration.* New York: Longman.

Parkinson, C. N. 1957. *Parkinson's law and other studies in administration.* Boston: Houghton Mifflin.

Parson, H. M. 1978. What caused the Hawthorne effect? *Administration & Society,* November.

Pascale, R. 1990. *Managing on the edge.* New York: Simon & Schuster.

Patton, A. 1974. To reform the federal pay system. *Business Week,* March 9.

Peirce, N. R. 1989. The secret of Boulder's success. *Houston Chronicle,* May 30.

Perry, J. L., and Rainey, H. G. 1988. The public-private distinction in organization theory. *Academy of Management Review,* 13:2.

Persinos, J. F. 1989. The return of Officer Friendly. *Governing,* March.

Peters, C. 1980. *How Washington really works.* Reading, Mass.: Addison-Wesley.

Peters, T., and Austin, N. 1986. *A passion for excellence.* New York: Warner Books.

Peters, T., and Waterman, Jr., R. H. 1982. *In search of excellence.* New York: Harper & Row.

Peterson, J. E. 1991. Managing public money. *Governing,* June.

Pious, R. M. 1979. *The American presidency.* New York: Basic Books.

Pomerleau, R. 1974. The state of management development in the federal service. *Public Personnel Management,* January–February.

Pressman, J. L., and Wildavsky, A. 1973. *Implementation.* Berkeley: University of California Press.

Public Policy Program, 1972. *Teaching and research materials, public policy 210 problem sets.* Cambridge, Mass.: Kennedy School of Government.

Quade, E. S. 1966. *System analysis techniques for planning-programming-budgeting.* Santa Monica, Calif.: Rand.

Quinn, J. B. 1980. *Strategies for change: Logical incrementalism.* Homewood, Ill.: Richard D. Irwin.

Rawls, J. 1970. *A theory of justice.* Cambridge, Mass.: Belknap Press.

Reddin, W. J. 1970. *Managerial effectiveness.* New York: McGraw-Hill.

Richardson, E. 1973. The maze of social programs. *Washington Post,* January 21.

Rivlin, A. 1971. *Systematic thinking for social action.* Washington, D.C.: Brookings Institution.

Rogers, C. R., and Roethlisberger, F. J. 1952. Barriers and gateways to communications. *Harvard Business Review,* July–August.

Rosenthal, S. R., and Levine, E. S. 1980. Case management and policy implementation. *Public policy,* Fall.

Sacco, J. F., and Ostrowski, J. W. 1991. *Microcomputers and government management: Design and use of applications.* Pacific Grove, Calif.: Brooks/Cole.

Sapolsky, H. M. 1972. *The Polaris system development.* Cambridge, Mass.: Harvard University Press.

Sayles, L. R., and Chandler, M. K. 1971. *Managing large systems: Organizations for the future.* New York: Harper & Row.

Savas, E. S. 1987. *Privatization.* Chatham, N.J.: Chatham House.

Schachter, S. 1959. *The psychology of affiliation.* Stanford, Calif.: Stanford University Press.

Schick, A. 1966. The road to PPB: The stages of budget reform. *Public Administration Review,* December.

Schlesinger, A. M. 1965. *A thousand days.* Boston: Houghton-Mifflin.

Schoemaker, P. J. H. 1990. *Decision traps.* New York: Doubleday.

Schultze, C. L. 1969. The role of incentives, penalties, and rewards in attaining effective policy. In The Joint Economic Committee, *Analysis and evaluation of public expenditures.* Washington, D.C.: U.S. GPO.

Schweiger, D., and Finger, P. A. 1984. The comparative effectiveness of dialectical inquiry and devil's advocate. *Strategic Management Journal,* 5.

Schweinhart, L. J., and Weikart, D. P. 1980. *Young children grow up.* Monographs of the High-Scope Educational Research Foundation, No. 7.

Selznick, P. 1949. *TVA and the grass roots.* New York: Harper & Row.

Sherrill, R. 1974. *Why they call it politics.* New York: Harcourt Brace Jovanovich.

Sherwood, F. P. 1990. The half-century's "great books" in public administration. *Public Administration Review,* March–April.

Siedman, H. 1980. *Politics, position, and power. The dynamics of federal organization.* New York: Oxford University Press.

Simon, H. A. 1957a. *Administrative behavior.* New York: Macmillan.

———. 1957b. *Models of man.* New York: John Wiley & Sons.

———. 1991. *Models of my life.* New York: Basic Books.

Slinger, B. F., Sharp, A. M., and Sandmeyer, R. L. 1975. Local government revenues. In J. R. Aronson and E. Schwartz (Eds.), *Management policies in local government finance.* Washington, D.C.: ICMA.

Sorensen, T. C. 1963. *Decision making in the White House.* New York: Columbia University Press.

Speer, A. 1970. *Inside the Third Reich.* New York: Macmillan.

Sproull, L., and Kiester, S. 1991. Computers, networks and work. *Scientific American,* September.

Starling, G. 1988. *The changing environment of business.* Belmont, Calif.: Wadsworth.

———. 1991. A framework for understanding commitment in the R & D organization. *Journal of Engineering and Technology Management,* 8.

Steinberg, A. 1972. *The bosses.* New York: Macmillan.

Steinberg, S. S., and Austern, D. T. 1990. *Government, ethics and managers.* New York: Praeger.

Stieglitz, H. 1969. What's not on the organizational chart. In D. I. Cleland and W. R. King (Eds.), *Systems, organization, analysis, management.* New York: McGraw-Hill.

Stone, D. C. 1981. Innovative organizations require innovative managers. *Public*

Administration Review, September–October.

Summers, H. 1982. *On strategy.* Novato, Calif.: Presidio Press.

Teltsch, K. 1989. Community initiatives. *New York Times,* April 20.

Terkel, S. 1972. *Working.* New York: Pantheon.

Tesler, L. G. 1991. Networked computing in the 1990s. *Scientific American,* September.

Thompson, F. 1976. Types of representative bureaucracy and their linkage. In R. T. Golembienski, et al. (Eds.), *Public administration.* Chicago: Rand McNally.

Toffler, A. 1980. *The third wave.* New York: Bantam Books.

Townsend, R. 1970. *Up the organization.* New York: Alfred A. Knopf.

Toynbee, A. J. 1946. *A study of history,* abridged ed. New York: Oxford.

Tullock, G. 1965. *The politics of bureaucracy.* Washington, D.C.: Public Affairs Press.

———. 1971. Public decisions as public goods. *Journal of Political Economy,* 913–928.

Ueberroth, P. 1986. *Made in America.* New York: William Morrow.

U.S. Civil Service Commission. 1974. *Guide to a more effective public service.* Washington, D.C.: U.S. GPO.

U.S. Congress. 1987. *The Iran-contra affair.* Washington, D.C.: U.S. GPO.

U.S. Department of Labor. 1988. *Opportunity 2000.* Washington, D.C.: U.S. GPO.

U.S. General Accounting Office. 1979. *Difficulties in evaluating public affairs government-wide and at the Department of Health, Education and Welfare,* LCD-79-405. Washington, D.C.: U.S. GPO. January 18.

———. 1987a. *DOD revolving door.* Washington, D.C.: U.S. GPO.

———. 1987b. *Human resources management: Status of agency practices for improving federal productivity.* Washington, D.C.: U.S. GPO.

———. 1990a. *Management of VA.* Washington, D.C.: U.S. GPO.

———. 1990b. *Coordination between DEA and the FBI.* Washington, D.C.: U.S. GPO.

———. 1990c. *Federal-state-local relations.* Washington, D.C.: U.S. GPO.

———. 1991. *Smart highways.* Washington, D.C.: U.S. GPO.

U.S. Office of Technology Assessment. 1990. *Critical connections: Communications for the future.* Washington, D.C.: U.S. GPO.

Van Horn, R. L. 1982. Don't expect too much from your computer system. *The Wall Street Journal,* October 22.

Venkatraman, N. 1990. Information technology and business transformation. Proceedings from Bull/*Computerworld* Forum Program, Houston, June 19.

Ventriss, C. 1985. Emerging perspectives on citizen participation. *Public Administration Review,* May–June.

Waldo, D. 1948. *Administrative state.* New York: Ronald Press.

Walters, R. W. 1972. Job enrichment isn't easy. *Personnel Administration Review,* September–October.

Ware, J. 1978. *Some aspects of problem solving and conflict resolution in management groups,* 9-479-003. Cambridge, Mass.: Harvard Business School.

Warwick, D. P. 1981. The ethics of administrative discretion. In J. L. Fleishman et al., *Public duties.* Cambridge, Mass.: Harvard University Press.

Webb, J. 1969. *Space age management.* New York: McGraw-Hill.

Weinberg, A. M. 1966. Can technology replace social engineering? *Bulletin of the Atomic Scientists,* December.

Weiss, C. H. 1972. *Evaluation research.* Englewood Cliffs, N.J.: Prentice-Hall.

Whitehead, A. N. 1929. *The aims of education.* New York: Macmillan.

Wholey, J. S., et al. 1970. *Federal evaluation policy.* Washington, D.C.: Urban Institute.

Wildavsky, A. 1978. A budget for all seasons? Why the traditional budget lasts.

Public Administration Review, November–December.

Williams, W. 1975. Special issue on implementation: Editor's comments. *Policy analysis,* Summer.

Wilson, J. Q. 1989. *Bureaucracy.* New York: Basic Books.

Wolfe, T. 1970. *Radical chic & mau-mauing the flak catchers.* New York: Farrar, Straus, and Giroux.

Wood, R. 1981. Managing a school system under court order. *The Wall Street Journal,* March 30.

Wright, D. 1982. *Understanding intergovernmental relations.* Monterey, Calif.: Brooks/Cole.

Wurman, R. S. 1989. *Information anxiety.* New York: Doubleday.

Yankelovich, D. 1983. *Work and human values.* New York: Public Agenda Foundation.

Zuboff, S. 1984. *In the age of the smart machine: The future of work and power.* New York: Basic Books.

Index

Optional:

Your name: ______________________________ Date: ____________________

May Wadsworth quote you, either in promotion for *Managing the Public Sector,* 4th Edition, or in future publishing ventures?

Yes: ________ No: ________

Sincerely,

Grover Starling

FOLD HERE

NO POSTAGE NECESSARY IF MAILED IN THE UNITED STATES

BUSINESS REPLY MAIL

FIRST CLASS PERMIT NO. 34 BELMONT, CA

POSTAGE WILL BE PAID BY ADDRESSEE

ATT: *Grover Starling*

Wadsworth Publishing Company
10 Davis Drive
Belmont, CA 94002

FOLD HERE

TO THE OWNER OF THIS BOOK:

We hope that you have found *Managing the Public Sector*, 4th Edition, useful. So that this book can be improved in a future edition, would you take the time to complete this sheet and return it? Thank you.

Instructor's name: ____________________

Department: ____________________

School and address: ____________________

____

1. The name of the course in which I used this book is: ____________________

____

2. My general reaction to this book is: ____________________

____

____

3. What I like most about this book is: ____________________

____

____

4. What I like least about this book is: ____________________

____

____

5. Were all of the chapters of the book assigned for you to read? Yes No

   If not, which ones weren't? ____________________

6. Do you plan to keep this book after you finish the course? Yes No

   Why or why not? ____________________

____

7. On a separate sheet of paper, please write specific suggestions for improving this book and anything else you'd care to share about your experience in using the book.

1949 **NORBERT WIENER**
CLAUDE SHANNON
P.M.S. BLACKETT

Emphasized systems analysis, operations research, and information theory in management

1955 **HERBERT KAUFMAN**
FRED W. RIGGS
WALTER R. SHARP

First course on comparative administration introduced at Yale University. Thi movement, which represented a broadening of public administration to other cultures, began to wane in later years as American foreign-aid programs were scaled back

1957 **CHRIS ARGYRIS**
DOUGLAS M. McGREGOR

Placed emphasis on social psychology and research in human relations in achieving a better fit between the personality of a mature adult and the requiremen of a modern organization. Argyris developed an open-system theory of organiza tion, whereas McGregor popularized a humanistic managerial philosophy

1959 **CHARLES A. LINDBLOM**

In his influential essay "The Science of Muddling Through," Lindblom attacke the rational models of decision making in government. In reality, the model di not work; decision makers, therefore, depend heavily on small, incremental decisions

1961 **AARON WILDAUSKY**

In an article, "The Political Implications of Budgetary Reform," Wildausky developed the concept of budgetary incrementalism and its political nature that le to his landmark work, *The Politics of the Budgetary Process* (1964)

1964 **ROBERT M. BLAKE**
JANE S. MOUTON

Proposed that every leader could be categorized in terms of two variables: concer for task and concern for people. Blake and Mouton's Managerial Grid was perhaps the best known of dozens of adaptations of this idea, which could be trace back to the Ohio State University leadership studies of the 1940s

1965 **CHARLES J. HITCH**
ROLAND N. McKEAN

In the same year that President Johnson ordered Planning-Programming-Budge ing System (PPBS) adopted governmentwide, the bible of government systems analysts appeared—*The Economics of Defense in the Nuclear Age*